Why You Need this New Edition

- The text has been updated to a more clear and concise version with the latest research literature and a revised list of chapters.

- New Illustrative Biographies: Sonia Sotomayor (Chapter 8) and Barack Obama (Chapter 13).

- Clearer presentation of some issues (e.g., recovered memory; hypnosis) (Chapter 2), additional references making comparisons with other religious traditions (Chapter 16), and a more concise history of Buddhism (Chapter 16).

- Expanded discussion, in the presentation of Erikson's biography, of the current state of child analysis. Clearer presentation of identity development and moratorium, and some longitudinal research about identity development. Expanded discussion of cross-cultural research (especially regarding the stage of generativity). Mention of terrorists as examples of a foreclosed identity (Chapter 5).

- Expanded content about research on relational approaches with respect to brain functioning and mental health issues (e.g., border-line personality; narcissism) (Chapter 6) and clearer presentation of psychological types (Chapter 3).

- Updated discussion of religious orientations, including more cross-cultural material (e.g., religious orientation in Muslim populations, and in American ethnic groups) (Chapter 7).

- Expanded discussion of the Big Five, and reduced focus on Cattell's older theory. Expanded discussion of cross-cultural studies of the Five Factor model. More studies of implications of the five factors for life outcomes (e.g., aging and retirement) (Chapter 8).

- Expanded discussion of behavioral genetics and new table on heritability of specific personality characteristics as well as cultural and cross-cultural issues as contexts (Chapter 9).

- The Behaviorism section has been updated with an abridged version of Dollard and Miller's theory along with Skinner's theory (also abridged) and Staats's theory. The Illustrative Biography of Tiger Woods has been updated, discussing how behavioral approaches are specific to particular behaviors, so that a behavioral interpretation of his success at golf (emphasized in the previous edition) shows the limitations of this approach, which does not present a broader view of personality that would have predicted his marital and infidelity problems, which are discussed in this edition (Chapter 10).

- Mischel and Bandura are each discussed in a separate chapter, instead of being combined into the same chapter (in the previous edition). Expanded discussion of the Wediko Camp study (included in this edition) that was the basis of Mischel's research on traits and situations. The CAPS model is presented as a distinct section. Discussion of the cultural learning and implications of cognitive affective units in the CAPS model (including race differences in response to the O. J. Simpson verdict, and interpersonal relationships in the context of prejudice). Discussion of cross-cultural studies of the CAPS model (the United States and Philippines). Discussion of the importance of measuring situations (Chapter 12).

- Expanded section on Positive Psychology, organized in terms of the "three pillars" of positive psychology, with attention to both the individual and social institutions. Also, a new discussion of why happiness is an important theoretical focus, based on an evolutionary argument (Chapter 15).

Theories of Personality

UNDERSTANDING PERSONS

Sixth Edition

Theories of Personality

UNDERSTANDING PERSONS

Susan Cloninger
The Sage Colleges

PEARSON

Boston   Columbus   Indianapolis   New York   San Francisco   Upper Saddle River
Amsterdam   Cape Town   Dubai   London   Madrid   Milan   Munich   Paris   Montréal   Toronto
Delhi   Mexico City   São Paulo   Sydney   Hong Kong   Seoul   Singapore   Taipei   Tokyo

Editorial Director: Craig Campanella
Editor in Chief: Jessica Mosher
Executive Editor: Susan Hartman
Editorial Assistant: Shivangi Ramashandran
Director of Marketing: Brandy Dawson
Executive Marketing Manager: Wendy Albert
Marketing Assistant: Frank Alarcon
Managing Editor: Denise Forlow
Project Manager: Marianne Peters-Riordan
Senior Operations Supervisor: Mary Fischer
Operations Specialist: Diane Peirano

Creative Director: Jayne Conte
Cover Designer: Suzanne Behnke
Cover Image: Shutterstock/Cheng See Yuan
Media Director: Brian Hyland
Lead Media Editor: Pete Sabatini
Full-Service Project Management: Shiny Rajesh
Composition: Integra Software Services
Printer/Binder: Courier Kendallville
Cover Printer: Courier Kendallville
Text Font: 10/12, ITC Garamond Std

Credits and acknowledgments borrowed from other sources and reproduced, with permission, in this textbook appear on appropriate page within text (or on page 403).

Many of the designations by manufacturers and seller to distinguish their products are claimed as trademarks. Where those designations appear in this book, and the publisher was aware of a trademark claim, the designations have been printed in initial caps or all caps.

Library of Congress Cataloging-in-Publication Data
Cloninger, Susan
  Theories of personality: understanding persons/Susan Cloninger.—6th ed.
    p. cm.
  ISBN-13: 978-0-205-25624-2 (alk. paper)
  ISBN-10: 0-205-25624-4 (alk. paper)
  1. Personality—Textbooks. I. Title.
  BF698.C543 2013
  155.2—dc23

                                          2012008176

10 9 8 7 6 5 4 3   [V0UD] 15

Student Edition
ISBN-10: 0-205-25624-4
ISBN-13: 978-0-205-25624-2

Instructor's Review Copy
ISBN-10: 0-205-26053-5
ISBN-13: 978-0-205-26053-9

To Nigel

BRIEF CONTENTS

CONTENTS

PART 3   The Trait Perspective   125

PREFACE

Writing this book, with its various editions, has been roughly a two-decade process (so far), and I've come to a realization that it will always be a work in process. What used to feel like "completion" now feels simply like a "milestone" as each edition is sent to production. That is fitting, as the field, too, is very much in process. Over the years, some of the hot topics (like the debate over traits versus situationalism, and the controversy over repressed memory of abuse) have faded into the historical past as theories have matured and research has guided reconceptualizations; and some topics have been dropped altogether, in order to make room for the new. The organization of this book has changed a bit to reflect these historical developments. Previously a full chapter, the Dollard and Miller contributions to a behavioral analysis of psychoanalytic theory are now part of a consolidated behavioral chapter, with Skinner and Staats. Behaviorism itself has been combined with cognitive behaviorism into one part (Part IV). Positive psychology is growing, and I have expanded its scope within the Maslow chapter, imagining that Abe Maslow would applaud psychology for finally heeding his vision, at least in part.

And while not reflected in the words I have crafted for this edition, I have frequently reminisced about the first term paper I wrote in my first personality course, where I explored all that I could find written by Gordon Allport. If there is a unitary statement, however vague and incomplete, for the field of personality, it seems—at least at this moment, to me—to be his personology. But the details are lacking in his statements, and for that, we need many other theories, ranging from the exciting findings of neuroscience to the very practical and socially important recognition of cultural contexts (e.g., challenges to the Protestant bias of Allport-inspired work on religious orientations). Researchers and theorists in personality have more contributions that deserve reporting than I can possibly report, or even (alas) read! So many things to say, it would take a whole series of books! I invite students to do as I have done, and make understanding personality a life's work.

One of the major challenges of this edition has been to reduce the total length of the manuscript. Students, both in my classes and in those taught by others who use this book, will undoubtedly be glad for the pruning, but many of those cuts nicked this writer's Muse as well. How can students of personality not be given more details of this, or of that, I ask myself—but then remember that there is only so much that can be absorbed on a first introduction to the field. All in all, the wisdom of my editors who requested this cutting is hopefully apparent in places that are easier to read. The choice of what to cut was only mine, though, and I apologize if I have made choices with which returning readers disagree. New editions, like nature herself, demand some clearing in order to make room for new growth.

NEW TO THIS EDITION

The following is a list of new items included in this edition:

- New Illustrative Biographies: Sonia Sotomayor (Chapter 8) and Barack Obama (Chapter 13), and an updated Illustrative Biography on Tiger Woods.
- A new chapter on Mischel, which addresses the delay of gratification, an easier concept for students to comprehend, before discussing Mischel's more complicated view of traits and the situational context of behavior.
- Expanded discussions of recovered memory and hypnosis, cross-cultural research (especially regarding the stage of generativity), child analysis in conjunction with Erikson's biography, and the Big Five.
- Expanded content about research on relational approaches with respect to brain functioning and mental health issues (e.g., borderline personality; narcissism) (Chapter 6) and clearer presentation of psychological types (Chapter 3).

- Expanded discussion of behavioral genetics and new table on heritability of specific personality characteristics as well as cultural and cross-cultural issues as contexts (Chapter 9).
- Expanded discussion of the Big Five, and reduced focus on Cattell's older theory. Expanded discussion of cross-cultural studies of the Five Factor model. More studies of implications of the five factors for life outcomes (e.g., aging and retirement) (Chapter 8).
- Updated research and discussion topics, such as religious orientations, including more cross-cultural material (e.g., religious orientation in Muslim populations, and in American ethnic groups), implications of the five factors for life outcomes (e.g., aging and retirement).
- The Behaviorism section has been updated with an abridged version of the theory, along with Skinner's theory (also abridged) and Staats's theory.
- Expanded section on Positive Psychology, organized in terms of the "three pillars" of positive psychology, with attention to both the individual and social institutions.
- New discussion of why happiness is an important theoretical focus, based on an evolutionary argument (Chapter 15).

SUPPLEMENTS

The following supplements are available to qualified instructors:

- **PowerPoints (0205260594)** The PowerPoints provide an active format for presenting concepts from each chapter and incorporating relevant figures and tables. The PowerPoint files can be downloaded from www.pearsonhighered.com.
- **Instructor Resource Manual with Test Bank (0205260578)** The Instructor's Manual includes key terms, lecture ideas, teaching tips, suggested readings, chapter outlines, student projects, and research assignments. The Test Bank is page referenced to the text and is categorized by topic and skill level. The Test Bank is available to adopters in both Windows and Macintosh computerized format.
- **MyTest Testing Software (0205260586)** This Web-based test-generating software provides instructors "best in class" features in an easy-to-use program. Create tests and easily select questions with drag-and-drop or point-and-click functionality. Add or modify test questions using the built-in Question Editor and print tests in a variety of formats. The program comes with full technical support.
- **MySearchLab with eText (www.mysearchlab.com)** This learning management platform has delivered proven results in helping individual students succeed. Its automatically graded assessments and interactive eText provides engaging experiences that personalize, stimulate, and measure learning for each student.

  - The Pearson **eText** lets students access their textbook anytime, anywhere, and any way they want—including listening online or downloading to iPad.
  - **Research and Writing tools** help students hone their skills and produce more effective papers. These tools include access to a variety of academic journals, census data, Associated Press news feeds, discipline-specific readings, and a wide range of writing and grammar tools.
  - **Discipline-specific resources** help students apply concepts to real-world situations.
  - **Assessment** attached to every chapter enables both instructors and students to track progress and get immediate feedback.

I am grateful to many people who, in various ways, have contributed to this work. Obviously, those who have reviewed the current edition, with often detailed suggestions (some taken, some not), deserve my thanks: David King (Mount Olive College), Eric Shiraev (George Mason University), Dan Segrist (Southern Illinois University, Edwardsville), Micah Sadigh (Cedar Crest College), Richard Mangold (Illinois Valley Community College), Todd Nelson (California State University–Stanislaus), John Roop

(North Georgia College & State University), Heather Long (NC A&T University), L. Sidney Fox (California State University, Long Beach), and Jutta Street (Campbell University).

Their advice adds to suggestions made by others, as reviewers of previous editions, and, less formally, those who have generously offered advice: Kurt D. Baker (Emporia State University); Melinda C. R. Burgess (Southern Oklahoma State University); Nicholas Carnagey (Iowa State University); Mary Louise Cashel (Southern Illinois University at Carbondale); George Domino (University of Arizona); Bernadette Tucker Duck (Chicago State University); Jeanine Feldman (San Diego State University); Beverly Goodwin (Indiana University of Pennsylvania); Ehsha G. Klirs (George Mason University); Elissa Koplik (Bloomfield College); Maria J. Lavooy (University of Central Florida); Thomas J. Martinez, III (private practice); Spencer McWilliams (California State University, San Marcos); Carol Miller (Anne Arundel Community College); Paul Murray (Southern Oregon University); Clay Peters (Liberty University); Tom M. Randall (Rhode Island College); Eric Shiraev (George Mason University); Arthur W. Staats (University of Hawaii); Eunkook Suh (University of California, Irvine); and Julie Ann Suhr (Ohio University). Others have also helped by sending papers and books.

Closer to home, several friends and colleagues have offered advice, loaned books, and given emotional support and encouragement when I needed it. So thank you: Russell Couch, Bronna Romanoff, and others in the Psychology Department at The Sage Colleges, where they have watched me juggle (not always successfully) the demands of a full teaching load, committee work, chairing the IRB, and other faculty responsibilities with "The Book." Special thanks to Nigel Wright, who not only appeared with a full box of books for me to read for an earlier revision (sorry, Nigel—I could not read them all!), but who also reminded me recently that I really indeed do love writing, at a time when exhaustion and an overdue manuscript led me to claim the opposite. His insatiable love of books inspires me. To my son John, thanks for all you have done by what you say and how you live—and one of these days, the other book that is dedicated to you will (hopefully) be ready.

My editors at Pearson have supported this project marvelously, with plenty of advance planning and organizing reviews—and patience for my delinquencies—and so special thanks to Susan Hartmann, Alexandra Mitton, Shiny Rajesh, and others with whom I have not had so much personal contact. Over the years and editions, they are joining others from Pearson in a larger personification of "My Editor," who makes me feel sometimes important, sometimes rushed, but always expanded to a larger project than my professorial role. Writing is, if not at every moment fun, at least always a challenge and a privilege.

Sue Cloninger
Troy, New York

Theories of Personality

UNDERSTANDING PERSONS

Introduction to Personality Theory

Writers and philosophers have reflected about personality for centuries. They describe various types of people.

> The true artist will let his wife starve, his children go barefoot, his mother drudge for his living at seventy, sooner than work at anything but his art. (George Bernard Shaw, *Major Barbara*, act 1)

> A fool uttereth all his mind. (Prov. 29:11)

They tell us about the dynamic motivations and emotions of human nature.

> We would all be idle if we could. (Samuel Johnson, quoted in Boswell's *Life of Johnson*)

> Unlimited power is apt to corrupt the minds of those who possess it. (William Pitt, speech, House of Lords, January 9, 1770)

Sayings tell us how personality develops down various paths.

> Train up a child in the way he should go: and when he is old, he will not depart from it. (Matt. 22:6)

> Spare the rod and spoil the child. (Samuel Butler, *Hudibras*, pt. ii, c. I, 1. 844)

With centuries of such commentary about personality, we might think that we may leave scientific investigation for other problems, perhaps to explore the mysteries of the physical universe and biological processes. Yet formal study is needed, perhaps here more than anywhere, for there are contradictions in culture's lessons about personality.

Virtue is bold, and goodness never fearful. (Shakespeare, *Measure for Measure*, act 3, line 215)

Boldness is a child of ignorance and baseness. (Francis Bacon, *Essays*, line 12)

How can we know, given such contradictory observations, whether boldness should be admired or pitied? Perhaps when we and our friends are bold, we will agree with Shakespeare and leave Bacon's skepticism aside until we confront a bold enemy. Such sayings, although charming, are disconcerting because there seems to be a saying to support any belief. Cultural sayings do not offer a systematic understanding of human nature. For that, we turn to psychology.

PERSONALITY: THE STUDY OF INDIVIDUALS

Psychology uses the methods of science to come to some clearer and less ambiguous (if, alas, less literary) understandings of human nature.

Definition of Personality

personality
the underlying causes within the person of individual behavior and experience

Personality may be defined as *the underlying causes within the person of individual behavior and experience.* Personality psychologists do not all agree about what these underlying causes are, as the many theories in this text suggest. They offer a variety of answers to three fundamental questions. First, how can personality be described? Personality **description** considers the ways in which we should characterize an individual. How do people differ from one another, and should we describe personality traits by comparing people with one another or use some other strategy, such as studying each individual separately? Second, how can we understand personality **dynamics**—how people think about and adjust to their life situations, and how they are influenced by culture? Third, what can be said about personality **development**—how personality changes over the life span, influenced by biological factors and experience? These three questions are so fundamental that each theory considers them in some way.

description
theoretical task of identifying the units of personality, with particular emphasis on the differences between people

dynamics
the motivational aspect of personality

development
formation or change (of personality) over time

DESCRIPTION OF PERSONALITY

The most fundamental theoretical question is this: What concepts are useful for describing personality? Should we concentrate on the differences between people? Or should we avoid comparisons, instead focusing on intensive understanding of one person?

Differences between People: Groups or Gradations?

individual differences
qualities that make one person different from another

Personality researchers have devoted considerable effort to identifying the ways that individuals differ from one another—that is, of describing **individual differences**. Essentially, we have the choice of classifying people into a limited number of separate groups, a type approach. Or we can decide that people vary in gradations and describe people by saying how much of the basic dimensions they possess, a trait approach.

type
a category of people with similar characteristics

TYPES   The *type approach* proposes that personality comes in a limited number of distinct categories (qualitative groupings). Such personality **types** are categories of people with similar characteristics. A small number of types suffice to describe all people. In ancient Greece, for example, Hippocrates described four basic types of temperament: sanguine (optimistic), melancholic (depressed), choleric (irritable), and phlegmatic (apathetic) (Merenda, 1987). Each person belongs to only one category.

TRAITS AND FACTORS   Nature often presents us with more gradual transitions (quantitative dimensions). Consider "cruelty": Between Mother Teresa and Stalin lie many intermediate levels of cruelty. Therefore, personality researchers generally

Table 1.1 Types, Traits, and Factors: Three Ways of Describing Personality	
Types	Type membership is an all-or-nothing thing (a qualitative variable).
	A person belongs to one and only one category.
	Theoretically, a small number of types describe everyone.
	A person fits into only one type.
Traits	Trait scores are continuous (quantitative) variables. A person is given a numeric score to indicate how much of a trait the person possesses.
	Theoretically, there are a great many traits to describe everyone.
	A person can be described on every trait.
Factors	Factor scores are also continuous (quantitative) variables. A person is given a numeric score to indicate how much of a factor the person possesses.
	Theoretically, a small number of factors describe everyone.
	A person can be described on every factor.

prefer **quantitative measures**, which give each person a score, ranging from very low to very high or somewhere in between. In contrast to types, **traits** are such quantitative measures. They describe a narrower scope of behavior. Traits permit a more precise description of personality than types because each trait refers to a more focused set of characteristics, and each person is a combination of many traits.

More traits than types are necessary to describe a personality. One classic study counted nearly 18,000 traits among words listed in the dictionary (Allport & Odbert, 1936). Do we really need that many? To eliminate unnecessary redundancy (e.g., by combining synonyms such as "shy" and "withdrawn"), researchers rely on statistical procedures that compute correlations among trait scores, and on that basis they have proposed broad **factors** of personality. Factors are quantitative, like traits, but they include a broader range of behavior. Factors are often thought to derive from underlying biological variables.

Types, traits, and factors all have a role in personality theory and research. The terms are sometimes used imprecisely, but knowing their differences (summarized in Table 1.1) helps us understand the variety of ways that personality can be described and measured.

Comparing People or Studying Individuals: Nomothetic and Idiographic Approaches

Personality traits and types allow us to compare one person with another: the **nomothetic** approach. Most personality research is nomothetic. Despite its scientific advantages, the nomothetic method has drawbacks. It studies many people and compares them on only a few numerical scores, which makes it difficult to understand one whole person (Carlson, 1971). Much personality research is also limited because it often investigates college students (Carlson, 1971; Sears, 1986), who are more conveniently available to researchers but who differ from the general adult population on many personality characteristics (Ward, 1993).

In contrast, the **idiographic** approach studies individuals one at a time. Strictly idiographic approaches are difficult because any description of a person (e.g., "Mary is outgoing") implies comparison with other people. Although implicit comparisons with other people are unavoidable, we call research idiographic if it focuses on the particularities of an individual case, for example, in a case study or a psychobiographical analysis. William McKinley Runyan reminds personality psychologists of Kluckhohn and Murray's (1953) classic assertion: "Every man is in certain respects (a) like all other men, (b) like some other men, (c) like no other man" (1988, p. 53). Personality psychology can discover truths about unique individuals, as well as typical group characteristics and universal principles.

quantitative measures

measures that permit expression of various amounts of something, such as a trait

trait

personality characteristic that makes one person different from another and/or that describes an individual's personality

factor

a statistically derived, quantitative dimension of personality that is broader than most traits

nomothetic

involving comparisons with other individuals; research based on groups of people

idiographic

focusing on one individual

PERSONALITY DYNAMICS

The term *personality dynamics* refers to the mechanisms by which personality is expressed, often focusing on the motivations that direct behavior. Motivation provides energy and direction to behavior. If you see a person running energetically toward a door, you may ask, "*Why* is that person running?" What is the motivation? Theorists discuss many motives. Some theorists assume that the fundamental motivations or goals of all people are similar. Sigmund Freud suggested that sexual motivation underlies personality; Carl Rogers proposed a tendency to move toward higher levels of development. Other theorists suggest that motives or goals vary from one person to another. For example, Henry Murray (1938) listed dozens of motives that are of varying importance to different people, including achievement motivation, power motivation, and nurturance.

Personality dynamics include individuals' adaptation or adjustment to the demands of life and so have implications for psychological health. Modern personality theory considers cognitive processes as a major aspect of personality dynamics. How we think is an important determinant of our choices and adaptation. In addition, culture influences us through its opportunities and expectations.

Adaptation and Adjustment

adaptation

coping with the external world

Personality encompasses an individual's way of coping with the world, of adjusting to demands and opportunities in the environment—that is, **adaptation**. Many theories of personality have historical roots in the clinical treatment of patients. Observations of their symptoms, and of increasing adjustment with treatment, suggested more general ideas about personality that have been applied broadly to nonclinical populations; conversely, studies of nonclinical populations have implications for therapy.

Cognitive Processes

What role does thinking play? Theories vary considerably on this question. Based on clinical experience, Sigmund Freud proposed that conscious thought plays only a limited role in personality dynamics; unconscious dynamics are more important in his psychoanalytic theory. Other approaches disagree, emphasizing conscious experience and investigating various thought patterns that predict behavior and coping. The ways that we label experience and the ideas we have about ourselves have substantial effects on our personality dynamics.

Culture

Historically, personality theories focused on the individual, leaving culture and society in the background. This left an incomplete picture of personality and prevented theories from adequately explaining gender, ethnic, and cultural differences. Influenced by greater awareness of cultural change, researchers have increasingly considered the role of culture in personality. Individualistic cultures, like the United States, emphasize individual differences in personality traits more than do collectivist cultures (Heine & Buchtel, 2009). There is also a difference in the personalities that are encouraged in various cultures. The individualism of U.S. culture encourages extraverted and assertive behavior that would be frowned on in more interdependent collectivist societies (Triandis, 2001). Personality traits also change from one generation to the next; for example, based on test scores, U.S. students have been increasing not only in self-esteem and extraversion but also in anxiety and neuroticism (Twenge, 2000, 2001; Twenge & Campbell, 2001). Much remains to be done to understand adequately the role of social influences on personality, but we can be sure that some of the motivations that direct people are shaped by their culture.

PERSONALITY DEVELOPMENT

Another major issue in personality theory concerns the formation and change of personality. To what extent is personality influenced by biological factors, such as heredity? To what extent can personality change as a result of learning? How critical are the childhood years for personality development, and how much change can occur in adulthood? How do we change personality in the direction we would like, to turn high-risk children toward healthier paths of development or to teach ordinary folk to be creative or to be leaders?

Biological Influences

Some children seem to be quiet or energetic or whatever from the moment of birth. Could it be that personality is genetically determined? The term **temperament** refers to consistent styles of behavior and emotional reactions that are present from infancy onward, presumably because of biological influences. As long ago as ancient Greece, philosophers and physicians believed that inborn predispositions lead one person to be melancholic and another sanguine (Kagan, 1994). Evidence supports the claim that personality is significantly influenced by heredity. With the explosion of research in genetics and neuroscience, personality researchers are identifying biological mechanisms that contribute to such aspects of personality as the tendency for some people to be outgoing and others to be shy. However, we should keep in mind that biology plays out its influence in the environment, and different environments can make quite different personalities out of the same biological potential.

temperament

consistent styles of behavior and emotional reactions present from early life onward, presumably caused by biological factors

Experience in Childhood and Adulthood

Personality develops over time. Experience, especially in childhood, influences the way each person develops toward his or her unique personality. Many of the major personality theories described in this text make statements about the development of personality. Theorists in the psychoanalytic tradition, for example, emphasize the experience of the preschool years in forming personality. Theories in the learning tradition focus primarily on change, but even some of them (e.g., Staats, 1996) propose that early learning can significantly influence the course of personality throughout life by developing essential skills on which later experience builds. In the emotional domain, early development of bonds of attachment with the parents is receiving considerable attention and is widely thought to influence relationships with people into adulthood. Although people do change, considerable evidence indicates the stability of personality over a person's lifetime (e.g., McCrae & Costa, 1984).

TO THE STUDENT   At the beginning of each chapter is a preview of its theory based on several of the issues just discussed. The issues often overlap. For example, cognitive processes not only are dynamic but also can be considered descriptive, because individuals differ in them, and developmental, because they change over time. You might begin your study of personality by considering what you believe about these issues based on your own life experience, trying to answer the questions in Table 1.2. Then, to get a preview of the field of personality, browse through the previews at the beginning of each chapter. Do some theories match your ideas more than others do? Do you find new or puzzling ideas in these preview tables? This formal study of personality ideally will offer you new ideas and help you think critically about those you already believe.

Table 1.2 Major Issues Addressed by Personality Theories	
Issue	**Examples of Approaches to These Issues**
Descriptive Issues	
Individual Differences	What are the traits that distinguish people?
	How can these traits be measured?
	Should we look at what people say, or what they do, to describe how they are unique?
	Are people consistent?

(continued)

Table 1.2 (Continued)	
Issue	**Examples of Approaches to These Issues**
Dynamic Issues	
Adaptation and Adjustment	How do people adapt to life's demands?
	How does a mentally healthy person act?
	What behaviors or thoughts are unhealthy?
Cognitive Processes	Do our thoughts affect our personality?
	What kinds of thoughts are important for personality?
	Do unconscious processes influence us?
Culture	How does culture influence our functioning?
	Does culture affect us by its expectations for men and women?
	For different classes and ethnicities?
Developmental Issues	
Biological Influences	How do biological processes affect personality?
	Is personality inherited?
Development	How should children be treated?
	How does childhood experience determine adult personality?
	Do adults change? Or has personality been determined earlier?
	What experiences in adulthood influence personality?

Note: These categories are presented for purposes of an overview. In many personality theories, the topics listed under each issue also are related to other issues.

THE SCIENTIFIC APPROACH

scientific method

the method of knowing based on systematic observation

determinism

the assumption that phenomena have causes that can be discovered by empirical research

Personality theorists, like psychology theorists more generally, test their assertions about people through the scientific method. The **scientific method** requires systematic observations and a willingness to modify understanding based on these observations. The assumption of **determinism** is central to the scientific method. Determinism refers to the assumption that the phenomena being studied have causes and that empirical research can discover these causes.

In the scientific method, two different levels of abstraction are important. In Figure 1.1, two abstract concepts are proposed at the theoretical level, "self-esteem" and "social responsibility." The theoretical proposition "High self-esteem causes social responsibility" asserts that a cause–effect relationship exists between these two concepts. Abstract concepts cannot be directly observed. They do, however, correspond to observable phenomena, indicated at the observable level in Figure 1.1. At the observable level, people who score high on a self-esteem test should like

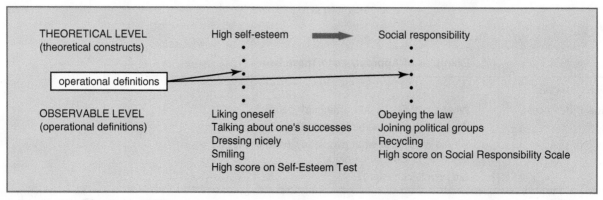

FIGURE 1.1 Levels of Thinking in Theory

themselves, talk about their successes, smile, and dress nicely; the opposite behaviors will be observable among people who score low on a self-esteem test. Furthermore, the high self-esteem people should also be observed engaging in behaviors that are observable evidences of the abstract concept of social responsibility. They should obey laws, join political groups, recycle, and score high on a test of social responsibility. People who are low in self-esteem should engage in the opposite behaviors. Clear scientific language makes explicit what we observe and what abstract theoretical ideas predict and explain those observations.

Theory

A **theory** is a conceptual tool for understanding certain specified phenomena. It includes concepts (theoretical constructs) and statements about how they are related (theoretical propositions). The concepts of a theory are called theoretical **constructs**. One kind of theoretical construct already mentioned is a personality trait. Traits are often considered to be the underlying units of personality. Examples of traits include shy, intelligent, and athletic. Because traits are assumed to remain constant and determine behavior, people are expected to behave consistently at different times and in different situations.

Traits, like all theoretical constructs, are not themselves directly observable. They are related to observable behaviors through **operational definitions**, statements identifying what observable phenomena are evidence of a particular trait. In Figure 1.1, the trait self-esteem is operationally defined to correspond to various observable behaviors: talking about successes (rather than failures), dressing nicely (rather than poorly), and scoring high on a self-esteem test (rather than scoring low). Each trait or other theoretical construct can have many different operational definitions. Because they all correspond to the same trait, we would expect these observations to be positively correlated with one another.

A theory contains various **theoretical propositions**, which tell how the constructs are related. For example, in Figure 1.1 the theoretical proposition diagrammed hypothesizes that "self-esteem causes social responsibility." Both self-esteem and social responsibility are theoretical constructs, and as such they are abstract conceptual tools that cannot be directly observed. Theoretical propositions are also abstract statements and are not themselves directly observable (cf. Clark & Paivio, 1989).

To test a theory, predictions about observable phenomena are logically derived from the theoretical propositions. Consider the example of a classic theoretical proposition in psychology that states, "Frustration leads to aggression." When this proposition is stated in terms of observable phenomena (i.e., in terms of the constructs as operationally defined), we have a **hypothesis**, which can be tested by **empirical** observation (see Figure 1.2).

Research tests whether hypotheses are confirmed by actual empirical observations. Does the abstract theoretical world accurately predict what actually takes place in the real world? The more reliably hypotheses derived from a theory are tested and confirmed by empirical research, the more confidence we have in the theory. When observations differ from prediction, the theory is disconfirmed. If this occurs often, the theory will be revised to make it more accurate, or it may even be abandoned.

Criteria of a Good Theory

Theories are always somewhat tentative. Elementary students of science know this when they differentiate between theories and facts, the latter being more definite and less arguable than theories. (Such elementary students commonly have the misconception that when we become certain of our theories, they will be considered facts. This misunderstanding stems from ignorance of the difference between the theoretical level and the level of observables presented earlier in this chapter. Facts are always at the level of observables; theories never are.) Because theories are abstract, a certain amount of ambiguity can be expected, compared to the concrete details that come as factual observations. Not all theories are equally valuable, however. How can we decide whether a theory is worthwhile?

theory
a conceptual tool, consisting of systematically organized constructs and propositions, for understanding certain specified phenomena

construct
a concept used in a theory

operational definition
procedure for measuring a theoretical construct

theoretical proposition
theoretical statement about relationships among theoretical constructs

hypothesis
a prediction to be tested by research

empirical
based on scientific observations

| THEORETICAL CONSTRUCTS: | Frustration |
| | Aggression |

| THEORETICAL PROPOSITION: | Frustration leads to aggression. |

OPERATIONAL DEFINITIONS:

Frustration	Losing 75 cents in a soda machine.
	Failing an exam.
	Losing one's job.

Aggression	Kicking the soda machine.
	Rating the instructor as "poor."
	Beating one's spouse.

HYPOTHESES:

1. Subjects who lose 75 cents in a soda machine (which is rigged by the experimenter) will kick the soda machine more often than a control group, which does not lose money.

2. Students who are told that they have failed an exam will rate their instructor lower than students who are told they have passed the exam

3. When unemployment rises, the number of reported spouse beatings will increase.

FIGURE 1.2 Hypotheses Derived from a Theoretical Proposition

Several criteria are generally accepted for evaluating scientific theories. That is not to say that individuals always base their personal theoretical preferences on these criteria. Psychology majors, for example, report that they prefer theories that help them understand themselves (Vyse, 1990). It may take effort to apply the more impersonal criteria that we discuss next, but the effort is worthwhile. These criteria guide psychology from intuitive knowledge toward a firmer scientific base.

verifiable

the ability of a theory to be tested by empirical procedures, resulting in confirmation or disconfirmation

VERIFIABILITY The most important criterion is that a theory should be **verifiable**, that is, testable through empirical methods. Theoretical constructs must be defined with precision so it is clear what is meant by the construct. The operational definitions must be clear and reliably measurable. Operational definitions may include written tests, clinical judgments, interpersonal ratings, observations of behavior, and other well-specified ways of making observations.

The theory must predict relationships among these measurements so clearly, in the form of hypotheses, that observations can be made to support or refute the prediction. If we specify what evidence would support a theory and what evidence would refute, or "falsify," it, we can use science to evaluate the theory. Philosopher of science Karl Popper (1962) elaborated on this criterion, and he criticized Freud's theory—which we will discuss in Chapter 2—as "pseudoscience" because it did not meet this criterion; however, his criticism is not without its own critics (Grünbaum, 2008). **Disconfirmation** is particularly important for advancing science. It is always possible to find supportive evidence for a vaguely formulated theory. The criterion of verifiability requires that we also identify evidence that would refute the theory.

disconfirmation

evidence against a theory; observations that contradict the predictions of a hypothesis

comprehensiveness

the ability of a theory to explain a broad variety of observations

COMPREHENSIVENESS Other things being equal, a good theory is characterized by **comprehensiveness**. That is, it explains a broad range of behavior. Most traditional personality theories are broad, comprehensive theories dealing with many phenomena: developmental processes in childhood, adaptation or mental health, self-image, social interactions with other people, biological influences, and so forth. In practice, however, if a theory attempts to explain too much, its concepts tend to become fuzzy and ill-defined so the theory cannot be tested adequately. Although comprehensiveness is a desirable characteristic in a theory, it is less important than empirical verifiability.

APPLIED VALUE   A theory that has **applied value**, offering practical strategies for improving human life, has an edge over theories that are simply intellectually satisfying. For example, personality theories may suggest therapeutic interventions, guide child care, help select the best employees for a particular job, or even predict what will happen in politics, based on the leader's personality (Immelman, 1993). As in many fields, personality psychology has both basic and applied interests that are not always integrated. **Applied research** is conducted to solve practical problems. **Basic research** is conducted for the purpose of advancing theory and scientific knowledge.

applied value
the ability of a theory to guide practical uses

applied research
research intended for practical use

basic research
research intended to develop theory

OTHER CONSIDERATIONS: PARSIMONY AND HEURISTIC VALUE   Besides the three important criteria of verifiability, comprehensiveness, and applied value, theories that are parsimonious and have heuristic value are preferred. A *parsimonious* theory is one that does not propose an excessive number of narrow constructs or propositions if a smaller number of broad constructs could explain the phenomena under consideration. To do so makes the theory unnecessarily complicated. However, humans are complex creatures, so a theory with too few constructs or propositions may be too simplistic to permit detailed prediction.

The ability of a theory to suggest new ideas for further theory and research is called its *heuristic value* or fertility (Howard, 1985). Scientific understanding is not static. Scientists build on the work of earlier scientists, moving toward an improved understanding. Just as artists replace rough sketches with more elaborate drawings, theories are replaced by their more polished successors.

Relationship between Theory and Research

Research and theory building in personality ideally go hand in hand. At the level of theory, constructs and theoretical propositions are proposed. By a process of deductive reasoning, hypotheses are derived and, through research, tested.

Theory leads to research. The converse is also true: Research leads to theory (Gigerenzer, 1991). Unexplained observations lead scientists to think inductively. They then suggest new or revised theoretical constructs and propositions. Theory without adequate research becomes stagnant. Research without adequate theory can wander aimlessly.

Scientific development of theories must advance against the complication that people are, in their everyday lives, informal personality theorists. Everyday unscientific beliefs about personality are sometimes called **implicit theories of personality**. We assume that certain phenomena that we have seen are accompanied by other personality characteristics. Attractive people, for example, are often assumed to be warm and trustworthy. Many undergraduates base sexual decisions on implicit personality theories, believing they can assess HIV status by appearance and other irrelevant factors (Williams et al., 1992).

implicit theories of personality
ideas about personality that are held by ordinary people (not based on formal theory)

Implicit personality theories are not necessarily incorrect. Physical attractiveness and interpersonal traits such as extraversion and agreeableness, for example, are correlated (Meier et al., 2010). Some researchers believe they often correspond to the formal theories that have been derived from extensive research (Sneed, McCrae, & Funder, 1998). There is no guarantee of their accuracy, though. Well-planned research studies are necessary to test, and sometimes to correct, errors emanating from implicit theories.

METHODS IN PERSONALITY RESEARCH

Throughout its history, personality research has used a variety of research methods: personality scales and questionnaires, projective techniques, observer judgments, and laboratory methods. In addition, biographical analyses and case studies permit investigations of individuals, and various biological measures, such as genetic analysis, attest to the increasing attention to biological aspects of personality.

Personality Measurement

Measurement of personality involves operationally defining theoretical constructs by specifying how they will be assessed. The most common type of measurement is the self-report personality test, which asks many questions, often in multiple-choice format, under a standard set of instructions. It is not difficult to write personality test items; you have probably seen so-called pop psychology personality tests on the Internet. However, establishing their value is more difficult. What constitutes sound measurement?

RELIABILITY   Measurement should yield consistent scores from one time to another. Such **reliability** is determined in several ways. *Test-retest reliability* is determined by testing the same subjects on two occasions and calculating the extent to which the two scores agree. Do the same people who score high on the first occasion also score high the second time? They will if the test is reliable. Could it be, though, that they simply remember how they answered the first time (even if they were guessing), which is why the scores do not change? The method of *alternate forms reliability* gets around this problem by giving different versions of the questionnaire on each occasion. What if subjects are tested only once? In this case, researchers can estimate reliability by calculating subscores based on two halves of the questionnaire. Generally, all the odd-numbered items are added together for one score and all the even-numbered items for the other score. The correlation between these two subscores is called *split-half reliability*.

    Problems of unreliability can result from several factors. Short tests are generally less reliable than longer tests. Tests combining unrelated items are less reliable than those composed of closely correlated items, or *homogeneous items*. Other factors that reduce reliability are ambiguously worded test items and uncontrolled factors in the test-taking situation that influence responses. In addition, real change can occur between the two times that the psychological characteristic is measured, although perhaps in this last case it would be better to speak of personality change rather than unreliability of measurement.

VALIDITY   Someone could claim to assess your intelligence by measuring the circumference of your head, or your morality by examining your skull for bumps in particular locations, as phrenologists once did. Undoubtedly, except in very unusual cases, these would be quite reliable measures. Yet we would not accept them. Such measures might be reliable, but they are not valid.

    Test validity is present if a test really measures what it claims to measure. Whereas reliability can be assessed straightforwardly, determining validity is more challenging. *Predictive validity* is established if a test predicts a behavior that the researcher accepts as a *criterion* for the construct being measured (e.g., if a test of assertiveness predicts the number of times a person initiates conversations). In the known groups method, a test is given to different groups of people who are known to differ in what the test measures. For example, a test of mental well-being should produce higher scores among college students than among psychiatric patients (Hattie & Cooksey, 1984). Employers use a variety of tests when they are deciding which job applicant to hire, and researchers have studied these tests to determine which have the best validity as predictors of effective employee selection. They have found that tests do improve selection over simply using employment interviews (Schmidt & Hunter, 1998). However, test validity can be reduced by several factors, including respondents' intentional distortion of responses (Furnham, 1990), their misunderstanding of test items, and their lack of knowledge or insight about the material being asked.

    Predictive validity focuses primarily on the validity of a particular test. What about the validity of the theoretical construct: **construct validity**? This question

reliability

consistency, as when a measurement is repeated at another time or by another observer, with similar results

test validity

desirable characteristic of a test, indicating it actually does measure what it is intended to measure

construct validity

the usefulness of a theoretical term, evidenced by an accumulation of research findings goes beyond measurement. If a theoretical construct is valid, it will be possible to define it operationally in a variety of ways, and we would expect these various measures to be correlated. Furthermore, the relationships of the construct with other variables, which are predicted by theory, should be similar regardless which particular measure is used. Consider this imaginary example: If a researcher finds that a new form of therapy reduces patients' anxiety when measured by a self-report but increases their anxiety when a behavioral observation is used instead, we would doubt the construct validity of anxiety. Perhaps one or both of the measures is defective. Perhaps anxiety is not the one unified combination of behavior and experience that we thought. Until compelling evidence indicates that two measures are comparable, it is best to limit our claims of validity to each measure separately, or, to use Jerome Kagan's apt phrase, "validity is local" (1990, p. 294). However, if several research studies using a variety of measures present converging lines of evidence for the usefulness of a theoretical construct—for example, if many studies using various measurement methods find that the new therapy reduces anxiety—we can make the important and bold claim that construct validity (of anxiety) has been established (Cronbach & Meehl, 1955).

MEASUREMENT TECHNIQUES   Various measurement techniques have been used in personality research. Usually, subjects are asked to provide some sorts of verbal statements that are analyzed.

Direct self-report measures ask subjects to respond to specific questions, generally in multiple-choice format. They may be either questionnaires (that measure one trait or construct) or inventories (that measure several traits or constructs, e.g., the California Personality Inventory and the Minnesota Multiphasic Personality Inventory). Self-report measures are easy to administer and often reliable, but they have disadvantages. Subjects may not have enough self-knowledge to provide accurate information. They may intentionally give false responses, or they may be influenced by response sets, such as the tendency to agree with items regardless of content.

Alternatively, personality can be measured through *indirect* methods. When people talk or write without having to pick a multiple-choice answer, many of the sources of distortion are reduced. *Open-ended questions* (e.g., "Tell me about your experiences at college") or other materials (journals, diaries, letters, etc.) can provide data for researchers to interpret (C. P. Smith, 1992). *Projective tests* present subjects with ambiguous stimuli (such as pictures or inkblots) to which they respond. The indirect approach can avoid some of the shortcomings of verbal reports. (What sort of imaginative story would you make up about an inkblot to look well adjusted, for example? It's hard to say!) The indirect approach may reveal material of which the person is unaware, and thus it avoids intentional deception and the limitations of conscious experience.

Behavioral measures are sometimes included in personality research. This type of measurement helps develop an understanding of personality in its real-world context. Observers may watch people in real life or in a laboratory, or subjects can be asked to provide information about their real-life experiences. We have to keep in mind, though, that such self-reports may not always be accurate reports of experience because of forgetting, inattention, distortion, or a variety of other reasons.

Objective measures sometimes play a role in personality research, though not generally for the measurement of personality itself. Consider the research finding that a person's anxiety level is correlated with self-reported allergies. Objective allergy tests, such as analysis of serum immunoglobulin E (IgE), find no relationship with anxiety. It seems that the self-reports were not accurate (Gregory et al., 2009).

Test scores are important data in personality research, but they can be misleading. Any test score may be inaccurate for a variety of reasons. Tests that are valid for adults may not be valid for children; tests that are valid for majority cultures may be biased when applied to minorities. Convergence across a variety of types of measures is more convincing than single method research.

Correlational Studies

correlational research

research method that examines the relationships among measurements

Correlational research, which measures two or more variables to study how they are related, is common in studies of personality. Sometimes two measures are used to operationally define a single theoretical construct; in such a case, these measures should obviously be correlated. At other times, two different theoretical constructs are predicted to be correlated because theoretical propositions describe one as causing the other (e.g., "Frustration causes aggression").

Causes and effects should be correlated; but there is no guarantee that when two variables are correlated, one is the cause and the other is the effect. Correlational research cannot provide strong proof of causation. Two observations can be correlated because one causes another, or because both are caused by a third variable. For example, suppose a correlational research study finds that two variables are associated in a study of elementary school children: number of hours of television watched (variable A) and children's aggressiveness, determined by observing behavior on the playground (variable B). What can we conclude based on this correlational research? First, it is possible that A causes B; that is, watching television increases the children's aggressive behavior. Second, it is possible that B causes A: Friends may reject aggressive children after school, and, having no one to play with, they watch television instead. Third, it is possible that another variable, C, causes both A and B, leading to their correlation without either causing the other. What might such a third variable be? Perhaps having neglectful parents causes children to watch more television (because they are not encouraged in other activities that would place more demands on their parents) and also causes them to be aggressive on the playground (because they have not been taught more mature social skills). The point is that correlational research is always ambiguous about the causes underlying the associations observed. From such a study it is not clear that aggressiveness could be reduced by limiting television, by increasing parental attention, or by changing any of the other potential causes that could account for the relationship. Causal ambiguities can be resolved through another research strategy: experimentation.

Experimentation

true experimental research

research strategy that manipulates a cause to determine its effect

independent variable

in an experiment, the cause that is manipulated by the researcher

experimental group

in an experiment, the group exposed to the experimental treatment

control group

in an experiment, the group not exposed to the experimental treatment

dependent variable

the effect in an experimental study

variable

in research, a measurement of something across various people (or times or situations), which takes on different values

In **true experimental research**, hypothesized cause–effect relationships are put to a direct test. An **independent variable**, which the researcher suspects is the cause, is manipulated by the researcher. An **experimental group** is exposed to the independent variable. A **control group** is not exposed to the independent variable. Everything else about the two groups is kept equal: their characteristics that they bring into the study, and the way they are treated during the research. The groups are formed by *random assignment* to make everything equal that they bring to the study, and care is taken to be sure that there are not extraneous uncontrolled variables that occur during the research, such as different expectancies based on knowing which group is expected to change. After the manipulation of the independent variable, the two groups are then compared to see whether they have different scores on the **dependent variable**, which is the hypothesized effect.

An experiment could be conducted for the preceding example to test whether watching a lot of television causes an increase in aggressive behavior. An experimental group would be assigned to watch a great deal of television. A control group would watch little television. Then their aggressive behavior on the playground would be observed. If watching television (the independent variable) is the cause, there will be differences between the two groups in their level of aggression (the dependent variable). If some other **variable** is the cause, the two groups will not differ in aggression, since all other variables were made equivalent between the groups by random assignment.

Logically, it is easier to imagine situations as independent variables in an experiment than personality. It is fairly easy to manipulate television viewing. In contrast, how could we manipulate aggressiveness, a personality trait, if we believe the trait of aggressiveness is the cause of aggressive behavior? Most often, this is not possible because research participants bring their personalities to the research, and all the researcher can do is measure them. Indeed, few personality studies use experimental methods (Revelle & Oehlberg, 2008). One strategy, however, is to change personality for an experimental group through some kind of situational manipulation or therapy program. Mischel (1992) and Bandura (1986b) have conducted experimental research in which situations or training interventions are manipulated to change aspects of personality and then effects on behavior are observed. Similarly, a program of research by McClelland and Winter (1969) changed businessmen's trait of "need for achievement" through a training program and found that this change brought about changes in their business activities. Experimental techniques have occasionally been used by psychoanalytically oriented researchers who have experimentally aroused unconscious material to investigate psychodynamics (e.g., Shulman & Ferguson, 1988; Silverman, 1976). Nonetheless, experimental research in personality is conducted less often than correlational research, in which personality is measured rather than manipulated.

Constructs derived from experimental research are not necessarily interchangeable with those derived from correlational research (Brogden, 1972; West, 1986). For example, a generally anxious person (with a trait of anxiety) may not be comparable to a generally calm person who is temporarily anxious because of a crisis (with a temporary *state* of anxiety).

Studying Individuals: Case Studies and Psychobiography

When researchers study individuals instead of groups, they often describe their observations in ways that remind us of people telling their life stories. These narratives are often rich in detail and imagery, and they can convey emotional insights in ways that more statistical data cannot. A **case study** is an intensive investigation of a single individual. For example, a clinician may describe an individual client (Gedo, 1999), or an educational psychologist may describe an individual child. When the focus is on theoretical considerations, case studies are called **psychobiography**. In psychobiography, the researcher often works from archival data, such as letters, books, and interviews, rather than directly interacting with the person being described.

case study
an intensive investigation of a single individual

psychobiography
the application of a personality theory to the study of an individual's life; different from a case study because of its theoretical emphasis

The analysis of individuals is occasionally prompted by practical, even political, considerations. For example, in 1943 U.S. government officials requested a psychological analysis of Adolf Hitler (Runyan, 1982), an analysis that was later published (Langer, 1972). In the early 1960s, a similar request was made for an analysis of the Soviet leader Nikita Khrushchev (Mack, 1971). When a person has died and suicide is suspected, a "psychological autopsy" may be carried out to help determine whether the case was a suicide, and if so, why it occurred (Brent, 1989; Kewman & Tate, 1998; Otto et al., 1993).

Studies of individuals using nonexperimental methods lack both the statistical advantages of large correlational studies and the advantages stemming from control of independent variables in the experimental method. Without these controls, alternate interpretations of the same material are possible (Runyan, 1981), making definitive analyses elusive. Despite the difficulties, case studies are invaluable if we are to be sure that our theoretical concepts do indeed help us understand individual personality dynamics.

William McKinley Runyan defines psychobiography as "the explicit use of formal or systematic psychology in biography" (1982, p. 233). Much psychobiography in the past has been based on psychoanalytic theory. The founder of psychoanalysis, Sigmund Freud (1910/1957), wrote the first psychobiography: a study of Leonardo da Vinci. Ironically, Freud did not follow the standards of sound psychobiography that he set out in the same work (Elms, 1988). Psychoanalysis warns that subjective factors (transference) can be a source of error in psychobiography (Schepeler, 1990). Psychoanalytic theory has been the predominant theory guiding psychobiographical analyses ever since Freud's initial effort (e.g., Baron & Pletsch, 1985; Ciardiello, 1985; Erikson, 1958; Freud & Bullitt, 1966). It has shortcomings, however. For one thing, evidence about childhood experience, which is important in psychoanalytic formulations, is often poor (Runyan, 1982). The theory often leads to overemphasizing a particular period, the "critical period fallacy," or specific life events, "eventism" (Mack, 1971). Also, psychoanalytic theory does not call attention to historical and cultural factors that influence personality (L. Stone, 1981).

Other theories have also guided psychobiography. For example, Raymond Cattell's theory has been used to analyze Martin Luther and other Reformation leaders (Wright, 1985), and Henry Murray's theory has been applied to a psychobiographical study of Richard Nixon (Winter & Carlson, 1988). Researchers have developed systematic ways to analyze existing materials, such as personal documents, diaries, letters, and dream records (Alexander, 1988, 1990; Carlson, 1981, 1988; Gruber, 1989; McAdams, 1990; Ochberg, 1988; Stewart, Franz, & Layton, 1988). Computer methods for analyzing verbal materials exist, but human judges are still essential in these narrative approaches, making such research extremely labor intensive.

ONE THEORY OR MANY? ECLECTICISM AND THE FUTURE OF PERSONALITY THEORY

eclectic

combining ideas from a variety of theories

paradigm

a basic theoretical model, shared by various theorists and researchers

Most personality psychologists prefer an **eclectic** approach, one that combines insights from many different theories. In the language of Thomas Kuhn (1970), no single **paradigm** serves as a theoretical model accepted by the entire field of personality. There are, instead, competing perspectives, including psychoanalysis, learning theory, trait approaches, and humanistic psychology. Some attempts have been made to integrate theories. For the most part, though, theories simply coexist, each developing its own theoretical and research literature. Why?

First, some of this fragmentation is related to larger divisions in psychology between what have traditionally been called the "two disciplines" (Cronbach, 1957, 1975) or "two cultures" (Kimble, 1984) of psychology. One side, which Kimble labels the *scientific culture*, emphasizes experimentation and studies groups of people (the nomothetic approach), often with respect to narrower aspects of personality. The other side, the *humanistic culture*, is more interested in individuals (the idiographic approach), especially the whole person, and is willing to compromise experimental rigor and to trust intuitive understanding. The conflict between these two cultures is illustrated by Lilienfeld's (2010) indictment of trust in intuition as one factor impeding the development of psychology as a science. Gregory Kimble (1984) undoubtedly spoke for many psychologists when he expressed pessimism about the chances for achieving an integration of the two orientations (see Table 1.3).

Second, theories may have different areas of usefulness. For example, one theory may be useful for understanding people's subjective experiences of life, another for predicting how people will behave in given situations. Some theories may help us understand the mentally ill or individuals distraught from overwhelming stress; other theories may be more useful in understanding the creative heights of those who have become highly developed. Theories developed in a middle-class North American or European context may not necessarily be valid in African or Asian cultures, nor help understand people who struggle to simply survive.

Table 1.3 Kimble's Analysis of "Scientific" versus "Humanistic" Psychology

	Scientific Culture	Humanistic Culture
Research Setting	Laboratory	Field study and case study
Generality of Laws	Nomothetic	Idiographic
Level of Analysis	Elementism	Holism
Scholarly Values	Scientific	Humanistic
Source of Knowledge	Observation	Intuition

Source: Kimble, G. A. (1984). Psychology's two cultures. *American Psychologist, 39,* 833–839. Copyright 1984 by the American Psychological Association. Adapted by permission.

Besides the different areas of application, theories specialize in different influences on personality. Some focus on early experience; others on the impact of thought; others on biological influences; and so on. Because diverse psychological processes influence individual personality, and because influences range from the biological to the social, the field of personality may always be more comprehensive than any single theory can encompass.

To be sure, it would be easy to get lost in such theoretical debates, but the subject matter of our discipline always brings us back to people. Past and current personality theories both help and hinder progress toward new theories that explain people. They help to the extent that they provide useful and heuristic concepts. They hinder to the extent that theoretical preconceptions, like implicit personality theories, blind us to new directions. How can we remove such blinders? One suggestion, to borrow advice from the British statesman Benjamin Disraeli, is to

Read…biography, for that is life without theory. (*Contarini Fleming*, pt. i, chap. 23)

Summary

- *Personality* is defined as the underlying causes within the person of individual behavior and experience.
- Three areas are addressed by personality theory: *description*, *dynamics*, and *development*.
- Personality can be described in terms of broad *types* or more numerous, and narrower, *traits*.
- Using statistical techniques, traits can be combined into personality *factors*.
- The *nomothetic approach* describes personality by making comparisons among people.
- Studies of single individuals use the *idiographic approach*.
- Personality *dynamics* refers to the motivational aspect of personality. Some theorists emphasize common motivations, which influence all people, whereas others focus on individual differences.
- Personality dynamics permit *adaptation* to the world and may be studied in terms of adjustment or mental health.
- Personality *development* in childhood and adulthood is also described by the various theories, recognizing biological and social influences on development.
- The scientific approach assumes *determinism* and makes systematic observations to test and revise theories.

- Theoretical *constructs* and *propositions* are made testable through operational definitions and hypotheses.
- Theories are evaluated according to the criteria of *verifiability*, *comprehensiveness*, and *applied value*.
- Theory and research mutually influence one another.
- Personality measurement, which should be *reliable* and *valid*, uses various techniques, including self-report measures, projective measures, measures of life experiences, and behavioral measures.
- Research techniques include *correlational* research, in which associations are examined among various measures, and *experimental* research, in which cause–effect relationships are tested by manipulating an *independent* variable to examine its effect on a *dependent variable*.
- Two methods, *case studies* and *psychobiography*, study one individual intensively. Psychobiography, in which theory is systematically used to understand one individual, can offer suggestions for theory development.
- People have informal *implicit theories* of personality with which they try to understand others.
- Personality psychologists use many *paradigms* for understanding personality. Many adopt an *eclectic* approach, whereas others seek to integrate competing theories.

Thinking about Personality Theory

1. Look again at the literary sayings at the beginning of the chapter. Discuss them in terms of the concerns of personality theory. For example, do they relate to description, dynamics, or development? Can they be verified? Can you think of any sayings about personality in addition to those quoted at the beginning of the chapter?
2. How important do you think it is for personality theory to be evaluated according to scientific criteria? Is the scientific method too limiting?
3. What implicit ideas about personality, besides those mentioned in the text, might produce bias when we think about personality?
4. Look at the preview tables for the coming chapters. Which of these theories most appeal to you? Why?

Study Questions

1. Define personality.
2. List and explain the three issues that personality theory studies.
3. Contrast types, traits, and factors as units of description in personality.
4. Explain the difference between idiographic and nomothetic approaches.
5. Explain what is meant by personality dynamics.
6. Explain the term *adaptation*.
7. Describe how cognitive processes and culture are related to personality dynamics.
8. What are some important influences on personality development?
9. Explain what is meant by temperament.
10. Describe the scientific approach to personality. Include in your answer theoretical constructs, propositions, operational definitions, and hypotheses.
11. List and explain the criteria of a good theory.
12. Discuss the relationship between theory and research.
13. Describe some ways in which personality can be measured.
14. Explain reliability and validity of measurement.
15. Explain the difference between correlational studies and experimental studies.
16. What is psychobiography? Discuss the strengths and weaknesses of this approach to understanding personality.
17. What is an implicit theory of personality? How is it different from a formal personality theory?
18. What is eclecticism? Why might someone prefer to have more than one theory?

PART 1

The Psychoanalytic Perspective

The psychoanalytic perspective on personality is one of the most widely known outside of psychology. Within psychology, it has steadfast adherents and forceful critics. The central idea of the psychoanalytic perspective is the unconscious. Simply put, this concept says that people are not aware of the most important determinants of their behavior. Self-understanding is limited and often incorrect. This concept of an unconscious gives us a way of thinking about behavior, moods, or other symptoms that seem out of touch with conscious intentions; thus it has been a valuable concept in the therapeutic setting (Piers, 1998).

All psychoanalytic approaches maintain the concept of a dynamic unconscious—that is, one that has motivations or energies and so can influence behavior and experience. Various psychoanalytic theories describe the unconscious differently. Sigmund Freud (see Chapter 2) proposed that the unconscious consists of sexual and aggressive wishes that are unacceptable to the conscious personality. For Carl Jung (see Chapter 3), the unconscious consists of more general motivations, which have spiritual content. Other theorists, including Melanie Klein (1946) and Harry Stack Sullivan (1953), have described the unconscious in terms of the self and relationships with other people, especially the mother as the first "other" the infant encounters—ideas that have influenced neoanalytic theories in Part II of this book.

Despite these variations, psychoanalysts share characteristic assumptions:

1. Personality is strongly influenced by unconscious determinants.
2. The unconscious is dynamic, or motivational, and is in conflict with other aspects of the unconscious and with consciousness.
3. Early experience is an important determinant of personality.

Psychoanalysis originated in the context of psychotherapy and clinical observation. It did not emphasize the scientific tradition of empirical research, but in recent years more effort has been made to test psychoanalytic ideas, such as repression and defense mechanisms, in controlled studies. The primary data for psychoanalysts consist of reports by patients in therapy. The fact that these inferences are not generally checked for historical accuracy with outside evidence has been the focus of considerable controversy. Psychoanalysts generally doubt that the complexities of personality, especially unconscious processes, can be measured by objective instruments. When formal measurement is used, psychoanalysts often employ projective techniques that present ambiguous stimuli, such as inkblots in the well-known Rorschach test, and ask the patients (or research subjects) to say what they see in them. Such techniques are generally less reliable than questionnaires, but their advocates claim that they provide access to deeper levels of motivation not available to conscious awareness.

Another objection is that psychoanalytic theorists have not clearly specified the types of evidence that would refute psychoanalytic theory. The theories often describe conflict between one kind of conscious motivation (e.g., self-control) and an opposite unconscious motivation (e.g., sexual freedom). Any observed behavior is consistent with the theory, simply by interpreting the observation flexibly. If a person behaves with self-control, the conscious is presumed to be the cause; if promiscuity is observed, the unconscious is said to determine this behavior. In potentially explaining every observation, psychoanalysis has weakened its scientific status. Scientifically, a theory cannot be tested if no observation is inconsistent with it. It is not verifiable, as explained in Chapter 1. Because its operational definitions are vague, empirical observations are not linked to theoretical constructs in a way that can be clearly specified in advance. Instead, intuition ("clinical insight") makes these links. Metaphorical thinking occurs where the hard-nosed scientist would prefer concrete, rigorous thinking. This criticism has been levied against psychoanalytic theory for many decades, but in recent years, research on defense mechanisms and other psychoanalytic constructs has increased, closing the gap between clinical theory and science.

Outside of psychology, psychoanalytic theory has influenced art and literature, film, and popular culture. With the decline of traditional religion and mystical thinking, psychoanalysis has, for some, become a way of contacting the irrational forces within the human personality, which is sufficiently "scientific" to be permissible today. Whether this is a legitimate function and whether psychoanalysis fulfills it adequately are matters to ponder.

Study Questions

1. What are the fundamental assumptions of the psychoanalytic perspective?
2. What objections have been raised against the psychoanalytic perspective?

2

Freud
Classical Psychoanalysis

Chapter Overview

ILLUSTRATIVE BIOGRAPHY
Adolf Hitler

Adolf Hitler was probably the most infamous tyrant of the twentieth century, perhaps of all time. This charismatic dictator was responsible for the deaths of millions of Jews and others in the extermination camps of Nazi Germany during World War II. Many biographers, often using psychoanalytic theory, have attempted to understand him. One of these analyses, commissioned by the U.S. government during the war in an attempt to learn how to overthrow Hitler, remained secret for decades (Murray, 1943).

Adolf Hitler was born in 1889 in Austria, near the German border. He aspired to be an artist but failed the entrance exam for art school, although he deceived family and friends into thinking he was a student. He earned a meager existence selling small paintings and postcards. Later he moved to Germany, which he adopted as his homeland, and where he served in the Bavarian army in World War I, although without much success. In the period of discontent following Germany's defeat in the war, he became active in politics and dreamed

Adolf Hitler

of a restoration of German glory. Elected as chancellor of Germany in 1933, he soon invaded neighboring countries; the hostilities escalated to become World War II. Far from restoring German glory, the result of Hitler's ambitions was the destruction of cities throughout Europe and the extermination of millions of Jews and other prisoners in concentration camps. In the face of defeat in May 1945, Hitler; his lover, Eva Braun; and some close associates committed suicide.

DEVELOPMENT

For Freud, childhood experience shapes personality. The conditions of physical drive satisfaction in early life determine character structure. A strong ego, capable of umpiring the forces of the unconscious, must develop gradually, protected from psychic trauma and supported by nurturant and guiding parents in areas it cannot yet master. From a Freudian perspective, the parents are credited or (more often) blamed for the child's personality. Three important stages

(continued)

(continued)

before the age of 5 shape personality. If a child's needs are met in these early years, and if there is not traumatic experience, then healthy development occurs. The third of these stages occurs from about age 3 to 5, a critical time for the development of masculinity (in boys) and a sense of morality (superego).

Hitler's abusive father and overprotective mother failed to nurture healthy development. His mother's overprotective-ness, in part a result of the death of her other children, con-tributed to what Freud termed "oral fixation," an exaggerated need for oral pleasure, evidenced by Hitler's cravings for sweets, his vegetarianism, his habit of sucking his fingers, and even his energy for public speaking, which is also an oral expression—in his case, primitive and tantrum-like, providing more evidence of its childhood basis. His father was a strict disciplinarian who frequently beat his son. When Hitler was 3 years old, he thought he saw his drunk father rape his mother, a traumatic incident because of the physical aggression and a premature exposure to adult sexuality. Hitler feared and hated his father and lacked the positive role model essential for normal development of a secure masculine identity and a moral sense (superego). Besides the abuse, Hitler's father lived apart from the family for a year when Adolf was 5, further depriving him of a male role model. Murray (1943) concludes that Hitler's love for his mother and hatred for his father constitutes a Freudian "Oedipus complex."

DESCRIPTION

Freud's theory describes people in terms of their failed or successful development through the psychosexual stages. Thus we speak of "oral characters" and "anal characters" and "phallic characters" (as explained in this chapter). Additional psychiatric labels can be applied to the seriously disturbed.

Hitler's personality is so disturbed that, although he does evidence problems at all of the first three psychosexual devel-opmental stages, he warrants a more serious label. Psychiatrist Henry Murray (1943) describes him as having all the symptoms of paranoid schizophrenia.

ADJUSTMENT

For Freud, the ego is the source of mental health and the hope of civilization. A strong ego can control impulses (id) and follow the rules of morality without being overburdened by guilt (superego). Evidence of health comes from two main areas of life: the ability to love (including sexual expression) and to work.

Hitler did not have a healthy balance between impulses (id) and conscience (superego). His ego wasn't strong enough to contain his destructive id impulses. According to the analy-sis that Henry Murray (1943) delivered to the American govern-ment, Hitler was periodically energized by impulsive outbursts from his id, whereas the superego, which in a healthy person would oppose such outbursts, was repressed. In terms of love, reports of his sexual encounters with women are replete with tales of perversity (Waite, 1977). According to Murray's (1943) report, before he came to power, several sexual incidents got Hitler into trouble and warranted a police record as a sexual per-vert. His perversions are described as masochistic (self-punishing) and anal, but their exact nature remained a government secret. Murray describes Hitler as impotent. He buoyed up his sense of self-worth by injecting himself with bull testicles and by project-ing onto women his fear of sexuality. Even the Nazi salute, a stiff

raised hand, has been described as a symbolic erect penis. Once Hitler boasted to a female visitor, "I can hold my arm like that for two solid hours. I never feel tired....I never move. My arm is like granite—rigid and unbending....That is four times as long as Goering....I marvel at my own power" (Waite, 1977, p. 49). He was, symbolically, claiming sexual potency.

COGNITION

If a person is healthy, then the world is perceived accurately. Mild disturbances may cause forgetfulness or wishful thinking, whereas serious pathology can leave a person in a fantasy world that has little resemblance to reality.

Hitler's unrealistic perception of the Jewish people is but one aspect of his distorted thought. He exhibited other delusions (false beliefs). Once, firmly believing the lottery ticket he had pur-chased would win, he responded to its failure to do so with a childish tantrum. Late in the war, he suffered delusions about the movements of fantasy troops. These false beliefs are typical of psychotics. It is possible, however, that some of his later symp-toms were caused by drugs prescribed by his doctor, reportedly made more powerful through tampering by spies. Interestingly, Henry Murray credits Hitler with skillful use of metaphor in his speeches. Metaphor, like art, can convey the primitive, nonlogical thoughts of the unconscious.

CULTURE

In Freud's theory, society restricts the individual's impulses for satisfaction of primitive drives. Learning to cope with these restrictions, by building a healthy ego, is essential to healthy development.

Hitler, however, did not learn to cope with society but rather projected his own pathology onto the external world. For Hitler, Germany, his "Motherland," symbolized his own mother (Murray, 1943), and his efforts to purify and defend her were motivated by his childhood perceptions of his family. Murray interprets Austria as symbolic of the father, so his military actions against that country are motivated by his hatred of his father. That he continued his delusional projections for so long without being institutionalized for mental illness is evidence that his projections resonated with the German people (Murray, 1943). Hitler echoed and amplified the anti-Semitic feelings of his era, and the Jewish people became projective targets for repressed characteristics. Some biographers have argued that Hitler's own grandfather was Jewish and denial of this ancestry intensified his persecu-tion of the Jewish people. Loewenberg (1988) suggests that Hitler was aware "the real enemy lay within" (p. 143); perhaps Hitler's projection of evil onto Jews was not entirely unconscious but rather a political strategy. Anti-Semitism was not unique to Hitler; it contributed to his popularity as a charismatic leader. Indeed, whenever the citizenry of a country feel frustrated (as the German people did because of the oppressive political conditions imposed on Germany after World War I), they are likely to elevate a leader who gives expression to their unresolved conflicts.

BIOLOGY

Freud turned to biology as the source of human motivation, pro-viding the energy that motivates behavior. Through development, this energy is transformed from its primitive urges (oral, anal, and phallic) to simply fulfill bodily functions, and it takes forms that are expressed in mature relationships and activities. In maladjusted people, impulses remain stuck in their primitive forms. The instinctual energy can be categorized as that which affirms life and love (*eros*) and that which propels toward aggression and death (*thanatos*).

The mass murders of the Holocaust give evidence of a greater measure of death instinct than life instinct. Hitler's difficulty with sexual love confirms this interpretation. His body was also inferior (a point that would be of even greater interest to one of Freud's followers, Alfred Adler). Hitler is famous for his single testicle, which, combined with a frail and effeminate body (Murray, 1943), accentuated his conflict over masculinity. In Freud's theory, the biological urges of an infant and toddler should be transformed into adult sexual expressions, but Hitler's masochistic anal sexual perversions are evidence that he was stuck with childish drives throughout adulthood, impotent and incapable of normal adult sexual behavior (according to Murray, 1943). His rhetoric about race and the importance of a pure Aryan gene pool stands in stark contrast to his own biological shortcomings.

FINAL THOUGHTS

The topic of many psychobiographical books, Hitler's personality is so disturbed that it shocks us even in the next millennium. We may analyze him from the perspective of personality theory, but the magnification of his pathology on the pages of history requires an historical understanding.

PREVIEW: OVERVIEW OF FREUD'S THEORY

Freud's theory has implications for major theoretical questions, as presented in Table 2.1. From a scientific point of view, this theory suffers from vague operational definitions that make it difficult to verify. However, recent research has tested some psychoanalytic propositions, as studies described in this chapter illustrate. Although the theory is in some ways comprehensive, including artistic productions and other symbolism, it is limited because of its limited focus on early life within the family, neglecting many environmental and social influences. Its applied value focuses particularly on psychotherapy and implications for childrearing.

Probably no theory of personality is as widely known or as frequently criticized as that proposed by Sigmund Freud. Freud compared his theory to those of Copernicus, who claimed that humans do not live at the center of the universe, and of Darwin, who discredited the idea that humans are a separately created species. Humanity was further humbled by Freud's (1925/1958, p. 5) assertion that reason does not rule behavior. He proposed that unconscious psychological forces powerfully affect human thought and behavior. These forces originate in childhood and continue their influence throughout life. Freud portrayed humans as driven by instincts that "in themselves are neither good nor evil" (p. 213) but have both kinds of effects, not only

Table 2.1 Preview of Freud's Theory	
Individual Differences	People differ in their ego defense mechanisms, which control expression of primitive forces in personality.
Adaptation and Adjustment	Mental health involves the ability to love and to work. Psychoanalysis provides a method for overcoming unconscious psychological conflict.
Cognitive Processes	Conscious experience often cannot be trusted because of distortions produced by unconscious defense mechanisms.
Culture	All societies deal with universal human conflicts and lead to repression of individual desires. Traditional religion is challenged as a shared defense mechanism.
Biological Influences	Psychiatric symptoms are explained in psychodynamic terms, instead of in biological terms. Biological drives, in particular sexual motivation, provide the basis of personality. Hereditary differences may influence level of sexual drive (libido) and phenomena such as homosexuality.
Development	Experience in the first 5 years is critical for personality formation. The oral, anal, and phallic (Oedipal) psychosexual conflicts are central. Adult personality changes very little.

Sigmund Freud

fueling the positive achievements of culture but also leading to war, crime, mental illness, and other human woes. Psychoanalytic theory has transformed our understanding of sex and aggression and has led people in the post–Freudian era never to quite trust their conscious experience.

Biography of Sigmund Freud

Sigmund Freud was born in 1856 into a Jewish family in predominantly Catholic Freiberg, Moravia (now part of the Czech Republic). By the time he was 4 years old, his family moved to Vienna, which remained his home until near his death.

Freud was one of eight children, including two older half brothers by his father's first marriage. Sigmund was the oldest and by all accounts the favorite of his mother. She expected him to be great, gave him the only oil lamp in the house, and did not permit his sister to disturb him by practicing the piano when he was studying. His father was a strict authority figure within the family.

Freud studied medicine at the University of Vienna, specializing in neurology. He intended to become an academician and had published five research studies by the age of 26. Realistically, though, academic medicine did not pay well, and discrimination against Jews made it unlikely that he would achieve a high position. Thus Freud turned to private practice as a clinical neurologist, and soon married his fiancée of 4 years, Martha Bernays. The union produced five children, including a daughter, Anna, who followed her father's footsteps as a psychoanalyst.

In his practice, Freud saw a variety of psychiatric patients, including many diagnosed as suffering from hysteria, a psychological disorder that produces physical symptoms without physical damage to the body. He developed new ways of thinking about these disorders, formulating the theory of psychoanalysis. His explorations were also turned to an understanding of his own symptoms; for example, he suffered a fear of travel and especially of flying, interpreted by one commentator (Scherr, 2001) as evidence that Freud feared women and sexuality, despite his psychoanalytic sophistication. His reputation grew beyond Vienna. He was well received in the United States, especially after his lecture series in 1909 at Clark University in Massachusetts. His theory was controversial because of its emphasis on childhood sexuality. It was also criticized as a Jewish science, dealing with psychiatric disturbances, then thought to affect Jews particularly. Undoubtedly, the anti-Semitism of his society greatly influenced both Freud and his patients (Blum, 1994). The Nazis burned the works of Freud and other Jews in 1933, and they raided his house in Vienna frequently in the years prior to World War II. Freud's personal health was failing at this time; he had cancer of the mouth, aggravated by his addiction to cigars. He finally fled Vienna in 1938, at the age of 82, and went to London, where he died in 1939.

FREUD'S THEORY IN HIS TIME, AND OURS

Before we delve into the details of Freud's theory, which strikes many modern readers as far-fetched, let's try to understand the assumptions about science in his time that shaped and constrained his thinking. First, he was trained as a medical doctor, so the search for biological causes was fundamental to his approach to mental dysfunction. Second, the broader understanding of science in his day was quite limited by modern standards. Physicists had not yet formulated understanding of the relationship between matter and energy, so Newton's assumption that matter was stable unless energy was applied to it became a metaphor for Freud's assumption that the psyche needed some kind of energy (Freud would call it "libido") to explain its dynamics. Finally, although heredity was recognized, Darwinian ideas of evolution had not been developed. So Freud's efforts to develop a scientific understanding of the psyche were based upon what we now see as an outdated metaphor from physics, a primitive understanding of the nervous system, and blindness to the possibility that some of the phenomena that he explained in terms of individual experience, such as repression, might in fact be part of our DNA. As we explore Freud's theory, let us not be too quick to judge it by modern standards.

THE UNCONSCIOUS

When people are asked why they did something, they usually can answer without much difficulty. Freud suggested that our explanations are often wrong. The most important determinants of behavior are not available to our conscious thought.

Psychic Determinism

At first, Freud looked for physical causes of psychiatric disorders. As a neurologist, he knew that damage to the brain and neurons could cause individuals to behave in strange ways, including physical symptoms, such as loss of sensation (anesthesia) or loss of motion (paralysis), and emotional symptoms, such as anxiety and depression. For some patients, though, physical causes could not be found. Forces outside of mainstream medicine were already preparing the way for another, psychodynamic approach (Ellenberger, 1970). Popular healers treated physical and psychological disorders by the laying on of hands and by "animal magnetism." In a Paris hospital where Freud studied for 4 months, he observed Jean-Martin Charcot induce psychiatric symptoms through hypnosis. Later, Josef Breuer discovered that a patient who recalled earlier memories while in a hypnotic trance was relieved of her symptoms. Breuer and Freud (1895/1955) published the case history of this woman, known as "Anna O.," to document the importance of catharsis in therapy.

These evidences of hypnosis converted Freud from the purely physical model of psychiatric disorder to "dynamic" (psychological) psychiatry (Ellenberger, 1970). Freud became convinced that unconscious forces have the power to influence behavior, an assumption called psychic determinism. At first, Freud (1895/1966b) tried to understand how psychic factors, such as traumatic events, produce physical changes in the nervous system, and then anxiety symptoms in later life. But these proposed physical changes could not be observed, so Freud turned to less direct investigative methods through the analysis of clinical material, an accepted approach within neurology, where nerve damage is often diagnosed on the basis of behavioral symptoms such as paralysis and pain. As his theory developed, Freud turned away from neurology, which rests on a physical model of human behavior, and founded a new science, based on mental causes (Sulloway, 1979). He named this new science **psychoanalysis**.

psychoanalysis
Freud's theory and its application in therapy

Levels of Consciousness

Some of our thoughts are easily known, and it may seem that that is all there is to our minds. Freud disagreed. He postulated three levels of consciousness and compared the mind to an iceberg floating in the water. Like an iceberg, only a small part of the mind is readily seen: the **conscious** mind. Just at the water's surface, sometimes visible and sometimes submerged, is the **preconscious** mind. Finally, most of the mind is hidden, like the bulk of an iceberg that is under water: the **unconscious** mind. Great dangers lurk in what is not seen.

conscious
aware; cognizant; mental processes of which a person is aware

preconscious
mental content of which a person is currently unaware but that can readily be made conscious

unconscious
mental processes of which a person is unaware

THE CONSCIOUS   The *conscious* level refers to experiences of which a person is aware, including memories and intentional actions. Consciousness functions in realistic ways, according to the rules of space and time. We identify with it.

THE PRECONSCIOUS   Some material that is not in awareness at a particular time can be brought to awareness readily; this material is called *preconscious*. It includes information that is not at the moment being thought about but can be easily remembered if needed—for example, your mother's middle name. The content of the preconscious is not fundamentally different from that of consciousness. Thoughts move readily from one to the other.

THE UNCONSCIOUS   The third level of consciousness is different. Its contents do not readily move into consciousness. The *unconscious* refers to mental processes of which a person is not aware. Such material remains in the unconscious because making it conscious would produce too much anxiety. This material is repressed; that is, it resists becoming conscious.

The unconscious includes forgotten traumatic memories and denied wishes. A child who has been sexually abused, for example, often represses this memory, having amnesia for the terrifying event. This protects the victim from the anxiety that would come from remembering traumatic experiences. Desires also may cause anxiety and be repressed if we are ashamed of what we wish. For example, a child may wish that a younger sibling were dead, so there would be no competition for the love of the parents. The unconscious becomes, in effect, the garbage pile of what consciousness throws away. It is emotionally upsetting and less civilized than consciousness.

A comment is in order about wording: What is the difference between "unconscious" and "nonconscious"? In this book, we use the term *unconscious* to refer to the unconscious or, literally, "unknown" (*Unbewusst*) as Freud used it: a dynamic unconscious, that is, one with forces that produce symptoms and motivation. A broader term, referring to everything of which we are unaware, is *nonconscious*. For example, we might say that people breathe and walk "nonconsciously" without implying any Freudian repression.

Effects of Unconscious Motivation

Behavior is determined by a combination of conscious and unconscious forces. These may act together smoothly so a person's actions appear comprehensible and rational, as though consciousness alone determined behavior. Alternatively, unconscious forces may interfere with conscious intentions. This conflict produces irrational thoughts and behavior.

conversion hysteria

form of neurosis in which psychological conflicts are expressed in physical symptoms (without actual physical damage)

PHYSICAL SYMPTOMS   Many of Freud's patients had physical symptoms for which no organic cause could be found. Influenced by his study of hypnosis under Charcot, Freud argued that cases of **conversion hysteria** represent the impact of unconscious forces on the body to produce physical symptoms of paralysis, mutism, deafness, blindness, tics, or other maladies that resemble physical diseases but occur in physically normal, undamaged bodies (Breuer & Freud, 1895/1955). The diagnosis is less often made today (M. M. Jones, 1980), and its appearance is influenced by beliefs about disease, which vary across time and culture (Fabrega, 1990).

One particularly striking example of conversion hysteria is *glove anesthesia,* in which a patient has no sensation of touch or pain on the hand in the area a glove would cover. Sensation on the arm above the wrist is normal. No pattern of damaged neurons could produce this disorder because nerves that serve the hand also extend to the forearm. So why does it occur? Freud argued that glove anesthesia is produced by psychological forces. A patient thinks of the hand as a unit and the arm a separate unit. A person who is very anxious about what the hand might feel or do might develop a symptom of glove anesthesia.

HYPNOSIS   In hypnosis, an individual experiences a highly suggestible state, a *trance,* in which the suggestions of a hypnotist strongly influence what is experienced or recalled. The hypnotist may suggest that the subject's arm will rise in the air automatically, without the subject intending it, or that the subject will be unable to do something that is usually easy to do, like bending an arm. Suggestions can also alter perceptions, causing subjects to see things that are not there, to not see things that are there, or to not feel pain.

Therapeutic benefits can occur from *posthypnotic suggestion,* in which the hypnotist suggests that a particular action or experience (sensation) will occur when the hypnotic trance ends. A hypnotist may suggest that a subject will feel a choking sensation when puffing a cigarette; after the trance is ended, the person can more easily quit smoking (Spanos et al., 1992–1993). Hypnosis is used to treat anxiety, asthma, skin diseases (psoriasis and warts), nausea, bulimia and anorexia nervosa, and other diseases (Frankel, 1987). It provides relief from headaches and other types of pain (Bowers, 1994; Kraft, 1992; Patterson et al., 1992; Primavera & Kaiser, 1992). Hypnosis can even reduce the length of hospitalization after surgery (Blankfield, 1991). Overall, research confirms that adding hypnosis to other forms of therapy improves treatment outcomes (Kirsch & Lynn, 1995; Kirsch, Montgomery, & Sapirstein, 1995).

Hypnosis remains a controversial phenomenon. According to Ernest Hilgard's *neodissociation theory* (1976, 1994), hypnosis is a state of consciousness that is dissociated from normal experience. That is, consciousness is divided into two (or more) simultaneous parts, and a barrier between them produces amnesia. As a result of this barrier, the part that acts out a hypnotic suggestion will not recall what happened when the person was in the other state of consciousness that received the suggestion from the hypnotist (Kirsch & Lynn, 1998).

Others have questioned Hilgard's proposed separate state of consciousness (cf. Kirsch & Lynn, 1998; Orne, 1959, 1971; Stava & Jaffa, 1988), arguing that social factors such as expectation must be considered to understand hypnosis and other alleged dissociative states such as multiple personality disorder (Spanos, 1994). Hypnotized subjects often behave similarly to people who are not hypnotized but are instructed to act as though they had been, raising the possibility that hypnosis could simply be a well-played role, not a separate state of consciousness. Furthermore, brain waves and other physiological measurements are not different under hypnosis than in normal consciousness (Silverstein, 1993).

Many phenomena reported under hypnosis could result from a desire to comply with the requests of the hypnotist (Orne, 1959, 1971; Spanos et al., 1993). For example, when researchers hypnotized experimental subjects and gave them a hypnotic suggestion for deafness, the subjects judged auditory tones to be less loud than when they were not hypnotized. If they were hooked up to a bogus pipeline apparatus that purportedly served as a sort of lie detector, subjects reported the tones more accurately (Perlini, Haley, & Buczel, 1998). Research such as this clearly shows that hypnotic reports are influenced by suggestion and that hypnotized subjects bias their reports to fit what they believe is expected of them. Such bias can produce errors in hypnotically recalled memories (Kihlstrom, 1994, 1995; Lindsay & Read, 1995; Lynn et al., 1997; Nash, 1987; Steblay & Bothwell, 1994; Yapko, 1994).

PSYCHOSIS   An extreme form of mental disorder is termed a *psychosis*. Psychotics lose touch with reality and experience the unconscious in raw form through hallucinations, seeing and hearing things that are not actually present. The irrationality of psychotic behavior, said Freud, reflects the underlying irrationality of the unconscious.

DREAMS   Freud praised dreams as "the royal road to the unconscious." In waking life, conscious forces control the unacceptable forces of the unconscious. During sleep, the restraints of consciousness are relaxed, and the unconscious threatens to break into awareness. This triggers anxiety, which threatens to awaken the dreamer. Sleep is protected by disguising the unconscious into a less threatening symbolic form in a dream.

Usually, a dream disguises the fulfillment of a repressed wish (S. Freud, 1900/1953). Consider this dream of a young man:

> I was on a beach with my girl and other friends. We had been swimming and were sitting on the beach. My girl was afraid that she would lose her pocketbook and kept saying that she felt certain she would lose it on the beach. (Hall, 1966, pp. 57–58)

The recalled dream (here, the story of the beach and the pocketbook) is termed the **manifest content** of the dream. *Dream interpretation* is the process of inferring the unconscious wishes disguised in the dream. Its hidden meaning, revealed by interpreting the dream symbols, is termed the **latent content** of the dream. A pocketbook is a Freudian symbol for female genitals, so the dream symbolizes the dreamer's wish that his girlfriend would lose her virginity on the beach.

manifest content
the surface meaning of a dream

latent content
the hidden, unconscious meaning of a dream

Although dreams respond to life's events, they do not do so in a clear and obvious way. To understand the meaning of dreams, it is necessary to follow the dreamer's associations to see where they lead. Freud, for example, asked an American woman who had written him a letter about a troubling dream to tell what the name "Mildred Dowl" meant. In the dream, the woman's romantic partner had sent her a cruel note saying he had married Miss Mildred Dowl, and she had (in the dream) stabbed herself in despair. As Freud said, without knowing the source of the name, only a limited interpretation of the dream was possible (Benjamin & Dixon, 1996).

People whose personality tests indicate they are repressors report dreams with relatively high levels of aggression, which supports the interpretation that dreams express what is repressed in waking life (Bell & Cook, 1998). Psychoanalysts emphasize the importance of dreams as ways of dealing with emotions, such as the anxiety and guilt that may follow traumatic events (Hartmann, 1998; Hartmann et al., 2001). Alternatives to Freud's model of dream interpretation have been developed by Carl Jung (see Chapter 3) and others (e.g., Blagrove, 1993; Hermans, 1987). One suggestion is that dreams function to promote attachment relationships (about which we say more in Chapter 6), for example by promoting mother–infant relationships and sexual pair bonding (Zborowski & McNamara, 1998).

Dreams have also been investigated from a biological viewpoint. During dream sleep, there is a shift from thinking to hallucination-like experiences, which brain researchers suggest comes from a different neurotransmitter pathway in the brain (Fosse, Stickgold, & Hobson, 2001). Dreams occur when lower brain centers stimulate activity in higher cortical areas (Hobson, 1988; Hobson & McCarley, 1977; Reiser, 2001). Although some influential neuroscientists deny that dreams have any significance (Crick & Mitchison, 1986), others suggest that physical and psychological explanations can coexist. Dreams could be expressions of a more primitive, emotional-narrative mode of functioning that has only been partially displaced by the development of higher human consciousness.

The characteristics of dream work that Freud described (condensation, displacement, and symbolism) represent the functioning of the unconscious more generally. Freud understood not only dreams and psychosis but also aspects of everyday normal behavior as results of unconscious motivation.

THE PSYCHOPATHOLOGY OF EVERYDAY LIFE   Freud described the impact of the unconscious in a wide range of behaviors of normal people. He termed such phenomena, in German, *Fehlleistungen*, which could be translated, according to Strachey (S. Freud, 1933/1966a, p. 25), as "faulty acts" or "faulty functions." We generally refer to them as **Freudian slips**, or "the psychopathology of everyday life."

Freudian slip

a psychologically motivated error in speech, hearing, behavior, and so forth (e.g., forgetting the birthday of a disliked relative)

One common Freudian slip is a misstatement, or slip of the tongue. For example, in parting from a boring party, one might say, "I'm so glad I have to leave now," intending to say, "I'm so sorry I have to leave now." The unconscious tells the truth, lacking the tact of consciousness. Other Freudian slips include errors of memory (e.g., forgetting the birthday of a disliked relative), errors of hearing, losing or misplacing objects, and errors of action. In 1935 Alfred Stieglitz wrote letters to his wife, Georgia O'Keeffe, and to his lover, Dorothy Norman, but he placed each letter into the wrong envelope so his wife received the letter intended for his lover (Lisle, 1980, p. 227). Was this merely an error, or did Stieglitz unconsciously wish to confront his wife with his other relationship? Such so-called accidents, to a Freudian, are motivated by unconscious wishes. Psychic determinism holds us strictly accountable for all our actions. An alternative cognitive explanation, however, holds that such slips result when actions become sufficiently automated that conscious control is not required, opening the possibility of feedback errors in the control of behavior (Heckhausen & Beckmann, 1990).

HUMOR   Freud (1916/1963b) described humor as a safe expression of repressed conflict, deriving its pleasure from the release of tension through a joke. We laugh at jokes if they express issues or conflicts that are unconsciously important but consciously unacceptable. A bigot, for example, finds racial jokes particularly amusing. Freud gave many examples of jokes in his writing. One that survives translation from the German is the following:

> Two Jews met in the neighborhood of the bath-house. "Have you taken a bath?" asked one of them. "What?" asked the other in return, "is there one missing?" (S. Freud, 1916/1963b, p. 49)

Like a dream, the joke is terse. Both dreams and humor often use the technique of **condensation**, in which two or more images are combined to form an image that merges the meanings and impulses of both. The humor of this joke is achieved by the double meaning of the word *taken*, providing a way of expressing the anti-Semitic attitude (or impulse) that Jews are thieves rather than clean. Because the anti-Semitism is indirect, the joke may be acceptable to those who would not consciously accept anti-Semitism. A research study supports the idea that humor makes prejudice acceptable, finding that sexist social interactions are more acceptable when they are presented as jokes (Ford, 2000). Political cartoons, too, often illustrate condensation; for example, cartoons of Italian dictator Mussolini with his arms drawn like the tentacles of an octopus graphically depict his power grabbing (Mascha, 2008).

condensation

combining of two or more images; characteristic of primary processes (e.g., in dreams)

PROJECTIVE TESTS   Both clinicians and researchers seek a method for revealing unconscious material on their request so they may diagnose individuals and test psychoanalytic hypotheses. For this purpose, they have developed **projective tests**. Among the most widely used projective tests are the Rorschach inkblot method and the Thematic Apperception Test (TAT), each of which can be scored in a variety of ways (Bornstein & Masling, 2005; Butcher & Rouse, 1996). Most (nonprojective) tests ask explicit questions. For example, a test may ask, "Do you feel happy most of the time?" In contrast, a projective test presents the client or research subject with an ambiguous stimulus, such as an inkblot or a picture, and gives only minimal directions for responding. "What do you see in this inkblot?" "Tell me a story about this picture." Responses reveal unconscious material, unknown even to the respondent. A person may tell a story that describes weeping and grief, despite having claimed to be happy.

projective test

a test that presents ambiguous stimuli such as inkblots or pictures, so responses will be determined by the test taker's unconscious

Sometimes the story told to a projective stimulus almost speaks for itself. Consider a man shown a picture of a boy with a violin, whose story included this: "Up on my wall there is a picture of a boy staring at a violin. I stare at my violin too and think and dream of one day playing the violin. On the table stretched out *like a dead corpse* is a music book" (Pam & Rivera, 1995; italics added). The evaluators, who had much more extensive information than this, concluded that the young man was seriously disturbed and potentially dangerous, perhaps suicidal, and recommended long-term hospitalization. Perhaps you agree; after all, not many people compare music books with corpses.

Researchers have used projective tests to investigate motives for achievement, affiliation and intimacy, power, and other social motives—not described by Freud, but theorized to be unconscious. These unconscious (implicit) motives are not correlated with people's consciously known (explicit) motives, and the unconscious measures are better predictors of various behaviors, including entrepreneurial business activity (McClelland, Koestner, & Weinberger, 1989; Winter et al., 1998).

Origin and Nature of the Unconscious

Where does this powerful, pervasive unconscious come from? Freud asserted that it was created primarily by childhood experience, through the mechanism of **repression**. According to Freud's hedonic hypothesis, people seek pleasure and avoid pain—a simple idea that occurs in many psychological theories (Higgins, 1997). In Freud's theory, impulses for pleasure often are accompanied by painful thoughts because pleasure would violate the moral restrictions we have learned. Repression is a mechanism for removing unpleasant thoughts, including unacceptable impulses, from consciousness, thus avoiding anxiety.

repression

basic defense mechanism that keeps threatening material in the unconscious, to avoid anxiety

STRUCTURES OF THE PERSONALITY

To state more clearly the tension between the unconscious, which seeks expression, and consciousness, which tries to hold back unconscious forces, Freud described three structures of personality. The **id** is the primitive and unconscious source of biological drives. The **ego** is the rational and coping part of personality, the most conscious and most mature structure (although not entirely conscious). The **superego** consists of the rules and ideals of society that have become internalized by the individual. Some of the superego is conscious, but much of it remains unconscious.

Each structure serves a different function. In the metaphor of Freud's day, the ego

> is like a man on horseback, who has to hold in check the superior strength of the horse.... Often a rider, if he is not to be parted from his horse, is obliged to guide it where it wants to go; so in the same way the ego is in the habit of transforming the id's will into action as if it were its own. (S. Freud, 1923/1962b, p. 15)

Like Freud's horseback rider, the ego may seem to be steering more than it truly is.

The Id

The *id* contains instinctive drives and is the only structure of personality present at birth. It functions according to the **pleasure principle**. It is hedonistic and aims to satisfy its urges, which reduces tension and thus brings pleasure.

PSYCHIC ENERGY: LIBIDO   Freud proposed that the id is the source of psychic energy, called **libido**, which is sexual. Motivation for all aspects of personality is derived from this instinctive energy, which must be transformed through socialization to energize other achievements, such as works of art, politics, education, and work. Conversely, repression ties up energy, making it unavailable for higher achievements.

LIFE AND DEATH INSTINCTS: EROS AND THANATOS   Psychic energy is of two kinds. **Eros**, the "life instinct," motivates life-maintaining behaviors and love. **Thanatos**, the "death instinct," is a destructive force directing us inevitably toward death, the ultimate release from the tension of living. It motivates all kinds of aggression, including war and suicide. Most often, Freud emphasized erotic, sexual energy and conflict over its expression. Death and conflict about it, according to some theorists, should receive more attention (Arndt et al., 1997; Becker, 1973).

CHARACTERISTICS OF INSTINCTS   Because Freud understood all personality functioning as derived from instinctive energy, knowing the fundamental principles regulating instincts provides a basic framework for understanding personality. These can be summarized as four basic aspects of instincts: source, pressure, aim, and object.

1. *Source*. All psychic energy originates as biological processes in some part of the body. The amount of energy does not change throughout a lifetime. At first, psychic energy is directed toward biological needs. Later, it can be redirected into other investments, such as interpersonal relationships and work.

2. *Pressure*. The pressure of an instinct refers to its force or motivational quality. It corresponds to the momentary strength of the instinctual drive; it is high when the drive is not satisfied and falls when the need is met. For example, a hungry infant has a high pressure of the hunger drive; one just fed has hunger at a low pressure. When the pressure is low, the instinct may not have noticeable effects; but when the pressure is high, it may break through, interrupting other activities. A hungry baby wakes up, for example.

3. *Aim*. Instincts function according to a principle of homeostasis, or steady state, a principle borrowed from biology. Instincts aim to preserve the ideal steady

---

id

the most primitive structure of personality; the source of psychic energy

ego

the most mature structure of personality; mediates intrapsychic conflict and copes with the external world

superego

structure of personality that is the internal voice of parental and societal restrictions

pleasure principle

the id's motivation to seek pleasure and to avoid pain

libido

psychic energy, derived from sexuality

Eros

the life instinct

Thanatos

the death instinct

state for the organism. Deviations from this state are experienced as tension. The aim of all instincts is to reduce tension, which is pleasurable. (Think of the good feeling of eating when you are hungry.) Instincts operate according to what Freud called the *pleasure principle*; they aim simply to produce pleasure by reducing tension, immediately and without regard to reality constraints. A chronic deviation from a restful homeostatic state occurs in individuals who have not found ways to reduce tension, such as neurotics.

Tension reduction occurs when the original biological instinct is directly satisfied—for example, when a hungry infant is fed or when a sexually aroused adult achieves orgasm. Some transformations of libido also allow tension reduction. An artist may experience tension reduction when a creative problem is solved. In his filmmaking, Charlie Chaplin (1964) stated,

> The solution [to a creative problem] would suddenly reveal itself, as if a layer of dust had been swept off a marble floor—there it was, the beautiful mosaic I had been looking for. *Tension was gone.* (p. 188; emphasis added)

4. *Object.* The object of an instinct is the person or thing in the world that is desired so the instinct can be satisfied. For example, the object of the hunger drive of an infant is the mother's breast: It brings satisfaction. The object of a sexually aroused adult is a sexual partner.

What kind of partner? It is with respect to the object of an instinct that experience matters. Some sexually aroused men look for a woman just like Mother; others look for a very different kind of woman or for a man, or even for clothing or a child or any of a vast assortment of sexual objects. Women, of course, also vary widely in their choice of sexual objects. The fact that libido is capable of being directed toward so many diverse objects, not fixed biologically, is termed the *plasticity* of the instinct. This plasticity is much greater in humans than in lower animals, who seem to come with instincts prewired to very specific objects.

PRIMITIVE FUNCTIONING: PRIMARY PROCESS   The id functions according to the purely instinctive **primary process**. Primary process is as blind and inflexible as the instinctive impulses that draw a moth to a candle flame, and its consequences can be as deadly. Primary process ignores time, recognizing no past and no future, only the present moment. It demands immediate gratification; it cannot wait or plan. If reality does not satisfy its urges, it may resort to hallucinatory wish fulfillment, that is, simply imagine that its needs are met. As a sexually aroused dreamer conjures up a lover, a psychotic individual might hallucinate a boat in a stormy sea. This, of course, is not adaptive in the real world.

primary process
unconscious mental functioning in which the id predominates; characterized by illogical, symbolic thought

Simple organisms in natural environments may be able to function quite well with only their biological drives (or id) operating according to the primary process. Humans, however, must adapt to a complex social environment, and the id, functioning according to primary process and blind instinct, cannot adapt or learn. It is the ego that can profit from experience.

The Ego

The ego resolves conflict and operates according to the **reality principle**, adapting to the constraints of the real world. The ego can delay gratification and plan. These abilities are termed **secondary process**.

reality principle
the ego's mode of functioning in which there is appropriate contact with the external world

Mental health requires a strong ego, one that can find acceptable ways to satisfy the id's demands, defending against anxiety while allowing the individual to thrive in the real external world. A weak ego may not adequately defend against anxiety, or it may require a person to behave in rigid ways to avoid anxiety. The ego uses *defense mechanisms* (discussed below) to adapt to reality. If the ego breaks down altogether, a psychotic episode occurs.

secondary process
conscious mental functioning in which the ego predominates; characterized by logical thought

The Superego

The *superego* is the internal representative of the rules and restrictions of family and society. Freud regarded it as the civilizing force that tames our savage nature (Frank, 1999). It generates guilt when we act contrary to its rules. In addition, the superego presents us with an *ego ideal*, which is an image of what we would like to be, our internal standards. But the superego is something of a tyrant.

Because the superego develops at a young age, it represents an immature and rigid form of morality. Our guilt is often out of touch with current reality, representing the immature understandings of a young child. Anna Freud (1935) illustrates the archaic nature of the superego with the case of a man who, as a child, stole sweets. He was taught not to do so and internalized the prohibition in his superego. As an adolescent, he blushed with guilt every time he ate sweets, even though they were no longer forbidden (p. 97). The superego failed to adapt to the adult situation.

Sigmund Freud dismissed much religion as similarly immature. For Freud, mature ethics are not achieved through the superego but rather through the ego, the only structure of personality that adapts to current reality. It may be helpful to think of the superego an early version of the ego, developing in childhood but not continuing to mature (as the ego does), limited to a child's comprehension.

INTRAPSYCHIC CONFLICT

intrapsychic conflict

conflict within the personality, as between id desires and superego restrictions

The id, ego, and superego do not coexist peacefully. The id demands immediate satisfaction of drives, whereas the superego threatens guilt if any pleasurable satisfaction of immoral impulses is attempted. Thus there is **intrapsychic conflict**. The ego tries to repress unacceptable desires, but it does not always succeed. The ego must use more advanced strategies than simple repression in order to reconcile the conflicting demands of the id and superego while at the same time taking into account external reality with its limited opportunities for drive satisfaction.

Energy Hypothesis

Freud proposed that personality has only a limited amount of energy. What is used for one purpose is unavailable for other purposes, so if energy is tied up in repression, there is less energy available for dealing with current reality. The repressed materials have energy, and this energy tries to return the repressed material to consciousness. Like an ice cube that is pushed under the surface of the water, it keeps bobbing up again, requiring energy to keep it down.

Although the energy hypothesis is a metaphor from outdated nineteenth-century physics, it aptly describes the exhaustion that can come from unresolved psychological stress or from the ego's need to direct activities (the "executive function of the ego," in Freud's language). Muraven, Tice, and Baumeister (1998) report that requiring experimental subjects to suppress their thoughts (about a white bear) or emotions led to impaired performance on a variety of experimental tasks (such as squeezing a handgrip and solving anagrams), as though their energy had been depleted by the effort of self-regulation. In another study, they found that experimental subjects gave up sooner when trying to solve problems if they had earlier forced themselves to eat radishes instead of chocolates—a choice that seems to have depleted their ego of energy (Baumeister et al., 1998). Emotional suppression impairs performance in laboratory tasks and in life.

Anxiety

Anxiety signals that the ego may fail in its task of adapting to reality and maintaining an integrated personality. *Neurotic anxiety* signals that id impulses may break through (overcome repression) and be expressed. A person who does not accept sexual desires would suffer from neurotic anxiety when aroused. *Moral anxiety* indicates fear that one's own superego will respond with guilt. *Reality anxiety* indicates that the external world threatens real danger.

Defense Mechanisms

Signaled by anxiety, the ego uses various strategies to resolve intrapsychic conflict. These **defense mechanisms** are adopted if direct expression of the id impulse is unacceptable to the superego or dangerous in the real world. All defense mechanisms begin with repression of unacceptable impulses, making them unconscious. However, repression ties up energy. To conserve energy, defense mechanisms disguise the unacceptable impulse, so that only partial repression is needed. By distorting the source, aim, and/or object of the impulse, they avoid the retaliation of the superego, allowing the impulse, in effect, to sneak past the censor. This reduces the energy requirements for repression, analogous to the way that letting steam out of a pressure cooker reduces the force required to hold on the lid. Furthermore, it avoids the experience of anxiety, which is an underlying issue in all defense mechanisms (Paulhus, Fridhandler, & Hayes, 1997; Turvey & Salovey, 1993–1994).

Defense mechanisms range from primitive ones, first developed in infancy, to more mature ones, developed later (Kernberg, 1994; Vaillant, 1971, 1992, 1993). The most seriously disturbed individuals, psychotics, use the most primitive defenses: denial and distortion of reality. Other immature defenses include projection, dissociation, and acting out. Less primitive (neurotic) defenses include intellectualization and isolation, repression, reaction formation, displacement, and rationalization. Finally, suppression and sublimation, as well as altruism and humor, are the most mature defenses (Vaillant, 1994). People who are better adapted use more mature defenses, and when patients with various diagnoses switch from less mature to more mature defense mechanisms, their functioning improves (Cramer, 2000, 2002). The maturity of defense mechanisms is unrelated to intelligence, education, and social class (Vaillant, 2000), and mature defenses help people overcome disadvantages in these areas. In a longitudinal study, 14-year-old inner-city boys who scored low (mean of 80) on an IQ measure were, nonetheless, likely to mature into well-adapted 65-year-olds with good incomes and educated children if they had mature defenses; those with less mature defenses fared less well (Vaillant & Davis, 2000).

Denial is a primitive defense mechanism in which an individual does not acknowledge some painful or anxiety-provoking aspect of reality or of the self. For example, a person may deny that smoking is contributing to health problems despite clear evidence. Denial is a normal defense mechanism in preschool children, but as they grow to 7, 8, and 9 years old, children turn to more mature defense mechanisms such as projection (Cramer, 1997; Cramer & Block, 1998). When denial continues to adulthood, it is maladaptive because it involves a major distortion of reality.

In **reaction formation**, an unacceptable impulse is repressed and its opposite is developed in exaggerated form. For example, a child who hates a younger sister may repress it and instead believe she loves the sister. The defense may be diagrammed thus:

I hate sister (*unconscious*) → I love sister (*conscious*)

When only love is acknowledged, but not its opposite, a psychoanalyst suspects that unconscious hatred is also present. Highly modest persons may be suspected of defending against exhibitionism. People who are raised to very strict moral codes, not allowed to enjoy the normal pleasures of childhood, sometimes turn against themselves and use reaction formation as a defense against impulses for gratification; thus they become excessively "good" and prone (by projection) to moral outrage against other people's flaws (Kaplan, 1997). The defense mechanism of reaction formation contributes to prejudice against homosexuals; that is, men who are unconsciously sexually aroused by other men defend themselves against this threatening impulse by exaggerated antigay attitudes. Researchers offer evidence of this; in a laboratory, homophobic men had erections when they watched sexually explicit erotic gay films, but nonhomophobic men did not (Adams, Wright, & Lohr, 1996).

In **projection**, the person's own unacceptable impulse is instead thought to belong to someone else. A woman who is tempted to shoplift but whose ethical sense

defense mechanisms
ego strategies for coping with unconscious conflict

denial
primitive defense mechanism in which material that produces conflict is simply repressed

reaction formation
defense mechanism in which a person thinks or behaves in a manner opposite to the unacceptable unconscious impulse

projection
defense mechanism in which a person's own unacceptable impulse is incorrectly thought to belong to someone else

(superego) will not allow her to even think of stealing may project this unacceptable impulse onto another person:

I want to steal (*unconscious*) → That person is stealing (*conscious*)

In experiments, people who have been misled to believe they possess an undesirable personality trait but asked not to think about it (which can be thought of as experimental repression) are likely to project their fault onto another person whom they are asked to rate on that trait (Newman, Duff, & Baumeister, 1997). In society, cultural scapegoats often become projective targets, accused of crimes and immoral acts that are really the accuser's own repressed impulses. In this way, individual intrapsychic conflict contributes to prejudice.

displacement

defense mechanism in which energy is transferred from one object or activity to another

The defense mechanism of **displacement** distorts the object of the drive. Displacement is less primitive than projection because the impulse is correctly seen as belonging to the individual; only the object is distorted. For example, a child who is angry with the father may not consciously be able to acknowledge the anger because of fear of retaliation and guilt. The aggressive impulse may be disguised by directing it toward a brother:

I want to hurt Dad (*unconscious*) → I want to hurt my brother (*conscious*)

We suspect that the feelings are related to displacement, rather than caused by the brother's actual behavior, if they are disproportionately strong compared to that which the current situation would warrant or if a person frequently has aggressive impulses in a wide variety of situations. Displacement of other emotions, such as dependency and sexuality, also occurs.

identification

defense mechanism in which a person fuses or models after another person

Identification is a process of borrowing or merging one's identity with that of someone else—avoiding the recognition of one's own inadequacies and wishfully adopting someone else's identity instead. It is part of normal development; boys identify with their fathers, girls with their mothers, and all of us with cultural heroes. Identification is important during the third psychosexual stage, when gender roles are an issue, and experimental research confirms that threats to gender identity (based on false information about scores on the Bem Sex-Role Inventory) increase the use of identification as coded from TAT tests (Cramer, 1998b). Identification sometimes functions to overcome feelings of powerlessness. Adopting the identity of someone who has power over us, even if that power is not used for our benefit, is termed *identification with the aggressor*. For example, children may identify with abusive parents or hostages with their captors.

isolation

defense mechanism in which conflictful material is kept disconnected from other thoughts

In the defense mechanism of **isolation**, unpleasant thoughts are disassociated from other thinking and thus do not come to mind. In addition, emotions that would ordinarily be connected with the thoughts are gone. For example, a person who has lost a loved one through death may isolate this experience, not thinking of the loved one because of the grief it might bring.

rationalization

defense mechanism in which reasonable, conscious explanations are offered rather than true unconscious motivations

The defense mechanism of **rationalization** involves giving plausible, but false, reasons for an action to disguise the true motives. A parent might rationalize spanking a child, saying it will teach the child to be more obedient, although the true motivation may be that the parent resents the child. Rationalization involves relatively little distortion, so it is considered a mature defense mechanism.

intellectualization

defense mechanism in which a person focuses on thinking and avoids feeling

The defense mechanism of **intellectualization** prevents clear, undistorted recognition of an impulse through distorted or excessive explanation. A person who overeats may give many reasons: "I need extra vitamins to deal with stress," "I always gain weight in the winter," and so on. Margaret Sanger described the loss of her newly built home to fire:

I was neither disappointed nor regretful.…In that instant I learned the lesson of the futility of material substances. Of what great importance were they spiritually if they could go so quickly?…I could…be happy without them. (1938/1971, p. 64)

This defense mechanism is adaptive, although defensive in that it distorts the grief of the tragedy.

Sublimation and Creativity

Sublimation is the most healthy way of dealing with unacceptable impulses. It occurs when the individual finds a socially acceptable aim and object for the expression of an unacceptable impulse. This allows indirect discharge of the impulse, so its pressure is reduced. Aggressive impulses may be sublimated into athletic competitiveness, and artists transform primitive urges into works of art.

sublimation

defense mechanism in which impulses are expressed in socially acceptable ways

Creative individuals are particularly interesting models of sublimation, and they have been of interest to psychoanalysis since Freud's study of Leonardo da Vinci (1910/1957). Creative persons retain the ability, lost by many adults, to access the fantasy world of the id. Unlike psychotics, they do not get caught irretrievably in the id, and unlike children, they can also function with a mature ego. Creative people are capable of what psychoanalysis describes as "regression in the service of the ego" (Kris, 1952/1964). Research confirms that creative artists can shift readily between controlled thinking (an ego function) and unregulated thought (the unconscious). Psychotic individuals can access unconscious material, too, but they have difficulty returning to controlled thinking (Wild, 1965). The schizophrenic, in contrast to the poet, cannot use metaphor as a bridge between reality and imagination (Reinsdorf, 1993–1994).

Empirical Studies of Defenses

Empirical studies of psychoanalysis are important for science, but it is challenging to design them rigorously. Consider gender identity disorders that lead people resort to sexual reassignment surgery to correct what they perceive to be the wrong-sex body. With sexuality so central to psychoanalytic theory, and identification so clearly described in the Oedipal stage, it is no surprise that psychoanalysts interpreted such disorders, and the voluntary castration that beckons as a cure, to result from a boy's excessive identification with his mother, especially in the absence of a strong father to serve as a model of the male role. Research designs to test these ideas, however, are marred by inadequate controls and measurements that permit researchers' preconceptions to bias their results (Midence & Hargreaves, 1997).

Measuring defense mechanisms is challenging. Observing defenses in clinical case histories is extremely time consuming, and because the therapist is both the interviewer and the interpreter of the material, it is unclear that another observer would have come to the same interpretations. Nonetheless, clinical interview methods are used to monitor changes in defenses over the course of therapy (Perry & Ianni, 1998).

Defense mechanisms can be scored from projective tests, including the TAT and the Rorschach test. Patients had healthier defense patterns, scored from the TAT, after therapy than before (Cramer & Blatt, 1990). Despite their limitations for measuring unconscious processes (Davidson & MacGregor, 1998), self-report inventories have also been developed to assess defense mechanisms (Bond, 1995; Gleser & Ihilevich, 1969). It has not been demonstrated, however, that self-report and projective tests are valid indicators of the use of defense mechanisms in everyday life. When researchers asked people to report coping in everyday life at the time when they were stressed, using a portable palm-top computer, these reports didn't correspond very well with later retrospective reports (Stone et al., 1998).

Researchers have explored defensive processes in experimental as well as correlational studies. Consider a repressive coping style: people whose bodies show physiological signs of anxiety but who score low on written self-report measures of anxiety. Repressors have fewer memories of adverse childhood events than do nonrepressors, even though more negative events happened in their childhood. Laboratory experiments suggest that they may be using emotional cues to signal repression. In one study, research subjects were directed to recall certain types of stimuli that they were shown and to forget others. Overall, they were able to do that, but most exciting for the study of defenses were differences between people. *Repressors* were especially able to forget stimuli that they had been told to forget when such stimuli were associated with negative emotions (Myers, Brewin, & Power, 1998). They seem able to use negative emotion as an unconscious cue.

In an extensive review of personality and social psychological research, Baumeister and colleagues concluded that there was substantial evidence for several defense mechanisms: projection, undoing, isolation, and denial. However, very limited evidence could be found for displacement and none whatsoever for sublimation (Baumeister, Dale, & Sommer, 1998).

Cross-cultural studies of defense mechanisms are relevant for testing Freud's claim that his theory describes universal aspects of personality. Although there is much to be done, a large-scale empirical study of defense mechanisms in Thailand, using self-report measures, found similar kinds of defenses to those in U.S. samples. Some, though, were used less frequently in Thailand (regressive or immature emotional behavior), and some were used more frequently (projection, reaction formation, and other indicators of a high level of control), reflecting different cultural values (Tori & Bilmes, 2002).

PERSONALITY DEVELOPMENT

One of Freud's legacies is that childhood experience potently influences adult personality. Personality development involves a series of conflicts between the individual, who wants to satisfy instinctual impulses, and the social world (especially the family), which constrains this desire. Through development, the individual finds ways to obtain as much hedonic gratification as possible, given these constraints. Consider the saying, "As the twig is bent, so grows the tree." Like a tree that has grown crooked under adverse conditions of wind and terrain, the adult human shows the permanent imprint of childhood struggles.

Freud proposed that the mucous membranes of the body could be the physical source of id impulses, the *erogenous zones* where libido is focused. These zones are highly responsive to sensation and can be associated with increased tension and reduction of tension, as the libido model requires. Different zones are central at different ages because of physical changes. For the adult, the erogenous zone is the genital area. In early life, other zones give more pleasure: in infancy, the mouth; in toddlerhood, the anus. Driven by maturational factors, all people develop through the same *psychosexual stages* (see Table 2.2).

The infant, under the tyranny of the pleasure principle, wants to be fed immediately whenever hungry. In reality, feeding is sometimes delayed, and ultimately the child is weaned. This is the conflict of the first psychosexual stage, the **oral stage**. In the second, or **anal stage**, the toddler enjoys controlling the bowels, retaining and expelling feces according to his or her own will; but conflict with the restrictive forces of society arises because the family demands toilet training. Conflict over drive satisfaction in the third psychosexual stage, the **phallic stage**, focuses on punishment

oral stage

the first psychosexual stage of development, from birth to age 1

anal stage

the second psychosexual stage of development, from age 1 to 3

phallic stage

the third psychosexual stage of development, from age 3 to 5

Table 2.2 Stages of Psychosexual Development

Stage	Age	Conflict	Outcomes
Oral Stage	Birth to 12 months	Weaning	Optimism or pessimism Addictions to tobacco, alcohol
Anal Stage	1 to 3 years	Toilet training	Stubbornness Miserliness
Phallic Stage	3 to 5 years	Masturbation and Oedipus/Electra conflict	Gender identification Morality (superego) vanity
Latency	5 years to puberty		
Genital Stage	Puberty to adulthood		

for masturbation and the child's complex fantasy of a sexual union with the opposite-sex parent—a wish that is frustrated because it conflicts with the universal taboo of incest.

Personality development occurs as the ego finds new strategies to cope with frustrations imposed by socialization. If socialization is too severe or too sudden, or if there is psychic trauma, the young ego cannot cope, and personality development is impaired. Such experiences produce **fixation**, in which impulses are repressed rather than outgrown. In normal development, growth of mental processes is assisted by language. But trauma stops that growth, and it may be helpful for therapists to use additional methods besides talking (e.g., symbolically reenacting traumatic experiences within the safety of the therapeutic setting) in order to heal such fixation (Rachman, Yard, & Kennedy, 2009).

fixation
failure to develop normally through a particular developmental stage

The Five Psychosexual Stages

Freud proposed five universal stages of development. He believed that personality is largely formed by the end of the third stage, at about age 5. By then, the individual has developed strategies for expressing impulses that constitute the core of personality.

THE ORAL STAGE   The oral stage of development occurs from birth to about age 1. During this stage, the erogenous zone is the mouth, and pleasurable activities center around feeding. At first, in the oral erotic phase, the infant passively receives reality, swallowing what is good or (less passively) spitting out what is distasteful. A second phase, termed *oral sadism*, involves the development of a more active role, epitomized by biting.

Because the infant's needs are met without effort, he or she is said to feel omnipotent. This feeling passes in normal development but is retained in some psychoses. The feeling of infantile omnipotence normally gives way to realization that needs are satisfied through loved objects in the world, not magically. As the infant learns to associate the mother's presence with satisfaction of the hunger drive, the mother becomes a separate object, and the first differentiation of self from others occurs.

Fixation in the first psychosexual stage results in development of an **oral character** personality type, whose traits are traditionally said to include *optimism*, *passivity*, and *dependency*. Conflicts can produce the opposite characteristics; for example, because of reaction formation, a person fixated at the oral stage may become pessimistic instead of optimistic, leading to depression (Lewis, 1993).

oral character
personality type resulting from fixation in the first psychosexual stage; characterized by optimism, passivity, and dependency

What does research find? Some research fails to confirm psychoanalytic hypotheses. An early and straightforward study found no association between mothers' reports of early feeding (including age of weaning and other indicators) and projective test scores for oral imagery on the Rorschach inkblot test in their college-age sons (Thurston & Mussen, 1951). Other studies suggest that oral concerns in the most literal sense, that is, "preoccupation with food and eating," are unrelated to dependency (Bornstein, 1992, p. 17), contrary to Freud's theory (Young-Bruehl, 1990).

Not all research is so discouraging. The hypothesized relationship between oral fixation and behavior that is conforming and dependent is sometimes supported. People with oral imagery on the Rorschach test conform more to others' judgments on an Asch-type judgment task, particularly in the presence of a high-status authority figure (Masling, Weiss, & Rothschild, 1968; Tribich & Messer, 1974), and they are more likely to indicate on personality tests the need for help (O'Neill & Bornstein, 1990). They are capable of disagreeing too, though, if that will create a favorable impression to an authority figure, according to Bornstein (1997), who advocates understanding dependency in terms of relationships with other people (object relations), instead of orality (Bornstein, 1996), a topic to which we will return in Chapter 6.

THE ANAL STAGE   During the second and third years, the toddler's pleasure is experienced in a different part of the body: the anus. The toddler's desire to control his or her own bowel movements conflicts with the social demand for toilet training.

anal character

personality type resulting from fixation at age 1 to 3, characterized by orderliness, parsimony, and obstinacy

Pleasure is experienced at first through the newly formed ability to retain feces, the anal retentive phase, and then in the experience of willful defecation, the anal expulsive phase. Lifelong conflicts over issues of control, of holding on and letting go, may result if there is fixation at this stage. The **anal character** is characterized by three traits, *orderliness, parsimony,* and *obstinacy,* which are correlated in many empirical studies (Greenberg & Fisher, 1978). Anal fixation may be expressed by issues related to money—hoarding it or spending it—as symbolic feces (Wolfenstein, 1993). As predicted by Freud's proposal that humor expresses unconscious conflict (described earlier), experimental subjects who score high on the anal traits (obstinacy, orderliness, and parsimony) find jokes on anal themes to be particularly funny (O'Neill, Greenberg, & Fisher, 1992).

THE PHALLIC STAGE   From age 3 to 5 (or a bit later), the primary erogenous area of the body is the genital zone. Freud called this stage of development the phallic stage, reflecting his male perspective. The child's desire for sexual pleasure is expressed through masturbation, which is accompanied by important (and, to critics, incredible) fantasies. At this stage, males and females follow different developmental paths.

Male Development: The Oedipus Conflict   According to Freud, the young boy wants to kill his father and to replace him as his mother's sexual partner. This **Oedipus conflict** is named after Sophocles' play *Oedipus Rex,* in which Oedipus unwittingly murders his father and takes his own mother as his wife. The young boy fears, however, that this desire will be found out and punished, and so he represses the incestuous desire. **Castration anxiety**, the fear that his penis will be cut off, is the motivating anxiety of the young boy at this stage. Although such castration anxiety may seem an incredible idea, threats of castration do occur. We are told that Adolf Hitler ordered artists to be castrated if they used the wrong colors for skies and meadows (Waite, 1977, p. 30). It has been suggested that some sexual problems are derived from castration anxiety. In other cultures, castration anxiety is expressed differently; for example, in Southeast Asia, the phenomenon of *koro* is the sudden anxiety that the penis (or, in females, the vulva and nipples) will recede into the body (American Psychiatric Association, 1994; Kirmayer, 1992). Freud asserted that the Oedipus complex was universal, but others argue that it reflects the father–son competition characteristic of Freud's cultural and historical time and is not universal (Wax, 2000; Winter, 1999). Incest itself, especially mother–son incest, is unusual among humans across the world, and also in animals, because it is maladaptive from an evolutionary viewpoint (Sugiyama, 2001).

Oedipus conflict

conflict that males experience from age 3 to 5 involving sexual love for the mother and aggressive rivalry with the father

castration anxiety

fear that motivates male development at age 3 to 5

In a healthy resolution of the Oedipal conflict, the boy gives up his fantasy of replacing his father and instead decides to become *like* his father. By this identification, the boy achieves two important developments: (1) appropriate male sex typing, and (2) the internalization of conscience, called superego. Conscience is fueled by castration anxiety: The stronger the castration fear, the stronger the superego. Or as Freud (1923/1962b, p. 38) phrased it, "The superego…is the heir of the Oedipus complex."

Female Development   Girls develop differently, according to Freud, as an inevitable consequence of their physical difference. Seeing that they lack a penis, girls believe they have been castrated, interpret their clitoris as inferior to a penis, and wish for the latter (penis envy). This biological inferiority sets girls up for psychological inferiority as well, in Freud's much-criticized theory (Lax, 1995, 1997). Like boys, girls fantasize sexual union with the opposite-sex parent. Unlike boys, girls must shift their erotic attachment from the mother (the first, pre-Oedipal love object for both sexes) to the father. This change of object is facilitated by the girl's anger toward her mother for not being powerful enough to protect her from castration.

Freud (1933/1966a, p. 590) lists three possible outcomes of the girl's castration complex: sexual inhibition or neurosis, a masculinity complex, or normal femininity. By *masculinity complex*, Freud meant that the woman strives for achievements considered in his day to be inappropriate for females, such as career advances to the exclusion of traditional feminine family commitments. Normal feminine development, according to Freud, results in accepting the role of wife and mother and developing the "normal" feminine traits of passivity and masochism.

Without castration anxiety to motivate their development, girls are theoretically less psychologically developed than males, with a weaker superego. Naturally, this assertion has been rejected by those who argue that cultural factors can adequately explain the acceptance of suffering that Freud described as biologically determined masochism (see Chapter 6). It also contradicts the empirical record of sex differences: that women report more shame and guilt (interpreted as evidence of moral development), have more empathy for other people's feelings (Tangney, 1990, 1994), and score higher than males on the level of ego development (Mabry, 1993). Women's morality can be described as an ethic-of-care orientation, contrasting with the justice orientation of men (Tangney & Dearing, 2004): a different, not inferior, moral perspective.

Incest: Freud's Abandonment of the Seduction Hypothesis Freud revised his theory over many decades. Freud first believed that actual incest was important in the histories of his female patients (the *seduction hypothesis*), and the father's sexual behavior with his daughter was responsible for her psychiatric problems (Freud, 1896/1962a; McGrath, 1986). In his final view, the girl's reports of a sexual relationship with her father were simply fantasy. Why did Freud change his mind? Could he have been defending himself against suspicion of sexual misbehavior in his own family or fear of rejection by his colleagues (Kupfersmid, 1992; Masson, 1984)?

Orthodox Freudians accept Freud's abandonment of the seduction hypothesis as the correction of an earlier error (Gleaves & Hernandez, 1999; Lawrence, 1988; Paul, 1985; Rosenman, 1989). Throughout Freud's theory, thoughts and wishes are central and actual events are less important. Recollections of abuse, regardless of accuracy, serve as narratives that are organizing metaphors for experience. Thoughts and fantasies can be changed through therapy, and so the analysis concentrates on what the abusive memory means for the patient. Even memories that aren't historically accurate can serve a therapeutic function, helping patients to develop a narrative of their lives that enable them to move forward (Birch, 1998; Gaensbauer & Jordan, 2009).

Effects of Fixation Psychoanalytic theory says that fixation at the phallic stage results in difficulties of superego formation; gender-role identity; and sexuality, including sexual inhibition, sexual promiscuity, and homosexuality. Freud argued that homosexuality is understandable because people all have some attraction to both men and women (bisexuality), but that a heterosexual outcome was more mature and healthy (Freud, 1905/1962c, 1920/1978; Jacobo, 2001). More recently, psychoanalysts have attempted to describe the dynamics of the Oedipus conflict in modified form to relate to gay men (Lewes, 1998; Schwartz, 1999). Other research implicates biological, rather than experiential, causes of sexual orientation, including prenatal hormone exposure (Meyer-Bahlburg et al., 1995) and brain structure (LeVay, 1991).

Freud asserted that personality is largely formed during these first three psychosexual stages when the basic ego mechanisms for dealing with libidinal impulses are established. If fixation has occurred, the specific neurosis will depend on the stage at which development was impaired. The earlier the fixation, the more serious the resulting disorder.

THE LATENCY STAGE Middle childhood is a period of relative calm for the sexual instincts, so Freud's model of libidinal tension says little about this stage. (It is, however, an important period of development according to other theories.)

THE GENITAL STAGE The **genital stage** begins at puberty. In contrast to the autoerotic and fantasy sexual objects of the phallic child, the genital adult develops the capacity to experience sexual satisfaction with an opposite-sex partner. The **genital character** is Freud's ideal of full development, requiring that fixations have been avoided or resolved through psychoanalysis. Such a person has no significant pre-Oedipal

genital stage
the adult psychosexual stage

genital character
healthy personality type

conflicts; enjoys a satisfying sexuality; and cares about the satisfaction of the love partner, avoiding selfish narcissism. Sublimated psychic energy is available for work, which brings enjoyment.

PSYCHOANALYTIC TREATMENT

In the healthy adult, both direct sexual satisfaction and indirect sublimation of sexual instincts occur, leading to Freud's famous criterion of mental health, *Lieben und Arbeiten*, that is, "love and work." Such an outcome is possible if there are no major fixations in development or if fixations are resolved through psychoanalytic treatment. Freud described psychoanalysis with the metaphor of archaeology. The analytic process tries to "dig up" primitive material long "buried" by repression and to bring it to the surface, to consciousness, so it can be considered with the skills of the more developed ego.

Psychoanalytic Therapy Techniques

Restoration of memory was a key throughout Freud's evolving understanding of therapy (Knafo, 2009). The psychoanalyst uses the principle of psychic determinism to discover the unconscious ideas and conflicts of the patient that originated in the past, thus helping the patient to become free of the neurotic compulsion to repeat the past, and able to live in the present (Covington, 2001). The basic technique of psychoanalysis is **free association**, which requires the patient "to say whatever came into his head, while ceasing to give any conscious direction to his thoughts" (Freud, 1935/1963a, p. 75). Suspension of conscious control allows the unconscious to be observed directing thoughts and memories. In addition, some clinicians also use psychological tests to guide their diagnosis (Jaffe, 1992).

Psychoanalytic treatment produces **insight**, that is, understanding of true motives, which are unconscious conflicts. To be therapeutic, insight must be accompanied by emotional awareness. The emergence of buried feelings from the unconscious is called **catharsis**. These feelings, including fear and grief, often accompany the recall of forgotten memories. Like the removal of infectious material when a wound is lanced, catharsis frees the unconscious of troublesome repressions.

Modern psychoanalysis recognizes that unconscious conflicts must be confronted again and again in treatment. The patient must "work through" the conflict, discovering the many circumstances that have been influenced by it and essentially reconstructing personality to replace these unconscious irrational determinants with mature motivations. Too much focus on a past traumatic memory, even in therapy, may not be the best approach. Instead, the aim should be some sort of cognitive restructuring, helping the patient to build a new life narrative that is broader than the traumatic experience and helps move in a healthy direction (Bonanno & Kaltman, 2000).

A major phenomenon in psychoanalytic treatment is **transference**. During treatment, the patient develops a relationship to the therapist based on unconscious projections from earlier life, experiencing emotions that were repressed when felt toward earlier significant others. For example, a female patient may "fall in love with" her male analyst because of transference of the love she felt for her father during childhood. Negative as well as positive emotions occur. Transference is, strangely enough, desirable, because it brings unresolved issues to the analytic process, where they can be resolved. More problematic are the analyst's unresolved issues triggering projective reactions to the patient, termed **countertransference**, which may interfere with treatment.

Psychoanalytic treatment is considerably more time consuming and expensive than alternative modes of treatment. Is it more effective, justifying the extra cost and commitment? Evidence is mixed, favoring psychoanalysis for psychosomatic disorders (Fisher & Greenberg, 1977) but not for anxiety and phobias (Goldfried, Greenberg, & Marmar, 1990) or depression (Westen & Morrison, 2001). Some research indicates that, if patients are assessed after a longer time period, the advantage of psychodynamic

free association

psychoanalytic technique in which the patient says whatever comes to mind, permitting unconscious connections to be discovered

insight

conscious recognition of one's motivation and unconscious conflicts

catharsis

therapeutic effect of a release of emotion when previously repressed material is made conscious

transference

in therapy, the patient's displacement onto the therapist of feelings based on earlier experiences (e.g., with the patient's own parents)

countertransference

the analyst's reaction to the patient, as distorted by unresolved conflicts therapy increases (Blomberg, Lazar, & Sandell, 2001), which makes sense if we grant that this approach aims at more fundamental personality change.

The Recovered Memory Controversy

A controversial technique that was used by a small minority of therapists has now been discredited: recovered memory therapy. The idea behind this therapy was that traumatic sexual experiences in childhood had led patients to develop a variety of symptoms (e.g., depression, promiscuity, and eating disorders) and also to repress the memory of the abuse. If memory for the traumatic event could be restored, it was thought, a therapeutic benefit would be obtained (Blume, 1995; Freyd, 1994, 1996; Whitfield, 1995).

There is no denying that childhood sexual abuse occurs and contributes to a variety of psychological problems (Cahill, Llewelyn, & Pearson, 1991; Finkelhor et al., 1990). Unfortunately, a few therapists jumped to a conclusion of sexual abuse with minimal evidence, even over the objections of patients, and through suggestion, therapists gradually convinced patients of a traumatic past that had not occurred in their cases. Occasional reports are so bizarre, including reports of Satanic ritual abuse, cult mass murders of newborns, and childbirth in women whose physicians find no evidence of pregnancy, that they are patently absurd. Some allegedly recalled memories of abuse are, in fact, the result of suggestion by therapists to gullible clients (e.g., Bowers & Farvolden, 1996). Such suggested memories are called the *false memory syndrome.*

Often there is no reliable way of knowing whether a particular client's memories are true or false or a mixture of truth and falsehood (Genoni, 1994; Lindsay & Read, 1995; Scheflin & Brown, 1996). The controversy moved to the courts, where trials pit children who claim to have been abused against their parents. The legal system, of course, requires knowledge about what behavior actually occurred, and psychoanalysis, because it is concerned instead with "subjective truth" and fantasy, is not well suited to provide the needed information (Birch, 1998). In those rare cases in which recovered memories can be objectively validated, they seem to be so different from the typical therapeutically recovered memory that one clinician suggests most recovered memory tales told in therapy are not really about the past at all but rather some metaphor for events that are actually happening within therapy itself (Brenneis, 2000). The challenge for clinicians and researchers is to identify and respond to real abuse, without the errors of false memories.

PSYCHOANALYSIS AS A SCIENTIFIC THEORY

Psychoanalysis is more than a therapy. It is a theory of personality. Does the personality theory fare any better than the therapy when subjected to the objective evaluation of the scientific method? Most psychologists today would say no. The main difficulty is that Freud's concepts were not described precisely enough to guide scientists toward a definitive test; that is, they fall short on the criterion of *verifiability.* For Freud, the psychoanalytic method of talking with an individual patient provided sufficient data to verify his theory, without worrying about potentially biased observations, and many analysts defend clinical observation as evidence, despite its difficulties.

Projective tests, such as the Rorschach inkblot test (Pichot, 1984), are commonly used to measure unconscious motivations, but they have low reliability compared to self-report questionnaires. Nonetheless, some striking results have been reported with the Rorschach method, and a variety of scoring methods based on empirical research have increased reliability and validity (Bornstein & Masling, 2005). In one study, Rorschach tests of women who killed their abusive husbands were found to be similar to tests of combat veterans suffering from posttraumatic stress disorder (Kaser-Boyd, 1993). Rorschach tests change as psychotherapy progresses; patients' scores indicate increasing adjustment over time and greater improvement with long-term than short-term therapy (Exner & Andronikof-Sanglade, 1992; Weiner & Exner, 1991).

Silverman's Experiments

Lloyd Silverman (1976, 1983) conducted a series of experimental tests of the unconscious. Calling his method *subliminal psychodynamic activation*, Silverman presented stimuli with a tachistoscope, a device that allows visual stimuli to be presented very briefly (4 milliseconds). Subjects reported that they could see only brief flickers of light. Although they could not consciously identify the subliminal messages, they were influenced by them. Schizophrenics exposed to a conflict-arousing stimulus, "I am losing Mommy," increased their psychotic symptoms. This response is predicted by Freud's theory because a schizophrenic uses hallucination, a primitive ego defense mechanism of infancy, to deal with unconscious conflicts about losing the mother, the object just developing in the oral stage.

When Silverman's tachistoscope conveyed the unconscious message, "Mommy and I are one," psychotic symptoms were reduced, presumably because the conflict was reduced by activating a symbiotic merger with the mother in the unconscious. Silverman later tested the cue, "Mommy and I are one," in a variety of populations and reported that it had many beneficial effects in reducing phobias (Silverman, Frank, & Dachinger, 1974), reducing homosexual threat (Silverman et al., 1973) and facilitating weight loss in obese women (Silverman, Martin, et al., 1978). The desire to merge with the mother thus is relevant for other populations besides schizophrenics. Building on Silverman's research, others have developed ways of measuring this fundamental desire to be merged with the mother, or with a later object, by coding projective stories for the Oneness Motive (Siegel & Weinberger, 1998).

Using different cues with other patient populations, Silverman claimed that unconscious arousal of the specific conflict identified by psychoanalytic theory to be associated with each diagnosis (e.g., oral conflict for schizophrenics and anal conflict for stutterers) could produce an increase or decrease of symptoms (Silverman, Bronstein, & Mendelsohn, 1976). Among women with eating disorders, subliminal arousal of abandonment conflict led to increased eating in a bogus cracker-rating task (Patton, 1992). An appropriate stimulus ("Beating Dad is OK") was even reported to improve dart-throwing performance in college males (Silverman, Ross, et al., 1978). If the stimuli were presented at longer exposures, so they could be consciously recognized, there was no effect on the symptoms; only unconscious dynamics produced changes.

Some researchers have not replicated Silverman's findings and have called for more stringent controls (Balay & Shevrin, 1988; Brody, 1987; Fudin, 1986, 2001; Malik et al., 1996). Other critics are more positive. One systematic statistical review of research using the subliminal activation technique concluded that it is effective in reducing pathology and that replications by other researchers not associated with Silverman's laboratory also confirm the effect (Hardaway, 1990). If it is effective, it is still unclear whether the mechanism is the hypothesized unconscious return to an infantile symbiosis with the mother, before the burdens of becoming a separate self. It might instead occur because this stimulus produces a positive mood, which in turn has a variety of beneficial effects (Sohlberg, Billinghurst, & Nylén, 1998). Further complicating the issue, other researchers report that the Silverman procedure sometimes results in suffering instead of comfort, presumably because for some individuals, increasing merger with the mother may arouse conflict (Sohlberg et al., 1998).

Nonconscious Cognition

Freud explored the unconscious from an assumption that consciousness was the usual mode of experience, and repression provides the energy to move material from consciousness to the unconscious. The unconscious and repression explained why emotional reactions in his patients, obvious from their behavior and physiological reactions, were not accompanied by appropriate awareness (Lang, 1994).

However, cognitive approaches suggest that material may not be conscious for other reasons besides repression, including lack of attention and competing associations. Several researchers have investigated nonconscious cognition without the assumptions of conflict that Freud's dynamic model describes (Kihlstrom, 1985,

1987, 1990; Kihlstrom, Barnhardt, & Tataryn, 1992; Natsoulas, 1994). While we are consciously paying attention to one thing, other information may be presented that does not become conscious but is still perceived at some level. When research subjects are asked to determine whether briefly presented stimuli are members of a specific category, such as "mammal," or not, their electroencephalograph (EEG) brain scans show different activity for category members ("horse") than for stimuli that are not members of the category ("apple"), even when they fail consciously to make the correct identification; this provides evidence of semantic processing of which we are not conscious (Stenberg et al., 2000). Subliminal presentations of smiling faces can cause experimental subjects to form more positive attitudes about people (Krosnick et al., 1992). Subliminal messages in advertising can change consumer's attitudes toward products, though not necessarily their actual purchases (Aylesworth, Goodstein, & Kalra, 1999; Trappey, 1996). Even under anesthesia, people may be influenced by auditory stimuli. One study reports that tapes of therapeutic suggestions played to patients during abdominal surgery reduced the amount of pain medication required after surgery, even though patients could not consciously recall the tapes (Caseley-Rondi, Merikle, & Bowers, 1994).

The cognitive interpretation of such nonconscious cognition does not require a sophisticated process of repression or censorship based on anxiety, such as Freud proposed. Instead of mental processes being conscious intrinsically, unless repressed to keep them unconscious, many modern theorists have proposed much the opposite: that mental processes are not conscious unless they are made to be so by some additional action (Natsoulas, 1993), such as focusing attention (Velmans, 1991). In one model, consciousness may occur when information in the nonconscious part of the brain (which is most of the brain) is represented again in a system of the brain devoted to consciousness (Olds, 1992). In this model, nonconscious suggestion is readily explained. Events that do not reach awareness can activate or strengthen neural networks that are related to certain ideas, so they are more easily activated by subsequent events and then become conscious (Greenwald, 1992), often aided by verbal representation. There is certainly a model that supports "talk" therapy.

The theory of a cognitive nonconscious offers an alternative to Freud's dynamic unconscious. It does not invoke questionable assumptions of psychic energy, and it can be reconciled with cognitive research and theory. Individual differences in defenses, such as repression, can be understood without a psychic energy model. Experiments show that people who are classified as repressors because written tests indicate that they avoid threatening thoughts are particularly attentive to emotional information, both pleasant and unpleasant. When circumstances allow, they distance themselves from emotional events (Mendolia, Moore, & Tesser, 1996). Individual differences in responses to emotion can be explained as differences in emotional reactivity, perhaps caused by a genetic predisposition or learned ways of behaving.

Nonconscious Influences and the Body

Freud's work began in neurology, and it became psychological because the clinical phenomena he confronted were incomprehensible with the medical knowledge of that time. Today, neurologists suggest that some of the clinical symptoms Freud observed do have a neurological basis. For example, consider traumatic memory loss. Neural imaging of the brain shows decreased functioning in the hippocampus, an area known to be important for memory, in people who have been exposed to combat stress and other traumas (Conway & Pleydell-Pearce, 2000).

When experimental animals are exposed to very high levels of stress, the brain responds physiologically in ways that can alter memory, producing amnesia. Rats who are stressed by a painful shock to their feet, forget how to escape from a tank of water. Stress causes an increase in the hormone glucocorticoid, which interferes with neural messages in the hippocampus (de Quervain, Roozendaal, & McGaugh, 1998). These or other biochemical consequences of severe stress, especially in an immature brain, could cause amnesia for biological reasons (Bremner et al., 1995, 1996; van der Kolk & Fisler, 1995). Perhaps, in focusing on the psychological significance of memories instead of the biological mechanisms of trauma, psychoanalysis has been incorrect.

Modern neurology has progressed considerably since Freud's time. It may be possible to understand some of the mind as Freud described it in terms of modern cognitive neuroscience (Kandel, 1999). Most likely, Freud's ideas cannot be fully reconciled with neuroscience (Frank, 2008), but will give way to a more biological, "neurodynamic" psychiatry (Hobson & Leonard, 2001; Shapiro, 2002).

EVALUATING FREUD'S THEORY

How are we to evaluate Sigmund Freud's theory from the perspective of today's understandings in psychology? On the negative side, many of his specific proposals do not seem consistent with observations. Yet his ideas have captured the imagination of many and are reflected in movies and popular culture. The big picture that he portrays is of individuals struggling with unconscious impulses that are incompatible with the demands of civilization and of maturity. This is, indeed, a story that triggers the imagination. And it can be retold, recast with the details of modern neuroscientific understanding. Many social behaviors that are rather complex are best understood by including the impact of evolutionary processes, as we shall see in Chapter 9. Individuals do not respond blindly to these unconscious impulses, at least not all of the time. But their conscious mind is not in control fully either. Rather unconscious impulses are modified through consciousness (cf. Baumeister, Masicampo, & Vohs, 2011).

Among Freud's enduring contributions is his basic idea that problems can be caused by reasons that are not conscious, although his descriptions of psychic energy and instincts are out of favor today (Frank, 2008). Research supports the idea that unconscious processes influence behavior, although this is a different unconscious than Freud proposed. Rather than criticizing him for being wrong about many of the details of personality and its unconscious foundation, it is more sensible to credit him with suggesting areas worthy of investigation and for opening doors for those who followed—those who were intrigued by the unconscious but dissatisfied with Freud's description of it. After all, theories are not meant to last forever. If they pave the way to better theories, is that not enough?

Summary

- Freud's psychoanalytic theory proposes that behavior is caused by psychological forces, according to the assumption of *psychic determinism*.
- Unconscious forces often overpower consciousness, producing symptoms of neurosis, dreams, and mistakes in everyday life.
- *Dreams* can be interpreted by seeking their symbolic meanings (latent content).
- The unconscious develops from *repression* of unacceptable thoughts.
- Personality can be described in terms of three structures: id, ego, and superego.
- The *id* functions according to primary process and the pleasure principle, unconsciously seeking immediate satisfaction of biologically based drives, and it is the source of psychic energy (libido).
- The *ego* functions according to secondary process and the reality principle; it adapts to reality by using defense mechanisms to cope with intrapsychic conflict.

- The *superego* represents society's restrictions and produces guilt and an ego ideal.
- Personality develops through five psychosexual stages. The first three stages are most influential. These are the *oral, anal,* and *phallic* stages, which occur from birth to age 5.
- The *latency* stage provides a lull before the final, *genital*, stage of adulthood.
- Fixation, especially at the first three stages, impedes development and may produce symptoms treatable by *psychoanalysis*.
- The basic technique of psychoanalysis is *free association*, which permits the discovery of unconscious material.
- Other key elements of treatment are dream interpretation, catharsis, and insight.
- Memory recovery in therapy is a controversial technique that may result in false memories.
- Although many psychoanalysts share Freud's belief that the observations of psychoanalytic treatment

provide sufficient evidence for the theory, others have attempted empirical verification through research, with mixed results.

- Alternative explanations of nonconscious phenomena have been offered, such as the cognitive (instead of dynamic) nonconscious.

Thinking about Freud's Theory

1. Have you observed behavior that fits Freud's description of unconscious motivation? Describe it. Could the behavior be explained in any other way, without referring to unconscious motivation?
2. Does Freud's idea that conflict over sexual motivation is central to personality make sense in our time, or have more permissive social attitudes toward sexuality made this idea obsolete?
3. Is Freud's theory biased against women? Why or why not?
4. Would you make any changes in Freud's description of mental health as the ability to love and work?
5. Consider recalled memories of sexual abuse that emerge during therapy and the decision by some to accuse their abusers through the judicial system. Do you think this is a wise action? What responsibilities should the therapist have to the patient and to the accused?
6. Can you suggest research to test some aspect of Freud's psychoanalytic theory, beyond the tests described in the text?
7. If neuroscience comes to demonstrate a physical basis for Freud's observations, such as the impact of traumatic childhood experiences on memory and defense mechanisms, do you think psychoanalytic theory should be replaced by neuroscience or integrated with it?

Study Questions

1. Describe what Freud claimed was revolutionary about his theory of personality.
2. Explain the concept of psychic determinism.
3. Briefly describe what is found in the conscious, preconscious, and unconscious levels of the mind. How are these levels like an iceberg?
4. How does conversion hysteria illustrate psychic determinism?
5. Describe a Freudian approach to dream interpretation. Explain, in your answer, the terms *manifest content* and *latent content*.
6. Describe how repression produces the unconscious.
7. List the three structures of personality. Describe each one.
8. List and explain the four characteristics of instincts.
9. Distinguish between primary process and secondary process.
10. What is intrapsychic conflict? Describe the roles of the id, ego, and superego in this conflict.
11. Explain the energy hypothesis. How does it interpret the benefits of psychoanalytic therapy?
12. List and explain the three types of anxiety.
13. What is the purpose of defense mechanisms? List several defense mechanisms and give examples.
14. Explain sublimation. Give an example.
15. Describe development through the five psychosexual stages.
16. Discuss the controversy over Freud's seduction hypothesis.
17. Describe psychoanalytic treatment. What is its basic technique?
18. What does research indicate about the effectiveness of psychoanalytic treatment?
19. Describe empirical evidence that tests psychoanalytic theory, including Silverman's studies of subliminal psychodynamic activation.
20. Explain the difference between Freud's dynamic unconscious and the modern cognitive nonconscious.

3

Jung
Analytical Psychology

Chapter Overview

ILLUSTRATIVE BIOGRAPHY
Martin Luther King, Jr.

Carl Jung's theory portrays an unconscious that is shared by all humanity rather than contained solely within an individual psyche. The impact of that collective unconscious is felt through powerful archetypal symbols that can be projected onto individuals and influence history. This is one interpretation of the larger-than-life events that surrounded the life and death of an American hero, Dr. Martin Luther King, Jr.

Born January 15, 1929, in Atlanta, Georgia, deep in the racially segregated South of the United States, M. L. (as he was called as a child) grew up the second child (first son) of a Baptist minister, Martin Luther King,

Martin Luther King, Jr.

Sr., a strict disciplinarian whose hard work had elevated him from poverty. His maternal grandfather, too, had been a minister, and eventually Martin, Jr., became minister in the same segregated Ebenezer Baptist church where his father and grandfather had served. His concern for civil rights was also a family legacy.

With the encouragement and support of his family, King attended Morehouse College, where he graduated with a degree in sociology, and then studied for the ministry at Crozer Seminary in Pennsylvania, where he was valedictorian, and at Boston University, where he earned his PhD in theology. He developed from these studies an intellectual foundation for integrating social justice concerns with religious beliefs. Early in the civil rights movement, Dr. King's potential for leadership was recognized, and in those divisive times, many thought of him as a safer alternative to those who advocated violence as a means to combat racism. His leadership role in the nonviolent civil rights movement was honored with a Nobel Peace Prize in 1964 (Garrow, 1986), although there were people who distrusted him, tracked his movements, and ultimately murdered him. Within less than 4 years (1968), at the age of 39, King was assassinated, leaving his widow, Coretta Scott King, to raise their four young children and his fellow civil rights activists to continue the struggle for racial justice in the United States.

DEVELOPMENT

Carl Jung's theory, unlike that of Freud, is little concerned with childhood. Instead, he focuses on the developments that occur in adulthood. During midlife, according to Jung, a person has the task of becoming a unique person whose unconscious qualities are now examined and revised. This is the *individuation* process, and it draws on the deep unconscious reservoir of personality that Jung called the *collective unconscious*, as well as on a strong ego.

Although Dr. King was still young when he died, he may have been further along in the individuation process because of his spiritual background. (For Jung, psychological and spiritual development had much in common.) During the individuation process, an adult explores aspects of his personality that were neglected earlier in life, and then integrates them into a more whole personality.

DESCRIPTION

Jung's theory describes differences between people along three dimensions: a fundamental attitude of introversion or extraversion, and two pairs of psychological functions. The first pair of psychological functions describe ways of making decisions: thinking and feeling. Finally, the remaining psychological functions are alternative ways of getting information: through the details of the five senses (sensation) or more intuitively (intuition). All combinations of these three dimensions are possible.

King, analyzing himself, claimed to be partly introvert and partly extravert: an "ambivert" in King's words (Oates, 1982, p. 40), but his greater strength is introversion, his connection with his own inner life. Within the types listed by Jung, King could best be classified as an intuitive introvert. Jung (1971, p. 400) said that introverted intuitive types are often *prophets* (see also Maidenbaum & Thomson, 1989), and many, including King himself, applied this term to his ministry. King drew richly from this symbolic realm in his sermons. He turned prayerfully inward at critical moments—for example, when deciding whether to take a leading role in the Southern Christian Leadership Conference, despite the conflicting demands of his congregation and his young family. King's most famous speech, delivered in August 1963, described his dream from the mountaintop, his vision of racial equality. King worked to make his dreams real in the world, but he described that as a future potential rather than a current reality. To be concerned with future potentialities is characteristic of intuitive types, using Jung's psychetype theory. On the third dimension of Jung's descriptive model, King may have emphasized thinking somewhat more than feeling, given his intense motivation for education, which prompted him to complete a doctorate degree, despite the early disadvantage of an inferior education in segregated schools. But the emotional richness of his speeches suggests that both of these poles, thinking and feeling, had been already well developed.

ADJUSTMENT

The healthy person, according to Jung, has developed all four of the psychological functions (thinking and feeling, sensation and intuition). The unconscious provides wisdom and creativity, and not only the maladjustment that Freud described. Consciousness alone is not sufficient. The challenge is to find ways to tap into this unconscious without being driven to pathology in the process.

King's success in his ministry and family are evidence of health, but along the way, there were times of great trouble. He attempted suicide twice, a biographer relates (Oates, 1982, p. 36). Until a person can forge a new relationship with the unconscious, the limitations of conscious life may seem unbearable, and the unconscious too dangerous and destructive. Once past this stage, though, King drew from his unconscious and spiritual side and found ways to make its energies available not only to himself but to others. The unconscious into which he tapped, Jung would say, was not only his personal unconscious but the collective unconscious of humankind; and so his journey was not only to heal himself but to help humanity. All the psychological functions came into play. With the help of others in the civil rights movement, he paid attention to the details of the campaign as well as the vision of the future, thus using the sensation as well as the intuition function. Feeling as well as thinking was clearly evident in his inspiring sermons and speeches. This ability to use all of the psychological functions is a characteristic of a healthy personality in Jung's theory.

COGNITION

Jung's theory values not only the logical, scientific way of thinking (drawing on the sensation function), but also, to a greater extent, the holistic way of thinking that derives from the intuitive function. He describes *archetypes* as basic cognitive units in the unconscious, on which symbols and mythology and religious imagery are built. One archetype is that of the *hero*, a person whose individuation process confronts the powerful forces of the unconscious and taps into their riches without being destroyed in the process.

Dr. Martin Luther King, Jr.'s success in mobilizing and challenging the moral conscience of the nation was possible because he functioned for many as a concrete representation of the *hero archetype*. Throughout his ministry, King spoke to his congregation and to the world in symbols that mobilized the energies of the unconscious, including many symbols from his Christian faith. In addition, the public's own unconscious hero archetype was projected onto him, recognizing that his work resonated with something not yet named (for many but not all of them) within their own psyche. Archetypes are powerful because of this shared nature, and they energize much human activity and history. Projection of the hero archetype onto King combined several components: a promise of a better life; the expectation that the hero will fight difficult battles on behalf of others; and in many myths, the tragic finale in which the hero, once crowned as king, must die. Jung recommended that people stay within the symbols and mythology of their own heritage, and King did so. He borrowed the ideas of nonviolence from Gandhi's teachings in India and South Africa, but he presented them within the framework of his own Baptist heritage.

CULTURE

Jung, himself an introvert, was more interested in the inner world of archetypes than in external social reality, and so he tended to regard social behavior as a consequence of inner psychological experience, rather than to think of social causes. He suggested that racial bigotry can occur when people project their own unacceptable unconscious qualities (their "shadow," in his terminology) onto cultural scapegoats, which is an argument with considerable merit. But is the solution to racism, then, to psychoanalyze the bigots? What about economic and legal reforms?

King, in contrast, actively worked in society on the front lines of the civil rights movement, and he paid dearly for that

(continued)

(continued)

effort. Among his other speeches is a noteworthy one in 1967, when he addressed a national meeting of psychologists about their potential contributions to the civil rights movement (King, 1968). To the extent that he can be considered not just an individual but a part of the collective whole of humanity, the benefit of his prophetic leadership lives on.

BIOLOGY

In contrast to Freud's emphasis on sexuality, Jung described a more psychological and even spiritual unconscious, but one that also is inherited as part of our biological nature. The unfortunate consequence of this proposed genetic basis for the collective unconscious was a certain blindness to racial issues, and he allowed his writing to be used to support racist Nazi propaganda.

FINAL THOUGHTS

From prophecy to assassination, King's life story reads as hauntingly archetypal. The myth of the hero, an archetypal story shared across cultures, seems to define the life and work of Martin Luther King, Jr., better than any strictly individual interpretation as he was cast into the role of a hero in the struggle against racial injustice in the United States. The fact that he has become world famous attests to the resonance in many people to the universal archetypal energies that he represents for us. It was Jung's life work to explore the archetypes so they could coexist with rational consciousness rather than blindly driving human experience. As long as masses of people are unconscious of the archetypal realm, we will continue to act out these various tragic scripts.

PREVIEW: OVERVIEW OF JUNG'S THEORY

Jung's theory has implications for major theoretical questions, as presented in Table 3.1. From a scientific viewpoint, Jung's theory contains some of the most elusive concepts to measure objectively, yet his theory of personality psychetypes has stimulated considerable empirical testing. The breadth or comprehensiveness of the theory encompasses not only individual functioning but also many cultural symbols and myths. The theory has been applied to psychotherapy and to business.

Like Freud, Carl Jung proposed a theory that gives a prominent role to the unconscious. For Jung, however, the libido was not primarily sexual but was a broad psychic energy with spiritual dimensions, and the most interesting personality developments occur in adulthood, not in childhood. He was concerned with future directions toward which personality is developing, in contrast with Freud's emphasis on the past. Jung allowed himself to experience the unconscious firsthand through dreams and fantasies, comparing his role to that of an explorer who was strong enough to make this dangerous voyage and come back to tell others what he found there.

Jung considered science an inadequate tool for knowing the psyche. He preferred the language of mythology. He rejected "rational, scientific language" in favor of "a

Table 3.1 Preview of Jung's Theory

Individual Differences	Individuals differ in their tendency to be introverts or extraverts, which is stable throughout life. They also differ in the extent to which they make use of four psychological functions (thinking, feeling, sensation, and intuition).
Adaptation and Adjustment	The unconscious has an important role in healthy maturity and should be explored through symbolism. Health requires a balance between conscious and unconscious functioning.
Cognitive Processes	Rational thinking, intuition, and emphasis on concrete details all provide useful information and should be developed. Unconscious images influence perceptions and may distort our perception of reality.
Culture	Cultural myths and rituals provide ways of dealing with the unconscious. Important differences exist among cultures and should be preserved.
Biological Influences	Mental contents (a "collective unconscious") as well as physical characteristics are inherited.
Development	Early experience was of little interest to Jung. Midlife change (individuation) involves exploration of the creative potentials of the unconscious.

dramatic, mythological way of thinking and speaking, because this is not only more expressive but also more exact than an abstract scientific terminology, which is wont to toy with the notion that its theoretical formulations may one fine day be resolved into algebraic equations" (1959, p. 13). This is ironic because Jung's international fame first came from his empirical studies of word associations (Naifeh, 2001).

This antiscientific attitude places Jung outside mainstream psychology, where some dismiss Jung's work as a "pseudoscience" (McGowan, 1994, p. 12). That is, it masquerades as science, although not using the scientific methods of empirical verification to determine what is true and what is not. (Other nonscientific areas, such as literature and art, are not pseudoscience because they make no pretense about being scientific.) Jung's perspective strengthens the bridge Freud had begun between psychology and symbolic expressions in literature, art, and religion. Jung goes further than Freud, though, in abandoning scientific constraints. Even Freud, who referred to the Oedipus story and other myths in his theorizing, opposed Jung's mysticism. Nonetheless, Jung's theory has attracted many followers. Jungian psychotherapy and applications of his ideas in career guidance, organizational development, and literary criticism attest to his influence.

Carl Jung

Biography of Carl Jung

Carl Gustav Jung was born in Switzerland in 1875, the son of a Protestant minister and perhaps the great-grandson of the renowned German poet Goethe. Jung had one sister, who was 9 years his junior. His father and several uncles were Protestant clergymen. Jung suspected, even as a child, that his father did not genuinely believe the church's teachings but was afraid to face his doubts honestly. Like many in her family, Jung's mother was emotionally unstable (Noll, 1994) and, according to Jung, psychic.

As a young psychiatrist, Jung lectured at the University of Zurich, developed a word association technique for uncovering the emotional complexes of his patients, and had a private practice. He greeted Freud's controversial work on psychoanalysis enthusiastically and supported it in his own professional writing. After a period of mutually admiring correspondence, the two met at Freud's office in Vienna. This first meeting lasted 13 hours, attesting to the breadth of their mutual interest and respect. They continued an active correspondence, which has been published (McGuire, 1974). Together they traveled to the United States in 1909 to present psychoanalysis at the G. Stanley Hall Conference at Clark University (Jung, 1910/1987). The trip, a long journey by sea, gave Jung and Freud plenty of time to discuss psychoanalysis and dreams. These discussions revealed a small crack in their relationship that later became a huge split. Freud, to protect his authority, would not reveal personal associations to a dream he was telling Jung. These mental connections would have disclosed a sexual indiscretion, and to protect his authority, Freud chose to violate a cardinal rule of psychoanalysis by censoring his associations (Rosen, 1993).

Jung presided over a psychoanalytic association in Zurich, and Freud intended to have Jung succeed him as president of the International Psychoanalytic Association, thinking it would be advantageous to broaden psychoanalysis beyond its Jewish circle. He conveyed this intent to Jung in a letter in which he referred to Jung as a "crown prince," and Jung responded with gratitude, referring to Freud as a father figure.

Before this could be achieved, however, the personal relationship between Freud and Jung was disrupted. There were intellectual disagreements, to be sure; Jung felt that Freud overemphasized the role of sexuality in his theory and underestimated the positive potential of the unconscious. However, it was a personal conflict as well (Goldwert, 1986; Marcovitz, 1982; Stern, 1976), part of a midlife crisis in which Jung withdrew from his academic pursuits and devoted himself to introspection and exploration of two personalities within his own psyche (Rosen, 1996; Ticho, 1982).

Jung had long been interested in mystical phenomena. His doctoral dissertation had reported experiments on his cousin, a spiritualistic "medium" (Ellenberger, 1991), one of many of Jung's relatives who experienced psychic tendencies (Las Heras, 1992). In later life, he continued subjective explorations of the unconscious, read esoteric texts on mysticism and alchemy, and built a primitive retreat at Bollingen, on

Lake Zurich. He reported several personal experiences of psychic phenomena, which he understood as manifestations of a broad, transpersonal "collective unconscious." For example, Jung is said to have dreamt of Winston Churchill whenever the English politician came near Switzerland, even though Jung had no conscious awareness of his arrival (Wehr, 1987, p. 357). Understanding the collective unconscious was Jung's major life task.

THE STRUCTURE OF PERSONALITY

Like all psychoanalysts, Jung recognized that personality contains both conscious and unconscious elements. Like Freud, Jung referred to the ego when describing the more conscious aspects of personality. His description of the unconscious, though, differed from Freud's id and superego structures. Furthermore, he did not seek to increase the role of consciousness in personality and to minimize unconscious influence, as Freud did. Rather, Jung sought a balance in which unconscious elements were given an equal role, complementary to that of consciousness.

The Psyche and The Self: The Personality as a Whole

Jung generally did not refer to personality but rather to the *psyche*, a Latin word that originally meant "spirit" or "soul" (Hall & Nordby, 1973, p. 32). This term suggested the integration of all aspects of personality. Jung referred to the total integrated personality as the **Self**. (In Jungian writing, Self is usually capitalized, which helps distinguish it from the more conscious and social self of other theorists.)

Self

the total integrated personality

Throughout life, we sometimes emphasize conscious growth (e.g., in developing a career identity); at other times we focus more on inner development. Jung compared this flow of libido outward (adapting consciously to the world) and then inward (to serve inner needs) to the ebb and flow of the tides. Jung did not believe it was possible or desirable to live entirely consciously; that would be like trying to build a dike to hold back the ocean. It is not healthy to give all energy to the unconscious either; that would be like a flood. Learning from the tides, people should expect sometimes to deal consciously with the external world and at other times to turn to the inner world for psychic rejuvenation.

compensation

principle of the relationship between the unconscious and consciousness, by which the unconscious provides what is missing from consciousness to make a complete whole

Consciousness and the unconscious coexist in individuals. In contrast to Freud's portrayal of conflict, Jung described this relationship as one of **compensation**. Consciousness is necessary for dealing with the real world, but it is not enough. The unconscious compensates for the one-sidedness of consciousness by emphasizing those aspects of psychic totality that have been neglected by consciousness. For example, a person who has developed a conscious attitude of rational and logical thought but who has neglected emotional issues will have these feelings in the unconscious. The unconscious has the "missing pieces" to allow the development of the Self toward psychic wholeness. A healthy condition requires both consciousness and unconscious, and compensation serves as a homeostasis-like mechanism to restore this balance, often through dreams (Beebe, Cambray, & Kirsch, 2001).

individuation

the process of becoming a fully developed person, with all psychic functions developed

INDIVIDUATION   People develop the various aspects of their psyche unevenly. Along the way, we may identify disproportionately with our ego or with some aspect or another of our unconscious; this excessive identification is often referred to as "inflation" (Edinger, 1972). Modern humans, according to Jung, are particularly vulnerable to ego inflation, and unlike our ancestors who lived more unconsciously, we suppress the unconscious to an unhealthy extent (Drob, 1999). **Individuation** is the process of restoring wholeness to the psyche in adult development. The psyche begins as a unified whole, although unconscious. During the course of development, various aspects of the psyche come into consciousness and are developed while other areas remain unconscious, creating an inevitable imbalance in the original wholeness.

This imbalance is restored during healthy adult development in midlife. Unconscious potentials are explored and reintegrated with the total Self in the individuation process, the goal of which is to move the center of personality from the ego to some midpoint between the ego and the unconscious. The person must develop a relationship with the experiences of the unconscious, including the collective unconscious (described below). Dreams may occur in which the dreamer questions the ego's perspective (Beebe, 2008). Dreams of mountains may symbolize the individuation process, often with the twist of climbing down (symbolizing the unconscious) before moving up (Perluss, 2008). In the later phases of the individuation process, the **transcendent function** integrates the diverse aspects into a unified whole.

Only through individuation can a person become truly an individual and not simply a carrier of unconscious images and other people's projections. When this developmental process does not proceed, tragic consequences can result. For example, Marilyn Monroe's inability to individuate herself left her trapped in her cultural image as a sex goddess, without a genuinely individual identity.

transcendent function
the process of integrating all opposing aspects of personality into a unified whole

Ego

Jung (1959), like Freud, described the ego as the aspect of personality that is most conscious. The ego is essential for a feeling of personal identity and is the center of our will, enabling us to strive for conscious goals. However, there are limits to willpower because of limitations to consciousness itself. To use Jung's metaphor, the ego is part of personality, but it is not the center of personality.

Probably the most common way of being out of balance, especially in the first half of life, is to identify too closely with conscious experience and intentions. Jung called this **ego inflation**. Growth forces within the psyche work to undo imbalance by such dramatic evidence of ego limitations as job burnout (Garden, 1991) or marital setbacks.

Less often, psychic inflation can result from overvaluing the unconscious. Mystics and spiritualistic mediums, as well as psychotics, suffer from this kind of psychic imbalance. The remedy for either type of psychic inflation is individuation, which involves finding a proper balance between consciousness and the unconscious.

ego inflation
overvaluation of ego consciousness, without recognizing its limited role in the psyche

Persona

The **persona** is the aspect of personality that adapts to the world, shaped by the reactions we elicit in other people. To the extent that people respond to us as good looking or bright or athletically skilled, that becomes our self-image, or persona. We strive to behave in ways that will earn for us a positive social image, emphasizing aspects of ourselves that are valued by others and trying to ignore or deny the rest. When social roles change, for example in graduation or retirement, we experience discontinuity in personality.

Changes in persona are celebrated with publicly visible symbols of the new status. During rites of initiation among primitive societies, members are given a symbol of their entry into adulthood. New clothes or costumes, as at a wedding or graduation, underscore a change in persona. An inadequate persona may be symbolized in dreams of being naked, and embarrassed, in a public place.

The persona is generally well established by young adulthood. Two other psychic elements, the shadow and the anima (in men) or animus (in women), are more problematic. Bringing these elements to awareness and integrating them with consciousness are major tasks of adult development.

persona
a person's social identity

Shadow

While consciousness has been occupied with creating a socially acceptable persona, other potentials in personality have been neglected or actively repressed. The term **shadow** refers to those aspects of the psyche that are rejected from consciousness by the ego because they are inconsistent with one's self-concept. Unacceptable sexual and aggressive impulses are especially characteristic of the shadow, reminiscent of Freud's theory of repressed id impulses. Other characteristics may be found: stupidity in a person who takes pride in intelligence, ugliness in one who is handsome, and so on.

shadow
the unconscious complement to a person's conscious identity, often experienced as dangerous and evil

The shadow is symbolized in literature and in dreams by various images of evil, disturbed, and repulsive people: criminals, psychotics, and others whom we despise or pity. In dreams, the specific repulsive qualities of a shadow figure give clues to the material that the person has repressed. Thus a man who is proud of his intelligence may represent his shadow in a dream as a mentally retarded man; a sexually controlled woman may symbolize her shadow in a dream of a prostitute. A classic literary portrayal of the shadow appears in Oscar Wilde's story, "The Picture of Dorian Gray," in which Gray maintained the outward appearance of a fine and upstanding citizen, while his hidden portrait, symbolizing his shadow, took on the hideous look of his secret crimes. Like Dorian Gray, we show our persona to the world and hide the shadow. As we do so, the split between persona and shadow, which disrupts our wholeness, widens. If we deal more consciously with shadow issues, as Jungians advocate (Zweig & Wolf, 1997), the shadow would not become so ugly.

The tendency to project shadow elements onto persons of other races in waking life, as well as in dreams, contributes to racial prejudice. Fanon (1967, p. 165) suggested that people project their instinctive animal characteristics onto blacks and their threatening intellectual qualities onto Jews, an interpretation that Jung would probably have accepted.

According to Jung (1959, p. 8), there are some rare exceptions to the general rule that the shadow is negative. A few people have an identity that is consciously evil and have repressed their own positive qualities into a positive shadow. For example, powerful tyrants may pride themselves on brutality and reject humane qualities as "weak."

The shadow mediates between consciousness and unconsciousness and can be regarded as "the gatekeeper to the unconscious." Our shadow is experienced as frightening or evil, and emergence of the shadow from the unconscious produces the experience of moral conflict. According to David Rosen (1993), a Jungian psychiatrist and scholar, the shadow assists psychological growth by helping to bring about an *egocide* (a symbolic suicide or an ego sacrifice); this helps the person find a center of personality that is more open to the unconscious. When a person comes to terms with the unconscious and recognizes that it has positive contributions to make to personality as a whole, experience changes. The shadow then is less repulsive and more playful, and it brings zest and liveliness to experience. When integrated with consciousness, the shadow is a source of creativity and pleasure.

Anima and Animus

People consciously reject not only qualities that are evil or inconsistent with their persona (the shadow) but also qualities they consider incompatible with their identity as males or females. These sex-inappropriate qualities, traditionally exemplified by traits such as emotionality for males and power for females, constitute the **anima** (a man's repressed or undeveloped feminine-type qualities) and the **animus** (a woman's repressed or undeveloped masculine-type qualities).

anima

the femininity that is part of the unconscious of every man

animus

the masculinity that is part of the unconscious of every woman

Sometimes a person becomes "possessed" by his anima or her animus, which is Jung's way of describing a condition in which unconscious qualities control behavior without being integrated into consciousness. Jung interpreted the anima to represent Eros, the principle of relatedness. Men possessed by their anima act moody and emotional. Jung referred to the animus as "the paternal Logos," claiming that logic and reason (Logos) are masculine qualities. He believed women were possessed by the animus if they were opinionated and preoccupied with power. These portrayals of gender leave Jung open to the accusation of sexism. Although Jung stressed the importance for each sex to develop psychological androgyny, he described women's animus development more harshly than men's explorations of the anima (Torrey, 1987).

PROJECTION OF THE ANIMA OR ANIMUS   The unconscious anima or animus is projected onto people of the opposite sex, including parents and lovers. These individuals trigger various emotions (such as fear, rejection, or longing), depending on one's attitude toward one's own unconscious anima or animus. A man who belittles a woman for her sentimentality is, by projection, rejecting his own unacknowledged sentimentality.

When he is ready to integrate it, he will stop criticizing women in whom he sees that quality. Similarly, women may project their own rejected animus by fearing or attacking qualities such as dominance and independence in men. These projections, too, will become more positive as the animus is integrated into consciousness.

One of the most common, and potentially healthy, instances of projection of the anima or animus is the experience of falling in love (Jung, 1931/1954). Falling in love promises to restore the missing piece of the psyche that was left behind in the unconscious when the conscious personality was developed. Each lover feels psychologically whole when with the beloved. Through the love relationship, the woman develops her own masculine potentials and the man becomes more conscious of his own repressed feminine qualities. In a psychologically healthy love relationship, the lover accepts the other in his or her entirety, even the shadow, which can now also be integrated. Thus love facilitates psychological development.

Collective Unconscious

The anima or animus and the shadow together constitute what Jung called the **personal unconscious**. This is the unconscious of each individual that is developed because of the person's unique experiences. Jung also described a deeper layer to the unconscious. It was symbolized, in a dream he reported, as a concealed basement deep below a house, approached down dusty stairs and finally to an ancient room below the ordinary cellar, filled with prehistoric bones and pottery (Jung, 1989; reported in Noll, 1994, pp. 177–178). Jung interpreted this dream as portraying a deep level of the unconscious, shared by everyone despite differences in personal experience.

Jung called this deeper level the **collective unconscious**. This is the core of Jung's mysticism and is the concept least accepted by mainstream psychology. Jung described the collective unconscious as inherited, contained in human brain structure and not dependent on personal experience to develop. The collective unconscious is shaped by the remote evolutionary experiences of the human species.

The collective unconscious contains "primordial images," called **archetypes**, which are similar in all people. These archetypes function as "psychic instincts" that predispose us to experience the world in certain universally human ways. Archetypes have both an emotional, psychosomatic component and a cognitive component of associated images and ideas, and they influence behavior. According to Jung, we have images that tell us what a mother is, what a spiritual leader is, even what God is. This is a particularly strange concept for modern psychology, which has been profoundly influenced by behaviorism and its emphasis on environmental determinism. A more palatable interpretation may be that archetypes are not themselves full blown and inherited, but rather that they are likely to emerge through the self-organization of the mind and brain, based on more fundamental emotional and cognitive processes that are inherited (Saunders & Skar, 2001).

Some suggest that archetypes can be reconciled with neuroscience (Stevens, 1995). Neuroscientists who do not discuss Jungian ideas at all sometimes use language that could be interpreted as referring to archetypes; in describing the role of the amygdala in the emotional reactions of monkeys, for example, one brain researcher (Amaral, 2002) referred to this brain center's theorized reaction to "innate templates of species-specific emotional elicitors (such as snakes)"—which certainly sounds like an archetypal image of a snake (in the monkey psyche). Furthermore, lesions of this brain area in the monkey sometimes produced fearfulness and sometimes unusual lack of fear, which varied with the age of the animal at the time of the lesion and the object or social stimulus to which the animal was exposed. Jungians describe an ambivalent aspect of archetypes, which seems to fit this still unexplained inconsistency in the role of the amygdala. It would be premature to draw definitive correspondences between archetypes and specific brain areas, but the possibility is intriguing.

THE SHADOW AND THE ANIMA OR ANIMUS AS ARCHETYPES As described earlier, the *content* of the shadow and the anima or animus, with associated emotional conflicts or complexes, is part of the personal unconscious. The content of the shadow would

personal unconscious
that part of the unconscious derived from an individual's experience

collective unconscious
the inherited unconscious

archetype
a primordial image in the collective unconscious; an innate pattern that influences experience of the real world

be different if a person were raised with different messages about what is right and wrong. (For a vegetarian Hindu, such as Mahatma Gandhi, eating meat is a shadow characteristic; for most Americans, it is not.) In a similar way, the content of the anima or animus varies according to the gender roles taught in a culture.

The predisposition to develop a shadow and an anima or animus, however, is collective and universal. Personal experience shapes its particular content for an individual, making one person's shadow a horrid satanic figure and another's a minor criminal. Besides the shadow and the anima or animus, in the collective unconscious there are many more archetypes.

OTHER ARCHETYPES   Because the shadow and the anima or animus are closest to consciousness, they are the archetypes with the most noticeable effects on experience. The other archetypes discussed here are said to be deeper in the collective unconscious and influence conscious experience less often. When they do, they feel more foreign. Archetypes may be experienced individually in dreams or projections onto other people. In addition, they are reflected in cultural stories and myths.

The Great Mother   The archetype of the Great Mother reflects the ancestral experience of being raised by mothers. The Great Mother is widely represented in mythology and art, from carved fertility symbols of ancient cultures to paintings of the Virgin Mary.

All archetypes have an ambivalent quality, with both positive and negative aspects. Sentimentality about motherhood and apple pie is positive, but the Great Mother also encompasses negative elements. Many primitive myths relate the fertility of the harvest and human reproduction with death, expressing both aspects of the archetype. The Hindu goddess Kali not only nurses infants but also drinks blood (Neumann, 1963, p. 152). The myth of Demeter and Persephone celebrates the coming of spring only after a woman's journey to the underworld. This underworld involves the powerful instincts of a woman's unconscious, which must be experienced as part of her full development (Perluss, 2008).

The Spiritual Father   In his descriptions of the father archetype, Jung contrasted instinctive qualities, which he claimed were more feminine, with the spiritual qualities of the archetypal father. The association of spirituality with masculinity did not originate with Jung; it has a long history in the Judeo-Christian tradition (Daly, 1978; Lacks, 1980; Patai, 1967), which has traditionally portrayed God and spiritual leaders as masculine. Even classroom teachers may be perceived to have more wisdom than they actually have because students project the archetype (sometimes called a "wise old man") onto them (Mayes, 1999).

The Hero   The hero of mythology and folklore conquers great enemies and wins mighty battles. Jung described this archetype as associated with the internal psychic struggle to become an individual, separate from regressive ties to the mother. It also relates to external battles with threatening forces in the world. The hero is often, like Daniel in the lion's den or Parsifal of the Grail myth, a relatively weak individual, but heroes and heroines are in touch with special forces that allow them to conquer mighty opponents. For Jung, the hero myth was central as a description of psychological development, a myth of continuing to confront the unconscious and emerge from it stronger and more developed (Haule, 2000). Many varieties of the hero myth are described by a Jungian scholar, Joseph Campbell (1949).

The Trickster   The Trickster appears in various cultures as a simple-minded prankster who seems to be outwitted but who ultimately brings good results. In literature, trickster figures disrupt (sometimes violently) an order that has become sterile and in so doing, they bring characters back to reality (Schaum, 2000). Trickster figures are less common in our culture than in some others (e.g., in Native American mythology), but they can be seen in the revelries of Mardi Gras and in circus clowns. Because of the frequent representation of mythic Trickster figures as criminals, such as murderers, rapists, and thieves (Carp, 1998), it seems possible that more cultural attention to Trickster figures could help transform psychic energies that are acted out as crime into more integrated and healthy forms. Jung (1969) referred to the trickster as "a collective shadow figure, a summation of all the inferior traits of character in individuals" (p. 150). Because they provide a symbolic expression of this shadow, trickster myths may assist individuals to incorporate the shadow to find creative energies for growth in previously repressed material. Carp (1998) suggests that clown therapy may be a way to help integrate the shadow.

Mandala   A **mandala** is an archetype of order, usually symbolized by a circle or a square or often a square within a circle. The "Golden Flower" of Buddhist meditation is one mandala image that Jung recognized (Beebe, 2008). Many religions include mandalas as symbols facilitating spiritual development (Coward, 1989). Examples are found in Tibetan Buddhism, the World Wheel of Hinduism, the Rose Window of Notre Dame cathedral in Paris, and many other places (see Figure 3.1).

mandala
symbolic representation of the whole psyche, emphasizing circles and/or squares

Dreams of mandalas often occur when people are experiencing great conflict, indicating that the unconscious has developed more of a solution to the conflict than the person consciously recognizes. The symbol anticipates the development of a more well-rounded, balanced Self (Coward, 1989). Because the mandala represents emerging psychic wholeness, the goal of the development of the Self, we can call it the archetype of the Self (Edinger, 1968) or the archetype of wholeness.

Transformation   **Transformation** is symbolized by many mythic and individual symbols. Alchemists, predating modern chemists, struggled to find the secret that would transform base metal into gold: the quest for the philosophers' stone. Myths of great journeys, such as Odysseus's wanderings in ancient Greece, are classic parallels to more mundane images of crossing bridges or crossing streets. Such crossings symbolize psychological transformation, the changes that occur with continued development (Jung, 1944/1968b).

transformation
modification of psychic energy to higher purposes (e.g., through ritual)

PSYCHOSIS: DANGERS OF THE COLLECTIVE UNCONSCIOUS   Jung's (1960a) theory interprets psychotic hallucinations and delusions as direct expressions of the collective unconscious. Without the conscious ego to act as a mediator, this powerful collective unconscious overwhelms the individuality of the person and makes manifest what is latent in the rest of us. Drugs can trigger psychosis by chemically inducing an

FIGURE 3.1   A Mandala, a Symbol of Psychic Wholeness
In Eastern religious tradition, these monks are preparing a mandala as an aid to meditation. For Carl Jung, this image affirmed the value of unconscious processes. He was influenced by Buddhist ideas.

encounter with images of the archetypal unconscious. Direct experience is dangerous, but the collective unconscious can be approached cautiously, with the aid of symbols and myths.

SYMBOLISM AND THE COLLECTIVE UNCONSCIOUS

Like Freud, Jung believed that the unconscious manifests itself in symbols. A symbol is formed at the meeting point between the unconscious and consciousness, shaped by both conscious experience and unconscious material, including archetypes. Symbols tap this shared archetypal substratum of the collective unconscious and thus have more or less universal meanings (cf. Chetwynd, 1982; Cirlot, 1971).

Jung delighted in finding similarities between the experiences of psychotic patients and symbols of ancient art and mythology. For example, he reported parallels between hallucinations and drawings of a psychiatric patient and symbols on a newly discovered Greek papyrus, which he interpreted as coming from the same collective unconscious. However, a historian suggests that the ancient Greek images were publicized before this patient's images and so could have been their source; other patients alleged by Jung to have spontaneously produced images like those of ancient peoples could also have learned of these images beforehand (Noll, 1994). Another critic finds several alternative explanations for this report, including simple coincidence, that challenge Jung's theory of archetypes (Neher, 1996).

Many of Jung's concepts, such as archetypes and the collective unconscious, are difficult or impossible to test empirically. Jung made no effort to do so by using well-controlled scientific procedures as we know them, and his followers likewise emphasize nonempirical methods. One exception, an experimental study of archetypal symbolism, is reported by D. H. Rosen and others (Rosen et al., 1991). They developed an Archetypal Symbol Inventory consisting of 40 visual images portraying symbols associated with Jungian archetypes. Undergraduate psychology students were administered a paired learning task in which they learned to associate these symbols with words. Half of the words matched the accepted archetypal meaning of the symbols, and half were mismatched (associated with the incorrect symbol). An image of a snake, for example, matched "health," as might seem sensible when we consider that the caduceus, the symbol of the medical profession, features a snake. Furthermore, the symbol of a crescent moon matches the word "feminine," as those aware of lunar imagery may readily see. When symbols were presented with their matching words, recall accuracy was significantly higher than recall of mismatched symbol–word pairs. Other analyses showed that subjects were not consciously aware of the meaning of the symbols (Huston, Rosen, & Smith, 1999). This research does not definitively demonstrate the Jungian assertion that archetypal symbols are innate because there may be other reasons why some pairs are more memorable than others, but it is, nonetheless, a step in applying scientific methods to the elusive concept of the collective unconscious.

numinous

experience of spiritual or transpersonal energies

The collective unconscious has a feeling that Jung called **numinous**, meaning "spiritual" or "awesome." It is not within an individual's will (Schlamm, 2007). It can never be totally assimilated into individual consciousness, but it is important for individual consciousness to have some relationship to this collective unconscious.

Myths and Religion

How can we tap the energies of the collective unconscious without being destroyed by them (as in psychosis)? That is the function of mythology, religion, and the arts, which provide cultural symbols, which give the conscious mind some access to the energy of the unconscious. Psychotherapist Bruno Bettelheim (1976) found that when he exposed young boys only to "safe" versions of traditional fairy stories, with all monsters, witches, and frightening episodes removed, the boys were much more disruptive than were children exposed to the traditional frightening stories by the Brothers Grimm. Symbolic representation of fearsome emotions through fairy tales brings these issues to consciousness, where they can be dealt with by ego strengths.

Some Jungian analysts use fairy tales as a way of encouraging creativity in developing new ways of thinking about life's issues (Kast, 1996).

Jung encouraged people to participate in the religious traditions in which they had been raised. (He discouraged Westerners from switching to Eastern religions, based on his premise that a somewhat different unconscious was represented in each.) Perhaps another caution in cross-cultural religious studies is the danger of distorting other traditions because we see the world through the lens of our own background, as one Jesuit priest is indicted for doing when he interpreted Native Americans' religious tradition of the Sacred Pipe from a Christian viewpoint (Bucko, 2000).

In this scientific era, we sometimes misinterpret myth as merely primitive science. A myth of the sun rising, for example, is dismissed as an outdated statement before people knew that the earth revolved around the sun. Fertility rites are, from this view, outdated by our increased understanding of biology. For Jung, however, myths are far more than primitive science because they deal with subjective experience. A myth of the sun "setting" expresses people's grief of seeing the departure of the sun and their fear of the dangers that come with the night. Science, which is intentionally neutral in the emotional sphere, cannot replace this emotional function of myth. Perhaps a sense of this loss has contributed to antiscience tendencies in our modern era.

Jung's theory is influenced by mystical thought in both Christian and Jewish religious traditions (Drob, 1999). The archetypal language of religious writing—for example, the apocalypse in the biblical book of Revelation (Edinger, 1999)—expresses symbolic insights. Interest in ancient gods and goddesses reflects a modern hunger for myths (May, 1991). Some people take offense at the labeling of religion as myth and try to defend religious assertions by scientific standards. The debate over creationism versus evolution is an example. To judge religion by scientific criteria is to misunderstand, and underestimate, the nature of myth and is really no more sensible than sending a dishwasher to the repair shop because it cannot bake a cake.

Modern Myths

Old myths, and the collective unconscious that they tap, contain "the wisdom of the ages lying dormant in the brain" and offer guidance for human life. Influenced by Jungian theory, many scholars are investigating old myths for wisdom. However, technological and social change have made some old myths obsolete and the consciousness they foster dangerous in the face of new perils, such as nuclear holocaust, that demand new ways of thinking (Kull, 1983; Mack, 1986; Perlman, 1983). We also need new myths to guide us through the new challenges of our age (Atkinson, 1991; DeCarvalho, 1992; May, 1991). At its best, myth making is an active and vital process in human culture. According to Jung, when humans lose the capacity for myth making, they lose touch with the creative forces of their being.

Modern myths are described by various Jungian scholars, including the mythologist Joseph Campbell (1972). Examples include the *Star Wars* films (Ryback, 1983) and other science fiction works. One of Campbell's students, George Lucas, produced several well-known movies that are modern myths, including *Raiders of the Lost Ark, Indiana Jones and the Temple of Doom,* and *Indiana Jones and the Last Crusade.* (The last of these extends a medieval legend, the Holy Grail.) Creative new myths, in the Jungian tradition, may be our guide to the development of new ways of relating to the collective human unconscious and to the historical experiences of our own time. A Jungian analyst, for example, praises Spielberg's (1993) film *Schindler's List* for its approach to the Holocaust. The story allows the viewer to experience mourning and shame without a confrontation with these emotions that is so direct as to be overpowering, providing "a healing rite of vision" (Beebe, 1996).

THERAPY

Jungian therapy assists the unconscious in claiming its rightful role, challenging the inflation of the ego (Singer, 1994). Like Freudian psychoanalysis, Jungian therapy focuses largely on dreams and symbolic material. Unlike Freud, Jung did not emphasize the past or childhood origins of psychological difficulty, and he regarded the unconscious as an ally rather than the enemy.

The direction of growth, in therapy and outside, is toward greater wholeness. Parts of the psyche that have been broken off from the whole must be retrieved and integrated with the rest of the personality. Often these isolated pieces take the form of **complexes**, that is, networks of unconscious conflicted emotions and thoughts. They center around a common theme (such as a mother complex or a hero complex), which is often archetypal (Edinger, 1968). Unresolved complexes cause maladaptive behavior, as when a complex based around an uninvolved father causes a person to become involved with distant spouses or bosses (Van Eenwyk, 1997).

Complexes may appear in symptoms or dreams. They also can be elicited through the **Word Association Test**, which Jung (1973) devised—an approach that brought him, at that time, international fame for his experimental work and has been described as a precursor of modern cognitive science (Noll, 1994). In this test, the patient listens to a word and is instructed to say whatever comes to mind. Unusual associations and delays in responding indicate that a psychological complex may have been activated. Jung's Word Association Test was, incidentally, an influence on Hermann Rorschach, Jung's colleague at the Burgholzli hospital, in his development of the famous Rorschach inkblot test (Pichot, 1984).

Dreams

Jung, like Freud, regarded dreams as products of the unconscious. Often patients have dreams early in analysis that, in effect, are statements by the unconscious of the therapeutic task. Because the Jungian unconscious contains multiple levels, personal and collective, various kinds of dreams can be distinguished. Many dreams reveal the individual's unresolved emotional complexes in the personal unconscious. These are comparable to Freudian dreams, although Jung (1974) did not interpret them sexually. Other dreams reach into the collective unconscious and incorporate archetypal imagery, especially when the dreamer's personality is intuitive and low in neuroticism (Cann & Donderi, 1986). Occasionally, according to Jung, dreams are not personal at all but are like the "big dreams" of Native Americans: messages to humanity at large, with the individual only a receiving medium.

Interpretation of dreams involves three stages. First, the dreamer recalls the dream, retelling it in detail. Second, in the **amplification** of the dream, the dreamer elaborates on the dream images, describing associations to the people and symbols (Mattoon, 1978). In the third stage, **active imagination**, the dreamer continues with the dream imagery in waking imagination, adding new episodes or otherwise continuing the symbolic work toward the personal growth that was begun in the dream. For example, if a dream includes a woman, who may symbolize unconscious potentials in the dreamer's psyche, then having an imagined conversation with that woman can further the psychological development begun by the dream (Beebe, Cambray, & Kirsch, 2001).

Jung interpreted all persons and symbols of a dream as aspects of the dreamer's psyche. The way they interact in the dream describes efforts and obstacles in the developmental task of individuation. For example, a dream of exploring a long-forgotten basement and being frightened at the monsters that live there may reflect a person's fear of exploring the unconscious. Many dreams can be interpreted according to the principle of compensation (Jung, 1974; Mahoney, 1966). That is, the dream presents ideas or emotions that supplement the limitations of consciousness, prompting the dreamer to have a more balanced approach to current life issues. Jung (1961) described one of his own dreams in which he looked across a valley and, straining to look up, saw one of his patients. He interpreted this dream, according to the principle of compensation, to mean that in real life he had been "looking down on" the patient with a condescending attitude. That interpretation, which he shared with the patient, prompted a change in Jung's attitude toward her, which facilitated therapeutic progress.

---

complexes

emotionally charged networks of ideas (such as those resulting from unresolved conflicts)

Word Association Test

method devised by Jung to reveal complexes by asking people to say whatever comes to mind when they hear a word

amplification

elaboration of dream images as a step toward dream interpretation

active imagination

technique for exploring the unconscious by encouraging waking fantasies

Other Symbolic Therapy Techniques

Besides dreams, other techniques are available to encourage a dialogue with the unconscious. Among both children and adults, artistic creations provide a way of expressing images from the unconscious, especially as they may have appeared in dreams. Sometimes visual images can be interpreted in a way that links the dreamer's experience to larger myths (Johnson, 1991; Nez, 1991). Play therapy is used with children by Jungians and therapists from other theoretical traditions (Allan & Brown, 1993).

Myths can provide meanings for patients' problematic behaviors, too. For example, the self-starvation eating disorder anorexia nervosa can be given larger meaning by interpreting this behavior as an unconscious acting out of the ascetic ritual of fasting, which is intended as a spiritual exercise (Barrett & Fine, 1990). Thus the symptom, the illness, provides an unconscious connection with larger, and potentially healthy, spiritual meaning.

Attention to symbols should not end with the conclusion of therapy. Further symbolic exploration through structured workshops (e.g., Progoff, 1975) may be useful. Through the power of symbols and myths, the psyche grows beyond the limitations of the ego to a larger consciousness (Hollis, 2000), centered not in the ego but in the Self. At its most desirable conclusion, Jungian therapy prepares individuals to create new symbolic forms. They actively participate in the ongoing human task of tapping the creative energies of the unconscious, thus contributing to an evolving human destiny. One who has successfully completed a Jungian analysis must lead a "symbolic life."

SYNCHRONICITY

Jung claimed that the collective unconscious forms the basis for paranormal phenomena that have no causal explanation in a deterministic science. Mainstream scientists dismiss phenomena such as extrasensory perception (ESP), spiritualism, and mental telepathy as superstitious or fraudulent. In contrast, Jung found them fascinating. He studied spiritualistic séances; he wrote in laudatory terms about J. B. Rhine's controversial experiments into ESP; he wrote about flying saucers (Jung, 1964).

Had Jung abandoned science and common sense altogether, as Freud feared? Writers sympathetic to Jung argue that he was not really a believer in these phenomena (e.g., Hall & Nordby, 1973). Rather, he felt that prescientific explanations offered a target onto which people projected their preexisting concepts and ideas, especially their archetypal images. Medieval alchemists described their search for the process of transforming base metal into gold, and their descriptions used symbols that provided clues to their archetypal patterns of thought (Jung, 1959, 1968a, 1944/1968b, 1970). This view of Jung, although it is accurate, is incomplete. It presents Jung as a more objective observer than, by his own account, he was. He experienced a world in which events sometimes had no deterministic explanation. Jung's (1961) autobiography reports many incidents of paranormal experience. He reported waking from sleep with a pain in his head at the time when, unknown to him, a patient shot himself in the head. He dreamed bloody forebodings of war. He discovered that a story he made up about fictitious criminal activity was actually the real-life story of a man he had just met. These are only a few of Jung's self-reported paranormal experiences. He did not dismiss such experiences as meaningless coincidences. In fact, he used such experiences in his work as a therapist, and they helped free his patients from being stuck in their apparently rational but limiting views (Haule, 2000).

Jung (1960b) proposed the term **synchronicity** to describe experiences that logically can be only coincidental but in a feeling sense have meaning. In short, these are meaningful coincidences. When he was talking to Freud, they both heard a loud, startling sound emanating from the bookcase and wondered what it was. Jung said it was the forces of their contact, and to prove it, he predicted it would happen again. It did (Jung, 1961). Jung interpreted such synchronistic events as manifestations of the collective unconscious. To most people, though, it is simply a coincidence that the bookcase settled or perhaps cracked at that moment.

synchronicity
the acausal principle in which events are determined by transpersonal forces instead of by causes generally understood by science

I Ching

*ancient Chinese method of
fortune-telling*

Jung was interested in the **I Ching**, a traditional Chinese method of "consulting an oracle" or, more bluntly, of fortunetelling (Wilhelm, 1960). The I Ching is based on a number system, with 64 hexagrams corresponding to various phases in the ever-changing conditions of human experience (Phillips, 1980). Traditionally, the Chinese draw straws to select the relevant answer to their question. Alternatively, Jung used a method of flipping coins; he carried a bag of special coins for this purpose. It was his way of transcending the limitations of ego consciousness when life posed difficulties irresolvable through reason. Even if an oracle provides random advice (although Jung was not so rationally cynical), there probably is something to be said for having a way out of the ever-deepening ruts of imperfect conscious decision-making strategies.

Jung's mystical side, like all paranormal thinking, is at odds with the deterministic assumptions of science (Blackmore, 1994; Gallo, 1994; Grey, 1994; Tart, 1992). When empirical studies of the I Ching have been reported, results are not convincing by traditional scientific standards; occasional significant results are reported (Storm & Thalbourne, 2001), but they do not replicate reliably from one study to another. Some have argued that most personality theory is based on a model of reality derived from outmoded physics. Developments in relativity theory and in quantum physics, they argue, provide a model that allows indeterminism and free will and is more compatible with subjective and even mystical approaches (Keutzer, 1984; Mansfield, 1991; Mansfield & Spiegelman, 1991; von Franz, 1964). Is a new philosophy of science emerging that will validate Jungian mystical ideas? Possibly. However this reference to new models of physics may also be a modern parallel to the medieval alchemists, whose objectivity was clouded by their own presuppositions.

Another way to interpret Jung's mysticism derives from his theory of psychological types (presented in the next section). Traditional science is based on logical and concrete thinking. Jung's theory of psychological types proposes that such thought represents only a partial use of the psyche. His mystical side can be viewed as exploring the implications of the other psychic potentials. Jung's theory of psychological types helps explain his orientation toward mysticism.

PSYCHOLOGICAL TYPES

psychological type

*a person's characteristic pattern
of major personality dimensions
(introversion-extraversion, thinking-
feeling, and sensation-intuition)*

Jung describes a person's **psychological type** in terms of three major dimensions of personality: introversion-extraversion, thinking-feeling, and sensation-intuition. The person is categorized on one side or the other of each dimension, resulting in one of eight possible psychological types.

To identify psychological type, it is first necessary to determine whether a person is oriented primarily toward the inner world (introversion) or toward external reality (extraversion). Jung called introversion or extraversion the *fundamental attitude* of the individual to emphasize its importance. Next, one assesses which of four *psychological functions* (thinking, feeling, sensation, or intuition) the person prefers. This is labeled the **dominant function**. The dominant function is directed toward external reality if the person is an extravert or toward the inner world if the person is an introvert (O'Roark, 1990). The fundamental attitudes (introversion and extraversion) can be combined with the four functions (thinking, feeling, sensation, and intuition) in eight different ways, constituting eight psychetypes (see Table 3.2).

dominant function

*a person's predominant
psychological function*

auxiliary function

*the second most developed function
of an individual's personality*

To give a more complete description, we can also identify the function that the individual uses for dealing with the less preferred direction (internal reality for an extravert, external reality for an introvert). This is labeled the **auxiliary function** (see Figure 3.2). Jung described the four functions as constituting two pairs: rational functions (thinking and feeling) enable us to make judgments or decisions, while irrational functions (sensation and intuition) provide us with information on which to base these judgments. If the dominant function is a rational (decision) function, the auxiliary function will be an irrational (information-gathering) function, and vice versa (McCaulley, 1990).

Table 3.2 Personality Psychetypes	
Introverted Thinking	Interested in ideas (rather than facts); interested in inner reality; pays little attention to other people
Introverted Feeling	Superficially reserved, but sympathetic and understanding of close friends or of others in need; loving, but not demonstrative
Introverted Sensation	Emphasizes the experience that events trigger, rather than the events themselves (e.g., musicians and artists)
Introverted Intuition	Concerned with possibilities, rather than what is currently present; in touch with the unconscious
Extraverted Thinking	Interested in facts about objects external to the self; logical; represses emotion and feelings; neglects friends and relationships
Extraverted Feeling	Concerned with human relationships; adjusted to the environment (especially frequent among women, according to Jung)
Extraverted Sensation	Emphasizes the objects that trigger experience; concerned with facts and details; sometimes with pleasure seeking
Extraverted Intuition	Concerned with possibilities for change in the external world, rather than with the familiar; an adventurer

Source: Adapted from Fordham, 1966.

Introversion and Extraversion

Even people with no psychological training use the terms *introvert* and *extravert* to indicate whether people are shy or sociable, and these concepts are included in many personality theories. Introverts turn their attention and their libido inward, to their own thoughts and inner states, whereas extraverts direct their energy and attention outward, to people and experiences in the world. Their orientations are so fundamentally different that they often do not understand each other. The extravert, unaware of his or her own inner dynamics, thinks the introvert is "egotistical and dull." The introvert, minimally concerned with other people, regards the extravert as "superficial and insincere" (Fordham, 1966, p. 33). Jung understood his conflict with Freud as an example of such a clash of types. Jung's introversion was unaccepted by the extravert Freud. Knowing the basis for such interpersonal conflicts cannot eliminate them, but it can at least provide a counterforce against the tendency to devalue the other type of person.

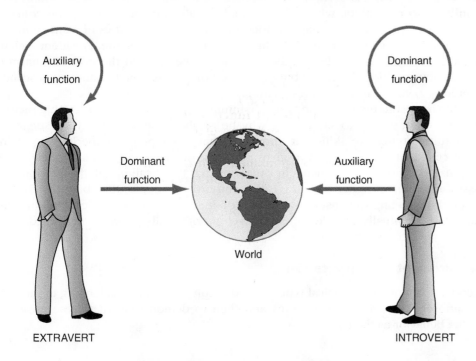

FIGURE 3.2 The Dominant and Auxiliary Functions in Extraverts and Introverts

An extraverted type uses the dominant function to deal with the external world and the auxiliary function to deal with inner reality. An introverted type uses the dominant function to deal with inner reality and the auxiliary function to deal with the external world.

Jung believed that a person remains an introvert or an extravert, without change, for a lifetime. Heredity determines whether the libido is directed to "flow inward" to the inner world or to "flow outward" to external reality. This hypothesized stability of the introversion-extraversion trait is consistent with empirical research using non-Jungian measures of introversion and extraversion.

The Four Functions

The four psychological functions describe fundamental cognitive processes that everyone uses (but to varying degrees). How do we make decisions—based on logical thinking or emotional feeling? How do we get information on which to base those decisions—do we look for details or focus on the big picture?

thinking

psychological function in which decisions are based on logic

feeling

psychological function in which decisions are based on the emotions they arouse

THINKING AND FEELING   Emotion and thought are not always consistent. **Thinking** and **feeling** are alternative ways of making value decisions or judgments. Some people decide what is worthwhile by how they feel emotionally. They make choices that increase positive emotions, such as excitement, pleasure, or joy and avoid negative emotions, such as anxiety, pain, or sorrow. Other people think things through logically, considering reasons and principles. The difference between thinking and feeling types is portrayed in the *Star Trek* television series by Mr. Spock, a logical and unemotional thinking-type Vulcan, contrasted with Dr. McCoy, a feeling-type human (Barry, 1991). Typical of opposite types, they struggle to relate to the other's experience, and their interactions tend to be abrasive because of their psychological differences.

Emotion and thinking are not necessarily in conflict. Emotion is not limited to the overpowering, undifferentiated force that results from early repression (portrayed by Freud) or that impels blind passion. Emotion can be developed and even intelligent; consider the concept of emotional intelligence (Salovey & Mayer, 1990). If development continues toward a healthy maturity, an adult should find a balance between thinking and feeling. A person who, in youth, makes decisions emotionally must learn to think things through logically as well, and a coldly logical person must learn to pay attention to feelings.

sensation

psychological function in which material is perceived concretely, in detail

intuition

psychological function in which material is perceived with a broad perspective, emphasizing future possibilities rather than current details

SENSATION AND INTUITION   **Sensation** and **intuition** are complementary ways of getting information about the world. Do we focus on specific details or the big picture? The sensation type pays attention to details and knows what comes through the five senses: what is seen, heard, touched, tasted, or smelled. The sensation type is unlikely to take hints, which require making an inference beyond the concrete details. This type risks becoming too focused on the particularities of a situation and missing the big picture. Perhaps if he had looked at the big picture, President Richard Nixon, a sensation type (Malone, 1977), would have grasped the potential harm of the infamous political Watergate burglary when there was time to handle this scandal differently, before it forced his resignation.

In contrast to the sensation type, the intuitive-type person grasps the big picture, although often unable to say exactly why he or she understands it. Jung suggested that intuitive types are skilled at knowing what other people experience, picking up on cues that the other person gives off, unconsciously and unintentionally. They recognize potential developments in situations that the detail-oriented sensation type misses. Intuition is higher among creative and artistic people (Sundberg, 1965). Like the thinking-feeling dimension, the sensation-intuition dimension develops through adulthood. Eventually, an adult should develop both skills, however one-sided he or she may have been when younger.

Measurement and Application

Theorizing about psychological type is not difficult. It is more challenging to measure the different personality dimensions and then to demonstrate that these measures predict behavior as the theory describes.

MEASUREMENT: THE MYERS-BRIGGS TYPE INDICATOR   The most commonly used psychological test for measuring the Jungian functions is the **Myers-Briggs Type Indicator (MBTI)** (McCaulley, 1990; Myers & McCaulley, 1985). This test gives scores for introversion-extraversion and the four paired functions (thinking-feeling and sensation-intuition). It determines which of the four functions is dominant by means of a fourth scale that measures whether the external world is approached by a judging function (thinking or feeling, whichever is higher) or a perceiving function (sensation or intuition, whichever is higher). For extraverts, the function identified by this judging-perceiving scale is the dominant function. For introverts, it identifies the auxiliary function because their dominant function is turned inward rather than toward the outer world (McCaulley, 1990). Because the MBTI specifies the auxiliary function in addition to the basic psychetype, it produces sixteen types rather than only eight.

Researchers have debated the best way to measure Jung's psychological functions. He proposed types, not traits (as described in Chapter 1); however, research supports continuous trait dimensions instead (Arnau et al., 2003; McCrae & Costa, 1989). In addition, the test's forced-choice format forces thinking and feeling and sensing and intuiting to be bipolar opposites, which may be less accurate than considering them as four separate traits (Cowan, 1989; Girelli & Stake, 1993; Lorr, 1991; J. B. Murray, 1990; O'Roark, 1990). Some people may have developed both of the supposed opposites in a pair; others may have developed neither.

Research using the MBTI confirms that it is a reliable and valid measure (J. G. Carlson, 1985; J. B. Murray, 1990; Thompson & Borrello, 1986) that correlates with other psychological tests as one would expect (e.g., Campbell & Heller, 1987). Extraversion is correlated with other psychological measures of that trait (Apostal & Marks, 1990; Sipps & Alexander, 1987). Extraverts are higher in self-monitoring than introverts (Hicks, 1985; Mill, 1984), are more likely to work in sales (Sundberg, 1965), and are happier with their lives than introverts (Harrington & Loffredo, 2001). Feeling types can perceive photographs of emotional faces more quickly than thinking types when the faces are presented very briefly using a tachistoscope (Martin et al., 1996). Higher scores on intuition are correlated with more frequent recall of archetypal dreams (Cann & Donderi, 1986), greater creativity (Myers & McCaulley, 1985; cf. Tegano, 1990), and innovation as business managers (Berr, Church, & Waclawski, 2000). Sensation types are overrepresented among people with coronary heart disease (Thorne, Fyfe, & Carskadon, 1987). Other analyses consider combinations of these dimensions: For example, thinking types score high on a psychological test of assertiveness—if they are also extraverted (Tucker, 1991). Overall, the Myers-Briggs instrument has stood up well to empirical testing.

BUSINESS AND EDUCATION APPLICATIONS   The MBTI has been used extensively in research, guidance, and especially in business (Bubenzer, Zimpfer, & Mahrle, 1990). By teaching people about their psychological type and its implications, trainers hope to make people aware that others may see the world quite differently than they do and to make allowances for this when they work and live together (Bringhurst, 2001; Olson, 1990; Rideout & Richardson, 1989). For example, financial planners are advised to present life insurance decisions to thinking types with numbers and data but to downplay this strategy in favor of an emphasis on personal values when selling to feeling types (Hanlon, 2000).

In business and other organizations, decision making can be improved by recognizing that a person's decision-making style varies with psychological type. Intuitive-type executives are particularly well suited for creative brainstorming about new ideas (Agor, 1991). Sensation types perform better than intuitive types on computer-simulated business decisions (Davis, Grove, & Knowles, 1990), although they prefer lecture-style classes over computer-assisted teaching (Wheeler, 2001). Despite such evidence, carefully controlled research measuring managerial performance in an international airline found no significant correlations with MBTI scores (Furnham & Stringfield, 1993).

Myers-Briggs Type Indicator (MBTI)
psychological test for measuring the psychic functions in an individual

The Myers-Briggs instrument has been used successfully in stress-reduction interventions, based on the assumption that different psychological types do not experience stress in the same way (Goodspeed & DeLucia, 1990). Depending on psychological type, students approach academic advisement differently, emphasizing details if they are sensation types, or breadth of information if they are intuitive types (Crockett & Crawford, 1989). Sensation-type students are more likely to choose applied fields than are intuitive-type students (Myers & McCaulley, 1985), and they also learn a computer program more quickly from videodisc instruction (Matta & Kern, 1991). Some evidence indicates that judgment types settle down to study with a more focused work ethic (Schurr et al., 1997) and use career services offered by the college more often than perceiving types (Nelson & Roberge, 1993). Jungian types help us understand the diversity of ways in which students experience the educational environment.

EXPERIMENTAL STUDIES OF JUDGMENTS The psychological functions have implications for phenomena studied by social psychologists, such as eyewitness testimony. Ward and Loftus (1985) reported that when eyewitnesses were questioned about what they had seen, introverted and intuitive types were particularly influenced by the wording of questions. If questions were misleading (e.g., referring to a stop sign that was not really there), introverted and intuitive subjects made more errors. However, if questions were consistent with what was seen, they gave more accurate testimony than other types. The researchers suggest that intuitive introverts are particularly unlikely to trust their own senses and hence are influenced by immediate information from questions.

Another experiment also demonstrates that psychological type influences attribution errors. A robust finding in social psychology is the fundamental attribution error (Ross, 1977), a finding of particular interest to personality psychologists. What is the fundamental attribution error? Most people attribute too much importance to personality and too little importance to situations when they give reasons for other people's behavior. For example, when they read student essays that take a position on a social issue (such as abortion or nuclear arms), research subjects typically judge that the essay accurately reflects the writer's attitude, even if they are told that the instructor assigned students to take a particular position in the essay (Jones & Nisbett, 1972). Hicks (1985) found that one personality type is less likely to make this error: the intuitive-thinking type. Another study suggests a consistent finding: Intuitive types, compared to sensation types, are less likely to exaggerate their control over the outcomes of their actions (Thomson & Martinko, 1995). Hicks (1985) notes that intuitive-thinking types are especially likely to enter scientific careers, which is consistent with their more objective judgments.

EVALUATING JUNG'S THEORY

Jung's theory broadened the scope of psychoanalysis beyond a sexual model, but into areas that are often dismissed as mystical and beyond the proper domain of scientific investigation. He argued that scientific thinking was too limited to understand the psyche. His understanding of complexes and their measurement by the Word Association Test and his description of psychetypes are the major scientific aspects of his theory. His psychetype model has been broadly applied in business and other areas. His views on mythology and symbolism have influenced cultural storytelling and psychotherapy, but have also met resistance within mainstream scientific psychology.

Summary

- Jung proposed a theory of personality in which the unconscious contains broad psychic energy, rather than simply sexual energy as Freud postulated.
- Consciousness and the unconscious exist in a relationship of *compensation*.

- During the *individuation* process of adulthood, unconscious aspects of personality are developed and integrated with those of consciousness in the development of a mature *Self*. In this process, the center of personality is shifted away from the ego.

- The *persona* is challenged by the emergence of the *shadow* and the *anima* or *animus* from the unconscious.
- Projection of the shadow contributes to racism. Projection of the anima or animus occurs in romantic love.
- The *personal unconscious* contains material repressed during individual experience.
- The *collective unconscious* contains transpersonal inherited material, including several *archetypes* that serve as patterns for experience.
- Jung encouraged people to encounter the unconscious through symbols in dreams, myths, religion, and cultural rituals. Modern myths, as well as ancient ones, are valuable and should continue to be developed by individuals leading a creative symbolic life.

- Jung discussed mystical, paranormal phenomena in his concept of *synchronicity*, or meaningful coincidence.
- Jung developed a *Word Association Test* to reveal complexes.
- He interpreted dreams as compensatory to conscious awareness.
- Jung's theory of psychological types comprises eight *psychetypes*, based on the dimension of introversion-extraversion and the functions of thinking-feeling and sensing-intuition. These dimensions can be measured by the widely used Myers-Briggs Type Indicator. Research in business, education, and laboratory settings has confirmed that the types vary in their experience and behavior.

Thinking about Jung's Theory

1. Do you think that the unconscious can be creative? If so, why does it sometimes lead to creativity and sometimes to maladjustment?
2. What observations about society (such as events in the news) can be understood through Jung's concept of the shadow?
3. Do you think that Jung's interpretation of religious mythology has any implications about the value of religion? (Is it an insult to religion? Does it make religion more important?)
4. Can you suggest a way to test Jung's archetypal theory through research?
5. Do you think that paranormal phenomena (such as ESP and astrology) should be included in a scientific theory of personality? If so, would you suggest any changes from Jung's description of the paranormal?
6. Does the concept of psychological types help you understand yourself or anyone you know? Does it have implications for your career plans?

Study Questions

1. Contrast Jung's description of the unconscious with that of Freud's.
2. Explain Jung's concept of the Self. What is the relationship between consciousness and the unconscious in the Self?
3. Describe the process of individuation.
4. What is ego inflation?
5. Explain the term *persona*.
6. Describe the shadow. How can it contribute to racial prejudice? What can it contribute, in a positive way, to personality?
7. Describe the anima and the animus. Discuss Jung's understanding of sex differences, androgyny, and falling in love.
8. Explain the term *collective unconscious*. List several of its archetypes.
9. Why are symbolism and mythology important for personality?
10. Describe Jung's understanding of religion.
11. Contrast Jungian therapy with Freudian psychoanalysis.
12. Describe the Word Association Test.
13. Explain Jung's approach to dream interpretation.
14. What is meant by the symbolic life?
15. Discuss Jung's mystical concepts, including synchronicity.
16. List the three dimensions Jung used to determine a person's psychological type (psychetype). Describe them.
17. Describe the MBTI. Describe a few research results from this instrument.

2

The Psychoanalytic-Social Perspective

Freud's psychoanalytic theory inspired many clinicians and theorists to consider personality in dynamic terms. They extended Freud's theory, emphasizing ego functions to a greater extent than Freud did (Hartmann, 1939/1958). They stressed the capacity of the individual to delay gratification, not simply to be driven by unconscious id impulses. Freud had developed the description of the ego in the later years of his theorizing, from the 1923 publication of *The Ego and the Id* onward (Rapaport, 1959), so these developments follow reasonably from his theory.

Many theorists who regarded themselves as orthodox Freudians are now labeled "psychoanalytic-social theorists." Freud's daughter, Anna Freud, elaborated on his concept of ego defenses in her classic book *The Ego and the Mechanisms of Defense* (Freud, 1936/1966). Heinz Hartmann (1939/1958) stressed the role of the ego in organizing or integrating personality. Alfred Adler, a member of Freud's inner circle, emphasized the striving aspects of personality and the social context of development, which are characteristic of the psychoanalytic-social perspective.

The ego's role includes adapting to relationships with other people. Infancy is reinterpreted to emphasize the development of a relationship with the mother (Erikson, 1950; Sullivan, 1953). An infant nursing at the mother's breast, for example, is viewed by Sigmund Freud as satisfying libidinal drives. In contrast, Alfred Adler and the ego psychologists emphasized the infant's relationship of cooperation with the mother, each needing the other (Davis, 1986). This emphasis on relationships with people is reflected in object relations approaches, so named because people are the "objects" of instinctive desire, or the related *relational approaches* in psychoanalysis (discussed in Chapter 6).

Theorists in the psychoanalytic-social tradition also call our attention to cultural factors that influence individuals. Social categories such as race and gender influence personality development and well-being, and these influences were not examined in Freud's and Jung's theories.

Theorists presented in the next three chapters—Alfred Adler, Erik Erikson, and Karen Horney, with later relational theorists—discussed interpersonal aspects of the ego's functioning, beginning in the family and extending to society generally. Culture, not simply biology, determines sex differences, according to Adler and Horney. Erik Erikson remained traditionally psychoanalytic in his biological explanation of sex differences, although he stressed cultural influences in other respects. Besides reinterpreting gender roles as cultural products, the social emphasis has encouraged the development of typologies of interpersonal behavioral styles. Adler ("getting," "ruling," and "avoiding" types) and Horney ("moving toward," "moving against," and "moving away" types) each offered such typologies. Thus, in addition to emphasis on the ego within personality, these theorists gave more attention to society, the context in which personality develops.

Psychoanalytic-social theorists agree with theorists in the psychoanalytic perspective on two important points: The unconscious is a useful concept for understanding personality, and childhood experience is important in determining personality. In addition, theorists in the psychoanalytic-social perspective have distinctive assumptions:

1. The *ego*, the adaptational force in personality, is more important than in Freud's theory.
2. The development of a sense of *self* is described.
3. *Interpersonal relationships*, beyond the relationships with one's parents, are important aspects of personality.
4. *Social and cultural factors* influence personality in important ways.

Most psychoanalytic-social theorists, like Freudian and Jungian psychoanalysts, have based their theories on clinical data. However, a research tradition in ego development has also emerged. Many studies of Erikson's theory have been conducted by using self-report data, as we see in Chapter 5. In addition, Jane Loevinger (1966, 1976, 1979, 1985) has developed an extensive theoretical and research program that measures ego development through questionnaires, thus enabling researchers to investigate ego development in nonclinical populations.

Theorists in the psychoanalytic-social tradition have presented an approach that is not so narrowly biological as classical psychoanalysis. They stress the adaptational and interpersonal aspects of personality and have provided concepts for understanding the ways society shapes human development.

Study Questions

1. What assumptions does the psychoanalytic-social perspective share with the psychoanalytic perspective?
2. What are the distinctive assumptions of the psychoanalytic-social perspective?

Adler
Individual Psychology

Chapter Overview

ILLUSTRATIVE BIOGRAPHY
Oprah Winfrey

Adler's theory focuses on choice and goals as more important than unconscious conflict. Oprah Winfrey's spectacular success as a television celebrity and her inspiration to help others to achieve their dreams make her a great example of the positive healthy functioning that Adler described.

Oprah Winfrey's own life and her role as a model for others focus on the theme of self-improvement by personal effort, a central idea in Adler's theory. Born in 1954 to an 18-year-old unmarried mother, Oprah's childhood environment was a mix of economic hardship, neglect, and abuse. As an adult, she is wealthy and loved by millions in her audience and by a longtime male companion. Her personal qualities were already apparent before school age—her intelligence and her strong will to succeed. The guidance that Oprah received from her father and from some of her teachers exemplifies a central lesson in Adler's theory: the importance of intervention to help a child find a socially useful lifestyle. Above all, his

Oprah Winfrey

theory would credit her own choices and personal striving for her success.

DEVELOPMENT

Adler called attention to parental behavior, which could influence a child to develop in either a selfish way or a healthy way that recognized other people's interests. He cautioned not only against pampering or giving in to the child's wishes but also against neglecting a child. The desirable path was to set standards and teach the child responsibility. Adler also recognized that a child interacts with sisters and brothers, and those interactions influence the developing personality, in part because of the different experiences of those who are the oldest, middle, or youngest in a family.

The parenting that Oprah experienced was varied. In her earliest years, she was raised by her grandparents on a poor farm. They were not demonstrative of affection and beat her frequently to punish her (as was the practice in that place and time), but they

(continued)

(continued)

encouraged her reading and church participation and so provided a solid base for her personality growth. At age 6 she went to live with her mother and a younger half sister in a one-room ghetto rooming house in Milwaukee (Mair, 1994), and she was sent back and forth a few times between that environment and her father's more disciplined home in Nashville. Her mother's neglect left her vulnerable. She was raped by an older cousin when she was 9 years old (King, 1987). She fell into undisciplined and promiscuous habits, having sex with several men, stealing money from her mother, and running away. She became pregnant, but the baby died. Faced with an increasingly out-of-control young teenager, her mother sent her again to live with her father. Vernon Winfrey and his wife gave Oprah the discipline that she needed: a curfew, advice about dealing with boys, restrictions about clothing, and homework. She thrived, becoming popular at school and responsible enough to earn the respect of her father and to set her on course for success in life. Her achievements have included spectacular fame and wealth in radio and then television, movies, and a magazine.

DESCRIPTION

In Adler's theory, each person develops a unique style of life that is formed early and remains consistent through life, directed by goals for self-improvement. He was particularly interested in the interpersonal style of the individual; for example, was the person too dependent, too domineering, or appropriately cooperative?

Oprah's life story attests to her intelligence and speaking ability and to her warmth toward other people. Already at age 3 she was able to read and write. She skipped first grade because of her ability and later was sent to a better high school than the neighborhood school, again because her achievement surpassed that of her classmates. She loved to give speeches—first to the barnyard chickens and pigs at her grandmother's farm and later to other children and to adults. She entered public-speaking contests. Her style of life seems to be one of getting attention, love, and admiration by speaking to a group of people—radio at first, and later the *Oprah Winfrey Show* on television. She talks easily with others, assertively interviewing them and expressing her opinion but with empathy.

ADJUSTMENT

Adler's theory describes compensation for previous inadequacies and disappointments as the motivating force behind healthy adjustments. In addition to love and work, the criteria that Freud proposed, he pointed out that social interaction is also an important component of good adjustment. A well-adjusted person does not pursue only selfish goals, but also contributes to society ("social interest").

Adler's criterion of social interest is fulfilled in Oprah's life. Her television shows frequently offer support and information to help others deal with adversity. Among the topics she has explored are divorce, homosexuality, transgender parents, terminal illness, sexual abuse and incest, as well as lighter themes like beauty and exercise. She is popular in part because of the generous gifts that she bestows on her television audience. Off air, she has been present for teenage girls to help them avoid unplanned pregnancy, with the life of poverty and despair that too often follows. She is helpful to others, especially in areas that draw from her own background. For example, she advocated for legislation to register child molesters as sex offenders. Over the years she has also conquered a problem with obesity, slimming down and exercising regularly. She has won acclaim and awards

for humanitarian work. Overall, these self-improvement efforts and contributions to others constitute what Adler would call a healthy style of life.

COGNITION

Although we do not always clearly think about it, each of us has an image of what would be desirable, what would make up for what is lacking (our "felt minus"). Adler called this our "fictional finalism" and suggested that it guides our efforts in life and gives a consistency to our motivation. Hints of what is felt to be lacking are often contained in a person's early memories. Over time, we may get a clearer idea of this goal. It's so important that once we understand a person's unique fictional finalism we understand that person's personality and choices.

The first descriptions of a "felt minus" that Adler proposed were based on physical features, and Oprah describes her dissatisfaction with her hair, which did not bounce like that of her white classmates; her nose, which she tried to reshape by pinching it with clothespins while she slept (Waldron, 1987); and her dark skin, especially upsetting because her lighter-skinned half sister was considered the pretty one. Later, her dissatisfaction focused on social class. She had few toys— only a doll made out of corncobs. One of her early memories is of "drawing water from the well every morning and playing with corncob dolls" (Waldron, 1987, p. 171), a clear indication that a simple and poor life was the situation from which she wished to rise. She describes seeing television images of privileged children, unlike her—white and not beaten—on friends' television sets (because their family had no television). Later, she saw upper-middle-class families in person when she visited friends from high school. These experiences helped focus her fictional finalism, her goal. She says, "Somewhere in my spirit, I always knew I was going to be exactly where I am" (Waldron, 1987, p. 18). Another important part of her goal was public performance. When she visited Hollywood and admired the sidewalk stars that commemorate celebrities, she told her father that she would be famous one day.

CULTURE

Adler's theory recognizes the society and culture to a greater extent than classical psychoanalysis. Influences from society, such as schools, offer opportunities for healthy growth. In turn, a healthy individual contributes to society. Adler criticized the way that society sometimes limits personal growth, for example through restrictive gender roles.

Although racial prejudice and unequal economic opportunity clearly existed, there were also positive influences concerning racial issues in Oprah's background. The small town where she lived in her early years (Kosciusko, Mississippi) had a history of supporting black opportunity. The town was, in fact, named for a Revolutionary War soldier who had left money on his death for the purpose of buying slaves to set them free (Waldron, 1987). She also lived at a time when antidiscrimination and equal opportunity laws made it easier for blacks and women to succeed in America, enhancing her early job opportunities in radio and television. Her movie roles, particularly the Oscar-nominated role of Sophie in *The Color Purple*, contributed to public awareness of the experience of black Americans. Another positive influence in her life was the church. As a preschooler, she spoke at church. Later, she gave impromptu sermons to kids on the playground, earning the nickname of "The Preacher." She considered, at one point, becoming a missionary. The church as a social institution presents a vision of a better world and provides guidelines to supplement the sometimes-inadequate parental guidance of its members. Education also contributed importantly to her success, and she has encouraged reading by suggesting books on her television show.

BIOLOGY

Adler's theory does not focus on biology as a determinant of personality but rather as one of the factors that creates the basis for positive striving. Feelings of inferiority about our physical bodies provide one source of motivation for self-improvement.

As just described, Oprah felt dissatisfied with her nonwhite physical features in childhood. In adulthood, she successfully, but not easily, battled obesity. These "felt minus" aspects of her body were the basis for positive striving, epitomizing a central theme in Adler's theory.

FINAL THOUGHTS

Adler's theory and his therapeutic work challenge people to take responsibility for their lives and not to blame others for what is lacking. He stressed the value of intervention to redirect troubled youth and urged people to contribute usefully to society. All these are major themes in Oprah Winfrey's life, which stands as a positive example of personality and an inspiration for many of her fans.

PREVIEW: OVERVIEW OF ADLER'S THEORY

Adler's theory has implications for major theoretical questions, as presented in Table 4.1. His theoretical ideas are easier to test scientifically than those of Freud and Jung, and researchers have developed tests to measure style of life, early memories, and other elements of his theoretical constructs. His hypothesized relationship between birth order and personality has generated many empirical studies. The theory extends the comprehensiveness of psychoanalytic theory by including more conscious thought and future goals. It has been applied to school interventions for troubled youth and has generated an Adlerian version of psychotherapy.

Alfred Adler was one of the earliest and most influential dissenters from Freud's inner circle. Unlike Freud, who emphasized universal conflicts that all people experience, Adler focused attention on the uniqueness of each person. He named his theory "individual psychology." Freud borrowed many Adlerian ideas, although often calling them by a new name: defense mechanisms (from Adler's safeguarding tendencies), ego-ideal (from Adler's self-ideal), and superego (from Adler's counter-fiction) (Ansbacher & Ansbacher, 1956, pp. 21–22). Adler's discussions of masculine protest contributed to Freud's postulate of the Oedipus complex.

Adler argued that people must be understood from a social perspective, not a biological one. He opposed Freud's exclusive emphasis on sex as a source of energy, and

Table 4.1 Preview of Adler's Theory	
Individual Differences	Individuals differ in their goals and in how they try to achieve them, their "style of life."
Adaptation and Adjustment	Health involves love, work, and social interaction and is the responsibility of each individual. Social interest, rather than selfishness, is required for health.
Cognitive Processes	Conscious experience and thought are important and generally trustworthy.
Culture	Society influences people through social roles, including gender roles. Schools are especially influential.
Biological Influences	Organ inferiority provides the direction of personality development as the individual attempts to compensate for the inferiority.
Development	Parents have an important influence on children, and better parenting techniques can be taught. Extensive guidelines for child rearing are provided, especially the caution to avoid pampering. Relationships with siblings are important; birth order affects personality. Throughout life, people create their own personalities through goal setting.

Alfred Adler

he asserted that any approach that does not consider the individual's goals is incomplete and cannot provide an effective therapy. His emphasis on growth and free will is an important counterforce to the deterministic attitude of Freud, and his emphasis on social interest and a holistic approach to personality is a historical precursor to the humanistic psychologists' concept of self-actualization (Runyon, 1984).

Biography of Alfred Adler

Alfred Adler was born in a suburb of Vienna, Austria, in 1870, the second son in a family of four boys and two girls. His family was financially comfortable and one of the few Jewish families in his village. In protest against the isolation of orthodox Judaism, Alfred later converted to Christianity.

As a child, Alfred was unhealthy and suffered from rickets. His earliest memory is as a 2-year-old, bandaged and barely moving, while his older brother moved freely about. His childhood, he said, was often made unhappy by the greater achievements of his older brother, with whom Alfred unsuccessfully competed. He was run over twice when he was 4 or 5. At the age of 5, Alfred heard a doctor tell his father that Alfred's pneumonia was so serious that he would die; treatment was useless. His younger brother had died 2 years earlier. On the advice of a second physician, however, treatment was given, and Alfred recovered. He decided to become a doctor himself "in order to overcome death and the fear of death" (Ansbacher & Ansbacher, 1956, p. 199).

Eventually, with the courage that he later was to urge on his patients, Adler overcame his physical difficulties. He became active in sports and popular with his classmates. He also compensated for early academic shortcomings. Throughout life, Adler loved music, attending various performances and singing in a wonderful tenor voice that, some thought, should have made him an opera singer.

Adler married a Russian émigré, a member of the intelligentsia whose ideas were far more liberal than those typical in Austria at the time. She undoubtedly influenced Adler to deplore the restrictions of traditional attitudes toward women. For example, he reported one study he conducted that found that successful girls often had mothers with careers. Adler and his wife, Raissa, had four children.

Adler received his medical degree from Vienna University in 1895. He was interested in the contribution of psychological factors to illness and its cure, but he did not limit his practice to psychiatry until 1910, after his break with Freud. As a general practitioner, his lifelong concern with the social context of illness is exemplified by his pamphlet *The Health of Tailors*, in which he exposed the working conditions leading to high rates of disease in this occupational group. During World War I, Adler served as a physician in the Austrian army, treating war neuroses (later to be called shell shock).

Adler was impressed by Freud's book on dreams and defended it against critics, although at the time he did not know Freud personally. In 1902 he joined Freud's weekly discussion group, and he became Freud's successor as president of the group in 1910 and coedited its journal. He took over many of Freud's cases and was Freud's personal physician.

In 1911, however, Freud broke with Adler, unable to reconcile Adler's theoretical contributions with his own. Freud questioned Adler's intellectual ability and accused Adler of failing to recognize the importance of the unconscious, thereby fundamentally missing the point of psychoanalysis. Adler, from his side, regarded Freud as a pampered child who had never overcome the self-indulgence of childhood and who clung to authority out of defensiveness. Adler had many supporters. When he resigned the presidency of the Psychoanalytic Society, 9 of the 35 other members left with him. In 1912 he established the Society for Individual Psychology, and in 1914, he founded his own journal.

Adler developed interventions to resolve problems with children, including the prevention of delinquency and of psychological difficulties related to physical handicaps, poor parenting, and problems in getting along with other children (Ansbacher, 1992). He set up nearly 50 child-guidance clinics in Vienna and elsewhere in Europe. He did not emphasize punishment but instead encouraged children's inherent creativity (Hoffman, 1997). He is reported to have established rapport with astonishing success. Surgeons summoned him to calm their juvenile patients, and he was especially effective with depressive patients. However, he directed his message more to the public than to medical experts and did not like empirical research studies. This popular orientation impeded his recognition among academicians, although it is echoed by those who urge psychologists to "give psychology away" (Miller, 1969) to the public.

Adler wrote extensively, publishing over 300 articles and books (Dinkmeyer & Dinkmeyer, 1989). His reputation spread internationally. Like many Europeans during the politically troubled times prior to World War II, Adler moved to the United States in 1935. He taught at the Long Island College of Medicine. In 1937, at the age of 67, he died of cardiac problems, with little forewarning and after a healthy adulthood, while on a lecture tour in Scotland.

Adler acknowledged that his theory drew on his own life experiences. It is easy to see how a boy who was ill would aspire to become a physician and would describe the overcoming of physical defects as a major motivating force.

STRIVING FROM INFERIORITY TOWARD SUPERIORITY

The fundamental motive in Adler's theory is the never-ending effort to move on to a better way of life. The struggle takes different forms for different people, and it seems impossible to some, who resign themselves to defeat.

Inferiority

Almost everyone has heard the term *inferiority complex*, which describes being overcome by a feeling of lack of worth. This concept was developed and popularized by Alfred Adler, although he may not have originated the particular term (Ansbacher & Ansbacher, 1956, p. 256). For Adler, the basic human motivation is to strive "from a felt minus situation towards a plus situation, from a feeling of inferiority towards superiority, perfection, totality" (p. 1). This is a process triggered by the dissatisfaction of the "felt minus."

ADLER'S EVOLVING IDEAS ABOUT STRIVING TO IMPROVE   What is this "felt minus"? All people begin life as infants, feeling inferior and helpless because their survival depends on others. Each person's sense of what is negative and what would be more positive emerges in a unique and personal way. Adler's terminology changed as he developed his theory over the years, grappling to understand this process. Throughout, Adler's message is that the fundamental motivation is to strive for something better.

Organ Inferiority   At first, influenced by his medical practice, Adler (1923/1929) referred to organ inferiority as the source of the felt minus. Inherited inferiorities intensify "the normal feeling of weakness and helplessness" all young children experience (p. 18). A person with weak limbs (like Adler himself, having suffered from rickets) considers his legs inferior. A child with hearing problems would feel inferior in auditory capacity. Delayed puberty can also be a source of this sense of organ inferiority, leading to the notion that one will always remain a child (Adler, 1921/1927, p. 72).

It is subjective experience that is important in determining the sense of inferiority. Severe socialization and environmental demands can produce a sense of inferiority that would be avoided, given the same physical condition, in a more benign environment. In healthy adjustment, the child strives to compensate for the organ inferiority. If compensation fails, the individual may instead develop an incapacitating sense that the inferiority cannot be overcome—hence an *inferiority complex*.

Aggressive Drive   The second term Adler used for this process, as his theory evolved, was **aggressive drive**. The struggle toward the felt plus may take the form of fighting and cruelty, or it may be expressed in a more socialized form as athletic competition or other striving for dominance, including politics. It is in this sense that

aggressive drive
one of Adler's terms for positive striving, emphasizing anger and competitiveness

we speak of "aggressive sports" or an "aggressive campaign" or even an "aggressive business deal." Consciously, the aggressive drive may be experienced as anger.

masculine protest

one of Adler's terms for positive striving, emphasizing manliness

Masculine Protest   In a third stage of his thinking, Adler referred to **masculine protest**, an assertion of manliness that implies greater competence, superiority, and control. Such traits as aggressiveness and activity are seen as masculine, whereas submissiveness and obedience are feminine. Adler did not accept the gender roles of his culture because they have adverse effects on both sexes (Adler, 1917/1988a), and he has been described as an early feminist (Stein & Edwards, 1998). Females, as well as males, are motivated by masculine protest as they struggle against the constraints of the less socially valued female role.

superiority striving

effort to achieve improvement in oneself

Superiority Striving   In yet another stage of thought, Adler spoke of **superiority striving**. He did not mean eminence so much as self-improvement. He meant striving to achieve one's own personal best, rather than striving to be better than others.

Perfection Striving   The final term Adler used for the process is *perfection striving*. Perhaps more than any of his previous terms, this connotes an inherent growth process within the individual. It refers to an effort to improve that is realistic, in contrast to a neurotic perfectionism (Lazarsfeld, 1991).

inferiority complex

stagnation of growth in which difficulties seem too immense to be overcome

INFERIORITY COMPLEX   When the felt-minus seems insurmountable and the growth process stagnates, a person may fall victim to an **inferiority complex**, accepting an exaggerated sense of inferiority as an accurate self-description. Contributing factors include physical disabilities, family dynamics, and societal influences (Stein & Edwards, 1998). All neurotics have an inferiority complex, according to Adler. Even non-neurotic people have inferiority feelings; but only in their exaggerated form, when they overwhelm attempts to move to the felt plus and stagnate growth, are they called a complex.

superiority complex

a neurotic belief that one is better than others

SUPERIORITY COMPLEX   Some neurotics repress their feelings of inferiority and believe themselves better than others. This unhealthy outcome is termed a **superiority complex**. It masks an unconscious sense of inferiority. People with a superiority complex often behave arrogantly; they exaggerate their achievements, which may be intellectual, athletic, or emotional, depending on the unique strengths of the individual. They may claim telepathic powers. Or they may claim superiority over other races and nationalities, as did Adolf Hitler (Murray, 1943).

Fictional Finalism

creative self

the person who acts to determine his or her own life

External factors present challenges, but Adler argued that people make choices and determine their own outcomes in life. To use an Adlerian phrase, the person is a **creative self** who is trying to discover or create experiences that lead to fulfillment. For Adler, each person is "the artist of his own personality" (Ansbacher & Ansbacher, 1956, p. 177).

This creativity is a way of compensating for feelings of inferiority (Lemire, 1998). In his or her life situation, each person imagines a better situation than the present. It is an image of the fulfillment of what is lacking at the present time: a strong healthy body, if the person is ill; a fortune, if the person feels held back by lack of money; admiration, if the person feels unappreciated; and so forth. Doctors, according to Adler, are often compensating for some early experience with death, trying to overcome it through their careers. Others are directed by a "redeemer complex," trying (not necessarily consciously) to save someone, perhaps by entering medicine or the ministry.

fictional finalism

a person's image of the goal of his or her striving

Adler called the imagined goal the **fictional finalism** of the individual. It gives direction to the individual's striving. Because an individual's fundamental motivation is to move toward this fictional finalism, a person cannot be understood without knowing the unique goal, which explains the consistency of a person's striving.

People do not ordinarily have a clear and complete idea of the fictional finalism that directs them. This goal is "dimly envisaged," partly known and partly not known (unconscious). Throughout life, the general direction of striving remains, but the specific understanding of the goal may change. A healthy person modifies the goal; a neurotic may have such an inflexible fictional finalism that behavior is not adaptive.

THE UNITY OF PERSONALITY

Adler (1937/1982b, 1932/1988b) emphasized the unity of personality, describing personality as held together by the fictional finalism and unique style of life. This contrasts sharply with Freud's description of conflict within personality. According to Freud, unity is a facade created by the defense mechanism of overcompensation; it masks deeper conflicts within the personality. Freud suggested that Adler did not understand the importance of repression and the unconscious. To be blunt, he missed the point of the psychoanalytic revolution. Adler rejected the idea of conflict between the conscious and the unconscious as "an artificial division…that has its origin merely in psycho-analytic fanaticism" (Adler, 1936/1964, p. 93), believing that the conscious and the unconscious work together more often than they conflict (Ansbacher, 1982).

Style of Life

A person's goal directs a unique **style of life**. Some people adopt antisocial styles of life, cheating and aggressively seeking their own satisfaction; others are cooperative and hardworking. The style of life begins as a compensatory process, making up for a particular inferiority. Besides the goal, the style of life includes the individual's concepts about the self and the world and his or her unique way of striving toward the personal goal in that world.

style of life
a person's consistent way of striving

EARLY MEMORIES   A person's style of life is established by the age of 4 or 5. A key to identifying the style of life is a person's first memory, which on average dates back to age $3\frac{1}{2}$ (Mullen, 1994), though many people remember nothing until 6 or 7 years of age. Early memories are often erroneous, and adults seem to confuse what they truly remember with what they have later been told about the past (Eacott & Crawley, 1998). Adler's perspective holds that the first memory sticks out because a person has thought about it repeatedly over the years, and it captures what has been subjectively important for that person. The key to the importance of this early memory is not the objective facts recalled but rather the psychological importance of the early memory for the individual.

Adler said that a person's "memories represent his 'Story of My Life': a story he repeats to himself to warn him or comfort him, to keep him concentrated on his goal, and to prepare him by means of past experiences, so that he will meet the future with an already tested style of action" (Ansbacher & Ansbacher, 1956, p. 351). Memories of accidents may suggest a lifestyle based on avoiding danger. Memories of one's mother may suggest issues concerned with her care or lack of it. Memories of the first day at school may suggest "the great impression produced by new situations" (p. 354).

Adler regarded patients' reports of incredibly early events, such as memories of their own birth or maternal care in early infancy, as factually suspect but psychologically revealing. Adler himself reported an erroneous early memory of running back and forth across a cemetery to overcome his fear of death. There was no cemetery in the place he described. Nonetheless, the false memory is an important clue to Adler's own consistent efforts to overcome death (Bruhn, 1992a; Monte, 1980).

Early memories are routinely assessed in Adlerian counseling and are useful with clients of all ages, including the elderly (Sweeny & Myers, 1986). The Early Memories Procedure (Bruhn, 1990) asks systematic questions about early memories and interprets these as clues to a person's current life attitudes. By briefly stating the essential structure of the memory, its meaning for one's current life becomes apparent (Bruhn, 1992a). For example, a memory of running away from playmates after falling off the jungle gym is restated more generally: "When I encounter difficulties with an achievement task…I withdraw" (Bruhn, 1992b, p. 327). Psychiatric patients (all men) who had committed felonies reported more early memories of abuse and aggression than did nondangerous psychiatric patients. Those who recalled early psychological abuse were almost 14 times more likely to be in the dangerous group than in the nondangerous group (Tobey & Bruhn, 1992).

Another measurement technique for early memories, the Adelphi Early Memory Index, assesses overall psychological health or distress (Karliner et al., 1996). Early memories are significantly related to vocational interest and vocational choice (Elliott, Amerikaner, & Swank, 1987), to delinquency (Davidow & Bruhn, 1990) and criminality (Hankoff, 1987), and to depression (Acklin, Sauer, et al., 1989; Allers, White, & Hornbuckle, 1990). Correlations with various clinical scales confirm that early memories express "relationship paradigms" and thus can reflect adjustment or maladjustment (Acklin et al., 1991).

While Adler focused on the individual and his or her autobiographical memory, later researchers have examined early memory from a cultural point of view. Individualistic Western cultures encourage an early sense of a separate self, and people in the United States report earlier first memories, and memories focusing on their individual self, compared to the later and more interpersonal first memories of Asian cultures (Fivush, 2010; Han, Leichtman, & Wang, 1998; Mullen, 1994; Wang, 2001).

Mistaken and Healthy Styles of Life

A person's style of life is unique. Adler did not like to present typologies because they ignore this uniqueness. For teaching purposes, however, he described four different types (Adler, 1935/1982a), including three "mistaken" (or unhealthy) styles of life and one that was to be recommended. His intent was not to classify people but to make it easier to grasp this concept; therefore, we should realize that these categories are only rough indications of the many styles of life that people adopt.

MISTAKEN STYLES OF LIFE   Sometimes, early in life, people develop strategies for improving their situations that are, in the long run, maladaptive. For example, a child may become overly dependent on doting parents or overly rebellious. Adler referred to these as "mistaken styles of life."

Ruling Type   Ruling types seek to dominate others. They may become "delinquents, tyrants, sadists" (Ansbacher & Ansbacher, 1956, p. 168). Adler (1998) described a schoolgirl who acted sarcastically and arrogantly toward her peers, seeking satisfaction there because she was unable to do her schoolwork. Not all people of this type are despicable. Some, with talent and hard work, are high achievers, but they are vain and overly competitive. They may express their sense of superiority over others by belittling them, a tendency that Adler (1921/1927, p. 161) called the **deprecation complex**.

deprecation complex

unhealthy way of seeking superiority by belittling others

Getting Type   Getting types lean on others. They are dependent, adopting a passive, rather than active, attitude toward life, and they may become depressed. Adler described pampered children and females as subject to environmental pressures that encourage this neurotic style, but it is always the choice of the individual that determines the style of life.

Avoiding Type   Avoiding types try not to deal with problems, thereby avoiding the possibility of defeat. Agoraphobia, an irrational fear that confines people to their homes, is one form of this maladaptive style of life. The avoiding type tends to be isolated and may strike others as cold. Whole classes, religious groups, and nations may adopt this style, which hinders the progress of civilization (Adler, 1921/1927, p. 186).

THE HEALTHY STYLE OF LIFE: THE SOCIALLY USEFUL TYPE   If the lifestyle is adaptive, Adler referred to it as a **socially useful type**. To be so characterized, a person must act in ways beneficial to others. This does not necessarily imply economic productivity or acts generally considered altruistic. Adler included artists and poets as people who "serve a social function more than anyone else. They have taught us how to see, how to think, and how to feel" (Ansbacher & Ansbacher, 1956, p. 153). Socially useful types have a well-developed sense of "social interest," which is described in a later section of this chapter. In addition, they feel a sense of internal control (Minton, 1968), an

socially useful type

a personality that is well adjusted

attitude that is especially important in the cognitive social learning theories of Rotter, Mischel, and Bandura.

Longitudinal research confirms Adler's prediction that style of life is consistent from childhood to adulthood (Pulkkinen, 1992). Identification of lifestyle in childhood is particularly important because intervention may prevent undesirable patterns from becoming resistant to change (Ansbacher, 1988).

THE DEVELOPMENT OF PERSONALITY

Although Adler said that each person was fully responsible for his or her own choices in life, he recognized that circumstances could incline people toward either undesirable or desirable styles of life. Societal factors that impede the development of a psychologically healthy lifestyle include restrictive gender roles, warlike orientations in government, and poverty. Because style of life is developed early, the family is a particularly important influence, including siblings as well as parents.

Parental Behavior

A child begins life in a helpless state. Parents can help or hinder the development of a healthy lifestyle to compensate for this fundamental felt minus. They can protect the child from tasks too difficult to be successfully completed and ensure that appropriate tasks are available. Parents err if they try to make their children always superior to everyone else, more symbols of parental worth than individuals in their own right. Dreikurs and Soltz (1964) have summarized Adler's advice for raising healthy children (see Table 4.2).

The mother, in particular, influences the development of social feeling, the cooperative attitude that distinguishes healthy from unhealthy styles of life. The father, traditionally the authority in the family, teaches the child about power and its selfish or socially responsible expression. (Adler, like Freud, developed his theory in the context of the traditional two-parent nuclear family.) However, the mother usually spends more time with children, and research suggests that maternal behavior is more closely linked with aggressive and other problematic behavior by children (Rothbaum & Weisz, 1994).

THE PAMPERED CHILD   Some of Adler's most critical remarks were directed toward parental **pampering**. Children who are treated with overindulgence come to expect that others will cater to their needs. Ultimately, because the real world is far less indulgent than they have come to demand, they will not be loved. Adler criticized Freudian theory as the construction of a pampered child. Who but a spoiled child,

pampering
parental behavior in which a child is overindulged or spoiled

Table 4.2 Advice for Raising Healthy Children, Derived from Adler's Approach
Encourage the child, rather than simply punishing.
Be firm, but not dominating.
Show respect for the child.
Maintain routine.
Emphasize cooperation.
Don't give the child too much attention.
Don't become engaged in power struggles with the child.
Show by your actions, not by your words.
Don't offer excessive sympathy.
Be consistent.

Source: Adapted from Dreikurs and Soltz, 1964.

he asked, would propose a universal Oedipus complex in which the child wanted complete possession of the mother?

neglect

parental behavior in which a child's needs are not adequately met

THE NEGLECTED CHILD   Parental **neglect** also contributes to maladaptive development. Children who have been neglected, including orphans and unwanted or illegitimate children, are likely to believe others will not support them. The tasks of life seem overwhelmingly difficult. Strangely, parental neglect can lead a child to adopt a pampered style of life. It is the desire to be pampered, the fictional goal of being cared for, rather than the fact of having been pampered, that characterizes the pampered style of life. Thus neglected children, as well as overindulged children, can become overly dependent on others for recognition and for nurturance.

PARENTING TRAINING PROGRAMS   Training parents to be more effective can prevent and help solve problems that might appear at school and elsewhere. Many parenting training programs based on Adlerian principles have been developed (Dinkmeyer & McKay, 1976; Dreikurs & Soltz, 1964). A major goal is to teach parents to understand the reasons for their children's misbehavior so they can more effectively influence it. Dreikurs (1950) identified four goals of children's behavior: "attention-getting, struggle for power or superiority, desire to retaliate or get even, and a display of inadequacy or assumed disability" (Dinkmeyer & Dinkmeyer, 1989, p. 28). Overall, the evidence suggests that parents can be taught more effective ways of parenting, based on Adlerian concepts (Utay & Utay, 1996), and that parent training programs have positive long-term effects on behavior, as well as mental and emotional outcomes (Sandler et al., 2011). Adding a parenting training component to a Head Start program taught parents to be more positive and less critical and punitive; children, in turn, became happier and more cooperative (Webster-Stratton, 1998).

Family Constellation

Interactions among sisters and brothers in childhood have important influences on the development of personality. Because other psychoanalysts have emphasized parent–child interactions, only infrequently considering sibling relationships (e.g., Agger, 1988), this emphasis on **family constellation** (the number, age, and sex of siblings) was an important and distinct contribution of Adler. In proposing the effects of birth order, Adler recognized that many other factors in any particular family would need to be considered. He offered general observations about birth order, but expected many exceptions.

family constellation

the configuration of family members, including the number and birth order of siblings

FIRSTBORN CHILD   The firstborn child begins life with the full attention of the parents and is often pampered or spoiled. When other children arrive, the eldest must share the parents' attention with the new baby. Only the oldest child has had the full attention of the parents, and so only the firstborn feels so acutely the loss of parental, especially maternal, love. Adler (1936/1964, p. 231) described the eldest child as "dethroned" by the arrival of later children, and they often, according to Adler, do not cope well. They are likely to become "problem children, neurotics, criminals, drunkards, and perverts" (Ansbacher & Ansbacher, 1956, p. 377). Most problem children, he claimed, are firstborns (although research, described later, does not generally confirm this prediction).

To compensate for having to share the mother with a new baby, the oldest child may turn to the father. Or he or she may take on a somewhat "parental," protective (and, not incidentally, powerful) role in relationship to the younger siblings. Eldest children may long for the past (i.e., the time before competition), and they tend to overvalue authority and hold conservative values.

SECOND-BORN CHILD   The second-born child, seeing the head start that the older sibling has on life, may feel envious, experiencing "a dominant note of being slighted, neglected" (Adler, 1921/1927, p. 127). This often makes him or her rebellious, even revolutionary. This experience presents a challenge that can usually be successfully overcome.

The older sibling serves as a "pacemaker," Adler's analogy with a racer. Thus the second-born child is stimulated to higher achievement. Observing the pace set by the older sibling, the second-born child does not waste energy by trying an impossible pace. (In contrast, the firstborn may become exhausted by trying too hard, like a long-distance runner without a pacer.) Unlike the oldest child, the second child always has had to share parental love and therefore is unlikely to have been spoiled. Adler regarded the second child as having the most favorable position.

YOUNGEST CHILD   Youngest children, said Adler (1921/1927, p. 123), often become problem children. As the baby of the family, the youngest is likely to grow up in a warmer atmosphere than the older children. This poses the risk of being pampered and, as a spoiled child, lacking the incentive to develop independence. With too many pacemakers, the youngest child may compete in many directions, leading to a diffuseness and sense of inferiority. Results can be more positive, though; success may be attainable if an area of effort not already claimed by other family members can be found.

ONLY CHILD   The only child never competes with siblings for parental attention. This child is likely to be pampered and overly attached to the mother, who is often overprotective, so the only child develops a "mother complex" (Ansbacher & Ansbacher, 1956, p. 381). Constant parental attention gives the only child an unrealistic sense of personal worth.

OTHER ASPECTS OF THE FAMILY ENVIRONMENT   In addition to sibling position, many particular aspects of the family environment may modify these outcomes. Children whose talents are quite different from those of their siblings are in a far different situation from those who compete more directly. The spacing between children is significant. If many years pass between the births of various children, they will all have some characteristics of an only child. The number of boys and girls also influences the encouragement of masculinity or femininity in each child.

RESEARCH ON BIRTH ORDER   Adler's observations about birth order have stimulated many studies. Research on birth order and personality has shown some relationships but not always in the direction hypothesized by Adler; the effects are weak and inconsistent (Guastello & Guastello, 2002; Jefferson, Herbst, & McCrae, 1998).

Several studies show that parents treat children in the various sibling positions differently. Parents are typically more anxious and critical of their first child than of later children, giving the firstborn more responsibility and pressure to live up to parental expectations (Falbo, 1987; Hoffman, 1991; Newman, Higgins, & Vookles, 1992). Lasko (1954), in a longitudinal study observing families at their homes, found that firstborns received a great deal of attention until a sibling was born, at which point the firstborn received very little attention, which is just what Adler's concept of dethronement describes.

Adler's expectation that firstborns would be oriented toward the parents is consistent with the research finding that oldest children are more likely than those born later to search the Internet for their genealogical roots (Salmon & Daly, 1998). Among Chinese American children, it is the eldest child who most often has a strong ethnic identity because this reflects the greater influence of parents on this sibling position (Cheng & Kuo, 2000).

Confirming Adler's prediction that firstborns have more difficulty than second-born children in pacing their work realistically, one study found firstborn teachers more susceptible to burnout (Forey, Christensen, & England, 1994). Firstborns are also more often type A (time-pressured, coronary-prone) persons (Ivancevich, Matteson, & Gamble, 1987; Phillips, Long, & Bedeian, 1990; Strube & Ota, 1982). Firstborns are reported to be higher in narcissism (self-absorption), which is consistent with Adler's negative portrayal of them (Curtis & Cowell, 1993; Joubert, 1989). Research using a Knowing Styles Inventory suggests that firstborns more often adopt a Separate Knowing style in which they distance themselves from others' ideas, which they challenge and doubt, whereas later-born children scored higher on a Connected Knowing scale, suggesting that they take the perspective of others (Knight et al., 2000).

Research does not support Adler's claim that second-born children are the highest achievers; firstborns generally achieve the most (Goertzel, Goertzel, & Goertzel, 1978; Schachter, 1963), are most intelligent (Sulloway, 1996), and are overrepresented among world political leaders (Hudson, 1990).

Only children tend to be similar to firstborn children: high achievers with high "locus of control, autonomy, leadership, and maturity" (Falbo, 1987, p. 165). In China, however, only children have undesirable social characteristics, including dependency and egocentrism, perhaps because of parental overindulgence (Falbo, 1987). This cultural difference stems, presumably, from the one-child policy of the Chinese government. Families are strongly encouraged to limit family size to one child because of the fear that overpopulation will lead to famine and other social problems. Parents tend to indulge rather than discipline this one precious child. No automatic and universal effect stems from being an only child (or any other birth order); the particular cultural and familial circumstances must be considered.

Research on sibling relationships sometimes looks at the quality of relationships among siblings. Sisters and brothers may be buddies, caretakers of one another, or have more casual relationships (Stewart, Verbrugge, & Beilfuss, 1998). When there is much conflict, adverse effects on psychosocial functioning result; when there is more support—to make up for parental shortcomings, for example, sibling relationships have more benign consequences (Brody, 1998). Although Adler described birth-order effects clearly, his theory was not as simplistic as it has often been presented, and he emphasized that external conditions do not determine outcomes. Ultimately, individuals create their own styles of life.

SULLOWAY'S ANALYSIS OF SCIENTIFIC REVOLUTIONS   Extending Adlerian ideas about birth order, Frank Sulloway (1996) theorizes that the history of science has been shaped by birth-order effects. He suggests that for their survival, as an evolutionary mechanism, different children in the same family develop divergent personalities because each child strives to compete for parents' attention and must find a unique way to do so. The oldest child may adopt parental standards and achieve within the established values of the parents' generation, but the next child needs to find a different strategy. Scientists who are later-born children are predisposed to rebellion, leading revolutions against the establishment. Copernicus rebelliously argued that the earth revolves around the sun, a revolutionary idea when the earth was considered flat, and Darwin's theory of evolution challenged the idea that humans are entirely separate from animals (Sulloway, 1996).

Although Sulloway presents impressive historical data to support his thesis—he is, after all, an historian and not a psychologist—history is subject to multiple interpretations, and his work has been criticized as scientifically biased to support his theory, selecting from among the myriad of data those that fit his predictions (e.g., Dalton, 2004; Townsend, 2000). Other research using self-report questionnaires does not support his predictions. Social attitudes on such issues as conservatism, support for authority, and tough-mindedness are not predicted by birth order (Freese, Powell, & Steelman, 1999). Similarly, a study of undergraduates found no association between birth order and various personality measures (Guastello & Guastello, 2002). So, although some biographical data and selected empirical research support the hypothesized rebelliousness of later-born siblings, it would be premature to accept the idea as proven. Birth order is only one factor that influences people's behavior. Overly simplified hypotheses may be easy to understand and exciting to ponder, but they do not do justice to human complexities (Rosenberg, 2000).

PSYCHOLOGICAL HEALTH

Adler's description of psychological health was phrased in more social, less purely individual terms than Freud's intrapsychic model.

Social Interest

Humans are inherently social. A sense of community is essential for human survival. The more **social interest** the person has, the more that person's efforts are channeled into shared social tasks, rather than selfish goals, and the more psychologically healthy that person is.

In German, Adler used the term *Gemeinschafsgefühl*, which has been translated as "social interest," "social feeling," "community feeling," and so forth. Perhaps "feeling of community" is the best description for social interest (Stein & Edwards, 1998). Social interest is the innate potential to live cooperatively with other people. It enables the person to value the common good above personal welfare. Although social interest is an inborn potential, it must be fostered, and the mother is an early influence for this. As a felt experience, social interest has been described as a distinct subjective condition as real as anger or grief (Hanna, 1996). Without social interest, life seems purposeless and the self feels empty (Richardson & Manaster, 1997). Social interest may even contribute to spirituality by encouraging a loving attitude toward all of life (Eriksson, 1992).

Social interest is a core concept for Adler, who says that all neurosis stems from inadequate social feeling. It is deficient in schizophrenics, criminals, and those who commit suicide, among others. Groups, as well as individuals, can be described by social interest or the lack thereof. Societies impede the development of social interest through the glorification of war, the death penalty, physical punishment and abuse, and failure to provide humane conditions for all classes and categories of people (Adler, 1936/1964, pp. 280–281). Researchers have compared Adler's concept of social interest to the teachings of various religious traditions, including Christianity, Judaism, and Buddhism (Kaplan & Schoeneberg, 1987; Leak, Gardner, & Pounds, 1992; Watts, 1992).

Adler assessed social interest through interview and history. Researchers have developed several self-report scales, though they have very low correlations with one another (Bass et al., 2002). The most commonly used are the Social Interest Scale (Crandall, 1975/1991) and the Social Interest Index (Greever, Tseng, & Friedland, 1973).

Although not all measures of social interest yield the same results, several studies confirm theoretical predictions. People who score high on social interest score low on narcissism (Miller et al., 1987), low on alienation (Leak & Williams, 1989), and low on MMPI scales that indicate maladjustment (Mozdzierz, Greenblatt, & Murphy, 1988). They score high on the Affiliation, Nurturance, and Aggression scales of the Personality Research Form and on scales of the Life Styles Inventory thought to be associated with self-actualization (Leak et al., 1985). Students high in social interest have attitudes toward love that emphasize companionship ("storge") and reject egocentric game playing ("ludus") (Leak & Gardner, 1990). Some studies report that measures of social interest correlate with prosocial behaviors: volunteering in legal advocacy agencies (but not other kinds) (Hettman & Jenkins, 1990) and having more friends (Watkins & Hector, 1990).

Overall, researchers in the area of social interest are convinced that this construct is useful and Adler's conceptualization was sound, although they have some unresolved questions about its measurement.

THE THREE TASKS OF LIFE

Life in society requires cooperation and, therefore, social interest. This is readily seen by considering the three fundamental tasks of life: work, love, and social interaction. Success in all three areas is evidence of mental health.

WORK Work refers to having an occupation, earning a living by some socially useful job. Division of labor is a means for organizing cooperation among people in providing for the necessities and wants of everyone. Any occupation that contributes to the community is desirable. When children describe their occupational aspirations,

social interest
innate potential to live cooperatively with other people

they provide insight into their whole style of life. Occupational aspirations may change as the child learns more about reality. This, said Adler, is a healthy sign (Ansbacher & Ansbacher, 1956, pp. 430–431). Criminals fail in the work task (as also in the other two tasks), and this failure can usually be observed from early in their life histories (p. 412).

LOVE   The love task refers to sexual relationships and marriage between men and women, including the decision to have children (Ansbacher & Ansbacher, 1956, p. 432). Adler recommended monogamy as the best solution to the love task (p. 132) and remonstrated against premarital sex, saying it detracts from "the intimate devotion of love and marriage" (p. 434). Someone who falls in love with two people simultaneously is, by doing so, avoiding the full love task (p. 437). More recently, Adlerians voice less traditional views about the love task, including the view that love tasks can be met in homosexual as well as heterosexual relationships (Schramski & Giovando, 1993).

Adler thought that many sexual dysfunctions and perversions, and even disinterest in one's partner, stem from lack of social interest rather than from purely physical causes. Equality between men and women is essential for success in the task of love, according to Adler. Successful love affirms the worth of both partners. In other ways, his attitudes sound less modern. Although he did suggest that birth control and abortion should be a woman's choice (Ansbacher & Ansbacher, 1956, p. 434), Adler criticized the decision of some women not to have children. It is interesting to speculate how he would resolve this issue now, on an overpopulated planet. Is there a conflict between his recommendation of parenthood as the norm of healthy individual choice and the need for humankind to maintain a habitable planet?

SOCIAL INTERACTION   The task of social interaction refers to "the problems of communal life" (Adler, 1936/1964, p. 42)—that is, social relationships with others, including friendship. People perform this life task better if they are high in social interest. All social relationships should be based on a strong sense of social interest, which prevents a self-centered, narcissistic attitude.

All three tasks are interrelated. None can be solved in isolation. None can be solved adequately unless there is sufficient social interest. If there is a fourth life task, Adler suggested, it is art (Bottome, 1947, p. 81). He even hinted at a fifth task, spirituality (Mosak & Dreikurs, 1967/2000).

INTERVENTIONS BASED ON ADLER'S THEORY

Like all psychoanalysts, Adler discussed the role of formal psychotherapy in overcoming psychological distress. Intervention is often needed to overcome developmental errors from childhood. We do not learn readily from life itself because we interpret life experience according to the often erroneous directions of our style of life (Adler, 1921/1927, p. 222).

Besides formal psychotherapy, the principles of individual psychology can be applied in other interventions as well, such as schools, making Adler a pioneer in modern community psychology interventions. In fact, Adler thought psychologists should advocate social change to prevent mental disorders (Ansbacher, 1990).

School

Adler's ideas have been applied in schools, where they are called *individual education* (Clark, 1985). Adler thought that schools had great potential for personality growth, but only if traditional authoritarian methods were replaced by practices designed to foster social interest. He opposed corporal punishment and favored cooperative learning strategies and clubs.

Adler taught his concepts of individual psychology in over 30 Child Guidance Clinics that he established in Vienna during the 1920s. In these clinics, he interviewed a problem child in front of an audience of teachers, using this demonstration to instruct them in the principles of his psychology. During the years the clinics operated, until political changes in Europe forced their closure in the early 1930s, court cases of juvenile delinquency and neuroses in Vienna substantially decreased (Bottome, 1947, p. 51).

The city of Vienna also established a public Individual Psychology Experimental School as a place for Adlerian ideas to be applied. The original school operated only from 1931 to 1934. Demonstration schools were reopened after World War II (Ansbacher & Ansbacher, 1956, p. 404). Subsequent generations of Adlerians have continued to develop new intervention programs in schools (Corsini, 1989; Dinkmeyer, McKay, & Dinkmeyer, 1982; Morse, Bockoven, & Bettesworth, 1988; Turk, 1990). Many of the democratic practices in education that focus on individual student needs stem historically from Adler's influence, even if that connection has been forgotten (Pryor & Tollerud, 1999).

Therapy

Adlerian therapy aims to change thinking, emotion, and behavior, with the encouragement of a supportive therapist. Q-sort ratings of a case study of a suicidal patient reveal that an Adlerian therapist sees the patient differently than therapists who are guided by other theories, including Freudian and Jungian (Stone, 2009). Because individual psychology believes all personality failures result from a lack of social interest, Adlerian therapy aims to foster the individual's social interest.

The client's style of life is assessed at the beginning of therapy, providing a context for understanding the patient's specific problem. By asking, "What would you do if you had not got this trouble?" Adler was able to determine what the patient was trying to avoid (Bottome, 1947, p. 148). The specific problem that the patient presents in therapy is often intertwined with the style of life, and can't be resolved without modifying the latter.

As discussed earlier, first memories are significant in therapy. Adler (1921/1927, pp. 30–31) gave the example of a man unrealistically distrustful that his fiancée would break their engagement. The man's first memory (always an important clue to the style of life) was of being picked up by his mother in a crowd but then put down again so his younger brother could be picked up. This memory suggests a lifestyle based on a sense of not being the favorite one, which of course would contribute to later doubts about the earnestness of his intended spouse.

Dreams in this approach are not concerned so much with the unconscious, but instead with present problems in life (Lombardi & Elcock, 1997). The key to understanding dreams is the emotion they create, which is what is needed to solve life's current problems. Adler cited the example of a man who dreamed that his wife had failed to take care of their third child, so the child became lost. He awoke feeling critical of his wife. This emotion, although triggered by a dream that was not accurate in terms of facts, was what the man needed to deal with his own dissatisfaction with his marriage (Ansbacher & Ansbacher, 1956, p. 361).

Adler tried to avoid developing a transference relationship, which he thought unnecessarily complicates and prolongs psychotherapy. Adlerian therapy is typically brief (Ansbacher, 1989). He avoided an authoritarian approach. The therapist can coach and advise, but it is the effort and courage of the client that determine the outcome (cf. Sizemore & Huber, 1988). He did not intimidate patients with his scholarly expertise, preferring to talk to them "like an old grandmother," according to a close friend (Bottome, 1947, p. 41). The atmosphere in Adler's sessions was supportive, with minimal tension.

Adler used humor frequently. Other therapists have agreed that humor can be effective in therapy (Baker, 1993; Richman, 2001). A formal therapeutic intervention using humor has been devised (Prerost, 1989) although not within a specifically Adlerian context. One therapist recounts the case of a 71-year-old man suffering from depression that stemmed from the death of a friend. A joke helped him overcome his own death anxiety. The joke tells of a physician who is trying, at the request of a patient's family, to inform his elderly patient that he had won $10 million in the lottery. The family was afraid that the shock of the good news would kill the old man. As the joke goes, "The doctor visited and said to the old man, 'What would you say if I told you that you won ten million dollars?' 'I would give half of it to you,' said the old man. And the doctor dropped dead" (Richman, 2001, p. 421).

Adler respected the religious commitments of his patients. He regarded the idea of God as a reflection of the basic human striving for a better condition. Many therapists avoid following up on mention of religion by their patients, thus conveying the idea that religious experience should not be a part of the therapeutic experience; in doing so, they miss therapeutic opportunities (LaMothe, Arnold, & Crane, 1998).

Physical as well as psychological improvement can result from therapy. Adler's claims of the importance of psychological factors in physical disease are persuasive because of his many years as a general practitioner preceding his specialization in psychiatry. We may regard Adler as a pioneer in the field of psychosomatic medicine, which recognizes psychogenic components in many physical illnesses.

Adler was innovative in his therapeutic techniques. He once got a patient whose speech was extremely slow, the result of depression, to speak more quickly simply by continuing to ask questions at a normal pace, whether the patient had finished responding yet or not (Dreikurs, 1940/1982). A behaviorist might say that he succeeded by withholding reinforcement (attention) for slow speech. Indeed, Adlerian therapy is essentially a primitive version of operant conditioning (Pratt, 1985). Behaviorists emphasize that it is important to analyze the function of a student's undesirable behavior, for example, how it influences the teacher (Taylor & Romanczyk, 1994). This functional analysis is essentially the same as Adler's advice to see what the problem child is trying to achieve. Behavioral psychology journals have been the major publication outlet for studies of one of Adler's emphases, parenting training programs (Wiese & Kramer, 1988). Behavioral psychologists have also applied their methods to interventions in schools, another of Adler's primary efforts (Kratochwill & Martens, 1994; Repp, 1994).

Adlerian therapists continue to explore new techniques, including hypnosis as a means of producing lifestyle change (Fairfield, 1990). O'Connell (1990) claims that his "natural high" approach encompasses Adlerian principles of holism and transcendence. Adler's therapeutic approach has been compared to various modern therapeutic techniques, including family systems approaches (Carich & Willingham, 1987), cognitive therapy (Elliott, 1992), and rational-emotive therapy (Ellis, 1989). In stressing the social nature of the human, Adlerians have also been highly involved in family therapy (Dinkmeyer & Dinkmeyer, 1989; Sherman & Dinkmeyer, 1987). These developments in therapy and in school psychology show that psychologists have judged Adler's ideas positively.

Summary

- Adler emphasized conscious striving and the *creative self*, in contrast to Freud's unconscious determinism.
- He described the fundamental motivation to strive from a *felt minus* to a *felt plus*.
- A person with an *inferiority complex* feels overcome by a lack of worth and ceases striving.
- In this striving toward a better condition, a person is guided by *fictional finalism*, the image of the goal.
- Adler viewed personality as a unity.
- A person's unique *style of life* is evidenced by *early memories*.

- Although he thought of each person as unique, Adler listed types of *mistaken styles of life*: ruling type, getting type, and avoiding type of person.
- In contrast, a healthy style of life is *socially useful*.
- Parents contribute to unhealthy styles of life by *pampering* or *neglecting* their children.
- Adler's theory has inspired training programs for parents.
- *Family constellation*, particularly birth order, influences personality development.
- Adler regarded the second-born position as the most desirable, although research does not generally

confirm his prediction of higher achievement for this sibling position.

- *Social interest* is the key factor in psychological health.
- A healthy person succeeds in *three tasks of life*: work, love, and social interaction.

- Adler intervened in schools to deal with problem children.
- Adlerian therapy supports self-esteem and aims to change the style of life to a socially useful one.
- Adler described physical as well as psychological benefits of therapy.

Thinking about Adler's Theory

1. Does Adler's emphasis on social aspects of personality problems have any particular relevance for today's problems?
2. How would Adler's concept of inferiority apply to people with physical disabilities?
3. Do you think Adler's use of the term *masculine protest* would be relevant to today's society?
4. Imagine that you are writing open-ended questions for a research project. What would you ask to assess people's fictional finalisms?
5. Do you have a first memory or an early memory that can be interpreted from the perspective of Adler's theory?
6. Families have changed considerably in many cultures since Adler wrote his theory. What additions to his theory would you suggest to describe the effects of these changes?
7. Western cultures emphasize individualism. How might Adler's theory help correct the problems created by too much self-interest?

Study Questions

1. How does Adler's approach to personality differ from that of Freud?
2. Describe a person's fundamental motivation, according to Adler. List five terms he used in the development of this idea.
3. Distinguish between a feeling of inferiority and an inferiority complex.
4. Explain the term *fictional finalism*. Give an example.
5. Explain how early memories are a key to personality.
6. What is a style of life? List three mistaken styles of life. What did Adler call a healthy style of life?
7. How do parents contribute to their children's development of unhealthy styles of life?
8. Explain how children can be helped by sending their parents to parenting training programs.
9. Discuss Adler's theory of the relationship between birth order and personality. What did he expect would be the typical personality of the oldest child? The middle child? The youngest child?
10. Describe how Adler's predictions hold up or are refuted by research on birth order.
11. Describe Sulloway's proposal about birth order and scientific revolution.
12. Explain what is meant by social interest.
13. List and explain the three tasks of life.
14. Describe Adler's interventions in schools.
15. Describe Adlerian therapy. Why is it compared to family therapy rather than to individual approaches?

Chapter Overview

ILLUSTRATIVE BIOGRAPHY
Mahatma Gandhi

Mahatma Gandhi was a political figure in nineteenth- and twentieth-century India when it was ruled by Great Britain. His nonviolent civil disobedience methods became a model for other civil rights activists, including Dr. Martin Luther King, Jr. Erik Erikson, an influential theorist in the fields of psychohistory (Pois, 1990) and psychobiography, analyzed our chosen personality in his book, *Gandhi's Truth: On the Origins of Militant Nonviolence* (1969), which won the Pulitzer Prize and the National Book Award.

Mohandas Gandhi (later called Mahatma, or "Great Soul," to honor his spiritual leadership) was born in 1869 in Porbandar, India. His father's family had for several generations served in government offices under British rule. According to the custom of his large Hindu family, Gandhi was married at age 13. Mohandas and his bride, Kasturba, lived together and conceived a child, who died shortly after birth, and later had four sons.

Gandhi went to England for his law degree. Members of his caste refused approval of this voyage. In leaving he became

Mahatma Gandhi

an outcast, and he was socially ostracized on his return. His mother consented only when he vowed to abstain from meat, wine, and women, to honor their religious values. Gandhi promised, not confessing that he had already eaten meat with a friend. He honored this vow in England and thereafter, refusing meat, meat broth, eggs, and milk even when doctors prescribed them. There was one exception, when he took goat's milk, legalistically reasoning that he had only promised his mother to refrain from the milk of cows and buffalo; but he regretted this action. In fact, his dietary restrictions expanded, so for the most part his diet consisted of fruit and nuts.

After earning his law degree, Gandhi worked for an Indian company in South Africa, where he was the victim of racial prejudice. Indians were resented for their economic threat and different living habits. Despite his British education, he was refused hotel accommodation and first-class train travel. Once he was beaten simply for being in the wrong neighborhood. Gandhi embarked on a career of public service and political activism on behalf of Indians in South Africa and, later, in India. He was influential in ending the practice of indentured labor. In India he founded an ashram (a traditional communal living arrangement) and boldly admitted an Untouchable family to membership, violating traditional Indian caste practices. He organized Indian fabric workers against exploitation by their employers, and he organized a civil disobedience movement to protest the British salt tax. He went to prison for his political activities. He fasted as a political strategy. Throughout, he was guided by the principle of *ahimsa*, or nonviolence, which seeks to do no harm to others (Gandhi, 1957, p. 349; Teixeira, 1987). He died by assassination in 1948, having lived to see India become independent from Britain.

Much in the life of this world-renowned leader invites psychoanalytic analysis. His focus on concerns of eating and sexual restraint match two of the areas of libidinal focus named by Freud. The other, anality, is also well represented in Gandhi's autobiography, with frequent concern about unsanitary conditions, which were prevalent in India because of lack of indoor plumbing. To explain how his personal psychology relates to the public and political arenas, however, it is necessary to theorize beyond the psychosexual level, as Erikson's psychosocial theory does. In addition, Erikson's approach to psychohistory finds creative strengths, and not only neurotic conflicts, in the analysis of historical figures (Pietikainen & Ihanus, 2003).

DESCRIPTION

Erikson's theory is a developmental theory, so it describes people by identifying the developmental stages that a person has experienced and suggesting whether growth was healthy or left personality flaws.

Mahatma Gandhi lived a long life, and so his personality could be shaped at all the stages of development that Erikson theorized. The major legacies of this development left him with a fervent commitment to a cause (as a result of identity development) but enduring difficulties about trust or nurturance and love for women. Erikson (1969) describes a personality he admires, but he describes it as also flawed.

DEVELOPMENT

Erikson's theory describes eight stages of development that occur in sequence throughout life (with a ninth stage added later, based on his ongoing revision of his model). Each has a typical age of occurrence, and Erikson believed these stages to occur in all cultures.

The concept of identity is the central concept by which Erikson attempted to understand Gandhi. Identity is the developmental issue that prevails in adolescence, according to Erikson's theory, and it typically involves career choice and racial identity issues. Erikson interpreted Gandhi's period of study in England as a psychosocial moratorium, a period in which he explored his identity, which is (in Erikson's theory) a healthy process. Gandhi's connection with his mother and with his Indian motherland was strengthened by his dietary vows, which continued to remind him of that connection in a strange land. (How ironic that Gandhi's return to India brought him the news of his mother's death.) Deciding to study law provoked identity issues

beyond those of career choice because it required travel to another country and invoked ostracism by his caste. His minority position in London made him more conscious of his identity as an Indian, which he explored by reading about vegetarianism and Hinduism. The greatest identity crisis, however, Erikson (1969, p. 47) suggested, occurred when Gandhi was first in South Africa. He was thrown off a train and denied the right to travel first class, despite having purchased a ticket, because of his race. His reaction was to devote himself to the political and religious cause of improving the life of poor Indians, solidifying his identity and illustrating Erikson's view of the interconnectedness of individual development and society.

ADJUSTMENT

In Erikson's theory, each stage of life involves a conflict between a positive pole and a negative pole, and if it is resolved in a healthy way, the ego is strengthened. His theory proposes that the identity crisis, if resolved well (as Gandhi did), enhances the ego with a stronger ability of what Erikson called "fidelity," by which he meant being faithful to a cause. Thus Gandhi's fidelity to the cause of nonviolent protest is a consequence of his identity development.

Although Erikson admired Gandhi, he also criticized him. Erikson suggested that Gandhi did not come to a good resolution of the next two crises, which typically occur in young adulthood (the crisis of intimacy) and middle adulthood (the crisis of generativity). Gandhi gave no evidence of psychological intimacy with his wife, Kasturba. According to Erikson (1969, p. 121), "one thing is devastatingly certain: nowhere is there any suggestion of joyful intimacy." On the contrary, Gandhi deplored his sexuality and treated Kasturba and other women as temptresses who aroused regrettable desires. He decided to give up a sexual relationship with her to devote himself to "higher" purposes (and, incidentally, to prevent conceiving another child) without consulting her. Erikson says that Gandhi retained "some vindictiveness, especially toward woman as the temptress" (p. 122) and even sadism (p. 234).

COGNITION

Like Freud, Erikson believed the major determinants of personality are not conscious. They are the result of conflict through the various stages of development.

In Gandhi's personality, the development of his identity as a lawyer and an Indian obviously had some conscious components. He could answer the question "Who am I?" appropriately and in ways that others would accept. The unconscious legacy of this stage, though, was the energy for his political efforts on behalf of Indians, and later of other oppressed people. His failure to resolve the young adult stage of intimacy adequately left more harmful unconscious tendencies to blame women for problems. Erikson relates one incident on Gandhi's commune as an example. Gandhi directed young boys and girls to bathe together, which to his naive surprise led to difficulties, with some boys making fun of the girls. (The details are not given in Gandhi's autobiography.) Gandhi's solution was to cut the girls' beautiful long hair, thus making them less tempting to the boys, a solution Erikson criticizes (1969, p. 237–242). Had Gandhi been able to confront his own sexuality more honestly, rather than denying it, he would not have, in essence, punished the girls for their sexual attractiveness.

(continued)

(continued)

CULTURE

Erikson (1958, 1975) proposed that the conflicts of the person studied in psychobiography are not simply individual conflicts but represent the conflicts of the society in which the person lived. Thus the study of individuals can enlighten historical understanding. Erikson (1969) honored Gandhi immensely for his work toward a more inclusive identity for humankind. Gandhi worked to rise above the divisions that mark what Erikson called *pseudospeciation* by envisioning a more inclusive identity. Pseudospeciation is inherent in colonialism, causing individuals to experience "guilt and rage which prevent true development" (p. 433). At this particular historical moment, then, Gandhi's solution to the problem of identity moved history forward toward greater peace and mutual acceptance.

Erikson (1969, p. 251) expressed disappointment that Gandhi's sexual renunciation would be unacceptable to the West, limiting the extent to which we could learn from his nonviolent political activism. We must ask whether Erikson's stages can be used, without modification, as universal developmental standards against which to evaluate someone from such a different culture. To criticize Gandhi for failing to develop all the strengths that Erikson outlined presumes that the strengths described in this Western theory apply in all cultures. Is intimacy, as described in the context of a tradition of Western love and marriage, to be expected in a culture where child marriage, arranged by parents, is accepted? Or would such a psychological interpretation be parallel to the economic colonialism against which Gandhi and other leaders of his country struggled so courageously?

BIOLOGY

Erikson's theory builds on that of Freud, presuming that biology provides the motivation for personality through the psychosexual stages that Freud outlined. However, biological sexual energy is not the only consideration. He also describes psycho*social* issues.

The linking of biological and social issues is evident in Gandhi's life in issues around eating and his mother. Gandhi sought throughout his life for a relationship to take the place of the disrupted relationships with his mother and father (cf. Muslin & Desai, 1984, who interpret this in terms of Kohut's psychoanalytic theory). Erikson (e.g., 1969, p. 110), noted that Gandhi did not acknowledge the extent of his dependency on his mother, even refusing to cry openly when he learned of her death. His dietary restrictions served as a ritual to preserve hope, the ego strength that develops in the first developmental stage, in which there is a conflict between trust and mistrust (p. 154). This stage

corresponds to Freud's psychosexual oral stage. The extremity of his dietary control suggests unacknowledged mistrust. His dietary restrictions can be considered obsessive (p. 152), though Erikson observes that "it is always difficult to say where, exactly, obsessive symptomatology ends and creative ritualization begins" (p. 157). Surely the physicians who urged Gandhi unsuccessfully to drink milk or eat meat for his health would have agreed with the more negative clinical label.

FINAL THOUGHTS

Erikson's approach to psychobiography emphasizes the immediacy of the person's experience, rather than reducing the person to an object to be studied with distancing and judgmental categories (Schnell, 1980). His theory calls attention to the cultural context in which an individual develops, and it acknowledges the potential of an individual, through a highly developed ego, to have an impact on culture (Nichtern, 1985), as Mahatma Gandhi did.

Erikson's (1969) respect for Gandhi and openness to learn from him is clear in his book. He even addressed a long section to Gandhi in conversational terms, as "I" to "you" (pp. 229–254). Erikson described his task in his analysis of Gandhi: "to confront the spiritual truth as you have formulated and lived it with the psychological truth which I [Erikson] have learned and practiced" (p. 231). Erikson suggested that psychoanalysis is the counterpart of Gandhi's philosophy of *Satyagraha* (roughly meaning "passive resistance" or "militant nonviolence") "because it confronts the inner enemy nonviolently" (p. 244). Lorimer (1976) suggested that Erikson's objectivity was compromised in this analysis. Erikson (1975), though, did not claim objectivity, instead characterizing his method as "disciplined subjectivity" (p. 25). It requires undistorted self-knowledge, which can be achieved by undergoing psychoanalysis.

Besides Gandhi, Erikson wrote brief analyses of George Bernard Shaw (1968), and of Hitler and Gorky (1963). His 1958 book, *Young Man Luther*, analyzed the Protestant theologian Martin Luther and triggered renewed interest in applying psychological theory to historical figures, becoming a model for psychohistorians (Coles, 1970; Hutton, 1983; Schnell, 1980). It helped move psychohistory beyond a stage in which it documented the impact of great people on history and toward a stage that recognizes the mutual influences of psychological and historical forces (Fitzpatrick, 1976). Erikson was a key figure in a research project devoted to psychohistory, the Wellfleet group, beginning in 1965 (Pietikainen & Ihanus, 2003). Thus we can credit him with helping to widen the intellectual impact of psychoanalysis beyond clinical settings.

PREVIEW: OVERVIEW OF ERIKSON'S THEORY

Erikson's theory has implications for major theoretical questions, as presented in Table 5.1. Like other psychoanalytic theories, it proposes a number of concepts that are not easily captured within the precise hypothesis-testing language of science. Some of his concepts, however, have been operationally defined in ways that have generated many research studies. Most notably, identity statuses are measured by interview and questionnaire. Additionally, empirical studies of racial and ethnic identity have tested theoretical ideas proposed by others but owing an historical debt to Erikson's groundbreaking work on identity. His theory is more comprehensive than classical psychoanalysis because it encompasses cultural phenomena. Erikson's theory has been applied to therapy with children and adolescents.

Table 5.1 Preview of Erikson's Theory

Individual Differences	Individuals differ in their ego strengths. Males and females differ in personality because of biological differences.
Adaptation and Adjustment	A strong ego is the key to mental health. It comes from good resolution of eight stages of ego development, in which positive ego strengths predominate over the negative pole (e.g., trust over mistrust).
Cognitive Processes	The unconscious is an important force in personality. Experience is influenced by biological modes, which are expressed in symbols and in play.
Culture	Society shapes the way in which people develop (thus the term *psychosocial* development). Cultural institutions continue to support ego strengths (e.g., religion supports trust or hope).
Biological Influences	Biological factors are important determinants of personality. Sex differences in personality are strongly influenced by differences in the "genital apparatus."
Development	Children develop through four psychosocial stages, each of which presents a crisis in which a particular ego strength is developed. Adolescents and adults develop through four additional psychosocial stages. Again, each involves a crisis and develops a particular ego strength.

Each person develops within a particular society, which, through its culturally specific patterns of child rearing and social institutions, profoundly influences how that person resolves conflicts. The ego is concerned not only with biological (psychosexual) issues but also with interpersonal and cultural concerns, which Erikson termed **psychosocial**.

psychosocial

Erikson's approach to development, offered as an alternative to Freud's psychosexual approach

Biography of Erik Erikson

Erik Homberger Erikson (as we now call him) was born near Frankfurt, Germany, in 1902. He was raised by his mother, who was Jewish and of Danish ancestry, and his stepfather, a Jewish pediatrician whom his mother met when she sought care for 3-year-old Erik. Erikson did not know that he was conceived illegitimately, believing his stepfather, whose name (Homberger) he was given, was his biological father (Hopkins, 1995). Erikson was not accepted as fully Jewish because of the physical appearance that was the legacy of his Danish parents: tall, blond, and blue eyed. Yet he had not been raised to think of himself as Danish. This somewhat confused background contributed to his own keen interest in identity, as he later said.

Erikson studied art and wandered through Europe in his youth, trying to become an artist (Wurgaft, 1976). In a job found at the suggestion of a friend, Erikson taught art to children of Freud's entourage. His future wife, Joan Serson, was studying to be a psychoanalyst, and she introduced him to psychoanalysis. Interestingly, in later years he became the psychoanalyst and she the artist. They had three children, including a son who suffered from Down syndrome and was institutionalized. After Erikson's death, his daughter published a critical memoir of her parents, faulting them for hiding from her the secret of her brother, whom they told her had died (Bloland, 2005).

Erikson was analyzed by Freud's daughter, Anna, for 3 years and was recruited as an analyst, a "lay analyst" because of his nonmedical training. In 1933 he and his wife left Germany, where anti-Semitism was becoming increasingly overt. They went briefly to Denmark, his ancestral home, and then to the United States. To mark the identity change in his own life, he took Erikson as a last name at this time.

Although he had no college degree (not even an undergraduate degree), Erikson became a child analyst and taught at Harvard. He was affiliated with the Harvard Psychological Clinic, under Henry Murray (Erikson, 1963), and was the author of the Dramatic Productions Test in Murray's (1938, pp. 552–582) well-known research report, *Explorations in Personality*. He was part of a team that prepared an analysis of enemy

Erik Erikson

leader Adolf Hitler for the American government during World War II. He also was affiliated, at various stages in his career, with the Yale Institute of Human Relations, the Guidance Study in the Institute of Human Development at the University of California at Berkeley, and the Austen Riggs Center in western Massachusetts. Besides his clinical and developmental studies, his association with anthropologists permitted him to observe development among two Native American cultures—the Sioux at Pine Ridge, South Dakota, and the Yurok, a California fishing tribe.

When Erikson was a professor at the University of California at Berkeley, the United States was undergoing a wave of concern about communist infiltration in schools. Faculty members were required to sign an additional loyalty oath, besides the oath in which they had already routinely pledged to uphold the national and state constitutions. Erikson and several others refused, resulting in their dismissal, although this was overturned in court. Because Erikson had become a U.S. citizen as an adult and conducted psychological research for the government during World War II, analyzing Hitler's speeches and conducting other war-related studies (Hopkins, 1995), he cannot be accused of anti-Americanism for his stance. Erikson (1951) argued that the anticommunist hysteria that had prompted the requirement of a loyalty oath was dangerous to the university's historical role as a place where truth and reason can be freely sought and where students learn critical thinking. Undoubtedly, his experience with German nationalism under the Nazis figured in his position.

Although he considered himself a Freudian, Erikson proposed many theoretical innovations that emphasized the ego and social factors. Most notably, he theorized that ego development continues throughout life. In his 80s, he and his wife were still active, interviewing a group of elderly Californians to learn more about this last stage of life (Erikson, Erikson, & Kivnick, 1986). He died in 1994, at the age of 91.

Although Erikson had "neither medical training nor an advanced degree of any kind except a certificate in Montessori education" (Fitzpatrick, 1976, p. 298), his contributions to psychology have transformed our understanding of human development and of the relationship between the individual and society. Erikson's most important contribution was a model of personality development that extends throughout the life span.

CHILD ANALYSIS

Like his mentor Anna Freud, Erikson became a psychoanalyst specializing in the treatment of children. He participated in the Seminar on Child Analysis held in Anna Freud's living room, and when he emigrated to the United States, he brought this specialization with him, as did others in that seminal group (Tyson, 2009a). Today, this specialization numbers few active practitioners (Hoffman et al., 2009). That does not necessarily indicate that psychoanalysis for children doesn't work. It competes with less expensive behavioral and pharmacological approaches for many childhood problems. Researchers have reported benefits from psychoanalytic treatment of children, not only for psychological problems, but also for medical problems such as the control of diabetes (Fonagy & Moran, 1990). Follow-up investigation of adults who had been psychoanalyzed as children suggests that the treatment helped to develop resiliency into adulthood, beyond what their troubled childhood would have predicted (Tyson, 2009b).

THE EPIGENETIC PRINCIPLE

epigenetic principle

the principle for psychosocial development, based on a biological model, in which parts emerge in order of increasing differentiation

Erikson (1959) based his understanding of development on the **epigenetic principle**: "that anything that grows has a *ground plan,* and that out of this ground plan the *parts* arise, each part having its *time* of special ascendancy, until all parts have arisen to form a *functioning whole*" (p. 52). This principle applies to the physical development of fetuses before birth (where it is easy to visualize the gradual emergence of increasingly differentiated parts) and to psychological development throughout life. For a healthy ego to develop, several ego strengths must develop sequentially. Each stage focuses on one aspect of ego development: trust in infancy, autonomy in toddlerhood, and so on.

THE PSYCHOSOCIAL STAGES

Erikson (1959) reinterpreted Freud's psychosexual stages, emphasizing the social aspects of each. Further, he extended the stage concept throughout life, giving a life-span approach to development in a classic set of eight stages. Erikson's first four stages correspond to Freud's oral, anal, phallic, and latency stages. Freud's genital stage encompasses Erikson's last four stages (see Table 5.2). Later (Erikson, 1997), his wife and collaborator Joan Erikson described a ninth stage that they had been discussing when her husband died.

Each stage involves a crisis, a developmental turning point, and conflict centers on a distinctive issue (Erikson, 1964). Out of each crisis emerges an ego strength, or "virtue," that corresponds specifically to that stage (Erikson, 1961). The strength then becomes part of the repertoire of ego skills for the individual throughout life. Each strength develops in relation to an opposite, or negative, pole. The strength of trust develops in relation to mistrust, the strength of autonomy in relation to shame, and so forth. In healthy development, there is a larger ratio of the strength (the syntonic element) than of the weakness (the dystonic element). Furthermore, these strengths develop in relationships with significant people, beginning with the mother and expanding more broadly throughout life (see Table 5.3).

Although each ego skill has its period of greatest growth at a distinct period in life, earlier developments pave the way for that strength, and later developments can, to some extent, modify an earlier resolution (see Figure 5.1). For example, being a grandparent offers many older people a second chance at developing the

Table 5.2 Stages of Psychosocial Development Compared with Psychosexual Development

Psychosocial Stage	Comparable Psychosexual Stage and Mode	Freudian Stage	Age
1. Trust vs. Mistrust	Oral-Respiratory, Sensory-Kinesthetic (Incorporative Mode)	Oral	Infancy
2. Autonomy vs. Shame, Doubt	Anal-Urethral, Muscular (Retentive-Eliminative Mode)	Anal	Early childhood
3. Initiative vs. Guilt	Infantile-Genital Locomotor (Intrusive, Inclusive Mode)	Phallic	Play age
4. Industry vs. Inferiority	Latency	Latency	School age
5. Identity vs. Identity Diffusion	Puberty	Genital	Adolescence
6. Intimacy vs. Isolation	Genitality	Genital	Young adulthood
7. Generativity vs. Self-Absorption	Procreativity	Genital	Adulthood
8. Integrity vs. Despair	Generalization of Sensual Modes	Genital	Old age

Source: Adapted from *The Life Cycle Completed: A Review,* by Erik H. Erikson, by permission of W. W. Norton & Company, Inc. Copyright © 1982 by Rikan Enterprises Ltd.

Table 5.3 Strengths Developed at Each Stage of Psychosocial Development and Their Social Context

Psychosocial Stage	Strength	Significant People	Related Elements in Society
1. Trust vs. Mistrust	Hope	Maternal person	Cosmic order (e.g., religion)
2. Autonomy vs. Shame, Doubt	Will	Parental persons	Law and order
3. Initiative vs. Guilt	Purpose	Basic family	Ideal prototypes (e.g., male, female, socioeconomic status)
4. Industry vs. Inferiority	Competence	Neighborhood, school	Technological order
5. Identity vs. Identity Diffusion	Fidelity	Peer groups and outgroups, models of leadership	Ideological worldview
6. Intimacy vs. Isolation	Love	Partners in friendship and sex	Patterns of cooperation and competition
7. Generativity vs. Self-absorption	Care	Divided labor and shared household	Currents of education and tradition
8. Integrity vs. Despair	Wisdom	Mankind and my kind	Wisdom

Source: Adapted from *The Life Cycle Completed: A Review*, by Erik H. Erikson, by permission of W. W. Norton & Company, Inc. Copyright © 1982 by Rikan Enterprises Ltd.

		1	2	3	4	5	6	7	8
Old Age	VIII								INTEGRITY vs. DESPAIR
Adulthood	VII							GENERATIVITY vs. STAGNATION	
Young Adulthood	VI						INTIMACY vs. ISOLATION		
Adolescence	V	Temporal Perspective vs. Time Confusion	Self-Certainty vs. Self-Consciousness	Role Experimentation vs. Role Fixation	Apprenticeship vs. Work Paralysis	IDENTITY vs. IDENTITY CONFUSION	Sexual Polarization vs. Bisexual Confusion	Leader- and Followership vs. Authority Confusion	Ideological Commitment vs. Confusion of Values
School Age	IV				INDUSTRY vs. INFERIORITY	Task Identification vs. Sense of Futility			
Play Age	III			INITIATIVE vs. GUILT		Anticipation of Roles vs. Role Inhibition			
Early Childhood	II		AUTONOMY vs. SHAME, DOUBT			Will to be Oneself vs. Self-Doubt			
Infancy	I	TRUST vs. MISTRUST				Mutual Recognition vs. Autistic Isolation			

FIGURE 5.1 The Epigenetic Chart

Source: Adapted from *Identity, Youth and Crisis* by Erik H. Erikson, by permission of W. W. Norton & Company, Inc. Copyright © 1968 by W. W. Norton and Company, Inc.

ego strength (generativity) that had its primary focus of development in the previous stage (Erikson, Erikson, & Kivnick, 1986).

Each stage must be considered not simply from the individual's point of view but also from a social point of view. An adolescent's identity develops in relationship to the older generation's ideals and values. Infant development implies not only the infant's needs but also the complementary need of the mother to nurture (Erikson, 1968; Erikson, Erikson, & Kivnick, 1986).

Stage 1: Trust versus Mistrust

During the first year of life, the infant develops basic **trust** and basic **mistrust**. Basic trust is the sense that others are dependable and will provide what is needed, as well as the sense that one is trustworthy oneself (Erikson, 1968, p. 96). It is based on good parenting, with adequate provision of food, caretaking, and stimulation. The infant approaches the world with an *incorporative* mode, taking in not only milk and food but also sensory stimulation, looking, touching, and so on. This begins relatively passively at first but becomes increasingly active in later infancy. This stage is one of mutuality, not simply of receiving; the infant seeks the mother's care and seeks to explore the environment tactilely, visually, and so on.

To the extent that the infant does not find the world responsive to his or her needs, basic mistrust develops. Some mistrust is inevitable because no parental nurturing can be as reliable as the umbilical connection. Some mistrust is even desirable. The world the individual confronts after infancy will not always be trustworthy, and the capacity to mistrust will be required for realistic adaptation. In a healthy resolution of the crisis between basic trust and basic mistrust, trust predominates, providing strength for continued ego development in later stages. In adult life, the ability to trust others, even though they could betray that trust, is an important quality that contributes to adjustment and happiness (Jones, Couch, & Scott, 1997).

trust
the positive pole of the first psychosocial stage

mistrust
the negative pole of the first psychosocial stage

Stage 2: Autonomy versus Shame and Doubt

During the second year of life, the toddler develops a sense of **autonomy**. This period includes not only toilet training, which Freud emphasized, but also broader issues of control of the musculature in general (becoming able to walk well) and control in interpersonal relationships. The toddler experiments with the world through the modes of *holding on* and *letting go*. He or she requires the support of adults to develop, gradually, a sense of autonomy. If the toddler's vulnerability is not supported by protective adults, a sense of **shame** (of premature exposure) and a sense of doubt develop. As in the first stage, a higher ratio of the positive pole (autonomy) should prevail, but some degree of shame and doubt are necessary for health and for the good of society.

autonomy
the positive pole of the second psychosocial stage

shame
the negative pole of the second psychosocial stage

Stage 3: Initiative versus Guilt

Four- and 5-year-old children face the third psychosocial crisis: **initiative** versus **guilt**. The child can make choices about what kind of person to be, based in part on identifications with the parents. Erikson agreed with Freud that the child at this age is interested in sexuality and in sex differences and is developing a conscience (superego). The young child acts in an intrusive mode, physically and verbally intruding into others' space. The child approaches the unknown with curiosity. For the boy, this intrusion is congruent with early awareness of sexuality, described by Freud's phallic stage. For the girl, awareness of her different physical sexual apparatus is significant at this stage, according to Erikson, who claimed that children reflect these different sexualities in their play. If the stage is resolved well, the child develops more initiative than guilt.

initiative
the positive pole of the third psychosocial stage

guilt
the negative pole of the third psychosocial stage

Stage 4: Industry versus Inferiority

industry

the positive pole of the fourth psychosocial stage

inferiority

the negative pole of the fourth psychosocial stage

The remainder of childhood, until puberty, is devoted to the school-age task of stage 4: the development of a sense of **industry**. The negative pole is **inferiority**. The child at this stage "learns to win recognition by *producing things*" (Erikson, 1959, p. 86). A child who works at tasks until completion achieves satisfaction and develops perseverance. If the child cannot produce an acceptable product or fails to obtain recognition for it, a sense of inferiority prevails. Teachers are especially important at this stage because much of this development occurs at school.

Stage 5: Identity versus Identity Confusion

identity

sense of sameness between one's meaning for oneself and one's meaning for others in the social world; the positive pole of the fifth psychosocial stage

Erikson's best known concept is the identity crisis, the developmental stage of adolescence. In this time of transition toward adult roles, the adolescent struggles to attain a sense of **identity**. Erikson (1968) defined the sense of ego identity as "the awareness of the fact that there is a self-sameness and continuity to the ego's synthesizing methods, the *style of one's individuality,* and that this style coincides with the sameness and continuity of one's *meaning for significant others* in the immediate community" (p. 50). The task is to answer the question, "Who am I?" in a way that is mutually agreeable to the individual and to others.

Exploring career possibilities is part of the process of achieving an identity, especially in the college populations that are typically studied. Other areas are also important, including religious beliefs and political ideology, and these can be measured by domain-specific instruments, based on the premise that identity is not necessarily achieved in all areas simultaneously (Goossens, 2001).

moratorium

period provided by society when an adolescent is sufficiently free of commitments to be able to explore identity; also, a stage of identity development when such exploration is occurring, before identity achievement

Society assists the healthy resolution of this stage by providing a **moratorium**, a period when the adolescent is free to explore various possible adult roles without the obligations that will come with real adulthood. Having the opportunity to study various fields, even to change majors, in college before settling down to a career commitment provides a moratorium. Erikson stressed the importance of exploration, fearing that too early a commitment to a particular identity would risk a poor choice. Furthermore, it would not provide an opportunity to develop the ego strength of this stage: *fidelity,* which he defined as "the ability to sustain loyalties freely pledged in spite of the inevitable contradictions of value systems" (Erikson, 1964, p. 125).

identity confusion

the negative pole of the fifth psychosocial stage

negative identity

identity based on socially devalued roles

Identity confusion occurs if a coherent identity cannot be achieved in a reasonable time. Another undesirable resolution of the identity crisis is the development of a **negative identity**, that is, an identity based on undesirable roles in society, such as a gang member. When young offenders are imprisoned with adult criminals, this mixing of the generations may encourage the development of such a negative identity (Erikson, 1962/1988). Culture, unfortunately, provides clear images of such negative identities, making them appealing for those who find that a positively valued identity seems unattainable (Erikson, 1968). Not all delinquent youth, to be sure, have attained a negative identity status. Many remain confused about their identity and are not as far along the developmental pathway as other adolescents (Klimstra, 2011). Finally, **identity foreclosure** (discussed later in the chapter) occurs if commitment is made too quickly, without adequate exploration.

identity foreclosure

inadequate resolution of the fifth psychosocial stage, in which an identity is accepted without adequate exploration

Stage 6: Intimacy versus Isolation

intimacy

the positive pole of the sixth psychosocial stage

isolation

the negative pole of the sixth psychosocial stage

The first of three stages of adulthood is the crisis of **intimacy** versus **isolation**. Psychological intimacy with another person cannot occur, according to Erikson, until individual identity has been established. Intimacy involves a capacity for psychological fusion with another person, whether a friend or lover, secure that individual identity will not be destroyed by the merger. The adult who does not satisfactorily resolve this crisis remains self-absorbed and isolated.

Intimacy increases during the early adult years (Reis et al., 1993). For many young adults, this crisis is experienced through the social role of marriage, although marriage is no guarantee that the crisis will resolve successfully. Furthermore, psychological intimacy is not the same as sexual intimacy, and a spouse is not the only significant other who may play a role in resolving this stage.

Stage 7: Generativity versus Stagnation

The seventh task is to develop the ego strength of **generativity**, "the interest in establishing and guiding the next generation" (Erikson, 1959, p. 97). Researchers offer this description of a high level of generativity:

> *Generative* individuals are highly involved in their work and the growth of young people, and are concerned about broader societal issues. They are tolerant of different ideas and traditions, and able to strike a balance between care and consideration for the self and for others. (Bradley & Marcia, 1998, p. 42)

Generativity is often but not necessarily expressed through the role of parenting. To be a teacher or a mentor may substitute. Failure to develop optimally in this stage leaves a person with a sense of **stagnation**, not being able to be fully involved in caring for others in a nurturing way.

generativity
the positive pole of the seventh psychosocial stage

stagnation
the negative pole of the seventh psychosocial stage

Stage 8: Integrity versus Despair

The task of old age is to resolve the crisis of integrity versus despair. The sense of **integrity** means being able to look back on one's own life and accept it as meaningful as lived. Periods of life when important transitions and choices were made are salient in this reminiscence. Among famous psychologists, according to researchers who analyzed their autobiographies, retrospection focuses on the college and graduate school years, which launched their professional lives (Mackavey, Malley, & Stewart, 1991). Not all focus is on the past, however; people at this stage who are successfully accomplishing the task of integrity also believe they have learned lessons that they can now apply (Brown & Lowis, 2003). The elderly, whose bodies are less robust than in the past, report to researchers that they feel less in control (Geppert & Halisch, 2001), so integrity is about the present, not only the past. In the absence of a sense of integrity, **despair** occurs instead, as well as unwillingness to accept death.

integrity
the positive pole of the eighth psychosocial stage

despair
the negative pole of the eighth psychosocial stage

A Ninth Stage: Dystonic Resurgence or Gerotranscendence

After his death, Erik Erikson's wife, Joan, described the ideas that they had been developing in their studies of the very old. Their observations and personal experience with aging suggested that people in their 80s and 90s face ego developmental issues beyond the integrity versus despair crisis (Brown & Lowis, 2003; Erikson, 1997). This period of life does not pose a new crisis comparable to those of the traditional eight stages. Rather, the very old return to the issues of earlier stages, confronting more directly the negative poles of those stages (mistrust, shame, guilt, etc.) as their frail selves and losses of loved ones no longer sustain the level of strength attained in their younger years. Shame, for example, may grow as a result of forgetfulness, incontinence, and other age-related declines. This stage is not simply disengagement from life, although people do typically withdraw from the busy activities of earlier stages. Now, the elderly struggle to accept death and kinship with those who have passed on. It is a time of spiritual, often but not always religious, reflection and growth. When the outcome is positive, grappling with the dystonic elements (mistrust, shame, etc.) as demanded by the physical declines of life but courageously maintaining the positive syntonic elements, it brings peace of mind and a concern with cosmic rather than material values, and it may be called **gerotranscendence**, or, as creative Joan Erikson playfully suggests with her image of dancing, *gerotranscendance* (Erikson, 1997).

gerotranscendence
the ninth stage of psychosocial development, referring to the very elderly

THE ROLE OF CULTURE IN RELATION TO THE PSYCHOSOCIAL STAGES

The stages themselves, Erikson said, are universal, but each culture provides the setting in which psychosocial crises are encountered and mastered and also provides continuing support for ego strengths when they are threatened in later life. Each stage has its own cultural institution to support continuation of the strength that emerges at

that stage. Influence goes both ways. The individual is supported by the social institutions. In addition, "each generation can and must revitalize each institution even as it
grows into it" (Erikson, 1963, p. 279).

The First Stage: Religion

hope

*fundamental conviction in the
trustworthiness of the world; the
basic virtue developed during the
first psychosocial stage*

Positive developments in the first psychosocial stage leave one with the capacity for
hope. Erikson (1959) observed that "religion through the centuries has served to
restore a sense of trust at regular intervals in the form of faith while giving tangible
form to a sense of evil which it promises to ban" (p. 65). Other cultural supports for
these ego strengths may substitute for religion. Erikson listed "fellowship, productive work, social action, scientific pursuit, and artistic creation" as sources of faith for
some people (p. 64). Erikson's respectful attitude toward religion stands in contrast
with Freud's earlier dismissal of religion as neurosis. For Erikson, religion makes the
wisdom of past generations available to support healing and growth (Erikson, 1958;
Simmonds, 2006).

Among the Dakota Sioux, a ritual Sun Dance, which includes prayer and atone-
ment, supports "the paradise of orality," the trust of the first stage (Erikson, 1963,
p. 147). The Yurok tribe, who depend on catching abundant salmon during the
brief period in the year when the fish can be netted in the river, practice rituals that
develop oral character traits, including strict eating rituals. These prepare them for the
unpredictability of each salmon catch. Such cultural rituals support the ego strengths
necessary for the specific needs of the culture.

The Second Stage: Law

will

*conviction that what one wants
to happen can happen; the basic
virtue developed during the second
psychosocial stage*

Positive developments in the second psychosocial stage leave one with the capacity for
will, or will power, which develops out of the toddler's struggle between autonomy and
shame. Institutional support for will is found in the law, which legitimizes and provides
boundaries for an individual's autonomy. The law also provides punishments. In the
past, punishment sometimes consisted of public shaming. Those caught misbehaving
could be locked in a pillory, hands and head immobilized in a wooden frame, exposed
to public scorn. Some have suggested that judges be permitted to order public shaming
as modern punishment, but the idea is controversial (Massaro, 1997).

The Third Stage: Ideal Prototypes

purpose

*orientation to attain goals through
striving; the basic virtue developed
during the third psychosocial stage*

The third stage of psychosocial development leaves the child with the basic virtue of
purpose. The corresponding element of the social order for this stage consists of the
ideal prototypes of society. Erikson said that primitive cultures provide a small number
of unchanging prototypes that are close to the economy of the tribe—for example,
the buffalo hunter of the Sioux. These provide models for children to channel their
initiative in play (e.g., playing at buffalo hunting with a toy bow and arrow) and for
adults to channel and support their initiative in the serious versions of these roles. In
contrast, in civilized cultures, prototypes are numerous, fragmented, and changing.

Americans value socioeconomic status, and they respond with guilt when it is
threatened, as third-stage development would predict (cf. Erikson, 1959, p. 28). Such
socioeconomic status is abstract and fragmented, however, compared with the whole
person of the buffalo hunter prototype. Another ideal prototype that Erikson discussed is the military prototype (p. 27), which channels the aggressive ideals important at this stage (1968, p. 122). Gender roles, central to psychoanalytic theory at this
age, provide ideal prototypes to support the ego strength of initiative. Perhaps it is
cultural confusion about other ideal prototypes that makes gender such a magnet for
controversy in our culture.

The Fourth Stage: Technological Elements

competence

*sense of workmanship, of perfecting
skills; the basic virtue developed
during the fourth psychosocial stage*

The sense of **competence** that develops in the fourth stage is supported by
technological elements in culture, particularly the way that labor is divided among
people. Opportunities unfairly limited by discrimination are particularly harmful to

the developments of this stage, as is an overemphasis on work as a basis of identity (cf. Erikson, 1968, pp. 122–128). The explosion of computer technology today provides a new cultural forum for supporting, or challenging, a sense of competence.

The Fifth Stage: Ideological Perspectives

The virtue of **fidelity**, which emerges from the fifth psychosocial stage, enables the individual to be faithful to an ideology. The ideological perspectives of a society support, sometimes even exploit, this ego strength. The cause may be political, social, or occupational, or it may take another form. Erikson (1968) outlined a complex relationship between developmental stages and cultural change:

fidelity
ability to sustain loyalties freely pledged; the basic virtue developed during the fifth psychosocial stage

> It is through their ideology that social systems enter into the fiber of the next generation and attempt to absorb into their lifeblood the rejuvenative power of youth. Adolescence is thus a vital regenerator in the process of social evolution, for youth can offer its loyalties and energies both to the conservation of that which continues to feel true and to the revolutionary correction of that which has lost its regenerative significance. (p. 134)

This stage permits reassessing issues of racial and ethnic identity (Erikson, 1968, p. 314). Because the individual and society are interrelated, identity cannot be solved wholly at an individual level. However, the personal identity developments of especially developed people, such as Mahatma Gandhi, may help point the way in which society should be directed.

The Sixth Stage: Patterns of Cooperation and Competition

Successful resolution of the sixth stage brings the ego strength that Erikson called a capacity to **love**. This strength is supported and channeled through what Erikson (1982) termed "patterns of cooperation and competition" (p. 33). For many, marriage serves this role, although cultures may provide other forms besides the nuclear family for shaping the sense of community. It can also be developed in homosexual relationships (Sohier, 1985–1986) and in nonsexual relationships. Cultural controversies today over the institution of marriage illustrate dynamic changes in the way culture relates to individual development over historical time.

love
ability to form an intimate mutual relationship with another person; the basic virtue developed during the sixth psychosocial stage

The Seventh Stage: Currents of Education and Tradition

The strength of **care** develops in the seventh stage of development. In this stage one plays the nurturing role of the older generation toward the younger generation, for example, as parents, teachers, and mentors. Societal involvement is clearly evident in such institutionalized forms as school systems. Erikson suggested that the psychosexual procreative urge (which he felt that Freud did not emphasize sufficiently) can be channeled into career paths like teaching if an individual does not become a parent. Even people who are biological parents can channel generativity into their careers. According to one analysis, Frank Lloyd Wright expressed his generativity more fully as an architect than toward his biological children, whom he neglected (de St. Aubin, 1998).

care
ability to nurture the development of the next generation; the basic virtue developed during the seventh psychosocial stage

Consistent with Erikson's claim that his stages are human universals, cross-cultural research finds generativity across diverse cultures (Cameroon, Costa Rica, and Germany) when people channel their power motivation in prosocial ways that can be helpful to the next generation. Cultures vary, though, in how much they value such generativity. After all, nurturing others can come at a cost to individual goals. Based on research reported so far, collectivist cultures such as the Sub-Saharan African country of Cameroon, and to a lesser extent Costa Rica, show higher levels of prosocial generativity than Germany, which is more individualistic (Hofer et al., 2008). Power in individualistic cultures may serve individual, rather than social, goals. Thus generativity, while it may be a universal developmental stage as Erikson theorized, is shaped by the values of each culture. Despite such cultural differences, in both Germany and Cameroon, the adolescents who scored higher on identity achievement were more likely than those who scored lower to show generativity and prosocial behavior, supporting Erikson's theory that the developmental pathway from identity to the next developmental stage was similar in the two cultures (Busch & Hofer, 2011).

The Eighth Stage: Wisdom

wisdom

mature sense of the meaningfulness and wholeness of experience; the basic virtue developed during the eighth psychosocial stage

Given demographic changes, our society has become more aware of its oldest members. What does society offer them for their continuing psychological development, and what do they have to offer society? The ego strength developed during old age is **wisdom**, described by Erikson as "informed and detached concern with life itself in the face of death itself" (1982, p. 61). The individual, ideally, becomes connected with the "wisdom of the ages," which seeks to understand the meaning of individual and collective human life. This interest is expressed in religious and/or philosophical areas. Elderly Californians interviewed by Erikson and his wife and a younger collaborator generally expressed this development by saying, in essence, "There are no regrets that I know of for things that have happened or that I've done" (Erikson, Erikson, & Kivnick, 1986, p. 70). Unfortunately, for many of the elderly, reminiscing about their lives brings unhealthy regret, instead (McKee et al., 2005). Undoubtedly, a culture that glorifies youth and turns a blind eye and deaf ear to the elderly contributes to such despair. Rapid cultural change contributes to such unfortunate tendencies.

These relationships, which Erikson proposed between individual ego development and cultural supports, are widely applauded, but should be explored empirically as well. Any theory that attempts to discuss cultural factors risks bias because of the experience and values of the theorist, and Erikson's list of ego strengths has been criticized as reflecting middle-class Western ideology (Henry, 1967). Some cross-cultural studies, as noted above, have been conducted, and more are needed.

RACIAL AND ETHNIC IDENTITY

Erikson remarked that identity first became noticeable to him in his psychiatric practice when he immigrated to the United States. People here, coming from diverse backgrounds, must define themselves anew, as Erikson did himself when he changed his name. This issue is particularly salient during adolescence. A study of Chinese immigrants to the United States, for example, found that those who came alone (without family) during adolescence emphasized their Chinese cultural orientation more than did those who came with family earlier in life or those who came when they were older when identity issues were not so acute (Ying, 2001). Even among those who have not themselves immigrated, racial and ethnic minorities have a distinctiveness to integrate in their identity formation. Erikson (1968, pp. 295–320), writing in the 1960s, observed that black Americans had particular difficulties with identity because of society's unresponsiveness to them. Recent history has, of course, changed this picture considerably.

Racism in society poses obstacles to the identity development of minorities. When others see the person's race through stereotyped eyes, they fail to validate the individuality of the person, which can contribute to an "invisibility syndrome" that interferes with a developing sense of self (Franklin, 1999). In the past, cross-cultural studies reported lower identity statuses among some national and ethnic groups, including black adults in South Africa (Ochse & Plug, 1986) and Mexican Americans (Abraham, 1986). With cultural change, however, minorities have more support for their identity formation. Black South Africans, for example, have more recently scored higher than whites on identity, probably as a consequence of more visible and respected black role models and a greater pride in their culture (Thom & Coetzee, 2004).

Since Erikson's introduction of identity as a seminal idea, others have expanded the concept to better understand racial and ethnic identities. A person may develop a strong identification with his or her ethnic, racial, or cultural group: an *ethnic identity*. This identification can provide the basis of strength and enhanced self-esteem, helping the person reject racism, instead of internalizing racism into his or her own individual identity when it is confronted in society (Alvarez & Helms, 2001;

Helms, 1990; Miller, 1999). Thus ethnic identity fosters psychological well-being and protects against depression and loneliness (Roberts et al., 1999). For those who can develop identities in both the majority culture and the minority culture—for example, mainstream American and a Native American tribe—self-esteem and psychological well-being tend to be even higher than those who develop identities in either culture alone or neither one (Moran et al., 1999).

Theorists propose that individuals may submerge their ethnicity and instead choose *assimilation* into the mainstream culture. They may emphasize their ethnicity. Or they may become bicultural or multicultural, celebrating unique and beneficial aspects of their ethnic background(s) and the mainstream culture, perhaps in different social groupings or contexts, without choosing one over the other, although this is more difficult to achieve (LaFromboise, Coleman, & Gerton, 1993).

Ethnic identity may be defined as "an enduring, fundamental aspect of self that includes a sense of connection in a social group ... or ethnic group, and the attitudes and feelings associated with that membership" (Yeh & Hwang, 2000). Most researchers have emphasized identity from an individual viewpoint, which is understandable in an individualistic culture, but misleading for understanding ethnic identities that emphasize interdependence, such as Hispanic, Filipino, African, Chinese, and Indian cultures (Yeh & Hwang, 2000). Explorations of identity development in such cultures promise new understanding of the mutuality of individual identity and cultural connection.

The study of ethnic and racial identity, inspired by Erikson's work, has burgeoned with theoretical and empirical advances beyond what can be fit into this description, which attests to the fertile power of Erikson's ideas. It's probably one of the areas where the interrelationships of individual personality and the social world are most clearly seen. His theory was developed at a time when race relations were a particularly hot political issue in the United States. Today, sexual orientation and transgender issues are the comparable focus of the dialogue between individual identity resolution and cultural recognition.

RESEARCH ON DEVELOPMENT THROUGH THE PSYCHOSOCIAL STAGES

Erikson's description of developmental stages has stimulated substantial empirical research, particularly in adolescent identity development.

Identity Status

The *identity status paradigm* has stimulated considerable research. Most frequently, identity is assessed from an interview. Questions probe crisis and commitment in the areas of occupation and ideology (Marcia, 1966), categorizing participants into one of four possible identity statuses. The least developed status is **identity diffusion**, when exploration has not yet seriously begun. (This corresponds to *identity confusion* described earlier in this chapter, and is the term Erikson was still using when James Marcia devised the identity status measure.) Second, an individual who is currently experiencing an identity crisis and is actively exploring possibilities but has not yet committed to an identity is said to be in *moratorium.* Two remaining categories describe final statuses. In the most mature outcome, **identity achievement,** an individual has experienced a crisis and has come through it with a commitment to an occupation and/or ideology. Less healthy is the status of *identity foreclosure,* in which a commitment has been made without a crisis and without much exploration of alternatives, often by simply accepting parental choices.

When researchers who have published in this field responded to a survey asking them to describe the prototypical person in each identity status (Mallory, 1989), these were among the most descriptive characteristics they chose:

> *Identity diffusion*: unpredictable; reluctant to act
>
> *Moratorium*: philosophically concerned; rebellious, nonconforming
>
> *Identity achiever*: clear, consistent personality; productive
>
> *Foreclosure*: conventional; moralistic

identity diffusion

the negative pole of the fifth psychosocial stage (earlier terminology)

identity achievement

status representing optimal development during the fifth (adolescent) psychosocial stage

Foreclosure is a permanent dead end, in Erikson's model. Fortunately, research indicates that some people move out of foreclosure to moratorium, and pick up the healthy exploration that Erikson endorsed. Strong identification with the father is typical of adolescents in the foreclosure identity status (Cramer, 2001). It occurs more often in cultures that emphasize norms and traditions, such as Greece, than in the United States, and is probably a less unhealthy alternative in such a cultural context (Vleioras & Bosma, 2005). Of more concern are cultures in which opportunities are so limited, and authoritarian tradition so glorifies this alternative, that the foreclosed identity of a terrorist appeals to youth, who sacrifice their lives for their ideology (Schwartz, Dunkel, & Waterman, 2009).

As individuals explore, they find that some options are more consistent with their motivations than other choices. For example, a motivation for affiliation with other people would be a better fit in a people-oriented profession such as sales representative than in a more isolated profession such as computer programmer. Affiliation motivation, like other motives studied through projective measures (including achievement and power motivation), develops early in life—long before identity issues are faced, and before the child has an awareness that can be expressed explicitly in language about what these motives are. Such *implicit motives* are measured by scoring TAT tests, a projective measure (McClelland, Koestner, & Weinberger, 1989). What happens if an adolescent has a low level of affiliation motivation in this sense, but comes to think of herself as a people-person, perhaps by adopting the values of her family and friends? This would be an example of *incongruence* between the earlier, less verbally available implicit level, and the later developed conscious self-concept. This later-developed motive is called an *explicit* motive, and it is measured by self-report questionnaires. In contrast, a person who is low in affiliation motivation at both the implicit and explicit levels, like a person who is high at both of these levels, is *congruent*. Students who have developed the more mature achieved identity status are more often congruent, indicating that their conscious (explicit) identity is a closer match to their deeper (implicit) motivations. Those who have a foreclosed identity status are at greater risk of incongruent motives, having not resolved the identity issues in a way that matches their core, unconscious motivations (Hofer et al., 2006). So identity achievement seems to bring unity within the personality, as well as solidifying the person–environment match.

Sexual orientation, too, has an impact on identity exploration. Evidence indicates that the sexual identity explorations of homosexuals could stimulate greater identity exploration overall, resulting in a more mature identity-achieved status (Konik & Stewart, 2004). More research is needed to see whether this result applies generally, or only to the atypical, politically aware group that was studied.

Other Psychosocial Stages

Erikson's proposal of stage sequences predicts that people will become more preoccupied with certain themes at appropriate periods in their lives: identity in adolescence, generativity in adulthood, and so on. Diaries and fictional writings by the British novelist Vera Brittain (1893–1970) have been analyzed for Eriksonian themes of identity, intimacy, and generativity. As predicted by Erikson's theory, as she became older, her writing turned from identity and intimacy issues to generative themes (Peterson & Stewart, 1990).

Age changes are also found using objective tests. George Domino and Dyanne Affonso (1990) developed a self-report questionnaire assessing positive and negative aspects of the original eight stages of development. This Inventory of Psychosocial Balance requires subjects to rate the extent to which they agree with each of 120 items. Sample items are as follows:

> *I can usually depend on others.* (Trust scale)
>
> *I genuinely enjoy work.* (Industry scale)
>
> *Sometimes I wonder who I really am.* (Identity scale)
>
> *Life has been good to me.* (Ego Integrity scale)

As expected, scores on the Inventory of Psychosocial Balance generally increased in older groups of people. In fact, longitudinal research using the Inventory of Psychosocial Development (another measure of Eriksonian stages) indicates that adults in their 20s continue to develop not only on identity and intimacy, as we would expect, but also on earlier stages, which would have been expected to be stable since childhood (Whitbourne et al., 1992). A meta-analysis of longitudinal studies supports Erikson's developmental model, with 36 percent of adolescents moving forward in identity status over time, and only 15 percent regressing; the other 49 percent remained stable (Kroger, Martinussen, & Marcia, 2010). Cross-sectional studies analyzed in the same report are consistent, with increasing numbers of adolescents achieving identities at older ages (though many still remained in process), after a peak number in moratorium status at age 19. Longitudinal research designs are particularly valuable for investigating developmental change over time, for obvious reasons. However, they are not used as often as would be desirable to test Erikson's theory (Bosma & Kunnen, 2008).

Correlates of Stage Measures

Higher scores on measures of the psychosocial stages are associated with better functioning in several studies. Howard Protinsky (1988) reported that problem adolescents scored lower on three of the first five psychosocial stages (trust, initiative, and identity) compared with other adolescents. Many studies report that subjects who score high on various measures of ego identity function better, not only in having chosen a career (Cohen, Chartrand, & Jowdy, 1995), but also in using more mature defense mechanisms (Cramer, 1998b) and performing better under stress (Marcia, 1966).

Intimacy resolution is correlated with self-reported interpersonal behaviors. College men who score low on resolution of the intimacy stage (isolates) report having had fewer friends when growing up (Orlofsky, 1978).

Generativity has been measured by a self-report scale, the Loyola Generativity Scale, which includes items like "I try to pass along the knowledge I have gained through my experiences" (Peterson, 2006). Fathers score higher than men who have not had children (McAdams & de St. Aubin, 1992), and high scores are associated with better parenting (Pratt et al., 2001). Generativity influences the style of parenting, compared to authoritarian parents, who are punitive, generative parents are more authoritative. That is, they guide rather than coerce and so have a better outcome (Peterson, Smirles, & Wentworth, 1997). They have children who are more conscientious and agreeable than others, and who themselves are high in generativity (Peterson, 2006). Adults who are highly generative describe their desire to help others (McAdams et al., 1997; Peterson & Klohnen, 1995). Some people express generativity through their work, others in their role as parents, and some channel their generativity into political activity and social activism (Peterson, Smirles, & Wentworth, 1997; Peterson & Stewart, 1996). Among younger adults, not yet parents, generativity is associated with attachment to pets (Marks & Koepke, 1994), perhaps as a way of practicing their nascent generativity potential.

Ego integrity (stage 8), as assessed by a written measure, is associated with less fear of death (Goebel & Boeck, 1987). The conflicts described by Erikson's stage theory do not begin and end at the times he described, but they have their precursors in earlier stages, and subsequent implications and developments later. In Erikson's stage theory, a person who does not successfully resolve the conflict at any one stage will be handicapped in following stages (somewhat like a student who does not master a basic math or language course and consequently finds later courses more difficult). Conversely, mastery of the earlier stages makes continued ego development more likely.

TOWARD A PSYCHOANALYTIC SOCIAL PSYCHOLOGY

Erikson envisioned a psychoanalytic approach that would consider social and cultural realities rather than focusing exclusively on the individual, as Freud had done. James Côté and Charles Levine have developed such a *psychoanalytic social psychology* in their research and theorizing (Côté, 1993; Côté & Levine, 1988a, 1988b, 1988c). How does society influence personality and its development? Conversely, how does personality influence society? These are core questions for a personality theory that includes the social context.

From such a perspective, psychological processes are affected by culture. James Côté (1993, pp. 43–44) speculates that social institutions reflect and direct psychic structures. For example, the id is expressed in music and dance, sports, and brothels; the superego in religion, the judiciary, and the military; and the ego in work, government, and education.

Personality development is influenced by culture, which, for example, provides a moratorium period for exploration of identity, especially for college students in the humanities rather than in technological fields (Côté & Levine, 1988a, 1988c). The moratorium is not simply a time to select an occupation. It is also a time for wrestling with questions of values, which in psychoanalytic parlance is a struggle between the superego (representing values presented to the individual by family and society) and the ego (representing the individual's own accepted values) (cf. Côté & Levine, 1989). The humanities encourage more pondering of the human condition and human dilemmas (Côté & Levine, 1992, p. 392). Studies of the individual in the social context fulfill Erikson's (1968) vision: "We are in need … of concepts which throw light on the *mutual complementation* of ego synthesis and social organization, the cultivation of which on ever higher levels is the aim of all therapeutic endeavor, social and individual" (p. 53).

Psychoanalytic social psychology should understand culture without being constrained by any specific set of cultural values, but that may not be easy. Heinz Kohut complained that Erikson's "description of the various developmental phases are really value judgments disguised in scientific terms" (Elson, 1987, p. 22; quoted in Cornett, 2000). These values are not simply Erikson's personal values but the values of Western culture: autonomy, industry, and individuality (Cornett, 2000; Eagle, 1997). As for Erikson's claim that the psychosocial ego strengths are not simply Western, but universal—we need more evidence before accepting that claim.

Summary

- Erikson proposed a theory of *psychosocial development* that described eight stages in the life span. A ninth stage was later added to reflect his final thoughts.
- According to the *epigenetic principle,* these stages build on one another and occur in invariant sequence across cultures.
- In each stage, the individual experiences a *crisis,* which is resolved in the context of society.
- The original eight stages are trust versus mistrust, autonomy versus shame and doubt, initiative versus guilt, industry versus inferiority, identity versus identity confusion, intimacy versus isolation, generativity versus stagnation, and integrity versus despair. The ninth stage is gerotranscendence.
- In each stage, culture influences development. Conversely, individuals also influence culture through the way they develop at each stage, particularly through their identity development.
- Considerable research has been conducted on the psychosocial stages. Predicted age changes have been found, and measures of identity formation show predicted positive personality correlates of higher identity status.
- Considerable research on racial and ethnic identity illustrates the relationship between individual development and culture.
- Erikson's cross-cultural studies of the Sioux and Yurok explored the relationship between individual ego development and the culture, a theme that identity status researchers have continued.

Thinking about Erikson's Theory

1. How do Erikson's stages help you understand the people you know who are older or younger than you are? Explain, giving a few examples.
2. Do you think your culture fails to provide adequate supports at any particular stage? What should it do better?
3. Do you think Erikson's theory is equally applicable to females and males? What do you think are the differences in the way the two genders develop in your culture?
4. Do you think that an early choice of a career and technological majors are obstacles to identity achievement

and that a delayed choice of major and humanities majors facilitate the process (as Erikson and Côté and Levine suggest)?

5. If you have lived in another country, compare that culture with your own. Does it have a different impact on the resolution of any of the psychosocial stages?

Study Questions

1. Contrast Erikson's view of motivation with Freud's psychosexual model.
2. Explain Erikson's epigenetic principle.
3. List Erikson's psychosocial stages. Describe the crisis of each stage. Describe the consequences of each stage for ego development.
4. List and explain various outcomes of the identity crisis. What is the healthiest outcome?
5. What is a psychosocial moratorium? Give an example.
6. Discuss the importance of the negative pole of the crisis at various Eriksonian stages. How does the negative pole contribute to healthy ego development?
7. Discuss the way culture contributes to ego development at various stages, from childhood to adulthood.
8. Explain Erikson's ideas about the relationship between identity and race.
9. Describe Marcia's measure of identity status.
10. Summarize research on Erikson's stages of development, including identity and other stages.

6

Horney and Relational Theory
Interpersonal Psychoanalytic Theory

Chapter Overview

ILLUSTRATIVE BIOGRAPHY
Marilyn Monroe

Karen Horney's theory is popular for its insights into gender. It confronted the male bias of the earlier generation of psychoanalysts. As an icon of femininity in twentieth-century American popular culture, Marilyn Monroe portrays a person trapped in the gender role of her time, and so she can be understood from the perspective of Horney's interpersonal theory and of the subsequent relational theory that further develops these ideas.

Although she has been dead since 1962, the movie actress Marilyn Monroe is a timeless embodiment of the image of femininity. She epitomizes sexual beauty; her picture on a nude calendar was admired by many men and envied by many women. She also had a tragic side, arousing sympathy for the helpless victim.

Marilyn Monroe

Born in Los Angeles, California, in 1926, Norma Jeane Mortenson (her birth name) was not told the truth about her paternity, the product of an extramarital affair. She grew up without a father or mother. Mental illness ran in her family, and her mother and grandmother were institutionalized (Steinem, 1986). After living in several foster homes and an orphanage and having no other stable home, Norma Jeane married at age 16 (a marriage that lasted 4 years). With her husband off to war, she worked in a factory until a photographer taking pictures to boost the troops' morale discovered her there. She quickly became a model, on her way to becoming a movie actress, under the name of Marilyn Monroe. Along the way, she posed as the first *Playboy* magazine centerfold, married baseball star Joe DiMaggio (a union that lasted only 8 months), and then married playwright Arthur Miller (for 4 years). She also was the lover of President John F. Kennedy (among others). Marilyn Monroe had many lovers and three, possibly four, husbands. As much as she sought love, her longest marriage lasted only 4.5 years. She loved children but never raised her own. Many were conceived; reportedly she had over a dozen abortions. (She reported that she bore an illegitimate child as a teenager, but it is unclear whether this is fact or imagination.) When motherhood was acceptable, as Arthur Miller's wife, she miscarried.

Throughout adulthood, Monroe took high doses of barbiturates and attempted suicide on several occasions. It is likely that her death was either an intentional suicide or an accidental overdose. Theories of murder are favored by some, who argue that the FBI, the Kennedys, and the Mafia all had reasons to be involved in her death. Whatever the circumstances, her death occurred on the fifth anniversary of her much-mourned miscarriage.

DEVELOPMENT

Karen Horney's theory emphasizes childhood parental love as essential for healthy development, whereas neglect produces a fundamental conflict that endures. Conflict is between basic anxiety (fear of not being loved or lovable) and basic hostility (anger about the lack of love).

Marilyn Monroe was neglected by her parents. She did not know her father. Her mother suffered serious depression and was institutionalized when Monroe was 7 and for most of her life thereafter. Monroe then grew up in foster homes and an orphanage, never experiencing a stable, loving family that would help her establish healthy interpersonal relationships. This insecure beginning, according to Horney's theory, would leave her with lifelong unconscious feelings of being unloved and angry.

DESCRIPTION

Horney's interpersonal psychoanalysis and subsequent theories of object relations emphasize that the most important aspect of personality is the relationships we have with other people. If they are not secure, then no amount of fame or success can replace them. Personality is described in terms of relationship styles. Some people have a style of an exaggerated need for love and acceptance ("moving toward" style). Others have exaggerated needs for competition or aggression ("moving against" style). A third style is an exaggerated need for isolation ("moving against" style).

Of these styles, Marilyn Monroe clearly had an exaggerated need for love. In her case, this need took the form of seeking sexual love and admiration for her physical beauty. She had a childlike innocence in her physical appearance and also a childlike hunger for love without the stabilizing anchor of mature self-esteem. Her childlike persona elicited love and protective impulses in others. Like many "moving toward" women, she chose for her male partners powerful men (including baseball player Joe DiMaggio, playwright Arthur Miller, and President John Fitzgerald Kennedy). Gloria Steinem describes her as "the child-woman who offered pleasure without adult challenge; a lover who neither judged nor asked anything in return" (1986, p. 22).

ADJUSTMENT

Mental health requires healthy interpersonal relationships, not immature relationships based on inadequate childhood experiences in object relations theory, and not limited in Horney's earlier theory to only one or two of the three interpersonal styles listed above. A poorly adjusted person creates a defensive idealized self that resists awareness and does not permit flexibility. A person whose idealized self demands always being loved will not be able to move against others by appropriate assertive behavior or to move away from them to be alone when that is needed. A variety of defense mechanisms maintain this style, defending against any unconscious impulses for the repressed material to emerge—in this case, for repressed anger that could lead to competitiveness or assertiveness.

Physical beauty can be a way of ensuring love; it therefore takes on great value for those with a neurotic need for affection (Horney, 1950, p. 138). Monroe's exhibitionist tendencies trace back to childhood (Steinem, 1986). Horney (1937/1967d, pp. 256–257) suggested that a neurotic need for love can also be expressed as a series of sexual relationships, surely characteristic of Monroe, whose promiscuity was legendary.

In people who have adopted this pattern of a neurotic, compulsive need for love, hostility is repressed, to avoid anxiety and the risk of being unlovable. One anecdote strongly suggests how much suppressed hostility must have pervaded Monroe's lovemaking. At a party, where a game required disclosing personal fantasies, "she said she imagined disguising herself in a black wig, meeting her father, seducing him, and then asking vindictively, 'How do you feel now to have a daughter that you've made love to?' " (Steinem, 1986, p. 144). How clearly this says that she thought her father's love could only be obtained by trickery, and she was mad about it. From an object relations theory point of view, this fantasy discloses an unhealthy pattern of relationships, and we would expect the fantasy to also contaminate her lovemaking.

COGNITION

As in other psychoanalytic theories, both object relations theories and Horney's theory describe defense mechanisms that distort thinking and interfere with accurate self-perception. Some of these defense mechanisms (e.g., repression) are the same as those described in previous chapters, whereas others (e.g., blind spots and externalization) are first described by Horney.

Marilyn Monroe showed an exaggerated concern for the suffering of animals and even plants that can be interpreted as a defense mechanism (externalization) that distorted accurate self-perception. She externalized her own sense of being unloved and helplessness in a hostile world, not realizing it was she herself who felt the need to be rescued. For example, when she found boys trapping pigeons to sell in New York City, she bought the birds every week and set them free. Another rather bizarre externalization occurred when she saw nasturtiums cut by a lawn mower. As her husband, Arthur Miller, tells it, "crying as if she were wounded," Marilyn demanded that they stop the car as they drove past. "Then she rushed about picking up the fallen flowers, sticking the stalks back into the ground, to see if they might recover" (Summers, 1985, p. 200).

(continued)

(continued)

CULTURE

Horney's most important contribution to psychoanalysis was her recognition that culture contributes significantly to mental health problems by encouraging certain neurotic tendencies. By relegating women into society's accepted gender roles, culture produces unconscious conflict and neurosis. Early psychoanalysts did not recognize this, and so their supposed expertise had the unfortunate effect of endorsing the unhealthy gender messages of society. Freud's theory describes masochism as part of normal feminine development, whereas Horney said this trait is a product of culture. It is not inevitably part of being a normal female, and it is not healthy.

The particular style of femininity that Marilyn Monroe epitomized, the sex goddess of her age, was a product of her culture. Marilyn Monroe paints, in bold strokes, themes that typify the feminine personality of her time, in her culture, suggests Gloria Steinem (1986). Her self-doubt and need to be loved, her inability to express anger appropriately, were widespread issues for women of that era. Marilyn Monroe was treated by a Freudian analyst Ralph Greenson, a psychiatrist internationally known for his scholarly publications and a former close friend of the Freud family. However, her therapist missed this opportunity to put her on a less dependent, healthier track (Steinem, 1986). Rather than challenging her need for love as neurotic, apparently he played along, at times even taking the patient into his home. He also intervened in her movie roles and other extra-therapy aspects of her life, to an extent that violated even his own teachings about proper therapy techniques (Kirsner, 2007). Of course, it is unfair to judge analysis from a distance; but if the therapy did not get beneath the neurotic need for affection, it was not addressing the core neurosis and could not hope to achieve a personality reconstruction. One suspects that Horney would even criticize the therapist for allowing "morbid dependency" in the doctor–patient relationship (cf. Horney, 1950, p. 243). Cultural assumptions can blind even the experts.

BIOLOGY

Although Horney added a cultural component to psychoanalytic theory, she did not deny the underlying assumption that biology provides the energy for personality. Thus she suggested that physical as well as psychological symptoms can be produced by unresolved unconscious conflict. She also realized that some people turn to physical substances to alleviate psychological suffering.

Marilyn Monroe tried to drown her hostility and anxiety with drugs. Horney (1950, p. 152) proposed that drug use stems from the underlying problem of self-contempt. Even Monroe's physical difficulties are consistent with Horney's theory. Monroe suffered extreme menstrual pain. She was reportedly frigid, compulsively seeking intercourse but not experiencing orgasm. If Horney's paper had not originally been published in 1926, we might have thought Horney had Marilyn Monroe in mind when she observed "that frigid women can be even erotically responsive and sexually demanding, an observation that warns us against equating frigidity with the rejection of sex" (Horney, 1926/1967c, p. 74). Horney reported that frigid women may convert their sexual functioning into a variety of menstrual disorders, including pain and miscarriage.

FINAL THOUGHTS

It took a woman, Karen Horney, to see cultural bias in misunderstanding women in the psychoanalytic theory that she otherwise admired and practiced. Her insights help us understand the psychological flaws of Marilyn Monroe, not simply to admire or desire her. The core conflict, in Horney's theory, stems from inadequate parental love. We may defend against that conflict in culturally driven ways, varying from one century to the next and from one subgroup within society to another, but our basic needs are the same.

PREVIEW: OVERVIEW OF INTERPERSONAL PSYCHOANALYTIC THEORY

Interpersonal approaches in psychoanalysis, raised by Karen Horney and continued in the subsequent relational approach, have implications for major theoretical questions, as presented in Table 6.1. Though closely related, Horney's theory and later developments in the relational approach are distinct enough so that they are presented as two major divisions in this chapter. Both Horney's theory and relational approaches have inspired empirical research, not only within clinical settings but beyond, studying infants and children as well as adults. In addition to implications for adjustment and therapy, interpersonal approaches help us understand the variety of interpersonal styles that occur in everyday life. Formal applications of the approach focus on therapeutic settings at this time.

INTERPERSONAL PSYCHOANALYSIS: HORNEY

The emphasis on society that Adler and Erikson contributed to psychoanalytic theory continued into the next generation of analysts, including Karen Horney. Like traditional Freudian psychoanalysts, Horney firmly believed that the unconscious is a powerful determinant of personality and that childhood conflicts are important. However, she questioned Freud's emphasis on sexual conflict. According to Horney, the most important conflicts are based on unresolved interpersonal issues. She argued that cultural

Table 6.1 Preview of Horney's Theory and Object Relations Theory

Individual Differences	Individuals differ in the way they define themselves in relationships. Horney described a balance among three interpersonal orientations: moving toward, moving against, and moving away (from people). People have different idealized selves and use different ways of adjusting to anxiety.
Adaptation and Adjustment	Healthy interpersonal relationships are a key to adjustment, and they are based on acceptance of the true self instead of some defensive idealized self. Horney provides full descriptions of neurotic trends. Therapy focuses more on the present time and on interpersonal relationships than on the past and libidinal conflict (contrasting with Freud's theory).
Cognitive Processes	Blind spots and other defense mechanisms limit insight, but courageous self-examination can lead to growth. Developmental and object relations theorists are studying specific cognitions, such as those related to emotion.
Culture	Culture is very important in shaping personality, especially through gender roles.
Biological Influences	Biology is far less important than orthodox psychoanalysis claims.
Development	Love and nurturance are key to a child's development. In Horney's theory, basic anxiety and hostility are the fundamental emotions of childhood. Without adequate parental love, the child develops unhealthy interpersonal modes and a defensive sense of self. Few major changes in personality occur after childhood (except through therapy).

forces must be considered and the personality differences between men and women are influenced more by society than by anatomy.

The interpersonal emphasis that Horney advocated has been the foundation of other psychoanalytic theories, as well. The *relational approach* draws from many of these theoretical developments and has forged connections with advances in developmental and social psychology. This approach, which has too many contributors to single out one "great name" with which to label it, is presented in this chapter.

Biography of Karen Horney

Karen Danielson was born near Hamburg, Germany, on September 15, 1885. She was the second child in an unhappy marriage of an often-absent Norwegian sea captain and his beautiful, somewhat higher-class wife. Danielson and her older brother Berndt were disciplined strictly by their tyrannical Lutheran father when he was home from long sea voyages around Cape Horn to the Pacific coast of South and Central America. She retained a strongly independent character, regarded her father's outspoken religious attitudes as hypocritical, and questioned the fundamentalist teachings of her church.

This was a time of social change in Germany, opening opportunities for women. Young Danielson entered the University of Freiburg in 1906, in a class of 58 women and 2,292 men. There she studied medicine, was popular, and married one frequent companion, Oskar Horney, in 1909. They moved to Berlin, where she continued her medical studies and he began a business career.

Karen Horney was a psychoanalytic patient of the Freudian analyst Karl Abraham. This was an avant-garde interest at that time. It was characteristic of her to explore new ideas, but she sought relief from personal problems as well: depression, fatigue, and dissatisfaction with her marriage. Her father died about this time, and she had ambivalent feelings toward him to sort out: anger because of the unhappiness of her parents' marriage, but also more fondness for him than she admitted. The demands of combining a medical education with family life, without much encouragement from her husband, also required coping.

Karen Horney

After receiving her psychiatric degree in 1915, she dared to lecture on the controversial Freudian theory and to defend it against critics including, interestingly, Adler and Jung (Quinn, 1988, p. 151). Her own challenges to the theory were still brewing. Unlike many psychoanalysts of this time, she did not visit Freud and so did not know him personally (Quinn, 1988). Freud did, however, chair a session in 1922 in which Horney presented a paper, "The Genesis of the Castration Complex in Women" (O'Connell, 1980).

Karen and Oskar Horney had three daughters. (One, Marianne Horney Eckardt, became a Horneyan analyst.) But the couple continued to have a troubled marriage and finally separated. Horney poured increasing energy into her career. She became one of the founding members of the Berlin Psychoanalytic Institute in 1920 and published several papers on male and female development, relationships, and marriage. Her 14 papers between 1922 and 1935 outlined a theory of female psychology that was clearly critical of Freud's theory. Horney's first suggestions were presented in a spirit of intellectual debate within classic Freudian theory, the sort of challenge that fosters the development of any science. The psychoanalytic community, however, dismissed her points and attacked her motivations. Freud is reported to have said of her, "She is able but malicious—mean" (Quinn, 1988, p. 237). He accused her of an inadequate analysis, saying that she did not accept her own penis envy (Symonds, 1991).

Given this hostile environment in Germany, it is no wonder that Horney accepted an invitation to become associate director of a new Institute for Psychoanalysis in Chicago, under Franz Alexander, in 1932. Then, in 1934 she moved to New York. Ironically, the same sort of professional debates over theoretical orthodoxy that had impelled her to leave Germany divided the New York Psychoanalytic Institute, which in 1941 voted to remove her from her role as a teacher and clinical supervisor, demoting her to instructor.

Horney and her followers quickly formed a new organization, the Association for the Advancement of Psychoanalysis, and founded the *American Journal of Psychoanalysis*. The announcement of the new training institute contained a statement of commitment to nonauthoritarian teaching:

> Students are acknowledged to be intelligent and responsible adults....It is the hope of the Institute that it will continue to avoid conceptual rigidities, and to respond to ideas, whatever the source, in a spirit of scientific and academic democracy. (cited in Quinn, 1988, p. 353)

It was not only the orthodox Freudians who were suspicious of her. The Federal Bureau of Investigation (FBI) kept a file on her because of her alleged communist sympathies, and she was for a while denied a passport (Quinn, 1988). She was ultimately granted the passport, and in Japan she stayed at several Zen monasteries (O'Connell, 1980). In Zen Buddhism, Horney found support for the idea of a striving, healthy *real self* within the individual that Freudian theory did not offer (Morvay, 1999). On December 4, 1952, within months of her return from Japan, she died of previously undiagnosed abdominal cancer.

As a person, Karen Horney seems to have had a capacity for enjoying life, despite the seriousness of her career and the disappointments of her marriage. She liked fine dining, concerts, and parties. She enjoyed relationships with men and had several affairs (Quinn, 1988). During Prohibition, she at least once spiked the punch by writing her own prescription for "medicinal" alcohol (Quinn, 1988).

Horney challenged Freud's claim that he had discovered universal developmental conflicts. Instead, she argued that personality and its development are influenced by culture and vary from one society to another. This energetic and nontraditional woman proposed new understandings of women, and of men, which today are more widely accepted than the classical Freudian theory she challenged. She is praised as an important role model for women and her writings had a major influence on feminist theory (Gilman, 2001; O'Connell & Russo, 1980).

BASIC ANXIETY AND BASIC HOSTILITY

Infants and young children are highly dependent on their parents for psychological security as well as physical survival. In the ideal case, the infant senses that he or she is loved and protected by the parents and therefore is safe. Under less-than-ideal circumstances, the child feels intensely vulnerable, experiencing **basic anxiety**, which Horney (1945, p. 41) described as "the feeling a child has of being isolated and helpless in a potentially hostile world."

Parental neglect and rejection make the child angry, a condition Horney called **basic hostility**. However, expressing the hostility would result in punishment or loss of love, so instead it is repressed, which increases anxiety. The neurotic, then, develops a basic conflict between "fundamentally contradictory attitudes he has acquired toward other persons" (Horney, 1945, pp. 40–41). On the one hand, the child needs the parents and wants to approach them but, on the other hand, hates them and wants to punish them. This is the driving force behind neurosis: an interpersonal conflict, in contrast to Freud's libidinal conflict between sexual desire and the restricting forces of society.

THREE INTERPERSONAL ORIENTATIONS

What is the child to do? Three choices are available: accentuate dependency and move toward the parents, accentuate hostility and move against them, or give up on the relationship and move away from them. The young child resolves the conflict with the parents by using whichever of these strategies seems best to fit his or her particular family environment. This choice becomes the person's characteristic interpersonal orientation.

Ideally, a healthy person should be able to **move toward** people, **move against** them, or **move away** from them, flexibly choosing the strategy that fits the particular circumstances. In contrast to healthy flexibility, neurotics are imbalanced in their interpersonal behavior. Some choices cause so much anxiety that they simply are not options. The young child who was never permitted to express any criticism of the parents, for example, is unlikely to be able to compete wholeheartedly against others in adulthood. The rejected child will continue to have difficulty depending on people.

Horney said that neurotics who emphasize moving toward people adopt the **self-effacing solution** to neurotic conflict, seeking love and minimizing any apparently selfish needs that could interfere with being loved. Neurotics who emphasize moving against people adopt the **expansive solution** to neurotic conflict, seeking mastery even if it impedes close relationships with others. Finally, neurotics who emphasize moving away from people adopt the **resignation solution**, seeking freedom even at the expense of relationships and achievement (see Table 6.2).

A measure of Horney's three interpersonal orientations, the Horney-Coolidge Type Indicator (HCTI; Coolidge et al., 2001) assesses three facets of each orientation, based on factor analysis (see Table 6.3). In a study of normal adults (Coolidge et al., 2004), scores on a scale measuring personality disorders were correlated with HCTI scores. Those with higher Cluster A (eccentric) scores, comprising the paranoid, schizoid, and schizotypal personality disorder scales, scored higher on the Detachment scale and, to a lesser extent, the Aggression scale. Those with higher Cluster B (emotional) scores, comprising the antisocial, borderline, histrionic, and narcissistic personality disorder scales, scored higher on the Aggression scale. People with higher Cluster C (fearful) scores, reflecting avoidant, dependent, and obsessive-compulsive personality disorders, scored higher on the Detachment and Compliance scales. These results are consistent with Horney's view that imbalanced interpersonal orientations are maladaptive, although the research needs to be replicated among clinically diagnosed individuals. Interestingly, the Malevolence facet of the Aggression scale was positively correlated with all three clusters of personality disorders, which, according to the researchers, "captures the maladaptive relational aspect of the personality disorders and suggests that underlying the differing relational postures of Horney's theory

Margin glossary

basic anxiety

feeling of isolation and helplessness resulting from inadequate parenting in infancy

basic hostility

feeling of anger by the young child toward the parents, which must be repressed

moving toward

interpersonal orientation emphasizing dependency

moving against

interpersonal orientation emphasizing hostility

moving away

interpersonal orientation emphasizing separateness from others

self-effacing solution

attempting to solve neurotic conflict by seeking love; moving toward people

expansive solution

attempting to solve neurotic conflict by seeking mastery; moving against people

resignation solution

attempting to solve neurotic conflict by seeking freedom; moving away from people

Table 6.2 Horney's Three Neurotic Solutions

1. Self-Effacing Solution: The Appeal of Love ("The Compliant Personality")

"Moving toward" people

Morbid dependency: the need for a partner (friend, lover, or spouse)

"Poor little me": feeling of being weak and helpless

Self-subordination: assumption that others are superior

Martyrdom: sacrifice and suffering for others

Need for love: desire to find self-worth in a relationship

2. Expansive Solution: The Appeal of Mastery ("The Aggressive Personality")

"Moving against" people

Narcissistic: in love with idealized self-image

Perfectionistic: high standards

Arrogant-vindictive: pride and strength

Need to be right: to win a fight or competition

Need for recognition: to be admired

3. Resignation: The Appeal of Freedom ("The Detached Personality")

"Moving away from" people

Persistent resignation and lack of striving: the aversion to effort and change

Rebellious against constraints or influences: the desire for freedom

Shallow living: an onlooker at self and life, detached from emotional experiences and wishes

Self-sufficient and independent: uninvolved with people

Need for privacy: keeping others outside the magic circle of the self

Source: Adapted from Horney, 1945, 1950.

is a basic belief that people hurt other people and cannot be trusted" (Coolidge et al., 2004, p. 372). Other research using this questionnaire examines its relationships to biological factor models of personality (see Chapter 9), suggesting that the Compliant scale is related to Eysenck's Neuroticism measure, and the Aggressive and Detached scales to his Psychoticism (or antisocial) scale (Shatz, 2004).

Table 6.3 Horney-Coolidge Measure of Interpersonal Orientations: Facets and Sample Items

1. Compliance Scale

Altruism	*"I like to help others."*
Need for Relationships	*"I feel better when I'm in a relationship."*
Self-Abasement	*"I am self-sacrificing."*

2. Aggression Scale

Malevolence	*"Beggars make me angry."*
Power	*"I like to be in command."*
Strength	*"I test myself in fearful situations to make myself stronger."*

3. Detachment Scale

Need for Aloneness	*"I prefer to be alone."*
Avoidance	*"I avoid questions about my personal life."*
Self-Sufficiency	*"I don't really need people."*

Source: Prepared from information in Coolidge et al., 2001; and Coolidge et al., 2004.

Moving toward People: The Self-Effacing Solution

Some people turn to others for the love and protection lacking in their early life and must be careful to do nothing to alienate others. Horney (1945) referred to these as *compliant types*. Some are dominated by a need for affection, living as though their motto were, "If you love me, you will not hurt me" (Horney, 1937, p. 96). Others are characterized by their submissive attitude, as though they felt, "If I give in, I shall not be hurt" (p. 97).

To be lovable, a person will do things to endear others: becoming sensitive to their needs; seeking their approval; and acting in unselfish ways, generous to a fault. The need for love may be expressed in an exaggerated need to be "in love" or involved in sexual relationships in which the partner takes control.

The compliant type of person makes few demands on others, instead playing a "poor me" role that emphasizes helplessness and subordination. This produces low self-esteem. Such a person "takes it for granted that everyone is superior to him, that they are more attractive, more intelligent, better educated, more worthwhile than he" (Horney, 1945, pp. 53–54).

Moving against People: The Expansive Solution

A second strategy for resolving the conflict over unmet early needs is to emphasize the mastery of tasks and power over others, which seem to offer protection from the vulnerability of being helpless. Horney (1945) refers to those who adopt this strategy as *aggressive types*, who seem to live by the motto, "If I have power, no one can hurt me" (Horney, 1937, p. 98). Less subtle domination over others, or more subtle power through competitive mastery, both achieve the desired protection against humiliation.

Career competitiveness and perfectionism tap this trend. In politics, the expansive solution can lead to vigorous campaigning or it can make military action seem more appealing (Swansbrough, 1994). From her clinical experience, Horney noted that patients of this type seem to have particular difficulty when they begin to come close to other people in love or friendship.

Moving away from People: The Resignation Solution

A third strategy for resolving childhood conflicts is epitomized by the fox in Aesop's fable who could not reach the grapes hanging over his head. After all attempts to reach them failed, the fox finally gave up, avoiding disappointment by telling himself that the grapes were probably sour anyway. In Horney's theory, some people try to do without other people, having given up on solving the problem of basic anxiety through love or power. Horney (1945) refers to these as *detached personality types* and says they seem to live by the motto, "If I withdraw, nothing can hurt me" (Horney, 1937, p. 99). In the effort to be self-sufficient, detached types may develop considerable resourcefulness and independence; Horney cites the example of Robinson Crusoe. Or they may restrict their needs and protect their privacy. Creative people are often detached types.

Healthy versus Neurotic Use of Interpersonal Orientations

Harmonious interpersonal relationships are an important source of life satisfaction cross-culturally, although to a greater extent in some cultures than others (Kwan, Bond, & Singelis, 1997). How do we achieve this? The healthy person adopts, when appropriate, any of the three orientations toward people because each is adaptive in certain situations. The neurotic individual is limited in using these orientations. Consider aggression. Although it is pathological to be aggressive toward everyone, the healthy person must be capable of "adequate aggressiveness," by "taking initiative; making efforts; carrying things through to completion; attaining success: insisting on one's rights; defending oneself when attacked; forming and expressing autonomous views; recognizing one's goals and being able to plan one's life according to them" (Horney, 1935/1967e, p. 228). The current term would be *assertiveness* rather than *aggressiveness*. Similarly, although excessive dependency (moving toward) is neurotic, the inability to ask for appropriate help (a deficit in the moving-toward orientation) is also maladaptive (cf. Bornstein, 1992).

Interpersonal orientations also influence physical health. Horney reported that repressed hostility may cause physical symptoms, such as headaches and stomach problems (1945, p. 58). Research confirms that high levels of hostility ("moving against" orientation) contribute to coronary heart disease (Miller et al., 1996; Roemer, 1987). Excessive dependency, too, puts people at increased risk for many physical diseases, including ulcers, asthma, epilepsy, and heart disease—perhaps in part because unmet dependency needs arouse anxiety, which impairs the immune system (Bornstein, 1998, 2000). If these relationships were found only after people became ill, we might dismiss them as only indicating that sick people become dependent. The fact that the relationships are also found in *prospective* studies (i.e., that earlier dependency predicts later illness) indicates that the dependency–illness relationship is not simply an artifact of the sick role. On the positive side, Robert Bornstein (2000) points out that dependency can have a protective effect, too, when it stimulates people to seek early treatment and to comply with medical instructions.

FOUR MAJOR ADJUSTMENTS TO BASIC ANXIETY

To solve conflicts over basic anxiety, an individual adopts defense mechanisms, including many of the defense mechanisms that previous analysts had described, such as repression, and Horney's expanded list of defensive maneuvers. All neurotics use some combination of four major strategies for resolving the basic conflict between helplessness and hostility. These strategies do not solve the conflict or lead to growth, but they may allow a person to adapt sufficiently to cope with daily life.

Eclipsing the Conflict: Moving toward or against Others

First, the neurotic may "eclipse part of the conflict [between helplessness and hostility] and raise its opposite to predominance" (Horney, 1945, p. 16). Some eclipse hostility and emphasize helplessness, seeking nonconflictful interactions and moving toward others. This style requires low self-esteem in order to avoid the distress that would otherwise result from holding back one's self-assertion (Robinson & Wilkowski, 2006). Others eclipse helplessness and emphasize hostility against other people. These constitute two of the basic interpersonal orientations: moving toward and moving against people.

Detachment: Moving away from Others

A second major adjustment strategy is to become detached from others. Because the conflicts are inherently interpersonal, simply moving away from people reduces the experience of conflict. If this tendency is much stronger than eclipsing, it leads to Horney's third interpersonal orientation, moving away from people.

The Idealized Self: Moving away from the Real Self

The third major neurotic adjustment strategy is to turn away from the real self toward some seemingly better (less helpless, less angry) **idealized self**. The **real self** is "the alive, unique, personal center of ourselves" (Horney, 1950, p. 155) and is involved in healthy psychological growth. It is the self that would have developed if we had been nurtured properly as we were developing or that we may become once we overcome our neurosis (Paris, 1999).

A healthy adult who is neglected or rejected can turn to other relationships, confident in his or her own self-worth, but the young child does not have the resources to do so. Consequently, the sense of self, which is just in the process of developing, emerges already wounded. The child develops a low self-esteem. The person may feel like a counterfeit, having "lost touch with essential aspects of self," that is, alienated from the true self (Ingram, 2001). Instead, the neurotic turns to an imagined idealized self, which would not be despised. The idealized self varies depending on the

idealized self

an image of what a person wishes to be

real self

the vital, unique center of the self, which has growth potential interpersonal orientation of the individual. "Perhaps if I am very, very good and kind, I will be lovable," thinks one child. "Or," imagines another, "if I impress people with my achievements and power, they will not be able to hurt me, and they may even admire me." "Or," muses a third, "maybe I don't need people after all; I can manage alone."

The profoundly disturbing consequences of turning from the real to the idealized self are suggested by the comparison Horney (1950) makes. The process corresponds to "the devil's pact…the selling of one's soul" (p. 155). The healthier choice is to turn away from false pride and instead to accept the "ordinariness" of one's real self (Horner, 1994).

However, neurotics try instead to strengthen the idealized self and avoid painful confrontation with the repressed real self. "I should be kind to everyone" or "I should not have to depend on other people." Horney called these sorts of demands the **tyranny of the shoulds**. They urge us ever closer to the idealized self but at the expense of increased alienation from the real self. Perfectionism can produce the sort of high performance that many jobs reward, but the cost is great, including emotional disorders and an elevated risk of suicide (Bieling et al., 2004; Blatt, 1995; Chang, 1998; Flett et al., 1998; Hewitt, Flett, & Ediger, 1996; Hewitt et al., 1997; Minarik & Ahrens, 1996; Orbach, 1997; Shafran & Mansell, 2001). Even if they succeed, perfectionists may feel like "impostors" (Henning, Ey, & Shaw, 1998). Bernard Paris (1999, p. 165) conveys wise advice: "Horney recognized that the absolute best is the enemy of the good, that we must not disregard our accomplishments because we have failed to attain perfection."

tyranny of the shoulds
inner demands to live up to the idealized self

Externalization: Projection of Inner Conflict

In the fourth major adjustment strategy, the neurotic projects inner conflicts onto the outside world, a process Horney called **externalization**. Externalization refers to "the tendency to experience internal processes as if they occurred outside oneself and, as a rule, to hold these external factors responsible for one's difficulties" (Horney, 1945, p. 115). It includes the defense mechanism of projection, as traditional psychoanalysis understands it, in which our own unacceptable tendencies (such as anger or sometimes ambition) are perceived as characteristic of other people but not ourselves. In one case study, for example, a woman was interpreted to have selected her ambitious but narcissistic husband because she could externalize onto him "power, competence, and a capacity for success" that she could not see in herself (Horwitz, 2001). This defensive choice by the self-effacing wife, combined with the husband's own expansive and narcissistic solution to conflict, led to considerable marital discord.

externalization
defense mechanism in which conflicts are projected outside

Externalization can also include our unrecognized feelings. Horney cited the example of a man unaware of his own feeling of oppression, who, through externalization, was "profoundly disturbed by the oppression of small countries" (1945, p. 116). Neurotics often externalize feelings of self-contempt, either by thinking that others despise them (projection of the impulse) or by despising others (displacement of the object of contempt). Compliant types (those who move toward others) are likely to externalize in the first way, and aggressive types (those who move against others) in the second way. In either case, the neurotic is unaware of deep self-contempt.

These four attempts at solution occur in all neuroses, although not with equal strength. The neurotic attempts only to "create an artificial harmony" (Horney, 1945, p. 16) rather than actually resolving the problem.

SECONDARY ADJUSTMENT TECHNIQUES

In addition to the major defensive strategies (eclipsing, detachment, the idealized self, and externalization), there are many auxiliary strategies for reducing anxiety. Horney believed these secondary adjustment techniques, like the major adjustment techniques, do not really solve the neurotic problem in any lasting way, as she made clear in the title by which she introduced the concepts: "Auxiliary Approaches to Artificial Harmony" (1945, p. 131).

blind spots

secondary adjustment technique in which a person is unaware of behavior inconsistent with the idealized self-image

compartmentalization

secondary adjustment technique in which incompatible behaviors are not simultaneously recognized

rationalization

secondary adjustment technique in which a person explains behaviors in socially acceptable ways

excessive self-control

secondary adjustment technique in which emotions are avoided

arbitrary rightness

secondary adjustment technique in which a person rigidly declares that his or her own view is correct

elusiveness

secondary adjustment technique in which a person avoids commitment to any opinion or action

cynicism

secondary adjustment technique in which the moral values of society are rejected

People are often unaware of aspects of their behavior that are blatantly incompatible with their idealized self-image. Horney (1945) cited the example of a patient who "had all the characteristics of the compliant type and thought of himself as Christlike" but who blindly failed to recognize the aggression expressed by his symbolic murders of co-workers. "At staff meetings he would often shoot one colleague after another with a little flick of his thumb" (p. 132). Such **blind spots** prevent conscious awareness of the conflict between the behavior and our self-image.

Another way to prevent the recognition of conflict is by **compartmentalization**, allowing the incompatible behaviors to be consciously recognized but not at the same time. Each is allowed to be experienced in a separate "compartment" of life: family or outsiders, friends or enemies, work or personal life, and so forth. For example, a person may be loving within the family but a ruthless business competitor outside the family.

Horney (1945, p. 135) called **rationalization** "self-deception by reasoning." We explain our behaviors so they seem consistent with what is socially acceptable and with our idealized self-image. Horney provided these examples: A compliant type who is helpful will rationalize this action as due to feelings of sympathy (ignoring a tendency to dominate, which may also be present); an aggressive type will explain his or her helpfulness as expedient behavior.

Excessive self-control prevents people from being overwhelmed by a variety of emotions, including "enthusiasm, sexual excitement, self-pity, or rage" (Horney, 1945, p. 136). When emotions threaten to break through, people may fear they are going crazy. Rage is particularly dangerous and is most actively controlled. People using this defense mechanism typically avoid alcohol because it would be disinhibiting, and they have difficulty with free association in psychotherapy.

Arbitrary rightness "constitutes an attempt to settle conflicts once and for all by declaring arbitrarily and dogmatically that one is invariably right" (Horney, 1945, p. 138). Inner doubts are denied, and external challenges are discredited. The rigidity of these people makes them avoid psychoanalysis, which challenges a person's core defensive beliefs.

Elusiveness is quite the opposite of arbitrary rightness. These people do not commit themselves to any opinion or action because they "have established no definite idealized image" (Horney, 1945, p. 139) to avoid the experience of conflict. The person who is elusive does not stick with a conflict long enough to really work at resolution. "You can never pin them down to any statement; they deny having said it or assure you they did not mean it that way. They have a bewildering capacity to becloud issues" (p. 138). They are reminiscent of the joke about the neighbor who, asked to return a borrowed bucket, says he did not borrow it, and besides it was leaking when he borrowed it, and besides he already returned it.

Cynicism avoids conflict by "denying and deriding...moral values" (Horney, 1945, p. 139). A Machiavellian-type person is consciously cynical, seeking to achieve his or her goals without moral qualms. Others use cynicism unconsciously; they consciously accept society's values but do not live by them.

CULTURAL DETERMINANTS OF DEVELOPMENT

Horney stressed cultural determinants of personality and neurosis, in addition to orthodox Freudian biological forces. Specific family experiences, such as having domineering or self-sacrificing mothers, only occur under particular cultural conditions (1937, p. viii). For Horney, even the Oedipal complex is not universal. Psychoanalysts have noted that family ties are closer and more central to the patients' sense of self in Asian countries influenced by Confucian values, including China, Japan, Korea, and Vietnam (Slote, 1992).

Horney (1937, p. 62) argued that sexual conflict was becoming less important as a source of anxiety at the time she wrote than in Freud's somewhat earlier era, and the conflict between competitiveness and love was becoming more important. "In our culture," she wrote, "the most important neurotic conflict is between a compulsive and indiscriminate desire to be the first under all circumstances and the simultaneous need to be loved by everybody" (1937/1967d, p. 258). This conflict is exacerbated by the feminine role. Because cultures can change, Horney's emphasis on culture appeals to feminists and others who advocate change.

Gender Roles

Whereas biology determines sex (male or female), it is culture that defines the accepted traits and behaviors for men and women. To recognize that we are discussing cultural rather than biological phenomena, it is customary to use the terms *masculine* and *feminine* instead of *male* and *female* and the term *gender* instead of *sex*. According to *social role theory,* cultures define what is masculine and what is feminine (Eagly, 1987; Eagly & Wood, 1991). For example, contrast the traditional value of machismo to the masculine identity of Chicano men (Segura & Pierce, 1993) with the high levels of dependency among males in China (Dien, 1992).

ACHIEVEMENT   Horney's description of gender roles concerning achievement stimulated later research. Women, she claimed, are especially likely to become compliant types who do not risk achievement because "our cultural situation…stamps success a man's sphere" (1937, p. 204). In her time, Horney (1939, p. 181) noted that a woman who sacrificed her own career for her husband's career was considered "normal," even if the wife was more gifted. Women may even develop a "fear of success" (pp. 210–214) that comes from a conflict between competition and the need for affection, leading her to believe that if she succeeds, she will lose her friends. Fear of success is measured for research purposes by a projective test (Horner, 1972), which has been used in many studies.

SOCIAL DOMINANCE   Traditionally, gender roles prescribe dominance or power for males and submissiveness or nurturance for females. This is true to such an extent that the short form of the Bem Sex-Role Inventory "masculine" scale is virtually identical to a scale derived by factor analysis called Interpersonal Potency, and the Bem "feminine" scale is virtually identical to an Interpersonal Sensitivity scale (Brems & Johnson, 1990).

Gender roles profoundly influence the development of social power or dominance. Masochism (the enjoyment of pain and suffering) was a biological characteristic of females, according to Freud. Horney disagreed, suggesting that "masochistic phenomena represent the attempt to gain safety and satisfaction in life through inconspicuousness and dependency" (1939, p. 113).

An empirical study of couples provides evidence that social power determines interpersonal behavior. The strategies people use to influence their intimate partners were found to vary with the person's structural strength or weakness in the relationship, as indicated by income, education, and age. The more powerful member of a couple was more likely to use bullying and autocratic tactics to influence the partner, whereas the weaker partner was more likely to use supplication and manipulation. This association held for both heterosexual and homosexual couples. In the former, the more powerful partner was usually the man, but it was power, rather than sex, that best predicted behavior (Howard, Blumstein, & Schwartz, 1986).

VALUING THE FEMININE ROLE   Horney rejected Freud's assertion that women reject their bodies as inferior. She argued that culture, rather than anatomy, is the important force behind the "penis envy" Freud had postulated. Women envy the power and privilege that humans with penises have, rather than the organ itself (Horney, 1926/1967a, 1923/1967b; Siegel, 1982). She countered, "Is not the tremendous strength in men of the impulse to creative work in every field precisely due to their feeling of playing a relatively small part in the creation of living beings, which constantly impels them to an overcompensation in achievement?" (quoted in Gilman, 2001). This argument, well known by the catchy term **womb envy**, questions the assumption that men have the enviable position.

Other supporters of women's roles emphasize the value of interpersonal connectedness and relationship-oriented values like nurturance and empathy (Gilligan,

womb envy

men's envy of women's reproductive capacity (the complement of Freud's penis envy)

1982; Lang-Takac & Osterweil, 1992; Miller, 1976; Symonds, 1991). This argument has not gone unchallenged. Marcia Westkott contends that women's valuing of relationships often takes the form of an idealized self, and that feminist theory and therapy, by affirming relationship values, unwittingly confirm a neurotic idealized self and perpetuate a cultural expectation that women should take care of men (Westkott, 1986a, 1986b, 1989). For example, when feminine nurturant values are emphasized, family members of alcoholics may inadvertently enable the alcoholic to continue drinking by taking care of the problems that the addiction creates, which is unhealthy for both the alcoholic and the codependent family member (Haaken, 1993).

MENTAL HEALTH AND GENDER ROLES In the past, the prevailing view among psychologists was that women who work and have professions suffer personality disturbances (labeled "penis envy" or otherwise) and that traditionally feminine women were psychologically healthier. Research does not support this view (Helson & Picano, 1990; Yogev, 1983). Psychological "masculinity" (as measured on sex-typing instruments such as the Bem Sex-Role Inventory), which reflects such qualities as assertiveness, is associated with better mental health in both men and women. Calling such healthy traits "masculine" reflects a cultural viewpoint.

Traditional gender roles bring a price. In women, they discourage assertiveness and individual development. People who overemphasize other people's needs compared to their own, in a pattern called unmitigated communion, are prone to later psychological maladjustment, such as depression (Aubé, 2008). The finding applies to both women and men, though gender roles make this style more common among women. In men, traditional gender roles contribute to defense mechanisms such as restrictions in emotionality (Mahalik et al., 1998) and to gender-related problems, including violence, fear of homosexuals, detached fathering, and neglect of health needs (Levant, 1996).

Cross-Cultural Differences

The emphasis on individual achievement is, as Horney hinted, particularly characteristic of Western culture. Harry Triandis and his colleagues have studied cultural differences in **individualism**, a value that emphasizes individual accomplishments and privileges. The United States and Britain are particularly high in individualism (Triandis, McCusker, & Hui, 1990). In contrast, countries that are less affluent, in which people depend on cooperation to share resources, are characterized by **collectivism**, which values the relationships between people and their shared goals and mutual responsibilities (Triandis, 1996). Collectivist cultures, like those in Africa, Asia, and Latin America, emphasize conformity, social harmony, group tasks, and family obligations.

The assumption that the self is separate rather than connected to others pervades Western thought and psychological theory and treatment, reflecting the individualistic values of its cultural founders. Having harmonious relationships with other people is less important as a source of life satisfaction in the United States, an individualistic culture, than in (for example) Hong Kong (Kwan, Bond, & Singelis, 1997). Individualistic cultures encourage Horney's moving-against orientation, emphasizing achievement and accepting aggressive behavior. Collectivist cultures are more supportive of a moving-toward orientation. For therapists dealing with clients from other cultures, it is important to not misperceive people whose behavior may reflect their different cultural values, rather than individual problems. For theorists, it's important to realize that our assumptions about what is healthy may be limited by our cultural vision, and that other cultures may provide correctives to cultural myopia.

HORNEY'S APPROACH TO THERAPY

In criticizing Freud's patriarchal biases, Horney set a model for later clinicians to question whether therapists could also fail to understand patients because of their own limited experience of race, sexual orientation, or other factors. Horney opened the

individualism

values, predominant in many Western cultures, of individual goals and achievement (in contrast to shared group goals and cooperation)

collectivism

values, predominant in some cultures, of social cooperation and group goals door for realizing that the therapist, too, is influenced by culture, bringing perhaps biased assumptions to the understanding of the client (Miletic, 2002).

Although orthodox in her acceptance of the importance of childhood experience in developing personality, Horney did not believe all psychoanalytic treatment required delving into childhood recollections. Horney criticized the Freudian overemphasis on the exploration of childhood origins of neurosis, although she would doubtless agree that interpersonal relationships based on faulty parent–child interacting can be mended in therapy (Morgan, 1997). Horney advised the therapist to keep bringing the patient back to the present, seeing how neurotic trends influence current life.

Inevitably, the patient's idealized image must he challenged, but this must be done carefully and slowly because it is the basis for the personality, wounded but not destroyed, that the patient brings to analysis. Eventually, the idealized image must be replaced by a more realistic self-concept. The term *shrink*, applied to the analyst, seems particularly fitting for this function.

PARENTAL BEHAVIOR AND PERSONALITY DEVELOPMENT

Neurotic problems begin early in life, within the family, where the "basic evil is invariably a lack of genuine warmth and affection" (Horney, 1937, p. 80). Parental behavior that undermines a feeling of safety will lead to neurotic development. This includes parental neglect, indifference, and even active rejection of the child.

One of the goals Horney described for psychoanalysis was to advise parents how to raise healthy youths, thus breaking the repeating cycle of neurosis through each generation. Psychoanalysts exploring these issues suggest it is important for parents to pay attention to their infants' emotional experiences. This requires that the mother (or other caregiver) be able to understand the infant's emotion and to respond appropriately, for example, by mirroring an infant's distress or joy. If this experience is deficient, the child will develop with deficits in affective regulation (Glucksman, 2000).

Research supports her ideas. The trait of neuroticism in parents contributes to their abuse of children, apparently by making the parents less able to tolerate the negative emotions that come from stressful interactions with their children (Belsky, 1993; McCrae & Costa, 1988). Longitudinal research shows that parental acceptance and nonauthoritarian punishment in childhood predict higher ego development at age 30, particularly for women (Dubow, Huesmann, & Eron, 1987). One particularly impressive study, using a longitudinal design, correlated parental behavior during preschool and the children's development as young adults. Fathers and mothers were evaluated according to the "poisonous pedagogy" formulation of psychoanalyst Alice Miller, whose ideas are similar to those of Karen Horney. As predicted, parents who treated their children with criticism and excessive control produced anxious, poorly adjusted children; parents who expressed affection and encouraged their children produced warm and socially well-adjusted young adults (Harrington, 1993). Other studies of parenting styles confirm that neglectful parents have children who have greater difficulties. Authoritative parents, who provide both direction and acceptance, rear better adjusted children (Lamborn et al., 1991).

THE RELATIONAL APPROACH WITHIN PSYCHOANALYTIC THEORY

Theories build on earlier theories. In contrast to Freud's emphasis on the unconscious and intrapsychic conflict, many of his successors today stress disturbances in the relationships that people have developed, beginning with early family experience, a theme that Horney and others emphasized (see Table 6.4). The relational model was presented as an alternative to Freud's drive model (Greenberg & Mitchell, 1983; Mitchell & Aron, 1999), and it influences even many therapists who were trained in the Freudian tradition (Sudak, 2000).

The **relational approach** emphasizes interpersonal relationships, especially the impact of early relationships with parents (Greenberg & Mitchell, 1983). The mother is more important in this approach, in contrast to Freud's emphasis on the father

relational approach

approach in modern psychoanalysis that emphasizes interpersonal relationships

Table 6.4 Important Persons in the History of the Relational Approach

Theorist	Theoretical Ideas
Melanie Klein	Young children are very needy; they relate to "part objects" (such as the breast) instead of the whole parent; their ambivalent feelings cause guilt about their negative feelings about their parents.
W. R. D. Fairbairn	People have a fundamental need for relatedness. Maternal indifference and lack of love for the child contribute to the development of child pathology. The child defensively splits the rejecting mother (which is internalized) from the hoped-for loving mother, which impedes development from immature to mature dependency.
Harry Stack Sullivan	Children attempt to avoid anxiety in interpersonal relationships by constructing an understanding of self that includes a *good me*, a *bad me*, and a *not me*.
Otto Kernberg	Borderline and psychotic patients suffer disturbed identity and interpersonal relationships. Early severe frustration leads to unmanageable aggression and narcissistic personality disorders. Especially in borderline personality disorder, narcissistic frustrations lead to a splitting of the "good" and "bad" self and object relations, which are kept isolated from one another, and a grandiose self is defensively formed.
Heinz Kohut	A *grandiose self* is part of normal, healthy development, based on a desire for merger with omnipotent caretakers, whose admiration is sought. A healthy, integrated self structure will be formed if the adults respond empathically to the child. If less-than-optimal parenting is available, the child will construct an *idealized parental imago* to support the grandiose self.
Mary Ainsworth and John Bowlby	Infants develop secure attachment, in which they derive comfort from the presence of the mother (or substitute); or insecure attachment, in which they are not comforted.
Nancy Chodorow	Children's gender development is influenced by the different roles that the mother and father play in caring for children (in contrast to Freud's proposed anatomical determinants of gender).

(Grotstein, 1993). Early relationships are particularly influential because the very young do not yet have a sense of themselves as separate persons. Early relationships are the basis for developing internal representations of self and others that will guide relationships throughout life, and that prepare us to expect love or rejection, nurturance or disappointment, from people. Whether people seek support from others in adulthood or avoid doing so and dwell on depression and self-criticism is related to the way they describe their parents, even though they are old enough to have moved on to new relationships (Mongrain, 1998). A relationship with an empathic, nurturant parent begins this process in a healthy way. But rejecting or abusive parenting sets the stage for internalizing much more negative images of others and of the self.

Some psychoanalysts argue relational theorists do not give Freud the credit he deserves for his insights about relationships. Besides the transference, Freud proposed that in seeking a marriage partner men seek someone similar to their own mother, and women seek someone like their father. This prediction finds some research support. A widely used test of personality (the Five Factor Inventory) was administered to participants (mostly college students) and to their parents, and on several traits, the participants' opposite-sex parent had a personality similar to their chosen romantic partner (Geher, 2000).

Relationships are often referred to as **object relations** in psychoanalysis, based on Freud's idea that other people serve as the objects that can satisfy libidinal desire. The relational approach considers the cognitive and affective processes that allow people to form healthy interpersonal relationships or that impede such relationships. For example, sociopaths have defective object relationships in that they exploit others

object relations

term used in psychoanalysis for relationships with people, based originally on the idea that people serve as objects to satisfy libidinal drives for their own selfish purposes. People suffering from borderline personality disorder have another kind of disturbed object relationship pattern: They manipulate others and may quickly become intensely attached to someone who is not suitable to meet this irrational need (Westen, 1991). Borderline personality disorder is associated with such a fundamental sensitivity to rejection that a brain area that reacts to such emotion, the amygdala, is activated by facial expressions that the general population sees as neutral (Westen, Gabbard, & Ortigo, 2008).

Emotions triggered in interpersonal situations are especially important in object relationships, as we might expect given the role of infantile anxiety and hostility that Horney described. Others may calm us when we are distressed or arouse anxiety when we are not. This effect depends on experience with early relationships. The emotions we expect from relationships can be measured by projective tests as well as by interview measures (Barends et al., 1990). By providing ways of measuring individuals' capacity for healthy relationships—methods that are more systematic than clinical impressions and can also be used to study people who are not in therapy—researchers are contributing to the dialogue between clinical and research-oriented psychologists (see Table 6.5).

Drew Westen and his colleagues have developed an instrument to measure affect regulation styles, using a Q-Sort technique in which clinical judges sort statements describing each patient's emotions into nine piles, according to how well they describe the person: the Affect Regulation and Experience Q-Sort (the AREQ). They suggest that psychological problems are more severe among people who have difficulty regulating strong negative emotions (Westen et al., 1997).

In a cross-sectional study of children, Westen and his colleagues (Westen et al., 1991) report evidence for increasing maturity from grade 2 to grade 5 (about age 8 to 11 years) on three dimensions of relationships: complexity of representations, capacity

Table 6.5 Measurement of Object Relations from TAT Stories

Scale	Description	Description of Low Score	Description of High Score
Complexity	Complexity, differentiation, and integration of representations of people	Poor differentiation between people	Complex, multifaceted, integrated representations of people's subjective experience and enduring dispositions
Affect-tone of relationship paradigms	Expectation that relationships will be safe and enriching or destructive and threatening	Expectation that relationships will be destructive and threatening	Expectation that relationships will be safe and enriching
Capacity for emotional investment in relationships and moral standards	Emotional orientation that is selfish, or that unselfishly invests in people, values, and ideals	Investment in one's own need gratification and desires	Commitment to values and relationships that acknowledge needs of self and others
Understanding of social causality	Logic, complexity, accuracy, and psychological mindedness of attributions	Absence of causal understanding	Complex understanding of the role mental events play in social causation

Source: Adapted from information in Westen et al., 1991.

for emotional investment, and understanding social causality. These results show that object relationships are not so fixed in the preschool years as Freud theorized, but instead they continue to develop for many years thereafter.

THE SENSE OF SELF IN RELATIONSHIPS

Our sense of self is rooted in relationships. Early disturbances, coming from relationships with inadequate parents, leave a person with a weakened or enfeebled sense of self (Kohut, 1984). In terms of relational theory, disturbed interpersonal relationships stem from early experience in which parents do not properly "mirror" the baby's experience and emotions, failing to provide the experience needed to develop a healthy sense of self. Thus the developing person lacks accurate awareness of his or her own self, identity, and emotions, producing unhealthy interpersonal behavior later in life (e.g., Vanheule & Verhaeghe, 2009). The sense of self is central to the understanding of defense mechanisms in relational theory. Defenses serve to protect self-esteem (Cooper, 1998).

Children who have not been adequately nurtured or loved develop a belief (which may be unconscious) that they are not worthy, and this impaired self is at the heart of much pathology. Patients diagnosed with borderline personality disorder report what Westen and his colleagues call "malevolent" early memories, in which people were injured (e.g., being pushed to the ground in an early school experience) and little help was given (Nigg et al., 1992). In contrast, adolescents who describe their parents as warm and fostering independence, as "ideal parents," are less likely to suffer from a variety of personality disorders than those who recall less benign parenting (Brennan & Shaver, 1998).

Relational theorist Stephen Mitchell (1970/1999) suggests that the early parent–child relationship is one in which parents' more or less distorted views of themselves and their child set up a distorted, grandiose self-image in the child. For example, the parents might create an unrealistically good and obedient image of their child, which is too limiting for a real child to have room to develop his or her full personality. Object relations theorist Fairbairn (Celani, 1999) describes the defense mechanism of "splitting" as a result of inadequate parenting. The parental object is seen as two separate objects: the bad object that has been rejecting or abusive and the good object that the child longs to please. The child develops both a despised self that in a warped sense justifies the parental rejection or abuse and a grandiose good self that could ideally be the basis for earning parental respect and love. These ideas are quite similar to Horney's description of the despised real self and the grandiose self, and in both theories, the split stems from bad parenting.

Our role relationships with other people throughout life are based on early relationships, and they recapitulate the weaknesses and the defective sense of self that are the legacy of the past. People whose early object relationships are unhealthy because of early physical, sexual, and emotional abuse or other mistreatment are vulnerable to self-destructive behaviors, including suicide (Twomey, Kaslow, & Croft, 2000). They remain in relationships that seem obviously unhealthy. Why would this be? The need to maintain a relationship with an important object, such as the parent, is so strong that extreme measures are taken to maintain the relationship, including blaming oneself (Grand & Alpert, 1993; Westen, 1991).

NARCISSISM

narcissism

unhealthy self-focus that impairs the ability to have healthy, empathic relationships with other people

Too much focus on the self can get in the way of healthy relationships. An unhealthy self-focus and self-admiration constitutes **narcissism**. In less than 1 in 100 people, narcissism is severe and impairs the person so much that it can be diagnosed as a mental disorder, *narcissistic personality disorder* (American Psychiatric Association, 1994). People who suffer from this disorder are extremely self-focused; they do not have much empathy for other people's experience. Their sense of being special, that they deserve attention and admiration, leads them to use other people as admiring audiences and supporters instead of as separate individuals. When undergraduates who score high on a measure of narcissism are asked to describe a shameful early memory (a manipulation theorized to confront the early basis of their narcissism), they subsequently express considerable hostility on an ambiguous projective picture of a child; but those in the experimental group asked to recall a positive memory projected much less hostility onto the picture. Nonnarcissists did not show these effects, which supports the interpretation that narcissists' hostility is tied to early shameful experiences (Heiserman & Cook, 1998). It is easy to see why narcissism, which is based on disturbed relationships, may lead to domestic violence (Zosky, 1999), and why narcissists sometimes react very strongly when they are insulted (Horton & Sedikides, 2009).

The insight that a disturbed sense of self is closely related to disturbed relationships with others helps us understand puzzling findings reported by researchers. High *self-esteem*, that is, thinking you are a worthwhile person, is generally a healthy characteristic. High self-esteem has its downside, though. For one thing, people with high self-esteem sometimes take on tasks that are too difficult, apparently trying to prove how much they can do (Baumeister, Heatherton, & Tice, 1993). They also may persist too long at tasks that cannot be finished and are prone to other self-defeating behaviors (Baumeister, 1997). Surprisingly, it has also been found that people with high self-esteem may also be more aggressive than other people (Baumeister, Smart, & Boden, 1996), at least under some circumstances—specifically, when they are also narcissists and they are insulted (Bushman et al., 2009).

Why? One factor to consider is that "self-esteem" is operationally defined as a person's score on a self-report measure. Some people who score high on such measures truly accept who they are, but others have a fragile, grandiose image of themselves hiding a deeper self-doubt. For them, high self-esteem scores are not so much accurate as they are defensive statements. When challenged, they feel vulnerable and so may behave aggressively in an effort to bully their way to being seen as worthwhile. That interpretation suggests that narcissism, not true self-esteem, leads to aggression when a person is insulted or provoked. This interpretation is supported by experimental evidence. Subjects who score high on a test of narcissism behave aggressively toward someone who has insulted them by criticizing essays they had written. When given the opportunity to do so in a laboratory setting, narcissists blast the other person with a loud noise in a computer game (Bushman & Baumeister, 1998). Narcissistic people are readily angered (Rhodewalt & Morf, 1998). Their self-esteem is insecure, subject to the supports and attacks of life's transient events (Rhodewalt, Madrian, & Cheney, 1998), and so they defend their self-worth aggressively.

ATTACHMENT IN INFANCY AND ADULTHOOD

Whether we turn to relational theorists, Horney, or even Freud, experts continue to point to the importance of early relationships between parents and children as a foundation for personality and relationships throughout life.

Infant Attachment

Infants develop bonds of affection with their mother, called **attachment** (Ainsworth et al., 1978; Bowlby, 1988). Attachment is based on an instinct (Eagle, 1996) that functions, in an evolutionary sense, to ensure children's survival by keeping them near to their parents, on whom they depend for survival. In historic observations, René Spitz (1945) observed that orphanage babies deprived of human touch and love became ill and even died, despite adequate food and medical care.

Mary Ainsworth (1972; Ainsworth et al., 1978) studied infant attachment to the mother (as the primary caretaker) by observing infants' responses to strangers. The development of a secure attachment between infant and parent provides a basis for emotional health and coping in later life. It facilitates cognitive development in childhood, presumably because the securely attached child has self-confidence to investigate the world (Jacobsen, Edelstein, & Hofmann, 1994). Later love relationships are also healthier when they build on secure attachment.

attachment

bonds of affection in which an infant turns to the mother or other caretaker for comfort and security; by extension, close interpersonal styles in adulthood

Table 6.6 Ainsworth's Description of Infant Temperament Types Compared with Horney's Model of Interpersonal Orientations

Infant Type	Infant Behavior	Horney's Interpersonal Orientation
Type A	• Resists being comforted	Moving Away
Type B_1	• Securely attached • Comforted by mother • Explores new environment	Balance of the three Interpersonal Orientations
Type B_4	• Securely attached • Stays near mother for comfort	Moving Toward
Type C	• Ambivalent toward mother • Shows anger toward stranger	Moving Against

Source: Adapted from Feiring, 1984.

In the infant attachment studies, researchers observed how infants behaved when in the presence of a stranger. Some infants were frightened; others seemed comforted by their mothers' presence. The various attachment patterns can be interpreted as confirming Horney's patterns of moving toward, against, or away from people (Feiring, 1984). One type (Type B_1) has the balanced interpersonal mode that Horney regarded as most healthy (see Table 6.6).

We should be cautious about blaming the parents entirely for attachment disturbances. Their ability to provide their children with warmth and support may be influenced by their own circumstances, including social position (Stansfeld et al., 2008). Furthermore, childhood temperament, produced by genetics, is partly responsible for the greater security of one child compared to another. The same parental behavior that is adequate for the average child may leave a temperamentally vulnerable child anxious about attachment. Fortunately, research on interventions shows that training parents how to be more responsive to their young children can improve attachment (Lyons & Sperling, 1996). And we know that attachment is mutual: babies' smiles influence the mother's brain activity in a unique way, different from her reactions to other infants (Strathearn et al., 2008).

Adult Attachments and Relationships

Attachment styles continue after infancy (Hazan & Shaver, 1994). Attachment in adulthood helps regulate emotion and reduce stress (Feeney & Kirkpatrick, 1996; Silverman, 1998). Securely attached adults feel more trust toward their partners than do those without secure attachment (Mikulincer, 1998b) and are able to resolve conflicts within relationships more maturely (Corcoran & Mallinckrodt, 2000). Adolescents hospitalized for psychiatric disorders are reported to be insecurely attached, as are their mothers (Rosenstein & Horowitz, 1996).

Various kinds of adult attachment resemble infant attachment styles. A person who falls in love, marries, and stays in a stable relationship throughout adulthood exemplifies secure attachment. Another who is hesitant about love, marries, but divorces not long after and thereafter avoids long-term relationships illustrates an avoidant attachment style (Klohnen & Bera, 1998). Laboratory research that asked college students to recall what they heard about a woman describing her relationships, suggests that avoidant people don't pay as much attention to such information as others (Fraley & Brumbaugh, 2007). Another type of insecure adult attachment is "desperate love," a style of love with high anxiety and the desire to be excessively close to the loved one (Sperling & Berman, 1991). Unhealthy attachment styles leave couples with the risk of being overly intrusive toward their partner (Lavy, Mikulincer, & Shaver, 2010).

Sperling and his colleagues have suggested a model of four types of adult attachment that emphasizes both dependence and anger. Their model corresponds well to Horney's three interpersonal styles, with an additional category reflecting ambivalence between moving toward and moving against (Sperling, Berman, & Fagen, 1992) (see Table 6.7).

Table 6.7 A Model of Adult Attachment Styles

	High Anger	**Low Anger**
High Dependency	Resistant-ambivalent attachment style (compare to Horney's description of conflict between achievement and love, that is, moving against and moving toward)	Dependent attachment style (compare to Horney's moving toward orientation)
Low Dependency	Hostile attachment style (compare to Horney's moving against orientation)	Avoidant attachment style (compare to Horney's moving away orientation)

Source: Adapted in part from Sperling, Berman, & Fagen, 1992. The comparisons with Horney's theory are added.

Other researchers have adopted a three-category model of adult attachment, corresponding to the infant research (see Table 6.8). It is not only simpler but more optimistic in that it includes a "secure" category (Hazan & Shaver, 1987). Personality tests show securely attached adults to be higher on extraversion and lower on neuroticism than anxious and avoidant adults (Shaver & Brennan, 1992). Securely attached adults are also less prone to anger and deal with it more constructively (Mikulincer, 1998a). Adults who are not securely attached have difficulty expressing anger toward their romantic partners; those who are securely attached, in contrast, can express anger appropriately and maintain the relationship (Sharpsteen & Kirkpatrick, 1997). Securely attached college students, as yet unmarried, look forward to having more children and are more confident about their ability to be effective parents, compared to insecurely attached college students (Rholes et al., 1997). In one study, anxiously attached male undergraduates wrote TAT stories describing violence of men toward female victims more than seven times as often as the secure group, perhaps reflecting the frustrations of anxiously attached men about intimacy (Woike, Osier, & Candela, 1996).

Longitudinal Studies of Attachment

Longitudinal studies of attachment verify that mothers' caregiving at 18 months predicts attachment in adulthood (Zayas et al., 2011). Furthermore, disturbed attachment relationships from early life carry over to adulthood. One study tracked down college students up to 31 years later when they were in their early 50s. In middle age, the

Table 6.8 Three Adult Attachment Styles

Secure Attachment Style

I find it relatively easy to get close to others and am comfortable depending on them and having them depend on me. I don't often worry about being abandoned or about someone getting too close to me.

Avoidant Attachment Style

I am somewhat uncomfortable being close to others; I find it difficult to trust them completely, difficult to allow myself to depend on them. I am nervous when anyone gets too close and often love partners who want me to be more intimate than I feel comfortable being.

Anxious-Ambivalent Attachment Style

I find that others are reluctant to get as close as I would like. I often worry that my partner doesn't love me or won't want to stay with me. I want to merge completely with another person, and this desire sometimes scares people away.

Source: Based on Hazan & Shaver, 1987.

women selected one of several paragraphs that best described them, allowing researchers to classify their attachment style. Those classified as "avoidantly attached" had already expressed more ambivalence about marriage and family when they were in college. As the years passed, they were less likely to marry than the securely attached group and more likely to be divorced if they had married. Researchers described the avoidantly attached as less interpersonally close, more defensive and repressive, and less tolerant to stress from college onward, compared to those who were securely attached (Klohnen & Bera, 1998).

Attachment difficulties are passed down from one generation to the next. For example, in a study of mothers who had a child born with a serious illness such as congenital heart disease, those mothers who were avoidantly attached had worse emotional and psychological outcomes in the coming 7 years for both themselves and their children (Berant, Mikulincer, & Shaver, 2008). In another study, which gathered data on subjects for 70 years of their lives, subjects whose parents had divorced (a major disruption of attachment relationships for a child) were adversely affected. They were more likely to become divorced themselves, and they were more likely to die earlier, at least in part because stable marriage tends to increase longevity (Tucker et al., 1997).

A representative sample of U.S. adults finds adults were less likely to be securely attached if, in childhood, their parents had suffered various forms of psychopathology (including depression, anxiety, and substance abuse), committed suicide, died, or were absent for long periods of time. Other traumas and hardships also were related to insecure attachment: physical and sexual abuse, neglect, accidents, natural disaster, financial adversity, and other distressing events (Mickelson, Kessler, & Shaver, 1997). Securely attached adults marry other securely attached adults; those insecurely attached also tend to marry people with similar attachment problems, which bodes ill for their ability to provide a secure relationship for their children (van Ijzendoorn & Bakermans-Kranenburg, 1996).

THE RELATIONAL APPROACH TO THERAPY

The relational approach to therapy contrasts with Freud's classic drive model by acknowledging a more significant role of the therapist's behavior as an influence in what happens in therapy sessions. In contrast to the traditional psychoanalytic drive model which emphasizes the patient's unconscious and defense mechanisms as the "one person" determinant of the sessions, the interaction with the therapist itself is influential (Altman, 1994).

Relational therapists suggest that the patient–therapist relationship provides an opportunity for transformation of old maladaptive relationship patterns to new healthy ones. The transference relationship should be similar enough to old patterns to put these disturbances in the arena of therapy, even if the old relationships were unhealthy, but different enough to stimulate change (Greenberg, 1986/1999). Paradoxically, a patient may need to cast the therapist in the role of the bad parent to experience that warped attachment—for example, acting out anger against a therapist perceived as hostile and rejecting like the patient's parent, before being able to move on to healthier relationships (Knight, 2005).

Looking back to the founder of psychoanalysis, it would seem that analysis has moved far away from the biological model that Freud proposed. Yet interpersonal relationships in the attachment approach can be understood from the perspective of a parent–child bond that begins with very physical connections, with attachments serving healthy development by a mirroring of the infant's physical experience in the responses of the other. Adult sexual relationships can provide, again, an echo of inner physical experience in the responses of the other (Fonagy, 2008; Fonagy & Target, 2007). And so interpersonal approaches in psychoanalysis, as this theoretical and therapeutic approach develops, may have more connections with Freud's early suggestions than we appreciated, after all.

Summary

- Karen Horney revised psychoanalytic theory to emphasize interpersonal factors, and this theme has been expanded by later relational theorists.
- The child experiences *basic anxiety* as a result of parental rejection or neglect.
- This anxiety is accompanied by *basic hostility*, which cannot be expressed because of the child's dependence on the parents.
- The child attempts to resolve the conflict by adopting one of three interpersonal orientations: *moving toward* people (the self-effacing solution), *moving against* them (the expansive solution), or *moving away* from them (the resignation solution).
- The healthy person can flexibly use all three orientations, but the neurotic person cannot.
- Horney described four basic strategies for resolving neurotic conflict: *eclipsing* the conflict, *detachment*, the *idealized self*, and *externalization*.
- The neurotic individual turns away from the real self, which has the potential for healthy growth, to an *idealized self*. The *tyranny of the shoulds* supports the idealized self.
- In addition, Horney described several *secondary adjustment mechanisms:* blind spots, compartmental-ization, rationalization, excessive self-control, arbitrary rightness, elusiveness, and cynicism.
- Horney emphasized the *cultural determinants* of development. Parenting patterns vary from society to society; even the Oedipus complex is not a universal human experience in her theory.
- Horney discussed gender roles as developments shaped by particular cultures, which can change if cultures change.
- Horneyan therapy seeks to uncover unconscious conflicts originating in childhood but emphasizes their implications for present life.
- *Relational theorists* (a newer approach than Horney's theory) also emphasize early parent–child relationships and their implications for a sense of self and for interpersonal relationships throughout life.
- Disturbances in *object relationships* contribute to many disorders, including narcissism, and to disturbed relationships in adulthood.
- In addition to contributors from psychoanalysis, developmental researchers investigating *attachment* have contributed to our understanding of object relations.

Thinking about Horney's Theory and the Relational Approach

1. Do you know people who represent each of the three interpersonal orientations that Horney describes? Which orientation best describes you?
2. Horney describes perfectionism critically, saying it can be a defense mechanism. Do you agree, or is it desirable to set very high standards?
3. How would you modify Horney's theory, given the changes in gender roles that have occurred since her work?
4. What can be done in society to give infants and children the kind of parenting that Horney and relational theorists recommend?
5. What are the characteristics of a narcissistic personality?
6. How do attachment styles provide a way of thinking about adjustment?

Study Questions

1. Contrast Horney's understanding of the unconscious with that of Freud.
2. Describe the emotional conflicts of early life. Include an explanation of basic anxiety and basic hostility.
3. List and describe the three interpersonal orientations. Give an example of each.
4. Explain the terms *self-effacing solution, expansive solution,* and *resignation solution* in relation to the three interpersonal orientations.
5. Explain the difference between healthy and neurotic use of the interpersonal orientations.
6. Discuss the research on Horney's interpersonal orientations.
7. List and explain the four major adjustments to basic anxiety.
8. Describe the neurotic's attitude toward the real self.
9. Explain the tyranny of the shoulds. Give a hypothetical example.
10. List and explain the seven secondary adjustment techniques. Give an example of each.
11. Discuss the role of culture in determining development. What did Horney say was the most important conflict of her time?
12. How did Horney explain female masochism?
13. Explain what is meant by womb envy.
14. Describe Horneyan therapy. How does it differ from other therapies we have considered so far?
15. Explain how parental behavior contributes to neurosis.
16. What is the relational approach?
17. What is narcissism?
18. Describe healthy and unhealthy patterns of attachment in infancy.
19. Describe healthy and unhealthy patterns of attachment in adulthood.
20. Discuss research on attachment from the perspective of relational theory.
21. How do attachment difficulties contribute to anger and aggressive behavior in relationships?

PART 3

The Trait Perspective

The trait perspective focuses on one of the most fundamental questions in personality: How will we describe people? Researchers begin with everyday language. People have been talking about one another, labeling one another, since before history was recorded. Raymond Cattell (1943a) asserted, "all aspects of human personality which are or have been of importance, interest, or utility have already become recorded in the substance of language" (p. 483; quoted by Borkenau, 1990). The "lexical approach" describes personality by systematically examining language, usually beginning with words in the dictionary (Allport & Odbert, 1936; Cattell, 1943b; John, Angleitner, & Ostendorf, 1988).

A *trait* is a theoretical construct describing a basic dimension of personality. Although they differ in many ways, trait theories agree on some basic assumptions:

1. Trait approaches emphasize *individual differences* in characteristics that are more or less stable across time and across situations.
2. Trait approaches emphasize the *measurement* of these traits through tests, often self-report questionnaires.

The attempt to find the basic, broad dimensions of personality has motivated many researchers. One popular model proposes five basic factors (the "Big Five"): extraversion, agreeableness, neuroticism, conscientiousness, and openness (Digman, 1990; McCrae & Costa, 1987). Another approach identifies 16 dimensions, rather than five (Cattell, 1979). Yet another approach proposes only three factors (Eysenck, 1990). The apparent discrepancy can be resolved by considering a hierarchical model, in which a larger number of more specific factors—not entirely uncorrelated with one another—correspond to a smaller number of more general factors (Boyle, 1989). By way of analogy, a person who claims there are only two things to study in college, liberal arts or professional training, does not really disagree with a person who says there are several dozen things to study and then lists all the departments in the university. They are simply speaking at different levels of generality. In the study of personality, the number of "basic dimensions" uncovered depends on how general or specific are the dimensions sought (Marshall, 1991).

Personality trait and factor theories have advanced considerably in recent years, seeking theoretical connections with our expanding understanding of the biological foundations of behavior. Some theories propose specific biological mechanisms that cause people to be introverted or extraverted, excitable or calm, and so on (see Chapter 9). It has been argued that a trait approach provides the basis for a coherent paradigm of personality theory in the natural science tradition because "in any science, taxonomy precedes causal analysis" (Eysenck, 1991, p. 774).

Whether trait research ultimately makes such theoretical contributions, it has great value for practical applications. For example, measurement of vocational-interest traits helps predict who is suited for particular occupations; those who enter careers that suit their personality are happier and more successful (Dawis, 1996; Hogan, Hogan, & Roberts, 1996; Holland, 1996). Using tests to screen applicants for employment, although it is a widespread and frequently beneficial practice, has sometimes resulted in lawsuits when candidates claim that tests are biased, resulting in racial or other discrimination (Tenopyr, 1995). Such lawsuits remind us of the importance of validity in testing (as described in Chapter 1), not only for abstract theoretical reasons, but also as a fundamental principle of fairness (Lubinski, 1995). Perhaps the prevalence of testing for traits indicates that, whatever theoretical debates remain unresolved, traits exist in the public's eye, and in our talking about one another.

Study Questions

1. What are the assumptions of the trait perspective?
2. Why do some models propose as few as three traits, whereas other approaches propose many more?

Allport
Personological Trait Theory

ILLUSTRATIVE BIOGRAPHY
Mother Teresa

Gordon Allport was interested in the healthy functioning of a whole person and particularly interested in the implications of religious attitudes for our behavior toward other people in the world. Clearly he would have found Mother Teresa an example of the positive contributions that he thought could stem from religious motivations.

Mother Teresa, born in Skopje, Serbia, on August 26, 1910 (Spink, 1997), was a world-renowned Roman Catholic nun, mourned worldwide when she died in 1997 (only a few days after the death of Diana, Princess of Wales). She was acclaimed by people of many faiths for her charitable work among those she called the "poorest of the poor" in India and elsewhere. Mother Teresa established a new order, the Sisters of Charity, to serve the very poor, including lepers and others whose basic physical needs were not being met. Over time, missions were established in many countries, and her concern for the sick and dying of the world mobilized charitable acts by others. Despite her personal humility, the

Mother Teresa

drive to declare her a "saint" officially has proceeded at an unusual pace.

DEVELOPMENT

Gordon Allport described personality development in terms of stages in the self-concept. Throughout life, he proposed, we move from lack of awareness of a self, to a primitive understanding that our body or physical self is who we are, and then include ever more details to this view. Our possessions (such as childhood toys) are concrete aspects of self, but as we grow to middle childhood we also "own" our intentions and goals, and by adolescence we can become reflective about a more inclusive view of self. Of course, our particular life experiences, especially in the social world, influence the content of this self-concept. We are influenced by social models, including our parents, but we come to take responsibility for our own behavior, no matter how it originated.

As a girl, Agnes Bojaxhiu (Mother Teresa's birth name) was the youngest of three children. She witnessed political upheavals in Albania that led to World War I, and her father died—possibly murdered for his political views—when Agnes was only 8. Her mother was devoutly religious in the minority Roman Catholic religion of Albania, and she modeled charity to her daughter by helping those who were even poorer than they were. The future Mother Teresa reports feeling called to the life of a nun when she was 12. At 18, with her mother's blessing, she left home and began the process of becoming a postulant and eventually a nun, learning English and traveling to India to help combat illness and poverty. She did not construe the missionary work as social work, however, but instead as a religious contemplation, in which she and the other nuns with whom she served encountered the divine and suffering Jesus through the needy persons they served. She witnessed suffering not only from poverty and illness, but also from violent conflict in Calcutta between Muslim and Hindu Indians.

DESCRIPTION

Allport emphasized the uniqueness of each person's traits as they develop ways of adjusting to the world, and he suggested that some people have such clear and cohesive styles of personality (cardinal traits) that their name conjures up a clear image of their personality. Surely that is so for Mother Teresa, world renowned for her life of charitable service toward the poor.

Allport's personological trait theory offered a less formal, more holistic version of trait theory than the more empirically focused trait models that followed. He would use the language of everyday life to describe Mother Teresa's traits: saintly, self-sacrificing, dedicated, well organized, and so on. Allport theorized religion can be used for self-serving reasons or it can inspire genuine love for others (and we would include Mother Teresa in this group). Allport envisioned traits within a model of humanistic development and integration of personality, and so he would emphasize the unifying vision of her religious commitment.

Allport's theory describes consistency of personality, because of a person's enduring traits. Throughout Mother Teresa's life we can find evidence of salient traits. Her trait of humility is evidenced in responses to public acclaim. For example, when she was awarded the much-esteemed Nobel Peace Prize in 1979, she traveled to Norway to accept the prize but stated that the recognition was for the poor, not for herself personally. Certainly Mother Teresa was pious in subjugating selfish pleasure for service to others.

ADJUSTMENT

Allport considered a healthy person to have a consistency or unity of personality (in contrast to conflicts among various parts of personality, as described by psychoanalytic theories). He suggests that unification is based on a person's philosophy of life, which for many is a religious philosophy. He suggested additional characteristics of healthy personalities: having interests beyond themselves, interacting with others warmly, emotional security, realistic perceptions, insight, and a sense of humor.

Mother Teresa's selfless concern for others is grounded on a unifying focus defined by her religious commitment and her conviction of the importance of love. In the sick and dying, she saw the presence of the suffering Jesus of her faith, and loving them was her calling. She viewed lack of love and prayer in the family as root causes of larger social problems, including loss of world peace (Spink, 1997, p. 132). Personality, in Allport's theory, provides a person's unique adaptation to the world, so we cannot expect that Mother Teresa's way of life is for everyone, but she has raised the world's awareness of the plight of the "poorest of the poor."

COGNITION

Besides self-concept and a realistic sense of self, already mentioned, Allport's theory includes other cognitive concepts. Social attitudes and values are often analyzed from a cognitive viewpoint. Allport developed a questionnaire to measure values on six scales: Aesthetic, Economic, Political, Religious, Social, and Theoretical.

It is clear that Mother Teresa would have scored high on the Religious scale. Despite her contributions to world social issues, she would likely have scored low on the Political scale; in fact, she avoided politics and is described by her biographer as having been uninformed about apartheid in South Africa (Spink, 1997, p. 214).

CULTURE

A social psychologist as well as personality psychologist, Allport studied some topics of interest to the war effort (World War II), especially rumor transmission, but the best-known social applications of his theory concern racial prejudice. Allport realized that people who proclaim themselves to be religious are sometimes cruel, and so he explored various kinds of religious orientation to see whether he could untangle the "brotherhood and bigotry" that he found intertwined. The result has been an influential analysis of religious orientation and prejudice. He predicted, and found, that people are less racially prejudiced if their religion is one in which they have accepted the religious teachings to give selflessly to others ("intrinsic religious orientation"). In contrast, people who see religion as a utilitarian means to improve their condition ("extrinsic religious orientation") are often racially prejudiced. Thus intrinsic religious orientation predicts love for one's neighbor (although, as the chapter points out, there are exceptions).

Mother Teresa's orientation is clearly the more favorable intrinsic religious orientation. Sometimes missionaries can be disrespectful of others' traditions, and because of that, there were some angry protests against the first arrival of her nuns in India. However, despite her own firm commitment to Roman Catholicism, Mother Teresa tolerated the religious views of others, providing for their own religious practices to also be included in celebrations at her charitable institutions (Spink, 1997, p. 123).

BIOLOGY

Allport taught that personality traits are physical as well as psychological, but at the time of his theorizing, he could not be more precise than that. He did suggest that an infant's first sense of self begins with the sense of the physical body, but soon cognitive and social issues rise into focus.

Mother Teresa obviously tended to the physical needs of the very poor, feeding them and caring for their wounded bodies. Most important from her point of view, though, was the love.

FINAL THOUGHTS

Allport envisioned a theory of personality that was comprehensive in scope, from the physiological to the social and even religious. In his time, he could not fill in all the details, including the physical aspect of traits. His ideas about religious orientation and prejudice, though, have inspired researchers to the present day, and we see that they help us understand Mother Teresa, who met the world as a place to act lovingly on her religious convictions, and not as a place to find converts or to punish evil others.

PREVIEW: OVERVIEW OF ALLPORT'S THEORY

Allport's theory has implications for major theoretical questions, as presented in Table 7.1. He contributed to theoretical discussions of traits and the self, and he stimulated empirical research on the relationship of religious orientation to behavior. He applied personality to social behavior and social problems, including prejudice, rumor transmission, and intergroup relations.

As an early personality theorist in an academic (as opposed to clinical) setting, Gordon Allport taught the first personality course in the United States and wrote a text for it. He was influential in establishing the field of personality as separate from clinical and social psychology (Barenbaum, 2000). In the preface to his 1937 text, *Personality*, he wrote that the study of personality was then a new and increasingly popular area in colleges. "The result of this rising tide of interest is an insistent demand for a guide book that will *define* the new field of study—one that will articulate its objectives, formulate its standards, and test the progress made thus far" (Allport, 1937b, p. vii).

Allport's theory is called *personological*, a term that emphasizes the development of a *person*, a unified and conscious whole (cf. Barresi, 1999). This theme is important for the humanistic movement in psychology (considered later in this book). In fact, Allport was one of the early founders of a formal humanistic organization in psychology. Roy DeCarvalho (1991a) reports that Allport was the first to use the term *humanistic psychology*, and his emphasis on the whole person, the self, has continued in the humanistic movement (Maddi & Costa, 1972), although his own theoretical focus could more accurately be portrayed as eclectic (Nicholson, 1997).

Allport's eclectic approach included contributions from various schools of psychology. Although he taught both psychoanalysis and learning theory, he viewed these approaches as limited. Psychoanalysis overemphasized the unconscious and did not pay enough attention to conscious motivation, whereas learning theory missed uniquely human qualities that cannot be understood through an animal model.

Allport conducted research as well as proposing theoretical ideas, and he hoped science would enhance psychology's contributions to human welfare. Nonetheless, Allport warned that it was a mistake for methodology to overshadow the content of a field, though he foresaw its increasing importance. In its early years, he said, personality was better served by paying attention to common sense and to philosophy and the liberal arts. To some, Allport's ideas are obsolete, but others defend the continuing value of his insights (e.g., Funder, 1991).

Table 7.1 Preview of Allport's Theory	
Individual Differences	Individuals differ in the traits that predominate in their personalities. Some traits are common (shared by various people); others are unique (belonging only to one person).
Adaptation and Adjustment	Psychology errs if it looks too much for illness. Allport listed several characteristics of a healthy personality.
Cognitive Processes	People's self-statements can generally be taken at face value.
Culture	Adaptation to society is of central importance. Allport made important contributions to our understanding of prejudice, rumor, and religion.
Biological Influences	All behavior is influenced, in some part, by heredity, but the mechanisms are not specified.
Development	The proprium (ego or self) develops through stages that are outlined but not researched in detail. Adult development consists of integrating earlier developments.

Biography of Gordon Allport

Gordon Allport was born in 1897 in Montezuma, Indiana, the fourth son of a sales-man who was changing careers to become a country doctor. The family moved several times, finally settling in Cleveland, Ohio, where Allport grew up in a hardworking, Protestant environment. His mother, a former schoolteacher, encouraged the educational and religious interests of her sons and hoped that Gordon would become a missionary (Nicholson, 1998). Allport remained, in adulthood, a devout Episcopalian (Pettigrew, 1999).

Gordon Allport

Allport followed an older brother, Floyd, to Harvard University, where he studied psychology and social ethics. After graduation at the age of 22, Allport stopped in Vienna to visit a brother, and he requested a meeting with Sigmund Freud, motivated by "rude curiosity and youthful ambition" (Allport, 1967, p. 8). In his naiveté, he had not prepared an introductory statement to Freud explaining the reason for the meeting. Freud sat in silence, probably expecting that this was a therapeutic consultation. As Allport tells it,

> I was not prepared for silence and had to think fast to find a suitable conversational gambit. I told him of an episode on the tram car on my way to his office. A small boy about four years of age had displayed a conspicuous dirt phobia. He kept saying to his mother, "I don't want to sit there…don't let that dirty man sit beside me." To him everything was schmutz. His mother was a well-starched Hausfrau, so dominant and purposive looking that I thought the cause and effect apparent.
>
> When I finished my story Freud fixed his kindly therapeutic eyes upon me and said, "And was that little boy you?" Flabbergasted and feeling a bit guilty, I contrived to change the subject…. Freud's misunderstanding of my motivation was amusing…. This experience taught me that depth psychology…may plunge too deep, and that psychologists would do well to give full recognition to manifest motives before probing the unconscious. (p. 8)

Freud's clinical intuition suggested that Allport felt "dirty." Allport argued later that this was not a therapeutic meeting, and that the incident should be interpreted at the manifest (conscious) level of his experience, which was simply a desire to impress Freud with his powers of observation. This theme, that psychology should pay more attention to conscious self-reports, became a major element of his theory.

Allport's graduate work continued at Harvard. His dissertation investigated personality traits, a new topic at the time, criticized by more traditional, experimentally minded psychologists. His first publication on personality traits was jointly authored with his brother Floyd (Allport & Allport, 1921). Gordon received his doctorate at the age of 24 and did postdoctoral study in Europe, learning about Gestalt psychology and the German doctrine of types, themes reflected in his later consideration of holism and his development of a type inventory.

Allport taught at Harvard for most of his professional life, and was respected for his helpfulness to colleagues (Winter, 1996). He developed what he reported was probably the first personality course taught in the United States, emphasizing connections with social psychology. He rose to prominence in national circles, edited the major journal in personality and social psychology, and served as president of the American Psychological Association and of the Society for the Psychological Study of Social Issues (SPSSI). The latter organization commemorates Allport's memory by awarding an annual prize for a paper on intergroup relations. Allport was one of several U.S. psychologists who assisted intellectuals in Europe to find work in the United States so they could flee Nazi Germany. Another contribution at the time of the war was his effort to help control wartime rumors, reflected in his daily newspaper column and a later book on rumors (Allport & Postman, 1947). Gordon Allport died of lung cancer on October 9, 1967, at age 69.

MAJOR THEMES IN ALLPORT'S WORK

Allport had a major influence on the developing academic field of personality. Here are some issues identified by Allport, which personality theorists have grappled with ever since.

Personality Consistency

The concept of personality consistency across time and across situations is central to the field of personality. Allport (1937b) argued strongly that from infancy on, humans are consistent, even though they vary from situation to situation and across time.

Social Influence

Allport studied many social issues. He wrote a book on prejudice that has become a classic text (Allport, 1954), and he studied rumor transmission (Allport & Postman, 1947). At a time when mass communication was quaint by modern standards, he and his former student Hadley Cantril wrote a book called *The Psychology of Radio* (Cantril & Allport, 1935; Pandora, 1998).

The Concept of Self

In an age when many other psychological approaches were reductionistic, Allport argued for the notion of self as a major focus of personality growth. The self is now a major theoretical concept in personality and social psychology, in areas as diverse as humanistic clinical psychology and cognitive social psychology.

Interaction of Personality with Social Influence

It is no surprise that a psychologist who was both a personality psychologist and a social psychologist would not think of personality and situations as either-or causes but would rather consider how they work together as joint influences. Situations influence people, but they influence individuals in different ways, as the interactionist approach to personality recognizes (Endler & Magnusson, 1976). In Allport's (1937b) words, "The same heat that melts the butter hardens the egg" (pp. 102, 325). He did not, however, develop the notion of the interaction between personality and environment beyond this brief sketch, acknowledging that in his focus on personality traits, he had "neglect[ed] the variability induced by ecological, social, and situational factors" (Allport, 1966b, p. 9). He recognized that further theoretical advances were needed to develop this concept of interactionism (Zuroff, 1986).

In summary, Allport anticipated many of the themes that would concern personality psychology in the decades since his classic personality text was first published. Current approaches are more sophisticated in their analysis of empirical data, certainly. Nonetheless, the themes of consistency, social influence, the self, and the interaction of personality with the environment have remained important foci.

ALLPORT'S DEFINITION OF PERSONALITY

After a review of 49 other definitions of personality in psychology, theology, philosophy, law, sociology, and common usage, Allport (1937b) proposed what has become a classic definition of **personality**: "Personality is the dynamic organization within the individual of those psychophysical systems that determine his unique adjustments to the environments" (p. 48; emphasis in original). Allport's explanation of the five major concepts in his definition of personality provides a broad outline of his theory.

personality

for Gordon Allport, "the dynamic organization within the individual of those psychophysical systems that determine his unique adjustments to the environment"

Dynamic Organization

Allport (1937b) referred to "the dynamic organization" of the healthy personality in order "to stress active organization" (p. 48). Dynamic organization evolves as a developmental process, and a failure of integration is a mark of psychopathology.

This theme of organization, or unity, is not shared by all theories. Traditional learning theories deal, instead, with discrete behavioral units, or stimulus–response associations. Psychoanalysis tends to fragment people into conflicting parts, which Allport attributed to studying clinical populations whose symptoms are not integrated with the rest of their personality. In contrast, healthy personality becomes an organized and self-regulating whole.

Psychophysical Systems

Personality is subject to biological as well as psychological influences. **Temperament** refers to biologically based differences in personality, often evidenced as emotional reactivity to new or potentially frightening stimuli. Allport (1937b) listed inherited physique and intelligence, together with temperament, as "the three principal raw materials of personality" (p. 107), and he recognized the need for genetic research to expand understanding of personality (Evans, 1981).

temperament
innate emotional aspects of personality

Regarding the classic nature–nurture issue, Allport illustrated that both are involved in every aspect of personality by a mathematical equation:

$$\text{Personality} = (\text{Heredity}) \times (\text{Environment})$$

"The two causal factors are not added together, but are interrelated as multiplier and multiplicand. If either were zero there could be no personality" (Allport, 1937b, p. 106).

Determinative

For some theorists, personality concepts are useful predictors that summarize behavior but are not themselves real causes. Allport disagreed, using the word *determine* to emphasize that personality is a cause of behavior. Allport (1937b) said that this term "is a natural consequence of the biophysical view. Personality is something and does something" (p. 48). Traits are real in a physical sense.

Allport's critics, noting that traits can't be observed independently of behavior, argued that using personality traits to explain behavior is a meaningless circular argument. For example, you see a man talking to a lot of people, so you infer that he is outgoing. Then, asked why he talks to a lot of people, you say it is because he is outgoing. If the same behavior that prompts inference of the trait is theorized to result from it, the trait cannot fail. Without the possibility of disconfirmation, a theoretical construct is not useful. Allport was not ignorant of the potential problem of circular reasoning. He discussed this issue in relationship to the question of whether the concept of a self is necessary in psychology (Allport, 1955, pp. 54–55), but he did not think that the circular reasoning argument invalidated the usefulness of personality concepts.

Unique

For Allport, traits are highly individualized, or unique. He explicitly disagreed with theorists who asserted that one or a few motives, or instincts, are determinative for all people (as, e.g., Freud attributed personality to sexual motivation). Rather, people are motivated by diverse traits reflecting the differences in their learning.

Adjustments to the Environment

Allport (1937b) emphasized the adaptive, coping functions of personality. He was far more interested in these, which would be called ego functions by psychoanalysts, than in the internal conflicts preventing adaptation that occur in the mentally unhealthy.

These adaptations are unique to each individual because of differences in heredity and environment.

PERSONALITY TRAITS

According to Allport (1931, 1937b), the primary unit of personality is the trait. Listing a person's traits provides a description of that person's personality.

Allport's Definition of Trait

trait

a characteristic of a person that makes a person unique, with a unique style of adapting to stimuli in the world

Allport (1937b) defined a **trait** as "a generalized and focalized neuropsychic system (peculiar to the individual), with the capacity to render many stimuli functionally equivalent, and to initiate and guide consistent (equivalent) forms of adaptive and expressive behavior" (p. 295).

In this definition, he reiterated themes from his definition of personality: the psychophysical emphasis, the uniqueness of the individual, the focus on adaptation, and the concept of the trait as a determinative entity. Traits develop over time. They may change as the individual learns new ways of adapting to the world (p. 146). They are, however, relatively stable, in contrast to *states*, which change quickly—for example, a moment of anger (state) on being cut off in traffic, in contrast with a chronic trait of hostility (cf. Chaplin, John, & Goldberg, 1988).

Can We All Be Described by the Same Traits?

individual trait

a trait that characterizes only the one person who has it (i.e., a trait considered from the idiographic point of view)

common trait

a trait characterizing many people (i.e., a trait considered from the nomothetic point of view)

Does everyone have different traits? Or can we all be described by the same list of traits, only in different amounts? Most researchers base their work on the second alternative, but Allport did not rule out either possibility. Based on the work of the German philosophers Windelband and Stem (Hermans, 1988), Allport distinguished **individual traits**, also called unique traits, which are possessed by only one person, from **common traits**, which are possessed by many people, each to a varying extent. He intended to distinguish "the study of *persons* on the one hand and the study of *person variables*, that is, variables with respect to which persons have been differentiated, on the other" (Lamiell, 1997, p. 123). The distinction may appear simple at first, but its implications are enormous.

In everyday speech, we often describe people by using common traits, comparing how much of a trait each person has. For example, we may describe Walt Disney as more creative than others or Albert Einstein as more intelligent than the rest of us. The trait dimensions of creativity and intelligence, and many others, too, can be applied to all of us in common, and we can measure how much of each trait a person has.

unique trait

a trait that only one person has (also called individual trait)

However, in Allport's theory, the real units of personality are **unique traits** (individual traits), which exist within an individual and are psychophysical realities. Traits are adaptive entities, unique to each person. Allport (1937b) argued, "Strictly speaking, no two persons ever have precisely the same trait" (p. 297). According to his argument, it is not possible to describe fully differences between people by simply scoring them on a set of universally applied traits. To understand an individual fully, it would be necessary to have a list of traits specifically chosen for that person. Only an idiographic approach (unique traits) can adequately describe an individual, although Allport accepted nomothetic research (common traits) as a rough approximation for research purposes (Allport, 1940).

A reviewer of his 1937 book complained that Allport's explanation of individual traits was not clear and that the examples he used were simply extreme scores on common traits (Paterson, 1999). It may be impossible to be genuinely idiographic because implicit comparisons with others are always made.

Understanding individuals' behavior and functioning is a primary task of personality theory (Lamiell, 1997; Runyan, 1983), and this requires studying individuals, not only groups. Allport emphasized the need to individualize trait conceptions. In one study (Conrad, 1932), which Allport described, teachers rated students on various traits. Reliability of these ratings was not particularly high overall. However, if teachers indicated with a star which traits particularly described the child, those starred ratings had a much higher agreement (Allport, 1937b, p. 301). Thus the same set of traits is not useful for describing every person, but the central traits of an individual can be rated reliably. Other researchers since Allport have essentially replicated this finding (Cheek, 1982; Markus, 1977), and Baumeister and Tice (1988; Baumeister, 1991) offer a statistical approach for dealing with unique traits when researchers collect nomothetic data, as they usually do.

Inferring Traits

How do we know what traits a person possesses? Allport suggested several methods, beginning, sensibly enough, with the wisdom of everyday language.

INFERRING TRAITS FROM LANGUAGE: THE DICTIONARY STUDY   Gordon Allport and Henry Odbert (1936) conducted a study in which they listed all of the trait words in the 1925 edition of *Webster's New International Dictionary* used to describe individuals. Excluding obsolete terms, they identified 17,953 trait names, which was 4.5 percent of the total words in the dictionary. They classified these trait names into four categories:

1. Neutral Terms Designating Personal Traits (e.g., "artistic," "assertive")
2. Terms Primarily Descriptive of Temporary Moods or Activities (e.g., "alarmed," "ashamed")
3. Weighted Terms Conveying Social or Characterical Judgments of Personal Conduct, or Designating Influence on Others (e.g., "adorable," "asinine")
4. Miscellaneous: Designations of Physique, Capacities, and Developmental Conditions; Metaphorical and Doubtful Terms (e.g., "alone," "Anglican")

They suggested that the first, purely descriptive, category would be most useful to personality psychologists as a compilation of nonevaluative terms for enduring traits. Researchers have developed this method further, as we shall see in Chapter 8.

INFERRING TRAITS FROM BEHAVIOR   Traits may also be inferred from behavior. People who talk a lot are judged to be outgoing; people who exercise regularly are called athletic. Behavioral inferences can be made in natural circumstances. For example, children can be observed in their everyday lives, using a time-sampling procedure (Allport, 1937b, pp. 315–316). Or observations can be made in an experimental setting if subjects are given a diverse set of tasks.

Allport and Vernon (1933) studied **expressive traits**, which are concerned with one's style of behavior—for example, how fast or slow, energetic, or graceful an action is. They found that 25 male subjects had consistent expressive traits, such as expansiveness or emphasis, that affected a variety of measures, including handwriting, walking, tapping, and reading. Few researchers have continued such research. One source of embarrassment is that Allport and Vernon provided personality sketches of people based on handwriting (graphology), which many in academic psychology banish to the realm of pseudoscience. A review of research finds that although handwriting analysis is popular in lay circles and even widely used as a part of personnel selection in European companies, it has not stood up to scientific tests of validity (Greasley, 2000).

expressive traits

traits concerned with the style or tempo of a person's behavior

Other expressive traits may have more value, for example, as predictors of coronary heart disease. Specifically, the expressive style with which interviewees respond to the structured interview, used to assess type A behavior (a coronary risk factor), is more important than the content of responses in predicting heart disease (Friedman & Booth-Kewley, 1987).

INFERRING TRAITS FROM DOCUMENTS: LETTERS FROM JENNY   We can infer traits from documents or records of people's lives, including diaries, letters, and public statements that are not produced specifically for research purposes. Allport devised guidelines for analyzing such documents and in collaboration with his wife, Ada, conducted such analyses himself, the best known of which is the case of Jenny (Barenbaum,

1997). Allport and his wife had received 301 letters from Jenny Grove Masterson, who was the mother of his college roommate. She had turned to Gordon as a "good son," in contrast to her own disappointing child (Winter, 1997). The letters covered a period of 11 years, beginning in 1926, until her death at the age of 70. They disclose a sad tale of a woman who found life difficult, worried about money, and complained frequently about her son's neglect. Allport and his students interpreted these letters from assorted theoretical perspectives, including various psychoanalytic approaches (Freudian, Jungian, Adlerian, and ego approaches) and learning theory.

Allport's own approach, which he called *structural-dynamic*, was in essence a content analysis of the letters. Allport and his research assistants and students read Jenny's letters and listed adjectives describing the personality traits they inferred from them. Combining analyses by 36 raters, Allport (1965, pp. 193–194) concluded that Jenny's personality could be summarized by eight traits: quarrelsome-suspicious, self-centered, independent-autonomous, dramatic-intense, aesthetic-artistic, aggressive, cynical-morbid, and sentimental.

One of Allport's students, Jeffrey Paige (1966), used a computer procedure called the General Inquirer to analyze Jenny's letters more quickly. Allport noted that his results were remarkably similar to the categories he had earlier derived "from common-sense interpretation" (p. 201).

Aided by computers, researchers can code material more quickly and reliably than by hand (Rosenberg, Schnurr, & Oxman, 1990), but even with computers, content analysis requires much more time than objective self-report questionnaires. Content analysis is a valuable method that permits analysis of existing materials from people such as political leaders, who would be unlikely to agree to fill out research questionnaires (e.g., D. G. Winter, 1993; Winter & Carlson, 1988; Winter et al., 1991a, 1991b), or historical figures long dead, who could not do so (e.g., Broehl & McGee, 1981; Craik, 1988).

INFERRING FROM PERSONALITY MEASUREMENT: THE STUDY OF VALUES   We can also measure traits by personality tests. Allport (1937b, pp. 227–228) said among the most important characteristics that distinguish people from one another are their values— that is, those things toward which they strive. With colleagues, he developed a scale to measure values, named (in its revised form) the Allport-Vernon-Lindzey Study of Values (Allport & Vernon, 1931; Allport, Vernon, & Lindzey, 1951) (see Table 7.2).

This self-report instrument consists of 60 questions. Scores are compared with normative data to determine which values are relatively high for an individual. Allport (1966b) reported that college students who entered different occupations had different value scores. For example, those who entered business scored higher on economic values. Later research confirms that scores on the Study of Values taken during college were associated with occupations of male students 25 years later (Huntley & Davis, 1983).

Despite considerable stability, values can change over time. Baird (1990) reported a 20-year longitudinal study indicating that Religious scale scores declined during the

Table 7.2 The Allport-Vernon-Lindzey Study of Values

Scale	Description of Value	Typical Occupation
Social	Helping people	Social work
Theoretical	Search for truth	College professor
Economic	Pragmatic, applied	Business
Aesthetic	Artistic values	Artist
Political	Power and influence	Politics
Religious	Religion, harmony	Clergy

4 years of college. In another study, talented 13-year-old students took the Study of Values at that early age and again at age 33. As these youth matured, they rated Aesthetic and Economic values more highly and decreased the relative emphasis on Political and Social values (Lubinski, Schmidt, & Benbow, 1996). Studies such as these demonstrate both stability and change in values.

ALLPORT'S ATTITUDE TOWARD METHODOLOGY   Allport raised serious concerns about methodology in trait measurement. Should psychology be based on methodologically rigorous experimental-positivistic philosophy or on humanistic experiential-phenomenological philosophy (DeCarvalho, 1990a)? Allport favored the latter. Animal research cannot, he argued (Allport, 1940), give complete understanding of human psychology. He distrusted complicated statistical procedures, such as factor analysis. He praised content analysis, such as he used to analyze Jenny's letters, because it kept researchers close to the data. He preferred to ask people rather directly about their traits and to take responses at face value. He expressed dismay at the decline in reporting individual case histories (Allport, 1940). Although acknowledging there is a place for methodological concerns within psychology, he argued, along with other humanistic psychologists such as Abraham Maslow, that psychology should be not method centered but problem centered.

The Pervasiveness of Traits: Cardinal, Central, and Secondary Traits

Some traits have a bigger impact than others. Allport categorized traits as cardinal, central, or secondary, depending on how extensively they influence personality. The most pervasive are cardinal traits; the least pervasive are secondary traits. The usual terms we use to describe someone are at the intermediate level: central traits.

CENTRAL TRAITS   A **central trait** affects many behaviors. Allport's analysis of Jenny's letters led to the inference that she had eight central traits, as we have seen. Someone who knows you well could summarize your personality in a small number of central traits, perhaps six to ten adjectives.

central trait
one of the half dozen or so traits that best describe a particular person

    Secondary traits describe ways in which a person is consistent but do not affect so much of what that person does as a central trait. Most tastes and personal preferences can be considered secondary traits: "John likes spinach"; "Sarah's favorite color is mauve." Of course, for some people a personal preference may be a central trait; consider Popeye's preference for spinach. In his case, the trait is not secondary; it is at least central or perhaps even a cardinal trait.

secondary trait
a trait that influences a limited range of behaviors

    A **cardinal trait** is so pervasive that it dominates just about everything a person does. Most people do not have such a highly pervasive single trait. When they do, the trait often makes its possessor famous, a prototype for a disposition that others may resemble to a lesser extent. Allport provided examples of traits so pervasive that they dominated all of their original possessors' behavior. Each of the following adjectives used to describe people originated as a cardinal trait in one person: *Calvinistic, chauvinistic, Christlike, Dionysian, Faustian, lesbian, Machiavellian, puckish, quixotic,* and *sadistic* (1937b, pp. 302–303). Very few people have a cardinal trait.

cardinal trait
a pervasive personality trait that dominates nearly everything a person does

Levels of Integration of Personality

Cardinal, central, and secondary traits are not three discrete types; they are markers on a continuum of pervasiveness (Allport, 1937b, p. 338). The continuum extends downward, to much less pervasive influences and upward to higher-order levels of integration (see Figure 7.1). At the lowest level of integration are simple conditioned reflexes. These become associated over time to form habits. A higher level of integration is the notion of self or, as sociologists sometimes refer to it, a subidentity—for example, one's sense of oneself as a sister, or as a professional. The fact that we can have multiple selves suggests that integration can occur on some higher level. At least some people have an even higher level of integration, "a thoroughly unified system of personality at the top of the pyramid" (p. 142) such as a unifying philosophy of life.

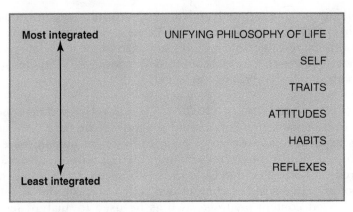

FIGURE 7.1   Levels of Integration in Personality

PERSONALITY DEVELOPMENT

In his description of personality development, Allport emphasized the later, more developed, stages.

Functional Autonomy

functional autonomy

a trait's independence of its developmental origins

Allport encouraged us to view the traits of an adult without being overly concerned with their developmental origins, whether those origins are adaptive strategies to satisfy needs, or identification with parents. In the adult, motivation becomes fully *contemporaneous* (Allport, 1937a) and its childhood origins are no longer relevant. This contrasts with the psychoanalytic approach that continues to describe a highly gullible adult, for example, as orally fixated. With maturity, earlier motives are transformed and the individual becomes more purposive, less pushed from the past (Allport, 1950b).

   In reaction to this preoccupation with the past, Allport (1937a, 1950b) proposed an alternative theoretical concept: **functional autonomy** of motivation. At some point, a motive or trait begins to function independently of its origins. For example, consider a woman who as a child really wanted to be like her mother and admired her. Allport argued that for the healthy adult, the motivation is no longer to "be like mother." The particular interests and values that began with maternal identification have been internalized. They are, Allport would say, "functionally autonomous" from their origins. Allport (1937b, p. 196) cited workmanship as another example of a trait that becomes functionally autonomous of its origins. Although one learns to do a job well because it brings praise or security, later the work itself is satisfying. Similarly, hobbies and artistic or intellectual interests show functional autonomy (p. 207).

   Allport (1955) criticized psychology for its preoccupation with the past. "People, it seems, are busy leading their lives into the future, whereas psychology, for the most part, is busy tracing them into the past" (p. 51).

Qualities of a Normal, Mature Adult

Allport (1937b, 1961) listed several characteristics of a mature (i.e., healthy) personality.

EXTENSION OF THE SENSE OF SELF   The developed person "has a variety of autonomous interests: that is, he can lose himself in work, in contemplation, in recreation, and in loyalty to others" (Allport, 1937b, p. 213). In explaining this capacity of a healthy adult for self-extension, Allport remarked that "the sign of cultivation in a man is his ability to talk for half a day without betraying [revealing] his occupation" (p. 218). Such an individual is not egocentric but rather is involved in goals that are "extensions of the self."

WARM HUMAN INTERACTION   The healthy person has a capacity for warm human interaction. Social interactions are sincere and friendly rather than prescribed by rigid roles and expectations.

EMOTIONAL SECURITY (SELF-ACCEPTANCE)   Healthy individuals are emotionally secure and accept themselves, having high self-esteem.

REALISTIC PERCEPTION, SKILLS, AND ASSIGNMENTS   The healthy person realistically perceives the world. Both unrealistic optimism, such as the conviction that this lottery ticket is going to be a winner, and unrealistic pessimism, such as the expectation of failing at everything, are avoided.

SELF-OBJECTIFICATION: INSIGHT AND HUMOR   Mature individuals are capable of self-objectification, seeing themselves accurately and insightfully, often with a sense of humor.

UNIFYING PHILOSOPHY OF LIFE   Finally, the mature person has a **unifying philosophy of life** (Allport, 1937b, p. 214). For many people this is a religious philosophy of life, but it need not be.

> ***unifying philosophy of life***
> *an attitude or set of values, often religious, that gives coherence and meaning to life*

Ravenna Helson and Paul Wink (1987) used Allport's criteria as a theoretical framework to examine maturity in a longitudinal study of women ages 21 to 43. Most of Allport's criteria were correlated significantly with two measures of maturity, one stressing adaptation to society (competence) and the other stressing intrapsychic development (ego level). However, some discrepancies suggest that Allport's criteria do not take into account the distress that may result from conflict between individual development and the demands of society.

Unity of Personality

Kenneth Craik (1988) credits Allport with envisioning personality "as that branch of psychology that takes the person as the unit of analysis, rather than selected processes (such as cognition, perception, learning, or interpersonal relations, etc.), and attempts to pull together the scientific achievements of these other branches of psychology, plus those from the biological and social sciences, to understand individuals and their fates" (pp. 196–197). In referring to the unity of personality, Allport used the Latin phrase ***unitas multiplex***, the "unity of multiples." He (1955) suggested a theoretical concept, the **proprium**, which "includes all aspects of the personality that make for unity" (p. 40). The proprium serves the functions that other theorists describe as belonging to the ego or the self. It is the striving part of our being that gives us our intentionality and direction.

> ***unitas multiplex***
> *the Latin phrase indicating that a person makes a unified whole out of many diverse aspects of personality*
>
> ***proprium***
> *all aspects of a person that make for unity; a person's sense of self or ego*

To some extent, of course, all of us are different in different social roles—as friend, student, worker, and so on—but we also develop consistency across these various roles (Roberts & Donahue, 1994). For Allport, to be healthy we must forge unity from within, because it is not guaranteed from society or from one's personal history. Integration occurs through the formation of "master-sentiments" (Allport, 1937b, p. 191). These may be religious or nonreligious philosophies of life that constitute a person's core consistency. Allport offered the example of Leo Tolstoy, who approached everything from his master-sentiment, the simplification of life (pp. 190–191).

For many people, such unification of personality is fostered by religious practice, which contributes to higher subjective well-being (Diener et al., 1999). People experience an unpleasant crisis of values when unification is threatened, but it can provide the opportunity for personal growth (Hermans & Oles, 1996). Research supports Allport's claim that integrated personalities are better adjusted and more effective (Behrends, 1986; Donahue et al., 1993), but he has been criticized for not recognizing that cultural messages make it difficult for minorities to achieve unity (Gaines & Reed, 1995), for ambiguity about how this unification is achieved, and for not realizing that some unifying goals are not mature or healthy (Marsh & Colangelo, 1983; Ryan, Rigby, & King, 1993).

Stages of Development

The proprium or self develops gradually through a lifetime. According to Allport (1937b), "The newborn infant *lacks* personality, for he has not yet encountered the world in which he must live, and has not developed the distinctive modes of adjustment and mastery that will later comprise his personality. He is almost altogether a creature of heredity" (p. 107), that is, temperament. On this inherited basis, personality develops through interaction with the environment.

Allport (1937b) suggested a list of stages of development, emphasizing the development of the self, but he warned that stages are somewhat arbitrary. "For the single person there is only *one* consecutive, uninterrupted course of life" (p. 131).

1. *Bodily Sense.* The proprium begins developing in infancy with the sense of the bodily self. An infant discovers, for example, that putting his or her own hand in the mouth feels quite different from mouthing a toy. This experience contributes to the development of a sense of "the bodily me."
2. *Self-Identity.* In the second year of life, the child develops a sense of *self-identity*, a sense of his or her existence as a separate person. Children begin to recognize themselves by name.
3. *Ego-Enhancement.* From age 2 to 3, the child begins working on self-esteem. The capacity for pride through achievement starts to develop, as well as the capacity for humiliation and selfishness.
4. *Ego-Extension.* Next, perhaps beginning as early as age 3 to 4, the child begins to identify with his or her **ego-extensions**, such as personal possessions: "That is my toy." Of course, this process continues into adulthood, especially in a consumer-oriented culture such as ours. Besides possessions, the maturing individual identifies with "loved objects, and later…[with] ideal causes and loyalties" (Allport, 1955, p. 45).
5. *Self-Image.* The self-image includes both evaluation of our present "abilities, status, and roles" and our aspirations for the future (Allport, 1955, p. 47). Children between the ages 4 and 6, Allport suggested, begin to become capable of formulating future goals and are aware of being good and bad.
6. *Rational Agent.* During the middle childhood years (age 6 to 12) the child may be thought of as a **rational coper**. The child is busy solving problems and planning ways of doing things. Allport contrasted his attention to the adaptive functions of the ego with Freud's emphasis on ego defenses.
7. *Propriate Striving.* **Propriate striving**, which begins in adolescence, is "ego-involved" motivation that has "directedness or intentionality," to use Allport's phrasing. At this time, some defining object becomes the "cement" holding a life together, as the person becomes capable of genuine ideology and career planning.
8. *The Knower.* The **self as knower** develops as the adult cognitively integrates the previous aspects of the self into a unified whole. Many other theorists have also referred to a self that integrates personality, including Cattell (see Chapter 8) Carl Rogers (see Chapter 14), Abraham Maslow (see Chapter 15), and others not presented in this book (e.g., Frick, 1993; Tloczynski, 1993).

Although Allport sketched out a description of personality development, he believed that psychology is very far from being able to predict outcomes. Ultimately, Allport (1940) asserted that a science of psychology ought to be able to predict individual outcomes more precisely and not settle for probabilities based on studies of groups.

RELIGIOUS ORIENTATION

Allport (1950a) criticized psychologists for ignoring the role of religion in personality. His theoretical contributions in this area continue to stimulate research. Allport distinguished two types of religious orientation, which he called intrinsic and extrinsic. People with an **extrinsic religious orientation** used religion for a selfish purpose— for example, raising their status in the community (Allport & Ross, 1967). They were likely to agree, on a Religious Orientation Survey, with such self-report statements as this: "One reason for my being a church member is that such membership helps to establish a person in the community."

ego-extensions

objects or people that help define a person's identity or sense of self

rational coper

a stage in middle childhood in which problem-solving ability is important to one's sense of self

propriate striving

effort based on a sense of selfhood or identity

self as knower

a stage in adulthood in which a person integrates the self into a unified whole

extrinsic religious orientation

attitude in which religion is seen as a means to a person's other goals (such as status or security)

Table 7.3 Concepts Associated with Intrinsic and Extrinsic Religiousness in Allport's Writings

Intrinsic	Extrinsic
Relates to all of life (a, b, c, d, f, g, h, j)	Compartmentalized (a, c, d, h)
Unprejudiced; tolerant (a, b, c, h, i)	Prejudiced; exclusionary (a, b, c, d, e, h)
Mature (a, d)	Immature; dependent; comfort; security (a, b, d, f, g, h, i, j)
Integrative; unifying; meaning endowed (a, c, d, f, g, h, i)	Instrumental; utilitarian; self-serving (a, c, d, e, f, g, h, i, j)
Regular church attendance (e, g, h)	Irregular church attendance (c, g, h, i)
Makes for mental health (f, g)	Defense or escape mechanism (d, f, g)

Note: Letters in parentheses refer to the following references: (a) Allport (1950a), (b) Allport (1954), (c) Allport (1959), (d) Allport (1961), (e) Allport (1962), (f) Allport (1963), (g) Allport (1964), (h) Allport (1966a), (*i*) Allport (1966b), (j) Allport & Ross (1967).

Source: From M. J. Donahue (1985). Intrinsic and extrinsic religiousness: Review and meta-analysis. *Journal of Personality and Social Psychology, 48*, 400–419. Copyright 1985 by the American Psychological Association. Adapted by permission.

Others held an **intrinsic religious orientation**, having presumably incorporated the religious values of loving others into their own belief system. Such people agree with self-report statements such as this: "My religious beliefs are what really lie behind my whole approach to life" (Allport & Ross, 1967) (see Table 7.3). An intrinsic religious orientation can have beneficial effects for an individual. It seems to protect against depression, at least in some studies (Genia, 1993; Park, Cohen, & Herb, 1990; Park & Murgatroyd, 1998).

intrinsic religious orientation
attitude in which religion is accepted for its own sake rather than as a means to an end

Building on Allport's theory, other researchers have distinguished two aspects of extrinsic orientation. One of these is socially oriented—for example, "I go to church because it helps me to make friends," whereas the other is personally oriented—for example, "What religion offers me most is comfort in times of trouble and sorrow" (Gorsuch & McPherson, 1989).

Since Allport, theorists have proposed additional dimensions of religious orientation. One that is much studied is **Quest Orientation**, describing people who are searching for answers to existential-religious questions, and who question the contradictions and tragedies of life, facing existential issues personally (Batson, 1976; Batson & Schoenrade, 1991a, 1991b; Batson, Schoenrade, & Ventis, 1993). A person with a high quest orientation is disinclined to depend on God to deal with the tragedy of a drive-by shooting of an infant who was held in the arms of her praying grandmother (Burris et al., 1996). For such a person, active questioning is part of religion's meaning. Another religious dimension is *immanence*, which involves "motivation to transcend boundaries [such as the boundaries among various religious groups], awareness and acceptance of experience, and emphasis on the present moment" (Burris & Tarpley, 1998, p. 55). Religious immanence is positively associated with other religious orientations that eschew traditional orthodoxy: extrinsic religious orientation and religion as a quest (Burris et al., 1996; Burris & Tarpley, 1998). Another area for expanded investigation would be to study *spirituality*, which is less focused on institutions, and more concerned with subjective experience, than religiousness (Saucier & Skrzypińska, 2006).

quest orientation
religious orientation that seeks answers to existential-religious questions

We may also ask whether the theoretical concepts about religious orientation that have been developed in largely Christian, Western samples are valid in other cultures. There is some evidence for cross-cultural validity, though more research remains to be done. Cross-cultural examination of questionnaires generally involves examination of the factor structure of instruments to see whether items intercorrelate similarly in other cultures. In addition, researchers look to see whether the measures predict outcomes similarly in the various cultures, providing evidence of similar criterion validity. Results are mixed.

Several studies investigate Islam, and while research with Muslim samples shows some similarities to that reported with Christian samples, there are enough differences to suggest studying various religious traditions in detail before assuming universals (Khan, Watson, & Habib, 2005). Intrinsic and extrinsic religious orientations, as well as quest orientation and religious orthodoxy, have been measured among Muslim college students, as a preliminary step toward more extensive research (Ji & Ibrahim, 2007). Intrinsic and Extrinsic Orientation, as well as Quest orientation, are useful measures in a sample of Muslim university students in Iran, though with the suggestion that prayer, which was tapped by the Extrinsic Orientation scale, may be particularly important in the Muslim religion (Ghorbani, Watson, & Mirhasani, 2007). Religious orientation measures correlate with interest and reaction to the important *Eid-ul-Azha* holiday that culminates the pilgrimage to Mecca (the Haj) among Pakistani Muslims (Khan & Watson, 2004).

Some researchers suggest that intrinsic religious orientation, which focuses on the individual, is a particularly Protestant phenomenon, and not a cultural universal. The emphasis on individualism is a particularly Protestant viewpoint, linked historically to the Protestant Reformation in the sixteenth century that forged a more direct link between individual believers and their God, with a decreased role of the church as an intermediary. Among major American religions, Protestantism is more individualistic, compared to more collectivist orientations in Catholicism and Judaism (Cohen & Hill, 2007). Furthermore, this assumption of individualism reflects the viewpoint of individualistic cultures and underestimates the importance of socially connected religious orientations in other traditions (Cohen et al., 2005). Contrary to Allport's negative attitude toward an extrinsic religious orientation, critics suggest that in many religions other than Protestantism, extrinsic components of religion are genuine and valuable, and in those traditions intrinsic and extrinsic religious orientations are not necessarily distinct factors. Such extrinsic components include religious community, ritual, and tradition (e.g., Flere & Lavrič, 2008). For some American ethnic groups, including those of Asian and African heritage, acculturation to American society brings an increase in intrinsic religious orientation, further suggesting cultural differences (Ghorpade, Lackritz, & Singh, 2006).

PERSONALITY AND SOCIAL PHENOMENA

Allport viewed humans as social beings, but his focus remained on the individual. Thus his contributions to the understanding of prejudice, religion, and rumor transmission emphasize personality rather than social causation. Personality influences how a person functions within a culture, and simply to focus on the "main effects" of culture without considering these variations is insufficient (Oishi, 2004).

Prejudice

Allport's classic book, *The Nature of Prejudice* (1954), examined such factors as in-group and out-group influences, ego defenses, cognitive processes, the role of language, stereotypes in culture, scapegoating, and learning prejudice in childhood. Allport understood prejudice from the point of view of the individual, instead of from a social historical viewpoint that emphasizes oppression of groups, such as the analysis by W. E. B. DuBois (Gaines & Reed, 1995). His ideas about loyalty to in-groups continue to be discussed by social psychologists (Brewer, 1999). Allport offered practical strategies for reducing prejudice, including equal status contact, common goals, no intergroup competition, and authority sanction, and subsequent research supports this analysis (Pettigrew, 1999). Allport's description of prejudice is a classic that is still applied to understand the persistence of the Israeli–Palestinian conflict (Kelman,

1999), prejudice against the elderly (Schwartz & Simmons, 2001), and the positive influence of models on minority academic achievement (Marx, Brown, & Steele, 1999).

Religion and Prejudice

Allport was particularly interested in how religion relates to racial prejudice. On the one hand, because religion teaches love, it should reduce prejudice. On the other hand, research shows that people who attend church, on the average, are more prejudiced than those who do not attend. How could these contradictory trends be reconciled?

Recognizing that brotherhood and bigotry are intertwined in religion (Allport, 1966a), Allport tried to understand when each would prevail. He expected that people with an extrinsic religious orientation, for whom religion served more selfish purposes, would be more racially prejudiced, and that is what he found (Allport & Ross, 1967). Other researchers have confirmed Allport's finding that extrinsic religious orientation predicts higher racial prejudice (Donahue, 1985; Herek, 1987). Intrinsic religious orientation, however, does not consistently predict low prejudice (Donahue, 1985).

When we consider other forms of prejudice besides racial prejudice, Allport's positive portrait of intrinsic religious orientation becomes even more sullied. Intrinsically religious people have been found to have higher-than-average prejudice against homosexuals (Herek, 1987) (see Figure 7.2). Because this group of intrinsically religious people was more tolerant of racial minorities in his study, Herek interpreted the prejudice against homosexuals as a direct result of intolerant religious teachings about homosexuality, and later research supports this interpretation (Veenvliet, 2008). Batson and colleagues found that intrinsically religious undergraduates discriminated against gays, in one experiment, by being less willing to help them win money in a contest, even when the prize would be used for personal needs unrelated to sexual orientation, namely, to visit grandparents (Batson et al., 1999). Another study reports an association between intrinsic religious orientation and antihomosexual prejudice on implicit as well as extrinsic measures of prejudice (Tsang & Rowatt, 2007).

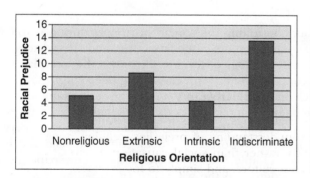
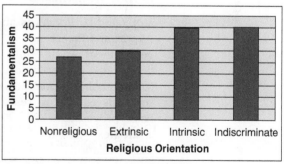
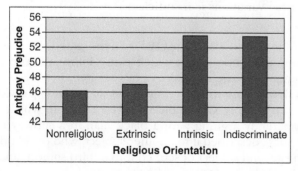
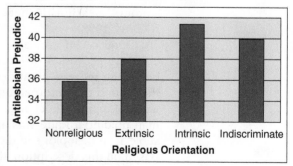

FIGURE 7.2 Religious Orientation as a Predictor of Religious Fundamentalism and Prejudice against Racial Minorities, Gays, and Lesbians

Note: Higher scores indicate more prejudice against racial minorities, higher religious fundamentalist ideology, and more prejudice against gay men and lesbian women. Prepared from data reported by Herek (1987).

In another experiment, however, intrinsically religious female subjects discriminated in apparently the opposite way; that is, they discriminated against those who are overtly antigay (Batson, Eidelman, & Higley, 2001). Studies of prejudice against homosexual persons have produced complex relationships with religious orientation, suggesting the need to measure various components of both religious orientation and prejudice (e.g., stereotyping and discriminatory behaviors) to understand the processes more accurately (Wilkinson, 2004).

Gender issues have also been studied. The traditional religions from which research samples are drawn have long been criticized for a patriarchal bias. One study reports that it is the subtler, protective paternalistic attitudes toward women that are typical of those high in intrinsic religious orientation; although these attitudes seem more benign than hostile sexism, they are also more difficult to challenge (Burn & Busso, 2005). In another study, undergraduates with high intrinsic religious orientation scores were more accepting of a man's abusive behavior toward a girlfriend who rejected his marriage proposal and said she might be a lesbian than those with other religious orientations, although they did not excuse such abusive behavior when he was rejected because of religious differences (Burris & Jackson, 1999). In yet another study, intrinsically religious people were less likely to devalue a rape victim (Joe, McGee, & Dazey, 1977).

The association of religious orientation with prejudice seems to depend, in part, on the target of the potential prejudice. Research casts doubt on Allport's suggestion that intrinsically religious people are wholeheartedly, unselfishly helpful to others. They are sometimes motivated by conscious impression management and unconscious self-deception (Leak & Fish, 1989) and by the desire to enhance their own esteem (Batson, 1990).

Batson suggests that a Quest Orientation comes closer to the nonjudgmental concern for helping others that Allport was trying to convey in his concept of intrinsic religious orientation (Batson et al., 1999; Batson, Eidelman, & Higley, 2001). In addition, religious fundamentalism is sometimes associated with increased prejudice (e.g., Fulton, Gorsuch, & Maynard, 1999). Though Allport's ideas about the association between religious orientation and prejudice have not been fully confirmed, the research he inspired continues.

Rumor Transmission

Motivated by concerns about controlling the spread of rumors during World War II, Allport and Postman (1947) studied rumors in the laboratory and offered advice to the government. Their book, *The Psychology of Rumor,* illustrates the interplay between history and psychological work, beginning with classifying the rumors that circulated following the Japanese attack on Pearl Harbor in 1941. It is an early example of applied social psychological research, and it interweaves experimental laboratory studies of basic processes with socially relevant descriptions of real rumors and intervention strategies. With his brother Floyd Allport and others, Allport considered broader public relations issues, too; for example, their work showed that newspaper headlines with a positive image about progress in the war were an impediment to recruiting soldiers; pessimistic headlines encouraged more soldiers to enlist (Johnson & Nichols, 1998).

One set of concepts Allport and Postman (1947) investigated concerned the cognitive processes of leveling and sharpening, which cause information to change, becoming more general or more specific as rumors are repeated. In a classic study, they found that information that begins with an eyewitness and then is passed on by word of mouth can change considerably. One subject viewed a slide in which a white man holding a knife was apparently arguing with a black man in a subway car. The subject, while looking at the slide, described it to another subject, who could not see it. Based on this description, the second subject described it to a third subject, and so on, until, like the child's game of telephone, the rumor had been passed on to several subjects. In over half the replications, participants incorrectly reported that the black man held the knife at some point in the rumor transmission. This study has become a classic one supporting the idea that stereotypes lead to erroneous eyewitness reporting.

Ironically, the original study is often exaggerated (Boon & Davis, 1987) and distorted (Treadway & McCloskey, 1987) in making this point.

ECLECTICISM

Allport recommended an eclectic approach in which psychology gain truths from many areas. According to Allport, we can distinguish "jackdaw" eclecticism from systematic eclecticism. A jackdaw is a bird that, like a pack rat, collects everything. **Jackdaw eclecticism** is not selective. *Systematic eclecticism*, in contrast, is selective and tries to make one unified whole out of all that is taken. Because most psychologists consider themselves eclectic with respect to personality theory, we should take Allport's advice to heart and consider how we select what to keep and what to discard from each theory.

jackdaw eclecticism

considering concepts from diverse theories, without making careful selection from and evaluation of these concepts

Summary

- Gordon Allport emphasized several major themes: personality consistency, social influence, the concept of self, and the interaction of personality with social influence in determining behavior.
- Allport defined *personality* as "the dynamic organization within the individual of those psychophysical systems that determine his unique adjustments to the environment."
- The primary unit of personality is the *trait*.
- Traits can be studied *idiographically* (individual traits) or *nomothetically* (common traits).
- Evidence of traits comes from many sources: language, behavior, documents (such as letters), and such questionnaires as the Study of Values.
- Allport emphasized that the subject matter should take precedence over methodological issues.
- Traits vary in pervasiveness. *Cardinal traits* have extremely pervasive influences but occur in only a few people. *Central traits* have broad influences and occur in everyone. In addition, people have *secondary traits* that influence only a few behaviors.
- Traits are in the middle of a spectrum of aspects of personality, ranging from very narrow reflexes through highly integrated selves.

- As personality develops, traits become *functionally autonomous* from their developmental origins. Thus the study of personality should focus on contemporaneous issues.
- Allport listed several characteristics of a mature, healthy adult: extension of the sense of self, warm human interactions, emotional security (self-acceptance), realistic perceptions, self-objectification, and a unifying philosophy of life. The healthy personality is unified, combining various elements into a *unitas multiplex*.
- Personality development, the development of the unifying *proprium* (or self), proceeds through stages: bodily sense, self-identity, ego-enhancement, ego-extensions, self-image, rational agent, propriate striving, and the self as knower.
- Allport studied prejudice, which he said was more frequent among *extrinsically religious individuals* and less frequent among *intrinsically religious individuals*. Subsequent research has found that Allport's predictions generally hold for racial prejudice but not for antihomosexual prejudice.
- Allport conducted applied social research on rumor transmission.
- Overall, Allport's approach was *eclectic*.

Thinking about Allport's Theory

1. Allport's point of view is quite different from that of psychoanalytic theorists. What implications does this have for the issues that we should concentrate on when trying to understand an individual's personality?
2. Do you believe it is possible to focus on one individual without comparing that person with others? That is, can we really do idiographic as well as nomothetic personality research?
3. Allport considered the relationship between personality and social psychology (e.g., in his description of prejudice). Are there other social issues or social phenomena that should also be studied in this way?
4. Do you think that expressive traits, such as the analysis of handwriting, have a place in a science of personality?

What research would you suggest to explore expressive traits?
5. Allport inferred personality by analyzing Jenny's letters. If you have access to personal letters or diaries or journals, look at them as a personality psychologist might. What inferences would you make from particular documents?
6. Propose a research hypothesis using the Allport-Vernon-Lindzey Study of Values as one measure.
7. Reflect on Allport's description of a normal mature adult. Do you think these criteria are adequate, or would you suggest any change?
8. How do you think religion contributes to prejudice or to the reduction of prejudice in today's world?

Study Questions

1. List and briefly describe some of the ways in which Allport influenced the study of personality.
2. How did Allport define personality? Explain the significance of this definition.
3. Discuss Allport's concept of a trait. Explain the difference between an individual trait and a common trait.
4. What sources provide evidence about traits? Discuss, in particular, Allport's *Letters from Jenny* and his Study of Values.
5. Explain how cardinal traits, central traits, and secondary traits differ in the pervasiveness of their influence.
6. Explain Allport's concept of functional autonomy.
7. List and explain the characteristics of a mature healthy adult.
8. Explain the importance of the unity of personality for good adjustment, according to Allport's theory.
9. List and explain the stages in the development of the proprium.
10. Explain what Allport meant by intrinsic and extrinsic religious orientation.
11. Discuss the relationship between religious orientation and prejudice.
12. Summarize Allport's advice about theoretical eclecticism.

8

Two Factor Analytic Trait Theories

Cattell's 16 Factors and the Big Five

Chapter Overview

ILLUSTRATIVE BIOGRAPHY
Sonia Sotomayor

A personality profile of an extraordinarily high achiever who has risen from poverty to one of the highest statuses within her eminent career has much to teach us. Such a person is Sonia Sotomayor, born and raised in a housing project in the Bronx, New York, who became a justice in the Supreme Court of the United States at age 55. In describing this appointment, President Obama emphasized not only her individual achievement but also her importance as a role model for others. "The historic moment was not just about her. It's about every child who will grow up thinking to him or herself, if Sonia Sotomayor can make it, then maybe I can, too" (Felix, 2010, loc. 3992–3993).

Born in 1954, Sotomayor was the child of immigrant parents from Puerto Rico, speaking Spanish as her first language and suffering the death of her father when she was nine.

(continued)

(continued)

She was diagnosed with Type 1 diabetes in childhood. Her mother, a nurse, continued the family tradition of hard work and economized to purchase the *Encyclopedia Britannica* and to send Sonia and her brother to private schools. An outstanding student, Sonia earned many honors at Princeton University and Yale Law School, where she edited the *Yale University Law Review*. She married her high school sweetheart shortly after college graduation, but later divorced. Her law career included serving as a prosecutor at the New York District Attorney's office (1979 to 1984) and private practice in a New York City law firm (1984 to 1992). She taught at New York University and at Columbia Law School, and lectured at various other schools. She actively advocated more opportunities for Latino students and faculty.

Sonia Sotomayor

Nominated by President George W. Bush, she was confirmed as a federal district judge in New York in 1992, the first Hispanic in that position. Five years later, President Bill Clinton offered her an appointment to the Second Circuit Court of Appeals, the highest federal court in New York. This was a path to the Supreme Court, where she was appointed in 2009 as the first Hispanic justice.

DEVELOPMENT

Factor theories are primarily descriptive, saying little about personality development. Personality factors are influenced by heredity, and they are generally stable over time.

Cattell's factor theory allows for the impact of experience (with the concept of "environmental-mold traits"). Many of an adult's motivations have been developed over time, by channeling basic motivations ("ergs") into sentiments and attitudes that influence specific behaviors. One sentiment that clearly influenced the course of Sonia Sotomayor's life was the positive value of education, learned from her mother. Education allowed expression of at least two of the basic motivations that Cattell listed: curiosity and self-assertion. As a prosecutor, she had the opportunity to channel other ergs, anger, disgust, protection, and security, in fighting crime.

DESCRIPTION

Cattell's theory lists 16 factors, but for purposes of this illustrative biography, we will consider the simpler Five Factor theory, which describes Extraversion, Agreeableness, Conscientiousness, Openness, and Neuroticism.

Sonia's leisure time was often spent with others, family and her many friends, as is typical of extraverts. Her Extraversion (a factor important in both of the theories described in this chapter) and Agreeableness (a factor that captures ease of getting along with other people) are evidenced by people's description of her as warm and generous, gregarious, easy to work with, and a team player (Felix, 2010).

This was not an agreeableness that stemmed from lack of self-confidence. Quite the contrary. Her brother described Sonia as "tough as nails" (Felix, 2010), and in court, she was direct and demanding toward lawyers and clerks. Any personality trait or factor is part of a broader profile, and it can be manifested in a variety of ways. Sonia's trait of Agreeableness influenced the way other aspects of her personality would be manifested. For example, as a student who became aware of the recruitment practices that in effect discriminated against Latino populations, she challenged the policies but in a friendly rather than antagonistic style, "without that personal edge that says I've been hurt, I need revenge" (Felix, 2010, loc. 1096). In her career as a judge, she had the confidence to rule against the Justice Department, ordering the release of a controversial suicide note by White House counsel Vincent Foster (Felix, 2010).

Her Conscientiousness (dedication and hard work) is evidenced by extraordinary effort and personal sacrifice to excel as a student and as a lawyer and judge. This work ethic likely was developed from the model of her mother. When nominated to the Supreme Court by President Barack Obama, Sonia pointed out her mother in the audience, saying, "I am who I am because of her, and I am only half the woman she is" (Felix, 2010, loc. 128).

The "fierce intellectual curiosity" (Felix, 2010, loc. 626) that has been attributed to Sotomayor suggests the factor of Openness in the Five Factor model. A passion for information is clearly helpful for a judge.

These are four of the Big Five factors. The remaining one is closely related to adjustment, to which we turn.

ADJUSTMENT

The Neuroticism factor in the Five Factor model assesses readiness to experience negative emotions such as anxiety or depression. Other models, including Cattell's, have similar factors. High levels of neuroticism are marked by readiness to experience negative emotions; low levels describe emotional stability. Likely, Sotomayor would score in the moderate range on this factor. She had enough emotional stability to thrive despite growing up in an environment where she saw crime and broken lives in her neighborhood, and to cope with the stresses of her career, sending criminals to prison for drugs and other offenses. On the other hand, she experienced enough negative emotion to voice concern about the personal costs of her demanding career and to strive for more balance.

Negative emotions have some benefits; they arouse enough worry to encourage better health behaviors. One study found that moderate Neuroticism combined with high Conscientiousness predicts better outcomes for Type I diabetic patients, presumably because of healthier behavior (Brickman et al., 1996). Undoubtedly the combination of negative emotions or worry with her trait of Conscientiousness contributes to the reliable control of Sotomayor's blood sugar levels, by frequent self-injection with insulin, that is necessary to maintain health.

Perhaps negative emotions are responsible, too, for her humility about the positions to which she has been appointed. About taking the oath for her appointment to the Supreme Court, she said, "I don't think any person can be assured that they are up to the task.... And so those moments are at one point incredibly meaningful and in a different way, incredibly frightening. It's hard to convey the coursing of emotions that goes through one at a moment like that" (Felix, 2010, loc. 3790–3792).

COGNITION

Cattell's theory describes intelligence, both innate potential (fluid intelligence) and that which has been learned (crystallized intelligence). Gifted by high innate intelligence, nonetheless Sotomayor had to work diligently in order to learn what was necessary to succeed as a scholar and as a lawyer. She also developed a capacity for deep concentration, so intense that she is reported to tune out even fire alarms while working (Felix, 2010).

Another aspect of cognition is the specific thoughts that a person has about various things. She was encouraged to think about current events and to express her views at school. Other theories would likely describe her self-affirming cognitions about herself, which theorists in the Five Factor model are now describing as part of an expanded view of their model that describes how the fundamental personality factors relate to other aspects of personality (McCrae & Costa, 2008).

Attitudes toward the social issues of the day are influenced by personality. Cattell's theory suggests that individuals learn to channel their basic motives into specific sentiments and attitudes. Sotomayor had a strong commitment to justice and to judicial institutions, which Cattell's model would describe as an enduring sentiment (a type of metaerg, in his model), that directed her striving. She described the tradition and the institutional role as "bigger than us" as individuals (Felix, 2010, loc. 3968).

CULTURE

For the most part, factor theorists have limited their cultural interest to comparisons across cultures, to verify that the same descriptive factors found in United States and other English-language populations are valid in other cultures. (They are, according to most research to date.) These underlying factors play out within individuals in their cultural environment, though the theories don't (yet) provide much specific guidance. The basic factors need to be supplemented by other aspects of personality in order to capture the cultural context that is so important in the narrative of Sonia Sotomayor's life.

Sonia Sotomayor's biographer highlights the importance of culture by subtitling the biography *The True American Dream* (Felix, 2010). This cultural environment provided educational and professional opportunities for a person with her traits to thrive. Sonia grew up in public housing, in one of the projects in the Bronx. To many today, such an environment connotes shame and crime, but at that time, and in her family, "there was no stigma attached to living in the projects…to the contrary, many residents took tremendous pride in the beauty of their surroundings" (Felix,

2010, loc. 353–354). When newspapers described her as coming from humble origins, she objected, focusing not on the economic deprivations but on the wealth of her maternal support. As she rose in socioeconomic status and prestige, she remained empathic to those who were less privileged; for example, she broke precedent by insisting upon being photographed with the cooks and wait staff at a formal dinner celebrating her appointment to the Supreme Court (Felix, 2010, loc. 3746).

Sonia also maintained her bicultural values, speaking of her "Latina soul." She describes her experience at prestigious Princeton University as making her aware of her identity as a Latina woman. The factor theories in this chapter do not describe such issues (as, for example, Erikson's identity model does), but we could interpret this identity awareness as a metaerg in Cattell's model, or as a self-related cognition in the expanding Five Factor model (McCrae & Costa, 2008). Though the theoretical connections can be outlined, in fairness we must confess that these cultural details are not detailed in factor theories. At any rate, her Latina identity motivated her to actively recruit Latino students in her work-study role, which can be labeled a sentiment in Cattell's model.

BIOLOGY

Factor theories that have developed more elaborate biological models are considered in Chapter 9. Even the factors in this chapter, though, are influenced by heredity, and so we can conclude that Sonia Sotomayor's fundamental personality traits were influenced by heredity. Intelligence is one obvious example. In addition, she was diagnosed in childhood with Type I diabetes, a potentially life-shortening disease. Fortunately, and probably in large part due to her trait of Conscientiousness, she has kept this disease well controlled with insulin injections and lifestyle precautions, avoiding the serious complications that can result when blood sugar levels vary too widely. Thus heredity influences broad predispositions, but the specific ways that these play out in an individual's life are not predetermined.

FINAL THOUGHTS

Factor theories are still developing. The established aspects of the theory provide reliable dimensions for describing personality. Although factor models can be intuitively applied to describe Sonia Sotomayor, we do not have the kind of systematic assessment, using tests, that factor theorists would prefer for a proper analysis. Nor do factor theories focus on the uniqueness of each person, so they can never fully capture an individual life.

PREVIEW: OVERVIEW OF FACTOR ANALYTIC TRAIT THEORIES

Cattell's theory and the more recent Big Five model, two of the most influential factor theories, both have implications for major theoretical questions, as presented in Table 8.1. Their major strength is their sophisticated description of personality through clearly defined factors assessed through questionnaires. This measurement provides clear operational definitions, contributing to the verifiability of the theory or model. Both Cattell's factor theory and the Big Five model emphasize description over theoretical statements about development, so in that sense the theories are less comprehensive than we might hope. Applied uses of the factor theories are a strength of this approach because empirically validated tests can be used to select people for various positions and to predict performance.

Table 8.1 Preview of Factor Analytic Trait Theories	
Individual Differences	Individuals differ in their traits, which are measured by personality tests. The two models considered in this chapter include 16 (Cattell) or five (Big Five) major personality traits.
Adaptation and Adjustment	Neuroticism, a predisposition to negative emotions, and its opposite pole, emotional stability, predispose people to maladjustment.
Cognitive Processes	Mental abilities can be measured objectively; culture-free intelligence can be measured. Specific cognitions, such as attitudes, are developed by experience.
Culture	Factor structures of tests are generally universal, across different cultures.
Biological Influences	Heredity affects many personality traits.
Development	Some traits are influenced by early experience, interacting with biological predispositions. For the most part, adult personality is stable.

FACTOR ANALYSIS

Factor analysis, the essential tool of factor analytic trait theories, is a statistical procedure based on the concept of correlation. A **correlation coefficient** measures the relationship between two sets of numbers. There is a positive correlation if high numbers in one set are associated with high numbers in the other set and low numbers in each set are associated with each other. If low numbers in one set go with high numbers in the other, there is a negative correlation.

A correlation coefficient may range from –1 to +1, indicating the direction and strength of the association between two variables. During the course of a factor analysis, the correlations among all pairs of items (questions on a questionnaire) are computed to form a **correlation matrix**. This immense amount of information is simplified by the statistical procedure called **factor analysis** to describe a smaller number of dimensions (factors).

Factor analysis is not a magical procedure, and even experts debate its proper uses. Still, factor analysis is a sophisticated mathematical tool for identifying patterns of related observations, and factor theorists use it to search for the fundamental traits of personality. Cattell (1957) considered factor analysis "a research tool as important to psychology as the microscope was to biology" (p. 4).

THE 16 FACTOR THEORY: CATTELL

A leader in the development of factor theories, Raymond Cattell (1979) claimed that the study of personality passed through two earlier phases before reaching its current scientific status. "From biblical times until the early nineteenth century," he wrote, "it was a matter for intuitive insights expressed in the realm of literature" (p. 6), marked by such giants as Plutarch, Bacon, and Goethe. Then came a century of clinically oriented theorists (Freud, Adler, and Jung), with some experimental work (Jung and McDougall). After that, the study of personality entered the third, "experimental and quantitative," phase.

Biography of Raymond Cattell

Raymond B. Cattell was born in 1905 in Staffordshire, England, the son and grandson of engineers. In college, Cattell studied science, but dismayed friends by pursuing psychology in graduate school. He completed his doctoral degree at the University of London (King's College), at the age of 23. There he learned Spearman's factor analysis, a mathematical procedure developed to study intelligence but that Cattell would later apply to personality research.

correlation coefficient

a measure of the association between two variables, in which 0 indicates no association, and +1 or –1 a strong association (positive or negative)

correlation matrix

a chart of the correlations between all pairs of a set of variables

factor analysis

statistical procedure for determining a smaller number of dimensions in a data set from a large number of variables

Prospects for a professorship in psychology were slight, so Cattell accepted an applied position in Leicester and set up a school psychological service. Of these 5 years of clinical work, he later said, "Though…I felt a charlatan it gave me many leads for personality research" (Cattell, 1984, p. 123).

Besides administrative work, Cattell conducted research in those years. He studied the relationship of intelligence to family size and social status (a research question that offended liberal critics). He developed a projective test at the same time as Henry Murray, who is generally credited for developing this testing strategy. Cattell commented that, to his best knowledge, he himself may be the one who first used the term *projective test.*

In 1937 Cattell accepted an invitation to work in social psychology in New York for a year, and remained in the United States permanently. He taught at Clark University and later at Harvard University, where his office was next door to Allport's (Cattell, 1984, p. 141). He remarked that "in personality theory, Allport and I spoke a different language, which…was tough on students" (Cattell, 1974, p. 71). During World War II, he developed objective personality tests for officer selection.

Raymond Cattell

In 1945, he moved to a research position at the University of Illinois. Freed from teaching responsibilities and with access to a new and (for the times) powerful computer, these were very productive years. To facilitate distribution of his many new psychological tests, Cattell set up a private organization, the Institute for Personality and Ability Testing (IPAT), in 1949. He founded the Society for Multivariate Experimental Psychology in 1960 to foster the kind of research he felt was necessary to advance personality theory scientifically.

Cattell retired to Hawaii, where he continued to advocate statistical approaches to theory development (Cattell, 1990) and to develop computer methods for personality research (McArdle & Cattell, 1994) until his death in 1998 (Horn, 2001). In 1997 he was recognized with an award for lifetime achievement by the American Psychological Association, which praised his work for its inclusion of many areas, saying, "Cattell stands without peer in his creation of a unified theory of individual differences integrating intellectual, temperamental, and dynamic domains of personality in the context of environmental and hereditary influences" (American Psychological Association, 1997, p. 797).

PERSONALITY MEASUREMENT AND THE PREDICTION OF BEHAVIOR

Earlier theories were rich in words and understanding but sparse in the specific predictions we would hope to make from a science. Cattell's (1950, p. 2) definition of personality emphasizes the importance of prediction:

> Personality is that which permits a prediction of what a person will do in a given situation.

Traits allow prediction. Cattell (1979, p. 14) defined a trait as "that which defines what a person will do when faced with a defined situation." Unlike Allport, he did not feel it was necessary to define traits in psychophysical terms. For Cattell, traits are abstract conceptual tools, not necessarily corresponding to any specific physical reality.

Cattell's most important contribution to personality is his systematic description and measurement of personality. He argued that a taxonomy of individual differences is essential before investigation of the causes of personality. To assess personality differences in the population at large, Cattell developed his best-known and most widely used test, the 16 Personality Factor Questionnaire (16PF), described later in this chapter. In addition, several tests have been specifically devised for clinical use, as well as intelligence tests.

Most personality tests ask a set of standard questions, requiring respondents to choose among multiple-choice or true-and-false answers. Such self-report tests provide "questionnaire data," which Cattell called **Q-data**. (To avoid confusing Cattell's terminology, you may find it helpful to call these questionnaires rather than

trait

that which defines what a person will do in a particular situation

Q-data

data from self-report tests or questionnaires

T-data

data collected from objective tests, such as reaction times

L-data

objective information about the life history of the individual

tests.) Although much useful information can be gained from such questionnaires, the procedure also has shortcomings. Respondents may attempt to present a certain image to the administrator, or their conscious self-understanding may be different from their true underlying personality. Dare we trust self-reports? Cattell looked for other evidence to support their validity.

A second type of data is **T-data**, or "objective test data." These are indirect measures; the purpose of the test is hidden. They cannot be faked because the subject does not know how answers will be interpreted. Projective measures, such as inkblot tests, fall into this category. So do objective behavioral measures observed in the laboratory, such as finger tapping and reaction time, and physiological tests, such as blood pressure and urinalysis.

Finally, Cattell measured objective information about the life history of the individual. Cattell called this **L-data**, or "life record data." School records, grade-point average, driving history, ratings by supervisors about job performance—all of these data can be obtained without requiring subjects to answer a questionnaire or respond to a test in a standard setting.

Cattell looked for patterns that could be confirmed in all three types of data. For example, a person with low emotional stability has distinctive responses in all three kinds of data: in Q-data, on Factor C of the 16PF personality questionnaire (ego strength); in T-data, on an objective test factor called self-sentiment control; and in L-data, in "low occupational stability, high automobile accident rate, and many clinical visits" (Cattell, 1957, p. 54). Confirmation across these three very different types of measures increases certainty that meaningful personality traits are being measured.

BECAUSE PERSONALITY IS COMPLEX: A MULTIVARIATE APPROACH

Personality is complex. Cattell cautioned against the oversimplification of predicting from one variable at a time—for example, predicting how well a person will do in school only from intelligence, ignoring motivation, educational background, health, and so forth. Life, of course, is multivariate, yet very few theories describe this in a formal sense.

multivariate

a research strategy that includes many variables

Cattell pioneered **multivariate** research methods, using several variables at one time to predict behavior. This would never have been possible before modern computers were available to do the tedious calculations, and such predictions are often difficult to grasp intuitively, since people can keep only a limited number of concepts in mind at the same time (Dawes, 1994; Grove & Meehl, 1996).

Surface Traits and Source Traits

surface traits

traits as defined simply at the level of observable behavior

The term *trait* roughly means "patterns of observations that go together." If we find sets of variables that are positively correlated, we have identified **surface traits**. Although they appear on the surface to be a trait, the pattern of correlations might not reappear under different situations—for example, in a different population, under different testing conditions, or at a different time.

source traits

basic, underlying personality traits

Through many studies, Cattell identified some correlation clusters that are quite *robust;* that is, they reappear over and over again, despite differences in population, in testing situations, and so forth. Cattell argued that such a robust pattern must have a single source of variance. It corresponds to one "cause" within personality, a fundamental trait of personality, which he called a **source trait**.

Measurement of Source Traits: the 16PF

16PF

Cattell's questionnaire designed to measure the major source traits of normal personality

Cattell developed questionnaires to measure the source traits as directly as possible. His best-known personality test, the **16PF**, represents the culmination of many factor analytic studies (Cattell, Eber, & Tatsuoka, 1970). It has 16 multiple-choice scales, each measuring one underlying source trait of normal personality (see Table 8.2).

profile

the pattern of a person's scores on several parts of a personality test

The set of scores on all factors is the **profile** of an individual. Average profiles of various groups, such as occupations, describe typical personalities of those groups. Other profiles can be computed. Based on correlations with an attitude toward

Table 8.2 Cattell's 16 Personality Factors (16PF)

A	Warmth
B	Reasoning
C	Emotional stability
E	Dominance
F	Liveliness
G	Rule-consciousness
H	Social boldness
I	Sensitivity
L	Vigilance
M	Abstractness
N	Privateness
O	Apprehension
Q_1	Openness to change
Q_2	Self-reliance
Q_3	Perfectionism
Q_4	Tension

Note: The names of these factors were different in Cattell's original descriptions. These names correspond to the current revision of the 16PF, as described in H. E. P. Cattell & Schuerger, 2003.

Christianity measure, religious youths have a profile that includes conformity (high factor G), tender-mindedness (high factor I), self-discipline (high factor Q_3), submissiveness (low factor E), and sobriety (low factor F) (Francis & Bourke, 2003).

Five Second-Order Factors

It is possible to reduce further the number of factors by a **second-order factor analysis**. Cattell (1957) described five second-order factors: extraversion, stability (low anxiety), receptivity (low tough-mindedness), accommodating (low independence), and self-control. These five factors are "strikingly similar to the Big-Five factors proposed today, and they are the basis for today's five-factor model" (American Psychological Association, 1997, p. 799), which is described later in this chapter.

It is tempting to focus on second-order factors because there are fewer of them; therefore, it seems easier to comprehend Cattell's research at this level. But Cattell maintained that they predict behavior less well than the 16 primary factors.

second-order factor analysis
factor analysis in which the data are factor scores (rather than raw data); produces more general personality factors

PSYCHOLOGICAL ADJUSTMENT

Some of the traits that Cattell measured contribute to a person's psychological adjustment. Neurotics differ from the general population on several traits, especially on the "controlling triumvirate" of three factors involved in impulse control and emotional adjustment: Factors C (Ego Strength), G (Superego Strength), and Q_3 (Self-Sentiment Integration). Anxiety is high among neurotics, partly because of family conflict, inconsistent discipline, and insufficient affection. Heredity also plays a significant role.

Psychosis is a more serious form of disturbance. There are several different types of psychoses, and Cattell found different patterns of traits for various diagnoses, including schizophrenia and manic depression. He criticized clinicians for not supplementing their unreliable diagnoses with empirically validated scales, which could improve the reliability of diagnosis (Cattell, 1979, p. 110).

THREE TYPES OF TRAITS

As is customary in personality theory, Cattell distinguished various types of traits, including dynamic traits (motives), temperament, and ability.

Ability Traits

Ability traits define various types of intelligence and determine how effectively a person works toward a desired goal. Cattell tried to measure innate intelligence independently of what a person has learned, expressing concern that existing intelligence tests are biased in favor of those with a good education.

Cattell (1971) described **fluid intelligence** as the innate ability to learn. It is "fluid" because it can be expressed in different kinds of learning, depending on the educational opportunities of the individual. Later researchers have suggested that fluid intelligence is related to the capacity of working memory (Engle et al., 1999) and perhaps even to brain size (Wickett, Vernon, & Lee, 2000). In contrast, **crystallized intelligence** includes the effects of education: what has been learned. Measures of crystallized intelligence predict scores on Advanced Placement tests and similar tests of knowledge better than the prediction from fluid intelligence tests (Ackerman et al., 2001).

In keeping with his aim to devise new and purer tests, Cattell devised the **Culture Fair Intelligence Test** to measure only fluid intelligence. It aims to provide a better assessment of the intelligence of people who may be educationally deprived. Contrary to his intent, however, research shows that experience does influence scores, so the test does not seem to measure simply innate ability (Flynn, 1987; Herrnstein et al., 1986; Horn, 1984).

Cattell concluded that about 80 percent of the variation in intelligence is determined by heredity (in other words, is fluid) and only 20 percent by experience (in other words, is crystallized). Based on this belief, he supported the eugenics movement, fearing a general decline in the intelligence of the British population because of the greater birthrate of less intelligent people (Cattell, 1937; Horn, 1984). Subsequent research has not confirmed Cattell's fears (Loehlin, 1984); intelligence among British children was found to be rising, rather than falling (Cattell, 1957; Lynn, Hampson, & Mullineux, 1987). Historical and cultural factors, in addition to genetics, influence intelligence.

Temperament Traits

Temperament traits are largely constitutional (inherited) source traits that determine the "general style and tempo with which [a person] carries out whatever he [or she] does" (Cattell, 1965, p. 165). Cattell (1950, p. 35) gave as examples "high-strungness, speed, energy, and emotional reactivity." Many researchers are seeking to understand the concept of temperament further because it is a key concept for understanding how biological influences, which are inherited, play a role in shaping personality (e.g., Bates & Wachs, 1994; Kagan, 1994).

Dynamic Traits

Dynamic traits are motivational; they provide the energy and direction to action. Like many other theorists, Cattell recognized that some motivations are innate and others are learned. He called these types of dynamic traits ergs (innate) and metaergs (learned).

ERGS Cattell accepted the concept from many previous psychologists that people have some innate motivational traits or, in his language, constitutional dynamic source traits. He called them **ergs** (from a Greek word meaning "energy") and compared them to animal instincts that involve "an innate reactivity toward a goal, though stimuli and means are learned" (Cattell, 1957, p. 893). Cattell listed several human ergs: anger, curiosity, fear, greed, hunger, loneliness, pity, pride, sensuousness, and sex.

METAERGS: SENTIMENTS AND ATTITUDES Ergs are channeled into learned patterns, called **metaergs**. Metaergs are environmental-mold dynamic source traits. These can range from the very general, like love of country and esteem of education, to the very specific, like opposition to a particular political candidate.

Sentiments are the more general metaergs, and are formed early and generally enduring. They include sentiments toward home, family, hobbies, and religion, among

---

fluid intelligence

the part of intelligence that is the innate ability to learn, without including the effects of specific learning

crystallized intelligence

intelligence influenced by education, so it measures what has been learned

erg

a constitutional dynamic source trait

metaerg

environmental-mold dynamic source traits; includes sentiments and attitudes others. The most important sentiment is the *self-sentiment* that Cattell referred to as a *master motive.*

Attitudes are the more specific expressions of sentiments that are responses to particular stimulus situations. Cattell (1965, p. 175) defined an attitude as "an interest in a course of action, in a given situation." An example would be "like to spend Thanksgiving with the family."

Ergs and metaergs are dynamic, motivational traits that are activated by situations (Boyle & Cattell, 1984). They help people select goals and provide the energy to pursue goals. They stimulate emotional responses to certain objects: hope, fear, expectation, and so forth.

SUBSIDIATION   Through a process of learning, basic drives (ergs) are satisfied by multistep sequences of purposive activities. Their energy is channeled through metaergs. The environment demands this kind of learning. Instrumental acts must be completed before basic goals can be met. Cattell (1950, p. 156) noted, for example, that we must work to eat. Working serves (or, to use Cattell's jargon, is "subsidiary to") the motivation to eat. Metaergs are subsidiary to ergs. Attitudes are subsidiary to sentiments because attitudes are more particular, more remote from the basic ergs.

This idea that the fundamental motivations are constitutional and that learning channels them into specific forms of expression is found in many personality theories. Freud, of course, assumed this (Herrnstein et al., 1986) in his assertion that all energy flows from the id and the ego channels this energy. Murray named the concept **subsidiation**, and it was from Murray that Cattell borrowed the idea. Even learning theory makes such assumptions with the concept of primary reinforcement. Hence the concept of subsidiation, although not always so named, is an idea that crosses theoretical boundaries.

subsidiation
the pattern of interrelationships among ergs, metaergs, and sentiments (as diagrammed in the dynamic lattice)

THE DYNAMIC LATTICE   Cattell diagrammed these subsidiation relationships in the **dynamic lattice**, a visual image that shows energy from ergs, flowing through sentiments and into attitudes. The dynamic lattice is unique to each individual, as a result of learned connections between ergs and the meta-ergs (sentiments and attitudes) through which they are channeled. He gave the example of a man whose basic ergs are channeled into sentiments and attitudes about money, marriage and business relationships, which he describes:

dynamic lattice
Cattell's diagram to show motivational dynamics

> The man's attitude…to his bank account has the direction that he wants to increase it. The lines of subsidiation…indicate that he wants to do so in order to protect his wife…to satisfy self-assertion…to assuage his fear of insecurity…and to satisfy hunger…. This attitude or sentiment to his bank account is served by an attitude of annoyance toward higher taxation…by an intention to keep company with his business friend…and by an attitude of avoidance to New York, where he spends too much money. (1950, p. 188).

We can visualize the motivational dynamics of Sonia Sotomayer, described in the Illustrative Biography for this chapter, using Cattell's dynamic lattice concept (see Figure 8.1). Her basic motivational ergs of self-assertion and curiosity (which are two that Cattell suggested as basic ergs for people in general) are, in her case, channeled as a result of learning into a sentiment of highly valuing education. Self-assertion and another erg that Cattell identifies, protection, are channeled into her positive sentiment toward justice. These sentiments, education and justice, in turn influence more specific attitudes toward legal opinions, advocacy for minority populations, and sympathy with lower social class people.

Certain types of learning involve reorganizing or coordinating various traits. We may learn certain behaviors that can satisfy many motivations (many metaergs and ergs) at the same time. This is called **confluence learning**. For example, learning to ski might satisfy various social and physical motivations. For Sonia Sotomayer, her legal opinions gave expression to both her education and her sense of justice.

confluence learning
learning behaviors that satisfy more than one motivation

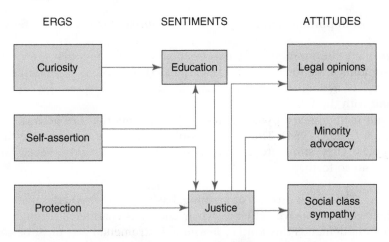

FIGURE 8.1 A dynamic lattice portraying Sonia Sotomayer's dynamics (based on the concept of a dynamic lattice described by Cattell, 1964, p. 187).

PREDICTING BEHAVIOR

Recall that Cattell defined personality as that which permits the prediction of behavior. Let us examine his model for making predictions about how individuals will behave in particular situations.

The Specification Equation

Various traits are combined in a predictive mathematical equation, called the **specification equation**. The specific terms, of course, would vary depending on the application. To predict which university football players would play the most games, an equation can be formed from four personality traits assessed by the 16PF (group-dependence, tough-mindedness, extraversion, and emotional stability) and five coaching variables (autocratic behavior, training and instruction, rewarding behavior, democratic behavior, and social support) (Garland & Barry, 1990). To predict the performance of airline cabin crew members, an equation would give positive weights to the 16PF factors of emotional stability, conscientiousness, and tough-mindedness (Furnham, 1991). These equations are determined by research in specific settings.

Traits are entered into the predictive equation if they are relevant for predicting the particular behavior. These may include ability traits, temperament traits, ergs, and metaergs (sentiments and attitudes). Situational factors (like the roles called for in a situation) and temporary factors (like fatigue) may also be added to the equation. Here is the full specification equation:

$$P_{ij} = S_{1j}T_{1i} + S_{2j}T_{2i} + \ldots + S_{Nj}T_{Ni} + S_jT_{ji}$$

The behavior being predicted, the performance of the individual i in situation j is referred to as P_{ij}. For example, if a person is running a race, P might represent the time to run the course.

Each predictive trait is referred to as a T in the specification equation. Subscripts identify the particular trait and the particular individual. Thus T_{2i} refers to the second trait and the ith individual. The letter S refers to a situational index, that is, the extent to which the trait T is relevant in predicting the performance P in this situation. Research determines which predictors are necessary and the appropriate weight of each.

In a theoretical article published after his death, Cattell and colleagues proposed a modification of the equation that would allow for some variation in a person's traits over time, reflecting the impact of learning on personality (Cattell, Boyle, & Chant, 2002).

Nomothetic and Idiographic Approaches: R-Technique and P-Technique

Most of Cattell's research involved the nomothetic method, or to use Cattell's terminology, the *R-technique,* in which many subjects are analyzed together, comparing their scores. Cattell also adapted his analysis to the intensive investigation of a single subject. This *P-technique* studies a single person, comparing scores across time. Thus, in theory, it can discover unique individual traits (though Gordon Allport was skeptical that Cattell's approach corresponded to his own concept of unique traits).

Cattell (1957, p. 643) suggested one promising application of the P-technique: the investigation of psychosomatic conditions in individuals. Simonton (1998), although not citing Cattell, found that King George III of Great Britain typically experienced ill-health about 9 months after times of extreme stress. Other researchers have, in effect, used the P-technique, without calling it by that term. It provides a method for investigating the dynamic relationship between some aspect of a person, such as life satisfaction (Heller, Watson & Ilies, 2006) and the changing environment.

DETERMINANTS OF PERSONALITY: HEREDITY AND ENVIRONMENT

Where do traits, so useful for prediction, originate? This is the familiar nature–nurture issue. Cattell distinguishes between **constitutional traits**, which originate in biological causes (especially genetics), and **environmental-mold traits**, which are the result of learning and social experience. He developed research strategies for untangling these two causes.

Cattell (1960) developed a statistical technique, the **Multiple Abstract Variance Analysis (MAVA)**, to analyze the effects of heredity and environment based on the similarity of relatives (identical twins, fraternal twins, siblings, and unrelated children) raised together and raised apart. To the extent that genetics determines a trait, relatives will be more similar than nonrelatives. The MAVA extends the twin method of studying heredity, which examines twins but not other relatives. Cattell (1973) estimated the **heritability** *(H)* of various traits, which he defined as "the fraction of the total measured variance of the trait X in the population that is due to hereditary differences in individual makeup" (p. 145). He found that many traits have high heritability.

THE ROLE OF THEORY IN CATTELL'S EMPIRICAL APPROACH

Cattell has been accused of being atheoretical, that is, of doing empirical work blindly and predicting without a guiding theory. He disputed this characterization, but remarked, "I have always felt justifiably suspicious of theory built much ahead of data" (1984, p. 158). Cattell (1979) aimed to be not simply a methodologist but also a psychologist who used statistical methodology to address substantive questions. He noted convergence of his results with several psychoanalytic concepts, a convergence that has concurrence from others (Campbell, 1988). Cattell's metatheoretical assumptions, which emphasize holism, motivation, and functionalism, are close to the mainstream theories, including Allport and Murray (Wiggins, 1984).

Not all researchers are satisfied with his factors, however. One of the biggest obstacles to consensus is disagreement about how many traits are necessary to describe personality. Currently, there is much enthusiasm for a Five Factor model sometimes referred to as the Big Five, to which we now turn.

THE BIG FIVE FACTOR THEORY

The method of factor analysis, which was the basis for Cattell's research, has been the tool of many other personality researchers. The grand scope of Cattell's vision—that of proposing an empirically supported model of traits that could encompass the full spectrum of personality—has been again captured in a more

constitutional trait
a trait influenced by heredity

environmental-mold trait
a trait influenced by learning

Multiple Abstract Variance Analysis (MAVA)
statistical technique for assessing how much of a trait is determined by heredity and how much by environment

heritability
the extent to which a trait is influenced by genetics

recent model: the **Big Five**. Since the late 1990s, the Big Five model has surpassed Cattell's model in number of research publications (John, Naumann, & Soto, 2008). Many researchers have studied these five factors, including Paul Costa Jr., Robert McCrae, and Oliver John.

As its name indicates, the Big Five model of personality asserts there are five basic factors of personality. The five factors originally were developed from factor analysis of the words people use in everyday language to describe personality, the *lexical approach* to personality (Goldberg, 1981, 1982; Norman, 1963). There is a good reason for starting with everyday language. If we assume people are tuned in to personality differences, because these differences are meaningful for everyday life, then the language of everyday speech should, over centuries, have come to reflect important dimensions of personality. (Recall that Allport had also analyzed everyday language for personality traits, as described in Chapter 7.)

The factors in this model have been called by various names and have been replicated by factor analyzing many different personality tests and ratings of personality by outside observers (see Table 8.3). Cattell's second-order factors have been compared to these five factors. Many researchers are convinced that these constitute the major dimensions of personality and thus a sensible descriptive foundation on which further personality research can be based (John, 1990). Other researchers, however, disagree: Cattell, because he prefers more narrow traits, and Jack Block (1995), because of methodological doubts.

The Big Five consist of five broad personality traits: Extraversion, Agreeableness, Neuroticism, Conscientiousness, and Openness. (Students may find that the word "ocean" is a convenient mnemonic for helping to remember the Big Five, if the letters are scrambled, because each factor begins with one of the letters in "ocean.") A self-report questionnaire has been developed to measure people's standing on each factor by asking how much they agree that various statements describe them. This questionnaire, the NEO-PI (Costa & McCrae, 1985, 1992b), was named for the three factors measured in its first edition (neuroticism, extraversion, and openness); soon conscientiousness and agreeableness were added.

Let's consider the five factors so central to the description of personality. Each factor has been studied extensively, and each is correlated with many behaviors.

Table 8.3 The Big Five Factors of Personality

Factor	Description of High Scorer	Description of Low Scorer
Extraversion (E)	Talkative	Quiet
	Dominant	Unfeeling
	Sociable	Passive
Agreeableness (A)	Good-natured	Irritable
	Soft-hearted	Ruthless
	Trusting	Suspicious
Neuroticism (N)	Emotional	Calm
	Vulnerable	Self-controlled
	Anxious	Sense of well-being
Conscientiousness (C)	Hardworking	Negligent
	Ambitious	Lazy
	Responsible	Irresponsible
Openness (O)	Creative	Uncreative
	Imaginative	Down-to-earth
	Prefers variety	Prefers routine

Source: Adapted from McCrae, 1990, p. 402; and McCrae, Costa, & Piedmont, 1993.

EXTRAVERSION

The first factor, **Extraversion**, has also been called both dominance-submissiveness and "surgency" (John, 1990). It is not surprising that extraversion is one of the Big Five. In fact, it is routinely found whenever factor analyses of personality questionnaires are conducted (Watson & Clark, 1997). Obviously an important dimension of personality, extraversion predicts many social behaviors.

Ask an extravert what he or she values in life, and the answer will often be cheerfulness and an exciting life (Dollinger, Leong, & Ulicni, 1996). Extraverted subjects, in a study in which they kept records of their social interactions, interacted with more people than did those low in extraversion; they also reported having more control and intimacy in those interactions (Barrett & Pietromonaco, 1997). Their peers consider extraverted people to be friendly, fun-loving, affectionate, and talkative (McCrae & Costa, 1987). Fellow group members perceive extraverted members as making valuable contributions to group projects (Barry & Stewart, 1997). Among both white and Asian American college students, extraverts are more willing to have sexual contact without commitment, and they report more sexual experience, compared to introverts (Wright & Reise, 1997).

Extraversion predicts the development of social relationships during college. Not surprisingly, those who are high on the trait of Extraversion make friends more quickly than those who are low. One facet of Extraversion, low *shyness,* also predicts falling in love. After a year in college, about one in three shy students, compared to three out of four nonshy students, reported being in love. Longitudinal research demonstrates that shy children in Sweden and the United States do not marry as early in adulthood as their less shy peers (Kerr, Lambert, & Bem, 1996).

Extraverts often seem happy, and it has been proposed that positive emotional experience is a core feature of Extraversion; perhaps the extravert is even biologically more responsive to pleasure than others are (Watson & Clark, 1997). It is not a serene happiness, but an active, energetic happiness that characterizes the typical extravert.

Extraversion

factor of personality, typified by sociability, cheerfulness, and activity

AGREEABLENESS

Agreeableness, which is sometimes instead called Social Adaptability or Likability (John, 1990), indicates a friendly, compliant personality, one who avoids hostility and tends to go along with others. Their friends find them sympathetic and softhearted, in contrast to those low in Agreeableness, who are described as suspicious, ruthless, and uncooperative (McCrae & Costa, 1987). On a survey of values, people scoring high in Agreeableness report that they value being helpful, forgiving, and loving (Dollinger, Leong, & Ulicni, 1996). They report little conflict in their interpersonal relationships; when conflict occurs, it reduces their self-esteem (Barrett & Pietromonaco, 1997). People high in Agreeableness avoid direct attempts to assert power as a means of resolving conflict with other people, but large sex differences have also been found. Men, even those high in Agreeableness (who use less power to resolve conflict than men low in Agreeableness), are more likely to assert power than women (Graziano, Jensen-Campbell, & Hair, 1996).

In one study, students high on the trait of Agreeableness reported more interactions with their family and very few open conflicts with opposite-sex peers. We can only speculate how this avoidance of conflict might affect the development of relationships over a longer period than the 18 months of this study (Asendorpf & Wilpers, 1998).

Agreeableness

factor of personality, typified by a friendly, compliant personality

NEUROTICISM

Neuroticism describes people who frequently are troubled by negative emotions such as worry and insecurity (McCrae & Costa, 1987) and is elevated among undergraduates who report deliberate self-injury (MacLaren & Best, 2010) and problem gamblers (MacLaren et al., 2011). The coping style of high scorers on Neuroticism, such as

Neuroticism

factor of personality, typified by negative emotionality

coping triggered by an experimental game in which they were socially ostracized, focuses more on managing emotion, rather than direct problem solving (Boyes & French, 2009). Emotionally, they are labile (readily aroused) instead of stable, like their low-scoring peers; thus the factor, turning attention to its opposite pole—low Neuroticism—has also been called Emotional Stability, Emotional Control, and Ego Strength (John, 1990). People who score low on Neuroticism are happier and more satisfied with life than those who score high (DeNeve & Cooper, 1998; Hills & Argyle, 2001; Schmutte & Ryff, 1997), and they are more satisfied with their marriage (Bouchard, Lussier, & Sabourin, 1999). Global well-being is higher among those with lower levels of Neuroticism in Germany and the United States (Staudinger, Fleeson, & Baltes, 1999).

In marriage, high Neurotics are unhappy and dissatisfied with life (McCrae & Costa, 1991). Besides difficulties in relationships and commitment (Karney & Bradbury, 1995; Kurdek, 1997; Malouff et al., 2010), they often suffer low self-esteem (Costa, McCrae, & Dye, 1991). A wide range of health problems, including diabetes, arthritis, kidney and stomach problems, and ulcers, are more frequent among people with high Neuroticism scores, though the cause–effect relationships aren't entirely clear (Goodwin, Cox, & Clara, 2006). People diagnosed with borderline personality disorder show a distinct pattern on the five factors that includes a high score on Neuroticism (Distel et al., 2009). Other psychiatric disorders, too, are being investigated to see whether they can be understood at least in part as inherited patterns of scores on the five factors. Attachment disorders are one example (Donnellan et al., 2008).

Another study reports that adults in the community who scored high on neuroticism also reported—in a diary in which they checked life events that had occurred each day—that more unpleasant events with family and friends, leisure, and finance had happened to them, which may explain why their mood was generally negative (David et al., 1997). Neuroticism is higher in people with diverse types of disturbances, whose specifics can be understood by considering their other personality factors (Claridge & Davis, 2001).

The emotional reactivity of those who score high on Neuroticism isn't always harmful. In some situations, it may provide the impetus for self-protective behaviors, such as taking care of one's health. That may explain, for example, why a group of elderly, highly intelligent men who years earlier had scored high on Neuroticism were less likely to fall ill and die when they were widowed, compared to their lower-scoring peers (Taga, Friedman, & Martin, 2009). It improves women's health by helping them to give up smoking (Ploubidis & Grundy, 2009). Also, as demonstrated in a laboratory experiment, when people who score high on Neuroticism can accurately identify threatening situations, this cognitive ability prevents them from experiencing the distress that they would otherwise feel (Tamir, Robinson, & Solberg, 2006). Whether emotional reactivity is harmful (leading to neurosis) or not, then, varies.

CONSCIENTIOUSNESS

Conscientiousness

factor of personality, typified by hard work, orderliness, and self-discipline

Conscientiousness, also called Dependability, Impulse Control, and Will to Achieve (John, 1990), describes differences in people's orderliness and self-discipline. Conscientious people value cleanliness and ambitiousness (Dollinger, Leong, & Ulicni, 1996). Described by their peers as well organized, punctual, and ambitious (McCrae & Costa, 1987), the student who has a neat notebook and list of assignments and who keeps up with reading and completes work on time would score high on Conscientiousness. Conscientious students are generally motivated to achieve; they achieve high grade-point averages (Digman, 1989; Kappe & van der Flier, 2010) and perform better in medical school (Ferguson et al., 2000). Conscientious students show increasing perfectionism over time (Stoeber, Otto, & Dalbert, 2009). School and many other settings reward conscientious individuals, contributing to their generally high self-esteem (Costa et al., 1991).

Conscientiousness predicts higher job satisfaction, income, and occupational status (Judge et al., 1999). Conscientious workers achieve more and set higher goals

(Barrick & Mount, 1991; Barrick, Mount, & Strauss, 1993), receive better evaluations from their bosses (Barrick & Mount, 1996), are less likely to be engaged in counterproductive work behaviors (Bolton, Becker, & Barber, 2010), and are also satisfied with their lives (DeNeve & Cooper, 1998). Conscientious employees have better attendance records (Judge, Martocchio, & Thoresen, 1997). Among police officers, low conscientiousness is associated with more job disciplinary actions for various kinds of misconduct, including sexual misconduct, insubordination, theft, and other unprofessional behavior (Sarchione et al., 1998).

We may note that, in addition to the strong evidence for Conscientiousness as a favorable personality contributor to job-related measures, other factors are also helpful for many jobs: low Neuroticism and Extraversion for jobs requiring social interaction and sometimes Agreeableness and Openness; when people are out of work, those high in Extraversion and Conscientiousness are more effective in searching for a new job (Kanfer, Wanberg, & Kantrowitz, 2001).

Beyond work and school, Conscientiousness also relates to other social attitudes, family relationships and health behavior. People who are low on this trait voice attitudes that are more accepting of shoplifting (Egan & Taylor, 2010). Young married people who score high on Conscientiousness are less susceptible to sexual infidelity than those who score low (Buss & Shackelford, 1997c). Conscientious mothers and fathers have better-adjusted adolescent children (Oliver, Guerin, & Goffman, 2009). Conscientious women with a family history of breast cancer are more likely to have a mammogram, despite the fear of breast cancer that is sometimes associated with fewer mammograms among less conscientious women (Schwartz et al., 1999; Schwartz, Taylor, & Willard, 2003).

OPENNESS

The factor **Openness** to experience is perhaps the most difficult to describe because it does not correspond to everyday language as well as the other factors (McCrae, 1990). Experts have given this factor various names: Culture, Intellect, Intellectual Interests, Intelligence, and Imagination (John, 1990; Sneed, McCrae, & Funder, 1998). Laypeople recognize it by the terms *artistic, curious, imaginative, insightful, original,* and *wide interests* (Sneed, McCrae, & Funder, 1998). Liberal values often go along with this factor (Costa & McCrae, 1992a). On the Rokeach Values Survey, people scoring high on Openness report that they value imaginativeness, broadmindedness, and a world of beauty. People low in Openness, in contrast, value cleanliness, obedience, and national security (Dollinger, Leong, &, Ulicni1996).

Openness
factor of personality, typified by artistic, imaginative, and intellectual interests

Openness is conducive to personal growth, according to questionnaires (Schmutte & Ryff, 1997). It seems to make people more receptive to guided imagery, such as that suggesting improved immune function (Thompson, Steffert, & Gruzelier, 2009). Creative achievements are greater among people scoring high on Openness and low in Agreeableness (King, Walker, & Broyles, 1996). People who are creative, curious, or open to experience are more likely to find intelligent solutions to problems. In the workplace, this creativity is most likely to be manifested when the high Openness employee has flexibility, or even ambiguity, in the goals to be achieved and the way to achieve them, instead of having a highly structured set of expectations (George & Zhou, 2001). There is even evidence that Openness is associated with more successful aging (Gregory, Nettelbeck, & Wilson, 2010).

A HIERARCHICAL MODEL

The Big Five factors are part of a hierarchical model of personality description. Each factor consists of components called **facets**, which can be measured separately. Each facet is a somewhat more precise and focused trait of personality than the larger factor to which it belongs, yet all the facets that belong to one factor are positively correlated with one another (see Table 8.4). This structure is similar to the relationship between Cattell's second-order factors (comparable to the Big Five) and his 16 primary

facet
a more precisely focused aspect of any of the Big Five factors

Table 8.4 Specific Facets of the Big Five Factors of Personality	
Factor	**Facets**
Extraversion (E)	Warmth
	Gregariousness
	Assertiveness
	Activity
	Excitement-seeking
	Positive emotions
Agreeableness (A)	Trust
	Straightforwardness
	Altruism
	Compliance
	Modesty
	Tender-mindedness
Neuroticism (N)	Anxiety
	Hostility
	Depression
	Self-consciousness
	Impulsiveness
	Vulnerability
Conscientiousness (C)	Competence
	Order
	Dutifulness
	Achievement striving
	Self-discipline
	Deliberation
Openness (O)	Fantasy
	Aesthetics
	Feelings
	Actions
	Ideas
	Values

Note: Each of the five factors in the left column is composed of the six facets of that factor in the right column. The facets are positively correlated with one another, and scores on the facets are summed to obtain a score on the corresponding factor.

Source: Adapted from Costa, McCrae, & Dye, 1991.

factors (comparable to the facets). Sometimes, because they are more precisely focused, particular facets are better predictors than the more general factors—for example, in predicting prejudice (Ekehammar & Akrami, 2007).

In addition to analyzing the more focused facets of the five factors, some researchers have asked whether they can be described as fewer, more general higher-order factors. Digman (1997) suggests that two such higher-order factors exist, one that reflects high Agreeableness, Conscientiousness, and Emotional Stability, and the other the factors of Extraversion and Openness.

ARE THE FIVE FACTORS UNIVERSAL?

Considerable research supports the universality of the Big Five factors across diverse cultures (McCrae, 2000; McCrae & Costa, 2008). Study people in different countries (Germany, Italy, the Netherlands, Spain, the Philippines, Turkey, the United States, and others), speaking different languages, and the same factors emerge, with perhaps more variation on Openness (Caprara et al., 2000; Church & Katigbak, 2000; De Raad, 1998; McCrae et al., 1998; Somer & Goldberg, 1999; Wiggins & Trapnell, 1997).

The Five Factor theory claims legitimacy in part because the same factors emerge in factor analysis despite variations in how data are obtained, across various ages and statistical techniques. Self-report questionnaires and peer ratings yield similar results.

However, some research identifies subgroups in which factor analysis yields a different number of factors. Among people who are particularly high in cognitive complexity (a trait described in Chapter 13), factor analysis yields 7 factors. Among those low in cognitive complexity, factor analysis yields only 3 factors. For those in the middle, the usual Five Factor model fits the data (Bowler, Bowler, & Phillips, 2009). Perhaps our reliance on self-report measures is constraining what we can learn about personality structure. After all, the method is based on people's perceptions of personality, and perceptive abilities can vary.

Saucier (2009) argues for a Big Six model across diverse languages and populations, and says that the sixth factor would have emerged earlier if researchers had included a broader number of personality descriptors in their research, instead of excluding adjectives such as "stupid, wicked, or outstanding" that are highly evaluative (p. 1581).

The HEXACO model includes the well-known factors of the Five Factor model (with some variations) and adds a sixth factor, Honesty-Humility, which distinguishes straightforward and unpretentious people from those who are self-centered and manipulative (de Vries, de Vries, & Feij, 2009). This model has been found in several languages (Lee & Ashton, 2008). A 7-factor model has been found in the Chinese language (Zhou et al., 2009).

Some researchers have even argued for one general factor of personality, to which all the other factors are correlated (e.g., Erdle et al., 2010; Rushton & Irwing, 2009a). Rushton and Irwing (2009b) suggest that this general personality factor predicts social efficacy; that is, it represents a cooperative tendency that has come about because of the selective pressures of evolution (Rushton, Bons, & Hur, 2008).

Though there is some debate about the details, in large measure the Big Five factors appear to be universal. Why should these particular factors be so robust? As described earlier, the factors originated from analysis of language, the rationale being that people will talk about the aspects of personality that are important to them as they interact (Goldberg, 1981). David Buss (1997), who offers an evolutionary approach to personality, reasons that people need to know how others will behave in their quest for social dominance. The factor Extraversion taps behavior, such as social assertiveness, related to social dominance, so it has become an important factor in all comprehensive trait models. Another issue is important in social interaction: our expectations that others will cooperate, perhaps to form alliances. The factor Agreeableness reflects cooperative tendencies, so it, too, has become an important factor when people talk about one another. It is not difficult to understand that people would also find it useful to label others as dependable or not (Conscientiousness) and as emotionally stable or not (Neuroticism). Openness is less well represented in everyday language than the other factors, but even here, knowing who is intellectual and aesthetic would be essential in any social group that values the mind and the arts.

VARIOUS MEASURES OF THE BIG FIVE

Alternative measures of these five factors have been developed. Adjective rating scales are based on carefully selected adjectives for each of the five factors (Goldberg, 1992), and make brief assessment possible. An interview measure for studying clinic populations permits the interviewer to follow up on personality trends to see whether they are maladaptive for the individual. For example, a person who seems high in the Agreeableness factor by affirmatively answering the question, "Do you often go out of your way to help others who are in need?" will then be asked, "Do you do this at the sacrifice of your own best interests?" (Trull et al., 1998).

Self-ratings, ratings by friends, and even ratings by interviewers who are just getting to know a person tend to agree. When people are trying to present themselves in a particular way—being conscientious for a mock job interviewer, for example—this strategic self-presentation may reduce the accuracy of an interviewer's impression (Barrick, Patton, & Haugland, 2000).

The Five Factor theory has prompted researchers to reexamine earlier personality tests to see whether they can be reinterpreted from this perspective. In many cases, they can. The five factors are found in analyses of the California Personality Inventory (McCrae, Costa, & Piedmont, 1993), the Eysenck Personality Inventory (McCrae & Costa, 1982), the Myers-Briggs Type Inventory (McCrae, 1991), the Personality Research Form (Costa & McCrae, 1988), the Adjective Check List (Craig et al., 1998), and other tests. Thus researchers can infer a person's scores on these five factors, based on data previously collected using other tests. Such recoding has permitted researchers to consider the Five Factor model in longitudinal research spanning 45 years. They concluded that these factors were relatively stable from the first test at the end of college to retest in the men's 60s and that they predicted adult adjustment and behavior (Soldz & Vaillant, 1999). Other longitudinal studies of the five factors not only support their general stability over time, but also suggest that they can change to some extent with life experiences. For example, neuroticism scores decrease when people become involved in relationships (Neyer & Lahnart, 2007). Generally, though, researchers report that the factors are stable over time.

FACTORS AND OTHER PERSONALITY CONSTRUCTS

Now that the validity of the separate five factors has been well established, many researchers have tried to see how these factors correspond to other personality constructs. In many cases, combinations of the five factors are correlated with other personality traits. For example, the combination of neuroticism with introversion yields a pattern that seems to correspond to Karen Horney's (see Chapter 6) "moving away" type of personality, while neuroticism combined with extraversion corresponds to her "moving against" type personality (Gramzow et al., 2004, p. 379). As noted above, Neuroticism is correlated with difficulties in relationships, but Introversion, low Agreeableness, and low Conscientiousness also contribute to such difficulties (Malouff et al., 2010).

Factors describe underlying personality traits, but a more complete understanding of a person requires more than assessing factor scores. McCrae and Costa (2008) suggest that the five factors describe basic tendencies that are influenced by biology, and that in turn influence an individual's characteristic adaptations (such as personal strivings) and self-concept. Combinations of the five factors predict a variety of behaviors and life outcomes, including thoughts about retirement (Robinson, Demetre, & Corney, 2010). The Big Five factors show significant associations with the ways that people tell their life narratives—for example, sad stories told by those high in Neuroticism (Raggatt, 2006). It's clear that trait and factor measures alone are not enough to convey the richness of an individual's personality as it is expressed in a person's life. But they are a fine starting point.

Summary

- Both of the theories discussed in this chapter, Cattell's 16 factor model and the Five Factor theory, use factor analysis to identify the major dimensions of personality description.
- Cattell defined *personality* simply as "that which permits a prediction of what a person will do in a given situation."
- Cattell developed a great number of *personality tests*.
- Cattell's research obtained data from three sources: self-report questionnaires (*Q-data*); objective tests, including projective tests and behavioral measures (*T-data*); and life history information (*L-data*). He sought convergence across these sources of data.

- Cattell used *multivariate* research methods.
- Cattell described the *surface traits* of people and, through more intensive statistical analysis, sought the underlying *source traits* that determine personality.
- Cattell's *16PF* personality test builds on this research and measures the 16 major source traits of personality. These scores can be presented in a *profile* for each individual.
- A *second-order factor analysis* of these scores results in five more general factors, including extraversion and anxiety.
- Cattell distinguished various types of traits: *dynamic*, *temperament*, and *ability*.

- Cattell differentiated *fluid intelligence* (innate potential) from *crystallized intelligence* (influenced by experience) and developed ways to measure fluid intelligence.
- Cattell's *dynamic lattice* presents the relationship among *ergs* (constitutional dynamic source traits) and *metaergs* (environmental-mold dynamic source traits), which include *sentiments* and *attitudes*.
- These are related according to the principle of *subsidiation*.
- In principle, behavior can be predicted by the *specification equation*, which includes traits, situational factors, and temporary factors.
- Although most of his research was nomothetic *(R-technique)*, Cattell also explored a *P-technique* for idiographic research.

- Cattell developed the *MAVA technique* to investigate the impact of heredity on personality.
- Although his approach has been criticized for being atheoretical, Cattell argued that extensive empirical work such as his had much to contribute to theoretical advances in personality.
- Another factor theory, the *Five Factor model,* includes Extraversion, Agreeableness, Neuroticism, Conscientiousness, and Openness as factors derived from analysis of language.
- The Big Five factors are found in many personality tests and have been compared to Cattell's second-order factors of personality.
- The Big Five factors, assessed by self-report or peer report, are correlated with behavior as would be expected, and researchers report that they are heritable.

Thinking about Factor Analytic Trait Theories

1. Gordon Allport had an office near Raymond Cattell's office, and students were often confused by the differences between their approaches to personality. Why might this be so?
2. What is your opinion about the causes of intelligence, especially the extent to which heredity and experience influence intelligence?
3. Discuss why people may have a difficult time being objective and unemotional when discussing the role of heredity as a determinant of intelligence and personality.
4. Cattell urges using mathematics in part because without it we have difficulty keeping several causes of behavior in

mind simultaneously. How multivariate can you be without math? Try to explain a particular behavior (e.g., working through the lunch hour), using as many variables as you can keep in mind at once.
5. Compare the Five Factor model with Cattell's model. Based on this comparison, does it seem broad enough to encompass all the major dimensions of personality?
6. Propose a research study to investigate the impact of the social environment on any one specific hereditary dimension of personality. For example, how might an inherited predisposition for high levels of anxiety lead to maladaptive personality in one environment but not in another?

Study Questions

1. How did Cattell define personality?
2. Describe Cattell's contributions to personality testing.
3. List and explain the three sources of data that Cattell included in his research. Give an example of each.
4. Explain what is meant by multivariate research.
5. Distinguish between surface traits and source traits.
6. Describe Cattell's 16PF. Why is it said to measure source traits rather than surface traits?
7. What is factor analysis? What is second-order factor analysis?
8. Summarize Cattell's contributions to the measurement of intelligence. Include a description of his concepts of fluid intelligence and crystallized intelligence.
9. What did Cattell report about the inheritance of intelligence?
10. Distinguish between ergs and metaergs. Give examples of each.
11. Explain the principle of subsidiation in Cattell's dynamic lattice. Give an example.
12. What is the purpose of the specification equation? What terms are included? (Explain in words.)
13. Explain the P-technique. How is it different from the more common R-technique? Which method would you use if you

wanted to study one individual in depth to determine what circumstances triggered that person's asthma?
14. What is the purpose of the MAVA technique of data analysis? What findings have resulted from this technique?
15. List the Big Five factors and describe each briefly.
16. How are the Big Five factors measured?
17. Summarize the behavior of a person who scores high on Extraversion. Summarize the behavior of a person who scores low (an introvert).
18. Contrast the interpersonal behavior of a person who scores high on Agreeableness with a person who scores low.
19. How is Neuroticism related to emotions? When is it adaptive, and when does it lead to less desirable outcomes?
20. How is the factor of Conscientiousness related to educational and work behavior?
21. List some of the behaviors that are related to Openness.
22. What are *facets* in the Big Five factor model?
23. Are the Big Five factors universal? Describe the evidence.
24. How does the Big Five factor model of personality compare with Cattell's model? How are they different?

Biological Theories
Evolution, Genetics, and Biological Factor Theories

ILLUSTRATIVE BIOGRAPHY
Hillary Rodham Clinton

Although personality theorists have long acknowledged that biological factors influence personality, only recently have detailed mechanisms described the variations that we find in normal personality. Why is one person shy and another bold, one anxious and another confident? Why does one person recoil from criticism, whereas another laughs it off? Now we are coming to understand the role that biology plays (in combination with environment and upbringing) to create this diversity of human personalities.

Hillary Rodham Clinton, the former First Lady who subsequently was elected as senator from New York and then appointed Secretary of State, has been an active and

Hillary Clinton

sometimes controversial public figure. Much in her life story speaks powerfully of the importance of upbringing and environment in determining personality. Yet these for her, as for all of us, did not act on a *tabula rasa* but rather on a person with a temperament, a biological potential that would interact with her experience to create a unique style of being human. Although the evidence is indirect—we have no bioassays or brain scans to offer—and the interpretations admittedly speculative, her life story illustrates the emerging biological models of personality presented in this chapter.

Hillary Rodham was born in 1947, the first child to hardworking parents in Illinois. She and her four brothers were disciplined with love and high standards for achievement. Impressive academic and extracurricular activities won her entrance to the prestigious Wellesley College, where she encountered liberal attitudes that contrasted with her conservative Republican upbringing. Graduating as valedictorian, she publicly criticized the conservative Republican speaker who had preceded her, receiving a 7-minute standing ovation (Brock, 1996) and nationwide attention as a voice of the liberal segment of the baby boom generation, those critical of the Nixon administration. She then attended Yale Law School, where she met her future husband, William Jefferson Clinton, whose career as Arkansas governor and then U.S. president (1993–2001) detracted (some say) from Hillary's own promising career as a young lawyer. Public controversy and defeat followed her ambitious proposal for national health care reform. This active role in government as an unelected First Lady was either a bonus or an intrusion, depending on the perspective of her supporters or opponents. Her husband, whose extramarital sexual activities had plagued their relationship for years, was publicly humiliated when a White House intern, Monica Lewinsky, exposed their liaison. After two terms in the White House, the couple reversed public roles; Hillary became the elected politician, winning the election to represent New York in the U.S. Senate (2001–2009). In the 2008 presidential election season, she was a major contender for the Democratic nomination, which went to Barack Obama, who won the election and recruited his former rival as Secretary of State. In that position, she traveled worldwide more than her predecessors and played an active role in world issues, including the troubled Middle East. And so the adolescent Republican was transformed into a Democrat, and the political wife into a politician in her own right.

BIOLOGY

Biological theorists describe the role of physical processes in personality. Much attention has focused on emotions, both positive and negative. These activate different brain areas (more left hemisphere activation for positive emotions and also for anger; more right hemisphere for negative ones), and they are implicated in the formation of memory, so they have particular promise for understanding development. Another biological approach, the evolutionary approach, is based on the adaptive implications of personality variations for our ancestors. This approach suggests different predispositions for women and men on sexual issues: a greater tendency toward sexual promiscuity among men than women because women who are more sexually selective have a greater chance of conceiving and raising more genetically fit children. Evolutionary theory also suggests an appetite for greater sexual promiscuity in men than women and more female concern with nurturing children.

Public images more often capture Hillary Rodham Clinton in smiling or assertive/angry poses than in sad ones, suggesting a prevalence of the positive and left hemisphere emotions. The implications of this require considering personality development, as we do in a moment. The evolutionary argument about gender differences in sexual promiscuity is consistent with the evidence. In this marriage, it is the husband who was the philanderer.

DESCRIPTION

Hillary Rodham Clinton, in the words of one biographer, "seems to have been born ambitious" (Olson, 1999, p. 23). Temperament refers to the innate biological predispositions of personality; some people are bold and assertive, whereas others are timid and shy (and many others, somewhere in between). An assertive personality is more influenced by rewards than punishment. For other people, the pain of punishment seems greater because negative emotions, such as fear, are accentuated by their brain functioning, and so they act more cautiously.

From childhood onward, Hillary Rodham was more assertive and bold than timid, although not to an extreme. She recalls a childhood incident in which, with her mother's encouragement, at age 4 she stood up to a neighborhood bully who teased her (Clinton, 2003). In elementary school, Hillary reports that she was considered a tomboy and had a reputation for being able to stand up to unruly male classmates (Clinton, 2003, p. 15). For a less assertive person, fear would have precluded many of the choices that Hillary made in her life: leaving her Illinois home for a distant, not-yet-seen college on the East Coast; approaching a male classmate (her future husband, as it turns out) in the Yale library to introduce herself; presenting an ambitious health care reform proposal to a skeptical audience; embarking on her own elective political career. But fear is muted in Hillary Rodham Clinton's personality, an innate temperamental quality. This quality is also helpful in dealing with events outside her own choices. Her husband's infidelity and the ensuing media frenzy could have produced retreat into the safety of a private life, but it did not. Her temperament also energized bold stances in the Senate and as Secretary of State.

DEVELOPMENT

Understanding the development of personality from a biological perspective highlights the impact of experience on diverse temperamental beginnings. Biological theories specify genetically based variants in the brain's functioning that predispose variations in the emotional responses that shape personality. All of us seek what feels pleasant and recoil from what is punishing, but the inner experience of these emotions is enhanced or muted, depending on our biological makeup. These subtle variations tweak personality in one direction or another.

Kagan's model of temperament, described in this chapter, says that the outcome of a hereditary predisposition can be one of good or poor adjustment, depending on the experience of an appropriate child-rearing experience for that temperament type. For temperamentally bold children, clear guidance and discipline are important, so the lure of rewards does not lead to ill-chosen behavior. That is the sort of environment that Hillary Rodham's loving and hardworking parents provided, according to her autobiography.

Still, it is the rewards rather than the punishments that seem to have made the greatest impression. Here is a childhood recollection that illustrates her attention to rewards. In sixth grade, Hillary was co-captain of the school safety patrol. A friend's mother commented that she would have fixed lunch for them instead of leaving them to make their own sandwiches if she had known of Hillary's status, which Hillary described as "my first lesson in the strange ways some people respond to electoral politics" (Clinton, 2003, p. 15). There are rewards to be gained from politics.

ADJUSTMENT

Emotional reactions cause adjustment problems if they are extreme. Those people whose anxiety or depressive reactions are predisposed by heredity will be at greater risk of developing adjustment problems. The same life experience may push one

(continued)

(continued)

person over a threshold to dysfunction, whereas another remains stable, depending on their different biological predispositions. In contrast, positive emotions provide the incentive for assertive behavior; however, if they are extreme and untempered by negative experiences, they can lock a person into maladapted addictive patterns.

Hillary Rodham Clinton's life attests to an ability to withstand the trials that provoke anxiety and fear and to be more strongly influenced by potential rewards and achievements. In part, the greater influence of positive than negative emotions is the product of heredity (as Gray's Behavioral Activation System and Behavioral Inhibition System, described in this chapter, explain). Society's judgments are influenced by role expectations, including gender roles, and there certainly was a time when Hillary's assertive style of behavior was judged maladjusted in a woman. Such judgments still occur in some circles.

COGNITION

Heredity influences cognitive as well as emotional aspects of personality. Intelligence is under genetic control (although of course it requires educational opportunity to fulfill its potential). Cognition, though, is more than simply intelligence. Researchers have even found that attitudes toward social issues, inclinations toward liberalism or conservatism, are influenced by heredity, although undoubtedly by indirect mechanisms, and in interaction with experience.

Hillary Rodham Clinton's academic credentials attest to high intelligence. She was near the top of her high school class, missing the top spot, according to one biographer, because some of her energies were expended on extracurricular involvements. She was the valedictorian of her class at rigorous Wellesley College. Attitudes of liberalism and conservatism are influenced by both heredity and experience. In studying a single case, it is not possible to know which of these influences was more important. Did Hillary become more liberal in college because of the experiences in that environment? Or could some of the suppressed heredity from her mother, a secret liberal Democrat in a conservative Republican family and town, have been freed for expression in that more permissive environment? We can only speculate, with one case.

CULTURE

Biology is expressed in a social context, and for humans, our shared biological predispositions have prepared us to play a role in a social environment. The ability to communicate with other people, to cooperate and to compete with them, is fundamental to our nature. We also learn from one another, and these lessons are passed down from one generation to the next, changing with each generation's experience, producing what can be called "cultural evolution." Thus the life experience of a person must be understood within a particular society and time.

The society and time that Hillary Rodham Clinton experienced is the postwar baby boom generation of America: a time of increased opportunities for women to participate in public life, and a time of disenchantment with the nation's political leadership that was particularly salient during Hillary's high school and college years, over the Vietnam War. As she points out in her autobiography (Clinton, 2003), women's colleges, such as her alma mater Wellesley College, have a track record of cultivating leadership in women. And so she emerged into young adulthood, prepared by her culture's influence to be more flexible than previous generations of women in the style of her femininity. Traditional maternal concerns for children are an example. She could try (although unsuccessfully) to care for the nation's children through expanded government health programs, in addition to nurturing her own daughter, Chelsea. Societal considerations can also help us to understand the intensity of anti-Hillary feeling that her critics voice. Dominance is characteristically a male trait, whether by evolutionary selection or cultural teaching or some combination of these. A woman with low levels of fear, who seizes the opportunities of this place and time to assert dominance, is thus unusual, and much psychological research indicates that people generally prefer the familiar to the new.

FINAL THOUGHTS

Although this chapter focuses on biological influences, it is clear from this brief analysis of Hillary Rodham Clinton that culture, too, must be considered. Theorists no longer present debates of nature versus nurture. They seek models to integrate the two. How does the environment enhance or suppress the possibilities that each person's biology predisposes? Thinking in these terms, the assertive, ambitious, and resilient Hillary Rodham Clinton is a product of both her biology and her familial and cultural environment. Using a phrase that is part of the curriculum in the women's college where I teach, we may call her a "woman of influence," as one who is not only product but also producer of our evolving culture.

PREVIEW: OVERVIEW OF BIOLOGICAL THEORIES

Biological approaches to personality have skyrocketed in importance as genetic methods and evolutionary theories have advanced. Biological theories have implications for major theoretical questions, as presented in Table 9.1. They have generated many empirical studies. The concreteness of many biological concepts further adds to the scientific status of this approach by suggesting clear operational definitions. The biological approach adds to the comprehensiveness of trait approaches by connecting personality to natural science. The potential for applied value in a biological approach is considerable, and the approach is already stimulating reconceptualization of many psychiatric problems. If reliable and valid assessments of personality predispositions in early life are developed, this approach may help identify the particular optimal "nurture" environment for people with different genetic "nature," thus permitting intervention.

Table 9.1 Preview of Biological Theories

Individual Differences	Individuals differ in their hereditary predispositions and in the traits that develop from the interaction of these predispositions with experience. Several factor theories describe individual differences.
Adaptation and Adjustment	Some biological factors, such as Neuroticism, are differences in emotional instability that predispose some people to anxiety and other adjustment problems. Differences in responses to rewards and punishments, based on biological differences, can predispose people to addiction, depression, and other problems.
Cognitive Processes	Evolutionary theory points to human language and cognitive abilities as adaptations characteristic of our species because of natural selection.
Culture	Society channels inherited traits and provides the cultural context for their expression through learning.
Biological Influences	Biological factors are the central focus of this approach, including evolutionary selection, heredity, brain, and neurotransmitter effects.
Development	Temperament is observable in infancy and later, as an early indicator of the individual's inherited biologically based personality. Some early experiences can sensitize particular neural pathways (e.g., for stress reactions).

EVOLUTIONARY APPROACHES

Imagine a small group of our ancient human ancestors. They are almost all related in some way, with a few women who have been coaxed or kidnapped from other clans. They seldom see other humans, and when they do, they are apprehensive and aggressive. One man is clearly the privileged one when it comes to food and mating. There is relative peace, except for occasional sexual jealousy or rivalry for status. The women gather food, with their superior memory for locations of fruits and berries, and care for their children. The men have gone to hunt, using their superior spatial abilities so useful for throwing spears. Children watch and imitate the skills their parents know. The adults tell tales of past hunting successes or talk about one another's social behavior.

These ancient ancestors are probably not so different from us, according to evolutionary theorists. The groups are much smaller—a few dozen people—and the advances that would come with the evolution of culture had not yet brought modern technology, but the fundamental emotions and behavioral impulses were remarkably like our own. This is the lesson of **evolutionary psychology**, which theorizes that natural selection—well known in biology because of the work of Charles Darwin (1859/1909) and others—has produced a human species with genetically based characteristics that affect personality and social behavior. The fundamental assumption is that genetic variations that enhance reproductive success become more frequent over generations as a result of natural selection.

Evolutionary theory has widespread applicability to many areas of personality (Michalski & Shackelford, 2010) and, according to its advocates, offers a genuinely new paradigm for the study of personality (Buss, 1995; Buss et al., 1998; Cervone, 1999). In fact, advocates claim that the evolutionary approach has the potential to provide theoretical coherence to psychology, avoiding the exaggerated dualisms of "body and mind, human and animal, and nature and culture" that burden much of psychology (de Waal, 2002, p. 187).

David Buss (1999) describes **evolved psychological mechanisms**, which are specific psychological processes that have evolved because they solve particular adaptive problems of survival or reproduction (see Table 9.2). Sexual jealousy evolved as a psychological mechanism to deal with the problem of uncertain paternity. Other

evolutionary psychology

the perspective that applies the evolutionary principles of natural selection to understanding human psychology, including personality

evolved psychological mechanisms

specific psychological processes that have evolved because they solved particular adaptive problems (e.g., sexual jealousy, dealing with the problem of paternal uncertainty)

Table 9.2 Examples of Evolved Psychological Mechanisms

Sexual jealousy	Functions to help ensure men that they are the genetic fathers of their mate's child
Sexual attraction based on physical appearance	Functions to ensure a healthy mate and one with effects of hormones (estrogen or testosterone) that indicate fertility
Sexual attraction based on man's ability to provide resources	Functions to ensure women that their mates will be able to provide resources needed for the survival of their children
Sexual attraction based on youth	Functions to optimize the number of remaining years of fertility
Imitation	Functions to enable children to learn culture and to profit from the experience of adults

psychological mechanisms include female preference for mates who can supply economic resources, serving the function of providing for children, and male preferences for youth and variety in sexual partners, serving the functions of increasing the fertility and number of sexual partners (Buss, 1995). Fears of snakes and of spiders evolved as mechanisms that increased survival for our ancestors, as did preference for certain landscapes that offer safety and resources (Buss, 2008). The tendency to imitate others makes social learning possible, and is evidenced at the neural level by *mirror neurons* in the brain that fire when we see someone else's motor behavior as well as when we ourselves are behaving (Iacoboni, 2009). Psychological characteristics such as these do not need to be learned, and they influence us without our conscious awareness.

Let's look at some of the areas where an evolutionary approach speaks to personality theory: aggression and sexual behavior (salient in Freud's theory); parenting; altruism and social behavior; and cultural evolution.

AGGRESSION AND DOMINANCE

Aggressive behavior, from an evolutionary point of view, not only defends individuals against physical attacks, but also establishes status hierarchies. In many species, low-status males are less likely to mate, as high-status ones fight them off, and as females choose higher-status reproductive partners (who presumably carry more favorable genes to pass on to the offspring). The competition for mates makes aggression and status concerns a particularly male domain, as studies of humans confirm (Fischer & Mosquera, 2001; Halisch & Geppert, 2001; Jones, 1999; Mesquida & Wiener, 1996).

SEXUAL BEHAVIOR

Reproduction is of primary concern to evolutionary theory, with a focus on passing on one's genes to the next generation, and with a partner whose genes will contribute the maximum survival potential for the offspring.

Much research on sexual attraction is consistent with evolutionary theory. The gene race is won by those who mate with fertile partners, and both sexes prefer physically attractive partners, whose good looks and symmetrical features are signals of health and genetic fitness. Men prefer youthful females, who have more reproductive years ahead. Studies of attraction in a variety of societies, both in laboratory environments and by analyzing such real-world evidence as advertisements for dating introductions, confirm these predictions (Buss, 1989; Campos, Otta, & Siqueira, 2002; Fink & Penton-Voak, 2002; Hume & Montgomerie, 2001).

Attractive features also serve as "hormone markers," indicating higher levels of estrogen in females and testosterone in males. Research generally supports the evolutionary hypothesis that men prefer women with a low waist-to-hip ratio, an observable cue to high estrogen levels associated with greater fertility (Bereczkei, 2000; Furnham, Moutafi, & Baguma, 2002). Women are attracted to men whose faces show masculine bone structure features, such as a strong chin, that are produced by higher testosterone levels—especially when the women respond to researchers' questions during their most fertile phase (Fink & Penton-Voak, 2002).

Besides sexual attraction, promiscuity has been interpreted from an evolutionary perspective, with particular attention to sex differences. The double standard that accepts multiple sex partners more readily for men than for women is, according to this view, a biological given. Having multiple sexual partners increases the number of children than a man can sire, though the survival of each is diminished if he does not remain present to protect them. So two male reproductive strategies have emerged as alternatives: promiscuity (to increase the number of offspring) and commitment (to ensure the survival of one's children).

For females, a promiscuous pattern is less advantageous because of different **parental investment** for the two sexes (Buss, 1988; Trivers, 1972). A woman can produce only a limited number of children in her lifetime because of the 9 months of gestation and, in ancestral times, diminished fertility after birth when the baby is being breast-fed. Because of the greater costs in time and lost alternative opportunities with each conception, it is adaptive for the woman to be particularly selective about her choice of mate. To conceive a genetically inferior child who might die or fail to carry on the genetic line would waste her reproductive opportunity, and natural selection would reduce such genetic tendencies. The woman, then, must be sure that she mates with the man who provides the highest-quality genes for her investment in maternity. In addition, because of the dangers to a vulnerable child and mother, she also looks for a man who will stay to help protect them and to provide resources.

parental investment
the expenditure of time and resources to reproduce, especially emphasizing the amount of one's reproductive potential that is expended for each child

In contrast, a man's reproductive potential is much greater because sperm cells are so much more abundant than ova and the reduced reproductive potential after each conception is measured in hours, not years. This view suggests that by their nature, men are more opportunistic and women more selective in their sexual behavior. Research confirms this observation. Buss and Schmitt (1993), for example, asked undergraduates on a questionnaire how long they would wait before being willing to have sexual intercourse with a hypothetical person of the opposite sex they had just met. Women would wait for 3 months before becoming as willing as the man was after only 1 day; by 3 months, the man was as ready as the woman would be after 2 years.

The promiscuous strategy is not a man's only choice, and it brings risks. His children may not survive, given the harsh environment for unprotected mothers and the danger of child killing by competing men. An alternative is available: to become bonded with the mother and stay to ensure that his children will survive. The increased survival of these children compensates for lost reproductive opportunities elsewhere.

Because all his reproductive potential is invested in this one relationship (with perhaps a few surreptitious exceptions, if opportunity permits—to increase his reproductive potential), a new issue arises: Are the children really his, or has another man conceived them? This **paternal uncertainty** has no parallel in a woman's experience (because she has carried the child during pregnancy), so sexual jealousy is greater in men. Confirming this idea, several studies find that male college students in a variety of countries report greater distress than women at the hypothetical scenario of their dating partner having sex with another man; in contrast, women were more disturbed at the prospect of their partner having an emotional relationship with another woman, theoretically because it might entice the male protector away from her (Buss et al., 1992; Wiederman & Kendall, 1999). Based on their actual personal experiences, though, another researcher reports no sex differences in the pain of emotional and sexual partner infidelity, either in heterosexual or homosexual respondents (Harris, 2002).

paternal uncertainty
evolutionary proposal that men cannot be sure they are the biological fathers of the children born to their mates

The image of the selective and committed female and the unselective, promiscuous male sexual styles is of course an oversimplification, even within evolutionary theory. Men are more willing to report infidelities on self-report measures, but actual behavioral measures show less difference between the sexes. Women, too, engage in sexual relationships outside of their primary relationship, especially when the alternative partner is superior and when they are fertile (Drigotas & Barta, 2001). Theoretical arguments explain that it sometimes is in the best reproductive interest of the woman to reproduce with a more genetically fit man, even if he is not willing to stay to protect the child (Buss, 1999; Gangestad & Simpson, 1990).

Most of the data supporting male promiscuity and female commitment come from questionnaires to undergraduates, whereas the actual behavior of adults shows more long-term relationships in both sexes. An alternative model suggests that both sexes are primarily drawn to long-term mating as an extension of the attachment process of earlier life. Under conditions of adversity, children are less likely to be raised in the sort of stable family that is conducive to secure attachment. This teaches them a strategy that is adaptive under conditions of scarce resources, that is, to mate opportunistically, instead of counting on stable pair bonds and high investment in parenting (Bereczkei, 2000). When the situation is more stable, both parents care for children, offering an evolutionary advantage in the survival of the offspring during a long period of immaturity.

In portraying this evolutionary picture, we should not oversimplify. After all, many behaviors have no simple, obvious evolutionary advantage, and many genes combine to produce a great variety of outcomes in various individuals. Consider homosexuality, a sexual orientation influenced by a number of genes. The component genes, it has been argued, produce such traits as empathy and sensitivity, which are attractive to women and enhance fathering. When a great many of these genes are present, they produce homosexuality, which confers no reproductive advantage on the individual but which, argues E. M. Miller (2000), is consistent with evolutionary selection because of the positive contribution of the component genes to cooperation and other social traits.

Celibacy is another sexual pattern that seems inconsistent with the evolutionary impetus to reproduce, but it, too, can fit evolutionary models. Our genes, after all, are not exclusively our own. If we enhance the survival of our siblings' children, these shared genes are well served. A celibate aunt or uncle (or other relative) whose relatives gain sufficient survival advantage from his or her altruistic behavior may more than compensate for the genes lost by celibacy. Consistent with this reasoning, religious communities that mandate celibacy, from diverse traditions that include Christianity, Buddhism, and Islam, often refer to one another using kin terms, such as "sisters" or "brothers," and they dress and groom themselves to appear similar, as relatives would. These behaviors invoke evolutionary kin recognition mechanisms to encourage altruistic behavior (Qirko, 2004).

PARENTAL BEHAVIOR

Parents who nurture their children enhance the survival of their genes. Other family members, aunts and uncles, grandparents, and others, who share some of these genes, also have an investment in the child's survival to reproductive maturity. Stepchildren, who are not the genetic offspring of the parent, are more often abused or neglected (Belsky, 1993) and they receive less financial support for education (Zvoch, 1999). Families can provide a supportive environment for the mother and child, with long-term consequences for the child's psychological health. In contrast, children who are exposed to stressed or depressed mothers during their preschool years have elevated cortisol levels later, indicating that they have developed a physiological sensitization to stress (Essex et al., 2002). Animal studies show that young rats who are deprived of maternal contact for as few as 3 hours per day develop permanent deficits in the hippocampus that could affect later learning and memory and make them (and humans too, if the result generalizes across species) more vulnerable to depression (Karten, Olariu, & Cameron, 2005). Clearly, not only survival but also the development of a psychologically healthy child depends upon good parenting.

ALTRUISM AND SOCIAL EMOTIONS

Groups that help one another have a survival advantage. Reciprocity in food sharing was likely essential to survival of our ancestors, as it is among hunter-gatherers today, and it seems likely that the importance of our own shared meals reflects the evolutionary importance of such sharing (Rilling & Sanfey, 2011).

The concept of **inclusive fitness** assumes that evolution will select for genes that increase the survival not only of the individual but also others who share his genes, through such social behaviors as nurturing children who are more distant relatives (Hamilton, 1964, as cited in Buss, 2008). Evolutionary approaches explain altruistic behavior according to two principles: kin altruism and reciprocal altruism.

The principle of **kin altruism** asserts that natural selection favors those who act altruistically toward their genetic relatives because the genes they save are (in part) identical to their own. Helping nonrelatives is explained by the concept of **reciprocal altruism**, whereby members of a group have evolved tendencies to help one another, even if they are unrelated. An individual's risk of harm while helping someone else is compensated by the increased benefit when others help him or her, so the net result is greater probability of survival. The maximum survival probability would belong to those who are surrounded by reciprocally altruistic others but who themselves would not help in an emergency.

These "cheaters" threaten others, whose risk by helping is not compensated by the benefits of being helped, and so mechanisms to control them are brought into play: scorn for free riders and honor to heroes. We are prepared by evolution to be on the alert for signs that people are not trustworthy by being skeptical about their motivations when there are reasons to think they may be deceiving us, and we are punitive toward those who don't contribute their fair share (Andrews, 2001; Price, Cosmides, & Tooby, 2002). Our brains come prewired to understand social nuances of cooperation and competition.

Altruism is not a rationally calculated act. It flows from a basic and unlearned psychological process, empathy. Shared with many other species, empathy arouses emotions that the individual sees in others, and thus provides the incentive to reduce the other's suffering and thereby one's own (de Waal, 2008). Emotions are essential for social behavior. We're prewired to understand others' facial expressions of emotion, with universally understood innate expressions of fear, happiness, anger, and other emotions (Ekman, 1993). But what triggers our own emotions? According to David Buss (2000), "Human anguish in modern minds is tethered to the events that would have caused fitness failure in ancestral times" (p. 18), that is, loss of social status, rejection by sexual partners, death of a child, and so on. Emotions and their communication make human social living possible.

CULTURE

Oddly, one of the most important evolutionary legacies is the ability of humans to form cultures. This irony illustrates how modern evolutionary theory challenges the biology–culture distinction that many take for granted. Cultural transmission of ideas from one generation to another includes elaborate symbolic representations, such as religion (Boyer, 2000). An evolutionary genetic change permitted humans to accumulate culture that continued to develop and change over many generations through learning, without the requirement of further genetic change (Tomasello, 1999).

Each personality develops in an environment shaped by cumulative **cultural evolution**. In fact, because biological evolution has continued among our human ancestors who had culture, including mystical and religious aspects, we may refer to both culture and biology in a conjoint way, as a *biocultural* paradigm or model (de Nicolas, 1998).

Evolutionary selective pressures can explain cultural practices. Consider the taboo against eating beef and oxen in cultures that needed those animals to plow fields. Over time, those who ate their animals were more likely to lose their farms and ultimately starve; those who kept the animals despite famine, if they survived, could plant the next crop (Alessi, 1992). Cultural practices coevolve with genetic evolution. Individual behaviors and societal-level cultural practices are mutually influential (Bereczkei, 2000).

inclusive fitness

the evolutionary principle that traits that increase the survival of the individual and his or her genetic relatives will become more frequent by natural selection

kin altruism

the principle that natural selection favors those who risk their own lives or welfare to improve the survival and reproductive prospects of their genetic relatives

reciprocal altruism

the evolutionary principle whereby members of a group take risks to help the survival and reproductive prospects of others, even nonrelatives, with the (not necessarily conscious) expectation of being helped in return

cultural evolution

evolution through transmitted learning from one generation to another

GENETICS AND PERSONALITY

behavioral genetic approach

approach that investigates the genetic and environmental contributions to behavior

Evolutionary theory portrays the big picture of our biologically based personality. For closer attention to detailed mechanisms, we turn to genetics.

The **behavioral genetic approach** studies genetic contributions to a variety of behaviors, including traits associated with both normal and pathological variations in personality. The research approach also provides estimates of environmental contributions, though these may be imprecise if the important aspects of the environment are not identified and measured. The strategy is to examine the similarity of twins, compared with other relatives, and taking into account whether or not they are raised together. Though this is not a new approach (Fuller, 1960), it is receiving increased attention today, despite some people's resistance to thinking of personality as determined by genetics (Johnson, Vernon, & Feiler, 2008).

heritability

the statistic that shows what proportion of the variability of a trait in a particular population is associated with genetic variability

Many personality tests show substantial genetic influences, usually with **heritability** estimates of about 0.50 (Bouchard & Loehlin, 2001; Clark & Watson, 1999; Loehlin, McCrae, & Costa, 1998). Intelligence, too, is substantially influenced by heredity (Deary, Johnson, & Houlihan, 2009). The heritability estimate is a description of how much of the variability of a trait, studied in a particular population, can be attributed to the genetic variation in that population. Studies that consider whether twins and other relatives have been raised together or adopted out into different homes make it clear that it is the genetic influence, and not the fact of having been raised by the same parents, that produces similarity among siblings.

One review concludes that "virtually every trait that has ever been examined . . . has a substantial genetic component" (Clark & Watson, 1999, p. 411). It is surprising how many characteristics, besides the usual personality factor tests, show significant heritability. Traits thought to be related to moral development, the "dark triad" of Machiavellianism, narcissism, and psychopathology, are significantly inherited, though moral development itself seems to depend more on experience, according to evidence so far (Campbell et al., 2009). Many other traits and attitudes show genetic effects (see Table 9.3).

Behavioral genetic studies not only show the impact of heredity on various traits, but also illuminate the ways that particular genetic profiles combine or interact with certain environmental experiences to produce outcomes. Such approaches are changing the way that experts think about personality disorders (Livesley & Jang, 2008). One promise of such research is to suggest ways to intervene for vulnerable individuals by taking care to provide them with the environmental support that they, in particular, need.

Beyond estimating the impact of heredity, researchers have also identified some of the specific genes and neurotransmitters that are involved in various personality dimensions, including Novelty Seeking and Harm Avoidance in the tridimensional model of Cloninger (described in this chapter) and Extraversion in the Five Factor model presented in Chapter 8 (Ebstein, 2006), as well as emotional intelligence

Table 9.3 Examples of Personality Characteristics for Which Significant Heritability Has Been Found

authoritarian attitudes (McCourt et al., 1999)

coping styles (Busjahn et al., 1999)

ego development (Newman, Tellegen, & Bouchard, 1998)

happiness, or subjective well-being (Lykken & Tellegen, 1996; Weiss, Bates, & Luciano, 2008)

likelihood of marriage and divorce (Jerskey et al., 2010; McGue & Lykken, 1992)

mental toughness (Horsburgh et al., 2009)

political views (Verhulst, Hatemi, & Martin, 2010)

sense of humor (Vernon et al., 2008; Vernon et al., 2010)

social attitudes (Tesser, 1993)

(Vernon et al., 2008), aggressiveness (Schmidt et al., 2002), and anger and impulsivity (Congdon & Canli, 2008; Joyce et al., 2009).

Sometimes individuals seem quite different from the rest of the family, and we may wonder how this can be. The inherited genetic profile, called the **genotype**, does not always correspond to observed characteristics, or **phenotype**. For one thing, genetic predispositions may be manifested differently, depending upon the environment. Genes are not always active. Like computer programs that do nothing until they are executed (much to the relief of those who find computer viruses on their machines that have not yet been activated), genes can be turned on and off in their expression by a variety of environmental factors that are just beginning to be understood.

In addition, combinations of many different genes are not simply additive in their effect on phenotype. In the case of **emergenic traits** (Lykken et al., 1992), a particular combination of genes produces a quite different phenotype from what would be anticipated by observing those with only some of the genes but not the unique combination. Among emergenic traits are extraordinary mathematical genius that can emerge in some individuals, such as Karl Gauss and the Hindu mathematician Srivinvasa Ramanujan, without evidence of particular talent in that area among other family members. Thus the impact of genetics on personality cannot be studied simply by documenting similarity in observable personality among those who are genetic relatives. Ultimately, we will need to understand the mechanisms by which genes, in their environmental context, influence personality.

TEMPERAMENT

Temperament is the biological foundation of personality, based on a child's inherited predisposition for certain behavior patterns. One typology, the EASI model, proposes four dimensions: emotionality, activity, sociability, and impulsivity (Buss & Plomin, 1975). Beyond infancy and childhood, other descriptors of temperament are useful. Some research points to a dimension that concerns negative emotion versus effortful control, and a second dimension that concerns extraversion and positive emotionality (Evans & Rothbart, 2008). Another temperament dimension, observed in adolescents, is a combination of self-esteem with low depression and low negative emotionality (Neiss et al., 2009).

Let's focus our attention on a childhood temperament model presented by Jerome Kagan (1994) because he proposes connections with specific biological variables. Kagan and his colleagues found a variety of behavior patterns when children are tested in standard novel situations (Garcia-Coll, Kagan, & Reznick, 1984; Kagan, 1994). In one study, 21-month-old children played with toys while their mother was with them. After a few minutes, an experimenter entered and played with the toys and then left. What would the child do? Some imitated the experimenter's play behavior (e.g., by having a doll talk on a telephone). Others did not; some even cried. Next, another woman entered and sat on a chair briefly, and then she spoke to the child and invited interaction on some developmental tasks. Most children at first stared at the strange woman; some approached and participated in the tasks, whereas others withdrew to their mother and would have nothing to do with the stranger. Then the experimenter returned and showed the child a robot; some children played with it, whereas others would not and stayed with their mothers. As a final test, the experimenter and the child's mother both left the room to see what the child would do when left alone.

The children's reactions varied depending on their temperament type. One pattern, the **inhibited type**, interacted less with the experimenter and with the strange woman, and they often cried and clung to their mothers during these novel experiences. Other children, the **uninhibited type**, interacted more with the experimenter, were more likely to approach the strange woman, and were more likely to approach and touch the toy robot that the experimenter showed them. (Some children did not fit into either of these two groups.)

These early behaviors predicted the child's behavior at age 7 when inhibited children shyly watched while other children played, and uninhibited children initiated interaction and seemed happier to play with other kids (Kagan, 1994, p. 132). Other

genotype

the inherited genetic profile of an individual

phenotype

the developed characteristics that can be observed in an individual, based on both genetic and environmental influences

emergenic traits

phenotypic traits caused by a constellation of many genes and so may not appear to run in families

temperament

the biologically based foundation of personality, including such characteristic patterns of behavior as emotionality, activity, and sociability

inhibited type

temperament type (described by Kagan) that is shy and nonassertive around strangers, proposed to have high levels of norepinephrine and an activation of the amygdala

uninhibited type

temperament type (described by Kagan) that is outgoing and low in fear, proposed to have lower sympathetic nervous system activity research also indicates relative stability of a child's behavior over time and suggests that children's talkativeness with people they do not know is a key behavior indicating whether they are shy, inhibited types or outgoing, uninhibited types.

These temperament types have a genetic basis, with heritabilities of 0.5 or higher (Kagan, 1994). Inhibited children are especially afraid of unfamiliar stimuli, according to Kagan, because their genetic makeup produces high levels of norepinephrine and/or corticotropin-releasing hormone. These in turn lead to stimulation of the **amygdala** and other brain areas involved in fear, which then produces greater sympathetic nervous system activity: acceleration in heart rate, rise in blood pressure, dilation of pupils, and evidence through urinalysis of more norepinephrine (see Figure 9.1).

Conversely, the uninhibited children have less activity in the amygdala and low levels of the neurotransmitter norepinephrine. Consequently, they are low in sympathetic nervous system reactivity, which makes them less fearful. Researchers have noted low heart rates in such adolescents and adults (Kagan, 1994, p. 53). As they develop through childhood and beyond, the uninhibited children are less affected by fear of punishment than their inhibited peers. Therefore, they are more disposed to become aggressive and antisocial, and in some cases criminals. Kagan warns that the uninhibited children, unless carefully disciplined, "may acquire a permissive superego" (Kagan, 1994, p. 240). Inhibited 3-year-olds, in contrast, are likely to become unassertive, depressed adults with little social support (Caspi, 2000).

Genetic inheritance does not alone determine personality. A child with an inherited tendency toward an inhibited temperament will not necessarily develop in that direction. Perhaps surprisingly, if the environment is very calming and predictable, with mothers who hold their infants a lot and do not call out warnings to them, the infants develop their predisposition toward inhibition. However, if the mothers give their infants more latitude to explore the world, by not holding them so much and by calling out explicit warnings when they do something forbidden, these clear limits produce a child who is less inhibited (Kagan, 1994, p. 205). Here's a comparison that may help make this clear: Imagine you are walking through a woods and some of the plants

amygdala

brain area involved in fear, theorized (by Kagan) to contribute to inhibited temperament

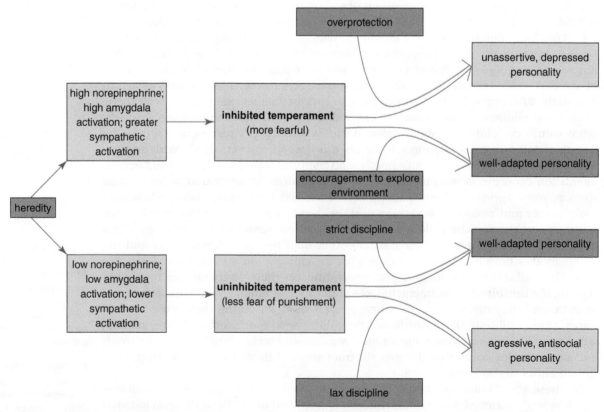

FIGURE 9.1   Inhibited and Uninhibited Temperament in Kagan's Model

have painful but invisible thorns. You would be inhibited, keeping a distance from all plants. But if you had a guide who reliably called out a warning when you got near the dangerous plants, you would explore more freely. Kagan's genetically inhibited group, then, seems to be the one for whom Alfred Adler's warning about the dangers of "pampering" is good advice.

The concept of temperament reminds us that in the parent–child interaction, influence goes in both directions. Temperament influences how parents respond to their child (e.g., Larsson, Viding, & Plomin, 2008), suggesting that if parents are to be blamed for poor child outcomes, perhaps we should point fingers at their genes, rather than their parenting style.

Children with different temperaments behave differently, and in turn they are treated differently by others, including their parents and other adults. This can produce ambiguities and errors when we interpret observations. If a genetically difficult child is behaving badly and, in turn, is treated harshly by parents, a person observing the parents and child might think the parents' behavior is to blame, overlooking the role of the child's temperament. On the other hand, simply looking at genetic studies may suggest little environmental effect, leading researchers to underestimate the impact of parents (cf. Maccoby, 2000). More nuanced research is needed to untangle cause–effect dynamics.

Increasingly, researchers are finding that particular combinations of a genetic predisposition and a particular environmental pressure work together to produce outcomes. For example, the combination of a gene for low monoamine oxidase A (MAOA) activity, combined with being maltreated in the family, makes boys more likely to develop child conduct disorder and adult antisocial behavior and criminality (Caspi et al., 2002, cited in Ferguson, 2010). Those with high MAOA activity are more resilient to maltreatment.

Furthermore, the effect of experience is not limited to behavior; it can change biology. Animal experiments show that experience influences the development of the brain. The density of glucocorticoid receptors in the hippocampus of newborn rats' brains is changed if they are handled by humans daily for 15 minutes for 3 weeks (Kagan, 1994, p. 35). Thus both genetic inheritance and early experience influence the physiology of the brain, and this combination of influences produces an individual's temperament.

EMOTIONAL AROUSAL

As argued above in relation to evolutionary theory, emotions are a key to human personality (Damasio, 1994). Neuroscientists study the brain mechanisms of emotion. Consider people's tendency to approach emotionally pleasant stimuli and to avoid emotionally unpleasant stimuli. Approach and avoidance, pleasure and pain, are not two extremes on the same scale; they are neurologically distinct. Studies of EEG brain wave recordings find that the left cerebral hemisphere is more active during pleasant emotional experiences and the right cerebral hemisphere during unpleasant emotional experiences (Davidson et al., 1990; Ekman, Davidson, & Friesen, 1990; Gross, 1999; Tomarken, Davidson, & Henriques, 1990). Not surprisingly, the left hemisphere is also more active when individuals are motivated to approach, and the right when they are motivated to avoid (Harmon-Jones & Allen, 1997; Sutton & Davidson, 1997). People with a history of depression, and those with family history of depression, have less activity in the left hemisphere (Harmon-Jones & Allen, 1997).

What is being registered, though: the pleasantness or the tendency to approach it, in the left hemisphere? Is it the unpleasantness or the tendency to move away from it, in the right hemisphere? Anger provides an important clue. Anger activates the left hemisphere, suggesting that motivation, not emotion, is the key to left–right asymmetry. Anger, among the emotions, may have a unique role in helping people confront fear, depression, and other inhibiting negative emotions, without being immobilized (Harmon-Jones & Allen, 1998; Izard, 1991).

Anger has been of interest to those who study the relationship between emotions and physical illness, such as cardiovascular problems (Hodapp, Heiligtag, & Störmer,

1990; Houston, Smith, & Cates, 1989). Important for personality, the asymmetries are not only activated during transient emotional experiences in a laboratory, but they are also stable over time and correlated with people's typical emotions (Tomarken et al., 1992). Research suggests that specific cerebral differences, observable from infancy onward (Dawson et al., 1992), make important contributions to personality.

CORTICAL AROUSAL

In addition to emotional arousal is another kind of arousal: from thinking. We respond to interesting or exciting stimuli by becoming aroused from our relaxed state. People vary in how rapidly this arousal of the brain's cortex (*cortical arousal*) occurs and to what extent. The idea of cortical stimulation is based on the work of the Russian physiologist Ivan Pavlov. Pavlov noticed that the dogs in his classical conditioning studies increased their conditioned responses with increasing conditioned stimuli up to a certain point; after that, increasing the strength of stimuli led to a decline in the strength of conditioning. Pavlov reasoned that when the stimulus was too intense, the nervous system protected itself by some sort of inhibitory process to counterbalance the intense excitatory process set in action by the stimulus. Pavlov made one more intriguing observation: Dogs varied in the point at which inhibition kicked in. Some—who Pavlov said had a **strong nervous system**—increased the strength of their conditioning to much more intense levels of the stimulus than others, whose inhibitory processes were already decreasing the strength of conditioning. Because these others could tolerate only weaker stimuli, they were said to have a **weak nervous system**. These types of nervous systems, however, were described by Pavlov in strictly functional terms (what processes occurred—activation and inhibition), and not in terms of the underlying brain structures (see Figure 9.2).

People, too, vary from one to another in whether they tend to overreact or underreact to stimuli, and this physiological difference has implications for personality. We seek to compensate for our nervous system variations by behavior. Several theories

strong nervous system

in Pavlov's theory, a nervous system that forms stronger conditioned responses and tolerates higher intensities of stimulation; said by other theorists to produce extraversion

weak nervous system

in Pavlov's theory, a nervous system that forms weaker conditioned responses and does not tolerate high intensities of stimulation; said by other theorists to produce introversion

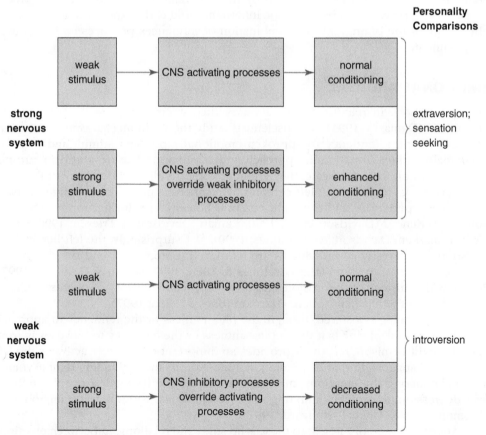

FIGURE 9.2 Pavlov's Model of the Nervous System and Implications for Personality

have proposed arousal-related personality concepts, including a trait called **sensation seeking** (Zuckerman, 1994). Sensation seeking is "the seeking of varied, novel, complex, and intense sensations and experiences, and the willingness to take physical, social, legal, and financial risks for the sake of such experience" (Zuckerman, 1994, p. 27). Highly influenced by genetics, this trait is thought to involve the enzyme monamine oxidase (MAO), which is low in sensation seekers, and two monoamine neurotransmitters that it regulates: dopamine (high) and serotonin (low) (Zuckerman & Kuhlman, 2000). College students who score high on the Sensation Seeking Scale typically prefer more arousing music (McNamara & Ballard, 1999). They are more likely to drink, smoke, use illegal drugs, gamble, and drive recklessly; and they are more likely to engage in risky sexual behaviors, such as unprotected sex and many sexual partners, that put them at risk for HIV infection (Hoyle, Fejfar, & Miller, 2000; Zuckerman & Kuhlman, 2000). Many problematical behaviors are correlated with sensation seeking. However, other individuals are able to channel their sensation-seeking tendencies into positive directions, such as curiosity leading to improved performance at school or on the job, instead of becoming delinquents or criminals, because of cognitions called Mastery Orientation (O'Connor & Jackson, 2008). Other theoretical approaches, including those presented by Hans Eysenck and J. A. Gray, also include arousal as a key concept, as we will see. Arousability is a core aspect of personality, present early in life as temperament, which is shaped by socialization into a variety of personality outcomes (Zawadzki & Strelau, 2010).

sensation seeking

trait, proposed by Zuckerman, of seeking varied, novel, complex, and intense sensations and experiences, even if that requires risk

BIOLOGICAL FACTOR THEORIES: EYSENCK, GRAY, AND OTHERS

Several theorists have proposed comprehensive factor models of personality that specify biological underpinnings of the major dimensions along which personality varies. In one sense, they correspond to the factor models we considered in Chapter 8, but instead of building only on a description of personality through verbal reports, they correlated it from the outset with biological variation.

EYSENCK'S "PEN" BIOLOGICAL MODEL

Hans Eysenck (1967; Eysenck & Eysenck, 1985) and others who expanded his approach (Gray, 1999) built their biological models of personality on Pavlov's analysis (described earlier) of strong and weak nervous systems (Strelau, 1997). Like Pavlov's laboratory dogs, each person has both excitatory and inhibitory processes in the nervous system that (respectively) respond to, or defend against, incoming stimuli. Physiological measures, such as brain scan recordings to varying flashes of light or auditory stimuli, have been used to measure these differences (Buckingham, 2002). Variations in excitatory and inhibitory processes produce interesting implications for personality. Specifically, people whose excitatory processes are stronger (who have a "strong nervous system") are extraverts, whereas those with relatively greater inhibitory processes (who have a "weak nervous system") are introverts.

Hans Eysenck

Extraversion is the first of Eysenck's three proposed factors of personality. The others, also based on biological differences between people that are inherited (Eysenck, 1990b), are Neuroticism and Psychoticism. (Rearranging the first letters of these factors gives the acronym "PEN.")

The first factor, **Extraversion,** with its opposite pole Introversion, illustrates how subtle differences in the balance of biological processes (excitation and inhibition, in this case) can have great implications for personality. A person with a "strong" nervous system can tolerate relatively intense stimuli without being overwhelmed by them, including the stimuli that come from social interactions. In fact, they crave such stimulation, and in seeking it, they act like extraverts. Introverts, in contrast, have a "weak" nervous system that is quickly overwhelmed by intense stimuli. In the presence of other people, they readily are stimulated above the level at which they can function well, so they take behavioral measures to control overstimulation; they withdraw from overly stimulating environments.

Eysenck identifies the ascending reticular activating system of the brain (ARAS), which senses arousal messages from the brainstem to higher brain levels, as a pathway

extraversion

tolerance for high levels of stimulation because of a strong nervous system that inhibits incoming stimulation, leading to sociability in Eysenck's theory for this arousal. We generally define introverts and extraverts in terms of their behavior, but Eysenck's assertion that they differ biologically as well is supported by laboratory observations (Eysenck, 1967; Stelmack, 1997). In one study, researchers monitored subjects' responses to auditory stimuli. Hearing a click automatically causes an evoked neural response in the brain, which the experimenters recorded through electrodes placed on the subject's head. Computers analyzed the recordings to focus on the brain's particular responses that are known to indicate activation by the brainstem (which Eysenck's theory identifies as important). Subjects who were extraverts, according to their personality tests, were slower to generate activity in response to the auditory stimuli (longer latency) and the waves were farther apart in time (greater interpeak interval)—in other words, extraverts were less reactive to the stimuli (Swickert & Gilliland, 1998). Also supporting the theory, when given an opportunity to choose the level of background noise during an experimental task, extraverts chose more noise than introverts, and they performed better at higher levels of noise (Geen, 1997). When tasks require a great deal of attentiveness—for example, keeping watch for a relatively infrequent stimulus to respond to it—extraverts perform poorly compared to introverts, who are better able to maintain attention with lower levels of stimulation (Brebner, 2000). Many studies support Eysenck's contention that introverts show more cortical arousal, and fewer relaxed alpha waves, compared to extraverts (Hagemann et al., 2009).

neuroticism

tendency toward high levels of emotional arousal; the second factor in Eysenck's factor model

The second factor in Eysenck's model is **Neuroticism**. Greater activity in the limbic system causes some people to become more emotionally aroused when they are threatened or placed in stressful situations. These people are high in the factor of Neuroticism. Others, low on that factor, do not become so emotional in the same situation. Greater emotional arousal can, in turn, cause neurotics to make use of defense mechanisms; hence the term *neuroticism*. (Notice that the factor of extraversion-introversion corresponds to cortical arousal, in contrast to the emotional arousal that is at issue in neuroticism.) On written personality tests, people with high neuroticism scores report that they are less self-accepting than those with lower scores (McCroskey, Heisel, & Richmond, 2001).

Psychoticism

in Eysenck's model, factor related to nonconformity or social deviance

Eysenck's third factor refers to a tendency toward nonconformity or social deviance (Zuckerman, Kuhlman, & Camac, 1988). Eysenck (1992) labeled this factor **Psychoticism**, an unfortunate label because it exaggerates the image of pathology. In fact, one study that measured the Psychoticism scores of college students found that, 10 years later, those scoring high had no increased risk of psychosis (Chapman, Chapman, & Kwapil, 1994). A better term may be *Disinhibition* (Krueger & Walton, 2008). People who are creative tend to have high Psychoticism scores (Eysenck, 1993, 1994). On average, those who score high on the Psychoticism scale do have characteristics that put them at risk for deviance: They are more impulsive, hostile, sadistic, and unempathic than those who score low (Eysenck & Eysenck, 1991). Those who score high on Psychoticism prefer to watch violent videos and find them more enjoyable and comical than those who score lower. Their physiological responses show quicker desensitization to the violence (Bruggemann & Barry, 2002). People trying to climb Mount Everest score high on Psychoticism, and also on Extraversion, but low on Neuroticism (Egan & Stelmack, 2003). Physically, Psychoticism scores are correlated with the gastrointestinal system. Those scoring high show more saliva flow in response to taste stimuli, and they are relatively unlikely to become seasick (Gordon et al., 1994).

Eysenck's theory has stimulated thousands of research studies (Geen, 1997). Many of them are noteworthy in that they find significant relationships between biological variables and personality. Caffeine, for example, makes people act more like introverts, with conditioning like those with a weak nervous system, and extraverts are quicker to become fatigued and make errors on a vigilance task (Pickering, 1997). High Neuroticism scores are correlated with greater limbic system activity, whereas lower Extraversion scores (introversion) are correlated with higher levels of cortical arousal. Other findings are summarized in Table 9.4. In itself, isolated findings are not momentous, but the accumulation of experimental evidence relating personality measures with biological measures and performance on laboratory tasks is nothing short of astonishing.

Slightly different from Eysenck's model is another three-factor model proposed by Clark and Watson (1999). They propose factors similar to Eysenck's Neuroticism

Table 9.4 Experimental Findings Relating Eysenck's Extraversion and Neuroticism Factors to Biological and Performance Measures

	high N (N+): neurotic	low N (N−): emotionally stable
Autonomic nervous system (ANS) reactivity	Greater (labile)	Less (stable)
Limbic system activity (hippocampus, amygdala, cingulum, septum, and hypothalamus)	High activation	Low activation
Emotions (response to emotion-arousing events)	More intense (moody, anxious, worried)	Less intense (calm, controlled, well adjusted)
Temporal lobe activity	Greater	Less
Preparation for novel stimuli	Reduce focus of attention	Do not reduce focus of attention
	low E (E−): introverted	**high E (E+): extraverted**
Brain's cortical emphasis	Excitation (rapid, strong response to stimuli)	Inhibition (slow, weak, brief response to stimuli)
Brainstem area responsible	Ascending reticular activating system (ARAS) leads to excitation	Descending reticular activating system (DRAS) leads to inhibition
Basal level of cortical arousal	Higher (leading to greater risk of overstimulation)	Lower (tolerates stronger stimuli)
Sensory response to low levels of stimulation	Greater	Less
Perceptual sensitivity, assessed by brain's event-related potentials (ERPs) to auditory and visual stimuli on vigilance tasks	Greater perceptual sensitivity; stronger ERPs; more attention; slower habituation to repeated stimuli; better performance at vigilance tasks	Less perceptual sensitivity; weaker ERPs; less attention (more lapses of attention); greater habituation to repeated stimuli; worse performance on vigilance tasks
Typical coping with incoming stimuli	Avoid overstimulation; focus on narrower range of stimuli	Augment stimuli; attend to a broader range of stimuli
Involuntary rest pauses (IRPs) during massed practice	Less frequent	More frequent

Source: Prepared from information in Taub (1998).

and Extraversion but emphasize the specific emotions involved in each. One factor, which they call Neuroticism/Negative Emotionality (N/NE), emphasizes negative emotions such as distress and threat, as well as instability of emotions. A second factor, called Extraversion/Positive Emotionality (E/PE), describes extraverts' cheerfulness and confidence in approaching life, one aspect of which is interpersonal involvement. As expected, college students with high scores on the N/NE factor report more negative moods currently in their lives, whereas those scoring high on the E/PE factor report more positive moods and more active social lives. The third factor, Disinhibition versus Constraint (DvC), focuses on impulsive behavior based on immediate feelings, as contrasted with carefully planned action that considers long-term consequences. Students scoring high on this scale are more likely than others to sleep late, stay up late, engage in casual sex with more partners, drive recklessly, and use alcohol, tobacco, and illegal drugs (Clark & Watson, 1999).

GRAY'S REINFORCEMENT SENSITIVITY THEORY

J. A. Gray (1987) proposes a biological theory of personality that builds on Eysenck's theory. Gray proposes that individuals vary in motivational systems related to positive and negative reinforcement (approach and avoidance). Some people emphasize approach and positive emotions, whereas others emphasize avoidance and negative emotions (Heubeck, Wilkinson, & Cologon, 1998).

Behavioral Activation System (BAS)

in Gray's model, tendency of personality related to the approaching of rewarding experiences

Gray describes a **Behavioral Activation System (BAS)** that comes into play when rewarding experiences happen, causing us to approach them. BAS scores are measured by responses to questions, such as "I crave excitement and new sensations" and "When I get something I want, I feel excited and energized." The BAS system is involved in extraversion, sexual behavior, and aggressive behavior and thought to be associated with the neurotransmitter dopamine, which stimulates the brain's reward and pleasure center in the nucleus accumbens. In fact, molecular genetic research confirms that BAS scores on a questionnaire are correlated with genetic variations that regulate dopamine (Reuter et al., 2006). This system produces greater happiness when research subjects anticipate a reward (Carver & White, 1994). The BAS can be expressed by impulsive behavior, especially in neurotic extraverts. It is improperly regulated in people who suffer from bipolar disorder, whose symptoms increase after they achieve goals that they have been striving toward (Johnson et al., 2000). High BAS scores are associated with greater craving for alcohol (Franken, 2002), which at least initially increases dopamine release and so enhances pleasurable emotion (Clark & Watson, 1999, p. 415). But when channeled through an orientation toward mastery in a work environment, particularly one that emphasizes rewards, BAS contributes to enhanced work performance as indicated by supervisor ratings (Izadikhah, Jackson, & Loxton, 2010). Low BAS sensitivity, in contrast, predisposes people to depression (Harmon-Jones & Allen, 1997).

Behavioral Inhibition System (BIS)

in Gray's model, tendency of personality related to reactions to aversive stimuli

Another system is measured by answers to questions like "Criticism or scolding hurts me quite a bit." Gray's **Behavioral Inhibition System (BIS)** comes into play when feared or aversive or surprising stimuli occur—for example, when a snake slithers across the path in front of you or when you touch a hot object and feel pain. When the BIS is activated, the person becomes aroused, attentive, and afraid, and inhibits behavior. Some people are particularly sensitive to punishment and activation of the BIS and are therefore anxiety prone, more impaired on an emotional Stroop test, and less able to disengage from tasks that involve aversive cues. They also are quicker to learn aversive associations (Avila, 2001). They become more nervous when anticipating punishment, and they are more vulnerable to anxiety disorders (Carver & White, 1994; Caseras, Torrubia, & Farre, 2001; Vervoort et al., 2010). Women who have been treated for breast cancer and who expect it to reoccur are particularly distressed if they also have high BIS levels (Carver, Meyer, & Antoni, 2000). The BIS is postulated to involve the neurotransmitter norepinephrine and the brain's hippocampus and septum.

The ability to inhibit behavior is essential for healthy psychological functioning. Underactivation of the BIS presumably contributes to impulsive behavior, excessive risk taking, and difficulty delaying gratification, and it has been suggested as a contributor to attention-deficit/hyperactivity disorder (ADHD) (Avila & Parcet, 2001; Quay, 1997). Violent criminal behavior is more common in youth who have low norepinephrine levels; physiologically, they seem calm (low heart rates), which may mean they have been less impacted by efforts to discipline them because their physiology makes them less afraid (Kagan, 1994).

BAS and BIS scores are not limited to emotional feelings; they also predict people's cognitive processing of emotional stimuli. In one study, subjects were presented with words that had some missing letters and told to fill in the blanks to make a word. On positive emotional words, such as *e_a_ed*, the approach-oriented (high BAS) scorers were more likely than the low BAS scorers to see *elated* instead of *erased*. Other emotional word tasks produced similar results (Gomez & Gomez, 2002). This finding is consistent with other research showing that emotional thoughts are more readily activated when the person is in the emotional state that corresponds to the thought or memory, so it makes theoretical sense. It also has practical implications, showing how people with strong approach orientation may, over time, build up cognitions that enhance this predisposition, and that conversely, avoidance-oriented people may become stronger in that direction through cognitions that emphasize the negative.

Fight-Flight System (FFS)

biological personality factor proposed by Gray that produces rage and panic

Gray also describes a separate **Fight-Flight System (FFS)** (Gray, 1987) that produces rage and panic (see Table 9.5).

According to Gray's theory, extraverts are more influenced by reward, introverts by punishment. As predicted by this theory, in an experimental task in which auditory

Table 9.5 Gray's Model of the Biological Basis of Personality

	BAS: Behavioral Activation System	BIS: Behavioral Inhibition System	FFS: Fight-Flight System
Neurotransmitter	Dopamine	Norepinephrine	
Implications for learning	Sensitivity to reward	Sensitivity to punishment (or nonreward)	
Psychological implications	Impulsivity; positive affect (in response to reward)	Anxiety; attention and arousal	Panic; rage

Note: The Fight-Flight System is less clearly described in Gray's model than the BAS and the BIS.

signals sometimes signaled reward and sometimes punishment, introverts showed more brain wave reaction to signals of punishment for an incorrect response, and extraverts showed more brain wave reaction to signals of reward for a correct response (Bartussek et al., 1993). Activation of the BAS and BIS does not simply produce pleasant and unpleasant emotion, but it also guides learning. Rewards and punishments are cues that teach us what to approach and what to avoid. In a study of male prisoners, physiological indicators were influenced by reward and punishment manipulations while subjects tried to earn money (reward) or avoid losing money (punishment) by determining which two-digit numbers were the "good" ones. When punishment was involved in the learning task, activation of the BIS produced an increase in skin conductance; when the BAS system was activated by the possibility of reward, heart rate sped up (Arnett & Newman, 2000). Because of their greater sensitivity to punishment, anxious subjects learn more quickly in a laboratory computer-learning task involving punishment (verbal feedback and loss of money), whereas low-anxious people learn more slowly (Corr, Pickering, & Gray, 1997).

Combining biological mechanisms with the impact of learning, as Gray's theory does, offers considerable promise for understanding personality as it is inherited and as it changes with experience.

CLONINGER'S TRIDIMENSIONAL MODEL

C. R. Cloninger's (1986, 1987a, 1987b) tridimensional model proposes three biologically based personality traits, each resulting from the relative level of a particular neurotransmitter in a person's central nervous system. These three dimensions can be considered temperament types, the biological foundation on which personality, through experience, is developed.

The first temperament trait, **novelty seeking**, is related to levels of the neurotransmitter dopamine (with low levels of dopamine producing greater novelty seeking). It serves as a behavioral activation system. In mice, exploratory behavior (which is analogous to human novelty seeking) increases when dopamine is increased (Sabol et al., 1999). People high in novelty seeking become more excited in response to novel stimuli, and they explore their environments more. They seek excitement and try new things for the thrill of it. In a double-blind placebo-control study, people with higher Novelty Seeking scores reported greater mood elevation to amphetamine than those scoring low (Sax & Strakowski, 1998). Novelty seeking is higher among those who abuse drugs, although sometimes substance abuse is produced by the second genetic trait, harm avoidance (Berman et al., 2002).

The second temperament trait, **harm avoidance**, is related to high levels of the neurotransmitter serotonin. It serves as a behavioral inhibition system. People high in this trait are highly influenced by aversive stimuli or by signals indicating they will be punished, and so they act to avoid pain. They report that they worry and feel tense. Conversely, low serotonin activity is associated with impulsive acts of aggression, including murder, suicide, and arson (Coccaro et al., 1989).

novelty seeking

biological trait proposed by Cloninger that activates people to explore new things; related to dopamine levels

harm avoidance

biological dimension proposed by Cloninger that inhibits behavior; related to serotonin levels

reward dependence

biological dimension proposed by Cloninger that maintains behavior through seeking rewards; related to norepinephrine levels

The third temperament trait, **reward dependence**, results from low levels of the neurotransmitter norepinephrine. It serves as a behavioral maintenance system, making people continue to behave in ways that produce reward, especially reward through warm social attachments (Stallings et al., 1996). People who are high in reward dependence report that they are hardworking and keep working even if others have given up.

These temperament dimensions are scored from a self-report measure, the Tridimensional Personality Questionnaire (TPQ). Here are some examples of items (listed by Stallings et al., 1996):

> *I do things spontaneously.* (Novelty Seeking)
>
> *I get tense and worried in unfamiliar situations.* (Harm Avoidance)
>
> *Others think I am too independent.* (disagree; Reward Dependence)
>
> *I often push myself to exhaustion.* (Persistence component of Reward Dependence)

These temperamental dimensions influence a person's risk for particular psychiatric diagnoses (Cloninger & Svrakic, 1997). Cloninger's theory helps explain different types of alcohol abuse. Type I alcoholics are high in harm avoidance and reward dependence and low in novelty seeking, and they become alcoholic in response to environmental stress. Type II alcoholics are high in novelty seeking and low in the other two traits, and they are likely to begin drinking earlier (Cloninger, Sigvardsson, & Bohman, 1988; Wills, Windle, & Cleary, 1998). However, traits in the tridimensional model do not have a direct, automatic influence on people's lives. Experience matters. One of the most important experiences for predicting adolescent substance use is having friends who use drugs. The trait of novelty seeking, in Cloninger's model, predicts having such friends, but without them, novelty seeking alone does not lead to substance use (Wills et al., 1998).

BIOLOGICAL MECHANISMS IN CONTEXT

Personality is influenced by heredity and biology, without doubt. The sense that we make of this, however, is challenging. Many traditional ways of thinking are not helpful. Much of Western philosophy presumed a separation between the physical and the mental, and that tradition does not help us integrate the two, as we must if we are to make sense of new findings in behavioral genetics and neuroscience. Nor is it helpful to turn to biology as a more developed science, replacing primitive psychology. Why not?

One consideration is that all psychological behavior is biological, requiring a body to occur. This does not mean we should try to understand it at the biological level, any more than a computer scientist would analyze a program at the level of electronic circuits. Turkheimer (1998) refers to this indiscriminant biological involvement as "weak biologism," in contrast to "strong biologism," which occurs when biological variables explain psychological phenomena. (A computer analogy of strong biologism is to understand a computer failure in terms of a defective hard drive, in contrast to a programming bug. Of course, the hard drive is not biological, but it is physical.)

Although we often presume that biology is basic and experience is added to it but does not change it (much as a computer program is added to a computer but does not change its hardware), this is not true. Experience changes biology. The brains of animals and humans develop greater differentiation when they are stimulated by enriched experience, and groups that begin with different biological characteristics (such as the two sexes) can exaggerate this difference by having different experiences—for example, the greater spatial abilities of males may become exaggerated when they spend more time on video games that involve spatial skills (Halpern, 1997). Harmful effects can come from experience. The brain's normal fear mechanisms can become sensitized so pathological anxiety results (Rosen & Schulkin, 1998). Animal studies show that maternally deprived monkeys develop abnormal norepinephrine systems that may have long-lasting developmental effects. Evidence suggests this also occurs in humans. Neglect also causes abnormalities in human dopamine systems. These findings mean that neglect of children in early life causes biological damage, which may help us understand the biological mechanism of its psychological effects (Galvin et al., 1991; Kraemer, 1992; Rogeness & McClure, 1996). Early mother–infant interaction, some theorize, is necessary for the normal development of the brain (Steklis & Walter, 1991) and for the personality that depends on the brain. Neuroscientist Joseph LeDoux (2002) argues that experiences (nurture) and heredity (nature) both have their effect by changing the synaptic organization of the brain; in this way, both nature and nurture "actually speak the same language" (p. 3).

The effects of individual experience, LeDoux acknowledges, build on innate species characteristics but shape them to the specifics of an individual's life. Monogamous pair bonding or attachment, for example, occurs in animals (although only a few species, including only 3 percent of mammals). Experiments with two species of voles suggest that bonding to the mate occurs because of the release of specific hormones during mating: specifically, oxytocin in the female and vasopressin in the male (LeDoux, 2002, pp. 230–233). Perhaps human pair bonding is influenced by the same hormones as in these small rodents. If it is, does that mean that oxytocin or vasopressin pills could cement a relationship? Clearly, that is an oversimplified idea. The hormone alone does not make for pair bonding; what it does is to prepare the nervous system to respond to experience with the mate by forming an exclusive and protective attachment, mediated by synaptic changes in the brain. In a similar way, as LeDoux describes it, when medication is effective in therapy for depression or schizophrenia, it works by preparing the brain to make permanent changes in response to specific learning, which must be provided by the experiences of life or of therapy. This is a reason why some medications take time to become effective: The learning that they facilitate occurs over time. Furthermore, LeDoux suggests that traumatic experience, such as childhood abuse, impedes brain development by limiting the emotional system, causing it to focus on fear systems at the expense of positive emotional systems; this limits the repertoire of neural circuits that are developed to prepare for future behavior.

Biological predispositions are shaped by experience to form adult personality. The same predispositions can be molded into a variety of outcomes, just as clay can be made into a pot or a vase or a plate. Consider the example of behavioral inhibition (Rubin, 1998). Cross-cultural developmental researchers have found that two children with this same biological predisposition—a wary, fearful reaction to unfamiliar people and situations—will develop quite differently in U.S. or Chinese cultures. In the United States, such a child has a difficult time because the cultural value for more assertive and competitive social interactions leaves the child on the sidelines or even a target of ridicule. They have difficulty with friendships and are at risk for loneliness and depression. In the People's Republic of China, however, such a reticent child encounters a more accepting reaction. This culture values collective outcomes, in contrast to the individualism of U.S. culture, and the shy child is not at a disadvantage here; in fact, this child's submissiveness and restraint may be an asset. In China, such a child is likely to have positive relationships with peers and high self-esteem.

Additionally, environments and genetics interact in complex ways. Genetic variations can cause individuals to seek out certain kinds of environments to which they are best suited, and that provide them with the stimuli that they need because of their particular predispositions, according to the Experience Producing Drive Theory (Bouchard & Loehlin, 2001; Johnson, 2010). And this is only one of several ways that environments and genetics interact (Loehlin, 2010). We need complex theories to avoid oversimplified thinking about either heredity or environment.

No doubt biological understandings will continue to transform personality theory, but they must be considered in relation to culture and experience. Biological explanations will not make personality theory obsolete by explaining all the phenomena of interest in terms of neuroscience. That would be *reductionism*. Carried to the extreme, reductionism would also make neuroscience obsolete by reducing all explanations to the level of physics (Gold & Stoljar, 1999). To understand personality, we will always need a multilevel theory that considers biological explanation in relation to cognition and experience.

Summary

- Biological understandings of personality have been offered from the evolutionary shared traits of our species to individual differences in genetic inheritance and brain functioning.
- At the level of *evolution*, natural selection based on reproductive success offers explanations for sexual selectivity and jealousy, aggression, altruism, and nurturance; many of these traits vary between males and females.
- The immaturity of human young, combined with human capacity for language and imitation, prepare for considerable influence of experience.
- *Cultural evolution* supplements biological changes.
- *Heredity* has widespread influences on individual differences in personality.
- *Temperament* differences are observable early in life, and they are the basis for adult personality differences.

- Studies of the brain and nervous system find specific areas for many human traits. Emotion and arousal are particularly important.
- Several biological factor theories have been proposed (including those by Eysenck, Gray, and Cloninger).
- Eysenck's *PEN model* describes Extraversion, Neuroticism, and Psychoticism.
- Gray's *reinforcement sensitivity theory* proposes a *Behavioral Activation System* (*BAS*) that emphasizes rewards and a *Behavioral Inhibition System* (*BIS*) that emphasizes punishments.
- Cloninger's *tridimensional model* describes three factors: Novelty Seeking, Harm Avoidance, and Reward Dependence.
- All of these biological aspects of personality are subject to influences from experience and culture.

Thinking about Biological Personality Theories

1. If an ancient human newborn were brought to our current time (by some science fiction time travel device) and raised with a contemporary family, would he or she fit in? How would this help us evaluate the evolutionary theory of personality?
2. Discuss how the concept of cumulative cultural evolution brings learning and experience into evolutionary theory.
3. Propose a research study to investigate the impact of the social environment on any one specific hereditary dimension of personality, such as a particular temperament type.
4. Considering the importance of biochemical influences (such as neurotransmitters) on personality from childhood on, do you think drugs should be used to modify or correct imbalances of these influences in children?
5. Many different biological factor theories have been described. What are the most important biological differences, considering all of the theories, in your opinion? Why?
6. Several biological models offer three components. Compare these models. In what ways are they similar? In what ways are they different?
7. Given the importance of biology for personality, do you expect there will be less attention to childhood experience and to culture in future theories?

Study Questions

1. In explaining personality (and other) characteristics in humans today, what does evolutionary psychology assume?
2. Describe the evolutionary explanation of social behaviors such as altruism and aggression.
3. What is an "evolved psychological mechanism"? Give examples.
4. How does evolutionary psychology explain the differences between men and women in sexual and parental behavior?
5. Why are people aggressive, according to evolutionary psychology?
6. What is cultural evolution? How is it related to language and symbolism?
7. How strong is the impact of heredity on personality, according to genetic research?
8. What is temperament? Describe Kagan's categories of temperament.
9. How does emotional arousal influence personality? Describe the distinction between positive and negative emotions and the emotion of anger.
10. Describe cortical arousal and its relationship to Pavlov's strong and weak nervous systems.
11. What is sensation seeking?
12. List and describe the three factors in Eysenck's PEN theory.
13. Summarize Gray's reinforcement sensitivity theory and the different functions of the Behavioral Activation System and the Behavioral Inhibition System. How does this theory interpret introversion and extraversion?

4

The Behavioral Perspective

Behaviorism has been one of the major perspectives in modern psychology for many decades. As an approach in psychology more generally, it focuses on observable behaviors as important in a scientific theory, and has stimulated personality theory to do the same. In terms of the model presented in Chapter 1, it is explicit about the observable level and offers clear operational definitions. Historically, behaviorism represented a departure from the introspective methods of Titchener and the psychoanalytic method of Freud (Rilling, 2000), and it still serves as a reminder to attend to what people actually do and to the circumstances in which they do it. Early in the twentieth century, John B. Watson (1924/1970) proposed that personality is determined by the environment. He made an often-quoted claim:

> Give me a dozen healthy infants, well-formed, and my own specified world to bring them up in and I'll guarantee to take any one at random and train him to become any type of specialist I might select—doctor, lawyer, artist, merchant-chief and, yes, even beggar-man and thief—regardless of his talents, penchants, tendencies, abilities, vocations, and race of his ancestors. (p. 104)

Read in context, it is clear that Watson was exaggerating to make a point of the importance of experience, which can overcome genetic predispositions. Habitual behaviors constitute personality. Personality change comes about through learning, which is more rapid early in life when habit patterns are forming. Watson believed the study of personality required extensive observation of individuals, as do other behaviorists.

Over the decades, behaviorism has remained an influential perspective in personality, including an ambitious attempt by Dollard and Miller to provide a behavioral explanation for the clinical phenomena that Freud described. Behaviorism has taken a variety of forms, ranging from the radical behaviorism of Skinner, who excluded all nonobservable phenomena such as thinking from a role as causes in his theory, to a variety of cognitive behavioral approaches that accept and elaborate upon such thoughts. Among these cognitive behavioral approaches are several theorists in the upcoming chapters, including Kelly, Staats, Mischel, and Bandura.

The behavioral perspective makes distinctive assumptions about personality:

1. Personality is formed through interaction with the environment.
2. Behavior, to a large extent, is environmentally determined and situation specific, influenced by stimuli or cues present in a given situation and by anticipated outcomes of behavior.
3. Change can occur throughout a person's life. It is possible to influence people for the better by changing environmental conditions, including social changes.
4. Behaviorism does not presume that situational factors influencing one person will necessarily have similar influences on someone else.
5. Research on animals is useful to understand basic learning processes, which can be applied to humans, with necessary elaborations based on unique human capacities (such as language).

Behavioral theories are diverse in other ways. Some de-emphasize cognition, focusing instead only on observable behavior and situations, while others present elaborate descriptions of cognition as causes of behavior. They vary in their assumptions about what constitutes reinforcement.

The behavioral approach has little difficulty explaining individual differences. Each person experiences a somewhat different environment, with different conditions of learning. Inevitably, different behaviors and (in most theories) cognitions are learned.

Study Questions

1. What are the distinguishing assumptions of the behavioral perspective?
2. How are individual differences understood from a behavioral perspective?

10

The Challenge of Behaviorism
Dollard and Miller, Skinner, and Staats

Chapter Overview

ILLUSTRATIVE BIOGRAPHY
Tiger Woods

Tiger Woods achieved unprecedented success as a professional golfer, with fame and fortune and status as an icon of racial integration in a previously "white" sport. Then his star faded, not because of golf failures, but because of personal behavior. Can these themes be understood from a behavioral perspective? His success in golf is easy enough to understand, since behavior theories propose that personality consists of well-specified learned behaviors, and athletic performance fits this mold. More challenging are the scandalous sexual indiscretions that destroyed his marriage, disrupted his golf performance, and toppled this heroic superstar. Behavioral approaches do not, alas, give an overview of the whole scope of a human personality, and so do not predict in advance what will happen in a new area of life; lacking that, the behavioral approach has significant shortcomings. Even here, though, there are lessons to be drawn.

Tiger Woods, by his extraordinary youthful achievements, transformed the image of professional golf. Consider these achievements in his first quarter century of life: He is the youngest player (by 2 years) to have won all four of modern golf's so-called major tournaments—the Masters, the U.S. Open, the British Open, and the PGA Championship. He is the only player in history to have won all four in succession, holding those championships simultaneously. His golf earnings have made him a multimillionaire. But golf is not all

Tiger Woods

of his life story, and in 2009 the world learned that Tiger Woods had been sexually involved with many women in extramarital affairs; this led to divorce the following year from his wife of less than 7 years and the mother of his two children. In subsequent years, plagued by physical injuries as well as emotional turmoil, his golf performance plummeted.

His golf achievements made him a celebrity, and that began very early. Already he appeared swinging a golf club on television at age 2, and he was featured in a golf magazine at age 5. At age 8, Tiger won the Junior World Championship, and he repeated this feat four more times by age 14 (Owen, 2001; "Tiger Woods Profile," 2006).

Tiger Woods was born on December 30, 1975. His ancestors are diverse: black, white, Native American, and Asian on his father's side and Asian on his mother's side (Owen, 2001, pp. 187–188). This diversity added to his media appeal as the world struggled to find models of diversity. Along the way, though, he was sometimes not permitted to play on golf courses that were restricted to whites.

From the start of his life, his father, Earl, fostered interest in golf, and the family continued to support Tiger both emotionally and materially. His parents sacrificed considerably for their son, taking out tens of thousands of dollars in loans to provide him with the opportunity to play golf competitively in his childhood and adolescence.

Tiger attended high school in Southern California and college at California's prestigious Stanford University (until he stopped to become a full-time golf professional). Woods married a former Swedish model, Elin Nordegren, in 2004. His father, who was so closely involved as a career mentor and—according to Tiger's description—best friend, died in 2006.

DEVELOPMENT

Personality develops by learning, through reinforcement and imitation. Repetition strengthens learning. For Tiger Woods, learning began early and continued intensively throughout life, insofar as golf is concerned.

Tiger Woods's father, Earl, directed his son's learning. He set up a high chair for Tiger while he practiced golf swings, and soon Tiger was climbing down from the chair to imitate him with a plastic golf club (Owen, 2001, pp. 59–60). In the beginning, we would expect the reward would be his father's approval, but

with time, as he learned to judge his own performance, reinforcement came from knowing he had hit well (i.e., the ball went where it was intended). In Staats's theory, motor activities such as golf provide reinforcement by directly seeing the effect of the swing on the movement of the ball and also by feedback from observers. Dollard and Miller's psychoanalytic learning theory would interpret his father's influence with the concept of imitation, a learning theory reinterpretation of Freud's identification, which is especially important for young boys. His father's approval would be a powerful reinforcement.

Frequency of behavior and of reinforcement also influence the strength of learning. The intensive practice that has been a routine part of Tiger's life provides reinforcement in the form of feedback with every swing of the club. As he puts it, "My dad always told me that there are no shortcuts,... and that if you want to become the best you're going to have to be willing to pay your dues" (Owen, 2001, p. 131). In addition, the approval of a greater audience and, after several years, the fame and financial rewards of golf achievement have contributed to the persistence of Woods's behavior in golf by increasing the reinforcement.

Staats's theory of psychological behaviorism describes the basic behavior repertoires (BBRs), which people learn early in life, that provide the basis for later personality. What we learn early is the foundation on which later learning builds. Golf is not the only thing a child needs to learn, as Staats's theory makes clear. While supporting his golf, Tiger's parents also were concerned that he might be missing other important experiences. Nonetheless, they let their son follow his own motivation and supported him. Tiger's mother, Kultida, used the time-honored method of reinforcement to get Tiger to do his school homework. She would not permit him to practice golf until the homework was done. Such a reinforcement procedure only works because practicing golf had itself become a reward, as a result of learning.

DESCRIPTION

Of the theorists in this chapter, Staats gives the most extensive descriptive categories for understanding personality. He proposes that personality consists of learned behaviors in three categories: behaviors that have to do with language and cognition, those that have to do with emotion and motivation, and those that have to do with sensory and motor behavior. Each of these groups is called a "repertoire," and the "Basic Behavioral Repertoires" learned early in life form the foundation for later personality.

Consider the Sensory-Motor repertoire. As a child, Tiger's ability to watch the ball (sensory) and to hit it (motor) established the foundation of this repertoire. Over time, it expanded to include all of his diverse golf shots, designed to propel the ball toward the hole in a variety of winds and other environmental

(continued)

(continued)

conditions. Tiger continued to develop new shots, which can best be appreciated by those who know the sport well, like keeping the ball low in windy conditions. His golf swing became so fast, 120 miles per hour, that even a camera designed to take stop-action photographs of missiles for the U.S. government had difficulty capturing an image of his club hitting the ball (Owen, 2001, pp. 124–125). The basic components of the Sensory-Motor repertoire were learned early. His biography is, alas, less revealing about the early foundation of language and cognition, emotion and motivation—the other basic behaviors upon which personality is formed. Perhaps deficiencies in those areas, in areas other than golf, may have left him vulnerable to the sexual temptations that became his undoing.

ADJUSTMENT

The behaviors that belong to Staats's Emotional-Motivational repertoire are relevant to adjustment. These include such skills as emotional control, including management of anxiety and anger. In a competitive sport such as golf, emotional self-management is essential for success. Golfers confront emotional situations when they miss a shot or when something disrupts their concentration, and learning how to manage these situations is an important behavioral skill.

To control his emotions, by adulthood Woods had developed an elaborate warm-up behavioral sequence before tournaments that he had learned made his swings more reliable. He arrived early at golf tournaments to go through a series of practice shots in a standard sequence, thus calming himself. He says this reduces his nervousness (Owen, 2001, p. 23). Skinner's theory (at least in its original formulation) would avoid such internal subjective states as "nervousness" that cannot be verified by external observers. Staats, however, permits emotional language in his expanded learning theory. A ritual sequence of behaviors like Tiger developed would produce a reliable stimulus environment for the golf shot, making the well-practiced behavior more reliably performed. He even learned to control his emotions and concentration under distracting conditions, as his father verbally hazed him and made distracting noises by jingling coins in his pocket, so that Tiger would learn to play through such conditions. When similar situations happened in a real tournament, Tiger's well-learned automatic self-control kept him focused.

Off the golf course, we now realize that there were inadequacies in the emotional-motivational behaviors that would be necessary for a trusting, faithful marriage. After disclosure of his infidelities, Tiger is quoted as saying, "I stopped living by the core values that I was taught to believe in....I convinced myself that normal rules didn't apply....I felt that I had worked hard my entire life and deserved to enjoy all the temptations around me. I felt I was entitled....I was wrong....I don't get to play by different rules" (ASAP Sports, 2010). Remorsefully, he recalled the values of Buddhism, his religious heritage, from which he had strayed, that he hoped would help him regain emotional stability. Behaviorism, though, teaches us that when situations change, behaviors are also likely to change. The childhood experiences that he recalled, with their stable behaviors, would not automatically generalize to adulthood with its new situation and opportunities. From a behavioral viewpoint, what is needed in situations like this is not a return to past behaviors, but rather new learning to behave in the current situation.

It is noteworthy that learning theories do not provide an overall description of personality unity. What is learned in one arena (e.g., golf) is specific to that area, and does not have implications for other areas of a person's life.

COGNITION

Cognitive elements of personality are included in what Staats calls the Language-Cognitive repertoire. These include intelligence and planning. There is no doubt about Tiger Woods's academic intelligence. He attended the highly selective Stanford University but left before graduating to turn professional.

As part of the Language-Cognitive behavioral repertoire he learned under his father's tutelage, Tiger was gradually taught to take responsibility for travel arrangements to his golf tournaments. In this, he not only learned the practical arrangements required to book transportation and hotels, he also learned the confidence that comes from being self-sufficient. Incidentally, such independence training is thought by researchers to be the basis for learning achievement motivation.

CULTURE

Learning is done by individuals, but the social context influences it, and a person's learned behaviors can also have an impact on society. Cultural factors in his parents' background undoubtedly made them better teachers of emotional self-control. Both his parents deserve credit for teaching him alternatives to aggressive outbursts. As described earlier, his father purposely made remarks and noises during practice sessions to give his son practice in putting up with such events. His mother, raised a Buddhist, taught him the nonviolent self-control that is better developed in that tradition than in the U.S. culture in which Tiger was raised. In an interview, Tiger praised Buddhism: "It's based on discipline and respect and personal responsibility. I like Asian culture better than ours because of that. Asians are much more disciplined than we are. Look how well behaved their children are. It's how my mother raised me. You can question, but talk back? *Never*" (Owen, 2001, p. 88).

Besides the usual emotional issues in golf, his race brought additional issues. As a minority in a predominantly white neighborhood in Southern California, he was targeted for attacks, like being tied to a tree on the first day of kindergarten (Owen, 2001, p. 87). Later, some golf clubs refused him permission to play because of race. Because of the emotional self-control he had learned, these societal obstacles were manageable.

Individuals can affect culture, as well as the reverse. The image of golf has been changed in the public eye, less what Tiger described as "a wussy sport" (Owen, 2001, p. 175), as it was when he was a kid and now attractive to young people who in the past might have been drawn to other sports, such as basketball. Golf was historically a whites-only sport. For nonwhite kids, biographer David Owen describes Tiger Woods as "the fearless conqueror of a world that has never wanted anything to do with them" (2001, p. 195). From a learning perspective, Tiger is a teacher as well as a learner. Since 1996, he has run the Tiger Woods Foundation, which teaches children about golf, career opportunities, and personal attributes such as courtesy and hard work that make people better off the golf course as well as on it.

BIOLOGY

Learned behavior can be limited by biological factors, especially when it requires an overt behavior, such as athletic performance. A combination of genetic gifts and lifestyle choices, including extensive practice, has been essential to developing this world-class athlete. Staats describes biological factors that can potentially affect a person before, during, and after learning (as we see later in this chapter). Numerous injuries have disrupted Tiger's golf performance after his peak in 2007. Overall, behavioral descriptions of the biological aspects of personality are incomplete. Other theories might also discuss the sexual drive and evolutionary selection for promiscuity that describe the infidelities that clash so severely with cultural norms, so central to his adult life narrative.

FINAL THOUGHTS

The particular behaviors that are learned vary from one person to another, creating a diversity of personalities. The behaviors, however, are specific—for example, golf performance—and do not generalize automatically to other areas of life. Tiger's father uttered only a partial truth when he said, "Golf is a game in which you learn about life" (Owen, 2001, p. 44). Other areas, such as developing a stable and trusting marital relationship, require a different curriculum. Tiger's life story, his success and downfall, exemplifies the lack of a holistic vision of personality in behaviorism that would tie together these disparate themes.

PREVIEW: OVERVIEW OF BEHAVIORAL THEORIES

Behavioral theories covered in this chapter have implications for major theoretical questions, as presented in Table 10.1. One of the greatest strengths of the behavioral perspective is its clear statement of scientifically verifiable hypotheses. Because the causes of behavior can be manipulated, this approach more closely approximates the models of science derived from laboratories in other scientific disciplines, and this was a major impetus for Dollard and Miller to recast psychoanalytic theory in ways that permitted animal testing of their model. Adding reinforcers, eliminating them, adding punishments—such manipulations are predicted to change the rate of responses, as

Table 10.1 Preview of Behavioral Theories	
Individual Differences	Individuals differ in their behaviors owing to differences in reinforcement histories. In Staats's theory, biological predispositions are also acknowledged.
Adaptation and Adjustment	Rather than considering "health" or "illness," it is more profitable to specify which behaviors should be eliminated and which increased, and to change them through learning therapies (behavior modification).
Cognitive Processes	Mental processes are difficult to study because the scientist does not have access to them. In principle, mental processes can be explained in behavioral terms. In practice, according to radical behaviorists such as Skinner, it probably is not worth the trouble; instead, the focus should be on observable behavior. According to Staats, cognitive processes can be studied by self-report measures, and thought processes are important behaviors.
Culture	Society provides the conditions of learning, and therefore shapes personality. Behavioral principles suggest that some aspects of society should be improved (e.g., education). A society can be envisioned in which more effective use of reinforcement makes people happier and more productive, using rewards rather than punishments or coercion to control behavior.
Biological Influences	Species differences influence response capabilities and the effectiveness of various reinforcements. According to Staats, individuals, too, have biological differences that influence but are also influenced by learning.
Development	Children learn which behaviors will lead to positive reinforcement and which to punishment, and they respond accordingly. Stimulus control and schedules of reinforcement influence this learning. Childhood development provides the basis for later learning, according to Staats. Adult development builds on earlier learning.

Skinner measured them. Staats's theory extends behavioral concepts beyond animal models, describing responses that have particular importance to humans, and explaining that development builds from basic early learning to adaptive or maladaptive adult behaviors. Behavioral theorists offer idiographic approaches, respecting that each individual is unique.

PSYCHOANALYTIC LEARNING THEORY: DOLLARD AND MILLER

John Dollard

Neal Miller

Like many in their time, John Dollard and Neal Miller were not only much impressed by Freud's work, but like many, they also found the theoretical statements to be unscientific. Could a more scientific description of psychoanalytic observations be offered? They thought so, and proposed such a theory based on behavior-learning principles.

Biographies of John Dollard and Neal Miller

John Dollard was born in Menasha, Wisconsin, in 1900. He did his undergraduate work at the University of Wisconsin and graduate work in sociology at the University of Chicago, where he was awarded a doctorate in 1931. He also studied psychoanalysis at the Berlin Institute.

Dollard taught anthropology, psychology, and sociology and for many years was a research associate at Yale University until his retirement in 1969. He died in 1980.

Dollard researched sociological issues of race relations and social class, biographical analyses, and various topics related to sociology and culture, as well as psychoanalysis. According to Dollard (1949, p. 17) much can be predicted without knowing anything about the individual, simply from knowing the culture into which the person is born. Dollard recognized the necessity of considering actual human social conditions, frequently ignored by psychoanalysts.

Neal E. Miller was born in Milwaukee, Wisconsin, in 1909. He studied psychology at the University of Washington and did graduate work at Stanford University and Yale University, where he studied learning theory from Clark Hull, whose concepts of drive reduction influenced Miller's later theorizing.

Like Dollard, Miller studied psychoanalysis. He went to Vienna in 1936, where he was analyzed for 8 months by Heinz Hartmann, an eminent Freudian. He couldn't afford the higher fees required to be analyzed by Freud himself (Moritz, 1974). Returning to the United States, Miller joined the faculty at Yale University (1936–1941), where he collaborated with Dollard and others, exploring a learning theory reconceptualization of psychoanalytic insights. In 1950, they published a more mature and comprehensive version of their theoretical work—*Personality and Psychotherapy: An Analysis in Terms of Learning, Thinking and Culture.*

After this theoretical work, Miller conducted basic research on physiological mechanisms of motivation that contributed to the development of biofeedback (Miller, 1985, 1989; Miller & Dworkin, 1977). In 1991, the American Psychological Association (1992) presented Neal Miller with one of its most prestigious awards, the Citation for Outstanding Lifetime Contribution to Psychology. He died in 2002.

LEARNING THEORY RECONCEPTUALIZATION OF PSYCHOANALYTIC CONCEPTS

Since the goal was to provide a behavioral explanation of psychoanalytic phenomena, Dollard and Miller described several such phenomena as learned behaviors, including identification and conflict.

FOUR FUNDAMENTAL CONCEPTS ABOUT LEARNING

Drawing on various theories of learning, Miller and Dollard (1941) summed up the primary concepts of learning theory by suggesting that "in order to learn one must want something, notice something, do something, and get something" (p. 2).

Drive: Wanting Something

Freudian theory regarded libido as the driving force behind all action, but Dollard and Miller preferred the more inclusive concept of **drive** to refer to the motivating force. Various drives exist, ranging from primary innate needs like hunger and sex, to learned motivations such as the need for approval. Drives can be learned. Their animal research demonstrated that rats who originally show no preference for a black or white experimental chamber acquired a drive of anxiety if they were shocked in the white chamber, and they learned to press a bar or turn a wheel to escape to the now-preferred black chamber (Miller, 1941, 1948/1992c). Many human drives are learned: anxiety, need for approval, ambition, and so on. Sensitive to cultural issues, Dollard and Miller suggested that ambition is fostered more in the middle class than in the lower class.

drive

what a person wants, which motivates learning

Cue: Noticing Something

Cues are discriminative stimuli that a person notices at the time of behavior. They include not only observable stimuli, such as lights and sounds in animal experimental chambers, but also intrapsychic stimuli, such as thoughts. Learning consists of strengthening the cue–response connection, so that a person's tendency to respond in a particular way in the presence of certain cues or stimuli is increased.

cue

what a person notices, which provides a discriminative stimulus for learning

Response: Doing Something

Any behavior that can be changed by learning can be considered a **response**. These include not only overt, readily observable behaviors, such as shouting or fainting, but also covert, or hidden, behaviors, like thinking. In any situation, some responses occur more frequently than others, and the likelihood of these competing responses can change with learning. For example, 2-year-old Jason, hearing it is bedtime (cue), is more likely to cry than to go quietly to bed. The challenge to his parents is to change these likelihoods so that the most likely or **dominant response** of crying will become less frequent, and a more desirable response will occur instead.

response

what a person does, which can be learned

dominant response

a person's most likely response in a given situation

Reward: Getting Something

Dollard and Miller defined **reward** in terms of Hull's learning theory, which says that drive reduction is reinforcing. This provides a ready link with libido in psychoanalysis.

reward

what a person gets as a result of a response in the learning sequence, which strengthens responses because of its drive-reducing effect (in Dollard and Miller's theory)

THE LEARNING PROCESS

If drives are satisfied by the dominant response, no learning will occur. If, however, the dominant response does not bring about drive reduction, there is a **learning dilemma**: a situation in which the existing responses are not rewarded. If a new response occurs and is rewarded (i.e., leads to reduction of the drive), it becomes more likely. Thus it is important to arrange the situation so the desired new response will occur. This may involve simplifying the situation (to reduce cues for competing responses), coaxing the desired response, providing models to be imitated, or any of a variety of strategies used by parents, teachers, and therapists.

learning dilemma

a situation in which existing responses are not rewarded, which leads to change

Learning is influenced by rewards, which increase the probability of behaviors, while extinction (withholding reward) and punishment reduce behaviors. The closer in time a reward or punishment is to the response, the greater its effect. Stimulus generalization and discrimination refer to the specificity of cues that trigger responses.

For human beings, the capacity to think and to use language makes learning possible in ways that animals don't experience. Language can provide cues for behavior, so that when parents talk to their children about desirable or undesirable actions, and then praise or punish, the talking can become an internalized cue that later will trigger the child's behavior in the desired direction.

Learning by Imitation

imitation

learning by observing the actions of others (a basis for identification, in Dollard and Miller's theory)

same behavior

a person's behavior being the same as that of a model, considering the cues and reinforcements as well as the response

copying

learning to behave in the same way as a model, but not in response to the same cues as the model, in order to be rewarded by perceived similarity to the model

matched dependent behavior

learning to make the same response as a model, in response to a cue from the model

Identification with the father is an important part of development at the third psychosexual stage in Freud's theory, leading to an internalization of the superego and gender roles. Dollard and Miller suggested **imitation** in an attempt to phrase the psychoanalytic concept of identification in terms of learning theory. Their analysis distinguished three specific processes, or varieties of identification.

To emit the **same behavior** as the person being imitated, it is necessary not only for the behavior to be the same but also for the controlling cues to be the same. Imagine a little boy playing basketball like his father, or engaging in any other behavior that we would say is evidence of identification. Has he really internalized his father's behavior? Not necessarily. What appears on the surface to be the same behavior may, if analyzed, actually be controlled by different cues.

In **copying**, the learner is cued by the discrepancy between his or her behavior and that of the model and is trying to reduce it. Often there has been a past reward for similarity. A young child who is trying to be like his father, talking like he talks, shooting baskets like Dad, and so on, is copying. Social conformity is produced by such copying (Miller & Dollard, 1941, p. 163), but it is not the same as an internalized conscience.

In **matched dependent behavior**, as in copying, the learner produces a response that matches the model's response and depends on the model to provide a cue for the behavior. Miller and Dollard (1941) provided the example of an older brother (model) who runs (response) to greet his father upon hearing his father's footsteps (cue). His younger brother runs just like the model (matched response) but has not yet learned to recognize his father's footsteps as an appropriate cue for the behavior. Instead, his response is cued by seeing his brother running (dependent cue). If the younger brother is rewarded by candy from his father (as his brother is also rewarded), this is a case of matched dependent behavior.

These distinctions indicate the conceptual clarity with which Dollard and Miller approached their task. Not all behaviors that we might loosely call imitation or identification stem from the same processes.

THE FOUR CRITICAL TRAINING PERIODS OF CHILDHOOD

Dollard and Miller credited Freud with pointing out the importance of childhood and its conflicts. They described the three psychosexual conflicts that Freud enunciated, translated into the language of learning theory. They also added a fourth important childhood conflict, focusing on anger. In considering these four stages, keep in mind that the learning analysis has not been tested systematically.

Feeding

Because eating reduces the hunger drive, it is rewarding. The circumstances of an infant's feeding determine what responses are reinforced. A hungry child who is consistently left to cry without being fed learns not to cry for food; crying as a response is extinguished. General character traits of apathy and apprehensiveness develop. A child fed appropriately (when hungry and in a warm interpersonal context) develops love for the mother and, by generalization, a sociable personality.

Cleanliness Training

This period, corresponding to Freud's anal stage, is a time of learning that may produce conflict between the individual and society's demands. Until now, the internal physical cues of a full bladder and bowel have triggered the responses of urinating and defecating. Now, toilet training requires more complicated behavior sequences: attending to external cues (e.g., seeing the bathroom) and doing more complex behavior (undressing and sitting on the potty) (Dollard & Miller, 1950, p. 137).

If this stage is rushed, excessive conformity and guilt may be learned. Additionally, the child may learn to avoid the parents in order to avoid punishment. Dollard and

Miller (1950, p. 141) suggest that the anxiety and guilt of this stage correspond to the early development of what Freud called the superego. The complex learning of this stage is easier and less likely to produce anxiety and anger if toilet training is delayed until language develops sufficiently to provide mediating cues.

Early Sex Training

Early sex training often consists of punishment for masturbation, which results in conflict; sexual impulses not only remain tempting but also arouse anxiety. Dollard and Miller (1950) favor a more permissive attitude because punishment simply "sets up in the child the same sex-anxiety conflict which the adults have" (p. 142). Dollard and Miller regard their learning analysis as consistent with Freud's ideas about Oedipal rivalry and castration fear. Besides developing conflict over sexual impulses, a child at this stage may learn a fear of authority figures, generalized from experience with the punishing parents (especially the father).

Anger–Anxiety Conflicts

Dollard and Miller thought that anger–anxiety conflict was sufficiently important to add it, as a fourth critical training period, to those that correspond to Freud's first three psychosexual stages. Because childhood produces many frustrations—including those that come from childhood dependency, mental limitations, and sibling rivalry—children must learn to deal with anger. Anger becomes a learned drive that motivates behavior. If it is unacknowledged and unlabeled, it is likely to lead to undifferentiated responses like repression. Angry feelings can be mislabeled; a child who has been punished for angry outbursts may come to label anger as "bad feelings" rather than "angry feelings." Guilt, rather than assertion, will follow. If properly labeled, anger can provide discriminative cues for behaviors appropriate in the real world.

FRUSTRATION AND AGGRESSION

Dollard and Miller's hypothesis relating frustration and aggression is probably their most often-cited idea. They acknowledged Freud's influence on this hypothesis, with his concepts of Thanatos and of the conflict between libidinal impulses and the restraining forces of civilization. Dollard and Miller, however, explained aggression as the result of frustration, that is, of failure to reach goals, rather than a death instinct.

Dollard and Miller began with the assumption that "aggression is always a consequence of frustration" and, in addition, "the existence of frustration always leads to some form of aggression" (Dollard et al., 1939, p. 1). They defined *frustration* as occurring when obstacles interfere with drive reduction. For example, it would be frustrating to be hungry and sit down to a meal, only to have the phone ring and call you away from the table. Might you be ruder toward the caller than usual? *Aggression* is defined as behavior intended to injure the person toward whom it is directed. Aggression is more likely when the blocked drive is strong, when the interference is more complete, and when the frustration is repeated.

The **frustration-aggression hypothesis**, that frustration causes aggression, has stimulated much research. Experimental evidence for the frustration–aggression relationship came from animal studies, in which mice that were shocked became aggressive against various targets (including other mice and dolls). Although in an abstract way these studies show that frustration (the shock) leads to aggression (attacking the target), in humans, it is more complicated.

Several studies have exposed people to frustration and then provided an opportunity for them to express aggression. Frustration often takes the form of blockage in meeting a desired goal, such as earning money in an experiment. Aggression is often operationally defined by having subjects administer electric shocks to another subject under the pretext that it is punishment being delivered in a learning experiment. By manipulating other variables, it is possible to investigate under what circumstances frustration leads to aggression and when it does not. Situational cues, such as the sight of weapons, increase aggression (Anderson, Benjamin, & Bartholow, 1998; Berkowitz,

frustration-aggression hypothesis

the hypothesis that frustration always leads to aggression, and aggression is always caused by frustration

1983; Berkowitz & LePage, 1967; Gustafson, 1986). Threats to a person's self-esteem often increase aggression (Baumeister, Smart, & Boden, 1996; Bushman & Baumeister, 1998). One kind of ego threat is a threat to masculinity, which can produce violence in relationships (Jakupcak, Lisak, & Roemer, 2002).

Research shows that the relationship between frustration and aggression isn't as simple as originally thought. People can learn other responses to frustration, such as by taking adaptive steps to change the situation that produced the anger (Tangney et al., 1996). By displacement, they can express aggression toward someone other than the source of the frustration (Marcus-Newhall et al., 2000). The psychoanalytic idea of indirect reduction of aggressive impulses through catharsis does not seem to be effective, however (Berkowitz, 1962, 1989; Lewis & Bucher, 1992). Aggression is influenced by situations and by individual differences in personality. Clearly people learn how to respond to life's frustrations.

CONFLICT

Intrapsychic conflict was a key idea in psychoanalytic theory. In the learning interpretation, if a situation provides cues for two incompatible responses (i.e., responses that cannot both occur at the same time), there is **conflict**.

conflict

a situation in which cues for two incompatible responses are provided

Conflicts assume many forms. We sometimes must choose between two desirable responses: Which favorite meal should we order at a restaurant? These are *approach–approach* situations, because we are motivated to approach two goals, but must choose. At other times the choices are unpleasant: Would you rather die by firing squad or lethal injection? Such choices are *avoidance–avoidance conflicts,* but if we can avoid either option, of course, there is no conflict. In a third case, the same situation may cue both approach and avoidance responses: Charlie Brown wants to flirt with the little redheaded girl, but his fear of rejection makes him want to run away. This is an example of an *approach–avoidance conflict.*

In their theorizing and animal studies, Dollard and Miller described how the strength of approach and avoidance tendencies increases as the person or animal comes closer to the point of actual behavior. Hunger is more tempting when the food is right in front of you—or the avoidance tendency greater if the food is something you dislike. These changing strengths of behavioral tendencies are called the gradient of approach and the gradient of avoidance. Dollard and Miller proposed that the avoidance gradient rises more steeply as the situation draws closer, so that someone who is brave at a distance may be overcome with fear and run away when the situation is right there.

Some of the ineffective behavior for which people seek therapeutic help can be understood as such conflict. A learning analysis offers change strategies. Avoidance tendencies can be reduced by medications that allow approach by reducing the avoidance tendency. For that matter, alcohol also has this effect; in animal studies, hungry rats who normally avoid a feeding area where they have been shocked will dare to approach it if they have been injected with alcohol, and frightened cats prefer a little alcohol in their milk (Dollard & Miller, 1950, pp. 185–186). Unfortunately, some of the avoidance tendencies that alcohol numbs in drunken humans are the inhibitions that are a necessary part of adaptive social behavior (Steele & Josephs, 1990).

The problem with drugs is that they are nonspecific, reducing avoidance tendencies generally. Thus they may have undesirable effects in other aspects of life. Psychotherapy, in contrast to drugs, can teach fear reduction that is specific to the problematic choice, although it is slower. It does this by language, which provides linguistic cues that signal what to approach and what to avoid.

LANGUAGE, NEUROSIS, AND PSYCHOTHERAPY

Language provides discriminative cues for learning how to deal with various situations and can be conceptualized as an important part of Freud's ego (Dollard & Miller, 1950, pp. 122–123). Unlabeled early, often emotional, experiences constitute the unconscious, and may be evidenced by physiological reactions (Miller, 1992b; Rendon, 1988).

Conscious, verbally cued behavior is quite different from the less-discriminating, less-future-oriented, timeless, and illogical prelanguage responses (cf. Dollard & Miller, 1950, p. 220). Learning implements Freud's recommendation, "Where there was id, there shall be ego," by providing words that correctly label experience.

Neurosis results from maladaptive learning, in which responses that could effectively reduce drives are not learned, so high drive remains undischarged. Thus neurosis can be called a *stupidity-misery syndrome.* Many neuroses can be understood as learned ways of avoiding anxiety. Phobias develop when a fear-producing experience generalizes to produce fear in similar situations. For example, a fighter pilot, after combat, became afraid of everything connected with airplanes (Dollard & Miller, 1950, p. 158). Compulsive hand-washing may be a way of avoiding anxiety about contamination. Alcoholism can result from the anxiety-reducing physiological effect of drinking.

Regression to immature behaviors occurs if a person confronts unresolved conflicts and returns to responses that worked in the past. Displacement is also understandable in learning terms, when behavior is directed toward a substitute target because of generalization based on similarity. For example, children seek and receive the love of their parents. When they are older, a romantic partner "just like" Mom or Dad is often chosen. Although this displacement may be the basis of a normal and happy outcome, it may also lead to maladaptive choices—for example, if the parent was abusive.

Psychotherapy provides relearning experiences. Powerful discriminations are possible with language, teaching the patient more adaptive ways to label situations and inner emotional states. Repressed experiences are made available to conscious control through free association and new labeling. The therapist allows patients to express feared material without reprimand, helping the fear to be extinguished, and uses approval strategically to reward specific aspects of the patient's behavior. Dollard and Miller comment that most therapists are not disciplined enough to be maximally effective at this.

SUPPRESSION

Suppression is willful control of thinking, purposely putting thoughts out of consciousness. Dollard and Miller thought this was a valuable skill, but subsequent research suggests caution about suppression.

suppression
willfully putting thoughts out of consciousness

For one thing, suppression often fails. Research subjects who were told to avoid thinking about a white bear found it difficult and experienced intrusive thoughts of white bears (Wegner et al., 1987), a rebound effect that has been reported by others and that also occurs when patients suffering from PTSD try to suppress traumatic memories (Abramowitz, Tolin, & Street, 2001; Kelly & Nauta, 1997; Wegner, Erber, & Zanakos, 1993; Wenzlaff & Wegner, 2000). Suppression of emotions, such as that aroused experimentally by viewing a film of an arm amputation or suppressing amusement, leads to increased sympathetic nervous system arousal (Gross & Levenson, 1993, 1997), which in the real world may have adverse health consequences.

Conversely, much research confirms that expressing emotions through writing has positive health benefits (Contrada, Cather, & O'Leary, 1999; Giese-Davis & Spiegel, 2001; Pennebaker, 1993; Pennebaker, Colder, & Sharp, 1990; Petrie, Booth, & Pennebaker, 1998; Richards et al., 2000; Smyth, 1998; Stroebe, Schut, & Stroebe, 2006). However, if the writing explores events that are too traumatic, opening them up without therapeutic support can backfire, leading to more visits to the health service instead of fewer (Honos-Webb et al., 2000). Sometimes, it appears, Dollard and Miller were right about the value of suppression.

RADICAL BEHAVIORISM: SKINNER

B. F. Skinner proposed an influential theory of behavior based on principles of reinforcement. Although most of his work was with animals, particularly rats, Skinner wrote extensively about the implications of behaviorism for humans. His model has, on the positive side, culminated in behavioral interventions that are widely practiced

B. F. Skinner

today, but most personality specialists are not convinced that his analysis can replace personality concepts.

Biography of B. F. Skinner

Burrhus Frederic Skinner was born in 1904 in Susquehanna, Pennsylvania. His younger brother died suddenly of an acute illness (probably a massive cerebral hemorrhage) while Fred Skinner, as he was generally called, was visiting home during his freshman year at college.

Childhood was happy for Skinner. He invented various devices, including a flotation contraption to separate ripe elderberries from green ones, a perpetual motion machine, and a device to remind himself to hang up his pajamas (Skinner, 1967, 1976). He was also interested in writing and majored in English. After college graduation, he took a year off to write a novel. The project failed, and he turned to psychology in graduate school at Harvard, from which he received his doctorate in 1931. He extended his studies by postdoctoral fellowships, and married Yvonne Blue just before beginning his first teaching job at the University of Minnesota (1936–1945). They had two daughters and raised the younger in her early years in a modified crib he called an Air Crib, designed to provide an environmentally controlled environment (Skinner, 1945).

Besides his scientific writing, Skinner wrote a novel, *Walden Two* (Skinner, 1948), and kept a journal for many years (1958). After a brief period as chair of the Department of Psychology at Indiana University (1945–1948), he returned to Harvard, where he continued his research, theory building, and teaching until his death in 1990, at age 86.

Skinner was one of the most influential psychologists of the twentieth century, according to surveys of psychologists (e.g., Heyduk & Fenigstein, 1984). He received many professional awards, including an unprecedented honor, the Citation for Outstanding Lifetime Contribution to Psychology, awarded by the American Psychological Association just before his death (American Psychological Association, 1990).

BEHAVIOR AS THE DATA FOR SCIENTIFIC STUDY

Skinner dismissed personality as a discipline that had not become fully scientific but was still contaminated with prescientific philosophical assumptions. The idea that behavior is caused by forces within an individual (traits, thoughts, needs, and so on) should be abandoned, according to Skinner, in favor of more scientific explanations outside the person.

Skinner (e.g., 1963, 1975, 1990) argued that scientific progress in psychology requires abandoning *mentalism,* which explains behavior in terms of internal mental states. External variables are convenient for science. The researcher can manipulate them so their status as causes of behavior is not in doubt. Skinner's approach is called *radical behaviorism* to distinguish it from learning theories that include some internal causes of behavior, such as drives (per theorists Dollard and Miller) and cognitive variables (per Staats, Mischel and Bandura). To most modern behaviorists, this radical refusal to consider intervening variables (variables not directly observable) is unnecessary and impedes the development of psychological theory (e.g., Kimble, 1994).

The Evolutionary Context of Operant Behavior

Evolution is a process by which adaptive characteristics are selected in response to the environment, through natural selection, but it is a slow process that takes generations. Skinner argued that adaptive behavior can also be selected within the experience of one individual. The basic idea is that behavior is determined by the environmental outcomes contingent on the behavior—that is, those that follow regularly from the behavior. Skinner described **operant conditioning** as the selection of behavior through its consequences.

operant conditioning

learning in which the frequency of responding is influenced by the consequences that are contingent on a response

The Rate of Responding

Skinner (1950, 1953b) argued that the best operant behaviors for research purposes are those that occur distinctly and repeatedly, so they can be clearly observed and counted. These **operant responses** are not forced by the environment (unlike salivation that is automatic when food is given to a dog in Pavlov's classical conditioning paradigm). Rather they are freely emitted by the organism. Learning is measured by changes (increases or decreases) in the **rate of responding**. To achieve control of extraneous influences, Skinner studied primarily lower animals, especially rats and pigeons, whose lives could be highly controlled. He invented a new apparatus, which has come to be known as a **Skinner box**, to provide an environment in which responses could be readily observed and automatically recorded.

LEARNING PRINCIPLES

Thousands of hours of observation resulted in Skinner's description of the fundamental principles of operant learning. The rate of responding can be increased by reinforcement and decreased by punishment or extinction, and the specific contingencies of reinforcement and punishment produce a variety of learning outcomes.

Reinforcement: Increasing the Rate of Responding

Most psychology students are familiar with Skinner's basic concepts. In brief, responses that are followed by reinforcement become more frequent, while those that produce no result, or that result in punishment, become less frequent. Laboratory rats press levers to obtain food reinforcers (an unlearned or *primary reinforcer*), and human students study to earn good grades (a learned or *secondary reinforcer* that has value only because of past experience).

Skinner insisted on studying individual organisms, which corresponds to the idiographic approach in personality research. People do not all respond in the same way to a specific environmental consequence of their action. If a teacher praises a student for asking a question, and if the frequency of asking questions increases, praise has reinforced the response of asking questions. The same praise, however, would not be called a reinforcer if it did not increase the frequency (rate) of the behavior. (Some students may prefer that the teacher not focus attention on them.) Only by observing the effects of a contingent outcome on the rate of behavior can we determine whether that outcome is a reinforcer in a particular situation for a particular individual.

It is the immediate short-term consequences of behavior that are influential. Often the immediate consequences of our behavior are different from the long-term consequences; for example, indulging in drugs brings short-term pleasure but long-term failure to achieve important life goals. Impulsive behavior can result, unless people learn to delay immediate gratification (Critchfield & Kollins, 2001).

Punishment and Extinction: Decreasing the Rate of Responding

In contrast, **punishment** reduces the rate of responding by presenting an aversive stimulus following a response. For example, parents reduce the frequency of their children's misbehavior by scolding.

The immediate effect of punishment is to reduce the frequency of an operant behavior. Animals in Skinner boxes learn quickly to stop doing whatever brings a punishing electric shock. Unfortunately, punishment also has unintended adverse effects that make it a generally undesirable technique. Punishment produces fear and anxiety, which remain even after the undesirable behavior has ceased and often generalize to other situations. For example, children punished for sexual exploration may experience anxiety later, even under circumstances when sexual behavior would be appropriate. Children punished for talking back to their parents may become nervous when they want to state an opinion later, even when speaking up would be desirable. In addition, unless the controlling agent is able to stay to administer continuing punishments as a "reminder," in the long run the behavior often returns.

operant responses
behaviors freely emitted by an organism

rate of responding
the number of responses emitted in a period of time; a change in this rate is taken as evidence of learning

Skinner box
a device that provides a controlled environment for measuring learning

punishment
a stimulus contingent on a response and that has the effect of decreasing the rate of responding

Another way to reduce the frequency of a behavior is to simply stop reinforcing it. For example, a child may tease a playmate, reinforced by the playmate's signs of embarrassment. If the playmate stops reacting, eventually the child will stop teasing. This reduction of responding when reinforcement ceases is called **extinction**. Skinner's first investigation of experimental extinction began when the food-dispensing apparatus on his Skinner box accidentally jammed (Skinner, 1979, p. 95). (Serendipity can be a fortuitous teacher!)

extinction

reduction in the rate of responding when reinforcement ends

Additional Behavioral Techniques

Behaviorists have many additional techniques available to change behavior, including shaping, chaining, discrimination, and generalization training. The net result of these strategies is to build up frequent responding, or to decrease undesirable behavior, based on learning principles. A few details are noteworthy for personality.

Skinner describes a technique called chaining to link together complex patterns of behavior, and suggests that this is how people learn a variety of adaptive behaviors, including self-control (Skinner, 1953a). The process of **discrimination learning** produces behavior that occurs in only certain situations, which is clearly important for adaptive behavior. In contrast, generalization occurs when we respond in the same way as in the past, despite somewhat different cues—for example, when our interactions with other people are patterned after childhood experience with parents.

discrimination learning

learning to respond differentially, depending on environmental stimuli

Schedules of Reinforcement

In adapting to the environment, the organism is exquisitely modifying its behavior in response to the frequency and timing of reinforcements. The term **schedule of reinforcement** refers to the specific contingency between a response and a reinforcement. Is every response reinforced? Are only some reinforced? If only some, which?

Responses that always produce reinforcement are said to be on a **continuous reinforcement (CR) schedule**. Continuous reinforcement schedules produce quick learning, but extinction is also rapid. How many college freshmen who had an easy time succeeding in high school have given up quickly when studying no longer brought the reward of good grades? Skinner's work suggests that a few earlier failures would produce greater persistence.

Partial reinforcement schedules occur when only some of the responses are followed by reinforcement. Although learning is slower, partial reinforcement schedules bring about greater resistance to extinction, which translates into more persistent behavior. Skinner described a variety of partial reinforcement schedules, depending upon whether reinforcements are contingent on the number of responses (ratio schedules) or their timing (interval schedules). By varying these schedules in laboratory animals, he could produce very high rates of responding, erratic responding, or other patterns. On a ratio schedule, for example, a pigeon pecked at a disk nonstop for 2 months (Skinner (1972, p. 134)! Doesn't that sound like a human compulsive behavior? Rather than explaining such behavior as the result of an inner drive or conflict, or (in the case of a desirable behavior) a trait of persistence, Skinner's theory explains it in terms of the external history of reinforcements.

schedule of reinforcement

the specific contingency between a response and a reinforcement

continuous reinforcement (CR) schedule

a reinforcement schedule in which every response is reinforced

partial reinforcement schedule

a reinforcement schedule in which only some responses are reinforced

APPLICATIONS OF BEHAVIORAL TECHNIQUES

Skinner's theory of operant behavior has been applied widely, particularly in therapy and in education, to design strategies for increasing desired behavior and decreasing problematic behavior. The key difference from most other therapy approaches is the focus on a well-defined behavior that is to be either increased or reduced in frequency. Such techniques do not require verbal sophistication and so can be used with children and nonverbal populations. For researchers, behavioral approaches have the advantage of providing straightforward measures of therapeutic effectiveness: the increased rate of desired behavior and the decreased rate of undesired behavior.

Behavior modification is the therapeutic approach that systematically applies learning principles to change behavior. The first step is to make a functional analysis

behavior modification

the application of learning principles to therapy

of the behavior to be changed by carefully identifying the stimuli and reinforcements influencing the behavior. Often such analysis shows that what people, including parents, are doing is the cause of problems. For example, one researcher (Fisher, 2001) reports that parents of autistic and mentally retarded children were making matters worse by paying more attention to the children's request for ice cream (or something else) after the children's self-injurious behavior caught their attention. The children had learned to injure themselves in order to get the parents' attention. The solution to such a problem is to change the parents' behavior. Only a careful behavioral analysis would identify such a subtle effect.

RADICAL BEHAVIORISM AND PERSONALITY: SOME CONCERNS

Skinner's work focused on animals and he argued against explanations in terms of thought and subjective experience, because these could not be objectively observed. Critics claim that Skinner's theory neglects the unique capacities of the human organism, such as language and intelligent thought. Skinner (1938, 1971) always intended his theory to apply to humans, and behaviorists have undertaken to explain social behavior (Schmitt, 1984) and even creative behavior by the operant conditioning model (Eisenberger, Armeli, & Pretz, 1998; Epstein, 1991; Winston & Baker, 1985). To most personality psychologists, however, such applications seem stretched, overestimating the potential of any behavior to be learned and underestimating genetic contributions to personality, such as inherited temperament and intellect (Todd & Morris, 1992).

Probably the most popular objection to Skinner's theory is that, with its emphasis on situational control, it describes people as not free (Garrett, 1985; Hillstrom, 1984). This objection is ironic because Skinner did not advocate highly controlling societies; in fact, he strongly objected to coercion (Dinsmoor, 1992). Societies should be designed, argued Skinner, in such a way that reinforcements cause people to behave in desirable ways, so that little coercion would be necessary. Skinner (1948) explored the question of how a culture should be designed in his utopian novel *Walden Two*, in which planned reinforcers coaxed people voluntarily to behave as good citizens. Although the community he described was fictional, it inspired actual communities designed more or less on his principles, including Los Horcones in Mexico (Holland, 1992).

Language is a particularly human characteristic. Skinner called it "verbal behavior" and valiantly tried to explain it from an operant behavior perspective. For 23 years, Skinner (1967), as he tells it, labored over his book *Verbal Behavior* (1957). The consensus among psychologists is that he failed, and that language and thought cannot be understood as operant behaviors (Chomsky, 1959; Paniagua, 1987) but require recognition of an innate linguistic ability in the human brain.

Many are convinced that Skinner's theory is not a theory of personality, focusing too much on the environment and too little on the person (Schnaitter, 1987; Zuriff, 1985). Yet his challenge to personality psychologists has stimulated other theorists and, in addition, Skinner always emphasized the importance of observing individuals, reminding us of the importance of a truly idiographic approach.

PSYCHOLOGICAL BEHAVIORISM: STAATS

Another behaviorist, Arthur Staats (1986, 1993, 1996), has developed a theory of **psychological behaviorism** (earlier called *paradigmatic behaviorism;* cf. Tryon, 1990) that contributes behavioral insights to an understanding of personality. Staats criticizes the Skinnerian radical behaviorism tradition for neglecting issues of personality: individual differences and psychological tests. His model addresses these ideas, and, in addition, it incorporates biological influences.

The framework that Staats builds is one he argues can provide a unified vision for many disparate fields within psychology (e.g., Staats, 1991). In his analysis, the study of personality rests on more fundamental levels that include biology, learning, social interaction, and child development. In turn, psychological measurement,

psychological behaviorism

behavioral theory, proposed by Staats, that includes traditional personality concerns (e.g., emotion, testing) as well as behavior abnormal psychology, and therapy draw on personality as a more fundamental level of psychological study (Staats, 1996, p. 19). The basic idea is that human personality is built up through learning. This learning occurs through the principles described by Skinner and other behaviorists: reinforcement, extinction, generalization, discrimination, and so on, and including classical conditioning as well as operant conditioning. Beyond that, Staats describes the extended and incremental nature of the learning process in far more detail than Skinner or other behaviorists.

Biography of Arthur Staats

Arthur Staats

Arthur Staats was born in New York in 1924, the youngest among four children. His Jewish mother, whose maiden name was Jennie Yollis, came from Tetiev, Russia. Her grandfather was a Talmudic scholar, devoted only to study. Her father, after his own study, became an atheist and radical thinker. When Staats was 3 months old, his father, Frank, died suddenly, several days after the family arrived in Los Angeles after a voyage through the Panama Canal; his mother never remarried.

Through primary and secondary schools he scored very high on standardized tests but remained, by his account, a bored underachiever and a disappointment to his teachers. An otherwise-happy childhood was devoted mostly to omnivorous reading and athletic play. With a family tradition of radical thought, he was exposed, especially by his sister and an uncle, to leftist progressive literature and discussions, and he began to form at a very early age a worldview and an interest in political-social-economic affairs that continued throughout his life. Raised in a family that was very poor, atheist in a Jewish ethnic tradition, vegetarian, and politically radical, Staats always felt different. He thought differently than his peers, he read different things, he questioned ideas that others accepted, and progressively he became a radical and original thinker, in ways that permeated every aspect of his life, including his various fields of study.

After serving in the navy in World War II, Staats became a serious college student. In graduate school at the University of California at Los Angeles (UCLA), his wide interests, combined with his drive for analysis in terms of basic principles, led him to complete the requirements for a PhD in clinical psychology while taking his degree in general-experimental psychology. With his objective view of human behavior, he found valuable elements in behaviorism's science philosophy and conditioning principles. However, he saw deep and widespread weaknesses also, including behaviorism's focus on animal research, its rejection of traditional psychology, and its divisive internecine rivalry. While still in graduate school, he began a research program to extend learning principles broadly in the systematic study of human behavior, a new development. The approach he constructed was a behaviorism, but not an ordinary behaviorism. It became "psychologized" because it incorporated essential elements of psychology, but it "behaviorized" those elements, so it remained a consistent, unified approach, later called psychological behaviorism.

In 1955 he became an instructor at Arizona State University (ASU), advancing to the rank of professor in 5 years. Beginning his own human behavioral program, within a few years he also succeeded in bringing in Jack Michael, Israel Goldiamond, and Arthur Bachrach to help begin the predominant center of the time for psychological behaviorism and radical behaviorism. While conducting intensive research in selected areas, he habitually placed it conceptually in a broad framework that lay the foundations for general development; then he would move on to the next needed development. For example, at ASU he began a human-oriented behaviorism that provided a critical foundation for the fields of behavior modification, behavior therapy, behavior analysis, and behavioral assessment. By the early 1960s, when others were just beginning to use reinforcement to change human behavior, he had been using it for 10 years. He was already laying the foundations for developments into areas such as cognitive behavior therapy, behavioral assessment, personality, and personality measurement.

He had met his wife, Carolyn, at UCLA. When he went to ASU, she became his assistant, completed her dissertation on a study in his research program, and contributed to two chapters in his first book. When they had a daughter in 1960, he soon devised training procedures to study and produce her language-cognitive and sensory-motor development, using his psychological behaviorism principles. He states that his children—Jennifer Kelley, a child psychiatrist, and Peter, an associate professor in pain medicine at Johns Hopkins—were the first children raised systematically within behaviorism. In this and other "experimental-longitudinal" child research, Staats claims invention of the "time-out" procedure that today is a household word, as well as the token reinforcer (token economy) system that he used in training dyslexic children.

His psychological behaviorism is set in a conceptual framework that involves unification with the biological sciences, from below, and the social sciences and humanities, from above. That perspective yields a philosophy of science, called unified positivism. Within the theoretical and philosophical paradigm, Staats projects significant developments for many areas of psychology, including personality. In 1998 the Arthur W. Staats Unifying Psychology Lecture was established in the American Psychological Association as an annual event to foster such developments.

REINFORCEMENT

Accepting behaviorism's assertion that behavior is maintained by reinforcement, Staats considered the implications of this concept for human behavior. Two of the interventions he used early on have become widespread. In a token-reinforcer or token-economy system, desired behavior is reinforced with tokens that can be exchanged later for other reinforcers (O'Leary & Drabman, 1971). The other is the popular **time-out procedure**. Staats reasoned that a child who is misbehaving is being reinforced for that behavior. Taking the child out of the environment where the problematic behavior occurs will often remove the reinforcer, and with a "time out from reinforcement," the troublesome behavior is diminished or eliminated. Staats reports introducing the concept of time-out with his own daughter in 1961–1962 and describing it to colleagues, who began using time-out procedures in their research (Staats, 1971). The procedure has become commonplace in elementary schools, where undesirable behavior can be controlled without using aversive punishment.

time-out procedure
a procedure or environment in which no reinforcements are given in an effort to extinguish unwanted behavior

In contrast to Skinner's (1975) radical behaviorism, which did not specify in advance what would be reinforcing but left that to empirical analysis, Staats asserts that stimuli that elicit emotional responses have the additional function of serving as reinforcers in new learning (Staats, 1988; Staats et al., 1973). If a positive emotional response occurs, behavior is strengthened; if a negative emotional response, behavior is weakened. In addition to reinforcing behavior, emotional responses can provide incentives that cause us to approach or, in the case of negative emotions, to avoid them. These basic principles make our emotional responding a very central determinant of our behavior. In addition, the theoretical recognition of emotions permits behaviorism to include classical as well as operant conditioning, and thus to be a more comprehensive theory (Staats, 1988).

BASIC BEHAVIORAL REPERTOIRES

The behaviors of interest to personality psychologists are built up through extensive learning experiences, beginning early in life and continuing onward for decades. Staats proposes that personality consists of *behavioral repertoires,* which, like traits, vary from one person to another and lead to different behaviors (see Figure 10.1). Most important are those repertoires that are the stepping-stones for subsequent learning: **basic behavioral repertoires (BBRs)**, built up through learning from birth onward.

basic behavioral repertoires (BBRs)
learned behaviors fundamental to later learning of more complex behavior, in three categories: language-cognitive, emotional-motivational, and sensory-motor

Although early learning has special importance for personality, it continues beyond these basic behavioral repertoires. Learning is "long term, cumulative, and very complex" (1996, p. 35). Typically, behavior is built up of combinations of component behaviors, including aspects from each of the three types of BBRs described in this chapter (Riedel, Heiby, & Kopetskie, 2001). Staats identifies three types of BBRs: the *language-cognitive,* the *emotional-motivational,* and the *sensory-motor* (see Table 10.2).

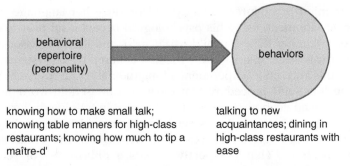

knowing how to make small talk;
knowing table manners for high-class
restaurants; knowing how much to tip a
maître-d'

talking to new
acquaintances; dining in
high-class restaurants with
ease

FIGURE 10.1   Personality as a Basic Behavioral Repertoire

Source: Adapted from Staats, 1996, p. 177.

Note: Personality consists of a person's basic behavioral repertoire
(BBR), which is produced by past environmental experiences.
Together with the current environment, personality influences
current behavior.

Table 10.2 Staats's Three Basic Behavioral Repertoires (BBRs)

Basic Behavioral Repertoires	Examples of Behaviors	Examples of Related Personality Tests
Language-Cognitive	Speech Reading Thinking Planning Social interaction	Intelligence tests (many items) Reading readiness tests
Emotional-Motivational	Responses to punishment and reward Emotional responses to social interactions with friends and family Sexual arousal Enjoying work and recreation Religious values Depression Anxiety Reinforcing or punishing self-talk Emotional responses to music and art Type-A behavior[a]	Interest tests (Strong Vocational Interest Blank) Values tests (Allport-Vernon-Lindzey Study of Values) Edwards Personal Preference Schedule Motivation tests Attitude tests Anxiety tests Depression tests
Sensory-Motor	Feeding Toilet training Writing Aggressive behavior Active-passive behavior Behavior judged "masculine" or "feminine" Athletic activities Social skills	Intelligence tests (some items, such as Geometric Design and Mazes) Behavioral assessments[a] Sensation-Seeking Scale[a] Expressive behavior measures[a]

Source: Adapted in part from Staats, 1986, 1993; Staats & Burns, 1981; and Staats & Heiby, 1985. Some
items, indicated by superscript a, are the suggestions of this author.

Behaviors in these categories provide the basis for later, more complicated learning. If the basics are not learned, later learning is necessarily compromised. Unless a child knows the fundamentals of holding a pencil, for example, learning to write will be impossible, and performance on intelligence tests will suffer. Fortunately, through carefully planned interventions, it is sometimes possible to teach the basics in remedial programs. Intervention to teach such fundamentals leads to improved scores on relevant intelligence scales (Staats & Burns, 1981). Furthermore, adolescents suffering from Down syndrome have been taught basic social skills, such as saying hello and introducing themselves, through a behavioral intervention that includes modeling and role playing (Soresi & Nota, 2000).

Whether because of a neglecting early environment or a neurological deficit, a child who does not learn basic experiences of pleasure in interpersonal situations will not develop normal social behaviors. Once we have analyzed the crucial basic behaviors, we are in a better position to deal with life tasks, such as raising children, as well as to develop appropriate interventions to change behavior, based on learning principles (cf. Staats & Eifert, 1990).

The Emotional-Motivational Repertoire

Each human, with a unique set of environmental conditions, learns emotional responses to a huge number of stimuli. That constitutes the individual's unique emotional-motivational BBR. Some emotional responses are innate: positive emotional responses to food, negative emotional responses to painful stimuli. Other stimuli come to elicit emotional responses in us through classical conditioning (Staats, 1996, p. 40). This emphasis on classical conditioning illustrates the greater breadth of Staats's theory, compared to Skinner's. It explains, for example, how people can develop learned fears.

The infant learns to love the parent because the parent is paired with food, warmth, caresses, play, and relief from negative stimuli. If a parent frowns when the infant feels pain, the parental frown becomes, by conditioning, a stimulus that elicits a negative emotion. Subsequently, because the child has a negative emotional response to seeing her parent frown at her, that will act as a punishment for whatever she is doing. Emotions aroused by concerts, religious activities, and other individual preferences vary from one person to another, reflecting the individual's unique emotional-motivational repertoire, and that repertoire plays a powerful role in determining the individual's behavior in almost every life situation that will be encountered.

As a result of learning, people approach pleasant stimuli and avoid unpleasant ones. A father's frown, because learning has made it elicit a negative emotion in the child, can now become the stimulus that teaches the child to avoid doing what makes Dad frown. Notice that fear and anxiety are not simply unpleasant remnants of past learning, but they also function as stimuli to direct current behavior. Whether they will be adaptive depends on the specific learning. A wise parental guide can direct adaptive behavior through smiles and frowns. An unwise abusive parent is the source of maladaptive learned behavior, instead.

Basic emotional-motivational responses build the foundation for more mature behavior. Early in life we learn to approach things that we enjoy or pull them toward us, as a baby grabs for a toy. We also learn to push away what is repulsive, spitting out undesired food or shoving a disliked object (or sibling!) away from us. These basic approach and avoidance behaviors form the foundation for more mature motivational-emotional processes.

An experiment illustrates this (Staats & Burns, 1982). Subjects were presented with stimuli, words associated with religion and words associated with transportation. Several weeks earlier, they had taken a personality test that allowed the researchers to classify each subject as high-religious or low-religious in values. They were then administered a learning task that required the subjects to learn to respond differentially to words related to religion and to a nonreligious topic (transportation). Some subjects were required to pull a handle toward them when they were shown a religious word and push the handle away for a transportation word. The researchers found that highly religious subjects responded quickly on this task. In another condition, the task

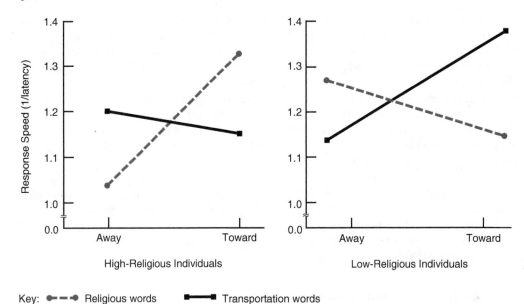

Key: ●– – –● Religious words   ■——■ Transportation words

Speed with which the religious and transportation words were approached or avoided by the high- and low-religious individuals, higher scores indicating a more rapid response.

FIGURE 10.2   Interaction of Religious Orientation and Task Demands on Performance on an Experimental Task

Source: From A. W. Staats & G. L. Burns (1982). Emotional personality repertoire as cause of behavior: Specification of personality and interaction principles. *Journal of Personality and Social Psychology, 43*, 873–881. Copyright 1982 by the American Psychological Association. Reprinted by permission.

was reversed: to push away when shown religious words and to pull toward when shown transportation words. Highly religious subjects were slower on this task. For subjects low on religious values, the results were reversed (see Figure 10.2). This study shows that reactions to religious values, which are part of the emotional-motivational repertoire, build on earlier, more basic behaviors in this repertoire: approach ("pull toward") and avoidance ("push away") behaviors. When the experimenters required a highly religious subject to approach what they value or a nonreligious subject to reject what they did not value, the task was easier than when the reverse was required. That is, we learn more quickly when our earlier learning, our basic behavioral repertoire, has prepared us for the new demands.

The Language-Cognitive Repertoire

Language is essential to human personality, enabling us to communicate with others and to think. Normal social interaction requires us to understand and respond to what others say. A person's own thoughts and self-directed speech can also direct behavior, permitting foresight and judgments. Consider the phrases "sex is dirty and sinful," and "abortion is murder" (Staats, 1996, p. 83). These statements elicit emotions and influence behavior.

Language is primarily cognitive. Words conjure up images. Analysis of education and the development of intelligence suggest that children who learn to visualize objects and ideas when they hear or read words can build on these basic responses with additional learning. Those who are less able to visualize verbal concepts will have a more difficult time understanding what they read, and so they will be handicapped in various educational tasks, including reading and mathematics (e.g., word problems). Parents, by speaking to their children, and by more self-conscious educational interactions such as flashcards for letters of the alphabet, teach these language skills. Children learn to imitate the words spoken by adults, and this basic response of imitation helps children learn more complex language. Building on language for concrete objects such as cookies and cars, children can ultimately develop concepts for more abstract ideas such as God and flying saucers (Staats, 1996, p. 95).

Artists, musicians, dancers, and others in specialized areas have particular strengths in concepts related to their fields. These competencies are learned. Staats challenges the necessity of proposing innate talents to explain why one person is an accomplished musician, another a reader, and so on.

The Sensory-Motor Repertoire

Using tools, performing work, combing hair, and cleaning the house are among the behaviors in our sensory-motor repertoire. Even our body movements, whether masculine or feminine, self-assured or timid, are learned motor patterns. Educators who teach the accents of foreign languages are training sensory-motor responses. In these various kinds of learning, the ability to imitate a model is an important basic response that facilitates later learning. Extensive practice is the basis for competent behavior—more important than genetic talent in producing champions, according to Staats.

Staats argues that children's early motor development is more influenced by learning, and less by innate predispositions, than most people believe. He illustrates this argument with pictures of his own children walking without support at 9 months of age, considerably earlier than most children, as a consequence of the learning opportunities provided by their behaviorist father (1996, p. 137). He also expresses the opinion that whether a child becomes right- or left-handed is largely a matter of early learning, not brain predisposition. Children also learn to be toilet trained, to avoid bed-wetting, to pay attention, to swim, and a variety of other behaviors that contribute to their social adjustment.

SITUATIONS

Situations can have three different kinds of implications on behavior, according to what Staats has variously termed "three-function learning theory" or "A-R-D theory" (Riedel, Heiby, & Kopetskie, 2001; Staats, 1975). Situations can arouse affects and attitudes ("A"), as when an exam room elicits anxiety. They can provide reinforcements ("R"), as when the attention of an audience reinforces a performer who is on stage. They can direct ("D") behavior, as when a well-organized study directs a student to the next academic task.

PSYCHOLOGICAL ADJUSTMENT

Staats describes his theory as one that "specifically aims to construct theory bridges that go from the scientific to practice in a bidirectional development, ... that ... has been formulated with respect to the goals of unification, including that of science and practice" (1993, p. 59). To function as a well-adjusted person, much learning is needed. People who fail to learn the basics, the important components of higher learning that constitute the basic behavioral repertoire, behave in ways that are maladjusted. Conversely, full-blown maladaptive patterns build on earlier components—for example, cruelty to animals in childhood is a stepping-stone to violence toward people (Miller, 2001).

Deficits in the emotional-motivational repertoire lead to many psychological disorders, including phobias (irrational fears), depression, and anxiety. Autistic children are deficient emotionally, lacking affection for their parents. Language-cognitive repertoire behavior is deficient in mental retardation, defense mechanisms, and paranoid delusions. The sensory-motor repertoire is inadequate in people who lack social skills and work skills, people who are violent, and in some excessive self-stimulation behavior of autistic children.

Behaviors in the language-cognitive repertoire include self-statements that lead to depression and other pathologies or that affirm health. A positive self-concept, core to health in many theories, occurs when favorable self-statements become habitual. Such mood-elevating positive statements must, however, be balanced with more cautionary statements, lest a person spiral into a maladaptive manic condition (Riedel, Heiby, & Kopetskie, 2001). A healthy person also learns reinforcing behaviors, corresponding to an effective emotional-motivational repertoire. Socially competent behavior requires appropriate learning. Our behavior functions as a stimulus to other people, so a child must learn to behave in a way that will produce desired responses in others: taking turns, sharing toys, and so on. If this happens, continued social learning with play-mates occurs; if not, such learning is stifled, and a cascade of problems may result. Later, learning the behaviors of adult friendship and love, of work relationships and leadership, builds on these childhood skills.

The defense mechanisms, as described by psychoanalysts (see Chapter 2), are products of learning. Repression, from a behavioral viewpoint, may be understood as the avoidance of making statements (including thinking) that elicit negative emotions. Maladaptive perfectionism occurs because of rigid rules, enforced through language directed toward oneself, that state unrealistically high standards for behavior (Slade & Owens, 1998). A behavioral interpretation has even been suggested for hallucinations (Burns, Heiby, & Tharp, 1983; Staats, 1996).

Over the years, behaviorists have developed interventions for many disorders: learning deficits, self-care among retarded and psychotic children and adults, social skills in various populations, depression, anxiety, and the whole gamut of psychological disturbances. Interventions often are planned in close conjunction with behavioral assessment of the problem, which facilitates planning of the intervention and evaluating its effectiveness. This perspective provides a different understanding of some issues described in other therapies: transference, for example, which occurs because of stimulus generalization, if the therapist resembles a parent or other important person from the patient's past (Staats, 1996, p. 329).

THE NATURE-NURTURE QUESTION FROM THE PERSPECTIVE OF PSYCHOLOGICAL BEHAVIORISM

Sometimes we think of learning and biology as competing explanations of personality: The more important one is, the less important the other. That competition between the two explanations is often called the *nature-nurture question*. Arthur Staats (1996) criticizes this position. He reasons that biological evolution has contributed to human survival by making our species highly adaptable. Biology has made learning important. In addition, learning can often influence biology, changing our hormonal and even neurological processes and structures.

Staats has also considered the impact of biological factors on learning as it affects individuals. His analysis provides a framework within which physiological approaches to personality may be integrated with behavioral approaches. Learning is stored in biological representations, and so biological factors can influence learning either by having an impact on the process of new learning or by influencing the biological storage of past learning. A stroke or other physical trauma can eradicate influences of past learning. Such interference can be permanent, as from a stroke, or temporary, as from the transient effects of many drugs (see Figure 10.3).

During the process of learning, biological factors may facilitate or impede certain types of learning. Many biologically based disorders, such as Down syndrome, affect learning. People with these biological variations may be able to learn more slowly or with different sequences of tasks and reinforcements than others. They can learn, however, if their environment provides the opportunity. By recognizing that biological differences do not directly cause the typical symptoms of these disorders but only change the circumstances of learning, the theory provides direction for effective intervention.

What about variations in intelligence among people who are not affected by Down syndrome or other known sources of low intelligence? Are such variations simply a matter of heredity (cf. Cattell, Chapter 8)? Without denying that heredity has an effect, Staats describes many ways of interacting with children that enhance their intelligence. He taught his daughter numbers by holding up one or two raisins and saying the numbers, rewarding imitation of these numbers with (naturally) the raisins (1996, p. 148). He taught letters of the alphabet using cards (p. 147). Children with preschool experiences such as these are likely to surpass their classmates in the earliest years of

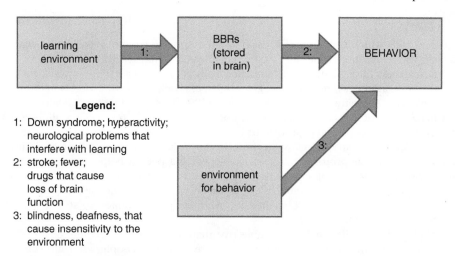

Legend:

1: Down syndrome; hyperactivity; neurological problems that interfere with learning
2: stroke; fever; drugs that cause loss of brain function
3: blindness, deafness, that cause insensitivity to the environment

FIGURE 10.3 Various Points at Which Biological Factors Influence Personality and Behavior from a Psychological Behaviorist Position

Source: Adapted from Staats, 1996, p. 182.

school, and this makes later lessons easier as well, compounding the advantage. Staats even argues that intelligence tests do not tap an innate ability to learn but rather the basic behavioral repertoire required for educational success—such as the effect of these preschool preparatory lessons. Systematic training of 4-year-old children from culturally deprived backgrounds resulted in improved reading, writing, and number skills and an average IQ score gain of 12 points (Staats, 1968).

As we saw in Chapter 9, whether a person is shy is thought related to a biologically based temperament. Staats challenges this view, however. He points out that parents vary in their interactions with children, and until we study more thoroughly the differences in such parenting—for example, in playful and reassuring interactions—he regards it as premature to assume that early differences in temperament must be biological and not learned. Even if partly biological, the impact of small differences in a child's sociability can be magnified by the different reactions of adults to a warm smiling infant or a hesitant shy one—and by different reactions of peers in childhood, adolescence, and beyond.

The Act Frequency Approach to Personality Measurement

Personality theorists assume that personality traits predict or cause behavior. Why not put a different angle on this relationship and use behavior to measure personality? If a person behaves in a distinctive way frequently, surely this is evidence of personality. Someone who frequently gives gifts and spends time helping others can be said to be generous. Managers may informally assess which of their workers are motivated by achievement needs and which by affiliation needs by watching to see who strives to do better than before and who chooses to work with friends rather than alone (Chusmir, 1989).

The **act frequency approach (AFA)** to personality measurement uses systematic procedures for assessing the frequency of prototypical behaviors to infer an individual's personality traits (Buss & Craik, 1980, 1983). Several steps are needed to be sure that the behaviors are relevant to the trait. First, research participants (undergraduates, typically) are asked to nominate acts that are good examples of the category under consideration. For example, they might be asked to describe an act by a friend that is typical of dominance or gregariousness. Next, a separate group of judges evaluates the nominated acts for their relevance, and their judgments are pooled. From the many acts nominated, a small number of prototypical acts are selected that have been judged characteristic of the particular trait (e.g., dominance) and not of any other. These acts then are used as the act frequency measure. Subjects are asked how often they have behaved in this way, or they rate the

act frequency approach

measuring personality traits by assessing the frequency of prototypical behaviors

(continued)

(continued)

frequency with which someone else, such as their spouse, has behaved in this way. This produces the act frequency measure of the trait (Buss & Craik, 1985).

Researchers have used the act frequency method to assess a variety of traits, including agreeableness, aloofness, dominance, gregariousness, helplessness, quarrelsomeness, and submissiveness (Angleitner, Buss, & Demtröder, 1990; Buss & Craik, 1980; Peterson, 1993). What behaviors would you nominate as typical of each of these traits? Some differences in judgments of acts as prototypical of particular traits have been observed cross-culturally, comparing West German subjects with those in the United States. West Germans are more likely to judge acts as prototypical of agreeableness if a person helps someone else more than duty requires, for example, "She tried to help a stranger with his problems." In contrast, Americans judged behavior as agreeable if a person yielded to someone else, for example, "He left the party when his date wanted to, even though he wanted to stay" (Angleitner, Buss, & Demtröder, 1990, p. 192).

Asking about behavior is more objective than asking about feelings or beliefs, but how do we know that self-reports of behavior are accurate? People, after all, sometimes overestimate the frequency with which they do desirable behaviors and underestimate their faults—especially people who are narcissistic (Gosling et al., 1998). Strict behaviorists have researchers observe behavior. Act frequency approaches often improve on the self-report method by having friends of subjects report the subjects' behavior (e.g., Moskowitz, 1990).

CONTRIBUTIONS OF BEHAVIORISM TO PERSONALITY THEORY

The behavioral approach has emerged from its early position of conflict with personality theory. As the act frequency approach illustrates, behaviorists have stimulated more precise operational definitions of personality concepts. Behaviorists remind us emphatically that situations matter.

Psychological theory has, since early behaviorism, become decidedly more cognitive, and versions of behaviorism such as that proposed by Skinner, which exclude considering people's thoughts, are thereby less integrated with theoretical advances in the field, despite their many applications (DeGrandpre, 2000). By contrast, Staats's theory explicitly includes meanings and is thereby more comprehensive and better able to be unified with other theoretical insights in psychology. The importance of cognition continues as a theme in the next two chapters.

Summary

- Dollard and Miller proposed a learning theory that could explain the clinical phenomena observed by psychoanalysts. Four learning concepts are fundamental: drive, cue, response, and reward.
- Behaviors are increased in frequency by reward and reduced in frequency by extinction and punishment. Reward and punishment have their greatest effects on behavior near the goal, producing approach and avoidance tendencies. The avoidance gradient is steeper than the approach gradient.
- Dollard and Miller reinterpreted several psychoanalytic concepts in terms of their learning theory, including identification, stages of development, and conflict. A fourth stage, concerned with anger–anxiety conflicts, was added.
- The frustration-aggression hypothesis described the cause of aggressive behavior.
- Language is an important species-specific human behavior that offers cues for behavior and permits a learning theory interpretation of levels of consciousness.

- Dollard and Miller's discussion of suppression has been followed by research that demonstrates its sometimes-adverse effects.
- B. F. Skinner proposed a *radical behavioral theory* of individual behavior in terms of environmental determinants, without referring to unobservable internal characteristics such as traits.
- He described *operant behavior* as behavior selected by the environment. This provides a mechanism for adaptation in the life of an individual, parallel to evolutionary selection that occurs over generations.
- Skinner's theory of *operant conditioning* describes the acquisition of behaviors through *reinforcement* and their elimination through *extinction* and *punishment*.
- Patterns of behavior can be understood in terms of chaining, discrimination and generalization, and *schedules of reinforcement*.
- Skinner's model suggested treatment interventions through behavior modification.

- Critics have argued that Skinner's model ignores important differences between humans and other species, especially language.
- Arthur Staats has presented a theory of *psychological behaviorism* that fills in many of the pieces missing in Skinner's theory to make it more precise as a behavioral approach to personality.
- Staats proposes that personality consists of *basic behavioral repertoires,* learned behaviors that have broad effects on personality and are the basis of later learning.

- Three categories of such basic behaviors are the *emotional-motivational repertoire,* the *language-cognitive repertoire,* and the *sensory-motor repertoire.*
- Effective learning produces psychological adjustment, whereas inadequate learning leaves a person maladjusted.
- Instead of regarding personality as innate, psychological behaviorism describes it as learned, leaving open the possibility that innate differences may contribute to personality but only through their effect on learned behavior.

Thinking about Behaviorism

1. If you were to apply learning principles to improve some aspect of life, what would you do? Describe the behavior(s) you would wish to change and describe the learning strategies that might achieve this goal.
2. Have you observed any use of operant conditioning techniques in education? Describe them. If not, what uses would you propose?
3. Of the three kinds of basic behavioral repertoires proposed by Staats, which do you think is most important for personality? Why?
4. Give examples of basic behaviors that you think are not sufficiently developed in the repertoire of people whose personalities are not well adjusted. Can you suggest therapeutic interventions or changes in child-rearing practices to deal with these problems?
5. Do you think it is possible to explain Freud's theory in terms of behaviorism? Why or why not?

Study Questions

1. Describe the relationship between Dollard and Miller's theory and psychoanalysis.
2. List and explain the four fundamental concepts about learning.
3. Explain the difference between a primary reward and a secondary reward.
4. What is a learning dilemma? Give an example.
5. Discuss how behaviors may be eliminated by using the techniques of punishment and extinction.
6. Discuss Dollard and Miller's analysis of imitation as a learning model for identification. Explain the differences among same behavior, copying, and matched dependent learning.
7. List the four critical training periods of childhood. Explain what is learned in each stage.
8. Summarize the basic principles of operant conditioning—that is, how do reinforcement, punishment, and extinction influence the rate of responding?
9. How might one schedule of reinforcement produce steady, frequent behavior and another produce inconsistent behavior?
10. Describe the application of operant conditioning to therapy.
11. Summarize the objections to Skinner's ideas as a theory of human personality. What are its strengths as a theory of human personality?
12. What is meant by the term *basic behavioral repertoire?*
13. Give examples of behaviors in the emotional-motivational repertoire, the language-cognitive repertoire, and the sensory-motor repertoire.
14. Using the "A-R-D" model, describe the three functions by which situations influence behavior. Give examples.
15. Describe Staats's psychological behaviorism as an approach for understanding personality adjustment in behavioral terms.
16. What are the implications of Staats's theory for the nature-nurture question?
17. Describe the act frequency approach to measuring personality.

11

Kelly
Personal Construct Theory

Chapter Overview

ILLUSTRATIVE BIOGRAPHY
Richard Nixon

Richard Nixon, remembered as the U.S. president who resigned from office in 1974 in the face of almost certain impeachment, provides an interesting case study for personal construct theory. The ideas that drove his personality are central to understanding how he succeeded politically and why he faced a disgraceful end to a long political career. George Kelly's personal construct theory provides a framework for understanding concepts such as these. It is distinct from many of the other analyses of this man because it focuses squarely on his thinking.

Richard Milhous Nixon, born in 1913, was elected the 37th president of the United States (1969–1974). His administration was widely praised for increasing contact with communist China, which earlier had been closed to Western visitors and business, but most Americans remember him for the disgrace that ended his presidency. He resigned under the threat of impeachment initiated by the Watergate scandal, a bungled act of political espionage, in which his Republican Party tried to steal documents from the Democratic offices at the Watergate Hotel complex and then lied in an attempt to cover up the burglary.

Richard Nixon

Richard Nixon was the second child of five boys. His older brother, Arthur, died of meningitis in 1925, and a younger brother, Harold, died of tuberculosis in 1933. Nixon was raised (after age 9) in Whittier, California, where he worked in the family store. His mother's family was Quaker, and this background influenced his upbringing by emphasizing emotional control, modesty, and hard work. His father (not a Quaker) was more emotional and punitive, and Nixon became interested in politics because of his influence (Ambrose, 1987). At times, Nixon avoided his father when the atmosphere became too tense, often going off somewhere alone to read.

Nixon enjoyed debate. His first formal debate was in seventh grade (Ambrose, 1987, p. 39). He continued with this interest at Whittier College. (Although he had been admitted to Harvard University and awarded a scholarship there, he could not afford to attend. His brother's bout with tuberculosis had been costly.) After college, Nixon attended Duke University Law School on a scholarship; he was an excellent student. He later became an attorney in California. During World War II, he volunteered for the navy, although as a Quaker he would have qualified for conscientious objector status. (At that time in history, there was a military draft in the United States, not a volunteer military.) Nixon was popular in this structured environment. He was also very good at poker, winning enough to start a political campaign for Congress when the war ended.

Elected to public office, Nixon became nationally known for his role in the House Committee on Un-American Activities, where he forcefully investigated Alger Hiss, who had served in the State Department, for secret communist associations and espionage. Nixon served in the House and then in the Senate before becoming vice president under Dwight Eisenhower (1953–1961). He had a reputation for dirty campaign tactics and was disliked by many because of his personality, seeming to be insincere and calculating (Ambrose, 1987). In 1960 he lost a close election for the presidency to John F. Kennedy, and 2 years later he lost a bid to become governor of California. He seemed to have retired from politics. However, he garnered the Republican presidential nomination in 1968 and won the general election that November. In 1972, Nixon was reelected by one of the widest margins on record, defeating Democratic presidential candidate George McGovern.

As president, Richard Nixon grappled with the Vietnam War, but like his predecessor, Lyndon Johnson, he could not easily end it. He opened diplomatic relations with communist China and signed an historic Strategic Arms Limitation Treaty with the Soviet Union. Despite these bold initiatives in foreign policy, most Americans remember Nixon primarily for the Watergate scandal. It began as a fumbled political espionage caper, with burglars hired by the Committee to Reelect the President breaking into the Washington, D.C., headquarters of the Democratic National Committee at the Watergate apartment-office complex. As the case developed, the break-in became less salient than Nixon's involvement in a coverup of the operation, a coverup documented in his own tape recordings of conversations in the president's Oval Office. Ultimately, threatened with impeachment, Nixon resigned from office on August 9, 1974 (Woodward & Bernstein, 1976). It is ironic that a third-rate act of domestic political espionage could bring down such a leader. During the years before his death in 1994, Nixon continued as an elder statesman and wrote about his public life and foreign policy.

DESCRIPTION

Personality, in Kelly's theory, consists of the ideas, the concepts, that a person uses to understand and predict his or her experience. He provided an elaborate description of the nature of such constructs, as we see later in this chapter. In Kelly's approach, there is no one objective, accurate way to construe situations. It is the unique concepts that each person applies that constitute personality.

Nixon's actions stunned many, who wondered what he could have been thinking, in the elaborate political espionage and coverup of Watergate. In foreign affairs, he thought differently about our then enemies, the communist countries of the Soviet Union and mainland China. (It was a different era then. Current students are not likely to appreciate how much distrust and fear those countries aroused.) People wondered how he could make overtures of peace and trade with these enemies. Obviously Nixon thought differently.

COGNITION

Kelly's theory offers an elaborate framework for describing a person's cognition. The concepts, called constructs, that we use to understand and predict the world are dichotomous, consisting of two opposite poles. We may not always know both sides of these concepts, consciously.

Richard Nixon's speeches give ample evidence of the dichotomous poles of his constructs. He described people by the construct of "we" (patriotic Americans; the working class; his supporters) versus "they" (the spoiled rich).

Hard work was a theme that resonated with the working class, especially when portrayed against the spoiled rich. Richard Nixon aimed for success, working long hours on his election campaigns and before that in law school, surviving on little sleep. Winter and Carlson (1988) concluded, from a content analysis of Nixon's first inaugural address, that he was high in achievement motivation. How did he define success? It was not in financial terms; he regularly gave speaking fees to charity (Ambrose, 1987). He considered success to be achievable by hard work. Some of his important personal constructs, then, concerned hard work. Perhaps his expression of this work ethic was a factor in his political success among middle-class and working-class voters.

Ambrose (1987, p. 614) describes the divisiveness of Nixon's campaign speeches: "He wanted to divide the community into 'us' and 'them,' and he succeeded." Nixon's construct of us versus them applied to domestic politics (Republicans versus the opposition) and to international relations (the United States versus the communists). Patriotism was an important theme, with the Vietnam war still on the nation's mind. Nixon's dogged investigations of communists early in his political career when he was a member of the House Committee on Un-American Activities reflects the *us* (patriotic Americans) versus *them* (communist sympathizers) construct. In his successful 1968 campaign for the presidency, Nixon defined *us* as "the Silent Majority, Middle America, the white, comfortable, patriotic, hawkish 'forgotten Americans'" (Ambrose, 1989, p. 222). *Them* included long-haired antiwar protesters and the elite who attended Ivy League schools. At other times, the press was the enemy (p. 250). Nixon's reputed vindictiveness also stems from an us-versus-them construct system. Ambrose described Nixon as "a vindictive man, with a long memory and a deep capacity to hate" (p. 172; cf. also p. 267). He maintained an "enemies list" of political opponents. Secretary of Defense Elliot Richardson suggested that Nixon was unable to stop thinking of others as enemies, which impeded his effectiveness as chief executive (White, 1975, p. 180). *We–they* may work as a construct in political campaigns (and Nixon was a dedicated campaigner), but it is a divisive construct for a sitting president.

How did he conceptualize the role of politician? Nixon's interpersonal manner was cold toward others, including his wife, at least in public. For Nixon, loneliness was inevitable for a politician. As he said, "Politics is not a team sport" (Nixon, 1990, p. 32). Yet Ambrose (1987, p. 618) argues that other politicians, including Dwight Eisenhower, were in fact gregarious, so there is nothing universal about Nixon's ideas. For Nixon, the construct of politician included, on the positive pole, loneliness; close interpersonal relationships belonged to the contrast pole, which for Nixon would also include the dimension of insecurity, given the death of two of his brothers and the absence of his mother during significant periods of his youth (Levey, 1986). The constructs of politician by others did not include this loneliness

(*continued*)

(continued)

component. It is noteworthy that in other conditions, in which he was not vulnerable, Nixon showed a friendly, considerate side of himself (Winter & Carlson, 1988). For example, he was especially considerate to hired help at the White House. Such fragmentation is consistent with Kelly's Fragmentation Corollary, which says constructs are applied in only some settings, not all.

Another aspect of Nixon's construct of a successful politician was pragmatism (Ambrose, 1989, p. 171; Nixon, 1990, chap. 32). Political realism or pragmatism could produce changes of opinion and illegal actions that others, with other construct systems, would regard as unprincipled (cf. Winter & Carlson, 1988). Nixon's construct system facilitated his bold initiatives in foreign affairs, most notably his visit to the People's Republic of China in 1972 and arms reduction negotiations with the Soviet Union.

The construct of privacy or secrecy was important for Richard Nixon. He seemed to regard secret activities as more effective and public ones less effective, the latter for show but not for effective action. Public behavior called for a politician to behave as an actor (Nixon, 1990). He often made executive decisions with little consultation. For example, his Secretary of State learned of his plan to visit China by reading it in the newspaper (Ambrose, 1989, p. 454). Nixon preferred to negotiate in "back-channel" communications, where fewer people were involved. He often acted through National Security Adviser Henry Kissinger rather than through the State Department. He is remembered for favoring covert operations, including wiretaps and the infamous break-in of the headquarters of the Democratic National Committee in the Watergate office complex in Washington, D.C.

Kelly's Sociality Corollary asserts that understanding another person's construct system makes possible a relationship with that person. Nixon and Kissinger understood one another. According to Ambrose (1989), "They shared a love of eavesdropping on others (the taps and the tapes), of secrecy, of surprises, of conspiracy, of backbiting, of power plays. They were alike in their utter cynicism, and in their contempt for everyone else, including each other" (pp. 490–491).

ADJUSTMENT

Constructs vary from one person to another, but some produce better adjustment than others. If we think of our constructs as ways of making predictions—what will happen, if I do thus and so—then some construct systems will produce more accurate predictions than others. A well-adjusted person has construct systems that make accurate predictions, and having a variety of construct systems ("cognitive complexity") suggests that the person is more likely to have one to fit any particular situation.

Nixon's greatest presidential achievements were, it is generally acknowledged, in foreign affairs. His knowledge was immense in this area. He eschewed simple tactics and criticized simplistic slogans about war and peace (Nixon, 1990, p. 346) and simplistic approaches to combating communism (Nixon, 1962, pp. 287–291). In Kelly's language, we may conclude that Nixon's construct system in foreign affairs was cognitively complex and served to predict accurately. In this area, he functioned commendably. In domestic affairs, his constructs did not lead to accurate predictions, or there would never have been the tragedy of Watergate. His "we–they" polarizations did not give him the flexibility needed to work with the people he needed to influence.

CULTURE

In Kelly's theory, you must understand the constructs of other people if you are to work effectively with them. It is not necessary that you have the same ideas, but you must understand the other.

The polarizing constructs of Nixon's construct system, just described, tended to dismiss the other's point of view, preventing effective dialogue, at least in the domestic arena. Nixon's success in opening new relationships with communist countries implies that he could understand their concepts. His own preference for secrecy and intolerance for dissent may be key to this understanding. Besides this theoretical point, when we are dealing with the actions of the president of the United States, it is obvious that his behavior has an impact on society both at home and abroad (e.g., the changed relationship with China).

DEVELOPMENT

Kelly's theory says relatively little about development. He does assert that constructs change with experience. If you use a construct and it makes a usable prediction (confirmation), you keep it. If the construct leads to a false prediction (disconfirmation), you abandon or modify it, although people do have ways of blinding themselves to disconfirmation.

Cognitive expectations influence our behavior, and if they are incomplete or inaccurate, adverse consequences may happen in the real world. This was the case in the infamous end of Nixon's presidency. Behavior that he thought of little consequence—approving domestic political espionage into the secrets of the opposing Democratic party and then ordering coverup of the crime of the Watergate break-in—led to public scandal and his forced resignation from office. Clearly, his constructs had been disconfirmed, but it was too late to take back those actions.

BIOLOGY

Kelly's theory says little about biology. One idea he offers is the idea of a "preverbal construct," which is not represented in language but rather in emotion or a physical symptom. Nixon's reported psychosomatic symptoms in times of crisis can be explained as preverbal constructs (Volkan, Itzkowitz, & Dod, 1997). They may have begun in his conflicted childhood.

FINAL THOUGHTS

In many ways, the life of Richard Nixon illustrates both the positive and the negative effects of our cognitively based personality. On the positive side, high beliefs in his potential for success inspired Nixon to climb from unremarkable origins to world fame. On the negative side, the fact that some of these cognitions were based on a shaky foundation led to his downfall. The great tragedy of Nixon's fall from the office of president came from a cognitive error, a miscalculation. He approved a scheme to steal political secrets, and when it was discovered, he misjudged that he could lie and make the accusations go away. These errors and their resultant behavior brought severe damage to his reputation, and they placed the federal government in disarray. The constructs by which he judged behavior such as domestic spying as simply expedient were judged by others to be unethical. If we want to know what another person will do, we must know what they think.

PREVIEW: OVERVIEW OF KELLY'S THEORY

George Kelly's theory has implications for major theoretical questions, as presented in Table 11.1. His fundamental lesson is that an individual's perception of the world determines his or her behavior. Kelly analyzed personality in a way that suggested measurement techniques, especially his Role Construct Repertory test. Predictions based on his theory are not always precise because of the difficulty of making allowance for idiosyncrasies, a problem inherent in all approaches that use an idiographic approach. The theory is primarily cognitive; although Kelly suggested preverbal constructs with bodily implications, explicit connections with particular biological functions have not been made. As an applied theory, Kelly's work on role constructs has been widely applied in business and organizations, as well as in therapy.

George Kelly proposed a theory of personality that emphasizes the individual's thoughts. When it was proposed, it was outside the mainstream of psychology. Despite psychology's increased attention to cognition (Cacioppo et al., 1996), Kelly's theory is still relatively isolated from other theories, perhaps because of its idiographic emphasis and its teleological orientation (Howard, 1988; Warren, 1991). It focuses on the individual, inspiring Kelly to refer to his theory as a **jackass theory** of personality. By this, he meant that the theory concerns the "nature of the animal" rather than environmental forces that push ("pitchfork theories") or pull ("carrot theories") the individual (Kelly, 1958). Of course, situations matter; but it is the individual's perception of them that is crucial. Like his unpretentious phrase, Kelly's theory is not caught up in abstract and unobservable theoretical constructs; rather, it focuses on the phenomenological experience of the individual (cf. Walker, 1990), as do humanistic theories (cf. Epting & Leitner, 1992). It is a difficult theory to pigeonhole into any one theoretical perspective (Benjafield, 2008). Despite the theory's emphasis on a person's thoughts, some argue that it is not a cognitive theory (Warren, 1990a, 1990b), and Kelly (1955) agreed. He argued for a holistic, even humanistic (Kelly, 1969) integration of cognition with other processes, usually separately considered as emotional and motivational. Broadly speaking, Kelly's view is similar to that of Alfred Adler. In fact, he published some of his work in the Adlerian journal *Individual Psychology* (Kelly, 1963b, 1964). People are not pawns in the face of reality. They make their own destiny by how they interpret events.

Table 11.1 Preview of Kelly's Theory	
Individual Differences	Individuals differ in the personal constructs (cognitions) they apply to experience. Other differences (emotions, behavior) follow from this.
Adaptation and Adjustment	Constructs that can predict a broad variety of experience accurately are more adaptive than constructs that predict only limited experience. Many therapeutic techniques are presented, including fixed-role therapy.
Cognitive Processes	Cognition is central to personality. Cognitive processes are elaborately described in Kelly's theory. Behaviors and emotions follow from cognitions.
Culture	Social relationships require that one person can understand the other's personal constructs. Kelly does not consider broader social institutions.
Biological Influences	Kelly does not consider biological factors explicitly. However, his concept of "preverbal constructs" and ideas about the relationship between construct change and emotions have potential implications for health and disease.
Development	Although Kelly does not focus on childhood, children develop constructs for making sense of their experience, especially their experience with people. Adults continue to use the personal constructs developed earlier, changing them when they do not predict accurately.

George Kelly

Biography of George Kelly

George A. Kelly was born in 1905 on a farm in Perth, Kansas, the only child in a family headed by a Presbyterian minister. In college, Kelly first studied engineering but then changed to education, completing his degree at the University of Edinburgh, Scotland, in 1930. In graduate school, he turned his attention to "learn[ing] something about sociology and labor relations" (Kelly, 1963a, p. 47). Kelly's first reading of Freud led to "the mounting feeling of incredulity that anyone could write such nonsense, much less publish it. It was not the pansexualism that makes Freud objectionable to some new readers, but the elastic meanings and arbitrary syntax that disturbed me" (p. 47). Kelly reported spending only 9 months studying psychology before completing his doctorate at the University of Iowa. This left him free to develop a theory that was quite original.

For 12 years, Kelly taught at a small college in western Kansas. Although his training was in education rather than clinical psychology, he saw many students in a free counseling clinic that he set up. This clinic became the laboratory for his emerging theory. He served as a traveling psychologist for many rural Kansas schools and so should be recognized as a school psychologist (Guydish et al., 1985). Also often forgotten is his early use of bipolar adjective ratings, which did not become popular until many years later (Jackson et al., 1988). Kelly (1963a) never charged for his consultations, aware of the impact of the Great Depression on his students, and he felt that psychology had an important role "to generate the imagination needed to envision…possibilities" of overcoming the limitations of circumstances (p. 50). As he alternated between seeing clients and supervising graduate students, Kelly came to view both as doing similar cognitive work. "Man-the-scientist" became his metaphor for therapeutic work.

After a year at the University of Maryland, Kelly moved to Ohio State University, where he took Carl Rogers's former position heading the clinical training program. It was there that Kelly (1955) wrote his two-volume work, *The Psychology of Personal Constructs*, explaining his theory and its clinical implications.

Kelly influenced the training of clinicians nationwide. He was president of the American Board of Examiners for Professional Psychologists from 1951 to 1953, a member of the Special Advisory Group for the Veterans Administration from 1955 to 1960, and a member of the Training Committee of the National Institute for Mental Health and the National Institutes of Health from 1958 to 1967. In the final year of his life, he accepted the invitation of Abraham Maslow to a position at Brandeis University. Kelly died on March 6, 1967.

CONSTRUCTIVE ALTERNATIVISM

Drawing on his experiences as both a clinician and a faculty member in a research discipline, Kelly developed a metaphor of personality that described a human being as a scientist. Just as a scientist uses theories to plan observations and make predictions, a person uses **personal constructs** to predict what will happen in life, especially in the realm of interpersonal relationships. When predictions are not confirmed, these personal concepts must be revised. This, then, is Kelly's (1955, p. 4) metaphor of **man-the-scientist**.

Kelly (1955, p. 15) makes the philosophical position behind his theory explicit: "We assume that all of our present interpretations of the universe are subject to revision or replacement." He calls this assumption **constructive alternativism**. Because we could construe the world differently, our beliefs do not have the status of objective truth, and should always be tentative and subject to revision (McWilliams, 1993). People are free to the extent that they are able to construct alternate interpretations.

The theory is stated clearly and explicitly in 12 succinct statements. These dozen statements consist of one Fundamental Postulate and 11 corollaries.

personal construct

a person's concept for predicting events

man-the-scientist

Kelly's metaphor for human personality

constructive alternativism

the assumption that people can interpret the world in a variety of ways

The Fundamental Postulate

Kelly's (1955, p. 46) **Fundamental Postulate** states that our expectations are of central importance. What we expect to happen, based on our cognitive assumptions, shapes all of our other psychological processes, including our emotions and motivations.

We prepare for the events that we anticipate. Our actions, thoughts, and emotions are determined by this anticipation, whether accurate or inaccurate. Imagine that you expect to win the lottery tomorrow; now, imagine that you expect the world to end tomorrow. Such anticipations have different effects, do they not? If events occur as they are anticipated, **validation** has occurred. If not, there has been invalidation (Landfield, 1988). This cycle of construing events and having the construction confirmed or not is repeated, sometimes with revision of the construct system (see Figure 11.1). Learning from experience through confirmation or disconfirmation of hypotheses is, of course, the scientist's way.

However, people are not very good scientists in their everyday lives. For one thing, they seek confirmation of their beliefs, whereas the scientist seeks evidence that could be disconfirming (Klayman & Ha, 1987). Life frequently offers enough evidence on both sides to permit the confirmation of mutually contradictory expectations, depending on where we look. This selective viewing is suggested by the popular image of the "half-empty, half-full" glass, which confirms either optimistic or pessimistic expectations. Optimism is maintained by a tendency to overlook negatives. Depressed people, in contrast, maintain their depression by self-confirmation (Andrews, 1989).

Beverly Walker (1992) suggests that the scientist metaphor is a goal, rather than a description, of human nature. By daring to test our beliefs, we can eradicate the errors and move toward more accurate understanding of ourselves and our world.

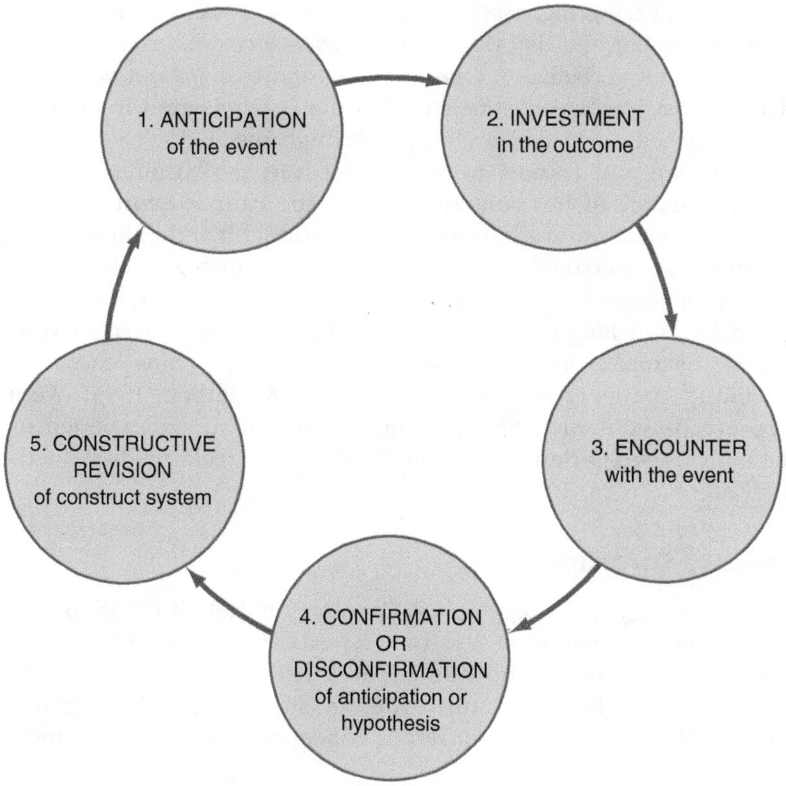

Fundamental Postulate

Kelly's main assumption, which stresses the importance of psychological constructs

validation

confirmation of an anticipation by events

FIGURE 11.1 The Experience Cycle

Source: Reprinted from "Personal constructs in clinical practice" by R. A. Neimeyer (1985b) in *Advances in Cognitive Behavioral Research and Therapy*, Vol. 4, pp. 275–339, edited by P. C. Kendall. Copyright © 1985 by Academic Press, with permission from Elsevier.

THE PROCESS OF CONSTRUING

Because anticipating (or construing) events is so important, Kelly described this process in detail. Four of Kelly's corollaries explain the process of construing (Neimeyer, 1987).

The Construction Corollary

Construction Corollary

Kelly's statement that people anticipate replications of events

According to the **Construction Corollary**, we make predictions about future events based on similar happenings that have occurred in the past. Whatever explanations make sense of the past are used to predict the future (Kelly, 1955, p. 50).

Like a scientist who anticipates that observations will confirm a stated research hypothesis, we anticipate confirmation of our constructs (cf. Mancuso, 1998). We base our expectations of the next football game on our experiences of previous ones, of the next concert by previous ones, and so on. Of course, events do not repeat themselves exactly. Nonetheless, adaptation would be impossible if we did not identify sufficient similarity among events to allow prediction of the future. We accomplish this by applying constructs to various events.

Events is a broad, inclusive term. It can be applied to events in the usual sense of the word; for example, "New Year's Eve is a time for celebration" applies the construct "a time for celebration" to the event "New Year's Eve." Most often, though, Kelly's concept of events is used to refer to people. Thus, if we say that "Hitler was disturbed," we are applying the construct "disturbed" to the event (in this case a person) "Hitler."

preverbal construct

a construct that is not conscious

The language of constructs and prediction has been criticized as being overly intellectualized, ignoring the emotional side of human experience (Bruner, 1956; Rogers, 1956). Kelly intended these processes to be understood more broadly (cf. Adams-Webber, 1990). Unverbalized and unconscious anticipations are also included. Kelly (1955, p. 459) refers to a **preverbal construct** as a nonverbalized anticipation that is not expressed in language. Constructs may be experienced as emotions (Landfield & Epting, 1987, p. 15). If a person becomes tense every time his or her father is present, that is evidence for a construct relating to the father, even if the individual cannot verbalize it. One therapist quotes a patient who has developed a preverbal construct as a consequence of sexual victimization in childhood: "When my husband touches me, I feel a chill go through me. I don't know why, as he is a really caring man and I know he would not hurt me" (Cummins, 1992, p. 360). The "chill" is evidence of her construct, which she cannot express in more precise language. Although such preverbal constructs are difficult and painful to uncover, they are important keys to personality. Many psychosomatic disorders (headaches, stomach or bowel problems, etc.) result from unverbalized constructs; the body expresses constructs in its own language. In therapy, the client may learn to verbalize such constructs. For example, one patient with frequent chest pains learned to verbalize her anger, and the pains rapidly improved (Leitner & Guthrie, 1993). We might compare such preverbal constructs with the unconscious emotional experiences described by psychoanalysts—experiences in which emotions occur without accompanying conscious content (Shean, 2001).

The Experience Corollary

Experience Corollary

Kelly's statement about personality development

Constructs can change. The **Experience Corollary** is Kelly's (1955, p. 72) statement of a developmental principle. It says that repeated events aren't always construed identically. The first time a child anticipates riding a two-wheeled bicycle will be construed differently than future rides. A student anticipating her first oral presentation to the class will use different concepts than the same student, several semesters later.

Briefly, people change with experience. The directions of this change vary and can be understood from the other corollaries, to be explained later (including elaboration of constructs, constriction, and slot movement). Perhaps Kelly's theory is as interesting for what he does not say about change. Unlike stage theorists (e.g., Freud and Erikson), Kelly does not propose that development must occur in a fixed sequence or toward a particular direction (Vaughn & Pfenninger, 1994). Nor does he emphasize the role of the environment in producing change. Nonetheless, personal construct theory as proposed by Kelly and expanded by others does describe development, particularly in adulthood as people use and revise their personal constructs (Berzonsky, 1992; Viney, 1992).

The Choice Corollary

How do we decide which of our constructs to apply to an event? Kelly's **Choice Corollary** is based on his metaphor of the scientist, motivated by intellectual curiosity, and so may seem overly optimistic to those who observe constrained and defensive people (1955, p. 64).

According to Kelly, people use the concepts that seem to permit expansion of understanding. As we will see later in the chapter, our constructs are bipolar or dichotomized, like "good-bad" or "interesting-boring." (This is explained later, when we consider the Dichotomy Corollary.) Like a scientist whose theory has worked so far, the individual seeks to extend his or her predictions. A person, in Kelly's terminology, makes the **elaborative choice** (p. 65). Sometimes the elaborative choice involves extending the construct system. The emphasis is on the action or choice, not on cognitive elaboration: on daring to do something different (Butt, 1998). Even drug use is, in a personal construct approach, a way of constructing meaning, of exploring a new, substance-centered self (Burrell & Jaffe, 1999). In the absence of threat we may explore and experiment, developing new constructs in the process. If threat is too great, however, a person will instead act in the same way as before, a choice called *sedimentation*. Although less healthy, sedimentation protects against the overly threatening choice of change, which feels as though it could destroy the system (Butt, 1998).

The Modulation Corollary

How extensively can a person's constructs be applied to new experiences? That is the question addressed by Kelly's (1955) **Modulation Corollary**, which says that only some of our constructs are available for interpreting new experience. Like a can of paint that may have turned to a hard glob over time and can no longer be used to paint anything, some constructs that worked in the past are no longer available. Others, like new paint, can still be used (p. 77).

A construct that can be applied to new elements is called a **permeable construct**. For example, imagine a person who thinks of many people as "able to read my mind" and of others as "not able to read my mind." Among his friends and acquaintances, each is categorized as a mind reader or not. Now the person meets someone new. Will he or she apply the construct of "mind reader or not" to the new person? If so, the construct is permeable.

The opposite of a permeable construct is a **concrete construct.** It is part of a person's construct system, but it is not open to new elements. An example of a concrete construct was suggested by George Kelly (1955, p. 1076): Most people regard the age of miracles as the past, even those who accept that miracles once occurred.

Kellian therapists sometimes deal with problematic constructs (or poles) by working with a client to make constructs more concrete, or impermeable, so that they, with their devastating effects, will not be applied to new experiences. Other types of construct system change are also made during constructivist therapy.

THE STRUCTURE OF CONSTRUCT SYSTEMS

Four of Kelly's corollaries explain the structure of construct systems (Neimeyer, 1987).

The Dichotomy Corollary

Constructs are always bipolar. Kelly's (1955) **Dichotomy Corollary** states that constructs are always bipolar, consisting of two alternatives (p. 59).

Choice Corollary
statement that people choose the pole of a construct that promises greater possibility of extending and defining the system of constructs

elaborative choice
a choice that allows a construct system to be extended; the Choice Corollary says this choice will be selected

Modulation Corollary
statement that the permeability of constructs sets limits to construction possibilities

permeable construct
a construct that can be extended to include new elements

concrete construct
a construct that cannot be extended to include new elements

Dichotomy Corollary
statement that constructs are bipolar

Good–bad, popular–unpopular, intelligent–stupid, and so on, are examples of dichotomous constructs. Either one pole or the other may be applied to an event (person). It is also possible for the construct itself to be deemed irrelevant (see the Range Corollary later). One side of the bipolar construct is typically used more often than the other. The nature of an individual's dichotomies may come as a surprise to the individual. It is generally the less used (contrast) end that is less available, or submerged.

When people change, the dichotomous nature of constructs has important predictive implications. Under stress, people often change from one pole to the opposite pole of a dichotomous construct. Such changes can be manifested as religious conversions, turning sober after being alcoholic, or in literature, the transformation of miserly Scrooge to a more generous soul in Dickens's *Christmas Carol* (Vaillant, 2002). Kelly (1955, p. 938) offers the example of a client who changes from kindly to hostile. Another example is the police officer who becomes a lawbreaker (Winter, 1993). Such changes from one pole to another are called **slot movement**. With a detailed understanding of the particular individual's constructs, a therapist can make an educated guess of the direction that person will move under stress, when current choices cease being validated. This offers an advance warning of dangerous change. On the positive side, a therapist armed with such information can use planned invalidation of currently operative constructs to trigger change in a client, when it is judged that such change would be in a safe and desirable direction.

Both poles of the construct must be understood from the individual's point of view. Often dichotomies are not strictly logical, and they vary from one person to another. The opposite of *ambitious*, for example, may be *lazy* for one person but *happy* for someone else. Alvin Landfield (1982) cites the example of two people with quite different contrasts to *liveliness*. For one, the contrast was *exhaustion*; for the other, *suicide*. The implications of these different dichotomous constructs are obvious.

The Organization Corollary

Constructs are arranged hierarchically. According to the **Organization Corollary**, constructs are arranged hierarchically. Compare this with the organizational chart of a business, with a chief executive officer at the top who has responsibility for the entire organization, and successive levels below—Vice Presidents, managers, office workers—each level with more limited areas of responsibility. In personal construct theory, at the top of the hierarchy are **superordinate constructs**, which apply broadly to several lower-order constructs, and are more abstract. The superordinate concept *vegetables* encompasses several lower-order concepts: carrots, beans, corn, and so on. If some things are true of all vegetables (e.g., they provide vitamins and little fat), it is more convenient to have a superordinate concept than to have only more limited constructs. Conversely, adding subordinate categories to break down a larger concept can lead to more correct anticipations. Consider mushrooms: Developing subcategories of edible mushrooms and poisonous mushrooms is potentially lifesaving. Similarly, constructs about people may need to be elaborated in such a hierarchical arrangement to improve adaptation. For example, we distinguish between trustworthy people and con artists. This sort of cognitive elaboration can be an important goal of therapy.

The term **core constructs** refers to constructs central to a person's identity and existence (Kelly, 1955, p. 482). They are superordinate constructs, encompassing others lower in the hierarchy. They constitute stabilizing elements within the personality, and are slower to change than less comprehensive **peripheral constructs**, though it may be possible for therapy to change them. Developing more superordinate, abstract concepts helps an individual to transcend contradictions. These higher-order constructs vary from person to person. For some people, the most important issue when facing conflicting choices is which will preserve wealth. For others, the deciding construct is which choice is ethical.

The Fragmentation Corollary

People are not always consistent, as Kelly's (1955) **Fragmentation Corollary** points out. Like Karen Horney (chapter 6), who described the defense mechanism of

slot movement

abrupt change from one pole of a construct to its opposite, often precipitated by stress

Organization Corollary

describes the hierarchical relationships among constructs

superordinate construct

a construct that applies broadly and subsumes lower-order constructs

core constructs

constructs central to a person's identity and existence

peripheral constructs

constructs not central to one's identity

Fragmentation Corollary

statement describing the inconsistency of people

compartmentalization, Kelly acknowledged that the constructs a person uses on one occasion may contradict the constructs used on another occasion (1955, p. 83).

Not all of a person's constructs are operative at the same moment. One moment we may be a ruthless competitor and the next, a loving friend. This potential for fragmentation suggests that observers may err if they infer personality from a limited sample of behavior.

The Range Corollary

Any construct has only limited usefulness. Kelly's (1955) **Range Corollary** states that some constructs have a broader "range of convenience" than others. When we are thinking about acquiring a pet, for example, we may apply such constructs as whether or not the animal would need a lot of attention, whether or not it would aggravate allergies, whether or not it would be fun to play with, and so on. These constructs would be irrelevant if we are choosing an insurance policy (p. 68).

The **range of convenience** of a construct refers to the events to which it applies. If either pole of a dichotomous construct describes the event (or person), that event is within the range of convenience of the construct. Apples, bananas, yogurt, and Cholesterol Clusters are all within the range of convenience of the dichotomous construct nutritious food versus junk food, but cement is outside of it. Examples with personal constructs are more problematic because each of us has somewhat different constructs. Most people would agree that Saddam Hussein, Adolf Hitler, and Mother Teresa are within the range of convenience of the construct villain versus saint. They might disagree about whether other individuals fall within its scope.

THE SOCIAL EMBEDDEDNESS OF CONSTRUING EFFORTS

Personal constructs are particularly important for understanding interpersonal behavior. Kelly's remaining three corollaries place the construing process in its social context (Neimeyer, 1987).

The Individuality Corollary

Kelly's (1955) **Individuality Corollary** states that different people use different constructs to anticipate events. That is, the way to understand personality differences is to identify people's different cognitions that guide their lives (p. 55).

It is in their constructs that individual differences, so important for any personality theory, are to be found. They are not to be found in different environments or different histories, although such factors may contribute to their formation. Only through the construction processes of individuals do such external events have an effect.

The Commonality Corollary

Although each person is unique, there are some similarities from person to person. Kelly's **Commonality Corollary** (1955) suggests where we should look for them. Not surprisingly, given the description of individual differences in the Individuality Corollary just explained, similarities are noted when people construe experience in similar ways. It's not shared DNA or shared traumatic experience; it's not similar education or nationality. What makes two people similar is their shared cognitive processes.

In contrast to what we might infer from other theories, similarity between persons is not a necessary consequence of similar experiences. It is the sense made of that experience that is critical.

The Sociality Corollary

Kelly's (1955) theory emphasizes interpersonal relationships. This last corollary addresses such relationships and allows Kellian therapists to establish a therapeutic relationship with their clients. The **Sociality Corollary** asserts that social role interactions require that at least one of the parties understands the other person's

---

Range Corollary
statement that a construct applies only to some events, not to all

range of convenience
the events to which a construct applies

Individuality Corollary
Kelly's assertion that different people use different constructs

Commonality Corollary
statement describing similarity between people

Sociality Corollary
statement that describes understanding another person or being understood as a prerequisite for a social process with that person

construction processes. I won't know how to relate to you if, because of ignorance about thought processes, I am constantly surprised by your behavior. Perhaps there is mutual understanding, but that is not required (p. 95).

Note that psychological similarity, addressed in the Commonality Corollary, is not necessary for a social interaction to occur. Understanding is necessary. This understanding may be mutual, as between two friends, or it may be unilateral, as between a parent and a child or a therapist and a client. For example, a therapist for clients who have problems with alcohol or other drugs will be more effective in the therapeutic role if he or she understands how the client thinks about alcohol and/or drugs. (This understanding is often greater if the therapist has personally recovered from problems with addiction.) If neither person in an interaction can "construe the construction processes" of the other, a social process is not possible. This construction failure may occur, for example, between a psychotic and a so-called normal person or between two people from vastly differing backgrounds.

Kelly (1955, p. 97) defines *role* in terms of understanding the other person's constructions or view of the world. The teacher role involves understanding students' concepts. An effective dog trainer must understand the dog's point of view (in this case, not expressed in language!). Psychotherapy involves role relationships, as the therapist comes to understand the client's construct system (Leitner & Guthrie, 1993). We also form role relationships with friends, lovers, and others, and in many cases the role constructions are mutual; each understands the other.

THE ROLE CONSTRUCT REPERTORY (REP) TEST

Role Construct Repertory (REP) Test

instrument for measuring a person's constructs

Kelly devised a measuring instrument to assess a person's constructs. This **Role Construct Repertory (REP) Test** has been widely used in research as well as in clinical and applied settings.

The REP test identifies the constructs a person uses to understand others. The first step is to list several particular people with whom the client or subject is acquainted. (See Table 11.2 for an example.) The subject is sometimes, but not always, included on this list. Next, three of the persons identified are selected by the researcher or therapist. The subject is instructed to identify one way in which two of

Table 11.2 Role Specifications for One Version of the REP Test
1. mother
2. father
3. brother
4. sister
5. spouse (or girlfriend/boyfriend)
6. same-sex friend
7. work partner who disliked you
8. person you feel uncomfortable with
9. someone you would like to know better
10. teacher whose viewpoint you accepted
11. teacher whose viewpoint was objectionable
12. unsuccessful person
13. successful person
14. happy person
15. unhappy person

Source: Adapted from Landfield & Epting, 1987, p. 33, who give more detailed descriptions of these roles.

RESPONSE SHEET

Column 1	Mother	Father	Happy Person	Successful Person	Andy (self)	Brian (son)	Mike (son)	Sharon (wife)	Beth (lover)	Therapist	Column 2	
1 Someone I love	1	1	1	1	2	1	1	1	1	1	Someone I hate	1
2 Lack sensitivity	1	2	1	2	2	2	2	2	2	2	Sensitive	2
3 Committed to family	1	1	1	1	1	1	2	2	2	2	Independent	3
4 Understanding	2	1	1	1	1	2	1	2	1	1	Impatient	4
5 Bright	1	1	1	1	2	1	1	1	1	1	Just average	5
6 Very inward	1	1	2	1	1	1	1	2	2	1	Very outspoken	6
7 Childlike inside	2	1	2	1	1	1	1	2	1	2	Get what you see	7
8 Have real communication	2	2	2	2	2	2	1	1	1	1	Aloof	8
9 Easy going	2	1	1	1	1	1	1	2	1	1	Emotional	9
10 Unaffectionate	2	2	1	1	2	2	2	1	2	0	Likes to touch	10

FIGURE 11.2 Example of One Client's Personal Constructs
Source: By Robert A. Neimeyer in *Handbook of Constructivist Assessment*, edited by G. J. Neimeyer.
Copyright © 1992 by Sage Publications, Inc. Reprinted by permission of Greg Neimeyer.

these individuals are the same and different from the third. The word or phrase used by the subject to identify how two individuals are the same is termed the *construct* (or sometimes the *likeness end*). The word or phrase used to describe how the third person is different is termed the *contrast*. These do not need to be logical opposites, and often they are not. Additional constructs are elicited by repeating the preceding step for several different triads of persons. Figure 11.2 shows examples of constructs elicited by one subject, a therapy client.

Under standard instructions, the circles in each row would nominate two individuals to the construct pole in column 1, indicated by "1" in the cell, and one individual to the contrast pole in column 2, indicated by "2." (The subject in Figure 11.2, however, refused to name anyone by the contrast pole, "Someone I hate.") A zero, as in the lower right of the figure, indicates that neither pole applies. After several constructs have been elicited, the subject is instructed to consider each person for every construct–contrast dimension and to indicate which pole applies. This creates a grid, rating each person on every construct.

Repertory tests provide counselors with qualitative impressions of clients as they progress through therapy. In addition, they can be scored in a variety of ways. For example, the discrepancy between the ideal self and the real, current self can be computed to look for change (Leach et al., 2001).

Even without further analysis, the grid and list of constructs may offer insights. The subject or client may be surprised to learn what constructs come to mind through this technique. A clinician may use these results to identify material for further exploration in psychotherapy sessions. For example, Robert Neimeyer (1992) notes that many of the client's constructs in Figure 11.2 refer to emotional reactions from other people (e.g., "sensitive," "impatient," and "emotional") and that a suggestion of conflict between being "committed to family" or "independence" could be relevant for the individual's current life decisions.

The grid, however, virtually begs for mathematical analysis. A variety of scoring methods have been devised. It is, however, advisable to seek empirical validation for the measures, for example, by comparing grid analyses with clinical judgments (e.g., Chambers et al., 1986). Constructs are judged to be similar or different not simply from the verbal labels but also from the way they are applied to the persons being rated.

For example, a person may propose two constructs, rich–poor and happy–unhappy. The words alone do not reliably disclose whether these are entirely different constructs. If all or nearly all of the individuals rated as rich are also rated as happy, whereas all or nearly all of those rated as poor are rated as unhappy, these are essentially the same construct, although with more than one way of referring to them in words. One pole of the construct is "rich and happy," while the contrast pole is "poor and unhappy."

COGNITIVE COMPLEXITY

cognitive complexity

elaborateness of a person's construct system, reflected in a large number of different constructs

The **cognitive complexity** of a person is reflected by the number of different constructs he or she uses in describing people (Bieri, 1955). Cognitively complex people are able to view social behavior from several different dimensions and thus have greater flexibility to adapt to challenges. They are less vulnerable to emotional swings than those with lower complexity (Linville, 1985). First-year university students who have greater cognitive complexity typically adjust to college more easily (Pancer et al., 2000). General Robert E. Lee won many military battles for the Confederate army during the U.S. Civil War, despite having fewer forces, because of his higher complexity, as inferred from his military documents (Suedfeld, Corteen, & McCormick, 1986). Peace overtures, as well as military victory, can come from cognitive complexity. During the 1970s, when Egyptian leaders spoke in more complex ways about their traditional enemy, Israel, their behavior became more cooperative (Maoz & Astorino, 1992).

Cognitive complexity is desirable, but it is not the sole criterion of an adaptive construct system. In addition, healthy development requires that people learn to integrate their various constructs. Complexity without integration is an unhealthy sign (e.g., Landfield & Epting, 1987). *Integrative complexity* can be developed as people think and write about the challenges of negative life events and explore ways to resolve contradictions (Suedfeld & Bluck, 1993). Complicating research on this topic, many measures of cognitive complexity based on the REP test and other instruments do not necessarily correlate with one another.

PERSONALITY CHANGE

Personal constructs can change. Sometimes change is necessitated by life events. When a loved one dies, for example, we grieve, not only mourning our loss, but also struggling to reconstruct a new set of meanings—that is, to revise our personal constructs to accommodate to a world without the one who has died (Neimeyer, 1999). Sometimes a person is not able to find new constructs for the new situation. This happened in the tragic case of a U.S. naval officer who had risen from a humble background to become chief of naval operations. When news reports accused him of wearing an unearned combat ribbon on his uniform, he was cast in the role of a liar and fraud. Unable to continue with his old successful constructs, he was also unable to find new constructs for his new situation. What to do? Unfortunately, he took the only course he saw available and committed suicide (Mancuso, 1998). Less dramatically but still tragically, people who have witnessed a mass murder or soldiers who have served in combat risk suffering posttraumatic stress responses if they cannot integrate these horrific experiences into their personal construct systems in an integrated, elaborate way (Sewell, 1996; Sewell et al., 1996).

Emotions Related to Change

threat

awareness of imminent comprehensive change in one's core structures

Personality change leads to strong emotions. **Threat** occurs when a person anticipates that core structures are about to undergo comprehensive change (Kelly, 1955. p. 489). Once we have become dislodged from our core role structures, we experience *guilt* (Kelly, 1955, 1962). Guilt, as used by Kelly, is not identical to its usual meaning concerning the violation of a culturally accepted standard of morality. Consider the case studies of two women who, having been sexually victimized themselves, were arrested or imprisoned for committing violent acts against the men in their lives. During therapy, as they came to think of themselves as victims as well as abusers, counterintuitively they experienced an increased sense of guilt (Pollock & Kear-Colwell, 1994).

Threat may be caused by major life changes, including the anticipation of death (Moore & Neimeyer, 1991; Neimeyer, Moore, & Bagley, 1988) and serious illness such as head and neck cancer (Turpin et al., 2009). Faculty evaluation of music students (Tobacyk & Downs, 1986) and counselors in training (Froehle, 1989) induces threat in students, which produces anxiety. Therapy that leads to changes in core constructs also arouses threat. Because people have different core structures, they find different situations threatening. For example, the possibility of becoming a homosexual is more threatening to some people than to others (Leitner & Cado, 1982). Threat is not always triggered by negative events. Kelly (1955, p. 490) supplies an example: standing at the gate to be released from prison after twenty years, and even though this is a desired event, a prisoner feels threatened. Personality developments in psychotherapy are (presumably) desired, yet still threatening.

Change in peripheral (rather than comprehensive) constructs produces *fear* (rather than threat). The less we think about a matter, the more likely we are to experience fear; the more we think about it, the more likely we are to experience threat. *Anxiety* occurs when we recognize that we are confronted by events outside the range of convenience of our construct system. Our constructs are not adequate to deal with events, and we know this. Anxiety is a sign of construct failure and the need for change.

People do not change their constructs easily and sometimes continue to try to make them work. Kelly (1955) understood **hostility** as an effort to force reality to confirm one's predictions, even though there has been evidence against those predictions in the past. One example is a man who became violent toward his wife when she wanted to divorce him, an idea he could not accept (Leitner & Pfenninger, 1994).

hostility

continuing to try to validate constructs that have already been invalidated

Effective Action: The C-P-C Cycle

A person who is making a decision about how to act typically engages in a three-step process called the **C-P-C Cycle**. In the first stage, **circumspection**, the person tries out several available constructs tentatively to see how they might fit in that situation. (For example, is a new teacher a slave driver, a mentor, or what?) The second phase, **preemption**, involves selecting which of the constructs to actually apply to that situation. (After the first exam, some students decide "slave driver" applies.) The third phase, **control**, involves action. (The student may study harder or drop the course.)

Each step contributes to effective action. Some people are less effective because they do not devote enough attention to the circumspection phase, deciding impulsively to act. Others continue pondering alternatives long after the time for decision has arrived. A therapist can help a client act more effectively by noticing which stages are inadequate and working on those.

C-P-C Cycle

the three-step process leading to effective action

circumspection

the first stage in the C-P-C Cycle, in which various constructs are tentatively explored

preemption

the second stage in the C-P-C Cycle, in which a construct is selected

control

the third stage in the C-P-C Cycle; the way in which the person acts

Loosening and Tightening Constructs: The Creativity Cycle

Although the C-P-C Cycle enables us to select constructs for action, it does not change those constructs. The **Creativity Cycle**, in contrast, involves the development of constructs. It occurs in therapy, which Kelly (1955, p. 529) describes as creative. Tight construing means that a large number of situations are construed in the same way, so the individual is insensitive to differences among them. Psychotherapy patients who use defense mechanisms (denial, rationalization, and turning against the object) show tight construing (Catina, Gitzinger, & Hoeckh, 1992). The first stage of the Creativity Cycle involves loosened construction, or **loosening**, which facilitates change. In therapy, techniques to loosen constructs include free association, fantasy, dream reporting, and silence (Kelly, 1955, p. 484).

In the next phase, one variation of the construct is selected, tightened, and applied in action. Without validation in action, the cycle is not complete, and the person is left with loose constructs that are too unclear to be adaptive. The creativity cycle occurs outside of therapy, too. It can be used in brainstorming sessions to aid problem solving. For example, the creativity cycle was invoked by a structured problem-solving exercise among graduate students to develop a strategic plan for the development of their educational program (Morçöl & Asche, 1993).

Creativity Cycle

the process of changing constructs by loosening and tightening them

loosening

applying constructs in ways that seem not to make sense, such as in brainstorming and free association

THERAPY

Personal construct theory traces disturbances to faulty constructs. Kelly's therapy requires the therapist "to understand the client in the client's own terms" (Landfield & Epting, 1987, p. 275) in order to be able to enter into a therapeutic role with the client (cf. the Sociality Corollary).

Although the therapeutic use of the REP test is individualized, some research illustrates its potential. One study, for example, finds that a few males with a history of having been sexually abused had REP grids that showed they identified themselves with their victimizer, rather than with the victimized child. Therapy changed this and helped relieve depression (Clarke & Pearson, 2000). Recently, patients with eating disorders were evaluated by a REP test that asked them to describe not people, but parts of their body (Borkenhagen et al., 2008).

Talk therapy is an obvious treatment for developing better constructs (Raskin & Epting, 1993). Kelly recommended a spirit of cooperative problem-solving techniques between client and therapist. Both therapist and client work to understand, test, and improve the client's constructs. This task-centered focus prevents the client from developing an overly dependent relationship. In fact, Kelly discouraged his own clients from disclosing too much personal material early in the therapy, until they came to understand what his mode of therapy was all about.

A variety of therapeutic techniques can be used to explore and then to change constructs. The REP test is used early in therapy to explore the client's construct system. Robert Neimeyer (1992) describes techniques for laddering constructs to explore their hierarchical organization into superordinate and subordinate constructs (see the Organization Corollary).

Later, when constructs are being revised, therapeutic techniques to tighten constructs include *time binding* and *word binding* (Kelly, 1955, pp. 484, 1074–1076). Elicited constructs can be made less harmful in the present by learning to say, for example, "That happened long ago and does not happen anymore" (an example of time binding) or "That is really exploitation, not love" (an example of word binding). Constructs are developed to be more complex and to have greater hierarchical organization.

Constructivist therapy is not a single method or school but has a variety of methods influenced by Kelly's work and emphasizing that the meanings are constructed (Neimeyer, 1993). Several therapists practice personal construct therapy based on Kelly's foundation (Bannister, 1975; Epting, 1984; Neimeyer & Neimeyer, 1987), and they have developed a variety of techniques (Walker & Winter, 2007). With children, puppets have been used (Dillen et al., 2009). Whatever the specific technique, the aim is to help clients improve their construct system.

One constructivist therapist undoubtedly speaks for many, in reminding us that therapy is not a process with a clear and unambiguous set of directions. He invites trust in the therapeutic process, even in the absence of definitive empirical results and the pervasive uncertainty of our postmodern era in which certainty is not to be found (Neimeyer, 2001).

Fixed-Role Therapy

fixed-role therapy

Kelly's method of therapy, based on role playing

One therapeutic technique suggested by Kelly is **fixed-role therapy**. In this technique, the client experiments with new constructs by role-playing a fictitious personality. For example, Linda Viney (1981) described a case study in which a bright and attractive female client, Susan, age 24, sought counseling for anxiety that focused on her limited social life. Her therapist worked with the client to devise the following fixed role for her, using constructs elicited from her REP test. As Kelly recommended, this fictitious personality was given a different name (Mary Jones), so that Susan could experiment with this role without losing her own identity or committing herself to change before she was ready.

> Mary Jones is a friendly young woman who is open and frank with the people she meets. She enjoys giving to these people and the feelings of companionship she has with them. She sees herself as united with her fellows, as part of the world with them.

Mary is a down-to-earth kind of person, and most of the time she is calm and relaxed. She is able to be patient with the people she knows and is not very critical of them.

Mary is also searching and inquisitive about her world. She can be forceful when the occasion demands it and lively too.

Mary is the kind of person people like to know. (pp. 274–275)

As therapy progressed, the client changed in the direction of this role, as was evident on the REP test and, although more subjectively, in life.

Development of the fixed role is a significant collaborative effort between client and therapist. It generally involves the discovery of new constructs and not merely the realignment of the individual in relation to existing constructs. The client practices the role in therapy. Sometimes the roles are reversed, so the client plays the other person while the therapist plays the role of the client. Besides teaching the client to view the situation from the other's viewpoint, this allows the therapist to model the new role. The new role is enacted in an exploratory way, and the attitude of experimentation facilitates self-directed change after the end of formal therapy.

Constructs in Context: Personal Stories

Roles are only one aspect of the drama of life. Robert Neimeyer (1994) emphasizes the importance of *narratives*, or stories that the client develops in therapy, often with the assistance of the therapist. They take many forms, ranging from personal stories and even poetry presented to the therapist to the self-discoveries that occur in a personal journal. Such narratives describe the context for one's personal constructs. They may function as a personal myth, giving meaning and predictability to life (cf. Howard, 1991; Mair, 1988). Because each person is unique, the meaning of a specific life event, like the death of a loved one, varies from person to person, and must be viewed with the meanings provided by an individual's personal life story (Romanoff, 1999). Narratives, like constructs, change in therapy (Gonçalves, Matos, & Santos, 2009; Hoyt, 1996).

RESEARCH FINDINGS

Kelly's theory has generated a great deal of research in a variety of settings, including therapy, business, vocational choice, and education (Walker & Winter, 2007).

Not surprisingly, the effectiveness of constructivist therapy is greater for patients with less severe symptoms, such as anxiety, than for those with more severe disturbance, such as psychosis; but effectiveness overall may be lower than other forms of therapy (Holland & Neimeyer, 2009). Various clinical populations, including those suffering from schizophrenia and paranoia, have different kinds of disturbed constructs (Lorenzini, Sassaroli, & Rocchi, 1989). Schizophrenics show impaired perceptions of themselves, as well as of others (Gara, Rosenberg, & Mueller, 1989), with greater distortion of constructs about people and psychological phenomena, compared to constructs about objects and the physical world (Bannister & Salmon, 1966; McPherson, Barden, & Buckley, 1970; McPherson & Buckley, 1970). Constructs have been studied in relationship to anxiety (McPherson & Gray, 1976), phobias (Huber & Altmaier, 1983), and eating disorders (Neimeyer & Khouzam, 1985). Physical disorders, too, are related to personal constructs. Hypertensive men have constructs about dependency that prevent them from turning to others for help that might reduce their stress (Talbot, Cooper, & Ellis, 1991).

Kelly's theory is popular in many business fields—for example, with industrial-organizational psychologists, management development specialists, and occupational counselors (Jankowicz, 1987; Stewart & Stewart, 1982). Market researchers use REP grids to understand consumers' preferences (Marsden & Littler, 2000). Many studies have used repertory grids to describe what experienced workers have learned, so that these lessons can be more readily taught to others (Jankowicz, 1987; Jankowicz & Hisrich, 1987; Salmon & Lehrer, 1989). In a complementary way, grid analysis shows how a new school psychologist learns the role of consultant under a mentor's guidance (Salmon & Fenning, 1993). An analysis of repertory grids completed by those who train counselors is useful for defining job requirements. They described good versus bad counseling trainees using the constructs "open–closed," "personable–aloof," "secure–insecure," and "professional skilled–unskilled" (Wheeler, 2000).

Several studies suggest that cognitive complexity is associated with a more appropriate vocational choice (Bodden, 1970; Harren et al., 1979; Neimeyer, 1988). People can evaluate careers on a repertory grid, instead of evaluating people on the REP test, to reveal the constructs they are using in making career decisions (Neimeyer, 1992). In addition, structured exercises based on personal construct theory have been developed to improve the vocational choice process (Forster, 1992). Job performance can also be enhanced by cognitive complexity; salespeople, for example, can be more effective because of a wider repertoire of sales strategies (Porter & Inks, 2000).

Personal construct theory has been extended to other topics as well, including biofeedback therapy (Zolten, 1989) and hypnosis (Burr & Butt, 1989). Researchers have explored the relationship between personal constructs and measures of identity (Berzonsky, 1989; Berzonsky & Neimeyer, 1988; Berzonsky, Rice, & Neimeyer, 1990); sex roles (Baldwin et al., 1986); and values and beliefs (Horley, 1991). In education, repertory grids document the changing concepts of elementary school students as they learn about science (Shapiro, 1991), as well as the concepts that university students learn, both personally relevant understanding and course facts (Fromm, 1993). In summary, Kelly's theory has implications for a variety of applied and theoretical issues.

Summary

- Kelly proposed a theory of personal constructs based on the fundamental postulate of *constructive alternativism*, which says that people can interpret any event in a variety of ways.
- His metaphor for personality was *man-the-scientist.*
- He elaborated on this model in a formal theory, which consists of a *Fundamental Postulate* and 11 corollaries. The *Fundamental Postulate* states that "a person's anticipations of events shape psychological processes such as motivation and emotion."
- The process of construing is described in four corollaries (*Construction Corollary, Experience Corollary, Choice Corollary*, and *Modulation Corollary*). These statements describe how constructs are formed and chosen to apply to a particular situation. People choose a particular way of construing events that offers the best possibility for extending the construct system.
- Four corollaries describe the structure of construct systems: *Dichotomy Corollary, Organization Corollary, Fragmentation Corollary*, and *Range Corollary.*
- *Dichotomous constructs* vary in their centrality and organization within the construct system.
- With development, constructs become expanded into hierarchical arrangements.
- Incompatible constructs may be applied in succession.
- Each construct has only a limited *range of convenience.*
- Finally, the social context of construing is described by the *Individuality Corollary, Commonality Corollary*, and *Sociality Corollary.*
- People have different construct systems, and personalities are judged to be similar if they use similar construct systems.
- Interpersonal relationships depend on at least one of the parties understanding the constructs used by the other.
- Personality change produces a variety of emotions, including anxiety and threat.
- The *C-P-C Cycle* describes the process by which a person selects a construct to apply in a particular instance.
- The *Creativity Cycle* describes the progressive loosening and tightening of constructs that occurs during change, including during therapy.
- Kelly developed a *Role Construct Repertory (REP) Test* to measure personal constructs.
- *Cognitive complexity*, which is considered adaptive, can be measured from the REP Test. It has been used to measure change as a result of therapy and has been modified for applications in industry.
- Kelly used *fixed-role therapy* to produce change through the development and practice of new constructs, and additional therapeutic techniques have also been developed.
- Besides therapy, Kelly's theory has stimulated research in business, group processes, social perception, and other areas.

Thinking about Kelly's Theory

1. The dichotomous nature of constructs emphasizes the importance of the opposite of usual experience. Have you noticed this theme in any other theorists (e.g., Freud's reaction formation or Jung's shadow)?
2. Kelly refers to identity as a core construct. What other theorists have had similar ideas about the importance of identity or a sense of self?
3. What are the implications of Kelly's Commonality Corollary for psychological testing? (In a nomothetic research study, one that compares individuals, what sorts of questions are consistent with the Commonality Corollary?)
4. Do you think that cognitive complexity is a general personality trait or a characteristic that can vary considerably,
   depending on the specific subject matter that a person is thinking about?
5. Based on Kelly's theory and the technique of fixed-role therapy, what do you think would be the effects of acting (as in movies or the theater)? How is such acting different from fixed-role therapy?
6. Have you observed or heard of anyone changing dramatically in ways that could be described by Kelly's concept of slot movement?
7. Propose a researchable hypothesis about cognitive complexity or some other concept from personal construct theory.

Study Questions

1. Explain Kelly's concept of constructive alternativism.
2. What is meant by Kelly's metaphor of man-the-scientist? In what ways are people like scientists? In what ways are they not?
3. Explain the difference between a verbal construct and a preverbal construct. Give examples to illustrate each.
4. What concepts from Kelly are relevant in understanding personality development? Contrast this approach with theories that propose stages of development.
5. Why do we make the choices we do, according to Kelly's Choice Corollary? Give an example to illustrate the idea of the elaborative choice.
6. Explain the difference between a permeable construct and a concrete construct. Give examples of each.
7. What concept from Kelly's theory would be relevant for understanding why a person makes a radical change in personality—for example, a criminal who repents and becomes a born-again Christian? Explain how this concept is relevant to the dichotomous nature of constructs.
8. Describe the hierarchical organization of constructs, from core superordinate constructs to peripheral subordinate constructs. How does this organization relate to identity?
9. What does Kelly's Fragmentation Corollary suggest about the situational stability of behavior?
10. What is the range of convenience of a construct?
11. According to Kelly's Individuality Corollary and Commonality Corollary, what is the main way in which individuals differ from one another? In what way can they be evaluated as similar?
12. How can personal constructs facilitate or prevent a social relationship from occurring?
13. Describe the REP Test. What information does it offer to a therapist to help understand a client?
14. Summarize research on cognitive complexity. Why is this an adaptive characteristic?
15. How does personal construct theory explain the emotions of threat, fear, anxiety, and hostility?
16. Explain the C-P-C Cycle of effective action. In what ways can it be distorted to interfere with effective action?
17. How does personal construct theory explain creativity?
18. How does a therapist learn about a client's constructs?
19. Describe techniques for changing constructs.
20. What is fixed-role therapy?
21. How do clients' stories (narratives) relate to personal constructs?
22. Summarize some research using personal construct theory or its measures outside of the clinical setting.

Chapter Overview

ILLUSTRATIVE BIOGRAPHY
Frida Kahlo

The cognitive social learning perspective, exemplified in this chapter by Walter Mischel, focuses on the cognitions that people have learned in their life experience. These cognitions, which may be quite nuanced in taking aspects of the environment into account, determine life choices and striving (or, for others, giving up). One woman whose life could have taken many directions but whose cognitions propelled her to an original and creative artistic life is Mexican painter Frida Kahlo.

Frida Kahlo was born on July 6, 1907, in an old residential area on the outskirts of Mexico City. Her childhood was a time of war. The Mexican Revolution broke out in 1910 when Frida was only 3 years old, and guerrilla armies led by Pascual Orozco, Pancho Villa, and Emiliano Zapata began an uprising that continued for a decade, finally leading to the inauguration of revolutionary president Alvaro Obregón.

Frida Kahlo

When Frida was 6, she contracted the crippling disease polio, and her right leg remained very weak for the rest of her life. Self-conscious of the deformity, she wore layers of socks and later long skirts to hide it. On the advice of doctors, she remained physically active. When Frida was 18 years old, an accident further damaged her body and changed her life. Riding in a bus home from school in Mexico City, a collision with a streetcar impaled her on a metal bar, fracturing her spine, crushing her pelvis, and breaking one foot. She nearly died. During her forced bed rest, she began to paint to relieve the boredom. For the rest of her life, she endured at least 32 surgeries, pain, and fear of infection. The accident left her unable to carry children to term successfully.

Frida left her small village in 1922 to attend the National Preparatory School in Mexico City, where she was offered an excellent education and the companionship of Mexico's intellectual elite. She was not intimidated, but actively participated, was somewhat of a prankster, and fell passionately in love with an artist commissioned to paint murals in the auditorium. She and Diego Rivera, more than 20 years older than Frida, later married (1929) and became internationally known as an artist couple. Frida painted colorful and symbolic images of herself and her family. Many self-portraits portrayed her physical deformities (crippled leg, injured spine) and contained symbols, including images of herself as a fetus in her mother's body and as a cactus flower being pollinated by the wind. She also painted cultural themes of native and colonial people in Mexico.

Frida's artistic fame was second to that of her husband's, whose career took him to the United States, where he was commissioned to paint murals for Henry Ford and others. And their physical appearance, petite Frida and immense Diego, conveys this discrepancy—except that Frida's behavior was outgoing and often outrageous, enlarging her in a metaphorical sense. She also wore unusual clothes for her circle: traditional Mexican long colorful dresses.

Her one art exhibition in Mexico came in 1953. In ill health, she was brought by ambulance on a stretcher to the gallery. Her typical good humor kept her joking and drinking with the crowd, who loved Frida and her art. Soon her health declined even further. Her right leg was amputated because of infection, and she became depressed. She died at home in bed at age 47, writing in her diary, "I hope the leaving is joyful and I hope never to return."

DEVELOPMENT

Personality develops by learning. We learn behaviors, and we learn what to expect when we behave in particular ways. Mischel also emphasizes that we learn to believe we have competence in particular areas (self-efficacy).

Obviously Frida Kahlo not only learned the technical craft of her painting, but she also learned what themes to paint. For Frida Kahlo, her father was an important teacher. She was his favorite child, and they were bonded not only by temperament but also by physical problems (he was epileptic). Her father was a photographer, and from his pictures she saw images of Mexican indigenous culture, undoubtedly inspiring her own great interest, which influenced her painting and also her choice of clothing. The long skirts also hid her legs, helping avoid embarrassment from her physical deformity. Her interest in self-portraiture likely stems from the many months of bed rest, when she could see little except her own reflection in a mirror that was hung over her bed. Whatever the origins of her nonconformist and extraverted social behavior, perhaps in part from the civil unrest that prevails during a revolution, her lively pranks earned attention, reinforcing her for nonconformity.

DESCRIPTION

Instead of listing traits, Mischel describes the cognitive and emotional constructs of a person, using detailed categories that are further explained in this chapter. These include beliefs about what he or she is capable of doing and expectations about what would be reinforcing.

Despite her physical suffering, Frida did not take on the role of a victim. Quite the contrary; behaviorally, she was assertive to the point of being abrasive. This strength derived in part from a feeling of connection with strong Mexican peasants and a rejection of the European-based influence. The personal construct she had of nurturance is beautifully portrayed in her 1949 painting *The Love Embrace of the Universe, the Earth (Mexico), Diego, Me and Señor Xolotl*. While she is being embraced by the Mexican earth mother, she in turn is embracing her husband, who seems more like an adult child. If a person does not think of herself as a victim, she is not, whatever misfortune has come to her.

Mischel's theory describes behaviors as situationally variable because of the different constructs that people apply in various situations. Frida's affectionate behavior toward close friends and audiences, contrasted with her abrasive incivility toward those she construed as overly ambitious and shallow, illustrates this situational specificity.

Another important aspect of Frida's life is her love relationship with Diego Rivera, her husband, through numerous sexual affairs by both and enduring despite a divorce and second marriage of the two. They seemed an unlikely pair, in part because of their physical differences in size (he was referred to as "The Elephant," in contrast to Frida as "The Dove"). Mischel refers to unique combinations of the cognitive affective components of two people that can produce a distinct "personality" of a long-term interpersonal relationship (2004, p. 16), like an interpersonal chemistry that bonds the two together. These two artists had such a chemistry, in part because of shared values (for art, for politics) and in part because her admiration of his artistic eminence and tolerance of his behavioral eccentricities, combined with her own talent, triggered a fascination in Diego.

COGNITION

As mentioned earlier, cognition is the central focus in this theory. A person's *competencies* describe what he or she is able to do. Mischel uses the term *self-efficacy* to refer to a person's confidence in being able to do something, asserting that without self-efficacy in a particular domain of behavior, performance will be limited. Knowing that one can do a behavior does not, in itself, ensure the behavior will occur. It also must be expected to lead to some desired outcome.

Frida Kahlo's competencies include her artistic ability, learned undoubtedly from observing her father's photographs and practiced in her long period of forced bed rest as she recovered from the streetcar accident that nearly took her life. The persistence of Frida's artistic effort attests to her sense of self-efficacy for painting. Experience taught Frida to expect approval from those in her artistic circle and from those who admired it without themselves being artists, and it was especially the opinion of the artistic elite whose opinion she valued. Without the approval of these, including her husband, Diego Rivera, her art might have languished.

Because there is such a gap between the tastes of the vanguard of artists and that of most of the population, it is no surprise that artists like Frida and Diego were particularly drawn to a bohemian circle of friends. Was it, perhaps, uncertainty about the less predictable reactions of those who did not really understand art but simply consumed it, as part of their lifestyle, that led Frida to be verbally aggressive toward them? That, at least, would lead to predictable outcomes of attention and awe.

ADJUSTMENT

Through elaborate learning, people develop self-regulatory systems and plans that permit them to pursue goals effectively. These enable delaying immediate gratification in the pursuit of long-term goals.

Given the severe physical limitations and pain resulting from her traumatic accident and preceding childhood disease, how could Frida Kahlo possibly sustain her pursuit of a career? As Walter Mischel (2004) puts it, "What are the … mechanisms and strategies that enable the individual to self-regulate and engage in proactive sustained goal pursuit?" (p. 13). His theory describes these mechanisms in detail, and they focus particularly on a person's cognitions.

(continued)

(continued)

The self-regulatory system that organized Frida Kahlo's striving was uniquely hers (as a cognitive social learning perspective would predict): her unique goals and values, her expectancies, her perceptions of situations. Her sexual promiscuity reflected her own values and those of her bohemian friends. Her artistic goals and self-judgments were obviously unique, as even casual examination of her paintings reveals. For despite similarities to surrealistic painters, she was obviously not trying to imitate someone else's style but rather exploring vividly colorful and symbolically haunting images of ancestors and political celebrities, deformed bodies and fetuses, and herself in many poses and costumes. (Cognitive social learning theorists do not engage in symbolic interpretation of artistic images, unlike psychoanalysts, but some of these are obvious, such as the portrayal of her damaged spine with the architectural image described in the title of her 1944 painting, *The Broken Column*.) Rather than perceiving her damaged body in only negative terms, she perceived it as inspiration for painting, and so did not languish in despair but made a good adjustment.

CULTURE

It is through behaving in a social and cultural context that a person develops and uses the cognitive constructs that are so important in Mischel's theory. Some of these are specific to an individual. Other cognitions are shared with members of a cultural community.

Throughout her life, Frida Kahlo's personality is intertwined with her cultural experience in Mexico. She adopted the dress of the indigenous peoples and incorporated much from their worldview, such as the connection to the earth, into her art. A child during the time of the Mexican revolution, she witnessed models of revolutionary rejection of established authority that neglected the interests of the people. Powerful established authority did not have legitimacy in these childhood lessons, and her communist and socialist sympathies later echoed this message of rebellion and the moral authority of the people at large, not the elite at the top. Participation in this circle must have provided predictable social rewards and a sense of fellowship, not to mention lovers.

Shared cultural views can bring together odd combinations of people: Frida and her husband Diego were politically active, supporting communism and liberal causes. As successful artists, they were invited to social functions by well-to-do society people,

where she acted outrageously, used obscene language, spoke disrespectfully of religion in the home of Catholics, and praised communism in the home of capitalist Henry Ford's sister (Herrera, 1983, p. 135). Frida did not share the cultural values she saw in the United States, especially the rampant ambitiousness which was even present in the art community. She did not think of her painting from the perspective of a business, even when she became financially successful. She seemed content to have her husband Diego be the publicly more esteemed artist, although it is not clear how much of this was a gender role restriction and how much a simple expression of her personal values. She tolerated his many sexual infidelities (and responded with her own, with both men—including Trotsky—and women). Without the cultural setting, neither the couple nor Frida would have had the same personality.

BIOLOGY

Mischel conceptualizes his social learning constructs as building on a biological basis, but the biological underpinning is not made explicit (unlike the biological approaches in Chapter 9). Although Mischel's theory does not focus on biological aspects of personality, he envisions a comprehensive, holistic approach to the individual as a goal of the field of personality, and notes that such an approach will include biological processes, including brain mechanisms (Mischel, 2004).

Thus we cannot say much about the biological basis of Frida's personality from this perspective, other than to say that her temperament (which seems to have been active and emotionally arousable) was channeled through her cognitions described above. And it is likely that Frida's efficacy expectations helped her endure physical pain and infections better than she could have done if she had adopted a victim mentality instead.

FINAL THOUGHTS

This theory makes a general point that is easy to grasp: Our beliefs are powerful determinants of our behavior. The elaborate details that follow are more at home in research journals than in life narratives. However, without knowing what a person, in this case Frida Kahlo, believes about herself, expects as a result of her behavior, and values, we cannot truly grasp her personality.

PREVIEW: OVERVIEW OF MISCHEL'S THEORY

Walter Mischel analyzes personality from a cognitive learning approach, focusing particularly on cognitive variables because the human capacity to think is central to personality. He substitutes cognitive affective units for global traits, and explicitly considers the role of the situation in predicting behavior, without assuming that situations affect everyone in the same way.

Mischel's theory has implications for major theoretical questions, as presented in Table 12.1. His views have stimulated considerable debate among personality psychologists, and he provides a personality model that has generated much collaborative research. Unlike some of the more historical theories, Mischel's model is being used to generate many hypotheses and to organize research in studies of diverse populations, ranging from young children to old people, and across various ethnic groups. The theory is comprehensive in covering various life stages and both normal and problematic behavior, although the relationship to biological variables

Table 12.1 Preview of Mischel's Theory

Individual Differences	Individuals differ in behaviors and in cognitive processes because of learning. The most important units of personality are cognitive affective units (CAUs).
Adaptation and Adjustment	Effective functioning requires that an individual be able to discriminate among situations, to know which behavior will be adaptive in each situation. In addition, a core adaptive skill learned early in life is the ability to delay gratification.
Cognitive Processes	Cognitive processes, that is, cognitive affective units (CAUs), which include competencies, expectancies, subjective stimulus values, and self-regulatory systems and plans, are central to personality.
Culture	Culture influences the formation and activation of cognitive affective units and thus affects people's beliefs and behaviors.
Biological Influences	Although the theory does not expand on biological phenomena, Mischel envisions a comprehensive view in which the cognitive aspects of personality build on a biological foundation.
Development	Learning occurs throughout life, as people encounter various situations. An important early ego development is the ability to delay gratification.

is not specified. The applied value of the perspective includes its suggestions for enhancing children's ego development (ability to delay gratification) and outlining a framework within which to understand interpersonal relationships and cultural issues.

Behaviorism emphasizes the importance of situations as determinants of behavior. This poses a challenge to traditional psychoanalytic and trait approaches, and Walter Mischel took on the challenge of recognizing the importance of situations without ignoring personality traits or dynamics. It was not an easy task, and his earlier work was often misunderstood as dispensing with personality. A heated theoretical controversy about the relative importance of personality traits and situations in predicting behavior stimulated personality researchers to ask how personality and situations both contribute to behavior, and Mischel's theoretical model provides guidance in this direction.

Biography of Walter Mischel

Walter Mischel was born in 1930 in Vienna, Austria. His Jewish family (he, his parents, and an older brother) fled Europe to avoid the Nazi persecutions in 1938 (the same year that Freud also left Vienna), thereby avoiding the fate of many of his friends and their families who were killed in the gas chambers (Mischel, 2007). Like many Europeans, they immigrated to New York City, working hard in a family store, where young Walter also worked (in addition to other jobs). In his autobiography, Mischel (2007) describes a love of the city that again drew him back many years later, and a passion for reading and painting.

Walter Mischel

Mischel attended college at New York University and did graduate work at the City College of New York, where he studied clinical psychology and completed a master's thesis linking psychology with his interest in art. While in the master's program, he worked as a social worker, focusing on juvenile delinquents. Mischel continued graduate work at Ohio State University (1950–1953) for the PhD, and this experience had an effect on his developing cognitive emphasis. In particular, he was influenced by the work of his mentors, George Kelly and Julian Rotter (Mischel, 1984b, 2007). From Kelly (see Chapter 11) he adopted the concept of personal constructs, and from Rotter's social learning perspective, he took expectancies and values.

Mischel's clinical and research experiences ranged from outpatient therapy, to a large state hospital (of which he was very critical), to observations of Orisha spirit possession ceremonies in Trinidad, where he and his wife spent several summers (Mischel, 2007). He reports (2007) observing two cultural groups in Trinidad, the Africans and the East Indians, who criticized one another over different values for future orientation (the East Indians) or enjoying the present (the Africans). This stimulated his interest in a research program on delay of gratification, which he began there and later continued with American children.

Mischel's teaching career began with brief faculty positions in Colorado (1956–1958) and at Harvard University (1958–1962), where Gordon Allport was one of his esteemed colleagues, and where he met his second wife. It was at Harvard that Mischel formally stated his criticism of personality assessment and its poor predictive value, based on a review of the existing literature and on his personality assessment research for the Peace Corps. Mischel then moved to Stanford University, where he taught and conducted research from 1962 to 1982, interacting with many esteemed colleagues, including Albert Bandura (see Chapter 13). Despite his clinical training, his career moved away from clinical populations and increasingly emphasized research. At the Stanford nursery school, Mischel conducted his "marshmallow test" research on delay of gratification, which has since become famous in reenactments on YouTube. This research demonstrated the early development of ego capacities by thinking, a major theme in his model of personality.

At Stanford he published his controversial criticisms of extant personality assumptions, challenging the idea of global traits that had broad effects on behavior despite changing situations. The research simply did not support this premise. This triggered a trait-versus-situation controversy in the professional literature that he characterizes as a false dichotomy. As he puts it, "The 1968 monograph traumatized the field of personality, because after a massive critical literature review I proposed that for a half century, researchers had been looking for personality in the wrong places, guided by untenable assumptions, and therefore could not find the expected results" (2007, p. 249). At the time, his ideas were not well received and threatened the established field of personality (though social psychologists welcomed his emphasis on the importance of situations). Over the ensuing decades, and as his theoretical formulations matured, the sensibility of his analysis has become more widely appreciated.

After 20 years in California while at Stanford University, Mischel returned to New York, first for a tentative year at New York University in 1980, and then he moved permanently in 1983 to Columbia University. There he continued collaborative research with many students and colleagues, enjoyed a family life with three daughters and six grandchildren, and relished the culture of Manhattan (Mischel, 2007).

DELAY OF GRATIFICATION

Although his clinical training taught Mischel about ego development, it was not until he investigated the actual thoughts of people facing conflict over temptation that he clearly understood how some people resist impulses and others do not. Modern culture offers instant gratification of many needs and tempts consumers with a barrage of advertisements for immediate happiness (Goldman, 1996). Our own impulses, too, beg for immediate gratification. In the face of these temptations, **delay of gratification**, the ability to defer present gratification for larger future goals, is an important adaptational skill that develops in childhood. Mischel and his colleagues explored this self-regulatory system in several studies (e.g., Mischel, 1966, 1974). They gave young children the choice of receiving a small reward (e.g., one marshmallow) immediately or a larger reward (two marshmallows) later. Some children were tested with pretzels instead of marshmallows. By manipulating aspects of the situation and by talking to those who could delay and comparing what they said with those who took the immediate but smaller reward, Mischel and his colleagues learned what facilitates delay of gratification and what prevents it. They were also able to teach the impulsive children better strategies for waiting.

Delay is more difficult if the rewards are visible (Mischel & Ebbesen, 1970) and if the child is thinking about how wonderful the marshmallow will taste (Mischel & Baker, 1975). If the marshmallows are out of sight (Mischel & Ebbesen, 1970) and if the child is thinking about something else (Mischel, Ebbesen, & Zeiss, 1972), delay of gratification is easier. Paying attention to pictures of the rewards (that is, symbolically presented rewards) instead of the actual rewards increases delay of gratification

delay of gratification

the ability to give up immediate gratifications for larger, more distant rewards

(Mischel & Moore, 1973). By age 5, children develop effective strategies that enable them to wait for rewards: covering the rewards (marshmallows) and thinking about something else (Mischel & Mischel, 1983). Children can be taught to think about other things, which improves their ability to delay gratification (Mischel, Ebbesen, & Zeiss, 1972). Adolescents who have difficulty controlling aggression can be taught to use imagery as a technique for increasing self-control (Lennings, 1996). The ability to delay gratification can also be improved by exposure to models who delay their own gratification (Bandura & Mischel, 1965; Mischel & Liebert, 1966).

Research on delay of gratification adds wisdom beyond that known intuitively by parents. When mothers of preschool children were asked to predict which techniques would be most effective, they underestimated the value of distraction in producing delay of gratification. They predicted that tasting a desired marshmallow would help children wait longer for it—when in fact that technique had the opposite effect (Hom & Knight, 1996). Fortunately, children can be taught to delay gratification. When mothers are more authoritative, providing direction, their children develop more ability to delay gratification, compared to those whose mothers are more permissive (Mauro & Harris, 2000). Children diagnosed with attention-deficit/hyperactivity disorder are prime candidates because of their impulsive behavior. An intervention with three children, ages 3 to 5, was successful in teaching them to forgo immediate rewards (such as a chocolate chip cookie) in favor of delayed but larger rewards (Binder, Dixon, & Ghezzi, 2000).

The delay of gratification research seems to be tapping a core ego strength (as it would be called in psychoanalytic language). When children learn to delay gratification, they are mastering a skill with important consequences for their future. Preschool children who waited longer for marshmallows or pretzels were rated higher by parents on cognitive and social competence years later when they were juniors and seniors in high school (Mischel, 1983b, 1984a; Mischel, Shoda, & Peake, 1988; Mischel, Shoda, & Rodriguez, 1989) (see Table 12.2). Preschoolers who delayed gratification longer had higher SAT verbal and math scores in high school. They were described by their parents as better able to concentrate and to cope with frustration and stress (Shoda, Mischel, & Peake, 1990). In contrast, children who are impulsive, who have temper tantrums more often than other children in late childhood (age 8 to 10), have poorer life outcomes later, with more frequent divorce and less successful occupational lives than their better controlled peers (Caspi, Elder, & Bem, 1987). Even among adults, some continue to choose small immediate reinforcers (such as briefly playing a video game) in favor of larger, delayed reinforcers (having a longer play time) (Navarick, 1998).

Longitudinal studies find that young children's ability to control their impulses, called *ego control*, is stable over time (Block, 1993). A related construct, *ego resiliency*, is the ability to modify one's behavior according to the demands of the situation (Block & Block, 1980). This ability helps people learn from experience, further developing their personality in healthy directions. For example, ego resiliency measured at age 7 predicts which children will have more advanced understanding of friendship and higher moral judgment 8 years later (Hart et al., 1998).

Table 12.2 Examples of High School Behavior Ratings Predicted from Preschool Delay of Gratification

Is attentive and able to concentrate.

Is verbally fluent, can express ideas well.

Uses and responds to reason.

Tends to go to pieces under stress, becomes rattled. (disagree)

Reverts to more immature behavior under stress. (disagree)

Source: From W. Mischel (1984a). Convergences and challenges in the search for consistency. *American Psychologist, 39*, 351–364. Copyright 1984 by the American Psychological Association. Adapted by permission.

Personality is adaptational, and the personality characteristics proposed by Mischel prepare an individual to cope with situations. Mischel's research inspires intervention programs for children who do not develop normal abilities to delay gratification, such as those who are aggressive or hyperactive (Mischel, Shoda, & Rodriguez, 1989; Rodriguez, Mischel, & Shoda, 1989). Inhibition of behaviors, although a valuable ego skill, sometimes comes at a price, resulting in emotional distress and even ill health (Polivy, 1998). Such costs underscore the importance of learning more about both healthy and inadequate development of people's capacity to seek gratifications in the long term as well as the short term.

The conflict over delay of gratification within the individual has been theorized as essentially a battle for cognition over emotion, with a hot "go" emotional system that urges the person to go for the immediate pleasure and a cool "know" cognitive system that inspires restraint (Metcalfe & Mischel, 1999). A tempting stimulus activates the "go" emotional system, so delay of gratification constitutes overcoming stimulus control. Adults can focus their attention on something other than the "hot" emotions in order to increase self-control. In an experimental study, for example, after imagining rejection, those who were assigned to focus their attention on the physical environment had fewer hostile thoughts and feelings than those who focused on their physical and emotional reactions (Ayduk, Mischel, & Downey, 2002).

Young children, because of their immaturity, have not yet developed the "cool" system sufficiently to be able to delay gratification. Metcalfe and Mischel speculate that this may be because the hippocampus and frontal lobes of the brain are not yet developed enough to take over this function, leaving the "hot" amygdala less controlled; but they do not commit to particular neural structures in their model. They also suggest that at very high levels of stress, the "cool" function becomes less effective, leaving more impulsive behavior. This model is exciting, not only because of the possibility of integrating with neuroscience, but also because it treats delay of gratification as a process and not simply a developmental level. That is, in addition to the many studies of individual differences in delay of gratification that have been reported, the model helps us understand why the same person will sometimes be able to delay gratification and other times (e.g., under high stress), will not.

PERSONALITY TRAITS: MISCHEL'S CHALLENGE

Mischel's best-known but often-misunderstood assertion about personality is reflected in a question on a licensing exam for psychologists that asked which theorist did not believe in personality. The answer (according to the test key): Mischel (Mischel, 2004). Like many exam questions and answers, this one was oversimplified, and only correct if the definition of personality is restricted to "broad traits described with situation-free adjectives" (Mischel, 2007, p. 260). Nonetheless, it does highlight an important difference between Mischel's approach as it evolved over the coming decades, and the traditional assumptions of trait theories.

Traditional personality theories, including trait and psychodynamic approaches, assumed that individual differences consist of global traits or dispositions affecting a wide array of behaviors, making people behave consistently across a variety of situations (Mischel, 1973). However, the research that he reviewed in his 1968 book *Personality and Assessment* did not support this assumption of cross-situational consistency. Mischel (1968) startled the field by questioning this fundamental assumption, contributing to a paradigm crisis in personality theory (Epstein & O'Brien, 1985; Mischel, 1973, p. 254). He stated, "With the possible exception of intelligence, highly generalized behavioral consistencies have not been demonstrated, and the concept of personality traits as broad predispositions is thus untenable" (1968, p. 140). The average relationship between self-report personality measures and behavior was only $r = 0.30$, which Mischel termed the **personality coefficient**. It is low, accounting for less than 10 percent of the variability in behavior.

The issue is often referred to as a ***trait-versus-situation debate***, pitting the concept of traits that should (it was argued) produce consistency across a variety of situations, against a situational argument that says behavior should vary with situations. Like the

personality coefficient

the average relationship between self-report personality measures and behavior, estimated by Mischel at $r = 0.30$

trait-versus-situation debate

the controversy over which explains more of the variation in behavior: traits or situations (i.e., personality or the environment) nature-versus-nurture debate, it turns out that the two sides only seem to be in conflict when the issues are oversimplified. The truth is a complex interaction between the two.

In a much-cited study, Walter Mischel and Philip Peake (1982) examined the trait-versus-situation issue directly by analyzing the consistency of college students on two characteristics, conscientiousness and friendliness. The trait model (as then understood) would predict that each student would behave consistently across situations, so that the most friendly students in one situation would also be the most friendly in other situations, and similarly for conscientiousness. However, the results indicated there was virtually no tendency for consistency between situations ($r = 0.13$). Critics objected that this result could be related to methodological faults, but Mischel believed that the lack of consistent behavior across situations was a real phenomenon and required revision of the theory of traits.

The Consistency Paradox

This discrepancy between the intuition that people are consistent, on the one hand, and empirical findings that they are not, on the other hand, poses a **consistency paradox**. People who are honest in the classroom may cheat on taxes; children who wait patiently in the presence of a parent may act impulsively when the situation changes. That is, behavior is not determined by general personality traits, but is situation specific. Even the religious beliefs and worldviews of elderly people, studied in longitudinal research, vary considerably from one testing to another (Kim, Nesselroade, & Featherman, 1996).

A learning approach does not predict that behavior will be consistent across situations. Behavior depends on the consequences (rewards and punishments) it produces. If the same behavior in different situations produces different consequences (e.g., talking in a restaurant or talking in a library), adaptive responses will vary from situation to situation. Consistency is expected in a behavioral model only when the same behavior is reinforced in a variety of situations or if a person is unable to discriminate among situations. For example, a child who is rewarded at play by friends, at school by teachers, and at home by parents for speaking will learn to speak in a great variety of situations. A child who cannot tell when speaking will result in punishment and when it will not may learn to be quiet all the time. When consistency is found, learning theory explains it as a consequence of a particular learning history, without resorting to a concept of traits, like extraversion or introversion.

That does not mean, though, that we must discard the concept of traits, provided we are aware of its limitations. Mischel pointed out that laypeople have always made trait attributions. Traits constitute summaries of multiple behavioral observations and may have some descriptive usefulness for salient characteristics, even though they exaggerate consistency and make inferences about unobserved behavior (Carlson & Mulaik, 1993; Hayden & Mischel, 1976; Mischel, 1973). For Mischel, traits are not causes but merely summary labels. They describe, but do not explain, personality.

The Situational Context of Behavior

Perhaps it will not surprise those who view the field from a distance that the consistency question has not bothered the average person as much as it distresses personality theorists. When people are given personality information in laboratory tasks, they can often reconcile inconsistent information readily. Told that a particular individual is both "generous" and "thrifty," observers do not find these traits inconsistent but reason that the individual is generous in situations that call for that, and thrifty when other circumstances make thrift sensible (Hampson, 1998).

Mischel's challenge to an overgeneralized conceptualization of traits was not intended to displace traits entirely from personality theory. Rather, he advocated replacing overgeneralized trait concepts with more refined analyses and to understand when people behave consistently and when they discriminate among situations (Mischel, 1983a, 1984b; Mischel & Peake, 1983; Peake & Mischel, 1984).

consistency paradox
the mismatch between intuition, which says that people are consistent, and research findings, which say they are not

Consider the following research that Mischel and colleagues conducted with college students. You are asked to vividly imagine yourself having gotten a poor grade on an important paper. Next, you fill in the blanks on a questionnaire, with items like: "I am ____ when ____" This procedure, the researchers assume, will put you in the frame of mind of imagining that your characteristics vary from one situation to another. Compared to other subjects, who go through the same imaginary exercise but have fill-in-the-blank questions that do not refer to situations ("I am ____."), you will be less extreme in thinking that one failure means you are overall a failure; the imaginary exercise will have a less-devastating effect on your self-concept. That is what Mischel and his colleagues predicted, and found (Mendoza-Denton et al., 2001). Keeping the situational context in mind helps prevent people from making overgeneralized conclusions.

Knowing that traits are oversimplified explanations unless they take situations into account, Mischel and his colleagues have developed sophisticated models of how traits affect behavior in situations (e.g., Mischel & Shoda, 1995; Wright & Mischel, 1987). For example, even aggressive people do not hit and yell all the time, and helpful people may act no different from others unless they see someone in need. The relationship between traits and behavior takes situations into account (see Figure 12.1). A given trait, such as aggressiveness, influences behavior only under certain conditions. For example, the trait of aggressiveness will influence behavior (hitting, yelling, etc.) only under certain conditions: when a person feels angry or frustrated and when people threaten or criticize.

This situational context for behavior makes a great deal of sense, if we think of traits as learned ways of adapting to situations. Situations activate thoughts and emotions that were developed as a result of prior experience with that situation (Mischel, 1973; Mischel & Shoda, 1995). Moods, fantasies, plans, goals, and other internal reactions are triggered by specific situations. The psychological situation that a person is in is therefore not simply the objective situation but the subjective amalgam of that, plus internal reactions to it. In fact, by ruminating about situations, people activate these dynamics themselves. In so doing, one individual may be particularly sensitive to rejection, responding to the slightest hint of abandonment with an exaggerated, even aggressive, response. Another may exaggerate the romantic possibilities of encounters (Mischel & Shoda, 1995).

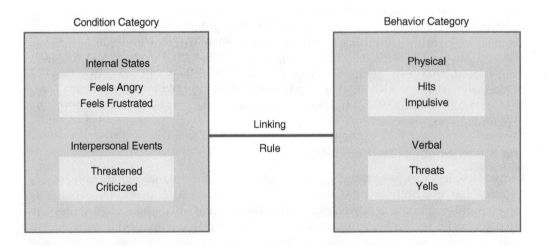

Behavior results from a set of conditions, rather than from a trait alone. Only under certain conditions does a trait of "aggressiveness" influence behavior.

FIGURE 12.1 Illustration of a Dispositional Construct (Aggressive) as an If-Then Linkage between a Category of Conditions and a Category of Behaviors

Source: From J. C. Wright & W. Mischel (1987). A conditional approach to dispositional constructs: The local predictability of social behavior. *Journal of Personality and Social Psychology, 53,* 1159–1177. Copyright 1987 by the American Psychological Association. Reprinted by permission.

The Wediko Camp Study

It is one thing to theorize person by situation interactions, and another thing to measure and analyze such phenomena to the satisfaction of research standards. Doing so requires an enormous amount of data. That opportunity was possible when Mischel returned to the East Coast and was able to study campers in New Hampshire over a 6-week period, at a summer residential camp for children with behavior problems (Mischel, 2007). Extensive observations recorded each child's behavior and also the situations in which they occurred, as they changed hour by hour over the 6-week camp session. Videotapes supplemented observer ratings. Extensive data like these are required to allow the detailed analysis of combinations of individual behavior with varying situations.

These data were analyzed idiographically, in the behavioral tradition, to show the behavior of each individual child separately for various kinds of situations. As Mischel expected based on prior evidence that people are not very consistent from one situation to another, the children who were aggressive in one situation (e.g., when teased by another child) were not necessarily the same children as those who responded aggressively in other situations (e.g., when warned by adults). So a general trait of aggressiveness, across situations, did not accurately describe the data.

Nonetheless, consistent individual differences emerged. One child, for example, was verbally aggressive when punished by an adult, across reoccurrences of similar situations. Another child was verbally aggressive when warned by an adult but less so when actually punished. A third child was verbally aggressive when approached by another child, time after time. Thus there are consistent individual differences in situation–behavior relationships. Furthermore, these consistent patterns were independent of the average level of the behavior (verbal aggression) across all situations, strengthening Mischel's contention that it is situation–behavior relationships, rather than overall behavior, that defines traits (Mischel, 2004; Shoda, Mischel, & Wright, 1994).

Learned Patterns of Situation–Behavior Relationships

While traits in the earlier tradition that Mischel displaced may have value as descriptions of the underlying and largely inherited predispositions of personality, they do not inform us about the way an individual will behave in a particular situation. That behavior is learned by experience, and so varies among people who may share underlying trait predispositions.

One intriguing finding comes from an unlikely source: a genetic study of temperament in twin toddlers. Although twin studies generally are cited to show the genetic contributions to personality similarity, sometimes even in person by situation interactions (Borkenau et al., 2006), in this case there was a difference between the twins that suggests consistent patterns that are not (in these twins) genetic. Experience can produce differences, even between twins. The children were observed in standard laboratory situations to see how they responded to toys, to adults, and so on. Emotional reactions, activity, and other behaviors were observed—not simply for overall traits of temperament but to find situation-specific reactions. For example, sometimes during the cognitive tests one twin became more sociable toward the experimenter, and the other became less sociable but more fussy. These individual differences were consistent with parents' reports of how the twins responded at home. Statistical analyses suggest that reactions to specific situations are influenced by both genetics and experience (Phillips & Matheny, 1997). In this case, each twin had apparently learned a different response to situations. Consistency is found, as Mischel emphasizes, at the granular situation by person combination.

The situational approach is consistent with people's everyday descriptions of behavior. When individuals describe other people's behavior, they hedge their statements with pronouncements about the conditions under which traits will be manifested (Wright & Mischel, 1988). For example, they may say, "Johnny will hit back [aggressive behavior] when he is teased [conditional modifier, or hedge]." Conditional statements about the expression of dispositionally relevant behaviors take the form

"Person does *x* when *y*." When people describe behavior, they do not use trait terms (e.g., aggressive) in a global, overly simplified manner that ignores the situation.

What happens when people are presented with information about behavior that occurs in situations in which it is unlikely to occur naturally? Data from such a study strengthen Mischel's argument that situations are always relevant to trait judgments. Accurate situational descriptions of children's behavior (e.g., "child hits when provoked") were perceived meaningfully. However, descriptions that distorted the situational context of behavior in unnatural ways (e.g., "child hits when praised") yielded descriptions of children as odd, withdrawn, or psychotic (Shoda, Mischel, & Wright, 1989). Judges labeled the children as aggressive or as odd depending on the situations that provoked the hitting. People have distinctive patterns of situation–behavior relationships.

In fact, the ability to discriminate among situations is characteristic of people who are well adapted (Mischel, 1968, 1973, 1984a). The assumption of global personality traits was an oversimplified theory that did not even include the wisdom of everyday people, who implicitly know that situations matter.

People are best described by a distribution of trait-related behavior across a variety of situations, and not by simply their typical behavior. Consider conscientiousness behavior, for example: An individual may be very conscientious sometimes (carefully proofreading a term paper), moderately conscientious at other times, and not at all careful at others (e.g., neglecting to return borrowed items). Conscientiousness varies from one situational context to another, but is consistent when situations are similar to one another. Our hypothetical student carefully proofreads all papers.

We may expand our notion of traits to include some of the old view and some of the new. The overall level of a trait, such as aggressiveness, is one aspect, which can be called the elevation or Type 1 component. The pattern or shape of aggressiveness (or another trait) across situations, for that individual, is the second aspect (Fleeson, 2001; Mischel, 2004).

The Consistency Question as a Continuing Theoretical Challenge

Mischel's posing of the consistency paradox opened a Pandora's box of theoretical ambiguities for personality. Where, indeed, should we expect consistency (Fleeson & Noftle, 2008)? One strategy would be to theorize a multilevel theory in which biological factors, such as those described by Eysenck and others, are the consistent foundation of individual differences for an individual, but this foundation is influenced by experience and situations to manifest behaviors that in some cases are situationally consistent, and in other cases not; that in some cases are consistent across time, and in other cases more changeable.

THE CAPS MODEL

CAPS model

the Cognitive Affective Personality System model that Mischel offers as an alternative to an overly generalized trait model of personality

cognitive person variables

cognitive factors within a person, less global than traits, which influence how an individual adapts to the environment

cognitive affective unit (CAU)

cognitive factors within a person, comprising cognitive and emotional aspects, that influence how a person adapts to the environment; (later terminology than cognitive person variables, in Mischel's theory)

Mischel's overall framework for describing the reconceptualization of personality is called the **CAPS model**, which stands for Cognitive Affective Personality System (Mischel & Shoda, 1995, 1998). In this model, instead of global traits, Walter Mischel and his colleague Yuichi Shoda describe a person's consistent cognitive and emotional patterns. These determine the individual's way of adjusting or responding to situations. Instead of trying to list all possible cognitive and emotional patterns, the model represents a general framework or metatheory (Mischel, 2007), to be expanded for a variety of applications.

Instead of global traits, Mischel (1973) proposes that personality psychologists consider several psychological processes within a person that determine how a particular situation will influence a person's behavior. As he distinguished his approach from trait theory, Mischel used the term **cognitive person variables** to distinguish his approach from trait theory. Later, the more inclusive term **cognitive affective unit (CAU)** was adopted. These aspects of personality enable adaptation to the environment, in the unique style of an individual. They come in various kinds.

Encoding Strategies and Personal Constructs

Trait terms, which people use to describe themselves and other people, are called **personal constructs**. They are personal both in the sense that they describe individuals and in the sense that they vary from one person to another. Personal constructs that people use to describe themselves may be termed a *self-system*. They are unique to each person.

personal constructs

trait terms that people use to describe themselves and other people

Besides personal constructs, people also have other kinds of **encoding strategies**, including concepts for describing situations and events. Because of their different learning histories, the meaning of situations varies from person to person. Behavior is influenced by environmental stimuli, but it is a person's unique interpretation of these stimuli, rather than objective aspects, that matters. Mischel (1968) suggests, "Assessing the acquired meaning of stimuli is the core of social behavior assessment" (p. 190). For this purpose, it is necessary to rely on subjects' reports because only they have access to their cognitions (Mischel, 1973).

encoding strategies

person variables concerned with how a person construes reality

Personal constructs are different from the traits of personality theories. Rather than judging personality consistency based on similar behavior across many situations (as a researcher might), the average person looks for consistency across time in a small number of behaviors that are seen as particularly characteristic (prototypical) of a given trait (Mischel, 1984b). In formal logic and in the simplified environment of a Skinner box, events either do or do not belong to a particular category. Logical reasoning demands that we are able to say that something either is A or not A, and it seems the two choices cover all options. In a Skinner box, a discriminative stimulus may consist of a signal light, which is either on or off. But what if the light is flickering? What if the thing we are judging as A or not A is an ostrich, and A is the category bird? Suddenly, things are not so easy, and we turn from logical categories to prototypes, which permit us to convey that some birds (robins and canaries) are more birdlike than others (ostriches and turkeys). A **prototype** is a typical example of a category.

prototype

a typical example of an object or type of person; a "fuzzy concept" typical of the categories people use in perceiving others

We also have "personality prototypes—abstract representations of particular personality types" (Cantor & Mischel, 1979b, p. 188)—such as introverts and extraverts. We judge whether a particular individual is an introvert or an extravert based on similarity to the prototype. Some people are difficult to classify, just as the ostrich is difficult to categorize as a bird or not a bird (Cantor & Mischel, 1979a). Prototypes include social stereotypes, such as redneck, and do-gooder, although researchers generally use more value-neutral labels, such as comedian type or pet-owner type (Andersen & Klatzky, 1987). We also have prototypes of various kinds of love: romantic love, maternal love, self-love, and so on (Aron & Westbay, 1996; Fehr & Russell, 1991).

Prototypes range from very broad categories (e.g., extravert) to narrow ones (e.g., door-to-door salesperson). Broader categories are distinctive, with little overlap among categories, and they correspond to broad personality types (cf. Chapter 1). Narrower categories are more vivid and concrete, conjuring up clearer visual images and trait descriptions (Cantor & Mischel, 1979a). It is more difficult to recall information about people who do not consistently fit a prototype (Cantor & Mischel, 1979b).

Competencies

What can a person do? What can a person think? These are the person's cognitive and behavioral construction **competencies**. These competencies "to construct (generate) diverse behaviors under appropriate conditions" (Mischel, 1973, p. 265) vary widely from person to person, "as becomes obvious from even casual comparison of the different competencies, for example, of a professional weight lifter, a distinguished chemist, a retardate, an opera star, or a convicted forger" (Mischel, 1977, p. 342). Leaders of neighborhood block organizations have higher construction competencies for skills relevant to leadership, including talking in front of a group and being able to get others to follow one's ideas (Florin, Mednick, & Wandersman, 1986).

competencies

person variables concerned with what a person is able to do

Table 12.3 Examples of Cognitive and Behavioral Construction Competencies
Sexual gender identity
Knowing the structure of the physical world
Social rules and conventions
Personal constructs about self and others
Rehearsal strategies for learning

Source: Adapted from Mischel (1973), p. 266.

Construction competencies include many learned behaviors and concepts (see Table 12.3). They refer to what a person knows or is able to do (not what the person actually does). Therefore, assessing competencies requires providing incentives for the performance of the behavior. Competencies have better stability across time and situations than do many of the personality traits that Mischel (1973, p. 267) criticizes because they are free of the variable factors that determine whether a person will do what he or she can do. Such factors include various expectancies about the situation.

Expectancies

expectancies

subjective beliefs about what will happen in a particular situation (including behavior outcomes, stimulus outcomes, and self-efficacies)

Whether people will behave in a particular way depends not only on whether they know how (their competencies) but also on their **expectancies**. Mischel said that internal subjective expectancies determine performance. Several kinds of expectancies can be distinguished: behavior-outcome expectancies, stimulus-outcome expectancies, and self-efficacy expectancies.

behavior-outcome expectancies

expectancies about what will happen if a person behaves in a particular way

Will racing to the corner in 11 seconds result in catching the bus, or will the driver ignore me and not stop? Will opening a door for a woman result in a "thank you" or a reprimand for sexist assumptions? A **behavior-outcome expectancy** is an expectation about what will happen if a person behaves in a particular way. Such expectancies are already evident in preschool children (Hegland & Galejs, 1983; Mischel, Zeiss, & Zeiss, 1974), although of course they can change with experience.

stimulus-outcome expectancies

expectancies about how events will develop in the world, that is, what events will follow other environmental stimuli

People also develop expectancies about how events will develop in the world, aside from their own actions. These are termed **stimulus-outcome expectancies**. "If the number 10 bus has just left, the number 23 must be coming soon." "If Jerry is shouting, he may soon hit someone." Although not always directly connected with immediate behavior, these expectancies are important in maintaining a person's ongoing awareness of the environment. I recall, when I was a little girl, riding with my family to visit cousins. It was a trip we often made, and on the way was a pony ride, on the right hand side of the road. For a small price, kids could ride around a ring on a pony in a circle—what a thrill that was! On the opposite side of the road was a place to buy landscaping materials—building stones and the like. One time my father called our attention—my sister and brother and me—to the building materials, in an effort to get past the ponies without our demands for rides. But I (the oldest child) recalled that the pony rides were near there, and asked, "Did we go by the pony ride?" Dad didn't realize that little Susie had developed a stimulus-outcome expectancy connecting the building materials with the pony rides, so his distraction effort failed! (I am pleased to report that he promised to stop at the ponies on the way home, which we did.) Developing stimulus-outcome expectancies helps us know what to expect in our environments. Sometimes, in addition, they may motivate an individual to change environments. (Dad could take another route, if he wished to avoid our demands.)

self-efficacy expectancies (or self-efficacy)

subjective beliefs about what a person will be able to do

"Can I even make it to the bus stop in 11 seconds, or will I fall flat on my face trying?" Expectancies about whether one actually can do the behavior are termed **self-efficacy expectancies**. They are different from behavior-outcome expectancies, as any student knows who not only believes that 12 hours of straight study would result in an A on an exam (high behavior-outcome expectancy) but who also believes that such a long study session would not be possible (low self-efficacy expectancy). Self-efficacy expectancies are central to the cognitive social learning approach and have been discussed by both Walter Mischel (e.g., 1981b, p. 349) and Albert Bandura (as we see in Chapter 13). An idea this important has, not surprisingly, been expressed in other theories as well, although not always by the same name and not always identical in meaning: Julian Rotter (1966, 1990) describes internal-external locus of control; Martin Seligman (1992) describes helplessness (which corresponds closely to low self-efficacy); Carol Dweck describes mastery orientation (Dweck & Leggett, 1988). All of these theoretical concepts share the idea that people's beliefs about what they can accomplish influence behavior in important ways.

These various types of expectancies that Mischel described—behavior-outcome, stimulus-outcome, and self-efficacy—develop from experience in specific situations. When a person is in a new situation, his or her expectancies are derived from past experience in similar situations (Mischel & Staub, 1965). Such generalized expectancies are replaced by specific situational expectancies when experience permits. A child will expect that a new babysitter will ignore obscene language if past babysitters have done so, but with experience the child may learn that she punishes such utterances.

Subjective Stimulus Values

Not all people value the same outcomes. The term **subjective stimulus value** refers to the extent to which a person regards an outcome as desirable or undesirable—that is, a person's goals or values. In learning terms, it is the value of the reward. Mischel (1981a) offers the example of a teacher's praise. This outcome may have high subjective stimulus value for a student trying to get good grades but would have quite a different value for a rebellious adolescent who rejects school.

subjective stimulus value
how much an outcome is valued by an individual

Self-Regulatory Systems and Plans

Among the most important cognitive person variables are **self-regulatory systems and plans**. These are internal mechanisms that have powerful implications for behavior. People set performance goals for themselves (whether it is running a 4-minute mile, skiing an advanced slope, or graduating with honors); they reward themselves; they criticize themselves; they pass by immediate pleasure for long-term goals (delay of gratification). All these are self-regulatory systems "through which we can influence our environment substantially, overcoming 'stimulus control' (the power of the situation)" (Mischel, 1981b, p. 350). One important self-regulatory system that we have already discussed is the ability to delay gratification. Mischel suggests that early development of self-regulatory competencies may contribute to resiliency against social rejection in later life, as follow-up of the "marshmallow test" children 20 years later suggests (Ayduk et al., 2000; Mischel, 2007).

self-regulatory systems and plans
ways that a person works on complicated behavior (e.g., by setting goals and by self-criticism)

APPLICATIONS OF THE CAPS MODEL OF PERSONALITY

The cognitive affective units in the CAPS model build on a biological base, on temperament and factors such as those described by the biological theorists (see Chapter 9). The specific cognitions of an individual are not only developed in part because of unique experience, but also are influenced by culture. Thus it is possible to study not only individuals, but also groups of people whose shared experience is hypothesized to give them similar cognitive affective units (CAUs), such as minority groups with a history of discrimination thought to make them vigilant for signs of prejudice. Also, groups may be formed for comparison based on their measured CAUs directly, rather than inferring similarity from their experience; for example, we can compare people who express sensitivity to interpersonal rejection with those who do not.

The insight that people who share similar experience will often have developed similar cognitive affective units helps us understand racial disparities in America (Mischel, Mendoza-Denton, & Hong, 2009). For example, the CAPS model explains why the verdict in the O. J. Simpson murder case was received differently by black and white Americans, on average. Their life experience led these two groups to have different evaluations of the trial testimony, based on different expectancies about police behavior (the likelihood that they may fabricate evidence, for one thing). When beliefs instead of race are considered, it is belief rather than race that correlates with acceptance or outrage about the acquittal verdict. Similar processes explain whether the two races blame deaths of a disproportionate number of minority victims of Hurricane Katrina on racist government programs (Mendoza-Denton & Goldman-Flythe, 2009). Addressing racial issues, then, requires attention to beliefs.

One aspect of situations and of shared or different experience is the social roles that we occupy, which are important contexts within which to understand personality (Roberts, 2007). Roles can activate the cognitive affective units important in Mischel's approach, including cultural roles such as those that discourage expression of emotion in Japanese culture, or that discourage conformity in individualistic cultures such as the United States (Matsumoto, 2007). But people respond to these role expectations, as they do to other kinds of situations, differently from one another. Sometimes, people suppress their individuality and shape their behavior to respond to what they believe is expected. Other times, they are less affected, or even react against what they perceive to be the role constraints. Furthermore, the same individual may respond to different roles differently—conforming, perhaps, to the expectations of a sports team but resisting the role expectations in a family. So there is the sort of *if . . . then* variation that Mischel and Shoda's model describes.

CAPS analysis also helps understand why people who are trying to hide their prejudice as they interact with others are sometimes not able to do so, while others succeed. The difference depends upon the thought processes that are activated in the person. Those who relax and enjoy the interaction are not perceived as prejudiced, while those whose fear of appearing prejudiced causes them to act in a constrained way, avoiding discussion of sensitive topics, don't successfully hide their prejudice (Butz & Plant, 2009). Perhaps if we could convince these folks to relax and not worry so much about how they are seen, they might present a less prejudiced image—but that is another research project.

Whether or not that suggested intervention would be effective, it illustrates the assumption in the CAPS model that a cognitive affective unit (CAU) influences behavior only when it is activated. The same objective situation will trigger a different behavior, if an individual construes it differently (activating different CAUs). Like the brain's neural networks in which disparate patterns are activated in complex ways (Mischel, 2007), the patterns of cognitive and emotional associations in an individual affect behavior when they are activated by situations or by one another.

In fact, the issue now has turned from looking for consistency across situations, to understanding the variation in an individual's expression of a trait. Why is John sometimes friendly and sometimes withdrawn? Why is Sarah sometimes conscientious and sometimes not? Fleeson (2007) investigated students' variation in expression of the Big Five traits four times each day, over several days, by having them record their "state" (temporary) scores on these traits on a handheld recorder. He found that individuals do indeed vary their momentary states of personality, and these variations were correlated with the changing situations that they were in.

Other researchers compared two cultures, the Philippines and the United States, to see how the person-situation relationships of the Big Five compared. They found considerable cross-cultural similarity in the "if-then" relationships that described what situations were conducive to expression of which traits, but there were a few differences. The Philippine respondents reported that more situations were conducive to negative emotionality (Neuroticism), compared to the Americans, which was consistent with their higher scores on this factor (Church, Katigbak, & del Prado, 2010).

Activation of cognitive-affective units can even influence our own self-image as a result of social interaction. Consider this finding: research subjects whose affiliation motivation is aroused, and who are led to believe that they will be interacting with a person who holds stereotyped views of their racial or gender group, change their self-views to be more consistent with that person. This increases their stereotyped view of themselves, at least temporarily (Sinclair, Pappas, & Lun, 2009). When sensitivity to others' opinions occurs frequently as it does in interpersonally sensitive East Asian cultures, a result can be decreased happiness (Suh, 2007).

The CAPS model has helpful implications for developing effective self-regulatory plans. Since activation of cognitive affective units influences our behavior, we can attempt to activate the relevant such CAUs to bring about the behavior that we desire, such as settling down to a serious study session. It might come from changing our physical context (e.g., going to a quiet room in the library), or by engaging in self-affirming self-talk. Becoming aware of the cognitive context that directs a particular behavior is an important insight; controlling that context is empowering.

Mischel's vision for a comprehensive model of personality continues to develop. An important challenge remains: can we describe situations more systematically? It would be helpful to have a taxonomy of situations that are relevant for personality. That is a task that Saucier, Bel-Bahar, and Fernandez (2007) tackled, based on listings of situations by undergraduates. Not surprisingly, many responses referred to locations, such as being at work or at home. Interpersonal situations were also frequently mentioned. In addition, many of the respondents listed subjective states, such as feeling confident or angry, though the researchers expressed reservations about including them as situational categories. Still, it does seem appealing to include "when alert" as a condition for answering "I am likely to be productive when _____." A productivity consultant, David Allen (2001), says that some of his clients find it useful to have a category like "when brain dead" to define a context in which they may not be able to accomplish demanding work, but they can attend to routine but still essential tasks such as filing or sorting mail. If the factor theorists (see Chapter 8) found it useful to attend to everyday language about traits, why not also listen to how laypeople describe their subjective situations?

Mischel's conceptualization of personality, which built on his studies with George Kelly, has taken the field beyond the study of people's perceptions of one another, which is the basis of the trait (or factor) theories based on the lexical model (see Chapter 8). He challenged the overgeneralized conceptualization of traits that he saw in those theories and argued that common sense is more sophisticated. People are aware of different situations when they choose their behaviors, though they differ from one another in the meanings they attach to particular situations. In their everyday lives, people do this intuitively, and may not be able to verbalize their underlying thought processes. The task for personality theory is to do just that, and to describe how unique cognitions about situations, and about themselves, cause individuals to vary from one to another as they adapt to their world. Mischel's theorizing has contributed substantially to that goal.

Summary

- Mischel investigated children's development of a capacity to *delay gratification*. Cognitive variables are important in this development, such as thinking about something else to avoid impulsive behavior.
- Mischel challenged the assumption of *global personality traits* that led to consistent behavior across many situations, finding inconsistency instead.
- Behavior is much more situationally variable than trait theory had assumed.
- Instead of traits, Mischel proposed *cognitive affective units (CAUs)*, or *person variables*, including *competencies, encoding strategies*, and *personal constructs*.
- His overall CAPS (Cognitive Affective Personality System) model has implications for individuals and also for interpersonal and cultural phenomena.

Thinking about Mischel's Theory

1. Do you think that cognitive social learning theory is capable of describing the most important human personality characteristics, or is it too focused on cognition?
2. Compare delay of gratification to what psychoanalysts meant by the ego.
3. Do you believe that people are consistent or not consistent? Explain.
4. How would you determine whether competencies and expectancies are the causes of behavior or the effects?
5. What cognitive affective units (CAUs) are widespread in your culture? In another culture with which you are familiar? Do you think these have changed over time, from one generation to the next?

Study Questions

1. Summarize research on delay of gratification. What evidence shows the importance of developing this capacity in early life?
2. Summarize the trait controversy and Mischel's role in it.
3. Explain the term *personality coefficient*. Why does it present a problem for traditional personality theory that this number is low?
4. Explain Mischel's concept of situational hedges. How is this concept relevant to the trait-versus-situation controversy?
5. Explain what Mischel meant by cognitive affective units (cognitive person variables) as alternatives to traits. Give examples.
6. Explain what is meant by competencies. How are they different from expectancies?
7. Define self-efficacy. Why are self-efficacy expectancies important?
8. Explain how expectancies can be influenced by experience.
9. What is the function of self-regulatory systems and plans in personality? Give an example.

13

Bandura
Performance in Cognitive Social Learning Theory

Chapter Overview

ILLUSTRATIVE BIOGRAPHY
Barack Obama

Albert Bandura's cognitive social learning perspective emphasizes a person's thinking and the mutual impact of a person and the environment on thinking—themes that are central to understanding the life and influence of Barack Obama.

Barack Hussein Obama Jr. was born August 4, 1961, in Honolulu, Hawaii, to a biracial couple, both college students at the time. His father, from Kenya, already had a wife and child in his native African country (though he kept that a secret) when pregnancy precipitated his marriage to Barack's white mother, Stanley Ann Dunham, from Kansas. (His African tradition permitted multiple wives.) Though described as goat-herders from Kenya, his father and grandfather were of high status and Westernized, but not entirely insulated from racial discrimination in colonial Africa (Remnick, 2010).

Barack Obama

Barack Hussein Obama Sr. left his wife and infant son to pursue graduate education at Harvard University before returning to his native Kenya to work in government, and Ann Dunham (as she was usually called) divorced him in 1964. He visited his son only once after that, when Barack was ten. Barack's mother portrayed his father in positive light and young

Barack—who went by the name Barry in his youth—took him for a positive role model. Only in adulthood did he learn that his father had several children by four different women, treated women abusively, and drank excessively. His father died in a drunk driving accident, not his first, in 1982 at age 48, while Barack was in college (Remnick, 2010). In an autobiographical work, *Dreams from My Father*, Barack describes his search for his father and his black identity, and the pain of realizing that the father he had idolized was, as his father's sister put it when he visited Kenya, "a miserable husband and a worse father" (Remnick, 2010, p. 146).

Barack spent his childhood in Indonesia with his mother and her second husband; the couple produced a half-sister for Barack, but that marriage, too, ended. Barack, his mother, and sister Maya, returned to Hawaii when Barack was 10 years old, welcomed back by his maternal grandparents. He chose to remain with them a few years later, when his mother, along with his sister, returned to Indonesia to continue her work in public service, finding with his grandparents the stability and support that he craved and enjoying the privilege of an excellent private

(continued)

(continued)

school education. Hawaii afforded a particularly accepting multicultural environment, so that his mixed race was less an issue than it would have been in many other states. Like many adolescents, Obama experimented with drugs during high school, which he later regretted.

When time came for college, Barack attended selective Occidental College in southern California, where he faced the age-appropriate issue of identity, working through what it meant to be black and transitioning from his more white nickname of "Barry" to his birth name of "Barack." After 2 years, he transferred to New York's Columbia University, studying political science and international relations in the more diverse atmosphere that he craved. After graduation, he worked for a few years with business firms, researching international economic opportunities, but he experienced moral qualms in that role, which was inconsistent with his public service values (Remnick, 2010). So he turned to a better fit for him: community organizing, working with a nonprofit organization on issues such as public transportation, voter registration, and recycling. He carried these interests to Chicago, working for a church-based group on job training and tenants' rights in impoverished and crime-laden neighborhoods, and gaining increased understanding of what it meant to be "black" in America for those whose experience of race was less inclusive and less economically advantaged than his own. In Chicago, he not only helped others but also experienced a sense of community that had been lacking in his life. Eventually, recognizing the limited potential effectiveness of the community organizer role, he decided to attend law school and aspired to elected political office.

He attended Harvard Law School (1988–1991), graduating *magna cum laude* and serving the prestigious elected position as editor of the *Harvard Law Review*—the first African American to achieve that honor. He met his future wife, Michelle Robinson, during a summer work experience in 1989 at a prestigious law firm in Chicago. Michelle had already graduated from Harvard Law and was assigned to advise him during this summer work. The relationship turned romantic, and they were married in 1992, settled in Chicago, and had two daughters, Malia (born in 1998) and Sasha (2001). Barack worked at a law firm on civil rights issues, participated in a voter registration campaign, and taught constitutional law at the University of Chicago (1992 to 2004). Beginning his elected political career, he served three terms in the Illinois state senate from 1997 to 2004 (Obama, 2004).

In 2004, then a candidate to represent Illinois in the U.S. Senate, Barack Obama catapulted to national attention by delivering the keynote address at the Democratic National Convention in Boston, where candidate John Kerry became the party's presidential nominee, subsequently losing the election to George W. Bush. Obama won the Senate seat, a position that he served until his successful presidential campaign, defeating Republican opponent John McCain in the November 2007 election. He was inaugurated in January 2008 as the 44th president, and the first black president in the country's history.

Early in his presidency, in 2009, Obama was awarded the Nobel Peace Prize, based on a hope for increased international diplomacy under his administration (Elovitz, 2010). Internationally, he struggled to win and end the war in Iraq and Afghanistan, which he had opposed before taking office. His administration grappled with domestic issues as well, enacting controversial health care reform and economic support for the banking industry.

DESCRIPTION

Instead of listing personality traits, Bandura's theory, like Mischel's (in Chapter 12), lists cognitions that are relevant to personality. So let's turn to cognition.

COGNITION

Beliefs about goal-seeking behaviors are central to this perspective. Behavior is predicted by knowing what a person believes he can do (self-efficacy) and expects to find rewarding (outcome expectation). Without self-efficacy in a particular domain of behavior, effort will lag and performance will be limited.

"Yes, we can!" was a theme throughout Barack Obama's presidential campaign—an assertion of competency and self-efficacy proclaimed loud and clear. Throughout his speeches, and in the title of one of his books, *The Audacity of Hope* (2006), Obama uses the word "hope," conveying the belief that action toward a desirable goal can be performed. Psychologists, too, have used the term *hope*; consider Erikson's description of hope as a positive outcome of the trust–mistrust crisis of infancy (see Chapter 5). But in Obama's usage, like Bandura's notion of efficacy, the hope is not the passive hope of a young child. This hope is accompanied by action. Furthermore, Obama's hope is not simply for individual gain, or else he would have turned his talents toward a lucrative law practice instead of investing his talents in exhausting, poorly paid community organizing. As Rowland and Jones (2007, p. 442) put it, "Hope is Obama's metaphor for a balance between individualism and communal responsibilities."

In using the plural "we" in his theme "yes we can," Obama illustrates a particular kind of efficacy expectation that Bandura calls "collective efficacy." In contrast to individual efficacy, which focuses on what the individual alone can accomplish (e.g., I believe I can shoot this basket), collective efficacy is a team effort. People working together can achieve something—win this game, or this election, or achieve certain political purposes. As Obama phrases it in *The Audacity of Hope* (2006, p. 356), the hope was that "we [Americans] had some control—and therefore responsibility—over our own fate." He explained his decision to run for president by saying, "I'm running for president because I believe it's possible" to bring about the changes in the economy, opportunities, and the environment that he envisioned (Obama, 2008, p. 3). Obama emphasizes belief, declaring "change is always possible if you're willing to work for it, fight for it, and, *above all, believe in it*" (Obama, 2008, p 6; emphasis added).

After seeing that community organizing could achieve only limited success toward his goals, Obama turned to another route: politics. In the language of social cognitive theory, although he had high *self-efficacy* for community organizing (he knew he could successfully do the organizing), the *outcome expectation* was low (he believed the goals of achieving significant reduction in social problems would not be reached). Knowing that one can do a behavior does not, in itself, ensure the behavior will occur. It also must be expected to lead to some desired outcome.

CULTURE

Bandura's theory encompasses the cultural context of personality, including role models and the assumptions and values of society. Reflecting American values, much research focuses on what a person can accomplish individually—for example, self-efficacy expectations. But collective efficacy and shared goals are also recognized.

Although American culture is more individualistic than collectivist, the balance of these two orientations varies among cultural groups. African Americans are among those whose cultural norms are more collectivist, and researchers report that, when he is talking to African American audiences, Barack Obama's rhetorical style increases the use of traditional cultural techniques such as call and response that emphasize the group (Howard, 2011). Perhaps it is the African American part of his multicultural heritage that contributes most to his skill in working with a community, and in listening to others' opinions in political and legal matters, before asserting his own opinion—a style that distinguishes him from many of his peers in the legal community (Remnick, 2010).

Obama's speeches present masterful combinations of the important American theme of individualism with the community-building theme of working together collectively. In a speech delivered in Denver on August 28, 2008, he described the "American promise" in this way: "Through hard work and sacrifice, each of us can pursue our individual dreams but still come together as one American family, to ensure that the next generation can pursue their dreams as well" (quoted in Jenkins & Cos, 2010, p. 189). He frequently used the collective pronoun "we" in his speeches (Jenkins & Cos, 2010), asserting that shared goals unite us, and that "we rise or fall as one nation; as one people" (from his speech on election night, 2007).

Bandura's concept of *reciprocal determinism* asserts that not only are people shaped by their environment, but they also have an impact on it. Indeed, Barack Obama was well aware of the interdependent processes that connect individual and societal change. Consider what he said about his former pastor Jeremiah Wright, whose racially divisive remarks triggered considerable criticism. "What my former pastor too often failed to understand is that embarking on a program of self-help also requires a belief that society can change" (quoted in Terrill, 2009, p. 374).

Some political differences in public discourse can be understood as emphasizing only part of the complex interplay between individual action and collective or societal perspectives. Political conservatives emphasize the individual, while liberals emphasize the societal (Rowland & Jones, 2007). According to Rowland and Jones (2007), Obama emphasized both the individual and the societal in his description of the American dream, which expanded his political appeal.

DEVELOPMENT

One of Bandura's most widely known concepts is that of modeling. His famous "Bobo doll" studies showed that exposure to aggressive or nonaggressive models influences children's behavior. Models influence behaviors that children learn and their standards for what level of performance is acceptable. In addition, the consequences of a model's behavior (whether or not it leads to reward) influence the child's own expectations of what is worth doing.

While the absence of his father while growing up did influence Barack Obama and stimulated his search for his father, described in his autobiography, in fact he did have other models while a child: his mother, whose public service and educational efforts are reflected in his own later activities, and his grandparents, who provided a stable and supportive family such as the one that he values in his own marriage. His grandmother, too, provided a model of persistence and hard work.

Although Obama's father was physically absent, his mother conveyed an idealized image of his father that served as a model, though vague, of education and engagement in society's issues (Fuchsman, 2009). When Obama later gained a more realistic understanding of his father and his human weaknesses, one biographer suggests that Obama developed contrasting positive qualities of his own, becoming "cool, rooted, polite, always listening," in order to not become like his father (Remnick, 2010, p. 52).

From his exploration of black history, Obama was exposed to dozens of role models beyond his own family, including Malcolm X, Frederick Douglass, Martin Luther King Jr., and Jesse Jackson, as well as whites such as the Kennedys, whose diverse perspectives on the shared goal of equality gave him much inspiration (Remnick, p.160). In Obama's own life experience as a young adult, Mayor Harold Washington of Chicago modeled a successful black elected official. Cultural models provided strong shoulders on which to stand.

ADJUSTMENT

Through elaborate learning, people develop self-systems that permit them to pursue goals effectively. Bandura describes these *self-regulatory systems and plans* and the goals toward which they direct a person as the stuff of which effective action is made. A laudable goal, without a self-regulatory system to direct a person, is unlikely to be reached.

Such systems require forgoing short-term gains in favor of longer term objectives, and there is ample evidence in Obama's life story of such a longer vision. His goals for education required hard work. His early job experience involved what he called a monk-like period of little time off and much sacrifice. He learned disciplined strategies for advancing his education and seeking his goals—though not without a period in his youth when he, like others in his generation, explored drugs and the immediate pleasure that they bring. Self-regulatory systems and plans (more briefly, the "self-system") develop over time. Reflection facilitates this, and Barack Obama's autobiographical writing provides ample evidence of his self-reflection and the development of his self-system.

Failures of self-regulation can result when people are carried away by their emotions, but Barack Obama, according to one psychobiographer, is particularly able to contain or even repress emotions, including anger—which is often positive but also has some negative political results, including failure to echo the public's anger about such troubling events as perceived economic abuses by businesses receiving government economic relief (Elovitz, 2010). Obama does, incidentally, credit his Indonesian step-father with modeling emotional self-management (Obama, 2004/1995, p. 38).

Self-regulatory systems include standards for performance, which affect people's aspirations and set the standards where they regard reinforcement as deserved. Obama's standards included not only individual standards, but also standards for the country as a whole. "Let's be the generation that ends poverty in America" (Remnick, 2010, p. 23), he challenged. Setting a standard higher than current achievement has a motivating impact, energizing activity toward an aspired goal. As Obama (2006) challenged, "A gap exists between our professed ideals as a nation and the reality we witness everyday" (p. 22). In his criticism of the country's economic recession, Obama described "a perfect

(continued)

(continued)

storm of irresponsibility and poor decision-making that stretched from Wall Street to Main Street" in which "short-term gains were prized over long-term prosperity, where we failed to look beyond the next payment, the next quarter, or the next election" (Fuchsman, 2009, p. 156). He called for greater fiscal discipline.

His way of framing the goal, as a reclaiming of the American dream (the subtitle of *The Audacity of Hope*), a "restoration rhetoric," presented a potentially unifying message to the American public (Harrell, 2010, p. 164), heightening the likelihood that a large number of Americans could share a collective task (though of course political differences remained and not everyone shared the collective goal).

Obama's political activities have been described as pragmatic. In community organizing, he sought alliances with those who could help move toward his goals (Jenkins & Cos, 2010). He is described as an excellent listener who gathers considerable information and reflects on it, before deciding upon a plan for action (Remnick, 2010, p. 137). His effective self-regulatory plan is neither impulsive nor overly rigid, and is open to input from a variety of others. His organizing in the black community was also open to considerations of fairness to whites (Remnick, 2010, p. 140). His answers to a reporter's questions about race and the economy during the state Senate campaign in 1995, for example, pointed to the need for a detailed plan: "Any solution to our unemployment catastrophe must arise from us working creatively within a multicultural, interdependent and international economy. Any African-Americans who are only talking about racism as a barrier to our success are seriously misled if they don't also come to grips with the larger economic forces that are creating economic insecurity for all workers—whites, Latinos, and Asians" (Remnick, 2010, p. 285). His explanatory system and plan for the future has obvious interconnections with a broad range of diverse people.

BIOLOGY

No theory can deny the impact of biology on personality, and cognitive social behaviorists—though their concern with biological phenomena is quite limited—have found some positive associations between high efficacy expectations and health.

It is consistent with these findings that President Obama, a man with high self-efficacy expectations, is healthy, as physicians report, and lives a generally healthy lifestyle, with exercise and

a healthy diet. One unhealthy habit that plagued him for years was cigarette smoking—a habit that he reportedly stopped with the help of his wife, Michelle, and nicotine gum within the first 2 years of his presidency. Bandura's theory recognizes that efficacy expectations can vary from one domain of behavior to another, so it is consistent with the theory that one unhealthy habit can coexist with others that are different.

FINAL THOUGHTS

This theoretical approach is particularly suited to understanding the mutual influences of a person and the society, an issue that is salient in trying to understand a person in such a powerful role as U.S. president.

Other theories could also be used in an attempt to understand Barack Obama. Psychoanalytic approaches (Elovitz, 2008; Fuchsman, 2009) would emphasize such issues as coping styles and the resolution of the Oedipal conflict for a boy whose father was absent. Erikson's notion of identity is particularly appealing for analyzing the identity resolution of a biracial youth. The election of Barack Obama as the first black president of the United States had a profound impact on the development of young African Americans, stimulating them to increased racial identity exploration (Fuller-Rowell, Burrow, & Ong, 2011). However, it would be an oversimplification to focus only on black identity. Although labeled "black," Obama's ancestry and his own personal narrative are more inclusive. He has been described as having developed a personal narrative of "cosmopolitan identity" (Hammack, 2010), helping to shift the country from polarized and separate racial identities toward a truly more inclusive viewpoint.

Although Barack Obama's rise to the presidency is (rightly) pointed to as a boost in black Americans' identity, the analysis of his personality from the perspective of Bandura's theory does not focus on his identity. The key issue is the effective attainment of goals: effective action in the social world. And it is about such issues that Bandura's theory provides such useful concepts. Barack Obama's rise to the presidency of the United States was not simply an individual achievement, but also a milestone in the country's change toward greater inclusion and an overcoming of racial discrimination. He represents a postracial period, in which previously divided racial and ethnic groups in America can unify behind a shared American dream (cf. Mastey, 2010).

PREVIEW: OVERVIEW OF BANDURA'S THEORY

Albert Bandura, like Walter Mischel (see Chapter 12), has advanced the social cognitive perspective of personality. Although Mischel and Bandura have many similar theoretical orientations, have cited one another's work, and have collaborated (Bandura & Mischel, 1965), most of their formal theoretical developments and research have been published independently. They both advocate cognitive person variables (including self-efficacy) in place of broad traits, and both emphasize the importance of the situation, which interacts with traits to produce behavior. This can be confusing for the student, since both theorists agree on broad theoretical issues, though each has developed, within this broad shared framework, some specific areas. While Mischel developed a theory of traits, Bandura has focused on how modeling produces the acquisition of behavior, and on how individuals set and pursue goals. Think of these

Table 13.1 Preview of Bandura's Theory	
Individual Differences	Individuals differ in behaviors and in cognitive processes because of learning.
Adaptation and Adjustment	Social learning builds ways of adapting to situations. New therapies using modeling and other techniques to treat phobias and other disorders have been found effective, because of the effect on self-efficacy.
Cognitive Processes	Cognition is central to personality. The theory describes many classes of cognitions (including expectancies and self-efficacy). Cognitions that are specific to particular situations are most predictive.
Culture	Culture influences the development of behaviors and cognitions. Modeling has major implications for society, including TV violence, which promotes aggression.
Biological Influences	Biology has prepared the human species for learning, rather than determining outcomes. Although the theory does not focus on biological mechanisms, Bandura found that self-efficacy improves immune functioning among phobic subjects.
Development	Children learn much through modeling, as demonstrated in research using children as subjects. Learning can occur throughout life. Expectancies and other cognitive learning variables can change as a result of experience.

two as playing on the same team, only in two different positions, rather than as theoretical combatants. Bandura's theoretical contributions permit personality theory to resolve a difficult dilemma: whether to treat people as pawns, whose behavior and experience are determined from the outside, or whether to treat them as the causes of their own behavior. Much is at stake. As Bandura puts it (2001b, p. 1), "The capacity to exercise control over the nature and quality of one's life is the essence of humanness."

Bandura's theory has implications for major theoretical questions, as presented in Table 13.1.

Like Mischel (see Chapter 12), Bandura's theory emphasizes learned behaviors and cognitions that are developed from experience. He emphasizes modeling as a way of learning by observing others, and criticizes culture for providing inappropriate (aggressive) models. Application of learning principles can improve individual functioning and contribute to the solution of social problems.

Biography of Albert Bandura

Albert Bandura was born on December 4, 1925, in northern Alberta, Canada, where his parents had immigrated from Europe to become farmers (Bandura, 2007). Elementary and high school were combined in one school in the small town of Mundare. Bandura worked on the Alaska highway (among other jobs) before entering the University of British Columbia, graduating in 3 years. He did his graduate work at the University of Iowa, finishing his doctorate in clinical psychology in 1952. There he met his future wife, Virginia Varns, who taught in the School of Nursing, at a chance encounter in a golf class, where he was fulfilling a physical education requirement (Bandura, 2007). After a postdoctoral internship at the Wichita Guidance Center, he went to Stanford University in California, where he has been on the faculty his entire career, becoming a full professor in 1964 and holder of an endowed chair from 1974. He headed the Department of Psychology from 1976 to 1977.

His interests have been broad, including not only the therapeutic concerns that might have been anticipated from his clinical training, such as application of his theory

Albert Bandura

to the treatment of phobias, but also broad issues in child development and social problems, including violence and environmental concerns. In applying his scholarship to the solution of the social problem of violence, he describes being blackballed by the television industry from participation on an expert panel to make recommendations, as on another issue the tobacco industry had been able to veto scientists from appointment to a government advisory panel (Bandura, 2007). He was president of the American Psychological Association in 1974 and has received many professional honors for his scholarly work, including the American Psychological Association's Award for Distinguished Scientific Contributions in 1980 (American Psychological Association, 1981). He continues his affiliation with Stanford University as professor emeritus (Bandura, 2007), actively engaged in several projects in his mid 80s.

RECIPROCAL DETERMINISM

reciprocal determinism

the interacting mutual influences of the person, the environment, and the behavior

Many psychological approaches deal with only some aspects of the complex network of interacting causes, describing how situations influence behavior (as behaviorism does) or how personality traits influence behavior (as trait approaches do). Bandura (1978, 1984b) expanded these more limited cause-and-effect models with his concept of **reciprocal determinism**. This concept recognizes that the person, the environment, and behavior all influence one another, as illustrated in Figure 13.1.

The concept of reciprocal determinism recognizes that the environment influences behavior, as behaviorism has always suggested. (Libraries are conducive to studying; the student lounge is not.) It also recognizes that characteristics within a person influence behavior, as trait approaches have traditionally emphasized. (Conscientious students study more.) Reciprocal determinism goes beyond these approaches, pointing out that behavior also causes changes in the environment (studying instead of spending time with friends reduces social pressures or invitations to go out) and in the individual (studying increases academic self-confidence). The environment is not only a cause of behavior but also an effect of behavior. One way in which personality influences situations is that people choose situations differently, depending on their personalities (Emmons, Diener, & Larsen, 1985).

A complete understanding of personality requires the recognition of all of these mutual influences among personality, situation, and behavior. In addition, fortuitous chance also plays a role in determining the paths that we take through life—as in the example of a professional who by chance took an empty chair at a conference presentation, whereupon he met, in the adjacent chair, the woman who was to become his wife (Bandura, 1998, 2007). But by arguing for the role of chance in determining life outcomes, Bandura did not present an image of people as pawns in the hands of fate. Instead, he argued that people should lead active lives and pursue interests, to increase the number of chance encounters, and then follow up on the opportunities that chance provides (Bandura, 2007). Determinist science must be salted with a few grains of unpredictability.

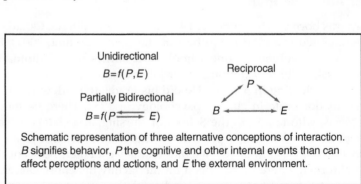

FIGURE 13.1 Reciprocal Determinism

Source: From A. Bandura (1978). The self system in reciprocal determinism. *American Psychologist, 33,* 344–358. Copyright 1978 by the American Psychological Association. Reprinted by permission.

SELF-REGULATION OF BEHAVIOR: THE SELF-SYSTEM

Bandura presents an empowerment model in which people are responsible for their own behavior, contrasting this portrayal of responsibility with deterministic models in neuroscience, psychoanalytic thought, and noncognitive versions of behaviorism that all describe people's behavior as determined by forces over which they have no control (Bandura, 2007). In his social cognitive theory, people have considerable control over their own behavior. They vary, of course, in how effectively they exert this control. Sometimes they procrastinate, putting off projects rather than working on them; sometimes people engage in self-handicapping, doing work in ways that make it difficult to succeed, such as trying to study in a place that has too many distractions (Lay, Knish, & Zanatta, 1992). In contrast, other people make the most of their potential. A study of gifted students reports that they are more likely than other students to take responsibility for their own learning. Thomas Edison, for example, read almost all the books in the local library, if his own report is accurate (Risemberg & Zimmerman, 1992). By teaching us about the processes by which people regulate their own behavior, Bandura's theory promises to give people more control over their own lives.

To contrast with the old behavioral model of a person who simply responds to the environment, or even a complicated information-processing system, Bandura speaks of *human agency*. In this mode, people act with intention, forethought, self-reactiveness, and self-reflectiveness (Bandura, 2001b). Humans are conscious beings, and we act intentionally, with a desire to achieve some end (although sometimes our intentional acts do not work out as we plan). By anticipating the future and adopting goals, people become, in essence, self-directed. As they progress toward these goals, they monitor their progress, evaluate how they are doing, and correct their course. Personal values and identity come into play here.

The processes are cognitive, and they are collectively called the **self-system**. "A self-system within the framework of social learning theory comprises cognitive structures and subfunctions for perceiving, evaluating, and regulating behavior, not a psychic agent that controls action" (Bandura, 1978, p. 344). These cognitive processes are outlined in Figure 13.2. Notice that self-regulation is more than simply giving oneself reinforcements, which alone does not work very well (Sohn & Lamal, 1982).

self-system

personal constructs that people use to describe themselves; cognitive structures and subfunctions for perceiving, evaluating, and regulating behavior (not a psychic agent that controls action)

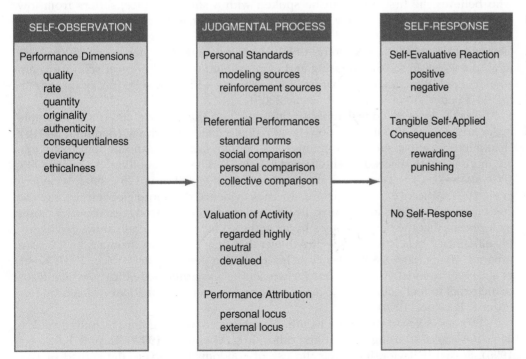

FIGURE 13.2 Self-Regulation Processes

Source: From A. Bandura (1978). The self system in reciprocal determinism. *American Psychologist, 33,* 344–358. Copyright 1978 by the American Psychological Association. Reprinted by permission.

Component processes in the self-regulation of behavior by self-prescribed contingencies.

Internalized guides toward desirable outcomes and avoidance of negative outcomes develop in childhood, as parents reward and nurture, and also threaten or punish, setting up patterns in the child for their own self-regulation (Manian et al., 2006).

Choosing goals is an important step in self-regulation. Higher goals generally produce higher performance. In the applied psychology research literature, one of the most replicated findings is that people who are given higher goals perform at a higher level than those given lower goals (Phillips & Gully, 1997). In many instances, people set their own goals. Setting subgoals generally enhances performance, especially if there is some flexibility about immediate tasks as we work toward longer-term goals (Kirschenbaum, 1985). Another way to think of goals is in terms of *possible selves,* the kind of self we want to become (a successful attorney, for example) and the negative possible selves that we wish to avoid (a college dropout, perhaps). These possible selves, like goals, can guide our self-regulation (Hoyle & Sherrill, 2006).

People can self-regulate their emotions as well as their behavior. Pursuing goals, whether in the laboratory or in life, sometimes requires taking steps to maintain interest in the task and to avoid boredom (Sansone & Thoman, 2006). Life's events surely contribute to our happiness or sadness, and other emotions, but we also can feel differently by internal processes of self-regulation. People in laboratory situations were shown unpleasant videotapes about mass destruction caused by an atomic bomb. Naturally, they experienced unpleasant emotions, but some of them defended against this unpleasantness by conjuring up pleasant memories (Boden & Baumeister, 1997). The ability to avoid thinking about unpleasant things can be adaptive; for example, it helps bereaved adults cope with the death of their spouse (Bonanno et al., 1995). At other times, putting a positive spin on events may prevent us from dealing with unpleasantries that need attention.

SELF-EFFICACY

Self-efficacy means believing "that one can organize and execute given courses of action required to deal with prospective situations" (Bandura, 1980). A person who has a high self-efficacy expectation in a particular situation is confident of mastery. For example, a tennis player who believes his or her serve is reliably excellent has a high self-efficacy expectation. A person who doubts that he or she can do the required behavior has a low self-efficacy expectation. A stage-frightened performer, who believes the first lines will be spoken with a squeaky voice, suffers from low self-efficacy. High self-efficacy leads to effort and persistence at a task and setting higher goals, whereas low self-efficacy produces discouragement and giving up (Bandura, 1989b; Phillips & Gully, 1997). Homeless people higher in self-efficacy are more persistent in seeking housing and employment; those with lower scores give up sooner (Epel, Bandura, & Zimbardo, 1999). Parents with high self-efficacy for parenting do a better job of it (Jones & Prinz, 2005).

Health depends considerably on lifestyle, and the lifestyle choices that people make are matters of self-regulation, largely determined by efficacy (Bandura, 2001b). Health interventions, such as programs for weight loss, exercise, and stopping smoking, are more likely to succeed if self-efficacy is high (Desharnais, Bouillon, & Godin, 1986; Dzewaltowski, 1989; Garcia, Schmitz, & Doerfler, 1990; O'Leary, 1985, 1992; Weinberg et al., 1984; Wojcik, 1988). Even when there is evidence that more global traits, such as conscientiousness, predict positive health behaviors (in this study, exercise), a closer look reveals that the benefit comes because these conscientious individuals are higher in self-efficacy beliefs about specific things that they can do to maintain an exercise program (Bogg, 2008). Self-efficacy helps people to control pain (Dolce, 1987; Kores et al., 1990). Self-defense programs for women increase their self-efficacy, which leads participants to feel safer so their mobility is no longer unreasonably restricted by fear (Ozer & Bandura, 1990).

Efficacy is key to successful health-related prevention programs, including adolescents' resistance to using alcohol and other drugs (Bandura, 1999b; Hays & Ellickson, 1990). Sexual behavior, including the use of condoms to prevent the spread of HIV and other sexually transmitted diseases, is influenced by self-efficacy (O'Leary, 1992).

Bandura (1990a) recommends developing AIDS-prevention programs that recognize the importance of self-efficacy, which is particularly low among runaway teens (Kaliski et al., 1990). Rehearsal of relevant behaviors—for example, through role playing of condom purchasing and HIV testing—can increase preventive behavior (Fisher & Fisher, 1992), perhaps by increasing self-efficacy for these behaviors. Among college students, self-efficacy about using condoms has been increased by a relay race that involved putting condoms on models of penises (Hayden, 1993), surely an illustration of two important concepts from Bandura's theory: Self-efficacy is specific to a particular behavior and self-efficacy can be changed through learning.

Although some researchers measure general self-efficacy, a broad trait applicable to a variety of behaviors (Shelton, 1990), Bandura recommends using measures of self-efficacy specifically for a particular domain of behavior (e.g., Wells-Parker, Miller, & Topping, 1990). Empathic self-efficacy, for example, is useful in understanding the dynamics that lead to prosocial behavior (Alessandri, et al., 2009). A measure of political self-efficacy has been developed, on which politicians score higher than the general population (Caprara et al., 2009). Unlike global self-efficacy measures that ask general questions, domain-specific questions are more precisely focused. For example, instead of asking, "Are you confident that you will be successful," a domain-specific self-efficacy item might ask, "Are you confident that you will study well enough to pass the MCAT exam?"

Health efficacy measures have proven very useful. A public health survey confirms that health self-efficacy comprises several specific dimensions (nutrition, medical care, and exercise), as Bandura predicted, rather than one global dimension (Hofstetter, Sallis, & Hovell, 1990). Measures of efficacy that refer to a particular situation predict better than global measures (Wollman & Stouder, 1991). If intervention programs, such as programs to reduce tobacco use in youth, are to succeed, they should target their teaching toward the specific problem—for example, teaching adolescents the cognitive and behavioral skills needed to resist pressure to smoke (Epstein, Botvin, & Diaz, 1999).

The concept of efficacy has been applied to many areas of life. Mothers who are higher in self-efficacy for specific problems in caring for their infants were rated higher in maternal competence by observers who watched them interact with their children (Teti & Gelfand, 1991). Low self-efficacy is associated with negative emotions, including depression (Bandura, 1989a; Davis-Berman, 1990). Politically active citizens scored higher on a measure of political efficacy (Zimmerman, 1989). People with high-efficacy expectations about computers are less anxious and use them more (Compeau, Higgins, & Huff, 1999). In organizations, where theories are evaluated by their practical contribution to corporate profitability, self-efficacy and other social cognitive concepts help predict career aspirations and job performance (Lent & Hackett, 1987; Stajkovic & Luthans, 1998).

Bandura (like Mischel) distinguishes between self-efficacy (the belief that one has the ability to perform the behavior) and **outcome expectations** (see Figure 13.3). The latter refers to the belief that if the behavior is successfully done, it will lead to desirable outcomes. If I am confident that I can put my coins in a soda machine but

outcome expectations
the belief about what desirable or undesirable things will occur if a behavior is successfully performed

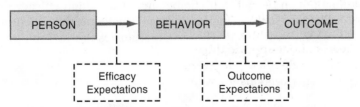

FIGURE 13.3 Diagrammatic Representation of the Difference between Efficacy Expectations and Outcome Expectations

Source: From A. Bandura (1977). Self-efficacy: Toward a unifying theory of behavioral change. *Psychological Review, 84,* 191–215. Copyright 1977 by the American Psychological Association. Reprinted by permission.

doubt the machine will deliver my chosen soda, I have low outcome expectations despite high efficacy expectations. Obviously, both types of expectations must be high for a person to attempt a specific behavior.

Efficacy and Striving Toward Goals

People vary in the goals that they value, whether health, wealth, a college degree, and so on; but striving toward goals is characteristically human and a major concern in personality, with implications for our emotional well-being (Austin & Vancouver, 1996; Brunstein, Schultheiss, & Grässmann, 1998; Emmons, 1997). Self-efficacy promotes striving toward goals. Students who have higher self-efficacy beliefs are more persistent in their academic work and achieve higher levels of academic performance (Multon, Brown, & Lent, 1991). Occupational choice is influenced by efficacy. In a study of high school equivalency students, those who had a broader generality of self-efficacy considered a wider possible range of occupations; they also had a greater range of interests (Bores-Rangel et al., 1990).

Athletes who are more confident perform better, and elite coaches use a variety of techniques to build such a sense of efficacy, including enhancing performance through drilling, modeling of confidence, and encouraging positive talk (Gould et al., 1989). Self-efficacy promotes good performance among graduate students in business in simulated managerial decision making (Bandura & Wood, 1989; Wood, Bandura, & Bailey, 1990). A sense of self-efficacy leads to persistence in the face of setbacks. Persistence, in turn, ultimately leads to greater success (Wood & Bandura, 1989b). Leading subjects in a managerial task to believe that performance is a skill that can be learned, rather than a stable ability trait, makes them more persistent, so early failures do not lead to giving up (Wood & Bandura, 1989a).

Efficacy is increased if subjects gradually improve their performance on a task. This efficacy, in turn, improves later decision making (Bandura & Jourden, 1991). At least under some circumstances, breaking a large task into smaller subgoals beneficially affects performance because it increases a sense of efficacy. Stock and Cervone (1990) found that subjects who worked toward proximal subgoals on complex problems had increased self-efficacy and persisted longer than those who worked only toward more remote goals. Students with low self-efficacy are especially likely to perform better if they are instructed to set goals for each day's work (Tuckman, 1990). Sexton and Tuckman (1991) studied female college students on a series of mathematics tasks. Based on changes over time, they proposed that self-efficacy beliefs are especially important at the beginning of a task. Thereafter, the behaviors themselves become more important than cognitive variables.

Considerable evidence exists that efficacy expectations and similar positive expectations (such as optimism) contribute to effective functioning in a variety of ways. Before signing up for a motivational "think positive" seminar, though, we should keep some cautions in mind. First, Bandura warns that efficacy expectations should be grounded in experience, or they may not last. Second, it is possible to have unrealistically high efficacy expectations that are harmful, for example, when we expect to be able to stop a bad habit cold and are therefore unprepared to deal with a relapse (Litt, 1988). Or unrealistically high efficacy expectations may cause us to commit to actions that are beyond our ability and therefore harmful or dangerous, such as skiing down a mountain beyond our competence. Third, high efficacy expectations for undesirable behavior (such as aggression) will facilitate those actions, unfortunately (Crick & Dodge, 1994). High efficacy expectancies are helpful, provided they are realistic and the behavior is desirable.

Physiological Correlates of Efficacy

When a person has low self-efficacy, the body, as well as the mind, responds. The autonomic nervous system is aroused (Bandura, Reese, & Adams, 1982). In one study, women phobically afraid of spiders confronted spiders in the laboratory. Sometimes the task was one that the subjects felt they had high efficacy to accomplish (e.g., seeing a spider at a distance); other tasks were more difficult. The women's level of efficacy predicted changes in plasma catecholamine secretion (epinephrine, norepinephrine, and DOPAC). When therapy increased their efficacy expectations, the physiological indicators also changed (Bandura et al., 1985).

Stressors can enhance or suppress immune system functioning. When subjects in a laboratory had low self-efficacy about performing the tasks they were given, their endogenous opioid systems were activated (Bandura et al., 1987; Bandura et al., 1988), which can interfere with the immune system. When subjects who had snake phobias developed self-efficacy to control phobic stressors (because of an experimental manipulation), immune functioning was enhanced (Wiedenfeld et al., 1990).

Although the relationship of efficacy and goal striving more generally to biological variables is only scant, this seems a direction for potential further developments. Self-directed motivated behavior, according to brain development research, plays a role in shaping the brain itself (Bandura, 2001b). Bandura clearly states, though, that psychological analysis cannot be reduced to biological explanation. Changes in such major characteristics as gender roles and a country's peaceful or warlike nature can occur rapidly, as a result of cultural change, not biological or evolutionary mechanisms (Bandura, 2001a; Bussey & Bandura, 1999). As part of an increasingly multilevel approach to theory in personality, the control beliefs described by Bandura (and others) serve an important bridge because they connect to both biological-level variables and societal-level outcomes (Haidt & Rodin, 1999).

PROCESSES INFLUENCING LEARNING

Bandura considered in some detail how cognitive person variables such as efficacy are developed. Much more occurs in learning than an automatic "stamping in" of preceding responses, based on reinforcement. His early studies, described here, showed that children could learn aggressive behaviors simply by observing models perform them, without reinforcement. Learning without reinforcement required a new theoretical explanation, which Bandura (1986b) offers: a set of theoretical concepts for understanding the complex events within people that must occur for observed models to produce changes in performance. Briefly, the learner must observe the behavior, remember it, be able to do it, and be motivated to do it. Let's examine these processes in more detail (see Table 13.2).

Attentional Processes: Observing the Behavior

Nothing will be learned that is not observed. People who have difficulty remembering names, for example, often simply do not pay attention to them in the first place. Several characteristics of the model and of the observer influence modeling. Models catch our attention more when they look distinctive because of their clothes or other aspects of their physical appearance, when they are liked or disliked, and when they are seen repeatedly, as advertisers well know. All these are examples of **attentional processes**. Characteristics of the observer, too, influence attention, including sensory capacities, arousal level, motivation, perceptual set, and past reinforcement.

attentional processes
noticing the model's behavior (a prerequisite for learning by modeling)

Retention Processes: Remembering It

As any student knows who has paid attention to a classroom lecture or film, not all that is observed is retained. The **retention process** occurs through imaginational representations (such as images of places or people that are familiar) and through verbal coding, which can be much more efficient. Symbolic coding facilitates retention, as cognitive psychology suggests it should. In academic settings, pedagogues teach students to work actively with material to remember it. The same advice applies in other settings as well (e.g., Bandura, Grusec, & Menlove, 1966). Additional factors influencing retention include cognitive organization, symbolic rehearsal, and motor rehearsal.

retention process
remembering what a model has done

Table 13.2 Processes in Observational Learning

1. ATTENTIONAL PROCESSES: Noticing the Model's Behavior.

The Model: Distinctive
Affective Valence
Complexity
Prevalence
Functional Value

The Observer: Sensory Capacities
Arousal Level
Motivation
Perceptual Set
Past Reinforcement

2. RETENTION PROCESSES: Putting the Behavior into Memory.
Symbolic Coding
Cognitive Organization
Symbolic Rehearsal
Motor Rehearsal

3. MOTOR REPRODUCTION PROCESSES: Being Able to Do It.
Physical Capabilities
Availability of Component Responses
Self-Observation of Reproductions
Accuracy Feedback

4. MOTIVATIONAL PROCESSES: Deciding It Is Worth Doing.
External Reinforcement
Vicarious Reinforcement
Self-Reinforcement

Source: A. Bandura (1986b). *Social Foundations of Thought & Action: A Social Cognitive Theory.* © 1986, p. 2. Reprinted by permission of Prentice Hall, Englewood Cliffs, New Jersey.

Motor Reproduction Processes: Doing It

motor reproduction process

being able to do what one has seen a model do

The behavior being modeled must then be reproduced from its remembered encoding **(motor reproduction process)**. No response can be emitted that is beyond the physical capacity of the individual. Complex behaviors can be reproduced by combining their component response elements, if they are known. Feedback about our performance, such as an athletic trainer's comments or videotaped images of our own play, improve this motor reproduction phase of learning.

Motivational Processes: Wanting It

motivational process

deciding whether it is worthwhile to behave as a model has behaved

Coaches also give pep talks, recognizing the importance of **motivational processes** to learning. Bandura clearly distinguishes between learning and performance. Unless motivated, a person will not produce learned behavior. This motivation can come from external reinforcement, such as the experimenter's promise of reward in some of Bandura's studies, or the bribe of a parent. Or it can come from vicarious reinforcement, based on the observation that models are rewarded. High-status models can affect performance through motivation. For example, girls age 11 to 14 performed better on a motor performance task when they thought it was demonstrated by a high-status cheerleader than by a low-status model (McCullagh, 1986).

OBSERVATIONAL LEARNING AND MODELING

We are so aware today of the importance of good models that it is easy to overlook the theoretical advance that occurred when modeling was introduced to the learning-theory paradigm within personality. Radical learning theory, in the Skinnerian tradition, required that responses must occur and be reinforced to be strengthened. Even Neal Miller and John Dollard (1941), for all their theoretical innovation, assumed that responses must be reinforced to be learned. Laboratory rats and pigeons in Skinner boxes were subjected to exhausting shaping interventions to bring about those necessary conditions for learning. If elaborate procedures were necessary to trigger relatively simple motor responses, how could learning theory possibly explain the much more extensive developments that occur in human personality formation?

Humans learn by observing. This is the simple answer that Bandura proposed. Intuitively, it is obvious. However, observational learning violates a traditional assumption of learning theory—that learning can occur only if there is reinforcement. Bandura asserted that learning and performance could be distinguished. Reinforcement provides incentives necessary for performance, but it is not necessary for learning.

Behavioral changes that result from exposure to models are variously called **modeling**, imitative learning, observational learning, or vicarious learning. These terms are interchangeable in Bandura's usage. He defines **vicarious learning** as learning in which

> new responses are acquired or the characteristics of existing response repertoires are modified as a function of observing the behavior of others and its reinforcing consequences, without the modeled responses being overtly performed by the viewer during the exposure period. (Bandura, 1965c, p. 3)

In everyday experience, a child may see a friend grab a ball away from a classmate and learn to grab as a result. Or a TV viewer may see a mass murder on television and later imitate the crime. More positively, exposure to competent and socialized adults teaches children desirable behaviors. Bandura's laboratory investigations show that exposure to adult models can lead to diverse effects, including the elevation of the level of moral reasoning (Bandura, 1969; Bandura & McDonald, 1963) or, conversely, an increase in aggressive behavior.

Bandura's interest in modeling had roots in other theoretical traditions. Psychoanalytic approaches emphasize identification with parents as the basis for much personality development. Previous researchers reasoned that children may identify with parents because of their power (as controllers of rewards) or because of their status (as recipients of rewards). Bandura designed a laboratory experiment to test these proposed causes of identification. Preschool children observed various kinds of models, some powerful, called *controller models* (because they controlled access to highly desirable toys) and some high status, called *consumer models* (because they received rewards). The children observed the models engaging in playful behavior with several distinctive components, such as putting on a hat backward or walking and saying, "Left, right, left, right."

Then the children played with the same toys, and observers counted the number of responses patterned after each model. Children modeled their behavior more after the controller models, not the consumer models. In a traditional family, with a working father and a homemaker mother, this would produce greater identification with the father, as much psychoanalytically derived research has suggested. Other family power structures exist, of course, and were explored in this study. Whether the controller model was male or female and whether the subjects were boys or girls, the controller model was imitated more than the consumer model. Overall, the research indicates that power leads to identification (Bandura, Ross, & Ross, 1963a). Other research has confirmed that models that dispense rewards to children have more effect on children's learning than nonrewarding models do (Grusec & Mischel, 1966).

modeling
learning by observing others; also called vicarious learning

vicarious learning
learning by observing others, without being directly rewarded oneself

Models also can influence children's development of standards for behavior (cf. Mischel, 1966). How good does a performance have to be before self-congratulations are deserved? Bandura and Whalen (1966) exposed 8- to 11-year-olds to models who rewarded themselves for their scores on a bowling task, giving themselves praise and candy according to a performance criterion that varied for different groups of subjects. Some models rewarded themselves only for superior performance; others demanded of themselves moderately good performance; and lenient models rewarded themselves for all but the very worst scores. When the children later played the game themselves, they demanded very high performance before rewarding themselves only if their models had set high standards. Even the most permissive models, however, produced self-reward standards higher than a control group of children who had not observed any model. Later research (Bandura, Grusec, & Menlove, 1967a) found that children were influenced by peer models who set high standards, as well as adult models.

Aggression, too, is learned by modeling (Bandura, 1965a, 1965b, 1973). Boys and girls, age 3 to 5, watched a film in which adults played with a variety of toys, including a large inflated Bobo doll. The adult models engaged in distinctive aggressive behaviors that the children would not have seen before to provide an opportunity to learn new responses.

> First, the model laid the Bobo doll on its side, sat on it, and punched it in the nose while remarking, "Pow, right in the nose, boom, boom." The model then raised the doll and pommeled it on the head with a mallet. Each response was accompanied by the verbalization, "Sockeroo... stay down." Following the mallet aggression, the model kicked the doll about the room, and these responses were interspersed with the comment, "Fly away." Finally, the model threw rubber balls at the Bobo doll, each strike punctuated with a "Bang." This sequence of physically and verbally aggressive behavior was repeated twice. (Bandura, 1965b, pp. 590–591)

For some children, this was the end of the film (no-consequences condition). Other children saw the film continue, ending with the model being punished by another adult for his aggression (model-punished condition) or with another adult praising the aggressive model for being a "strong champion" and rewarding him with food (model-rewarded condition).

To test for modeling, the children were brought to a playroom similar to the one they had seen on the film. Observers counted the number of aggressive responses the children imitated from the film. As predicted, there was less imitation in the model-punished condition than in the other two conditions. There was no difference between the model-rewarded condition and the no-consequences condition. These modeling effects were similar for boys and for girls, although the girls behaved less aggressively overall (see Figure 13.4), consistent with other studies finding greater aggression in boys. Whether these sex differences were caused by different learning experiences for boys and girls or from the influence of biological differences such as hormones (Collaer & Hines, 1995) could not be answered from this study.

It is tempting to conclude that aggressive television is no danger as long as the villain is punished in the end. Although observing a model who is punished can sometimes inhibit aggression (Bandura, Ross, & Ross, 1963b), such a conclusion is not always warranted. Bandura included another feature in this study, which discredits this erroneous conclusion. For some children in each condition Bandura offered incentives (stickers and juice) if they could behave like the model they had seen. These children showed high levels of learning of the aggressive behaviors in all conditions. Thus punishing the villain may temporarily suppress the performance of imitative aggression, but the behaviors have been learned and may emerge later when incentive conditions change.

In his autobiographical essay, Bandura (2007) recalls that his efforts to apply his research in order to reduce the amount of violence in television programs and commercials met with considerable resistance from the television industry. Ever since

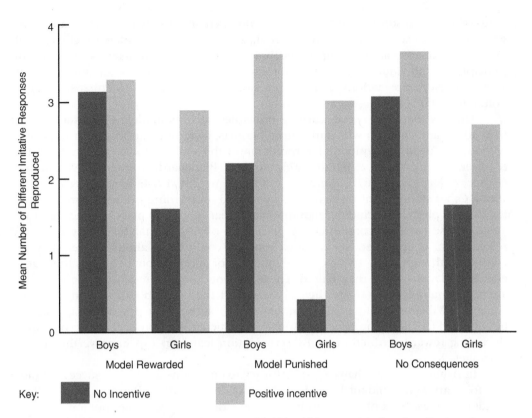

Mean number of different matching responses reproduced by children as a function of positive incentives and the model's reinforcement contingencies.

FIGURE 13.4 Modeling of Aggression

Source: From A. Bandura (1965b). Influences of models' reinforcement contingencies on the acquisition of imitative responses. *Journal of Personality and Social Psychology, 1,* 589–595. Copyright 1965 by the American Psychological Association. Reprinted by permission.

Bandura's early research, hundreds of studies using a variety of research methods have examined the relationship between TV violence and behavior. The overwhelming finding is that in the real world, as well as in the laboratory, models do teach aggression. Fortunately, as other studies show, models can also teach high standards and other positive social behaviors. A social drama television series on Mexican television uses social cognitive principles to model strategies for attaining a better life (Sabido, 1981; cited in Bandura, 2007).

Modeling is not limited to childhood. Industrial psychologists use principles of learning through modeling to train workers (Decker & Nathan, 1985). In a field experiment, female college students who were in a car were more likely to use a seat belt if the driver did so (Howell, Owen, & Nocks, 1990). Even the Philadelphia Zoo has increased the attention of visitors to its exhibits, causing them to linger instead of moving quickly on to the next by placing strategic models who expressed interest in various exhibits (Koran & Camp, 1998). Modeling is a powerful determinant of the sorts of behaviors that have traditionally interested personality theorists. Bandura's clear theoretical specification of the processes involved in modeling and other forms of learning makes a precise, verifiable theory.

THERAPY

Bandura (1961) criticizes therapy based only on talking, when known learning principles could improve outcomes. This evaluation is widely shared; cognitive behavioral approaches in therapy have been the most rapidly growing citations in recent years (Killgore, 2000), and cognitive behavioral therapy has demonstrated success in treating a variety of problems, including depression, eating disorders, and several kinds of anxiety disorders, and it even has value in treating sexual offenders and those who suffer from schizophrenia (Butler et al., 2004). Programs to increase clients' ability to avoid relapse after giving up alcohol have been devised, using social learning principles to individualize treatment for each alcoholic's high-risk situations (Annis, 1990). Efficacy expectations help people stop using marijuana (Stephens, Wertz, & Roffman, 1995).

Therapy that uses social learning principles such as modeling can successfully treat adults and children who suffer from phobias, including excessive fear of snakes, without any need for symbolic interpretation of the snake phobia (Bandura, Adams, & Beyer, 1977; Bandura & Barab, 1973; Bandura, Blanchard, & Ritter, 1969; Bandura, Grusec, & Menlove, 1967b; Bandura, Jeffery, & Wright, 1974; Bandura & Menlove, 1968). Other studies confirm that therapies based on learning principles are effective for various phobias, including agoraphobia, a fear of public places (Bandura et al., 1980). These findings contradict the prediction of psychoanalytic theory that only resolution of deep-seated unconscious conflicts could bring about a cure. They are consistent, though, with a study of the thoughts of agoraphobic people as they faced enclosed places, which they feared. These patients thought much more about their ability or inability to manage their anxiety than they did about any danger in the situation (Williams et al., 1997). Bandura (1961) argues that psychotherapy should be regarded as a learning process. More systematic application of learning principles (including reward, extinction, and discrimination learning) can improve therapeutic outcomes.

In Bandura's view, changing self-efficacy expectations are key to successful therapy for fears and avoidant behavior (Bandura, 1977, 1984a; Bandura et al., 1980). Bandura suggests that phobias result from low efficacy expectations, not low outcome expectations. A person with a fear of flying may be convinced that, if only it were possible to get on the plane, life would be improved by desirable recreational and business outcomes (high-outcome expectation). But as long as it seems impossible to board the plane and sit calmly in a seat during a flight (low-efficacy expectation), that person will not be able to fly. Bandura stated, "treatments that are most effective are built on an empowerment model. If you really want to help people, you provide them with the competencies, build a strong self-belief, and create opportunities for them to exercise those competencies" (Evans, 1989, p. 16). Therapy will succeed if it increases self-efficacy. Bandura suggests that various therapy techniques, including talk therapy, are effective for a common reason: They change dysfunctional expectancies. People avoid actions that they do not expect they are able to do (Bandura, 1986a, 1989a, 1991a). Behavioral therapies, according to Bandura, are the most efficient and effective ways to raise efficacy expectations and therefore are the treatment of choice for phobias. Other techniques may be effective but only to the extent that efficacy expectations are raised. Even depth psychoanalysis can change dysfunctional expectancies but slowly. After many months or years, a patient may come to expect that adult life will be improved because problems are seen as stemming from childhood conflicts that are considered resolved. Figure 13.5 lists some of the therapeutic alternatives for increasing efficacy expectations.

Sometimes increasing efficacy is simple but nonetheless effective. Naval cadets who were simply told that they would probably not become seasick, and that if they did, it would probably not interfere with their work, in fact experienced less seasickness as a result (Eden & Zuk, 1995). Usually, though, more extensive therapeutic intervention is required to modify efficacy expectations. Knowing its importance, researchers who evaluate the effectiveness of therapies, such as interventions to help people with disabilities, now include measures of empowerment as one desirable outcome of their interventions (Zimmerman & Warschausky, 1998). We can think of increased empowerment or efficacy as a *nonspecific* outcome of therapy, in contrast to *specific* outcomes, such as a reduction in fear (Frank, 1982; Keijsers, Schaap, & Hoogduin, 2000).

Research has made it clear that a sense of self-efficacy or empowerment, whichever we call it, has benefits in fostering healthy behaviors (among other things), and

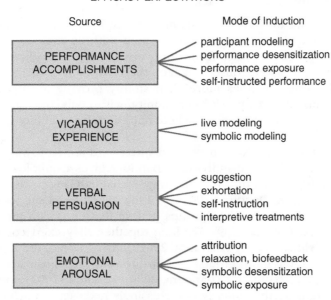

EFFICACY EXPECTATIONS

FIGURE 13.5 Changing Efficacy Expectations Through Therapy

Source: From A. Bandura (1977). Self-efficacy: Toward a unifying theory of behavioral change. *Psychological Review, 84,* 191–215. Copyright 1977 by the American Psychological Association. Reprinted by permission.

Major sources of efficacy information and the principal sources through which different modes of treatment operate.

that efficacy beliefs that are specific to the behavior targeted for change (like not smoking) make better predictors than general self-efficacy measures. As Cervone and his colleagues observe (2008), though, we have less understanding of the causes of these beliefs. As the studies mentioned above indicate, we can sometimes intervene to change beliefs, but a broader understanding of their causes would give a better context for planning interventions. Cervone and his colleagues have looked in detail at how a smoker, wanting to quit, makes self-efficacy appraisals about quitting that are particular to situations that are unique from the situational context for other people. One person may find it particularly difficult to resist the craving to smoke when at a social gathering, while for another person, it is work pressure that brings the most craving. Similarly, each smoker has some contexts in which it is easier for them to resist the urge to smoke. In their research, Cervone and colleagues (2008) found that they could temporarily increase each person's self-efficacy about quitting if they primed them by having them work on a memory task that evoked word associations related to their unique situation where resisting the urge to smoke was easier. For example, if a research subject had reported that it was easier to resist smoking when with family members, then a word association task with family-related words to remember primed them for this beneficial context, and on a subsequent self-efficacy assessment, they expressed more confidence about refraining from smoking. The same context would not necessarily be helpful for others. Some, in fact, would find that priming of these thoughts would increase their vulnerability instead. The implication is that prediction and intervention must take into account each individual's characteristic thought patterns—in other words, the approach must be idiographic. This finding is consistent with the lesson about person–situation interactions that are so important in cognitive social learning theory, including both Bandura's and Mischel's theories. It has important implications for interventions that must be tailored to individuals. Perhaps (though this would need to be tested) a smoker could put individually affirming messages or photos in a place where they would be seen, to ameliorate the temptations in situations that are high-risk for smoking, to give a temporary needed "I can do it" boost to their resolve to quit. What this research shows is that no mass-produced, one-size-fits-all message would be as effective as one individually tailored to the particular individual.

THE PERSON IN THE SOCIAL ENVIRONMENT

Many of the terms we have been using—*self* and *goals*, for example—conjure up images of the individual pursuing selfish goals with no thought of others, but that misperception probably comes from the overwhelming individualism of the culture in which most of us were raised. In fact, the environment in Bandura's three-part reciprocal determinism does more than simply provide an arena for individual accomplishments. It is a place of community, with goals and values that we share with others; of social responsibility, where our efficacy and ability can be put to work on behalf of others.

Individual self-efficacy can be, and often is, directed toward goals that benefit society, rather than the individual. Bandura gives examples of people whose sense of self-efficacy was directed that way: Mahatma Gandhi, Nelson Mandela, and Martin Luther King Jr. (Bandura, 2002). In addition, Bandura suggests that a sense of **collective efficacy** occurs when groups believe that they, as a group, can do what needs to be done (Evans, 1989). Working together, they exert collective agency, in contrast to individual agency (Bandura, 2001b). As expected, the higher the sense of collective efficacy, the more groups mobilize toward their goals and resist obstacles, and the more they accomplish (Bandura, 2000). Bandura (2002) notes that in an era of globalization, collective efficacy is increasingly necessary to achieve shared goals. In addition, he (2002) names a third type of efficacy, *proxy efficacy,* in which the individual is dependent on others to take action on his or her behalf. What the three types of efficacy beliefs share (self-efficacy, proxy efficacy, and collective efficacy), is the belief that effective action can be taken.

Bandura (1990b, 1991b) warns that individuals often fail to regulate their own behavior in ways that live up to high moral standards. They exploit others, commit aggressive acts, pollute the atmosphere, and engage in many other behaviors that violate moral standards. This is a problem of **moral disengagement** (Bandura, 1978, 2001b; Evans, 1989). People can turn off, or disengage, their moral standards by a variety of techniques: convincing themselves that the ends justify the means, using euphemistic language that does not convey the immorality of the action, comparing with far worse behavior, displacing responsibility onto others, dehumanizing the victims, and so on (Bandura, 2001b). Like defense mechanisms described by psychoanalysts, these maneuvers protect from guilt. What is more, though, the social sensitivity of this theory makes a point that intrapsychic psychoanalytic theory does not: The moral disengagement mechanisms facilitate immoral behavior against others. Measures of moral disengagement (e.g., agreeing with the statement "If people are careless where they leave things, it is their own fault if they get stolen") predict that people will commit more transgressions (Bandura et al., 2001). Bandura (1999a) argues that societies must exert social control to supplement individuals' undependable moral self-control.

Fortunately, there is not a conflict between individual efficacy and moral responsibility. In fact, Bandura (2001b) reports that children who are high in efficacy are more cooperative and helpful to others, not less.

collective efficacy

the sense that a group can do what is to be done

moral disengagement

failure to regulate one's behavior to live up to high moral standards

Summary

- Bandura's concept of *reciprocal determinism* describes the mutual influences among the person, the environment, and behavior.
- Bandura has divided learning into four processes, allowing more precise prediction of when learning will occur. These are *attentional, retention, motor reproduction*, and *motivational processes*.
- Bandura demonstrated that children are influenced by *models* of desirable and undesirable behavior.

They can learn to delay gratification or to be aggressive by watching adults in real life and on television.
- *Self-efficacy* refers to the belief that one can perform a particular behavior.
- Extensive research shows that *efficacy beliefs* affect the choice and persistence of behavior.
- Efficacy beliefs can be increased in *therapy*, and this is the mechanism by which therapy is effective, according to Bandura.

Thinking about Bandura's Theory

1. How would you describe the differences between Bandura's theory and that of Mischel (in Chapter 12)? How would you describe the similarities?
2. How would you apply research about the need for individually tailored interventions, to some behavior that you personally would like to change?
3. How would you determine whether competencies and expectancies are the causes of behavior or the effects?
4. Compare modeling with identification.
5. Do you believe that media violence contributes to aggression in the real world? What advice would you give to parents and/or lawmakers?

Study Questions

1. Diagram and explain Bandura's concept of reciprocal determinism. Discuss how this concept is different from Skinner's concept of environmental determinism.
2. What is a self-system, in Bandura's theory?
3. What is self-efficacy? How is it related to behavior?
4. What evidence has Bandura presented to indicate that self-efficacy affects the body?
5. List and explain Bandura's four processes that influence learning. Give an example of each process as it might influence a person who is learning to act like a famous athlete.
6. Summarize Bandura's research on modeling. Explain the relevance of this research for personality development.
7. Describe the evidence Bandura presented that indicates a relationship between seeing aggressive models and behaving aggressively. Why can aggression still result, even if the aggressive model is punished?
8. What has cognitive social learning theory contributed to psychotherapy?
9. How does self-efficacy change during therapy?
10. What is collective efficacy? Give an example from your own observation.
11. Explain what Bandura meant by moral disengagement. How does this process raise problems that must be solved by society, and not simply by changing individuals?

PART 5

The Humanistic Perspective

The humanistic perspective in personality theory represents a "third force" (Maslow, 1968b), established to combat the deterministic and fragmenting tendencies of psychoanalysis and of behaviorism. It began as an informal network of psychologists who, organized by Abraham Maslow, exchanged mimeographed papers representing ideas not welcome in the established psychology journals (DeCarvalho, 1990b). Several of these humanists held their first meeting in 1957 and formally organized in 1961, founding the organization now known as the Association of Humanistic Psychology (Moustakas, 1986). Among the first members were Gordon Allport, Erich Fromm, George Kelly, Abraham Maslow, Rollo May, Henry Murray, and Carl Rogers (DeCarvalho, 1990b; Wertheimer, 1978). Although Gordon Allport is generally classified as a trait psychologist, he is probably the first to have used the term *humanistic psychology*, and he was closely involved with the movement until his death (DeCarvalho, 1990c, 1990d).

The early self-proclaimed humanistic psychologists had a close affinity with Adlerians. The two humanists we consider in the following chapters, Abraham Maslow and Carl Rogers, both studied with Adler, and both acknowledged Adler's influence on their ideas, especially Adler's emphasis on holism, choice, and the intentions and subjective experience of the individual. Other significant influences included Karen Horney and Kurt Goldstein, who found that brain-injured patients can best be understood as striving whole organisms rather than as collections of part-brain processes. Furthermore, the early developments of humanistic psychology were closely connected with the academic developments in personality by Gordon Allport, George Kelly, Henry Murray, and others (Taylor, 2000).

The major distinguishing characteristics of the humanistic perspective derive from its commitment to the value of personal growth:

1. The humanistic perspective focuses on "higher," more developed, and healthier aspects of human experience and their development. Among these are spirituality, creativity, and tolerance.
2. The humanistic perspective values the subjective experience of the individual, including emotional experience. This is sometimes called a phenomenological approach.
3. Humanistic psychologists emphasize the present rather than the past or the future.
4. Humanists stress that each individual is responsible for his or her own life outcomes. No past conditions predetermine the present. A person's capacity for self-reflection enhances healthy choice.
5. The humanistic perspective seeks to apply its findings to the improvement of the human condition by changing the environment. It assumes that, given appropriate conditions, individuals will develop in a desirable direction.

Humanists describe a "true self" that contains the potential for optimal growth. Alienation from this true self results from unhealthy socialization when other people define what one should do. The view of humanism that one should be guided by one's true self, or "daimon," is an old idea, with roots in eudaemonistic philosophy as old as Aristotle (Waterman, 1990). Humanistic psychology has sometimes served as an ideology (Geller, 1982; Smith, 1990) and has been compared with religious traditions (Smith, 1985), including Hinduism and Buddhism, although these Eastern approaches describe self-actualization as requiring considerably more effort than humanism (Das, 1989). Closer to home, humanism is compatible with the individualism and optimism of U.S. culture (Fuller, 1982). In contrast to psychoanalysis, which regards instincts as dangerous and needing suppression for civilization to function, humanists assume human nature is inherently good and that suppression itself causes difficulties (Wallach, 2004).

Humanists have been criticized for underestimating the evil in humankind (Das, 1989). Some critics suggest the idea of self-actualization fosters selfishness or narcissism rather than promoting what Adler called "social interest" (Geller, 1982; Wallach & Wallach, 1983). Rogers (1982b) expressed dismay at this indictment, which he regarded as undeserved.

Humanistic psychologists are more interested in process and change than in measuring individual differences. In clinical settings, humanistic therapists prefer not to make a diagnosis if possible (e.g., Munter, 1975). By emphasizing the goals of behavior rather than the mechanisms by which behavior occurs, humanists are teleological (future oriented) as opposed to deterministic. The challenge to humanism is to be able to be rigorously, scientifically teleological (Rychlak, 1977).

Humanists are generally uncomfortable with the constraints of the traditional scientific method. Seligman and Csikszentmihalyi (2000) criticize humanistic psychologists for failure to produce a cumulative, empirical body of research. The tension between the constraints of the scientific method, on the one hand, and interest in the whole healthy human, on the other, will be felt throughout our consideration of the humanistic perspective. Ongoing efforts to add science to the humanistic emphasis on well-being are consolidating under a movement called *positive psychology* (Seligman & Csikszentmihalyi, 2000).

Study Questions

1. What are the fundamental assumptions of the humanistic perspective?
2. Should the humanistic perspective be considered a scientific approach, an ideology, or both? What considerations will be relevant as you consider this question while reading the following chapters? (Chapter 1 presents criteria for a theory that may apply.)

14

Rogers
Person-Centered Theory

Chapter Overview

ILLUSTRATIVE BIOGRAPHY
Maya Angelou

Maya Angelou, writer, actress, civil rights activist, and more, struggled with some of the issues that are central to Rogers's theory: issues of self-acceptance and esteem and fulfilling her potential despite life's challenges. Her writings and teachings inspire affirmation of life and love for all beings.

Maya Angelou is a U.S. writer of prose and poetry who has published several autobiographical works (1969, 1974, 1976, 1981, 1986, 1993, 1998, 2002). Her vivid descriptions of her own experience make it rather easy for the reader to understand life from her point of view, as Rogers urges for those who would truly understand another person. She was born in 1928 to parents who soon divorced and sent her at age 3 with her 4-year-old brother, Bailey, from Southern California to live with their grandmother in Stamps, Arkansas. They grew up in the black section of this poor community, helping their grandmother in her grocery store. From her they learned pride and discipline. Although poor, they were relatively better off than the other blacks, who picked cotton. For a time, they lived with their other grandmother and then with their mother and her boyfriend, Mr. Freeman, in St. Louis. Angelou (1969) describes being raped

Maya Angelou

by him when she was 8 years old. For this, he was convicted and sentenced to jail, but he was lynched before serving time. Afterward, Maya developed psychogenic mutism, and after a time she and Bailey were sent back to Stamps.

During her adolescence and young adulthood, Angelou lived in various places: in Stamps with her grandmother, in Los Angeles with her father, and in San Francisco with her mother (a prostitute). For a while she lived in an abandoned car in a junkyard. At 16 she had a son. She held a variety of jobs: waitress, cook, dancer, singer, prostitute, music store clerk, and San Francisco cable car operator. She worked for Martin Luther King Jr.'s Southern Christian Leadership Conference (SCLC). She has been an actress. Above all, she is a writer. She lived for a time in Ghana, where her son attended college. She married and divorced a Greek, Tosh Angelos, and later an African freedom fighter, a relationship that also ended but taught her about her African heritage. After the end of another marriage, she moved from the San Francisco Bay Area to North Carolina, where she is a professor at Wake Forest University. Throughout these varied experiences, her primary career is writing.

(continued)

(continued)

DEVELOPMENT

In Carl Rogers's theory, the most important childhood experience is to be loved, wholly and unconditionally. As a young child, only 3 years old, when she and her brother were sent from their mother's home to live with their grandmother, Maya could not have understood that this abandonment was not her fault. Experientially, it was rejection. Once in Arkansas, she experienced a loving and stable environment from a protective grandmother who loved her granddaughter with few "conditions of regard." That is, as Rogers advocates, she was loved for who she was, providing a solid foundation for self-esteem. She returned to her grandmother's home later, during a difficult time when she needed that love again. Throughout her varied careers and love relationships, Maya Angelou has tasted richly of life's opportunities, exploring many facets of her own evolving self and resisting the limitations that would be imposed if she abandoned her own voice.

DESCRIPTION

A person's sense of self is key to Rogers's theory. He describes most people as split, aware of a part of themselves that is acceptable to others but unaware of a deeper "real self" that has the potential for health and vitality. Self-esteem suffers when the real self is not affirmed by others.

Intelligent, talented as a dancer and actress as well as a writer, Maya Angelou frankly reveals her multifaceted self in autobiographical books that are also noteworthy for their artistic merit. The tension between the true self and the self that others can accept has been part of her life journey, with the real self prevailing, as Rogers would advocate. Being nonwhite in America places people at risk for alienation from the true self because of prejudice. Maya Angelou describes some of the cruelties of white children that she experienced in childhood, the sort of discrimination that assaults self-esteem. Her grandmother insisted that Angelou act courteously toward whites, even when she felt angry. Such incongruence between felt emotion and overt behavior is inconsistent with Rogers's advice, but it was adaptive under the social conditions of racial prejudice in which Maya grew up because blacks who expressed their feelings openly risked attack, even lynching. As a child, when Maya met some whites who treated her as an equal, she found that "the old habits of withdrawing into righteous indignation or lashing out furiously against insults were not applicable in this circumstance" (Angelou, 1976, p. 75). Positive regard, as Rogers would say, can be transformative.

ADJUSTMENT

Rogers's concept of process proposes that at higher levels of development, people become more spontaneous in discovering and accepting aspects of themselves and their feelings. They censor less, both from others' view and from themselves. Self-acceptance is more likely if a person has been accepted unconditionally by others (the parents, ideally; if not, then remedially in therapy). This acceptance helps a person maintain touch with the inner voice from the self, called the *organismic valuing process*.

Maya Angelou's self-disclosures, rich in emotional feeling, fit the higher levels of process (as measured by the Process Scale that is described later in this chapter). They do so in a way that is not self-indulgent, as some autobiographical works can be, but that reflects on the wisdom gained from her family and African and American culture. Her self-acceptance is clear from the

way she rejoices in even the aspects of her life that seem like mistakes—the passions that led to failed marriages, for example.

She describes seeking therapy, in young adulthood, and finding that the white male therapist had little help to offer (Angelou, 1976). She quickly concluded that the wealth and social class of this man would make it impossible for him to understand her, and she turned instead to a friend. Rogers insisted that a therapist, to be effective, must empathically understand as well as accept the client. This is more difficult when ethnicity or other differences separate the life experience of the client and therapist.

COGNITION

Accurate awareness of the true self is impeded by other people's messages about what is acceptable, what sort of self we must be to be loved by them.

Along the way, though, Angelou did not always follow her organismic valuing process; it conflicted with her need to be loved. For example, she decided to marry Thomas Allen, a bail bondsman, despite misgivings about his presumption that he could make all the important decisions. "I ignored the twinge which tried to warn me that I should stop and do some serious thinking" (Angelou, 1981, p. 103). Soon, though, another man won her heart and prevented the practical but subjectively troublesome marriage from taking place. Another relationship, too, conflicted with her inner sense, when her African lover, Sheikhali, demanded that she become less impatient, more submissive, more traditionally female (Angelou, 1986).

Often, though, Angelou was guided by her organismic valuing process, which not only made her a nonconformist but also saved her from mishap. When the singers in the cast of *Porgy and Bess* had their hair straightened in Italy, Angelou insisted that the chemicals, which burned intensely, be washed out of her hair; she was the only one who did not have her hair fall out as a consequence of this overly harsh chemical treatment. The lessons of the healthy nature of that inner voice, the organismic valuing process, are usually not quite so concrete as this!

CULTURE

In Rogers's approach, society's problems can be addressed by helping people accept their true selves. This would reduce racial prejudice and international conflict and transform educational institutions by giving students more responsibility for their intellectual explorations.

In exploring her own identity as a black American, both in the United States and in travel to Africa, Maya Angelou describes the importance of society's messages about race. In Africa, Angelou (1986) met proud black tribal leaders and learned from these models to accept being black with pride. The power of her feelings attests to the importance of the acceptance of other people as nourishment for self-actualization. In contrast, in America she encountered blatant racism. As an active participant in the civil rights movement, she has helped change that blight. She reminds us of our history, of slavery, of continuing poverty, and also of the tremendous strength that black Americans have shown and continue to show. The brutal honesty of her own self-examination is a model for a societal honesty that can also help us discover truth and healing. She asserts, "If it is true that a chain is only as strong as its weakest link, isn't it also true a society is only as healthy as its sickest citizen and only as wealthy as its most deprived? I think so" (1998, p. 108)

BIOLOGY

Rogers uses a biological metaphor when he describes self-actualization as an innate tendency to grow, to fulfill one's potential. His theory, though, does not describe the actual biological details of this process.

Like Rogers's therapy clients, Angelou wrestles with biological urges, particularly sexuality, in her journey toward self-actualization. She celebrates that aspect of selfhood and urges that it continue into old age (Angelou, 1998). Psychologists sometimes emphasize our intellectualization of the self, forgetting its biological reality. The self is biological in more than a metaphorical sense.

FINAL THOUGHTS

Rogers's theory teaches us that health requires self-understanding and self-acceptance. Maya Angelou's autobiographical self-explorations and her explicit lessons about poverty and race not only exemplify Rogers's theory, they also extend its promise.

PREVIEW: OVERVIEW OF ROGERS'S THEORY

Rogers's theory has implications for major theoretical questions, as presented in Table 14.1. Among personality theories that have major relevance for psychotherapy, Rogers's theory holds a special place. It is the one theory of therapy that was first extensively tested by empirical research. The theory is not limited to therapy but is comprehensive enough to have also been extended to other settings, including business organizations, and it offers advice to parents about how to be effective. The applied value of the theory also extends to the political arena, offering suggestions for reducing conflict.

Carl Rogers, probably the best-known spokesperson for humanistic psychology, was one of the first members of the Association of Humanistic Psychology. Like other humanists, his ideas built on Alfred Adler's belief that people have a fundamental tendency to develop in healthy directions. This is particularly understandable in that Rogers, as an intern, studied with Adler, a visiting professor, in 1927–1928 in New York (Watts, 1996).

Biography of Carl Rogers

Carl R. Rogers was born in Oak Park, Illinois (near Chicago), on January 8, 1902. The family valued hard work and fundamentalist Christianity, adhering to strict rules of behavior. "We did not dance, play cards, attend movies, smoke, drink, or show any

Table 14.1 Preview of Rogers's Theory	
Individual Differences	Rogers did not focus on stable individual differences, although individuals can be said to differ in their level of development and in the conditions they perceive must be met to be approved by others. Other researchers have recently developed scales to measure aspects of his theory that may be comparable to personality traits.
Adaptation and Adjustment	Rogers describes in detail his client-centered therapeutic technique. Individual therapy and group therapy, including encounter groups, lead to progress through stages of functioning, leading to greater openness to feelings, the present, and choice.
Cognitive Processes	Thought and feeling may be impeded by accepting others' messages about what we should be.
Culture	The person-centered approach has implications for the improvement of society, including education, marriage, work roles, and group conflict (including conflict among nations).
Biological Influences	Rogers did not consider biological factors, though his actualizing process is based on a biological metaphor.
Development	Children become alienated from the growth forces within them if they are raised with conditions of worth. Parents should raise their children with unconditional positive regard. People can change in adulthood, becoming freer.

Carl Rogers

sexual interest" (Rogers, 1967, p. 344). The family moved to a farm so the children would not encounter the temptations of close contact with others in the city or suburbs. This "gently suppressive family atmosphere" (p. 352), however, took its toll. Rogers and two siblings developed ulcers.

Rogers read at a fourth-grade level when he first entered school, and he loved to be alone and to read when he was growing up. As one might expect, his grades were always high. Chores on the family farm led to his interest in scientific farming, and he enrolled in the agriculture program at the University of Wisconsin. He was active in a church-related student volunteer movement and spent more than 6 months in China on a YMCA (Young Men's Christian Association) program for young people. This was the first time he was distant from family members and their influence. Letters at that time moved by ship, so communication took months. He grew increasingly tolerant of different customs that his parents could not challenge.

Rogers graduated from college in 1924 with a bachelor's degree in history (having lost interest in agriculture). Ironically, he had taken only one psychology course as an undergraduate. That summer he married his fiancée of nearly 2 years, Helen Elliot, a commercial artist, and they went to New York City, where they both entered graduate school. Rogers studied at Union Theological Seminary, continuing his religious interest, and also took courses at Teachers College at Columbia University and decided to do graduate work there in psychology. For his dissertation, Rogers developed a test to measure children's personality adjustment, which researchers used for many years (Cain, 1987). Carl and Helen had two children—David and Natalie, who became a person-centered expressive art therapist, further developing many of the person-centered principles that her father pioneered (Sommers-Flanagan, 2007).

Rogers worked with children for several years, first at the Rochester (New York) Society for the Prevention of Cruelty to Children, where he worked with delinquent and underprivileged youths, and later as head of the Rochester Guidance Center when it first opened in 1938. He struggled for many years over the status of psychologists within the mental health care establishment, traditionally headed by medically trained psychiatrists (Rogers, 1974c). He felt alienated from the mainstream of psychology, which emphasized animal laboratory studies. Not constrained by disciplinary loyalty, Rogers felt more akin to social workers and participated actively in their professional organizations.

In 1940, after 12 years at Rochester, Rogers and his family moved to Ohio, where he took his first academic appointment: full professor at Ohio State University. It is highly unusual for a faculty member to begin at the top academic rank, but Rogers had just published an influential book, *Clinical Treatment of the Problem Child*. In his lectures, he came to realize that his ideas about therapy were new, and he developed these ideas in another book, *Counseling and Psychotherapy* (Rogers, 1942a), which became a classic. It contained the first published verbatim transcript of a therapy case, opening this private process for study (see also Rogers, 1942b). His students learned not only in the classroom but also through practicum experience, which was revolutionary at the time (Rogers, 1967).

In 1945 Rogers went to the University of Chicago to establish a new counseling center. An active and collegial atmosphere developed there, and during this time Rogers (1951) wrote another of his influential books, *Client-Centered Therapy*. In 1957 he accepted a joint appointment in psychology and psychiatry at the University of Wisconsin, where he found a competitive and nonsupportive atmosphere that conflicted with his own humanistic convictions. He protested in 1963 by resigning his appointment in the Department of Psychology, retaining his position in psychiatry and suggesting a more humanistic approach to education (Rogers, 1969).

His next move was away from university life. In 1964 he went to the Western Behavioral Sciences Institute in La Jolla, California. With others, he formed the Center for Studies of the Person, where he explored encounter groups and sensitivity training. According to one biographer, these group experiences were times of personal exploration and problems for Rogers (Cohen, 1997). His efforts turned, too, to international issues of peace and conflict resolution in Central America, South Africa, Northern Ireland, and the Soviet Union (Bondarenko, 1999).

Rogers was a leader in professional organizations throughout his career. He served as president of the American Association for Applied Psychology (1944–1945) and of the American Psychological Association (1946–1947). He received two prestigious awards from the American Psychological Association: the Distinguished Scientific Contribution Award in 1956 (American Psychological Association, 1957) and the first Distinguished Professional Contribution Award in 1972 (American Psychological Association, 1973). He was the first (and as of 1987, only) psychologist to receive both honors (Cain, 1987). Rogers was also nominated for the Nobel Peace Prize in 1987. A little-known fact is that Rogers, like some other prestigious psychologists, was recruited by the Central Intelligence Agency to provide scientific advice and respectability during the tense international period following World War II, though the details of his activity are subject to conjecture (Demanchick & Kirschenbaum, 2008). Rogers died in 1987, at age 85, of a heart attack.

THE ACTUALIZING TENDENCY

Rogers (1961) theorized that all motivation is subsumed under a fundamental process, the **actualizing tendency**, that is:

> the directional trend which is evident in all organic and human life—the urge to expand, extend, develop, mature—the tendency to express and activate all the capacities of the organism, or the self. (p. 351)

actualizing tendency
the force for growth and development that is innate in all organisms

The broad, general tendency toward development in nature he called the *formative tendency*. He contrasted it with a tendency toward randomness (entropy) and suggested that the tendency to move from simpler to more complex forms is just as powerful in nature (Rogers, 1979).

The specific human aspect of the formative tendency is the actualizing tendency. It includes not only biological motivations, such as hunger and thirst, but also "higher" human motivations, leading to differentiation (complexity), independence, and social responsibility. We do not behave irrationally, but rather toward goals of enhanced development (Rogers, 1983). For Rogers (1986a), the motivation intrinsic to each person is basically good and healthy. Contrasted with the more negative views of human motivation that prevail in psychoanalysis, Christianity, and educational institutions, Rogers's optimism "is profoundly radical" (p. 127).

The Organismic Valuing Process

A self-actualizing person is in touch with inner experience that is inherently growth producing, the **organismic valuing process**. It is a subconscious guide that draws the person toward experiences that produce growth and away from those that inhibit it. Even activities that might seem fun or profitable to conscious experience will be avoided if they feel wrong to this inner guide. This inner valuing process is natural in the infant, who values food and security. Although this is not usually emphasized, some have interpreted Rogers's organismic valuing process in terms of the body, interpreting physical symptoms and healthy functioning as evidence of contact with the organismic valuing process (Fernald, 2000).

organismic valuing process
inner sense within a person, which guides him or her in the directions of growth and health

With development, people unfortunately substitute external rules for inner experience as they learn values from society that interfere with psychological development (Rogers, 1964). When people are unhealthy and immature, or even criminals, Rogers blamed social forces that cause them to lose touch with inner growth processes. Messages from parents, schools, and even psychoanalysts repeatedly warn that feelings are bad, and so people come to distrust their inner feelings.

The Fully Functioning Person

A person who pays attention to the organismic valuing process is self-actualizing or **fully functioning**. To be in that state, a person must tune out adverse socialization messages. A potentially creative person may lose touch with that capacity by being

fully functioning
Rogers's term for a mentally healthy person

taught that idle drawing is a waste of time. Similarly, a potentially empathic person may lose touch with that capacity by being taught that showing feelings is a sign of weakness.

The person who is fully functioning, who is most healthy, has several characteristics, which Rogers lists. These characteristics can be interpreted as signs of mental health.

OPENNESS TO EXPERIENCE The fully functioning person is *open to experience*, receptive to the subjective and objective happenings of life. Others may censor experience through defenses (e.g., not recognizing an insult or the anger it provokes). In contrast, the fully functioning person accurately perceives such events. In this sense, one might describe such a person as having an expanded consciousness including tolerance for ambiguity.

EXISTENTIAL LIVING A person open to experience shows "an increasing tendency to live fully in each moment" (Rogers, 1961, p. 188). Each moment allows the real self to emerge, possibly changed by new experience. Part of the person is participating in each moment of existential living, but part is an observer of the process. The self is experienced as a fluid process rather than a fixed entity.

ORGANISMIC TRUST A person with *organismic trust* (also called the "organismic valuing process," described more fully later in this chapter) relies on inner experience at each moment to guide behavior. This experience provides accurate perception of inner needs and emotions and of the external social situation. The individual integrates all these facets of experience and comes to an inner sense of what is right for him or her, not depending on outside authorities to say what is right.

EXPERIENTIAL FREEDOM The fully functioning person experiences freedom, in each moment, to choose. Such *experiential freedom* is subjective and does not deny there is determinism in the world. Viktor Frankl described concentration camp prisoners, each free to choose at least an attitude toward the experiences of life (Rogers, 1969). In most circumstances, there is considerable behavioral freedom as well.

CREATIVITY The fully functioning person lives *creatively*. He or she finds new ways of living at each moment, instead of being locked into past, rigid patterns. Rogers (1961a, p. 194) described fully functioning humans as the best able to adapt to new conditions, the "vanguard of human evolution."

Subjective Experience and Science

Rogers experienced a conflict between the model of science, in which the therapy client would be viewed objectively, and his experience as a therapist, in which a subjective stance worked better (Barresi, 1999; Rogers, 1955). In his later writing, Rogers (1973, 1979, 1980) went further in his emphasis on subjectivity and suggested that he might have underestimated the "mystical, spiritual dimension" of experience. Participants in his workshops sometimes described the experience in terms of spirituality (Benjamin & Looby, 1998; Van Kalmthout, 1995). In this vein, a scale measuring belief in Transcendental Mental Powers has been developed from Rogers's theory (Cartwright, 1989).

Values are explicitly important in Rogers's theory (DeCarvalho, 1989), as in humanistic theory generally. Rogers (1964) argued that values emerge for each individual, and for humankind as a whole, from the process of experiencing. This position offends those who hold that science should be value free and others who regard it as an invitation to selfishness, in which no one is held to an external standard of right and wrong. His approach challenges us to consider the role of subjectivity and values within a scientific framework, even in areas that seem to contradict science.

THE SELF

One of the legacies of Rogers's work has been increased recognition that self-esteem is important. Much of personality growth, including that occurring in therapy, involves changes in the self. Rogers hesitated to introduce this term into his theory, but clients would say, for example, "I'm not sure I'm being my real self." Walter Mischel (1992), reviewing the history of the study of personality, credited Carl Rogers with his influential recognition of the importance of the self as an organizing unit of personality.

The self that is healthy, though, is not the self that is carefully built up by success and approved by others. That self can, in fact, be an impediment to health (Van Kalmthout, 1995). We are familiar with the terms *ideal self* and *real self* from psychoanalytic theory (especially Karen Horney's theory). Rogers used these terms too. He observed that many people experience a discrepancy between the two. They wish to be like the **ideal self**; perhaps they even pretend to be like it, but that is a path to disturbance. The **real self** is different; it contains a person's true or real qualities, including the actualizing tendency, and leads to health. Rogers used the term *incongruence* to describe the experience of conflict between the real self and the ideal self. When a person is incongruent, he or she experiences the real self as threatening, and uses defense mechanisms that distort and deny experience, trying to be like the ideal self. "Me? Angry? Never!"

Most people use the term *self-actualization* loosely to refer to the healthy actualizing process. Rogers (1951) himself did not distinguish between *self-actualization* and *actualization* in his early work. Later, however, he described self-actualization as a "subaspect" of the actualization process. If the person has forsaken the real self, actualization and self-actualization are in conflict. A phony self-actualization impedes the healthy actualization process. *Self-actualization*, in the more precise sense of the term, is an unhealthy tendency when a person is in a state of incongruence because the self that is being actualized is defined by society, not by the individual. Actualization, the more general tendency, is always healthy (Ford & Maas, 1989; Rogers, 1959).

ideal self
what a person feels he or she ought to be like

real self
the self that contains the actualizing tendency

DEVELOPMENT

To understand why incongruence occurs, consider how the self-concept develops. Adults tell children to "be good." Rogers described such pressures in his own childhood: Be hardworking, be respectful to adults, and so forth. "Bad" behavior leads to punishment or is simply ignored. Rogers called this kind of socialization *conditional positive regard*. That is, parents will love (regard positively) children only to the extent that the children live up to their **conditions of worth**. As a result of this socialization, children disown the "bad" qualities. Unfortunately, some of the "bad" qualities parents discourage are really healthy potentials.

Parents have different styles of raising their children. Some, called *authoritarian parents*, place a high priority on respect and obedience (Baumrind, 1971). Although well intentioned, such a style of parenting works against the child's inherent tendency toward self-actualization. College students who report that their parents used authoritarian parenting techniques were less self-actualized than those whose parents gave them direction without harsh restrictions, an *authoritative parenting style* (Dominguez & Carton, 1997).

A growth-producing parenting style is to give the child **unconditional positive regard**, which means loving the child regardless of his or her behavior. This allows the child to explore all his or her potentials. Because Rogers viewed human beings as essentially good, the outcome is the development of a fully functioning person. Critics argue that such advice is impractical and neglectful. Indeed, parents who have humanistic values are more likely to have children who report experimenting with drugs, although they are unlikely to engage in delinquent behaviors (Garnier & Stein, 1998). Surely, Rogers did not advocate abdicating parental responsibilities to direct and teach their children. His daughter, Natalie, described her father as someone who listened to her experiences, but who set limits. She told

conditions of worth
the expectations a person must live up to before receiving respect and love

unconditional positive regard
accepting and valuing a person without requiring particular behaviors as a prerequisite

an interviewer, "I think the permissiveness often has been misunderstood. He said that any thoughts and feelings are OK, but not all behavior is acceptable. Unless that is really made clear, both in the theory and in the practice, it can be disastrous" (Sommers-Flanagan, 2007).

Development of Creativity

Creativity emerges from healthy development. Rogers (1954) considered what sort of environment encourages creativity. Creativity requires three psychological qualities: "openness to experience, an internal locus of evaluation, and the ability to toy with elements and concepts" (Harrington, Block, & Block, 1987). Harrington and colleagues studied 106 children and their parents from preschool through adolescence. Results confirmed predictions based on Rogers's ideas. Parents of preschool children who about a decade later were creative agreed with statements such as these:

> "I respect my child's opinions and encourage him to express them."
>
> "I encourage my child to be curious, to explore and question things."

They disagreed with statements such as these:

> "I do not allow my child to get angry with me."
>
> "I feel my child is a bit of a disappointment to me."

In the research laboratory, parents taught tasks to their preschoolers. Creativity-facilitating parents encouraged and praised their children. Parents who criticized and who controlled or structured the tasks instead of allowing the child to work independently raised less creative children. Because the study was correlational, we cannot be certain whether the parents caused their children to become creative or not. For example, the children may have already been different, causing the parents to behave differently, rather than vice versa.

Later in life, too, exposure to Rogerian-type leadership enhances creativity. Students at a technological university were assigned to groups with a Rogerian leader, a structured leader, or a considerate leader, and they worked on an engineering problem, designing a way to provide fresh water to their dog, who was left at home while the family went on a vacation. The group with Rogerian leadership solved the problem more creatively (Fodor & Roffe-Steinrotter, 1998).

THERAPY

Not everyone is fortunate enough to have been raised by ideal accepting parents and to have developed according to the innate actualizing potential. Can remedial therapy help overcome unhealthy tendencies? Carl Rogers developed a new therapeutic approach, and he pioneered the scientific investigation of the effectiveness of therapy. Surveys of therapists over a span of a quarter century (Cook, Biyanova, & Coyne, 2009; Smith, 1982) find Rogers named the most influential on their practice.

Client-Centered Therapy

Rogers considered therapy to be an experience that could help people reconnect with their organismic valuing process, which guides healthy development. In contrast to therapies based on the medical model, which objectifies those who are to be treated and presumes that wisdom comes from the authority of the therapist (Kahn, 1999), Rogerian therapy is a noncoercive approach that honors the client's experience.

Rogers described an early encounter when he was still following his training in psychoanalytic theory. He helped a pyromaniac boy discover that his motivation for setting fires stemmed from sexual desire, only to be crushed when this insight did not prevent recurrence of the behavior. Psychoanalysis maintained that *insight* brought a cure; clinical experience taught otherwise. And so, Rogers dropped theoretical formulas and instead listened to what his clients were telling him. Rogers called his technique **client-centered therapy**.

client-centered therapy
therapy based on the belief that the person seeking help is the best judge of the direction that will lead to growth

Table 14.2 Necessary and Sufficient Conditions for Therapeutic Process

1. Two persons are in psychological contact.
2. The first, whom we shall term the client, is in a state of incongruence, being vulnerable or anxious.
3. The second person, whom we shall term the therapist, is congruent or integrated in the relationship.
4. The therapist experiences unconditional positive regard for the client.
5. The therapist experiences an empathic understanding of the client's internal frame of reference and endeavors to communicate this experience to the client.
6. The communication to the client of the therapist's empathic understanding and unconditional positive regard is to a minimal degree achieved.

Source: From Rogers (1957a).

Drawing on his therapeutic experience, Rogers (1957a) listed six conditions that lead to therapeutic progress (see Table 14.2). Foremost among these conditions were *unconditional positive regard, congruence,* and *empathic understanding,* conditions he regarded as necessary and sufficient for therapeutic progress. His emphasis on the relationship between the client and the therapist was revolutionary, but has since become generally accepted within the therapeutic community, even by those who practice therapies called by other names (Goldfried, 2007).

UNCONDITIONAL POSITIVE REGARD Rogers found that clients are most likely to make progress when they feel accepted by the therapist. Obviously, a therapist cannot approve of maladaptive behaviors. Yet it is possible to convey a feeling of warmth and acceptance, of *unconditional positive regard,* offering the client acceptance as a person. (This is the same quality that Rogers advocated for effective parenting, described earlier.)

Rogers expressed his **prizing** (another term for unconditional positive regard) of a patient, Gloria, in a training film when he said to her, "You look to me like a pretty nice daughter" (Shostrom, 1965). Feeling positively valued by the therapist, the client becomes more accepting of herself. Aspects of the real self that were previously repressed because of childhood conditions of worth become available. The client begins to trust the inner organismic valuing process, and therapeutic progress ensues.

What about clients whose behavior is despicable? How is a therapist to prize a wife batterer, for example? The key is to distinguish between the behavior and the person. The therapist suspends judgment about the client's behavior and feelings, while prizing the whole person (Weaver, 2008). Without this unconditional positive regard, a judgmental attitude would impede the deeper personality change that therapy can facilitate. Of the three conditions for effective therapy, one therapist argues that unconditional positive regard is the most important one; the other two conditions simply make it credible (Wilkins, 2000). If the therapist does not seem to be genuine (congruence) or does not seem to understand the client emotionally, then positive regard may not be credible. In fact, in the unusual case where a therapist simply does not like the client, Rogers recommended that the therapist acknowledge anger or even dislike of the client rather than pretend acceptance. That sort of dishonesty would violate the second condition of effective psychotherapy.

CONGRUENCE A second condition for successful psychotherapy is **congruence** in the interaction. That is, the therapist's behavior should match his or her inner experience. The therapist should be genuine and to a large extent transparent, so the client sees the therapist's experience rather than only a facade or mask that hides the real person of the therapist. As one expert explained it, "Through the therapist's willingness to risk [being genuine in the relationship], and his or her confidence in the client, the therapist makes it easier for the client to take the plunge into the stream of experiencing" (Friedman, 1994, p. 50). How can one expect the client to become a person open to experience if the therapist is not? This congruency or genuineness or authenticity does not mean, though, that the therapist passively lets every thought be known; it is an active disclosure, taking the client's well-being into consideration (Tudor & Worrall, 1994). Genuineness becomes easier as a therapist matures (Goldfried, 2007).

prizing
characteristic of a good therapist, which involves positively valuing the client; also called unconditional positive regard

congruence
a feeling of consistency between the real self and the ideal self

EMPATHIC UNDERSTANDING A third condition for successful psychotherapy is **empathic understanding**. That is, the therapist should understand the experience of the client. Whereas other approaches seek to reduce a client's pain, the client-centered approach also seeks to share that experience empathically (Gruen, 1998). Largely because of Rogers, empathy has become a major topic of discussion among therapists (Bohart & Greenberg, 1997). Empathic understanding is easier to teach than the other two therapeutic requirements, according to Rogers. It often involves restating the client's communications in a way that has been criticized as "parroting" plus a change of pronoun. (Client: "I am sad." Therapist: "You feel sad.") The criticism is too hasty. Empathic understanding involves more than mechanical restatement. Consider Rogers's reflection of one client's statement, "[I]t would be much better for me to ...": he reflected back "'I need and must have...,' thus placing more emphasis on the client's underlying need" and taking her deeper into experience that she brought as unfinished business from her past (Gundrum, Lietaer, & Van Hees-Matthijssen, 1999, p. 472). We may think of a person as having many inner voices that aren't integrated. A depressed patient, for example, may voice self-doubt (perhaps internalized from critical parents) and also have a more self-assertive voice that speaks in self-defense. Empathic reflection by the therapist helps the client to attend to neglected aspects within the self; the depressed client, for example, may benefit by increasing strength of the self-assertive voice that was previously neglected (Goldsmith et al., 2008).

One client said of her therapist, "Jack understood me more than I understood me" (Myers, 2000, p. 162). Research suggests that it is not so much what the therapist does but rather the client's perception of being understood empathically that matters (Hill & Corbett, 1993). Because of the empathic response of the therapist, the client is treated as "a self that is an authentic source of experience" (Bohart & Greenberg, 1997, p. 6), and thus comes to accept as valid his or her own experience.

Empathy as a counseling technique may need to be augmented when the counselor and client come from different cultural backgrounds. In many cases, minority clients, treated by therapists from the majority white culture, experience "empathic failure" and so do not form effective working alliances with the therapist (Jenkins, 1997). Rogers conducted a videotaped therapy demonstration with a black man in the 1970s that has been used as a training film, demonstrating that effective therapy can be conducted across racial lines (Moodley, 2000). Some strategies for dealing with cultural differences are selecting counselors whose background matches that of their clientele, additional training about cultural issues, and explicitly asking clients about their culture (Laungani, 1997; Scott & Borodovsky, 1990).

Research on Therapy

The concepts in Rogers's theory are challenging to study scientifically. Self-actualization is an elusive potentiality. Empathy and genuineness refer to phenomena within an individual; how is an observer to record them? Despite these formidable challenges, Rogers (1959) was committed to empirical research and criticized therapists who did not test their theories (Rogers, 1968, 1986a).

Rogers described his theoretical constructs with as much precision as possible to make it possible for them to be operationally defined, focusing on what was immediately present (1986a). Rogers especially objected to interpretations of the therapeutic relationship in terms of transference (Bohart, 1991; Rogers, 1986c; Weinrach, 1991), which denies the real and present relationship between the client and the therapist. Rogers tape-recorded therapy sessions to open the process for examination by researchers, as well as to provide training material for therapists-to-be. This opening of therapy does, of course, require the consent of the client. Even with that consent, publicizing therapeutic material brings risks of adverse consequences for the client and those in her life, as the daughter of Rogers's famous patient, Gloria, testifies (Burry, 2008).

Guided by his vision, many of Rogers's students and colleagues developed measuring instruments to study the events that occur during therapy (Hill & Corbett, 1993). Using these instruments, judges code the behaviors of the therapist and of the client. For example, are feelings expressed? What tone of voice is used? Other instruments ask the client and the therapist to describe their experiences of therapy sessions. Scales to assess therapist effectiveness made it possible to evaluate and improve counselor training programs (Carkhuff, 1969; Ivey, 1971).

Early research supported Rogers's "necessary and sufficient conditions" for therapeutic progress. Rogers asserted that if these conditions (unconditional positive regard, congruence, and empathic understanding) were present, regardless of the theoretical orientation of the therapist, progress would occur. He was correct. Therapists from other orientations produce these same conditions, to a large extent, and the three conditions lead to improvement in therapy (Keijsers, Schaap, & Hoogduin, 2000).

According to some researchers, other factors may also be necessary (Hill & Corbett, 1993; Lockhart, 1984). For example, it may be helpful to more actively encourage clients to reflect consciously on their goals and evaluate means of reaching them (Watson & Rennie, 1994). Or, according to one critic, there may be therapies that need to emphasize new knowledge or new experiences that don't require the conditions that Rogers outlined (Mahrer, 2007).

Rogers and other therapists modeled their therapeutic techniques in instructional films. Rogers was, as we would expect, distinctively different from other therapists in what he said to clients in these films (Essig & Russell, 1990; Mahrer et al., 1988). He frequently reflected or restated what the client said, and he often offered encouragement, approval, and reassurance (Lee & Uhlemann, 1984). He offered more interpretation than we might expect (Weinrach, 1990; but see the rebuttal by Bohart, 1991), and he was not always so nondirective as client-centered therapy typically is portrayed (Bowen, 1996). In one case, for example, he was uncharacteristically directive in his counseling of a black man, thereby helping the client to express his anger about society's mistreatment of him, aided by Rogers's empathic connection with that unexpressed anger (Brodley, 1996).

Detailed microanalyses of client and therapist behavior help us understand how therapists can get clients to focus on the internal subjective experiences that are critical to growth (Wiseman & Rice, 1989). Rogers and other client-centered therapists do a great deal of reflection of clients' statements, as expected (Tomori & Bavelas, 2007). Therapy sessions that therapists rate as indicating improvement tend to be preceded by sessions in which there is a particularly positive emotional bond between therapist and client and are followed by sessions in which the client reports insight (Sexton, 1993). The most important question, though, is whether the effects of therapy carry over to life after therapy.

Rogers examined the outcomes as well as the process of psychotherapy. In one study, self-concept was measured by a Q-technique. Subjects sorted 100 self-perception statements—for example, "I often feel resentful," "I feel relaxed and nothing really bothers me"—into nine piles, indicating how well the statements described themselves. These sortings were done for the actual self (as perceived by the subject) and for the ideal self (how the subject would like to be). Before therapy, the real self and the ideal self were quite different ($r = -0.47$). After therapy, they were much more similar ($r = 0.59$). Thus therapy produced greater self-acceptance (Butler & Haigh, 1954). This heightened self-acceptance sprang from changes in both the actual self, which came to have more desirable qualities, and the ideal self, which came to include previously unappreciated qualities that the person already possessed.

Personality change in psychotherapy occurs gradually. Rogers devised a way of measuring the types of changes that occur in psychotherapy: a Process Scale that constitutes a seven-stage description of the process of change. At the outset of therapy, the client generally experiences problems in the past and external to the self. As therapy progresses, the client experiences a greater immediacy and ownership of experience. These changes are carried over to life outside the consulting room, so the client increasingly lives according to the organismic valuing process rather than according to rigid ideas that may not correspond well to subjective experience.

Humanistic therapists have a vision of therapy that emphasizes healthy growth from the subjective point of view of the client. A client should come to feel more free, more self-accepting, more willing to experience life as it presents itself. Such goals are not shared by all therapies, and they are not well represented as outcome criteria in studies that compare the effectiveness of various types of therapy, so the contributions of humanistic therapy may be underestimated by such studies (Bohart, O'Hara, & Leitner, 1998; Rychlak, 1998).

Encounter Groups

Therapeutic change may be brought about in groups, as well as in individual psychotherapy. Groups often serve as growth-enhancing experiences for healthy people rather than as a means of treatment for those with emotional problems.

encounter group

growth-enhancing technique in which a group of people openly and honestly express their feelings and opinions

facilitator

the leader of an encounter group

Rogers offered **encounter groups** to provide experiences that would produce personal growth and improve interpersonal functioning. The groups have a **facilitator**, who directs participants. Rogers (1970) preferred a relatively unstructured format, opening his groups with something as simple as the statement, "Here we are. We can make of this group experience exactly what we wish" (pp. 46–47). Too much structure through highly programmed group exercises, according to Rogers, is essentially a power play by the group leader. It keeps the locus of responsibility for the group with the leader instead of sharing it with the members.

Betty Meador (in Rogers, 1970) reported the study of an encounter group that met for 16 hours over an intensive weekend. Each of the eight participants was filmed in ten 2-minute segments, two during each of the five sessions. On the average, participants moved up one and a half stages on the Rogers's Process Scale during this weekend. Of course, these data do not address the question of whether this change affected behavior when participants returned to their everyday lives.

Treatment groups have become accepted modes of intervention for a variety of personal problems, including drug and alcohol abuse. Just as acceptance by a therapist facilitates change in individual psychotherapy, acceptance by group members promotes healing. Acceptance by other group members can help alcoholics acknowledge their drinking problem, an important first step toward change (Rugel & Barry, 1990).

OTHER APPLICATIONS

Principles that guide client-centered therapy have also been applied outside of the therapy setting, to a greater extent than some other therapy traditions (Kahn, 1996). Rogers (1986a, p. 138) commented, "I find a deep satisfaction in discovering that some of my basic learnings in psychotherapy apply to other areas of life." Let us examine some of these other areas.

Humanistic Education

person-centered

Rogers's orientation to therapy and education, which focuses on the experience of the client or student rather than the therapist or teacher

Rogers wrote at length about the implications of his **person-centered** approach for education (DeCarvalho, 1991b; Rogers, 1957b, 1969, 1974a, 1974b). (Outside of therapy the term *person centered* is more appropriate than *client centered*.) Humanistic education has implications for both the relationship between teacher and student and the content of education. It nurtures the personal as well as professional development of unique individuals (Shapiro, 1997, 1998).

Traditionally, the teacher decides what should be learned, and students are treated as though they would do nothing productive if not motivated by external demands and threats of poor grades. Such an atmosphere can undermine the motivation of even competent, creative scholars such as Albert Einstein (Rogers, 1969). By focusing on the authority of the teacher, rather than on the needs and experience of the learner, traditional education violates the fundamental value advocated by Rogers: namely, making each person the evaluator and guide to his or her own experience.

In the ideal classroom, the authority of the teacher would be reduced. A better term for that new role would be *facilitator of education*, someone who would provide resources to students based on students' interests. In a humanistic educational environment, the teacher would have the characteristics of an effective therapist (DeCarvalho, 1991b; Roscoe & Peterson, 1982).

Traditional education ignores feelings and distrusts experiential learning (Rogers, 1973, 1987). Rogers argued that feelings are part of the whole person and to educate only the mind is unnecessarily limiting. This contrasts with the emphasis on content, such as that exemplified by Skinner, who emphasized educational technology (Rogers & Skinner, 1956). Humanistically oriented educators use such strategies as values clarification exercises (Richards & Combs, 1992). Another strategy is the use of narratives—for example, teaching students about gerontology through the stories of older people, an approach that engages students emotionally as well as intellectually (Gattuso & Saw, 1998). Some even claim that "the *real* purpose of higher education [is to develop] self-actualizing personalities" (Cangemi, 1984, p. 51).

Marriage and Relationships

Rogers's humanistic approach also has implications for relationships. He noted that modern marriage occurs in a new context, compared to past generations, in which people live longer, have more choice to limit family size, face less stigma if divorced, have changes in gender role expectations, and have greater sexual freedom (Rogers, 1977). Rogers advocated a person-centered relationship with mutual trust, tolerance of separate as well as shared interests, and focus on the uniqueness of each partner.

Humanistic openness may produce more mature interaction, but there are risks (as in any change). Partners may form **satellite relationships**, significant secondary relationships that sometimes involve extramarital sex. Although these seem, to the individuals who choose them, to meet significant growth needs, they obviously challenge trust and risk jealousy.

satellite relationships
side relationships, which supplement a person's primary committed relationship

Among dating couples, being loved and supported helps partners to grow toward self-actualization, becoming closer to their ideals (Ruvolo & Brennan, 1997). In several studies, Duncan Cramer (1985, 1986, 1990a, 1990b) has examined both romantic relationships and friendship. These studies support the growth-producing qualities of relationships identified by Rogers. Cramer (1990a) reported that high school and college students had higher self-esteem if their romantic partners, and also their friends, possessed the characteristics that Rogers identified as facilitating growth (unconditional acceptance, empathy, and congruence) (Cramer, 1990b). Friends appear able to be relatively directive—that is, giving advice—while still having growth-facilitating qualities, in contrast to the nondirective mode advocated by person-centered therapists (Cramer, 1986). Having a friendship characterized by understanding, congruence, and unconditional acceptance is (at least among women) correlated with higher scores on measures of psychological adjustment and self-esteem (Cramer, 1985). Of course, in correlational studies, the direction of causality is debatable. Perhaps psychological adjustment produces better friendships rather than the other way around.

Business

Rogers and other humanistic psychologists have also influenced industrial-organizational psychology, providing business managers with a model to guide their dealings with employees (Massarik, 1992). Rogers reasoned that relationships between administration and staff, like those between therapist and client, parent and child, and teacher and student, will be growth promoting if the three characteristics of genuineness (congruence), acceptance (prizing), and empathic understanding are present (Rogers, 1979). Traditional authority patterns must change. In addition to encounter groups (described earlier), Rogers described an industrial experiment in sharing power and decision making with workers that was so successful it boosted the profit margin substantially, so much so that it was regarded as a trade secret (Rogers, 1977, pp. 101–102).

Political Conflict, War, and Peace

With his focus on the individual person and abhorrence of authority, Rogers presented a perspective that was essentially democratic (Kahn, 1999). In the political realm, Rogers (1982a) suggested ways of dealing with conflict through encounter groups: to facilitate discussions between the National Health Council, made up of representatives of medical professions, and poor people concerned with their access to health care; in Northern Ireland, between Protestants and Catholics in their long-standing conflict; and in 1985, when government officials, academicians, and others from 17 countries met in Austria, aiming to reduce political tensions (Rogers, 1986b). Rogers suggested that psychological principles, including those discovered in his encounter groups, could even help avert the threat of nuclear annihilation (Rogers & Ryback, 1984).

CRITICISMS OF ROGERS'S THEORY

Although it has enthusiastic supporters, and has provided a solid research foundation for psychotherapy, Rogers's theory has been dismissed by others as naive about human nature. Carl Rogers the therapist reminds some of Fred Rogers, the sensitive, accepting neighbor on children's television (Palmer & Carr, 1991). Such optimism about people attracts many but critics attack Rogers's naïveté in failing to acknowledge the reality of evil in human nature (Friedman, 1982, 1994; May, 1982; Rogers, 1982b). Existential theorist and therapist Rollo May blames the humanistic movement in general for this failure, and Rogers in particular for repeatedly referring to people's supposed innate goodness (Hoffman, 2009). Rogers has clearly hit a deep chord in our fundamental assumptions about human nature.

Summary

- Carl Rogers offered a theory in which the person actively seeks higher development, motivated by the *actualizing tendency* rather than being passively determined by external forces.
- He described the characteristics of a healthy person, whom he called a *fully functioning person*.
- His client-centered therapy emphasized three factors that contribute to therapeutic success: *unconditional positive regard, congruence*, and *empathic understanding*.

- Rogers specified his theoretical constructs in ways that could be measured, so the theory could be *empirically verified*. Furthermore, he conducted groundbreaking research on the therapeutic process.
- Rogers elaborated on the change process in therapy, groups, education, and political conflict.
- One issue that troubles critics is whether people are innately good, to the extent that Rogers assumes.

Thinking about Rogers's Theory

1. Discuss the experience of freedom, contrasting Carl Rogers's concept of experiential freedom with B. F. Skinner's criticism of the concept of free will.
2. Imagine you are talking to a person who is about to become a parent, who asks your advice about how to raise a well-adjusted child. Based on Rogers's theory, what would you recommend? Give examples of particular issues that are likely to become potential problems in your cultural setting. How would you recommend resolving them?
3. Do you believe it is important for a therapist to come from the same ethnic and cultural background as the client? If someone from another background were to be your

therapist, what would it be important for that therapist to understand to be able to act with empathy toward you?
4. Recall Adler's concept of social interest. Do you agree that Rogers's concept of unconditional positive regard is similar to saying that a therapist should have an attitude of social interest toward the client (cf. Watts, 1996)?
5. What values from Rogers's theory are relevant to marriage and other intimate relationships? How do your own ethical beliefs compare with the implications of these values?
6. Do you believe that political conflict can be reduced by using encounter groups or other humanistic techniques? Or does this suggestion reflect political naïveté?

Study Questions

1. Explain what Rogers meant by the actualizing tendency.
2. Discuss Rogers's idea that people are basically good, and the criticism this optimism has elicited.
3. Describe the organismic valuing process. Give an example.

4. List and explain the characteristics of a fully functioning person.
5. Discuss Rogers's attitude toward subjective experience.
6. Explain how Rogers used the concept of self to understand personal growth.

7. Explain Rogers's concept of congruence and incongruence. Include the terms *real self* and *ideal self* in your discussion. What are the implications for psychological well-being?

8. Describe the confusion between self-actualization and actualization.

9. What does it mean to be raised with unconditional positive regard? What are the effects of such child rearing?

10. What sort of environment encourages the development of creativity?

11. Why is Rogers's theory called client centered?

12. List and explain the three major conditions necessary for therapeutic progress.

13. Discuss the difficulties of therapists in using empathy as a counseling technique when treating clients with different backgrounds from their own.

14. Describe research on client-centered therapy.

15. Describe an encounter-group experience. List some of the uses of these groups.

16. Describe Rogers's approach to education. Why is it called a person-centered approach?

17. How did Rogers's humanistic approach influence his beliefs about marriage and relationships? What are satellite relationships?

18. Describe the implications of Rogers's approach for business.

19. Describe the application of Rogers's theory to problems of international tensions.

20. Summarize the major criticisms of Rogers's theory of personality.

21. Describe research outside of the clinical setting that investigates Rogers's theory.

15

Maslow and His Legacy
Need Hierarchy Theory and Positive Psychology

ILLUSTRATIVE BIOGRAPHY
David Pelzer

Abraham Maslow's theory describes an ordered sequence of human needs. When each one is met, the person may move to a higher level of motivation, ultimately reaching the highest level (self-actualization). Deprivation of a need holds one back. Positive psychology, building on the foundation laid by Maslow and other humanists, describes being drawn toward what will bring happiness. The case of David Pelzer is an inspirational life in which the force to move upward to higher potential is shown to be extraordinary because he has endured unspeakable childhood abuses and still found the courage to move on.

David Pelzer grew up in an abusive home in Daly City, just south of San Francisco, California. His alcoholic and mentally disturbed mother singled him out, among his brothers, for abuse that was one of the most extreme in California history. Ultimately, in 1973, at the age of 12, school officials intervened

David Pelzer

and he was removed from the home and placed in foster care. His life story after that epitomizes a heroic struggle for healthy development against immense obstacles. Dave Pelzer describes his life in four autobiographical works, describing his childhood abuse (1995), his rescue to foster care (1997), his adolescence (2004), and his young adulthood (1999).

His mother's abuse was extreme. She forced David to sleep in the cold basement. He was commanded to get up before her in order to sweep and do other household chores. She deprived him of food, so he stole from other children's lunch boxes at school, from a grocery store, and even ate from garbage cans and from the family dog's dish. His clothes were ragged and dirty, causing other children to make fun of him. His mother assaulted him physically, once in a drunken rage stabbed him with a knife, forced him to drink spoonfuls of ammonia and breathe toxic fumes from an ammonia and Clorox mixture, and pushed him down the stairs, leading to a neck injury that made it difficult for him to breathe. He was regularly at the school nurse's office to be examined for cuts and bruises and relate fabricated explanations of accidents that his mother devised to keep the abuse secret.

Along with the physical abuse, his mother belittled him and told him he was bad and less than human. She called him "It" instead of using his name. David was the designated scapegoat; his four brothers were treated more humanely. (Once he was removed by social services from the home, however, his other brothers became targets of abuse.)

His father was a firefighter, and David admired him as a hero and cherished memories of his attention. In truth, though, such moments were rare. His father retreated to alcohol and was powerless to protect his son or to maintain semblance of a loving family. Memories of better times in his early life seem to have given Pelzer hope through the difficult times that came later, as he struggled to escape the abusive side of his mother that he refers to as "The Mother," in contrast to the better, "Mommy" side of her (Pelzer, 1999, p. 107). Like many abused children, he fantasized both escape and rescue.

David was fortunate to spend some of his time in foster care in the home of a loving and supportive family, beginning at age 13. This was no easy time, though. He got into trouble with stealing, which he did to impress other kids, and was suspected of starting a fire at school (although he claims to have been trying to put it out). He was placed in a juvenile detention facility for a while. During high school, he worked long hours, trying to save enough money to make something of his life (because he knew that when he reached age 18, he would be done with the foster system and be on his own), which detracted from his academic efforts. After many difficulties, including a brief stay at a reform school, he dropped out of high school to work. He joined the Air Force at age 18 and served for 13 years, beginning as a cook and finally working on a flight crew to refuel the F-117 Stealth Fighter and other aircraft, serving in Desert Storm and other combat operations. He also worked assiduously on behalf of abused children in several capacities, as a counselor, lecturer, adviser, and board member. He has received several national and international awards for his activities, including one of The Outstanding Young Persons of the World.

DEVELOPMENT

The fundamental idea behind Maslow's need hierarchy theory is that satisfaction of lower-order needs leads, inevitably, to movement toward higher-order needs. It would seem that if lower-order needs are not met, the human spirit would be kept from developing, but that prediction is difficult to reconcile with the story of Dave Pelzer's life.

His most basic needs for safety and food were chronically dissatisfied by his mentally ill, alcoholic mother. In fact, she actively impeded the satisfaction of those needs. Instead of providing adequate food, she deprived him and made him vomit what food he may have eaten at school. Instead of keeping him safe, she burned him on the gas stove, pushed him down the basement stairs, and stabbed him in a drunken accident. Instead of providing satisfaction of his need for love, she hated him. Instead of fostering his esteem needs, she mocked him and told him he was worthless. His father had little power to protect him. The force for growth posited by Maslow and positive psychologists must be strong, indeed, to endure such an environment.

DESCRIPTION

Maslow's theory does not list descriptive traits at the lower levels of the need hierarchy (although it does give descriptors of self-actualized people, which we consider later.) He does mention that, as they develop, people often must choose between safety and growth.

From the outside, the boy Dave Pelzer must have seemed wretched: disheveled, smelly, skinny, isolated, furtively seeking to steal food. He had obvious unmet needs at many levels. But another aspect of his personality must also be described: the courage, the will to live, that enabled him to use his wits to keep alive in childhood and then, with help, to become a proud and loving adult. As he describes his childhood experience, this courage is apparent: "Mother can beat me all she wants, but I haven't let her take away my will to somehow survive" (Pelzer, 1995, p. 4). In the language of positive psychology, he would be described as resilient.

ADJUSTMENT

Adjustment is built on need satisfaction and motivates movement up the hierarchy to concentrate on the next sequential need. Maslow's theory describes many characteristics of self-actualized (very healthy) individuals, including accurate perception of reality, spontaneity, creativity, and many others described in the chapter.

It was not until he was removed from his parents' home that David Pelzer could move beyond a survival mentality. Ultimately, school officials contacted the police and judicial system and had Dave removed from his abusive home, finally protecting his most basic needs for food and safety. As Maslow's theory predicts, this finally opened the possibility of healthy growth. He was placed with loving foster parents who, through words and deeds, gave him love and support. In adolescence, he made friends. Later, as a member of the U.S. Air Force, he describes achieving a "sense of pride and belonging that until then, I had never known" (1995, p. 158), reflecting movement toward satisfaction of Maslow's third and fourth stages.

A social worker offered him safety and love, and loving foster parents provided the child and adolescent Dave with what he needed to break free from fear and self-loathing. They not only provided food and shelter but love and compassion. Not uncommon for abused children, Dave's behavior tested this love through misbehavior, including minor theft. His foster father, even when facing the accusation that Dave had been involved in setting a fire at school (which he denied), for which he was to be sent to reform school, said, "No matter what happens, I want you to know that we care for you" (Pelzer, 1995, p. 187). It takes many instances of such support, though, to heal deep wounds, and when David was old enough for marriage, his low self-esteem left him vulnerable to an unwise marriage, which depleted his savings and challenged his self-discipline. However, this experience also taught him something of love and fatherhood, which he took quite seriously as he strove to be a better father for his son Stephan than his own father had been for him, and his second marriage was more successful.

COGNITION

The lower four stages of the need hierarchy can be described as cognitions: I know I have food (or not); I know I am safe (or not); I know I am loved (or not); I know I am worthwhile (or not). At the highest stage, self-actualization, Maslow describes some cognitive elements more explicitly: accurate perception, creativity, and peak experiences. Positive psychologists would point to his optimism that things could improve.

(continued)

(continued)

Pelzer (1997) describes his low childhood self-esteem: "I have no home. I am a member of no one's family. I know deep inside that I do not now, nor will I ever, deserve any love, attention, or even recognition as a human being. I am a child called 'It' " (p. 5). He describes "standing in front of the bedroom mirror yelling at myself, 'I'm a bad boy! I'm a bad boy!' over and over again" (Pelzer, 1999, p. 121). Even at age 23, with an Air Force career, he describes himself as having "the self-esteem of an ant" when dealing with women (1999, p. 143). Fortunately, as the positive psychology movement says, interventions can produce a change in these important cognitions about the self.

CULTURE

Abraham Maslow envisioned a utopian society in which people's needs would be adequately met so they would naturally move toward healthier personalities. Both Maslow and the positive psychologists who built on his theory suggest that schools and the workplace are among social institutions that can support healthy growth, and in David's case, they helped where his family had failed.

In addition, the foster care system provided the support that Dave Pelzer needed. It was not, of course, the "system" that turned the tide but the particular loving foster parents to whom he expresses gratitude. In turn, Pelzer has contributed to many abused children through speeches and programs. He became an autobiographer and a motivational speaker, inspiring others to improve their lives. Instead of narcissistically focusing on his own needs, he serves the needs of others—of his son, with a parental protection that he had not experienced (until foster care), and

of others through his service and speeches. This giving toward others is an important contributor to life satisfaction, according to positive psychology research.

His books do not detail all of the abuses he suffered, according to his second wife (although he tells enough to bring tears), and they only hint at the help he received from therapy. The message is consistent with the perspective of Maslow and of the positive psychologists: Turn away from the forces that diminish the human spirit and toward growth and health. Pelzer (2000) emphasizes the importance of choice and of positive emotions, consistent with current themes in positive psychology and Maslow's theory.

BIOLOGY

Maslow's theory considers biology only from the need-fulfillment viewpoint, and is most easily related to the deprivations in David's childhood. While genetic research on the heredity of traits might have predicted a less positive outcome, the positive growth theme of this perspective stands against determinism and asserts the growth potential of everyone. Consistent with that emphasis, Dave Pelzer's life story begins with severe deprivation of biological needs, and then moves on to the "higher-order" needs with a resiliency that inspires.

FINAL THOUGHTS

Maslow's humanistic vision and the positive psychology movement that followed emphasize the growth potential within each person. They point to forces within the person, such as resiliency and choice, that can draw a person to fulfill his unique potential. Maslow urged psychology to look to those positive examples—among which we include David Pelzer.

We will begin with Maslow's theory, and then later in the chapter, turn to the more scientific positive psychology theory that built on his foundation.

PREVIEW: OVERVIEW OF MASLOW'S THEORY

Maslow's theory has implications for major theoretical questions, as presented in Table 15.1.

Table 15.1 Preview of Maslow's Theory and Positive Psychology	
Individual Differences	Individuals can be said to differ in their position in the need hierarchy, that is, their level of development toward self-actualization. Individuals differ in positive traits and subjective states, such as optimism and life satisfaction.
Adaptation and Adjustment	Only a few people reach the highest developmental stage, self-actualization. Maslow describes these individuals in detail. Positive psychologists describe interventions that enhance well-being.
Cognitive Processes	Self-actualized people perceive the world accurately and are creative. Thought patterns, such as optimism, influence behavior, and happiness.
Culture	Changes in schools, work settings, and other institutions can be made to foster healthy development and happiness.
Biological Influences	Biological motivations are the foundation of personality, but once satisfied, they become unimportant.
Development	Children's basic needs should be met. Changes in schools could facilitate growth. Few adults develop to their full potential. Transformations in the workplace and elsewhere could change this.

In contrast to recognition of the importance of scientific verification that Rogers expressed and that is reemerging in current *positive psychology* (see later in this chapter), Maslow thought the methods of science were far too restrictive to be useful for his vision of a growth-oriented psychology. This has seriously detracted from his role in mainstream psychology, although humanistic theoretical ideas remain appealing. Because of his focus on the most healthy (self-actualized) individuals, Maslow's theory is less comprehensive than one would want, neglecting detailed description of the vast majority of people who do not attain his goal of self-actualization. The theory is comprehensive enough to apply to business and to ideas about adult healthy functioning, and to set the stage for later theoretical developments by positive psychologists.

NEED HIERARCHY THEORY: MASLOW

Abraham Maslow believed that people develop through various levels toward their full potential. While most stop at a lower level along the way, stuck in needs that are not adequately met, a few reach the highest level of development and are called self-actualized. He saw these few as beacons, directing humankind toward its full potential.

Biography of Abraham Maslow

Abraham Maslow was born on April 1, 1908, in Brooklyn, New York. His parents were Russian immigrants, poor and uneducated, but hoping for something better for their son. Abraham was the oldest of seven children, in the only Jewish family in the neighborhood, and he "was not always sure where his next meal was coming from" (Maddi & Costa, 1972, p. 159). He described the experience as lonely: "I grew up in libraries and among books, without friends" (Maslow, 1968a, p. 37). In his family, too, he was regarded as physically ugly and so developed a sense of inferiority (Nicholson, 2001).

Maslow was intellectually gifted. His IQ was measured at an astonishing 195 (Maslow, 1954/1987, p. xxxvi). In college, he at first studied law, as his father wished, but abandoned it after 2 weeks. He turned to a broader course of studies at Cornell and then transferred to the University of Wisconsin in 1928 to study psychology. While still in college, he married his high school sweetheart, an artist, who undoubtedly fostered Maslow's respect for more global and integrative approaches to knowledge.

Ironically, given the later direction of his theorizing, Maslow was at first excited about the behaviorism he was studying under the supervision of Harry Harlow (famous for the "cloth mother" studies that established the importance of contact comfort for monkeys).

Maslow's interest turned for a time to psychoanalysis and Gestalt psychology and philosophy, and these paved the way for an experiential conversion.

Abraham Maslow

> Then when my baby was born that was the thunderclap that settled things. I looked at this tiny, mysterious thing and felt so stupid. I was stunned by the mystery and by the sense of not really being in control .... I'd say that anyone who had a baby couldn't be a behaviorist. (Maslow, 1968a, p. 56)

Maslow remained at the University of Wisconsin as assistant instructor and teaching fellow (1930–1935) before going to Columbia University (1935–1937), where he interviewed female college students about their sex lives (Maslow, 1942), extending to humans his earlier observations of monkeys. This research caused some controversy and may have inspired the Kinsey studies of sexuality that began several years later. Later, as associate professor at Brooklyn College (1937–1951), he was especially popular among the many students who came from immigrant families.

Besides his academic career, Maslow also was plant manager in a family company from 1947 to 1949 (Maddi & Costa, 1972). He became professor and chair of the Psychology Department at the new Brandeis University (1951–1969).

Despite his success, Maslow experienced anxiety about his academic work in graduate school and public presentations later, for which he sought psychotherapy briefly. While on a leave of absence, working on the implications of humanistic psychology for broader social values, Maslow died of a heart attack (Frick, 2000) in 1970, at age 62.

Abraham Maslow was a member and officer in several professional organizations, including the American Psychological Association (of which he became President in 1968), and of course the Association for Humanistic Psychology (of which he was one of the founding members).

Maslow (1987) supported the human potential movement, in particular the Esalen Institute in Big Sur, California, "the world's first growth center" (p. xi). His work was directed toward society at large, which he hoped to improve, more than to academic audiences, whose methodological rigidity and lack of vision he criticized. He described himself as having a "missionary" concern for improving the world and pointed to the utopian concerns of his own Jewish background (Frick, 2000).

MASLOW'S VISION OF PSYCHOLOGY

Abraham Maslow (1966) distrusted the methods of mainstream psychology. Rather than enlightening us, he said, traditional scientific methods prevent full knowledge of human nature. Psychological theory and research are not focused on the most important areas of human nature, the higher functions that raise us above the animals. It is not enough for psychology to study animals and neurotic individuals.

Maslow argued that scientific constraints had undermined the purpose of psychological work. Traditional scientific methodology is **method centered**. Human experiences that cannot be investigated in the traditional fashion are ruled "nonscientific." Maslow recommended, instead, a **problem-centered** approach in which the issues to be investigated would be given higher priority than would the methods.

For psychology to understand the profound meaningfulness of life, the "ultimate aloneness of the individual" (p. 14) and the real uncertainty of the future, it must go beyond the more limited deterministic theories available in behaviorism and in psychoanalysis. A **third force** psychology, humanism, was being developed with Maslow as its spiritual father.

Maslow (1966, p. 95) described his vision as **Taoist Science**, which he contrasted with "Controlling Science." Taoist Science would be subjective and experiential, not objective and abstract. It would be interpersonal, truly engaged in a meaningful interaction with the object of study. Furthermore, it would be explicitly concerned with values. All of these notions violate traditional assumptions of objective scientific methods that, Maslow argued, cannot study healthy personalities adequately.

HIERARCHY OF NEEDS

Maslow postulated that people begin development with basic needs (motives) that are not noticeably different from animal motivation. As they mature and as their lower-order needs are satisfied, people develop more uniquely human motivations. Thus motivation changes as we progress upward through a **hierarchy of needs**, or motives. This hierarchy consists of five levels: four levels of deficiency motivation and a final, highly developed level called being motivation, or self-actualization. In his later writing, Maslow proposed additional levels beyond self-actualization—levels that have been expanded by those who write about transpersonal psychology, such as Ken Wilber (Rowan, 2007). Maslow's model of personality suggests that we must take into account the qualitative differences among people who are functioning at different levels—for example, when we measure large samples of people and statistically describe these data (Rowan, 2007).

method centered

an approach to science that emphasizes procedure over content

problem-centered

an approach to science that emphasizes subject matter over procedure

third force

Maslow's term for his theory, emphasizing its opposition to psychoanalysis and behaviorism

Taoist Science

Maslow's alternative to the traditional scientific method, emphasizing values and subjectivity (instead of objectivity)

hierarchy of needs

ordered progression of motives, from basic physical needs upward to motives of the most developed human beings

Deficiency Motivation

The first four levels of the need hierarchy can be understood as motivation to overcome the feeling of a deficiency and are collectively called **deficiency motivation**. A **basic need** at any of these four levels, if unmet, leads to a craving, and it directs action to get the need fulfilled. This fulfillment brings pleasure or happiness (which emotion, we will note later, is central to the positive psychology movement that followed).

deficiency motivation
motivation at lower levels of development

basic need
a fundamental deficiency need

What are these basic needs? Maslow listed four of them and asserted that they emerge in a particular order (see Figure 15.1). Each need must be met, more or less adequately, before the individual is free to move on to a "higher" need. "More or less adequately" is not so precise a statement as one might prefer. The same events might satisfy one person's need but not another.

PHYSIOLOGICAL NEEDS   At the lowest level of the need hierarchy are physiological needs—the needs for food, water, sleep, and sex. These needs are essential to human and animal survival. If unmet, they dominate motivation, regardless whether other, higher-order needs are also unmet. "For the man who is extremely and dangerously hungry, no other interests exist but food," Maslow (1943) asserted (in Lowry, 1973, p. 156).

Lower animals may always live at this level, but humans, under normal conditions, have their physiological needs predictably met. If these needs are met adequately, the next need level becomes salient.

Maslow (1943) suggested that a person's history—as well as the current level—of need satisfaction is important. He hypothesized that "it is precisely those individuals in whom a certain need has always been satisfied who are best equipped to tolerate deprivation of that need in the future, and those who have been deprived in the past will react differently to current satisfactions than the one who has never been deprived" (in Lowry, 1973, p. 157). Research on the effects of dieting on food metabolism offers support for his claim at the physiological level; those who have dieted in the past convert food to fat more quickly than those who have not dieted. Could those who have been deprived of love or of security also hoard these satisfactions when they are available?

SAFETY NEEDS   At the next level, the person's predominant motivation is to ensure a safe situation. Familiarity is perceived as safe, so the young child feels threatened when new situations occur (loud noises, strange animals, parental quarrels or divorce, etc.). Physical violence, of course, also threatens safety for both children and adults.

Maslow interpreted some neuroses as attempts to ensure a feeling of safety. Compulsive and obsessive neurotics, especially, try to keep life quite predictable, although it impedes their higher-level functioning. For others, money seems to promise safety. For example, someone whose business enterprises bring great wealth but little love may continue to strive for a feeling of safety through compulsive financial dealings.

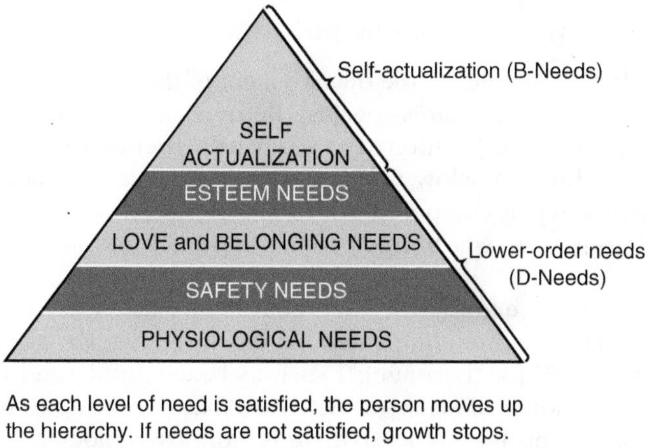

As each level of need is satisfied, the person moves up the hierarchy. If needs are not satisfied, growth stops.

FIGURE 15.1   Maslow's Hierarchy of Needs

BELONGINGNESS AND LOVE NEEDS   If safety and physiological needs are met adequately, the next level to become salient is the need for love and belongingness. At this level, the person seeks love and friendship. Maslow included the need to give love, as well as to receive it. He described these needs as a frequent source of maladjustment in our society.

Sex is an issue at this level to the extent that it is an expression of affection; but sex can also function at a purely physiological level (i.e., the first level of the hierarchy). Maslow was interested in human sexuality, extending his doctoral studies in which he observed sexuality in animals. His work pre-dated the rise of sexology, and it was less statistical than the later work of Alfred Kinsey and others. He described sexual dissatisfaction as an important "deficiency need."

ESTEEM NEEDS   The next need to emerge in the hierarchy is the need for self-respect and the esteem of others. Esteem should be "stable [and] firmly based," by which Maslow meant that it should result from our actual abilities and achievements.

We can interpret achievement strivings as manifestations of the esteem needs because society honors those who achieve. Many successful entrepreneurs, for example, whose physiological, safety, and love needs are met sufficiently, turn their motivation to career success. Maslow's hierarchical conception also suggests that people who feel unloved, perhaps sensing parental rejection, continue to function at the third level of the hierarchy and are not motivated by esteem needs.

Although esteem needs are the highest of Maslow's deficiency motivations, they are still only the fourth of five developmental steps. The highest level, self-actualization, is so different from the others that it stands alone as a nondeficiency motive.

Being Motivation

being motivation

higher-level motivation in which the need for self-actualization predominates

Once the deficiency needs are more or less adequately met, the person functions at a higher level, which Maslow called **being motivation**, as opposed to deficiency motivation. This level is the pinnacle of development and the primary focus of Maslow's theory. It is described briefly here and more fully later in the chapter.

THE NEED FOR SELF-ACTUALIZATION   At this highest stage, the person is no longer motivated by deficiencies but rather by the need to "actualize" or fulfill his or her potential. "A musician must make music, an artist must paint, a poet must write, if he is to be ultimately happy" (Maslow, 1943; in Lowry, 1973, p. 162). It is the desire "to become everything that one is capable of becoming" (p. 163). Subjectively, the person feels bored if lower-order needs are met, and this boredom motivates and is relieved by self-actualization striving.

Because humans have different potentials (compared to their similar physiological needs), the particular behaviors motivated by self-actualization needs vary from person to person. For Maslow (1968b, p. 33), "self-actualization is idiosyncratic since every person is different."

Differences Between D-Motivation and B-Motivation

Lower-order needs occur earlier in the development of the individual and lower in the phylogenetic chart (which compares species). Because they are necessary for survival, lower-order needs cannot be postponed as easily as higher-order needs, and they feel more urgent when unmet. Maslow (1954/1987, p. 57) cited an example: "Respect is a dispensable luxury when compared with food or safety." Luxury or not, living at the level of higher-order needs brings better physical health and greater subjective happiness and serenity.

metamotivated

motivated by needs at the top of the hierarchy

To stress the difference from deficiency motivation, Maslow described people at the level of self-actualization as **metamotivated**. At this level they are motivated by "meta-needs" or "B-values" ("B" for "becoming") such as beauty, truth, and justice. They are not motivated in the traditional sense of the term—that is, seeking to reduce a need to restore homeostasis. At this highest level, there is more psychological freedom (Maslow, 1955). Perception is no longer focused, looking for objects to satisfy needs; it can be more passive and receptive. This is B-motivation, in contrast to D-motivation (deficiency motivation). Interpersonal relationships take on a very different quality at the level of B-motivation. Maslow described **B-love** as nonpossessive and enjoyable. In contrast, **D-love** is often contaminated by jealousy and anxiety. B-love allows the partners more independence and autonomy and it facilitates the growth of each person (Maslow, 1955).

SELF-ACTUALIZATION

Maslow preferred the term **self-actualization** to such terms as *psychological health* (or illness). His term connotes the full potential of being human. Unlike the term *adjustment,* it does not mean adjusting to a particular situation. Maslow (1968b, p. vii) suggested that instead of referring to "illness," we should speak of "human diminution or stunting." Illness strikes if the person denies his or her inner potential, going against one's own nature. Maslow credited Karen Horney, who made a similar point in describing the alienation from the real self in neurosis.

When a person's basic needs (the first four levels of the need hierarchy) have been met, motivation is directed toward self-actualization, which Maslow (1968b) defined as

> ongoing actualization of potentials, capacities and talents, as fulfillment of mission (or call, fate, destiny, or vocation), as a fuller knowledge of, and acceptance of, the person's own intrinsic nature, as an unceasing trend toward unity, integration or synergy within the person. (p. 25)

Maslow (1954/1987) was convinced that it was necessary for psychology to study its healthiest, most developed people if it was to learn about human potential.

Maslow reported a study of self-actualized people, selected from his personal acquaintances and friends and from public figures, both current and historical. In a survey of some 3,000 college students, he found only one subject who met his criterion for being self-actualized. Maslow (1968b) estimated that fewer than 1 percent of all people are self-actualized.

His decision about whether a person was self-actualized was subjective, of course. He included Rorschach tests when practical (obviously not for historical figures). Early in his observations, he found that "possible subjects, when informed of the purpose of the research, became self-conscious, froze up, laughed off the whole effort, or broke off the relationship. As a result, since this early experience, all older subjects have been studied indirectly, indeed almost surreptitiously" (Maslow, 1954/1987, p. 127).

Among the public figures, Maslow included Abraham Lincoln and Thomas Jefferson, both "fairly sure" to have been self-actualized, and seven others whom he said were "probably" self-actualized: Albert Einstein, Eleanor Roosevelt, Jane Addams, William James, Albert Schweitzer, Aldous Huxley, and Benedict de Spinoza. Describing individuals as self-actualized is a risky strategy. Everett Shostrom (1972), writing for a popular audience, named Richard Nixon, then at the height of his prestige as president, as an example of a self-actualized person. The later scandal of Watergate, leading to Nixon's resignation to avoid impeachment, discredited this assessment and highlighted the danger of equating public success with self-actualization (Anderson, 1975; Shostrom, 1975).

Characteristics of Self-Actualized People

Based on his observations, Maslow identified a number of characteristics of self-actualized people.

EFFICIENT PERCEPTION OF REALITY   Self-actualized people have "an unusual ability to detect the spurious, the fake, and the dishonest in personality, and in general to judge people correctly and efficiently" (Maslow, 1954/1987, p. 128). They are less likely than others to be misled by their own defense mechanisms, wishes, expectations, or stereotypes. This accuracy perhaps develops because they are not threatened by the unknown and because their focus is not narrowed by unfilled needs (Maslow, 1955).

B-love

nonpossessive love, characteristic of a self-actualized person

D-love

selfish love, characteristic of a person who is not self-actualized

self-actualization

development of a person's full potential

Einstein:
"The most beautiful thing we can experience is the mysterious"

loving yourself

accept their flaws! embracing yourself

ACCEPTANCE   Maslow's self-actualized subjects were more accepting of themselves, of others, and of nature than the average person, including acceptance of their "animal level"; they eat well, sleep well, and enjoy sex. They accept both the bad and the good and are thus tolerant. Research suggests that self-actualized people (measured by low discrepancies between the self and the ideal self) have less fear of death (Neimeyer, 1985a).

SPONTANEITY   Self-actualized people behave spontaneously, simply, and naturally, and are in touch with their inner impulses and subjective experience. They do not hide behind a social mask.

PROBLEM CENTERED   Self-actualized people focus on problems outside themselves. They are problem centered, not self-centered. The tasks may come from a sense of social obligation.

NEED FOR PRIVACY (SOLITUDE)   More than most people, self-actualized individuals like privacy. Maslow hypothesized that they would endure sensory deprivation (conducted by experimental psychologists) more easily than others. They are capable of high levels of concentration, and they make up their own minds rather than letting others make decisions for them.

INDEPENDENCE OF CULTURE AND ENVIRONMENT (AUTONOMY)   Self-actualized people do not depend on other people or the world for need satisfaction. They are "self-contained" and resilient in the face of difficulties. Because the self-actualized person is motivated by internal needs, rather than responding to the external world, such a person feels more "psychological freedom" (Maslow, 1968b, p. 35).

grateful

FRESHNESS OF APPRECIATION   The sense of awe and wonder at life remains always fresh with self-actualized individuals. This may come from aesthetic experiences, social encounters, or other sources, including sexual pleasure.

PEAK EXPERIENCES   Probably the best known characteristic that Maslow described is the capacity for mystical experiences, which he called **peak experiences**. Maslow (1954/1987) described these as

peak experiences

mystical states of consciousness, characteristic of many but not all self-actualized people

> feelings of limitless horizons opening up to the vision, the feeling of being simultaneously more powerful and also more helpless than one ever was before, the feeling of great ecstasy and wonder and awe, the loss of placing in time and space with, finally, the conviction that something extremely important and valuable has happened, so that the subject is to some extent transformed and strengthened even in daily life by such experiences. (p. 137)

A variety of events may trigger such experiences. Sometimes they occur in response to nature; sometimes they are religious experiences; sometimes they occur during meditation; sometimes they are even sexual encounters. According to one study, Japanese adults' retrospective reports of childhood peak experiences more frequently involve interpersonal experiences, in contrast to the individualistic reports typical of Westerners (Hoffman & Muramoto, 2007). "Peakers" are more poetic, musical, philosophical, and religious. In addition, Maslow said that some self-actualized people are nonpeakers; these are more practical, working in the social world through reform, politics, and other real-world arenas. Maslow expressed more admiration for peakers, whom he called "transcending," than for nonpeakers, whom he called "merely healthy" (p. 138).

HUMAN KINSHIP   Self-actualizing people identify with human beings in general, feeling a sense of kinship with the human race. Because they identify with all humans rather than only one particular group, they are not prejudiced.

HUMILITY AND RESPECT   Self-actualizing people are humble, feeling they can learn from many different people, even those of a different class or race. They are democratic, rather than authoritarian, and do not insist on maintaining their status over others.

INTERPERSONAL RELATIONSHIPS   Self-actualized people are capable of "more fusion, greater love, more perfect identification, more obliteration of the ego boundaries than other people would consider possible" (Maslow, 1954/1987, p. 140). They seek out other self-actualized people, so they have deep relationships with a few people rather than many more superficial relationships.

ETHICS AND VALUES   Self-actualized people have strong ethical standards, although their standards are often not conventional standards of right and wrong. They are not concerned with what Maslow (1954/1987) regarded as trivial ethical issues, such as "card playing, dancing, wearing short dresses, exposing the head (in some churches) or not exposing the head (in others), drinking wine, or eating some meats and not others, or eating them on some days but not on others" (p. 147). Their values emerge from acceptance of human nature and of their own nature, including their unique potentials.

DISCRIMINATION BETWEEN MEANS AND ENDS   Maslow's subjects were clearly focused on the ends or goals of their efforts and subordinated the means to the end. Nonetheless, they could appreciate the pleasure of the means.

SENSE OF HUMOR   Self-actualizers have a nonhostile sense of humor, not laughing at other people's expense. Their sense of humor is more philosophical than that of most people, laughing at the human condition. Overall, though, Maslow's subjects were more serious than humorous. *laughing of you not at you*

CREATIVITY   Creativity is the one characteristic Maslow claimed was present in all of his self-actualized subjects, without exception. He did not mean creativity in the sense we often use it. It does not necessarily involve any creative product such as a work of art or music, which Maslow (1954/1987, p. 160) calls "special talent creativeness," as contrasted with "self-actualizing creativeness." "There can be creative shoemakers or carpenters or clerks....One can even see creatively as the child does" (p. 143).

   Although Maslow's creativity does not require expression in the traditional arts, the arts can foster such creativity and self-actualization for many people. One study, for example, reports that artistic activities foster self-acceptance and openness, two important aspects of self-actualization (Manheim, 1998). Researchers report correlations between measures of self-actualization and creativity (Buckmaster & Davis, 1985; Runco, Ebersole, & Mraz, 1991). The creativity of a self-actualized person emerges naturally out of the other characteristics: spontaneity, resistance to enculturation, efficiency of perception, and so forth. It is a capacity in all children but is lost by many, as both neurosis and what psychoanalysts call secondary process displace earlier creativity (Maslow, 1958).

RESISTANCE TO ENCULTURATION   Self-actualized people do not "adjust" to society at the expense of their own character. They are conventional when it is easier or less disruptive to be so, but this is a superficial adaptation that readily gives way to their autonomous nature. *not allowing themselves to be passively molded by culture.*

make up their own minds — some made by their parents or news so on...

RESOLUTION OF DICHOTOMIES   Self-actualized people do not see in either-or terms, as less healthy people often do. Maslow (1954/1987, p. 149) offered several examples of dichotomies that to self-actualized people no longer seem so—for example, reason versus emotion, selfish versus unselfish, serious versus humorous, active versus passive, and masculine versus feminine. Rather than seeing conflict between what is good for the individual and what serves others, the two operate together, with "synergy" (Maslow, 1964). This fusion of self-interest and social interest can occur at a cultural level, too, leading to a better society, a utopia, or to use the term Maslow preferred, **Eupsychia.** Consciously thinking and acting in terms of synergy,

Eupsychia

a utopian society in which individual and societal needs are both met and where society supports individual development highly developed people can help solve some of the social problems that have been produced by less developed, dichotomous thinking (Carlsen, 1996).

Measurement and Research on Self-Actualization

Maslow did not devote much effort to the development of measuring instruments, preferring for the most part to observe people more holistically, in keeping with his concept of a receptive or Taoist scientific method. He did, however, collaborate with his wife to devise the Maslow Art Test "to test for holistic perception and intuition by testing the ability to detect the style of an artist" (Maslow, 1966, p. 62). This may be described as an intuitive cognitive style.

Maslow (1968b) realized that his ideas were in the early stages of scientific validation, merely hypotheses. Others have carried these ideas the logical next step. The key concept in Maslow's theory is self-actualization. Whereas Maslow explored this construct through observation, others have attempted formal measurement by a questionnaire.

Personal Orientation Inventory

the most popular measure of self-actualization

Inner Directed Supports

scale of the Personal Orientation Inventory measuring a person's tendency to obtain support from himself or herself rather than from other people

Time Competence

scale of the Personal Orientation Inventory that measures a person's concern with the present rather than the past or future.

PERSONAL ORIENTATION INVENTORY The **Personal Orientation Inventory (POI)** (Shostrom, 1964) is a 150-item multiple-choice inventory that provides two primary scores derived from Maslow's theory. The **Inner Directed Supports** scale measures the degree to which the subject provides his or her own support (as opposed to turning to others). The **Time Competence** scale measures the degree to which the subject lives in the present. In addition, there are subscales to measure self-actualizing values, existentiality, feeling reactivity, spontaneity, self-regard, self-acceptance, the nature of people, synergy, acceptance of aggression, and capacity for intimate contact.

Everett Shostrom (1964) reported that his inventory distinguished between groups nominated by clinicians to be self-actualized or not, and that scores changed during the course of psychotherapy. Several studies have validated the POI through criterion group studies; that is, groups thought to be more self-actualized score higher than those assumed to be less self-actualized (Hattie & Cooksey, 1984). As a criterion measure of mental health, scores increase as a result of various therapeutic interventions (Duncan, Konefal, & Spechler, 1990; Elizabeth, 1983; Peterson-Cooney, 1987) and less formal interventions to improve psychological health, such as meditation, reading self-help books, and even exercise (Delmonte, 1984; Forest, 1987; Gondola & Tuckman, 1985). Some evidence indicates that self-actualization on the POI is correlated with greater spirituality, as measured by a written test (Tloczynski, Knoll, & Fitch, 1997).

Obstacles to Self-Actualization

If self-actualization is an innate potential, why is it not universally developed? Human beings repeatedly confront situations in which they must choose between growth and safety. Safety choices are appealing, but only growth choices move us toward self-actualization. To encourage growth choices in children, parents are wise to avoid both overprotection (which orients the child toward safety) and excessive approval (which focuses the child on others' opinions rather than on his or her own experience). When all goes well, the child finds that the growth choice offers delight, and the safety choice leads to boredom. Under less ideal circumstances, the growth choice seems dangerous and the safety choice offers approval (see Figure 15.2).

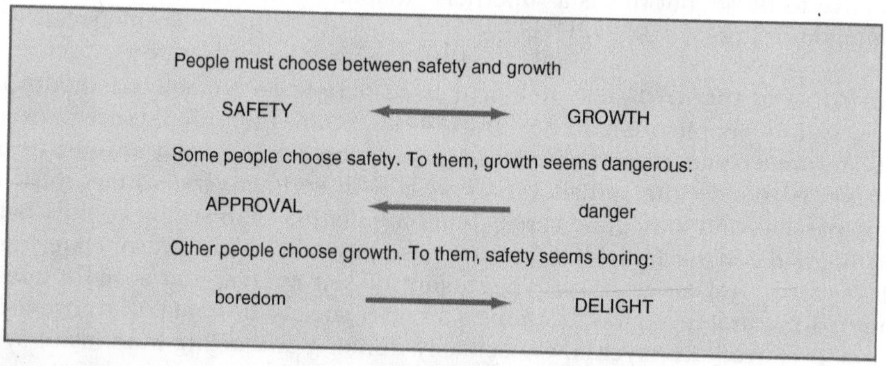

People must choose between safety and growth

SAFETY ⟷ GROWTH

Some people choose safety. To them, growth seems dangerous:

APPROVAL ⟵ danger

Other people choose growth. To them, safety seems boring:

boredom ⟶ DELIGHT

FIGURE 15.2 Choice between Safety and Growth

Source: Adapted from Maslow, 1962, p. 44.

Besides this intrapsychic pull against self-actualization, there are other reasons why self-actualization is not more frequent. Higher-order needs emerge only if favorable external conditions (such as adequate food and housing) allow satisfaction of the earlier needs. Also, higher-order needs are weaker than lower-order needs; hence they must compete with them.

APPLICATIONS AND IMPLICATIONS OF MASLOW'S THEORY

Maslow's ideas have been applied to diverse areas. These applications are part of the **human potential movement**, which strives to improve the human condition by fostering the development of individuals to their highest potential through growth centers (including the Esalen Institute in Big Sur, California) and through the transformation of social institutions like places of employment and schools. His emphasis on growth is also reflected in new approaches to therapy.

human potential movement
social trend to foster the full development of individuals, reflected in the development of growth centers and in transformation of social institutions

Therapy

Many people, according to Maslow, turn to psychotherapy because their love and belongingness needs are unfulfilled. Therapeutic progress requires that these needs be met. Maslow believed the therapeutic approach should be tailored to the particular patient. For seriously disturbed neurotics, a traditional clinical approach might be appropriate. For more healthy individuals, group therapy and encounter groups would be more suitable.

Building on the ideas of Maslow and others, *transpersonal therapists* work with a worldview that encompasses a larger domain than the individual who is suffering. There are many varieties of transpersonal therapy (Boorstein, 2000). They draw not only from traditional therapies but also from religious and spiritual traditions and techniques of healing, valuing states of consciousness that are outside of everyday experience. Sometimes meditation techniques are included in therapy. Claims of paranormal insights are sometimes offered to support the validity of the transpersonal approach. In keeping with Maslow's emphasis on the higher human functions, transpersonal therapists are concerned with positive emotions as well as painful ones: "Transpersonal psychotherapy attempts to open awareness to … psychic realms where joy, love, serenity, and even ecstasy are present" (Boorstein, 2000, p. 413). At times, these therapeutic methods push the boundaries of what is professionally and culturally accepted, as when Maslow permitted his reputation to be used to support controversial nude therapy sessions offered in the 1960s by Paul Bindram (Nicholson, 2007).

Workplace

Maslow's need hierarchy has become a major concept for industrial-organizational psychologists (Massarik, 1992). Those who help people choose their careers can counsel more effectively, even helping people become more self-actualized in the process, by taking into account clients' levels on the need hierarchy (Sackett, 1998). The workplace is a major area for the development of self-actualization, and workers are more effective when they function at the level of the higher needs while avoiding dissatisfaction based on unmet lower-order needs.

In 1962 Maslow was a visiting fellow at a high-tech corporation in California, NonLinear Systems. Among self-actualized managers, he found positive, supportive interpersonal relationships with subordinates and more productive and creative work. These managers were more likely to believe that people are trustworthy, responsible, curious, open to change, and intrinsically interested in work (cf. Payne, 2000). Unfortunately, many managers are not self-actualized but rather are motivated by neurotic power needs. The challenge for business is to fill management positions with the most highly developed individuals, despite the fact that self-actualized people may not be particularly attracted to those positions (Schott, 1992).

Customer satisfaction is important in the business realm, and Maslow's theory offers suggestions to satisfy not only employees but also customers and to maintain loyalty: Businesses should aim to meet lower-order needs while also appealing to higher-order needs (Maslow, 1998; Tuten & August, 1998).

Maslow's need hierarchy provides a framework for reaching potential customers (Kahle & Chiagouris, 1997). Many products can be considered from various need levels. Food, for example, fulfills physiological needs but also is relevant to esteem needs, as a friend of mine recognized when choosing a gourmet brand of bottled mushrooms instead of a less expensive, but equally nutritious, store brand of mushroom stems and pieces.

Religion and Spirituality

Maslow urged a more spiritual approach within psychology, adding his voice to a chorus of advocates of a spiritualized psychotherapy, often one that added insights from Eastern religious tradition to the Judeo-Christian backgrounds of Western psychotherapists. Although there are similarities in their concern for growth and healing, self-actualization and spirituality are not interchangeable concepts (Benjamin & Looby, 1998; DeHoff, 1998). Clinical and counseling psychologists who agree with Christian beliefs generally prefer other (cognitive-behavioral) therapy orientations, instead of humanistic or existential approaches to therapy, which are preferred by those whose religious beliefs are more mystical and Eastern (Bilgrave & Deluty, 1998). Maslow strongly opposed dogmatic views in religion, as in other fields. He interpreted the experiences of religious prophets as peak experiences that bring important insights to humankind in general and not simply to the individual. Unfortunately, institutionalized religions are often filled with "nonpeakers" who cannot communicate prophetic experiences and who substitute dogmatic rigidity for vision (Maslow, 1970).

desacralization

loss of a sense of the sacred or spiritual

Although he did not support traditional institutionalized religion, Maslow lamented the **desacralization** of human experience by professionals (including psychologists and physicians) as well as others. Removing a sense of the sacred was a profound loss. He hoped that psychology would contribute to the "resacralization" of human experience, even if it meant experimenting with new forms, such as publishing poetry and personal testimonials in professional journals.

Education

Maslow (1976) described the goal of education to be "the 'self-actualization' of a person, the becoming fully human, the development of the fullest height the human species can stand up to or that the particular individual can come to" (p. 162). This is surely a different aim from the mere acquisition of technical skills and knowledge. Maslow realized that his theory implied drastic changes in educational practice, similar to the changes proposed by Carl Rogers. Humanistic education should foster, rather than sedate, the natural curiosity of children. In most classrooms, children learn to behave in ways that please the teacher rather than being encouraged to think creatively.

The ideal college would have much more self-directed learning. Students would follow their own inner directions in meaningful and honest dialogue with faculty. "There would be no credits, no degrees, and no required courses" (Maslow, 1976, p. 175). For such a system to succeed, of course, students and faculty would need to be self-actualizing so their choices would indeed be directed toward growth.

MASLOW'S CHALLENGE TO TRADITIONAL SCIENCE

Humanistic psychology, because of its emphasis on subjective experience and its valuing of experience and growth, regularly faces the dilemma of a scientific method that seems inadequate to study the phenomena that really matter. Maslow articulated this problem, and he went further than many humanistic psychologists—certainly further than Carl Rogers—in questioning the relevance of traditional science for the study of human psychology.

Maslow has been accused of allowing his own values to dictate his description of the concept of self-actualization. His list of characteristics of self-actualized persons may simply be a list of qualities that Maslow admires (cf. McClelland, 1955). For example, his emphasis on mystical, nonrational experience, rather than reason, may reflect personal bias (Daniels, 1988; Smith, 1973). It has also been suggested that the values represented in the need hierarchy are Western cultural values only. An alternate hierarchy has been proposed to reflect Chinese values, in which the highest level is "self-actualization in the service of society" rather than individual self-actualization (Nevis, 1983).

Maslow responded to accusations of not following traditional methodology, not providing statistics to support his assertions, and allowing values to influence his work so blatantly. He claimed it did not bother him:

> I have a secret. I talk over the heads of the people in front of me to my own private audience. I talk to people I love and respect. To Socrates and Aristotle and Spinoza and Thomas Jefferson and Abraham Lincoln. And when I write, I write for them. This cuts out a lot of crap. (Maslow, 1968a, p. 56)

Maslow was aware of the powers of science to persuade. In his preface to his book *Toward a Psychology of Being*, he remarked, "Science is the only way we have of shoving truth down the reluctant throat" (Maslow, 1968b, p. viii). Or as his former student assistant, Kendler, puts it more diplomatically, "Maslow considered psychology to be a *prescriptive* science, capable of providing moral values that should guide human conduct…[as opposed to] a *descriptive* science …, which describe[s] the world as it is, not as it ought to be" (Kendler, 2002, p. 56).

POSITIVE PSYCHOLOGY

A number of psychologists who currently endorse the emphasis on health and self-actualization that Maslow and other humanists advocated have rallied behind the term **positive psychology**. A key similarity between Maslow's theory and current positive psychology is the emphasis on immediate experience as an aspect of healthy functioning (Rathunde, 2001). An important difference is the expanded emphasis on scientific research within positive psychology. The positive psychology movement brings increased methodological rigor to areas, such as psychological well-being and the study of spirituality, that humanists studied previously, for example by developing measuring instruments (Emmons, 2006).

Martin Seligman and Mihaly Csikszentmihalyi (2000) describe positive psychology this way:

positive psychology
current movement in psychology that emphasizes healthy functioning, with concern for immediate experience and positive emotions such as happiness

> The field of positive psychology at the subjective level is about valued subjective experiences: well-being, contentment, and satisfaction (in the past); hope and optimism (for the future); and flow and happiness (in the present). At the individual level, it is about positive individual traits: the capacity for love and vocation, courage, interpersonal skill, aesthetic sensibility, perseverance, forgiveness, originality, future mindedness, spirituality, high talent, and wisdom. At the group level, it is about the civic virtues and the institutions that move individuals toward better citizenship: responsibility, nurturance, altruism, civility, moderation, tolerance, and work ethic. (p. 5)

Positive psychology has had a particularly strong influence on health psychology, emphasizing the development of healthy lifestyles and cognitive habits that contribute to resiliency in the face of threat, and not merely focusing on disease. Positive emotions are also important as people seek to improve health. A review of research finds that various positive psychological states and traits (such as happiness, positive mood, self-esteem, active coping, and religiosity or spirituality) are associated with less physiological reactivity to stress, which contributes to cardiovascular health (Chida & Hamer, 2008). In one longitudinal study of the effectiveness of interventions to reduce tobacco use, researchers found that the positive emotion of vitality was a better predictor of tobacco abstinence than negative emotion, that is, depression (Niemiec et al., 2010).

Positive psychology has spurred developmental psychologists to focus on strengths, and not only to predict negative outcomes for people in adolescence and other life stages. Positive psychology is also having an impact on studies of therapy, schools, and the work environment.

Table 15.2 Three Pillars of Positive Psychology	
"Pillar" of Positive Psychology	**Examples of Concepts Studied**
Positive subjective experience	Life satisfaction
	Subjective well-being
	Happiness
	Positive mood
	Flow
	Meaningful life
Positive traits	Optimism
	Hope
	Positive thinking
	Active coping
	Religiosity or spirituality
	Resiliency
Positive institutions	Workplace
	Schools

The field is often described as resting on the *three pillars of positive psychology*: positive subjective experience, positive traits, and positive institutions (Donaldson & Ko, 2010; Peterson, 2006). As we consider these three areas, we will sample some of the research in positive psychology that ranges, as the categories imply, from the phenomenological experience of a person, to comparisons among people, to our social institutions that have the potential, at least, to support positive development. (See Table 15.2.)

POSITIVE SUBJECTIVE EXPERIENCE

Positive emotional states are a major concern of positive psychology, and the popular media has embraced this easily understood concept, for example, with a *Time* magazine cover story on happiness research in 2005 (Wallis, 2005) and a continuing supply of advice. Newspapers and magazines entice readers with assessment tools to rate themselves—including questions from the Satisfaction with Life Scale (in the next section). And there is much to be told!

Happiness and Satisfaction with Life

subjective well-being

how happy or satisfied an individual is with his or her life

Are you happy? Satisfied with life? "Don't worry, be happy!" goes a popular song, and who can argue? **Subjective well-being** measures affect, with a balance of more positive than negative emotions, and also includes judgments about life satisfaction (Linley et al., 2009). A related construct is *psychological well-being*, which includes additional factors (positive relations with others, self-acceptance, purpose in life, autonomy, environmental mastery, and personal growth) (Linley et al., 2009; Ryff, 1989).

An overall assessment of life satisfaction or subjective well-being is straightforward. The Satisfaction with Life Scale, simply asks questions such as "I am satisfied with my life" and "In most ways my life is close to my ideal" (Diener et al., 1985, p. 72). It has high face validity, and an accumulation of research evidence supports its construct validity as well. It's consistent with the assumptions of humanistic psychology to take people's self-reports at face value.

Happiness may be desirable in and of itself, to be sure. It has captured the attention of professionals, though, for additional reasons. Happiness and other positive emotions frequently predict outcomes that are of interest to society and to policy makers. It predicts better physical and mental health, which means less cost for health care. It predicts socially responsible behavior. For employers, positive subjective states predict higher worker productivity and improved profits.

Benefits like this make sense if we think of positive emotions from an evolutionary perspective, as signals that adaptation is working, to encourage continuing in that direction. Negative emotions are our evolutionary warnings to do something different. The humanistic perspective maintains that we inherently are directed toward growth, and positive emotions signal the path we are to take. So happiness and positive emotions aren't just pleasurable, but reward and direct our good choices. That's why it is so important to avoid short-circuiting this function by misusing drugs that produce a false euphoria that does not direct us to where we must go.

Long-term subjective well-being may often require temporary pain and sacrifice. A sound theory and research base of positive psychology will help us know which choices will pay off in the long run. Some further and more objective consideration, taking into account critical thinking and normative values, and drawing on philosophy and empirical evidence, may be helpful (Tiberius & Hall, 2010).

Flow

A quintessential example of activities that inherently contribute to satisfaction and happiness is Csikszentmihalyi's (1996) concept of **flow**. This is a state of deep engagement in an activity that is characteristic of creative individuals. The experience of flow is most easily visualized in the solitary experience of creative individuals, such as artists and musicians immersed in their work. In addition, a *social flow* experience has been proposed, which occurs when groups working together, such as sports teams, experience joy in their interdependent activity (Walker, 2010). Among professional rugby players, a state described as "rigid persistence paradox" or "obsessional passion" (Sheard & Golby, 2009) seems comparable, in that the negative emotions usually associated with obsessions don't play a role, but the athlete is totally engaged in the activity, which motivates persistence despite obstacles, leading to outstanding performance. Positive psychology focuses on identifying and helping facilitate such valuable potentials in human personality.

flow
a state of deep engagement in an activity that is characteristic of creative individuals

Intrinsic Striving

Sometimes goals are attained by some action or good fortune that has nothing inherently positive about it. Money, for example, may be obtained by various means. The pathway to attaining the money may be extrinsic (like the good luck of winning a lottery) or intrinsic to our own effort (like working at an unpleasant job that pays well), but the happiness that comes from the goal (getting money) is separate from the effort. Contrast that with activities in which the effort toward the goal is enjoyable in itself: the musician immersed in a composition, whose joy comes as much from the work itself as from the outcome. That is, sometimes the means and the end can be separated, and sometimes they are inherently interrelated.

Positive psychology is particularly concerned with helping people to find those activities in which the joy is intrinsic to the effort, rather than tacked on as an external reward or incentive. This desirable state has been compared to the good life as described in ancient Greece by Aristotle, whose concept of eudaimonia refers to "a life comprised of actions that are worthwhile in themselves" (Fowers, Mollica, & Procacci, 2010). For example, a questionnaire devised to assess eudaimonic well-being includes the item, "I find I get intensely involved in many of the things I do each day" (Waterman et al., 2010). A meaningful life, and the quest for meaning in life, is not always happy (Schnell, 2009), but it does bring a deep sense of satisfaction.

A theoretical precursor to this interest is Edward Deci's concept of intrinsic motivation (Deci, 1975), which led to a more refined theoretical model, *self-determination theory* (SDT) (Ryan & Deci, 2000). Deci's best-known theoretical concept, **intrinsic motivation**, refers to "doing an activity for the inherent satisfaction of the activity itself" (Ryan & Deci, 2000, p. 71). Self-determination theory proposes that people innately have three important psychological needs: competence, autonomy, and relatedness (Ryan & Deci, 2000). All of these needs must be satisfied if an individual is to thrive. When these basic needs are satisfied, self-motivation is enhanced: People work more persistently, perform better, and are more creative. They

intrinsic motivation
motivation to perform an activity for its inherent satisfaction (rather than as a means to some other goal)

have a higher self-esteem and sense of well-being. Mental health improves. However, when these needs are not satisfied, well-being suffers and motivation decreases.

Money Does Not Bring Lasting Happiness

Researchers have shown us that money isn't as important for happiness as most people think. Fantasies of a happy future often involve money, whether won by chance or conscientiously saved. Yet when people win money in a lottery, their increased happiness is temporary, and soon it drops back to the level of happiness they experienced before their good fortune (Lykken & Tellegen, 1996; Myers & Diener, 1995). External good fortune, such as coming into money, doesn't bring lasting happiness; we get used to our new fortune and it no longer brings a pleasure boost, as the concept of *adaptation level* explains. Once you're used to designer handbags or state-of-the-art computers, you take them for granted.

Money generally does not raise people's level of happiness as much as they expect. To some extent, it increases happiness for the poor, by permitting satisfaction of needs (King & Napa, 1998; Myers & Diener, 1995). However, national surveys show that people with very low incomes in the United States are not as unhappy as most people think they would be (Aknin, Norton, & Dunn, 2009). Although there may be some methodological shortcomings (e.g., those with low incomes may include more retirees and students who are less vulnerable financially than underrepresented homeless people), the researchers believe the effect to be real. Those with less money take joy in things that money can't buy, like family and friendships.

Other research finds that when money is spent on material goods, such as clothing, it brings less satisfaction than when it is spent on life experiences, such as tickets to a concert or ski slope (Van Boven, 2005). One of the differences is that life experiences are more likely to bring interpersonal interactions, and this relationship satisfaction contributes to subjective well-being (Howell & Hill, 2009).

In social circumstances that are economically secure, a movement toward "voluntary simplicity" often emerges, in which people voluntarily turn away from consumption toward other values, including the arts and education—choices that have beneficial consequences for the environment and for the economic well-being of those less well off (Etzioni, 1998), as well as directing attention toward the true causes of happiness.

A Meaningful Life

One important contributor to life satisfaction is people's sense that their life has meaning. People who report that their lives are meaningful are more satisfied than those who do not find meaning (e.g., Bronk et al., 2009). Positive affect and satisfying relationships are among the factors that contribute to the judgment that life is meaningful (Hicks & King, 2009).

As Gordon Allport (see Chapter 7) described, one basis for finding a coherent sense of meaning in life is religion. Positive psychology has found that some religious values, such as forgiveness, contribute to a person's well-being, so it is perhaps not surprising that people who become more religious over time also increase their well-being, based on a longitudinal study in Germany (Headey et al., 2010). The ability to forgive others, including one's spouse, is one beneficial trait contributing to well-being (e.g., Miller & Worthington, 2010). Both forgiveness and religion contribute to a sense of community, and it is well established that supportive interpersonal relationships contribute to well-being, so perhaps it is the relationships that are the key. As a species, we depend upon others for survival, and forgiveness, according to an evolutionary explanation, is an adaptive mechanism that helps restore disrupted relationships with those close to us, thus enhancing survival (Hogan, 2010; McCullough, 2008). Its centrality to survival explains why forgiveness feels so good. Besides forgiveness, positive psychology research affirms that happiness is increased by intentionally performing acts of kindness toward others (Lyubomirsky, Sheldon, & Schkade, 2005) and by "doing good" for others by, for example, giving blood (Piliavin, 2003). Whether framed by individuals in a religious context or not, these altruistic social behaviors enhance happiness by contributing to a meaningful life.

Altruism is motivated by empathy for the other person's suffering. A slightly different concept has been proposed, emphasizing justice. *Civil courage* is defined as "brave behavior accompanied by anger and indignation which intends to enforce societal and ethical norms without considering one's own social costs" (Greitemeyer et al., 2007, p. 115). In the face of an injustice against others, a person with civil courage may protest or take other action.

Culture and Happiness

People seek happiness in a variety of ways, whether directly pursuing pleasure (hedonism), or emphasizing a meaningful life; and there seem to be some cultural differences as well (Park, Peterson, & Ruch, 2009). Based on their review of positive psychology interventions in clinical practice, for example, Sin and Lyubomirsky (2009) suggest that prevention of depression in collectivist cultures should emphasize activities focused on other people, such as performing acts of kindness and writing a letter of gratitude, in contrast to interventions such as reflecting on personal strengths, which is more suitable for individualistic cultures.

POSITIVE TRAITS

Traits, as the term is generally used in personality, are stable characteristics that describe individual differences. While the descriptive emphasis of the trait perspective (Part III of this text) aimed, as much as possible, to be neutral as to values, positive psychology is unabashed about valuing some traits more than others. What traits are desirable that contribute to well-being? We'll see that optimism, among others, earns the endorsement of positive psychologists. Among the Big Five factors, emotional stability (low neuroticism) and extraversion are correlated with fewer negative emotions and higher life satisfaction (Pavot & Diener, 2008).

As we saw in Chapters 8 and 9, many traits are influenced by genetics. But as we will see, behaviors associated with traits can also be cultivated or learned, and positive psychology suggests interventions to accomplish this. Thus the predictions of positive outcomes from traits are but a stepping-stone toward teaching people how to live a good and happy life.

Optimism

Optimism is the tendency to expect positive rather than negative outcomes. It contributes to health and helps protect against depression. Longitudinal research shows that pessimistic explanatory style predicts poor health some decades later (Peterson, Seligman, & Vaillant, 1988). Other traits closely related to optimism, such as hope, also have beneficial effects on well-being (Gallagher & Lopez, 2009). To some critics, optimism is overrated, reflecting American cultural values, as a psychological value. Nonetheless there is a strong body of evidence relating optimism to mental health, justifying its role in models of mental health (Vaillant, 2003), as well as physical health.

Among people suffering with the debilitating disease of multiple sclerosis, those who are more optimistic have a variety of better outcomes, including less anxiety and depression, more positive expectations about the future, and better adjustment on physical and social as well as psychological measures (Dennison, Moss-Morris, & Chalder, 2009).

Optimists expect the future to be better than the past (higher in anticipated life satisfaction), but at least one study of undergraduates finds that pessimists do, too (Busseri, Choma, & Sadava, 2009). In this study, optimists reported higher life satisfaction throughout time (past, present, and future) than pessimists. Intriguing was a finding that pessimists expected the future to be better than the present, while optimists reported that their life satisfaction in the present was already as high as it would be in the future. It isn't clear whether this study of undergraduates will be replicated in other samples and at other ages, but it seems wise to not assume that optimism can be equated with future expectations.

Other research examines the social behavior of optimists compared to those who score lower on this trait (pessimists). Do optimists just feel better, or do they do better as well? Research supports the second alternative. For example, under certain conditions when white undergraduates who hold egalitarian values have heard a racially prejudiced remark, optimists were more likely than pessimists to challenge it (Wellman, Czopp, & Geers, 2009).

Values and Strengths

Psychology draws on traditions of thought that preceded the establishment of our separate discipline, and we can look there for guidance. An examination of philosophical and religious teachings worldwide suggests six "core virtues" that are positive traits: "courage, justice, humanity, temperance, wisdom, and transcendence" (Dahlsgaard, Peterson, & Seligman, 2005).

Positive values such as these contrast with an emphasis on negativity and problems that has characterized much of mainstream psychology. A project spearheaded by Christopher Peterson provides an inventory of strengths, in contrast to the typology of weaknesses in the *Diagnostic and Statistical Manual for Mental Disorders*. This Values in Action (VIA) Classification of Strengths describes positive qualities that will enable a person to fulfill values that are deemed desirable. The classification lists six categories of strengths: wisdom and knowledge, courage, love, justice, temperance, and transcendence (Peterson, 2006). Each of these strengths can be measured, indicating whether a person has sufficient strength in that area (e.g., kindness, as one of the love values), or perhaps too little (indifference) or too much (intrusiveness). A disorder, from this perspective, is the lack of a desirable strength (in contrast to the presence of an illness, such as schizophrenia, listed in the *DSM*). With this model, Peterson is suggesting how positive psychology can contribute to understanding psychological disorders.

Defense mechanisms (see Chapter 2) provide ways of coping with psychological problems, but in addition, the mature defenses include such virtues as altruism and humor. George Vaillant (2000) integrates his influential research on defense mechanisms with positive psychology by noting that in contrast to immature defenses, the mature defenses—such as altruism, suppression, humor, anticipation, and sublimation—are quite relevant to positive psychology. Other positive psychologists have begun to examine types of humor (Beermann & Ruch, 2009), which can help differentiate positively valued, nonhostile humor from that which is hurtful to others.

Another healthy defense mechanism is *positive reframing*. Looking at what is generally thought of as a negative event through different eyes, to see the positive aspects of the situation, contributes to well-being by enhancing people's sense of coherence, that is, their belief "that life is manageable, meaningful, and comprehensible" (Lambert et al., 2009).

Resiliency

resiliency

the strength to survive stressful situations or those in which one is mistreated, without experiencing the usual negative consequences of such experiences

An important concept in health psychology, resiliency focuses on strength, as is characteristic of positive psychology. **Resiliency** is the strength to survive stressful situations or those in which one is mistreated, without experiencing the usual negative consequences of such experiences. One aspect of resiliency is the ability to bounce back from stress, which contributes to emotional well-being and physical health (Smith et al., 2010). Resilient responses to terrorist attacks include an enhanced sense of solidarity with others in one's country who are targeted (Vázquez & Hervás, 2010).

Some individuals are unusually resilient in coping with very stressful life events, such as the loss of a spouse or life partner (Bonanno et al., 2005). Even in the face of major loss, they are not overcome with grief but express positive emotions, according to their friends. That is, they create meaning out of adverse life events, which is a different process than simply finding meaning when good things happen to us (King & Hicks, 2009).

An exciting feature of the positive psychology approach to resiliency is that it is not simply a trait, but a set of habits or skills that can be taught. Several examples of such interventions will be described here, but they are only a sampling. Learning about the specific ways that resilient individuals differ from those who are less able to cope with adversity can provide hope for those who wish to make *intentional change* in their lives. Based on concepts from complexity theory (which will be discussed briefly in Chapter 17), researchers studying ways to help patients with diabetes to better manage their chronic disease argue that there is particular value in focusing on positive emotions rather than negative emotions—an idea that is consistent with both positive psychology and with the idea of "positive emotional attractors" in complexity theory (Dyck, Caron, & Aron, 2006). Their argument suggests that there is more than a psychological reason for the superiority of positive thoughts, including "one's personal values, dreams, hopes, ideal sense of self and/or strengths" (p. 673). In addition, their theory suggests that such positivity activates the parasympathetic nervous system, with its calming and health-producing effects (in contrast to the sympathetic nervous system activation of negative thoughts). Negativity may back us into a corner of stressful immobilization, but positivity can pull us (as an "attractor" in complexity theory) to new habits.

A variety of *positive psychology interventions* have been developed to help people attain enhanced well-being (see Table 15.3). Interventions, ranging from writing letters of gratitude to thinking optimistically to socializing, have been shown to increase subjective well-being in nonclinical samples, and interventions with clinical samples are also effective in reducing depression (Sin & Lyubomirsky, 2009). For example, college students who were trained to improve their hardiness in a college course not only scored higher on written measures of hardiness after the training, but also improved their grades in a 2-year follow-up period after the course, showing that hardiness training improves college achievement (Maddi et al., 2009).

Another study explored an intervention to deal with being insulted. Ruminating on interpersonal insults prolongs the suffering. There are better ways to cope, and to some extent, people can be taught how to cope more effectively with interpersonal offenses. College students were asked to recall a situation in which someone hurt and offended them. They were taught to have compassion for the offender, or to find benefits for themselves in the offensive situation. This intervention led to improved emotional states and reduced tension in cardiovascular activity and facial expression (vanOyen Witvliet, Hinman, & DeYoung, 2010).

Positive psychology encourages the development of positive emotions as a strategy for improving subjective well-being. Indeed, increasing life satisfaction among youth may be an important step toward for subsequent psychological, social, and behavioral benefits (Proctor, Linley, & Maltby, 2009). An intervention that had children and adolescents write and deliver a letter expressing gratitude to someone who had

Table 15.3 Examples of Positive Psychology Interventions to Enhance Well-Being

Best possible self exercise	Imagine yourself in the future, when everything has gone as well as it possibly could, and you have reached your full potential. Write about this and reflect on it.
Blessings exercise	At the end of the day, reflect on three things that went well that day, for which you are grateful.
Gratitude visit	Write a letter expressing gratitude to someone you have never properly thanked. Visit the person and read the letter to him or her.
Life summary	Write a summary of your life as you would like to be remembered. Reflect on what you could change to bring this about.
Savoring exercise	Take a few minutes to reflect on a pleasurable experience and enjoy the positive emotions.
Strengths exercise	Identify areas of your personal strength. Find new ways to use these strengths in your life.

Source: Prepared from information in Peters et al. (2010); Schueller (2010).

been kind to them, seems to have increased feelings of gratitude (compared to a control group that wrote about daily life events), particularly among those who began with more negative emotions (Froh et al., 2009). *Behavioral activation*, an approach also used to treat depression, is engaging in activities that an individual values and enjoys, which vary from one person to another (Mazzucchelli, Kane, & Rees, 2010). This increases positive well-being even among nondepressed people.

Overall, then, positive psychologists have studied individual differences in traits and behaviors to identify those that contribute to well-being, and then have been able to develop effective interventions to teach these behaviors to others.

POSITIVE INSTITUTIONS

Just as Maslow earlier had discussed work, education, and other institutions from the perspective of his needs hierarchy theory, so have positive psychologists. Positive psychology has developed many interdisciplinary connections that foster applications to diverse fields, including organizational behavior, education, health care, and political science (Donaldson & Ko, 2010).

The Workplace

Following through on Maslow's suggestion, positive psychology has been applied to improve the work environment, humanizing its atmosphere for workers and bringing improved health and reduced stress that also benefit the financial bottom line.

In work organizations, positive outcomes including job satisfaction, performance, and organizational commitment are predicted by such positive psychology traits as optimism, hope, and resiliency (Donaldson & Ko, 2010). It isn't all a matter of mental attitude, of course. Having needed resources and support and avoiding excessive job demands are among the organizational factors that foster well-being at work, including the experience of "flow" that was described above (Donaldson & Ko, 2010).

When positive psychology principles are applied in the workplace, employee engagement increases, and this may increase productivity and profits, as well as contributing to lower employee turnover and higher customer satisfaction (Harter, Schmidt, & Keyes, 2003). Many of the contributing factors to such a desirable outcome are within the power of supervisors: conveying clear expectations, providing adequate resources, showing appreciation, ensuring that the employee's characteristics are a good fit with the job, and so on.

One line of study examines *executive coaching* for managers or supervisors. This one-on-one support for leaders is different from group-based leadership training, and can assist executives with the unique challenges of their work at a particular point in time. Techniques may draw on various theories, including cognitive behavioral approaches (which emphasize setting goals and developing ways of attaining them) and even psychodynamic approaches (dealing with interpersonal issues), as well as positive psychology. Positive psychology contributes attention to subjective well-being and resiliency, which are enhanced by executive coaching, along with more objective measures of work productivity (Grant, Curtayne, & Burton, 2009).

Schools

Schools have the potential to support children's development of resiliency and other healthy traits and habits (Baker et al., 2003). From the perspective of positive psychology, schools should aim to develop the strengths of all children, as reflected in measures of life satisfaction, and should avoid the practice of focusing only on children who are at risk (Gilman & Huebner, 2003). This is analogous to the need to focus on mental health, and not simply the absence of disease.

From a positive psychology perspective, school counselors are advised to take an approach called Developmental Advocacy, supporting the strengths that develop resiliency in students (Galassi & Akos, 2004). Gifted students have particular needs that positive psychology can address, such as the need to be provided with a sufficiently challenging curriculum to avoid boredom (Reis & Renzulli, 2004).

Qualities identified by positive psychologists make teachers more effective. Among teachers in public schools without adequate resources, those who began their first year of teaching with a trait that the researchers called "grit" and with high life satisfaction, produced the best learning outcomes in their students during this first year (Duckworth, Quinn, & Seligman, 2009). In addition, as Maslow argued, the qualities of students contribute to positive educational outcomes when the environment is conducive to growth.

THE PROMISE OF POSITIVE PSYCHOLOGY

Positive psychology aims to expand on the humanistic legacy by making it more scientific. Building a foundation of solid research can provide more certain guidance for actualizing the positive visions of humanism in the real world where personality lives.

Why should we—as people living our lives, and also as psychology investigators—pay attention to the qualities emphasized by positive psychologists? A Native American legend from the Cherokee people is sometimes invoked to explain this. It describes a conversation between an old Cherokee and his grandson. The story describes a fight between two wolves: an evil wolf who is resentful, greedy, and full of other flaws, and a good wolf who is generous and compassionate. Grandfather says all of us experience a similar fight within us. The grandson asks "Which wolf will win?" Grandfather's answer: "The one you feed" (First people, n.d.).

Positive psychology, building on its humanistic psychology foundation, reminds us to feed our understanding of the human potential for good.

Summary

- Maslow proposed a third force humanistic psychology that is less deterministic and more focused on values than psychoanalysis or behaviorism.
- Maslow proposed that people develop through five levels of a *need hierarchy:* physiological, safety, love and belongingness, esteem, and self-actualization.
- At the four lower stages, a person is motivated by deficiencies. At the highest stage, *self-actualization*, the person is motivated by *being motivation* and has distinctive characteristics, foremost of which is creativity.
- Peak experiences are mystical states of consciousness that are particularly common among self-actualized people.
- Maslow's theory has implications for many fields and is closely associated with the *human potential movement.*
- Maslow urged religion to be less dogmatic and more concerned with growth. In addition to psychotherapy, his work prompted the development of growth centers, where people could live in a community that promoted self-actualization.
- Maslow urged employers to be more concerned with the growth needs of their employees and educators to encourage personal growth and creativity among students. He urged psychology to be more concerned with human values.
- Maslow criticized mainstream psychology for being method centered rather than problem centered, and he argued that scientific investigation of the highest human potentials requires the development of new models of science.
- Positive psychology has built on Maslow's emphasis on subjective experience and growth, adding scientific research to the humanistic base.
- Positive subjective experience, like happiness, life satisfaction, and flow, has benefits for individuals that include improved health and productivity.
- Positive traits, like optimism and resiliency, predict beneficial outcomes. Furthermore, they can be developed by positive psychology interventions.
- Positive institutions, like properly functioning work and school environments, have the potential to improve individual outcomes and to function more effectively.

Thinking about Maslow's Theory and Positive Psychology

1. Maslow found only 1 out of 3,000 undergraduates to be self-actualized. Do you think there would be fewer, more, or the same number today, considering changes in the student population (such as more students returning to school at later ages and a greater ethnic and racial diversity)?
2. Discuss the implications of Maslow's hierarchy of needs for current society. Are there factors (e.g., poverty or crime) that can be interpreted in terms of deficiency motivation?
3. Maslow suggested that sexuality is partly a physiological need and partly a belongingness need. Are any other levels of the need hierarchy relevant to understanding sexuality in the context of current society? Explain.
4. Are any of the listed characteristics of self-actualized people not indicators, in your opinion, of a high level of development?
5. Contrast Maslow's description of Taoist Science with the description of science in Chapter 1.
6. Thinking about all the psychology you have studied (in this and other courses), is the emphasis on positive psychology and healthy functioning unusual?
7. Can you suggest other areas where positive psychology could conduct research and/or offer interventions?
8. How would you reply to someone who knows about positive psychology only through superficial media reports, and who says it is a waste of time and money to study something as inconsequential as happiness?

Study Questions

1. What is third force psychology?
2. Contrast Maslow's view of psychology with that of mainstream psychology. In particular, how important is scientific methodology? What else is important?
3. Discuss the role of values and experiential knowledge in Maslow's theory.
4. List and explain the levels of Maslow's hierarchy of needs. What is implied by having them arranged in a hierarchy?
5. Contrast deficiency motivation with being motivation. Include the differences between D-love and B-love.
6. What is self-actualization? How is it different from mental health? From public success?
7. List and explain characteristics of a person who is self-actualized.
8. What are peak experiences? Discuss the types of people who experience them.
9. From his description of self-actualized people, discuss Maslow's attitude toward both religion and ethics.
10. Explain what Maslow meant by creativity as a characteristic of a self-actualized person. How is this different from musical or artistic talent?
11. How is self-actualization measured?
12. How common is self-actualization? Why is it not more common?
13. Discuss implications of Maslow's theory for the workplace.
14. Explain what Maslow meant by desacralization.
15. Discuss implications of Maslow's theory for education.
16. What is positive psychology? What is its relationship to Maslow's theory?
17. List the three pillars of positive psychology. Give an example of each.
18. What is life satisfaction and why is it important?
19. What is flow?
20. What is intrinsic striving (or intrinsic motivation)?
21. Does money bring happiness? What is the research evidence?
22. What contributes to a meaningful life?
23. How is optimism related to health?
24. Describe Peterson's Values in Action model.
25. What is resiliency?
26. Describe a workplace that is desirable, from the perspective of positive psychology.
27. How does positive psychology apply to schools?
28. According to the Cherokee legend, how do we cultivate positive characteristics?

Buddhist Psychology
Lessons from Eastern Culture

ILLUSTRATIVE BIOGRAPHY
The Dalai Lama

Dalai Lama

Buddhist approaches to personality are derived from a religious tradition dating back two and a half millennia. This rich tradition has many practices and writings that are closer to personality theory than to what we in Western cultures think of as religion. Buddhism emphasizes exploration and control of the mind, so it is a cognitive approach. It also has much to say about ethical behavior. The current leader of Tibetan Buddhism, the 14th Dalai Lama, travels widely and collaborates with psychologists and others.

In the remote and mountainous Asian country of Tibet, a succession of Tibetan Buddhist leaders, whose title "Dalai Lama" means "Ocean of Wisdom" (Bstan-dzin-rgya-mtsho, 1989), lived in isolation from the rest of the world and provided spiritual and political guidance for their people. This changed with the invasion of the country by China in the middle of the twentieth century. After many failed attempts to keep Tibet free from Chinese rule, on May 31, 1959, the 23-year-old 14th Dalai Lama (whose personal name is Tenzin Gyatso but spelled Bstan-dzin-rgya-mtsho in conventional library usage and so in the references at the end of this book) fled his palace in Lhasa, Tibet. With a group of supporters, he established a community of refugees in neighboring India, where the city of Dharamsala has become the seat of the Tibetan government-in-exile (Bstan-dzin-rgya-mtsho, 1990). Thrust into the larger world, unlike all the earlier Dalai Lamas, he has met with political and religious leaders throughout the world and has engaged in dialogues on political freedom, modern science, and religion, bringing the tradition of Buddhism with its insights to the problems of the modern world. Tibet, too, has lost its isolation, with the completion of a railroad connection between Lhasa, Tibet, and Qinghai, China, in the summer of 2006 (Kahn, 2006).

(continued)

(*continued*)

DESCRIPTION

Because the emphasis is not on stable personality—the very idea of which is considered an illusion (Kamilar, 2002)—but rather on spiritual progress, personality description is closely connected with ideas of development and adaptation (or spiritual progress). People who have risen to higher levels of development are calm and compassionate. Those who remain less developed have more troubled traits.

The Dalai Lama would certainly be described as highly developed, which translates into the trait term of *compassionate*. Those who have observed him and his effect on people give many examples of this compassion: listening to people with a variety of troubles; taking time to greet hotel staff individually instead of looking past them as invisible persons of no consequence, the way so many guests do; turning from a crowd of people to offer individual attention to a man showing the telltale physical tremors of long-term mental illness treatment. Despite his high status, he is unpretentious and lives the humble, celibate, reflective life of a Buddhist monk. He is described as approachable and practical, answering questions in thoughtful and often commonsense ways, and unafraid to say, "I don't know" when that is the case. He frequently smiles and makes jokes. In his autobiographical writings, the Dalai Lama also reports aspects of his personality that would be of interest to other personality theories: an interest in mechanics that from childhood had him tinkering with mechanical things, including watches and cars, and led him to comment that if he had another career than Dalai Lama, he might be an engineer (Knight, 2004). His interest in science made him receptive to some cultural modernization trends, and he muses that this scientific interest led to Chairman Mao of China's underestimation of spiritual dedication when the two met, before the Chinese invasion and occupation forced his exile from Tibet (Bstan-dzin-rgya-mtsho, 1990).

ADJUSTMENT

Buddhism describes adaptation and adjustment in spiritual terms. Poor adjustment is reflected in ways familiar to Western psychologists: impulsive and addictive behavior, selfishness, anxiety, and other adverse emotional states. In Buddhist teaching, healthy growth requires clear and undistorted perception of reality as it is, which requires giving up the illusory notion of a separate self and recognizing the interrelationships of all people and all that exists in the natural world. Other theories have described narcissism as unhealthy self-absorption, but the Buddhist approach goes much further, teaching that the individualism generally regarded as normal and healthy in our culture is inherently unhealthy and a cause of suffering. Selfish acts are evidence of shortcomings. Happiness is the reward for spiritual growth and ethical living.

In both Buddhist teaching and Western psychotherapy, healthy functioning requires undistorted perception. Much that the Dalai Lama says reflects his openness to new information. Instead of adhering to a dogmatic viewpoint, he welcomes dialogue with modern brain researchers to explore the relationships between meditation and brain functioning (as described later in this chapter). Emotional well-being reflects adjustment, and he claims to be happy, despite a variety of adversities, including exile from his homeland and the death of many family members and friends. The Dalai Lama recounts childhood impatience and conflict with his brother, confessing that he was the aggressor, and he notes that in childhood he played with toy soldiers. As an adult, however, his patience and calmness are well known.

COGNITION

Cognitive processes receive considerable emphasis in this ancient discipline. Through meditation, with disciplined examination of the contents of consciousness, centuries of insights detail people's distorted thinking that leads them to act foolishly or unethically. The fundamental error is "our passionate desire for and attachment to things that we misapprehend as enduring entities" (Bstan-dzin-rgya-mtsho, 1989). We do not realize how transient everything is. We must become aware of suffering (the first of the Four Noble Truths), including the reality of death. Buddhist tradition urges people to meditate, to be aware of their perceptions, and to question the validity of what they think they know, to come closer to true reality.

In keeping with Buddhist practices, the Dalai Lama spends considerable time in meditation. He prays 4 hours a day (Bstan-dzin-rgya-mtsho & Cutler, 1998). He connects with suffering humanity, bringing the pain of others into his own consciousness. The Dalai Lama describes his education as rich in many ways but without exposure to modern science. His writings convey an unusual degree of intellectual curiosity and open-mindedness to new ideas. For example, earlier in his life, he saw visible shadows on the moon's surface, and so acknowledged that the moon did not emit light as classic Buddhist texts said but rather reflected it. Now he engages in enthusiastic dialogues with modern neuroscientists about the nature of consciousness. One place that such interchange between Buddhism and science occurs is at the Mind and Life Institute in Colorado, established to promote such a dialogue (http://www.mindandlife.org).

Despite his openness to scientific analysis of Buddhist practices, the Dalai Lama rejects the Western tendency to see biology as the fundamental cause of mental processes. Instead, he argues for the Buddhist emphasis on thought as a cause and challenges the tendency of reducing it to biological or neural processes as a Western prejudice. Science and Buddhism, he argues, can each learn from the other. Scientists can learn more about consciousness by including, among their research participants, those who have developed their consciousness to high levels through Buddhist meditation. Conversely, he expresses openness to integrating the findings of modern science into his Buddhist beliefs, and he says he would change those beliefs if science can prove them wrong (Goleman, 2004).

BIOLOGY

Buddhist sages and Western neuroscientists are now actively collaborating to understand consciousness. In contrast to the tendency in modern psychology to think of the body and brain as determinants or limiters of psychological functioning, Buddhism suggests a more interactive model. Mental processes can be truly causal, changing biology, in this model. This does not deny the role of biology, though. Diet and behavior are the first line of treatment for disease, and Tibetan medicine also uses organic medicines, acupuncture and heat treatments, and surgery (Bstan-dzin-rgya-mtsho, 1990, p. 219). The Buddhist worldview regards a person's status and characteristics in this lifetime as bearing the results of past lives, so that whatever Western approaches describe as the hereditary aspects of personality would, from a Buddhist viewpoint, be the moral legacy of past lives.

According to this doctrine, the selection of Tenzin Gyatso as the next Dalai Lama recognized his entitlement to this high position. Buddhist rebirth teaching says that the previous

Dalai Lama chose to be reborn in this child. In the context of a tradition that regards the idea of a separate individual self or soul as illusory, this is a difficult idea to conceptualize. The attitude created by the doctrine, however, is clear: The Dalai Lama's high position is an entitlement and so should not provoke envy, in the way that random genetic gifts can seem unfair. In terms of his own biology, the Dalai Lama has led a healthy life, following the Buddhist practices of healthy eating, avoiding alcohol, and practicing meditation. He confesses that his diet is not strictly vegetarian, his health having suffered when he tried (after observing a chicken being slaughtered) to give up meat (Bstan-dzin-rgya-mtsho, 1990). Tibetan people have traditionally incorporated meat in their diet, because of the harsh mountain climate that makes a purely vegetarian diet inadequate.

CULTURE

Although individuals are responsible for their behavior and development, society is also important in Buddhist teaching. The individual influences others and has a responsibility to help reduce others' suffering. Buddhists are concerned with ethics; in modern times Buddhists are involved in such humanitarian concerns as peace and environmentalism. The individual's relationship to society goes in the reverse direction also. The society in which the individual is developing can help or hinder individual development, so it is important to put oneself in a healthy community environment (*sangha*).

The invasion of his homeland by the Chinese impelled the Dalai Lama to deal with larger social issues. He has voiced insights about some of the world's most difficult problems, including war, starvation, the environment, sexuality, and abortion. His identity and loyalty for his homeland, Tibet, have prompted him to advocate that it be restored to independence, and he tries to maintain Tibetan culture through education and cultural practices in the exile communities in India and elsewhere. He proposed a peace plan between Tibet and China in 1987 that would have (among other provisions) removed armaments from Tibet, stopping its use as a place to produce nuclear weapons and store nuclear waste. His proposal would have preserved Tibet's cultural identity by stopping the influx of Chinese people, who now outnumber native Tibetans. Although not implemented, this proposal was influential in his nomination for the Nobel Peace Prize, awarded in 1989. His discussions of peace do not satisfy some critics because he stops short of demanding full political independence of Tibet from China, and once the United States invaded Iraq, he did not demand cessation of hostilities there either, despite having objected to the war ahead of time (Goodstein, 2003; Zupp, 2004). These positions, however, can be understood from the Buddhist principle of accepting reality as it is. Once China invaded Tibet and the United States invaded Iraq, he accepted those realities and discussed, as a realist, what should happen next.

Although embracing Buddhism for himself, the Dalai Lama recognizes the value of many religious traditions, and he does not wish for everyone to become a Buddhist. Other religions may be better suited for other people (Bstan-dzin-rgya-mtsho & Cutler, 1998). His tolerance extends to the nonreligious as well, recognizing the secularization of society, and he argues that individuals can be spiritual even if they do not identify with a formal religious tradition.

DEVELOPMENT

Buddhist psychology emphasizes continued growth. The emphasis is not on external determinants, such as the influence of family or society, but rather on the individual's own choices and actions. In the model of development that Buddhism accepts, development spans not only one lifetime but also time before birth in past lives and after death in the next rebirth. Intentional acts that are virtuous boost the individual toward higher states, according to the principle of moral causality (karma), and also have beneficial consequences for others.

Other approaches to personality development would find, in the 14th Dalai Lama, evidence of an active, assertive childhood. The Dalai Lama reports that he fought with his brother, resisted school lessons, ate what was not permitted, and only in adolescence fully appreciated the Buddhist legacy and its scholarship. (This nicely fits the stage of identity formation, in Erik Erikson's theory.)

Beyond this normal developmental pattern, the Buddhist approach outlines a larger developmental perspective, spanning multiple lifetimes. On the issue of rebirth, the Dalai Lama describes his life from the perspective of the Buddhist tradition, telling anecdotes from childhood that seem premonitions of his high destiny. For example, as a child he insisted on sitting at the head of the table, and he fantasized a trip to the city of Lhasa, location of the palace of the Dalai Lama (Bstan-dzin-rgya-mtsho, 1990). Despite being chosen for his leadership role, he still faced many years of demanding education and examinations before officially becoming a Buddhist monk. As an adult, his continued study and service to humanity are evidence of ongoing development. In the Buddhist worldview, if that development reaches a sufficient level, after death he would be free of the cycle of rebirth.

FINAL THOUGHTS

This is a unique illustrative biography, not only because of the cross-cultural focus of the subject matter, but also because the Dalai Lama is a spokesperson for the theory and so mixes teaching with his life story. An issue to consider, which will not be resolved here but only suggested, is this: Are the concepts about personality universal in their application? That is, do Buddhist insights apply to a Western audience? Conversely, could we apply our Western theories to the Dalai Lama (as in the identity suggestion earlier), or are the cultures so different that they require different theories?

PREVIEW: OVERVIEW OF BUDDHIST PSYCHOLOGY

Buddhism has become a popular influence in personality and clinical psychology. Buddhism has implications for major theoretical questions in personality psychology, as presented in Table 16.1. It presents an elaborate model of psychological development with traditional practices, especially meditation, to foster healthy growth. It emphasizes universal potentialities in the human condition, rather than individual differences in stable characteristics. Buddhism teaches nonjudgmental acceptance of experience, including the experience of human suffering, and

Table 16.1 Preview of Buddhist Personality Theory

Individual Differences	Buddhist approaches emphasize the commonalities among people. Differences occur in the specific content of consciousness, but these are transient, and the emphasis is on a common developmental progression.
Adaptation and Adjustment	Buddhism explains suffering and its causes, and offers an Eightfold Path to alleviate suffering and bring happiness. It offers detailed practices for improving mental functioning, through various kinds of yoga and meditation.
Cognitive Processes	Wrong thinking is a fundamental cause of suffering. Meditation improves cognitive functioning. The idea of a stable, enduring self is seen as an illusion with adverse consequences.
Culture	The individual is not separate from others or the world as a whole, and individual development has positive consequences for the world. Conversely, a supportive community improves individual functioning.
Biological Influences	The Buddhist worldview does not see the body and mind as separate but rather as closely related, so improved consciousness has beneficial health effects.
Development	Development results from systematic and intensive spiritual practices, and is an individual responsibility. In contrast to other approaches, Buddhism does not look to external causes, such as the family or the environment, as the cause of development or developmental failures.

emphasizes change and the transitory nature of experience, including the experience of the self. Its influence on Western psychology, especially therapy, is increasing.

THE RELEVANCE OF BUDDHISM FOR PERSONALITY PSYCHOLOGY

William James, one of the primary founders of American psychology, admired the psychological ideas contained in Buddhism and predicted that psychology would soon be influenced by Buddhism (Michalon, 2001). His prediction was premature but not wrong. Several of the theorists described in earlier chapters in this book mentioned Buddhist concepts in their own writing. Karen Horney studied Zen Buddhism at the end of her life (Morvay, 1999; Westkott, 1998). Carl Jung was visited in 1958 at his home by Buddhist Zen master Hisamatsu Shin'ichi, and the two discussed their areas of common interest, although the difference between the two views was immense (Haule, 2000; Heisig, 2002); Zen Buddhism goes much farther than Jung in questioning the value of the ego and goes even deeper into the unconscious (Steffney, 1975).

As a religion, Buddhism has been neglected by researchers who have developed measures of religious orientation, such as those presented in Chapter 7 (Tsang & McCullough, 2003). Here we study it as a psychology, not a religion. Buddhism is in many ways more comparable to Western psychotherapy than to Western religion (Muramoto, 2002). It provides ways of knowing about reality based on personal experience, and it does not ask people to accept the idea of a god or the teachings of a dogma or of any particular teacher. The separation between the sacred and the secular, which has been part of Western culture for hundreds of years, is not characteristic of Eastern cultures. Additionally, Buddhism takes as a major goal the task of alleviating suffering, which makes it comparable to psychotherapy.

Many of the concepts in Buddhism, including the self, are also important ideas in theories of psychotherapy and personality. Buddhism urges self-control and disciplined understanding of the self through meditation. In contrast to humanistic approaches that are sometimes criticized as simplistic, urging people simply to become aware of their true self and follow its guidance, the Buddhist approach emphasizes mental discipline and restraint.

A BRIEF HISTORY OF BUDDHISM

Buddhism is one of the major Eastern world religions, with roots in the older Hinduism. Buddhism began in India about 2,500 years ago, when a man on a spiritual quest, named **Siddhartha Gautama**, reportedly reached enlightenment after years of searching. Siddhartha rejected many aspects of Hinduism, and he emphasized compassion and an individual quest for enlightenment. The name of the religion is based on the name, the **Buddha**, meaning "the Awakened One" (Richards & Bergin, 1997). Buddhism is not a deistic religion; it does not depend on a divine presence for wisdom or salvation. It is quite psychological, describing human nature and emphasizing ethics (Finn & Rubin, 2000).

One fundamental idea that Buddhism and Hinduism share is the concept of **rebirth**. Existence is continuous, extending beyond death and before birth. The condition in which a person is born depends on intentional actions in past lives. Cause and effect continue beyond the death of the individual. It is not the individual that continues beyond death, however. Buddhism teaches that the individual self is an illusion, a false perception; what continues beyond death is a broader reality, of which the individual is only one brief and fleeting component. This idea is often conveyed by the metaphor of a wave on an ocean: The individual self is like a wave that rises and falls, but that is in reality not separate from the ocean but only a transitory form.

Biography of Siddhartha Gautama

Buddhism traces its origins to a man whose spiritual path inspired others to follow. About 2,500 years ago, in or around 563 BC, a wealthy and privileged young prince in northern India ventured out from his overprotective paternal home, leaving his wife of 13 years and his child. He saw, for the first time, people suffering and dying. Instead of retreating back into his shelter, as his father wished, he began a quest for understanding suffering and happiness that ultimately led to his enlightenment and to the founding of a new religious tradition. This man was Siddhartha Gautama (Knierim, n.d.).

According to legend, Siddhartha's father had a particular incentive to protect his son because prophecy predicted one of two destinies: He would become either a political leader or a religious ascetic. The father, Suddhodana, thought that preventing Gautama from seeing life's misery would preclude the religious ascetic path, but he did not succeed. Siddhartha left the palace to see the world, and to his shock, he realized that the sheltered life of the palace was not all there was to existence. Outside, people were ill. People became old, and they died. Now that he had witnessed human suffering, it troubled him. He also saw a religious man, who seemed at peace— suggesting a path that could provide an alternative to disillusionment. So he left his home, abandoning his family, and began a spiritual journey.

For 6 years Siddhartha wandered, studying under Hindu teachers and subjecting himself to strict discipline as a monk. He was brutal at self-mortification. But this did not satisfy his spiritual quest, and he tried other approaches. At one point, he indulged in the opposite extreme, enjoying many pleasures in a life of luxury. Neither extreme satisfied. He turned to a life of meditation and self-examination. Tradition has it that while meditating in the lotus position under a Bodhi tree, he finally and suddenly achieved **enlightenment**, understanding how to get rid of suffering by giving up illusions and desire. During his remaining long life, Siddhartha taught his insights to many disciples in northern India, dying at the age of 80.

THE BUDDHIST WORLDVIEW: THE FOUR NOBLE TRUTHS

Siddhartha Gautama conveyed the wisdom of his enlightenment through teaching the **Four Noble Truths**. Buddhism does not expect these truths to be accepted on the basis of authority. Instead, the approach is one of natural law, and people are encouraged to test the truths for themselves.

We are ignorant of the true nature of things, the **dharma**, mistaking appearances for reality (Mahathera, 1982). This ignorance is often called **delusion**. The true nature of things can be discovered through Buddhist teachings and practices, especially

---

Siddhartha Gautama

the historical Buddha, whose spiritual journey provided the foundation for Buddhism; also called Sakyamuni

Buddha

Awakened one; the term often refers to Siddhartha Gautama (Sakyamuni Buddha), who lived in India about 2,500 years ago; in some forms of Buddhism, it is held that everyone can attain buddha status (become a buddha) by following the path, although it may take more than one lifetime to achieve this

rebirth

continuation of the effects of karma in previous lifetimes into the present

Enlightenment

higher stage of consciousness that results from following the Eightfold Path; sometimes also used synonymously with Awakening

Four Noble Truths

that there is suffering, that it has a cause, that suffering can cease, and that there is a path to end suffering

dharma

the true, intrinsic nature of things

delusion

ignorance or false beliefs about the nature of reality

meditation. To an enlightened person, the dharma appears everywhere: in beautiful natural objects, in a baby crying, and even in unexpected places such as horseshit because nothing is rejected (Nhat Hanh, 1996, p. 24). Even suffering is part of the dharma. This approach accepts reality in its entirety.

The First Noble Truth: There is Suffering

The first fundamental lesson is that "there is suffering." The original Pali language word, **duhkha**, has other possible translations, including "unsatisfactoriness," "disharmony," "painfulness" (de Silva, 1990) and "frustration" (Hayes, 2003). Referring to being blocked in attaining what we want, frustration seems a particularly apt translation for psychology because so many of our theories describe human "needs" or "drives" and the efforts to satisfy them. Most people are not aware of the extent of suffering. They are not yet aware, in a traditional Buddhist image, that "the pretty, colored rope that one has found and treasures is actually a very poisonous snake" (Chen, 1999, p. 15). We are under the illusion that things are better than they are. The realization and acceptance of the fact of suffering motivates following the Buddha path.

Karen Horney (see Chapter 5) compared *duhkha* with the "basic anxiety" that she proposed in her own theory (Westkott, 1998). What is distinct is the Buddhist attitude of permitting suffering into consciousness, rather than suppressing or repressing painful experiences (Sumedho, 1992). Furthermore, we are not permitted to indulge in feeling sorry for ourselves.

The Second Noble Truth: The Origin of Suffering

The Second Noble Truth identifies the origin of suffering: craving, or **attachment** to desire. At root, the problem is ignorance because we are deluded about what would make us happy, and so we crave the wrong things (Bstan-dzin-rgya-mtsho, 2000). Consider addiction: If a craving for tobacco (or another drug) can be eliminated, the suffering of not having it will disappear. Similarly, if a desire for fame and fortune can be eliminated, the suffering of being ordinary and poor will disappear. Ordinary people, not yet enlightened, are caught up in **samsara**, the "wheel of suffering" in which the consequences of ignorant craving and bad behavior cause continued suffering and prevent attaining nirvana and liberation from the cycle of rebirth.

Buddhism lists three kinds of desire: for sensory pleasure (*kama tanha*); to become or continue to exist (*bhava tanha*), including ambitions; and for annihilation (*vibhava tanha*), or to get rid of something, such as annoying people or a troubling emotion (de Silva, 1990; Sumedho, 1992). These three desires are similar, respectively, to libido, ego, and thanatos in Freud's theory (de Silva, 1990).

The Third Noble Truth: The End of Suffering

Ending the craving will end the suffering. *Detachment* from craving is the key. This includes detachment from the craving for material goods. It also includes detachment from possessiveness of other people, but it does not imply giving up on loving them (Ghose, 2004). Psychological studies of unhealthy or "desperate" love are easily reconcilable with this teaching; it is not healthy to cling possessively to another person, even in the name of love. We must also give up attachments to fixated ideas and attitudes to be more open to present experience and new information. The individual ego or self is relinquished because it is not real but only an illusion. This difficult concept is more fully discussed later.

Attachments do not disappear easily. Meditation allows them to appear, be examined, and be released. Some of the persistent intrusions in meditation come from previously unacknowledged attachments, fears, ideas, and so on. They must be allowed to become conscious before they can be let go.

The Fourth Noble Truth: The Eightfold Path

Suffering exists; it will end if craving ends; craving can end. How? The Fourth Noble Truth outlines an **Eightfold Path** for achieving this: right view, right intention, right speech, right action, right livelihood, right effort, right mindfulness, and right

---

duhkha

suffering, which is accepted in the First Noble Truth

attachment

craving for a variety of things, including physical objects and even the self; the source of suffering (according to the Second Noble Truth)

samsara

the wheel of suffering, in which the consequences of unenlightened action lock a person into a cycle of rebirth instead of permitting liberation to nirvana

Eightfold Path

the method for achieving an end of suffering, described in the Fourth Noble Truth

	Table 16.2 The Eightfold Path

Step	Description
Right view	Accurate perception, not distorted by prejudice or prior conceptualization, such as a negative self-concept or inaccurate assumptions about other people
Right intention	Intention based on acceptance of what really is, rather than wishing for something better (intending to achieve unrealistic goals) or believing that things are worse than they really are (intending to avoid exaggerated or inaccurate dangers)
Right speech	True and direct, assertive, respectful statements
Right action	Living simply and behaving respectfully toward others (not in a spirit of self-denial but out of our basic goodness)
Right livelihood	Work that is meaningful and consistent with ethical and spiritual principles
Right effort	Being disciplined but not overly severe toward oneself, so that there is room for playfulness and rejuvenation
Right mindfulness	Maintaining awareness of the larger picture, instead of only the immediate perception or project
Right concentration	Full involvement in the moment, in a nondualistic way that does not see the self and the other or the environment as separate entities

concentration (see Table 16.2). This path is sometimes called "the **Middle Way**" because it avoids the extremes of either self-indulgence or self-mortification (de Silva, 1990), as Siddhartha learned when he realized that neither extreme asceticism nor extreme indulgence brought lasting satisfaction. He nearly died from an excess of asceticism by not eating enough to sustain life; he then accepted food, even asking for more—although other monks criticized his weakness (Nhat Hanh, 1996).

Middle Way

description of the path to Enlightenment by avoiding extremes, such as extreme asceticism or extreme self-indulgence

The responsibility for following the path and attaining the goal of nirvana rests with each person. Teachers show the way, but neither they nor any higher power grants salvation. This is one instance in which Buddhism is much closer to Western psychology than religion.

BUDDHISM AND PERSONALITY CONCEPTS

Buddhism's understanding of human personality is rich indeed. It offers insights into many topics that personality psychologists have included in their theories, including the self, behavior, emotions, and social relationships.

Self or Ego

Thinking positively of our selves seems so very important, and predicts positive outcomes in much personality research, yet many people lack self-esteem. The Dalai Lama was astonished when he asked a gathering, including many psychology professionals, how many of them had experienced a lack of self-esteem, and many raised their hands (Kamilar, 2002). Self-esteem requires self-acceptance, yet our culture teaches self-doubt. In Western culture, self-esteem must be earned, and can be lost when we fail. (Carl Rogers's concept of conditional positive regard makes this point.) Buddhism suggests an alternative to the Western conceptualization of self-esteem: *self-compassion*, which "entails treating oneself with kindness, recognizing one's shared humanity, and being mindful when considering negative aspects of oneself (Neff & Vonk, 2009). Self-compassion provides an alternative pathway to mental health, without the pitfalls of narcissism and aggression that are sometimes associated with self-esteem. Self-compassion accepts shortcomings as part of the human condition, thus fostering well-being and serving as a buffer against depression. Self-compassion varies cross-culturally, with higher levels in the traditionally Buddhist culture of Thailand, than in the United States. Eastern cultures are diverse, however. Taiwan is more influenced by its Confucian traditions, which demand proper behavior, and surveys there show even lower levels of self-compassion than in the United States (Neff, Pisitsungkagarn, & Hsieh, 2008).

In contrast to the idea of a stable self, one that is reflected in the self-concept, Buddhism teaches that the self, like everything in the universe, is impermanent (Paranjpe, 1998). The self can be compared to a wave on an ocean; it appears, then disappears, and is part of the whole, not a separate entity.

Buddhism teaches that we do not know ourselves. We may not be quite as wrong as a deluded mental patient who claims to be God, but we are nonetheless deluded. We are not our thoughts, not our wishes, not our reputation. All these are fleeting. The Buddhist idea of **anatta**, or "no-self," says that in reality, there is only a sequence of changes and not a stable, permanent self. Buddhist monk and teacher Choǧyam Trungpa (2005) describes the Buddhist view as "egolessness." Attachment to illusory ideas of self impedes progress toward the goal of liberation from the cycle of rebirth (e.g., Williams & Tribe, 2000). The goal of development is **nirvana** "which represented the final annihilation of all 'selfhood' and attachments, the causes of suffering" (Dudley-Grant, 2003, p. 108).

Western tradition, including psychology, emphasizes the development of an independent, autonomous self. Cross-cultural research finds many differences between Eastern and Western personality processes. Westerners are much more likely to enhance themselves and to emphasize their independence (Heine & Buchtel, 2009). This sense of separateness from others, although it has been central to traditional views of psychological health in our individualistic society, is coming under attack. Harris (2004) asserts that "Almost every problem we have can be ascribed to the fact that human beings are utterly beguiled by their feelings of separateness" (p. 214). Depression is one common form of suffering that can be understood as stemming from a cultural overemphasis on individualism. Even so, because the self has been so central to a person's development in our culture, renouncing the self by precipitously adopting a Buddhist perspective can be threatening because there is so little to replace it (Michalon, 2001).

Transience and Mortality

In contrast to the illusion of, and the longing for, a stable self, Buddhism teaches that things are constantly changing. Our perception, for example, is a sequence of transient moments in sequence. Thought, too, is one transient image after another. Meditation allows a person "to deconstruct the apparent stability of things, and to see directly the world as a *process*, a *flow*" (Williams & Tribe, 2000, p. 85). This is true not only on the scale of everyday life, and of the seasons, and of the life span. It is also true on a cosmic scale. Instead of one origin of the universe—a point about which even literal creationists and "big bang" cosmologists agree—Buddhism teaches that the universe has been created and destroyed many times, and this continues to occur.

The awareness of mortality is one of the primary reasons why people turn to religion. But whereas most religions deal with this by describing an immortal soul that does not die, Buddhism does not, and in this way it is more comparable to modern psychology, which is silent on the issue of a soul (cf. Loy, 2002). Psychoanalyst Erich Fromm, one of many Western psychoanalysts who studied Buddhism, described a Zen-inspired meditation in which he practiced his own death, merging with the great cosmic oneness that psychoanalysts call an "oceanic feeling" of infantile unity with the mother, and which Buddhists conceptualize as relinquishing the illusion of an individual self (Maccoby, 1995). Not surprisingly, those who work with dying patients in hospice are finding, in our increasingly secular world, that Buddhism is helpful (Garces-Foley, 2003).

Behavior: Its Causes and Consequences

Behavior is produced by thought and intention, whether wise or unwise. Behavior, including antisocial or maladaptive behavior, can be changed by stopping the underlying thoughts. Buddhist practices include various techniques that are similar to

anatta

no-self; the doctrine that there is, in reality, no fixed, stable, enduring self (although the illusion of one may be constructed from fleeting impressions)

nirvana

the goal of spiritual development, in which there is no attachment, and therefore suffering has ended some cognitive behavioral methods of control, including rewards, modeling, aversion, and thought stopping (de Silva, 1990; Dudley-Grant, 2003). But for Buddhism, it is not simply a matter of substituting other thoughts, as some Western psychological techniques suggest. Rather change requires ceasing the chronic egoistic self-observation that is the habit of an undisciplined mind.

Action is not always necessary. When one Western academician met the Tibetan Buddhist teacher Chogyam Trungpa and remarked that, because of upheavals in his life he did not know what to do, the monk's reply was, "Why do you want to do something? How about doing nothing?" (Goleman, 2004, p. 308).

CONSEQUENCES OF BEHAVIOR: KARMA   Buddhism assumes that people have free will and make choices about their lives and these choices have consequences. The term **karma** refers to intention and to volitional activity. Such willful action has consequences, called *Vipaka*. (Many people use the term *karma* to refer to both the action and its consequences—as when a child climbs on a stool to take a forbidden cookie—karma—but falls down and gets hurt in the process.)

karma

intentional or willed activity, which produces consequences (positive or negative, depending on the action)

Intentions, good and bad, have results, not only in this lifetime but beyond. Buddhism (like Hinduism) assumes rebirth. The circumstances of rebirth depend on the karma of the prior life. Depending on one's karma, rebirth can be to various states: in hell or purgatory, as an animal, a ghost (these three being lower than human, a result of bad karma), a human, a god, or a jealous anti-god (Williams & Tribe, 2000). The gods in this worldview are not perfect or enlightened, although some are higher than others; many have some of the same faults that humans possess: anger, pride, and so on. From the human state, if enlightenment is attained, then the cycle of rebirth ends.

Westerners have difficulty understanding rebirth because we assume an individual self. Buddhism, in contrast, views the idea of a fixed individual self as an illusion. What is reborn is not what we know as the individual person, not a "fixed soul," according to Paranjpe (1998, p. 124), but rather the karmic consequences of the past life. The physical death of an individual does not stop the karmic consequences of that person's intentional behavior.

The idea of karma provides an incentive for good behavior, but it can also be used to tolerate the plight of those who are unfortunate in social status, reasoning that they deserve their suffering. Survey data of Indian college students indicate that those from higher castes are more likely to accept statements like this: "It is proper to bear without complaining our current miseries as rightful dues for our deeds in a previous life" (Paranjpe, 1998, p. 340). Lower-caste college students reject such statements, which after all would undermine their dissatisfaction with their unfairly low status.

DEPENDENT ORIGINATION   Although karma states an important causal principle, the result of intentional action, it is not the only cause–effect relationship. Another principle is that of *dependent origination*. Everything is interconnected; nothing is separate (e.g., Thomson, 2000). In Buddhism, the doctrine of dependent origination emphasizes that many interconnected factors determine any condition. The individual's attitude is one factor in this field of interconnected causes, and it is one that the individual can and should control by free will (cf. karma). But the idea of dependent origination also acknowledges other causes, which may include biological predispositions, social factors, and so on.

Mind and Body

Buddhism asserts that the physical world and consciousness are not distinct, in contrast to the general assumption in the West of the separation of body and mind. Neuroscientists and philosophers, sometimes in discussions with Buddhists, have been deliberating how physical processes in the brain are related to conscious experience. Is the physical process primary, with consciousness an effect? Is consciousness primary? When I think that my choice is causing me to act in a particular way (as common sense tells me), is that true or perhaps only an illusion (Nahmias, 2005; Wegner & Wheatley, 1999)?

Psychology and medicine recognize that psychological factors influence the body. Stress predisposes to illness, for example, and psychological factors influence recovery from illness (e.g., Nelson et al., 1989). The Buddhist worldview goes further. Because mind and body are not two separate entities, there does not need to be a physical intermediary as part of every explanation. For example, the Buddhist monk Thich Nhat Hanh (2001) asserts that anger can be caused (in part) by eating angry chickens, those who have been caged inhumanely and who suffer from confinement. Our Western mentality would either take this statement as a metaphor or would look for some physical mechanism for the connection—a molecule in the chicken that can be ingested and absorbed by people, for example. In the Buddhist view, in contrast, the body and the mind are not separate but linked as a "body/mind formation *namarupa*... the psychesoma, the body-mind as one entity. The same reality sometimes appears as mind, and sometimes appears as body" (Nhat Hanh, 2001, p. 14). Furthermore, the separateness of the chicken and the chicken eater is questioned.

CONSCIOUSNESS   Ordinary consciousness is chaotic, with ideas rapidly jumping from one thought to another. The undisciplined mind can be considered to be like a wild horse (Trungpa, 2005) or a drunken monkey that has been stung by a scorpion (cf. Saraswati, 2002). This undesirable condition can be improved by meditation (discussed later). Buddhism does not confine itself to ordinary waking consciousness, unlike most Western approaches, which are suspicious of "mystical" thought (Paranjpe, 1998). Buddhism encourages altered consciousness through meditation, and according to Walsh (1988), Tibetan Buddhists have practiced lucid dreaming, in which the dreamer is conscious of dreaming and able to exert some control over the dream, for over 1,200 years.

Buddhism advocates a transformation of consciousness, conveyed by the metaphor of awakening. A classic story of the Buddha conveys this awakening image. After attaining his insight, he seemed to radiate some special quality, causing people to ask what he was—some kind of special spirit, a god, a wizard, or what? His response: "I am awake."

Awakening

a transformation from ordinary consciousness in which a person recognizes the true nature of things and the path to spiritual progress

At other times, the change is called "enlightenment." Others describe enlightenment as a higher stage than awakening. **Awakening** involves recognizing the true nature of things and the path to achieving Buddhahood (one's true nature), whereas enlightenment comes later, when one has overcome imperfections and delusions by following the path (Chen, 1999).

The puzzle of what is real is not easily resolved. Like many traditions, Buddhism offers explanations through stories. Consider the following traditional story, recounted by Shore (2003, p. 30):

> Once Chuang Chou dreamt he was a butterfly, a butterfly flitting and fluttering around, happy with himself and doing as he pleased. He didn't know he was Chuang Chou. Suddenly he woke up and there he was, solid and unmistakable Chuang Chou. But he didn't know if he was Chuang Chou who had dreamt he was a butterfly, or a butterfly dreaming he was Chuang Chou. Between Chuang Chou and a butterfly there must be *some* distinction! This is called the Transformation of Things. (*Chuang Tzu*, chap. 2; quoted in Watson, 1968: 49)

Am I a butterfly? A man dreaming of a butterfly? Escape from the presumptions of the familiar self, upon awakening, can be quite confusing—an identity crisis beyond the usual sense of the term.

Emotions

All personality theories deal with emotion in one way or another. Buddhism offers insights as well. Emotions can interfere with growth, but happiness is the natural consequence of following the right spiritual path. Emotions can be made more healthy through learning, and a collaborative project between Buddhists and Western scientists and educators has developed a curriculum, called Cultivating Emotional Balance, to teach emotional health in eight sessions that include both meditation and Western psychological techniques (Mind and Life Institute, 2006).

HAPPINESS The goal that individuals should seek, according to the Dalai Lama, is happiness. By this he means not momentary pleasure but the lasting happiness that Tibetan Buddhism calls *sukha*. This happiness comes from an internal source, not from external things or experiences. It requires long years of discipline to achieve (Ekman et al., 2005). Although it sounds simple—after all, who doesn't want to be happy— Buddhist tradition teaches that genuine happiness is not easily obtained. Things that seem to bring happiness in the short run often have opposite consequences farther along: junk food, drugs, and passionate encounters, to name a few. If only we knew the true nature of reality, we would make wiser choices and so would be happier.

Current psychological research supports Buddhist teaching that happiness does not come, in any lasting way, from material possessions. However, there are differences, too, such as psychology's current emphasis on biological mechanisms of happiness, including genetics and brain biochemistry (e.g., Davidson, 2003; Klein, 2006).

ANGER Buddhism is labeled as one of the world's "unangry religions," according to a classic analysis (Stratton, 1923/2005). Buddhism strives for tranquility and peace. It regards anger as a form of suffering (Hook et al., 2010). In contrast, religions categorized as angry religions, including Christianity and Islam, accept and even encourage some aggressive acts. Holy wars have been fought in both religious traditions, whereas Buddhism has a history of pacifism. A cross-cultural empirical study of emotions typical of various religions reports that Buddhists are typically moderate in the levels of a variety of emotions, compared with other religions, consistent with the Buddhist quest for moderation. In this study, Christians reported high levels of love (but low levels, in this study, of anger); Muslims reported high levels of sadness and shame; Buddhists and Hindus reported lower levels of pride than Christians, Muslims, and Jews (Kim-Prieto & Diener, 2009). Although it seems clear that different religions value and encourage different emotions, we need to bear in mind that some of these effects might change as history unfolds.

Buddhism describes people who are possessed by anger as being in a "hell realm" marked by aggression against enemies and their retaliation. Looking at the world today, it does feel very much like such a hell realm. How can this end? As Buddhist teaching is summarized by Scott Kamilar, "the only way out of this realm is to observe one's feelings of anger and hatred clearly. This is symbolically represented by the Boddhisattva of Compassion holding a mirror" (p. 93). Anger diminishes when a person's sense of self expands to include compassionate identification with others. Without clinging to desires and without protecting an individual self, the individual is not provoked to anger.

Buddhism offers techniques for dealing with anger: "the method of mindful breathing, the method of mindful walking, the method of embracing our anger, the method of looking deeply into the nature of our perceptions, and the method of looking deeply into the other person to realize that she also suffers a lot and needs help" (Nhat Hanh, 2001, pp. 24–25). Notice that none of these techniques rejects the anger. Instead, it must be brought to awareness and treated with compassion, as one would a loved but immature brother or sister (Nhat Hanh, 1996).

Brain scans show that people are able to regulate their emotions, at least to some extent, when they choose to do so. People who have been instructed to continue thinking about the negative emotion elicited by a picture they have just seen, compared to those who turn their thoughts elsewhere, show different brain activity. Neuroscience expert Richard Davidson suggests that people who have difficulty controlling their anger have been influenced not only by physical causes such as genetics, but also by early social experience; he proposes that training experiences could be developed, based on understanding the brain circuitry involved, to teach such people to control their emotions better (Davidson, Putnam, & Larson, 2000). In one case, an institutionalized, mildly mentally retarded adult learned to control his aggressive impulses so successfully that he was released to the community. He was taught to focus attention on the soles of his feet instead of on whatever had triggered his anger (Singh et al., 2003). Another study found that Buddhist accommodative Cognitive Behavioral Therapy (which incorporates meditation with behavioral principles) reduced anger among male prisoners in a low-security facility (Vannoy & Hoyt, 2004). Like other studies that use religious or spiritual techniques, however, it isn't demonstrated that the Buddhist component added to the effectiveness of the already established benefit of traditional therapy (Hook et al., 2010). More research is needed.

LOVE AND OTHER EMOTIONS   It's not only negative emotions like anger and hatred that are eschewed in Buddhism, however. Even pleasant emotions can be problematic, under some conditions, because they interfere with an accurate perception of reality. In linking our positive emotions to some person or object in the outside world, we lose touch with the truth that happiness truly comes from within (Ekman et al., 2005). Buddhism warns against sexual passion (although accepting sexual relationships in the context of love and commitment), and even attachment to family and friends, because all of these disturb the calm and unattached mind. Early Buddhism rejected even joy and love, but modern Buddhism is more accepting of these emotions (Stratton, 1923/2005). Emotion, like so many other aspects of human experience, needs to be guided by the Middle Way, avoiding excesses.

Interpersonal Relationships and Society

People who have come to grips with emotions and have grown beyond the illusion of a separate self are also transformed in their interpersonal relationships.

COMPASSION   Compassion (*karuna*) is a central concept in Buddhism. Compassion is similar to the term *love* in Western approaches (McDargh, 2000). We might also compare compassion to empathy, the term more often used by psychologists, or to Adler's concept of social interest.

Compassion for others comes as a natural consequence of realizing that the separate self is an illusion (Loy, 2002). When there is no separate self, the suffering of others is not separate from the self. The Dalai Lama portrays a mother breastfeeding her infant as a powerful symbol of this love, conveying the innateness of compassion to human nature (Bstan-dzin-rgya-mtsho, 2001). Intriguingly, the relationship of early life social experience to happiness has additional support from neuroscience. Researchers measured the prefrontal brain activity of 10-month-old infants. Those whose right hemispheres were relatively more active were more likely to cry when they were briefly separated from their mothers, whereas left hemisphere activity predicted not crying (Davidson & Fox, 1989). In rats, those exposed to early maternal licking and grooming—care that is more frequent when the mothers are themselves less stressed—developed physiological changes (including increased receptors for benzodiazepine in the amygdala and locus ceruleus) that made them more able to cope with stress in later life (Davidson, 2000; Francis & Meaney, 1999). Early social experience shapes the brain.

In the tradition of Mahayana Buddhism, the individual self and the universe are the same. One should not seek so much to deny the self as to expand or enlarge one's concept of self so it is connected with all others (Dudley-Grant, 2003). This begins with smaller networks of friends and gradually expands to include more and more people, all humans, and all creatures (Hayes, 2003). The environmental concerns of Buddhists today flow from this compassion because harm to the earth produces harm to living creatures.

Spiritual progression is accompanied by increased compassion, not only for fellow humans but also for other creatures. Perhaps the ultimate compassion is shown by a **bodhisattva**, one whose spiritual progress would enable him or her to be released from the cycle of rebirth, out of the world of suffering, but who remains back out of compassion to help those who have not attained that degree of development. Intergroup prejudice, understood from a Buddhist perspective, stems from attachment to difference—in the language of social psychology, to social identity and in-group bias (Dockett & North-Schulte, 2003). Activists in India have found support in Buddhism for efforts to eliminate caste-based prejudice (Chappell, 2003).

bodhisattva

a spiritually enlightened person who remains in the world to help others on their spiritual path

PEACE   Although the focus of Buddhist practice is on individuals, its impact permeates throughout the world. An individual who personally moves toward inner peace creates a more peaceful world. To scientific ears, this is a metaphorical statement that requires specifying the mechanisms. Does a peaceful world come about through certain kinds of interpersonal interactions, for example, such as the greater ability of the more peaceful individual to listen empathically to others, producing in turn their reduced animosity?

Some claims for the peace-producing potential of meditation cannot be reconciled with science as we know it. For example, some researchers report that by assembling a critical number of meditators in a violent area of the world, they can change the collective consciousness or stress level enough to produce a measurable reduction in acts of violence. Such a strategy was reported in the Middle East, where meditators in locations as distant as the United States were credited with reducing war-related acts of violence and death in Lebanon and Israel (Davies & Alexander, 2005).

Buddhist monk Thich Nhat Hanh, one of several monks who became engaged in humanitarian and peace efforts as a result of the war in Vietnam, left his native Vietnam and he has applied Buddhist ideas to the search for peace and offered many workshops to Westerners. He has met with world leaders, including Pope Paul VI, Dr. Martin Luther King Jr., and American secretary of defense McNamara (Nhat Hanh, 1996), and he was nominated for the Nobel Peace Prize. He has offered retreats and workshops to help peace activists learn how Buddhist practices, including the anger management practices described earlier, can help reduce the suffering of war, which is one facet of his Engaged Buddhism movement (Tamdgidi, 2008).

COMMUNITY   Although Buddhism stresses the development of the individual's consciousness, this is not done in isolation, and its benefits are not limited to the individual. The term **sangha** refers to "the community that lives in harmony and awareness" (Nhat Hanh, 1996). A lesson about community may be drawn from the story of Siddhartha, described earlier. Recall that he practiced extreme asceticism before finding the Middle Way. He learned to be needy in relationship to other people and to accept their support. Nearly starving, he accepted milk from a milkmaid. A young boy tending buffaloes thought he had nothing to give, but at Siddhartha's suggestion, he gave him grass from which to make a cushion to sit on (Nhat Hanh, 1996). Only after accepting these gifts did Siddhartha's meditation result in his final enlightenment. This may be a noteworthy lesson for those who seem to be more psychologically advanced than others, to whom others turn for help (including psychotherapists). We must receive as well as give. Sometimes this insight is easier to understand in the language of self or identity; if one's self-perception is focused on being strong and helping others, then clinging to this self-image is one sort of attachment that must be let go.

sangha

a community living in harmony and awareness

SOCIAL ISSUES   Americans, consistent with the individualism of our culture, have focused more on Buddhism's implications for personal development than on its implications for social transformation, although environmentalism and the peace movement have strong Buddhist support. Yet some Buddhists work actively for social change in political and economic spheres, and in that aspect of their work they may be closer to community psychologists than to psychotherapists (Dockett, 2003). The later Mahayana school of Buddhism is more involved in such social action than is the older, more introspective Theravada Buddhism (Jason & Moritsugu, 2003).

Environmental problems stem from human selfishness, from attachment to individual desires that lead to exploitation of the environment. This attitude reflects ignorance of the interdependence of all things, which is a fundamental Buddhist teaching, a teaching that in Chinese and Japanese Buddhism describes aspects of nature, including plants and mountains, as having a Buddha-nature (Yamamoto, 2003). A higher consciousness would not spew toxins out of smokestacks or degrade the landscape with strip mining or clear cutting of forests. Most Buddhists do not eat animals, either, although some Tibetan Buddhists are not vegetarian (owing to the harsh mountain climate that makes nutrition more problematic).

SPIRITUAL PRACTICES

Eastern religions offer various paths to spiritual development. Meditation is a basic practice that has been the focus of considerable research and has been incorporated into Western psychotherapies, so it receives particular attention here.

In a broad sense, the term **yoga** refers to any of several spiritual self-development paths. The most familiar to Westerners are the paths that involve physical postures, but there are other yoga types. Even the physical posture types of yoga are not solely, or even mainly, about physical fitness but are paths to spiritual development (see Table 16.3).

Buddhism, like Hinduism, provides guidance through various exercises and the direction of a **guru**, a spiritual teacher. Various teachers offer different kinds of practices to stimulate awareness. Zen Buddhism calls our logic into question by posing riddles, or **koans**, that cannot be resolved through the usual methods of logic. One famous example: What is the sound of one hand clapping? (The traditional answer is for the student to slap the teacher's face.) The goal is not to engage in scholarly Olympics, though, but to cut through obstacles that arise because of thinking. Simple actions, unimpeded by thought, are encouraged. Often stories make the point:

> A monk said to Chao-Chou, "I have just entered this monastery. Please teach me."
> Chao-Chou said, "Have you eaten your rice gruel?"
> The monk said, "Yes I have."
> Chao-Chou said, "Wash your bowl." (Aitken, 1990, p. 54; quoted in Gaskins, 1999, p. 209)

Meditation

Meditation is a fundamental practice in Buddhism in which attention is consciously regulated to achieve insight and enhance well-being. Depending on the form of meditation, consciousness may be focused on a particular object (such as breathing) or it may be more passive, attending to whatever thoughts and sensations arise spontaneously. With practice, the "drunken monkey" of consciousness is tamed, and power of the mind over consciousness and the body increases. With meditation, the grosser layers of consciousness driven by passions and by outside stimuli are calmed, and more "subtle" layers of consciousness can be experienced. These can harness powerful forces (Bstan-dzin-rgya-mtsho, 1989).

Many varieties of meditation exist, each with particular practices and, to some extent, distinct outcomes. In general (with some exceptions), they have a calming and joyful effect. Meditation focuses on regulating attention, producing calmness and enhanced awareness, without harmful distractions. Because much everyday thought is nonproductive and even counterproductive, with worry and distraction, the result is improved cognitive functioning. The Dalai Lama quotes an ancient Buddhist saying: "If the problem is such that there is a solution, there is no need to worry about it; if there is no solution, then there is no point in being overwhelmed and paralyzed" (Bstan-dzin-rgya-mtsho, 2003). This focus on only productive thought may be the basis for his response, when asked how he could not be angry at all that the Chinese had taken from him and from his country: "Why should I give them my mind as well?" (Lefebure, 2005, p. 84).

Two major types of meditation—concentrative and mindfulness meditation—are often distinguished (although there are variations that cross these categories).

yoga

spiritual practice; various forms exist

guru

teacher; spiritual adviser

koan

in Zen Buddhism, a riddle that is posed for the purpose of overcoming preconceptions and so furthering spiritual enlightenment

meditation

a practice in which attention is consciously regulated to enhance serenity and well-being

---

Table 16.3 Some Types of Yoga Practices

Yoga Type	Description
Bhakti yoga	Cultivates love by contemplating a saint, teacher, or God
Hatha yoga	Disciplines the body through exercises and postures
Karma yoga	Serves others, thus relinquishing egocentric motivation and addiction
Jnana yoga	Through contemplation, relinquishes false self-concepts and explores reality

Concentrative meditation focuses attention on an object, often the breath, but sometimes a sound or an image. This helps reduce distractions that come from external stimuli and from one's own distracting thoughts. One form of concentrative meditation, *Transcendental Meditation* (TM), was developed a half century ago and is copyrighted and marketed; it aims to convey ancient practices to the modern world in schools, businesses, architecture, and other settings (The Transcendental Meditation program, 2005). **Mindfulness meditation** allows thoughts to appear as they will and observes them without judgment. Zen meditation, called **zazen**, and Vipassana meditations are types of mindfulness meditation.

THE PROCESS OF MEDITATION   Meditation frequently focuses attention on breathing or sometimes an external object. An advantage of breathing as a focus is that it is always present, and it comes to be a conditioned stimulus for the meditative mind-set, carrying some of the benefits into everyday life. The body is held in a position that aids concentration, typically a seated, cross-legged lotus position. During meditation, awareness is maintained and monitored, but the usual duality of self and other is removed. A frequent metaphor for the effect of meditation on the mind is water. Without meditation, the surface of the water is full of waves and turmoil that prevent us from seeing what is below. With meditation, the surface of the water becomes calm and still. The depths can now be seen. Thus meditation permits knowing the deeper contents of the mind, the "subtle" consciousness, that is obscured by the frenzy of unregulated attention.

Meditation turns focus away from external objects, inward. The goal is "pure consciousness" in which the person is alert but not disturbed by specific content of consciousness. Physiological correlates include decreased autonomic activity and increased peak power of the EEG, a sign of alertness (Travis & Pearson, 2000). The blissful state reported by experienced meditators has been compared to that produced by opiates; perhaps it results from a release of these endogenous brain chemicals, the endorphins (Austin, 1998).

Although the experiential reporting of meditators is rich, it is hard to quantify. Researchers have devised a scale consisting of Likert-type items to measure mindfulness, the Freiburg Mindfulness Inventory. It consists of items such as this: "I watch my feelings without getting lost in them" (Walach et al., 2006, p. 1553). Scores increased, as expected, with meditation practice.

MEDITATION AND THE CONTROL OF ATTENTION AND PERCEPTION   Some research supports the idea that focused attention improves after meditation. In one study, a group who had practiced meditation twice daily for 3 months became more accurate on two perceptual tasks: judging whether a vertical rod was exactly vertical, despite the distraction of a misaligned surrounding frame (the Rod and Frame Test), and locating hidden pictures in the Embedded Figures Test. A wait-list control group that simply sat quietly, without meditating, did not change (Austin, 1998). Meditation also improves performance on tests of creativity, practical intelligence, field independence, and other cognitive tasks (So & Orme-Johnson, 2001) and it helps the elderly maintain their intellectual abilities (Nidich, Schneider, et al., 2005).

Subjective experience is not determined by external input alone but by a person's response to it. The practice of meditation teaches a person to observe and change that response, thereby gaining control over subjective experience. Ordinarily, when sensory input—what we see or hear, for example—comes in, we immediately respond to it. In the language of psychology, *sensation* (the incoming light or sound waves that trigger neural response) is immediately followed by *perception*, the meaning we impute to those sensations (perceiving a snake or a rope, for example). It is so immediate that the sound of a class-ending bell and the perception "class is over" have no pause in between for reflection!

Perceptions, however, can be wrong or incomplete. Consider the familiar story, told in Buddhism and other cultures, of several blind men who touch various parts of an elephant. The specific details vary from one telling to another, but the point is clear: Each perceives a different reality, based on partial information. The man who

concentrative meditation
a form of meditation in which attention is focused on a particular object, such as the breath or a word or phrase (mantra), one of the best known being the mantra om

mindfulness meditation
a form of meditation in which thoughts are observed but not judged

zazen
meditation; sitting meditation; practiced in Zen Buddhism

touches the elephant's leg describes the beast as like a pillar or a tree trunk; the one touching the elephant's side says it is like a wall. The one who touches the ear likens the elephant to a large basket or a huge leaf. The one at the tail end describes a snakelike animal. The tusk led another other to say it was like a plowshare. Each has only a partial view of the elephant; perception is limited. The story is often used to encourage the listener to honor other people's perspectives, which may be based on information that they themselves lack.

Consider another interpretation of this story of the blind men and the elephant: that if each of the blind men had not been so hasty to identify the incoming sensations, he might have remained open himself to more information, perhaps exploring more of the elephant's body. By pausing longer between sensation and perception, we may make fewer errors. We should not remain fixated or attached to our perceptions of reality. In a translation of the original story, the Buddha is said to have characterized the quarreling blind men, and the quarreling religious scholars about whom the parable was told, as "attached" (Bhikkhu, 1994). Attachment to perception is one of the kinds of attachment that must be forfeited in following the Buddhist path to enlightenment.

Attachment to the self, as discussed earlier, must also be given up. Measurement of brain changes during meditation help us conceptualize the experience of being conscious and aware but not focused on the self or on any specific content of experience—that is, "pure conscious experience," or awareness of only consciousness itself. Brain studies show that when meditators report being in this state, they show increased alpha waves, increased frontal blood flow, and decreased blood flow in the visual regions of the brain; they are more autonomically aroused by sudden, unexpected stimuli (Taylor, 2002).

Self and nonself, brain chemistry and the like, are interesting but a bit abstract. Consider the following very concrete and somewhat amusing study of perception. This study, not surprisingly, caused some of the Tibetan Buddhist monks who were research subjects to express "mild bewilderment towards the study's aims and motivations" (Carter et al., 2005b, p. R1). Researchers presented monks, during meditation, with a binocular rivalry task. Horizontal lines were presented to one eye and vertical lines to another, through a device strapped to their heads. Typically people perceive each of these images sequentially, and the perception fluctuates back and forth as the brain tries to coordinate the input from the left and right eyes. Could the monks, experienced through meditation in controlling incoming stimuli, experience something different? Indeed they did. The meditating monks reported that the images stabilized in one or the other (horizontal or vertical) form for much longer periods of time than was typical for this task. One reported that he could hold one of the stabilized images indefinitely. These effects occurred for only one type of meditation, one that focuses attention on an object. Compassion meditation did not produce the effect, even in the same monks (Carter et al., 2005a). It seems clear that meditation practice, lasting for several decades in some of these monks, does indeed alter perception.

The 17 Moments of Perception   The distinction between unprocessed incoming sensation and meaningful consequent perception is analyzed far more extensively in Buddhist teaching than in psychology. According to Buddhist teachings, mental processes create the illusion of something that is solid and permanent, from transient sensations. The classic Buddhist texts describe 17 successive moments of perception, which can be made known through carefully trained introspection (Lancaster, 1997). Beginning with unawareness or unconsciousness of the object of sensation, it is not until the 6th moment in this sequence that the person "receives" the object, described by Lancaster as "a simple feeling tone... which at this stage is merely 'agreeable,' 'disagreeable' or 'neutral'" (p. 126). At this point, the person has not yet identified the object. At stage 8, the mind responds to the object but has still not identified it (Lancaster, 1997).

Consistent with this ancient teaching, current psychological studies have found that research subjects can respond to the emotional tone of a stimulus without knowing consciously what the object is. If emotional reaction to an object comes before identification of the object, then psychoanalytic defense mechanisms become more understandable, particularly because the process of perception can be stopped at this stage, without progressing to full awareness (Lancaster, 1997).

Observations by neurologists document kinds of mental functioning that may correspond to the Buddhist description of the earlier stages of perception, including blindsight and implicit memory (Lancaster, 1997). In Western science, though, these phenomena are observed through cases of people with brain damage (blindsight) or through contrived experimental tasks (implicit memory), not through trained introspection. Lancaster (1997) proposes that Buddhist descriptions of incomplete processes, where sensory input does not proceed all the way to conscious perception, correspond to various phenomena that have been observed in modern psychological studies. The sort of implicit processing that happens in amnesia, he suggests, corresponds to the *abhidhamma* tradition of a "great object," in which perception proceeds only to the 15th stage. The last two stages, when conscious awareness of the object would occur, do not happen. Lacking the last two stages, which involve the concept of self (or "I"), memory is impaired. Nonetheless, enough perception has occurred to affect behavior. Another correspondence is to the phenomenon of subliminal perception, which corresponds to the *abhidhamma* tradition of a "slight object," in which processing is incomplete at an even earlier stage, before the sensory stimulus has been interpreted and before its self-relevance has been interpreted.

Emotions do not require full progression through all 17 stages of perception. Positive and negative emotions are activated at earlier stages. As research continues, we may discover that mood disturbances, such as depression, could be treated by teaching specific kinds of control over these stages of perception. We may learn that the dissociation of consciousness that occurs in hypnosis and in some diagnostic categories reflects a condition in which part of the perceptual process stops earlier while a related process continues further. Meditation may provide a way to understand and make therapeutic use of the discrepancies between what people know consciously and how they feel and behave, allowing clearer understanding of defense mechanisms.

BRAIN MEASUREMENT DURING MEDITATION   The meeting of Eastern spiritual traditions with Western scientific technology has resulted in many observations of brain activity during meditation. Benson and his colleagues (1990) reported that Tibetan monks living in India were able to reduce their resting metabolism to 64 percent, or increase it by 61 percent, through meditation. In 1992 the Dalai Lama (Tenzin Gyatso, the 14th Dalai Lama of Tibet) and the American neuroscientist Richard Davidson began studying longtime meditating monks (Hall, 2003). The brain's functioning may well be different in a person who has only been meditating a few weeks or months and a person who has been meditating for decades.

Meditation generally produces slower EEG activity, increased alpha wave activity (and increased feelings of calmness associated with this pattern), both during meditation and thereafter, and also increased theta waves during meditation. Over time, meditation changes the way that the brain responds to stimuli (Cahn & Polich, 2006).

Although alpha and theta waves are the usual finding, EEG gamma waves, too, have been reported elevated among long-term meditators (Lutz et al., 2004). In this study the type of meditation was one of compassion and loving kindness, without a specific object. Different forms of meditation produce a variety of neural activity patterns, and results are also affected by the experience of the meditators and the particular tasks presented (Cahn & Polich, 2006). One meditator was being recorded when he experienced a state of ecstasy, and the recordings showed a sudden increase in autonomic activation (Andresen, 2000).

Researchers have explored the metabolism of various brain areas using positron emission tomography (PET) techniques, functional magnetic resonance imaging (*f*MRI), and blood flow using single-photon emission computed tomography (SPECT) imaging. Many brain areas change during various meditation studies, including the thalamus, the basal ganglia, the frontal, temporal, and parietal lobes, and others. The specific findings vary depending on the type of meditation and the experience of the practitioners (Andresen, 2000; Ritskes et al., 2003). Brain scientists have even suggested that brain functioning is reorganized as a result of meditation practice (Manna et al., 2010). Clearly meditation has effects on the brain.

Habituation   *Habituation* means that, with repetition, the same stimulus no longer triggers the response that it earlier did. Typically, when a relaxed person with high alpha activity is confronted with a stimulus, such as a noise, there is a decrease in alpha activity (*alpha blocking*) as the brain's cortex processes the stimulus. (Relaxation interrupted; what was that stimulus?) With repetition of the stimulus, these brain changes diminish (habituation). Meditation, though, can change this. A classic study of Zen meditators found that with repeated auditory click stimuli, the meditators continued to respond with alpha blocking, evidence that they remained open to the moment and continued to respond to each new stimulus. In contrast, control subjects became habituated to the stimulus quickly and it no longer triggered the alpha blocking (Kasamatsu & Hirai, 1973).

Later studies had mixed results, attributed at least in part to the kinds of meditation. Those that focus on fully experiencing each moment (mindfulness meditation, including Zen meditation) do not show alpha blocking habituation. Those that emphasize concentration do show alpha blocking habituation as the meditator tunes out the interruption and focuses on the object of meditation (Cahn & Polich, 2006). More detailed brain monitoring suggests that meditation using focused attention methods develops control over brain regions that monitor and attend to stimuli (including the dorsolateral prefrontal cortex, the superior frontal sulcus, the intraparietal sulcus, and the visual cortex); in contrast, mindfulness meditation left the brain functioning as it did when at rest, not meditating (Manna et al., 2010). Thus the choice of meditation technique tells the brain how to respond.

Processing Emotional Stimuli   What about emotional stimuli? According to Richard Davidson (2005), who has frequently discussed Buddhist meditative practices and their relationship to science with the Dalai Lama, happiness can be increased by meditation. People can, at least to some extent, regulate their emotion, and doing so increases their resiliency to adversity (Davidson, 2005). He has confirmed this using brain-imaging studies. Research subjects who were shown upsetting pictures, such as a infant with a tumor on its eye, showed more activation of the amygdala when they focused on the negative emotions and less activation when they were instructed to think positively, that the tumor was successfully removed (Davidson, 2005). Another study shows that subjects who were instructed to continue the negative emotion induced by a stimulus (such as a picture of a gun pointed toward them), after the picture was removed, maintained their elevated amygdala activity longer, confirming the impact of voluntary focus of conscious attention (such as occurs during meditation) on brain activity (Schaefer et al., 2002).

A Russian laboratory found that experienced Sahaja Yoga meditators (a form of mindfulness meditation) were less affected by an emotionally distressing video clip (a scene in which two young people are abusing a family), compared to a control group of nonmeditators (Aftanas & Golosheykin, 2005). Both subjects' subjective ratings and their brain activity showed the meditators to be less distressed. Brain EEG recordings showed that the meditators had larger alpha and theta waves (indicative of relaxation, bliss, and inward concentration or the meditative goal of thoughtless awareness). These differences occurred even though the meditators were not instructed to meditate during these film viewings, which is consistent with other evidence that the effects of meditation endure into ongoing life.

Clearly meditation produces change in the functioning of the brain. Could it also change its structure, as (by analogy) exercise changes not only the functioning of muscles but also their bulk? Comparing a group of Western meditators who regularly practiced Buddhist insight meditation with a control group of 15 nonmeditators, MRI showed that the meditators had greater cortical thickness in certain brain areas, those associated with attention, interoception, and sensory processing (Lazar et al., 2005).

Ongoing collaboration between experienced meditators and neuroscientists promises to identify more rigorously specific brain mechanisms that have been brought under voluntary control through the discipline of meditation. What an exciting

Table 16.4 Examples of Conditions for which Meditation Has Been Used as Treatment

Anxiety	Infertility
Asthma	Insomnia
Atherosclerosis	Irritable bowel syndrome
Cancer	Learning disabilities
Chronic pain	Muscle and joint pain
Criminal behavior	Premenstrual dysphoric disorder
Diabetes	Psoriasis
Drug abuse	Psychiatric conditions (inpatients)
Fibromyalgia	Stress disorders
High cholesterol	Stuttering
Hypertension (blood pressure)	

Source: Information from several sources, including Carlson et al. (2004); Grossman et al. (2004); Kamilar (2002); Keefer & Blanchard (2002); Monk-Turner (2003); Seeman, Dubin, & Seeman (2003); Walsh & Shapiro (2006).

expansion of biological approaches that promises: biology not as simply the cause of subjective experience (as in the attribution of depression or anxiety to an imbalance of neurotransmitters) but as the mechanism by which human will and practice can achieve control of subjective life.

PSYCHOLOGICAL AND HEALTH EFFECTS OF MEDITATION Meditation has been used as a method for treating an astonishing variety of medical and psychological problems (see Table 16.4), and a meta-analysis confirms its overall value in improving health (Grossman et al., 2004). Some claim that meditation can reduce the cost of health care (Herron & Cavanaugh, 2005).

Meditation offers an alternative, nonpharmacological approach for the treatment of attention deficit disorder (Arnold, 2001). Perhaps it is not surprising that improved ability to concentrate attention, achieved through meditation, has also been found to improve memory, intelligence, and academic performance (Walsh & Shapiro, 2006). Meditation seems to increase mindfulness, which contributes to well-being (Falkenström, 2010).

Meditation has become a popular alternative treatment for a variety of stress-related disorders, including hypertension, headaches, and insomnia, and it is reported to also reduce pain (Andresen, 2000).

During meditation, physiological indicators typically (but not always) show reduced stress and increased relaxation: lower heart rate and respiration rate, lower levels of cortisol, plasma lactate, and catecholamines (e.g., MacLean et al., 1997; Travis, 2001). Immune response improves (Aftanas & Golosheykin, 2005). An experimental study of healthy biotechnology employees documented reduced stress and improved immune activity as a result of meditation. Some were trained to meditate and then compared with a randomly assigned wait-list control group (Davidson et al., 2003). After only 8 weeks of mindfulness meditation training, these new meditators not only reported that they were less anxious; they also showed a significantly greater rise in antibody titers when they were given an influenza vaccine, evidence of improved immune system functioning. The immune system improvement is particularly impressive because self-reported anxiety reduction could theoretically be an artifact of demand characteristics, a potential source of error in research that occurs when subjects respond (consciously or not) in ways that they think the researcher expects or wants (Austin, 1998).

Meditation produces physiological changes that indicate reduced stress and lower arousal of the sympathetic nervous system: lowered blood pressure and heart rate, reduced oxygen consumption, slower breathing, and reduced levels of lactic acid (Barnes, Treiber, & Davis, 2001; Barnes, Treiber, & Johnson, 2004; de Silva, 1990; Wenneberg et al., 1997). Most impressively, the death rate of hypertensive older people who were randomly assigned to Transcendental Meditation interventions was significantly decreased, by 30 percent for cardiovascular causes and also significantly for cancer (Schneider et al., 2005).

The dramatic results of meditation surprised researchers who were monitoring, for research purposes, the impact of a drug that increases sympathetic nervous system functioning. One subject showed an unprecedented dramatic drop in heart rate of 17 beats per minute at a time in the procedure when it should have been increasing by about 21 beats. What was going on? She reported that she had been meditating. When the procedure was repeated without meditation, her heart rate increased instead, as it had for the other subjects (Dimsdale & Mills, 2002).

Meditation has psychological as well as physical effects. The goal of a meditative retreat described by Davidson (2001) is to enhance one's own personal happiness and to cultivate compassion toward other people, especially those with whom one has had conflict and those who are suffering. Meditation produces a change in the sense of self, moving the experience away from the experience of a self separate from others, and toward a state that encompasses all that is around (Cahn & Polich, 2006). This state of consciousness, it is argued, moves people to higher levels of moral development (Nidich, Nidich, & Alexander, 2005). Other studies suggest that meditation produces gains in ego development and moral reasoning (Chandler, Alexander, & Heaton, 2005) and improvement in maturity of defense mechanisms and stress tolerance (Emavardhana & Tori, 1997).

Effects of meditation can permeate everyday life. We generally think of meditation as a very separate activity: sitting in a special position, stopping our regular activity. However, a meditative state of mind can be present during everyday activities, increasing mindfulness. An experimental study (Kohlmetz, Kopiez, & Altenmüller, 2003) found that an experienced musician and meditator could play complex music (Erik Satie's *Vexations*) on the piano while meditating, and brain recordings indicated a trance. People who practice Transcendental Meditation regularly have reported that the states of consciousness first experienced in such meditative states then begin to coexist with their waking and sleeping states of consciousness, and EEG recordings are consistent with these reports of experience (Mason et al., 1997; Travis et al., 2002). So meditation does not necessarily mean stopping everything else. In fact, some spiritual advisers recommend maintaining a meditative state during everyday activities.

BUDDHISM AND PSYCHOTHERAPY

Among psychologists, psychotherapists are among the most enthusiastic supporters of the Buddhist viewpoint and of meditation. This seems reasonable; both approaches expect dramatic improvements in a person's well-being to come from changes in consciousness. Jungian psychoanalyst Polly Young-Eisendrath (2002) succinctly describes the similar goals of therapy and Buddhism as a decrease in personal suffering and an increase in compassion for others. Both psychotherapy and meditation encourage a nonjudgmental stance (Kamilar, 2002; Miller, 2002). Meditation is useful for therapists to cope with their own stress and avoid burnout, and to listen more effectively to their clients (Finn & Rubin, 2000; Michalon, 2001; Shapiro et al., 2005; Thomson, 2000).

Psychotherapists are increasingly incorporating meditation, mindfulness, and other Buddhist ideas into their practice (O'Driscoll, 2007), and Buddhism also has the potential to prevent the development of disorders (Kelly, 2008). Cognitive behaviorists have incorporated aspects of meditation into their treatments for a variety of disorders, including eating disorders, phobias, addiction, and obsessive-compulsive disorders ("Integrating," 2002; "Meditation in Psychotherapy," 2005). *Dialectical behavior therapy* treats borderline personality disorder by integrating Zen Buddhist principles, including acceptance and mindfulness meditation, to a cognitive behavioral approach (Robins, 2002).

Addiction can be treated, recognizing the Buddhist assertion that desire or craving produces suffering. Surely addiction can be thought of as a problem of unhealthy craving, which cannot be satisfied (Dudley-Grant, 2003), whether we are talking about alcohol and drug addictions or behaviors, such as "sex addiction" or "workaholism,"

Table 16.5 The Six Realms of Experience

Realm	Characteristic Emotions and Experience
Realm of the gods	Pride; ego striving; self-consciousness
Realm of the jealous gods	Paranoia; distrust; defensive pride
Realm of humans	Passion; striving for high ideals; intellectual concerns
Realm of animals	Lack of self-consciousness; egocentrism; stubbornness
Realm of the hungry ghosts	Neediness; vulnerability to addictive substances and behaviors
Realm of hell	Anger; aggression; hatred

Source: Prepared from information in Trungpa (2005).

that do not have an obvious physiological component. Both kinds of craving are included in a level described in Buddhism as the realm of the **hungry ghosts** (*preta*), one of six realms or styles of experience (see Table 16.5). The hungry ghosts have gigantic and empty bellies, but they cannot eat enough to be satisfied because their mouths are tiny. In addition to physiological cravings that cannot be satisfied, and behavioral "addictions," interpersonal attachments, the desire for fame and fortune, or any compulsive hoarding can be encompassed in this model of unhealthy craving.

hungry ghosts

(pretas) one of several realms of existence in Buddhist teaching, characterized by persistent, unsatisfied cravings

Buddhism offers advice about dealing with cravings, and so it has practical value for alcoholism and other addictions. One intervention to treat addiction and consequent HIV-risky behavior was developed by integrating Buddhist principles, such as mindfulness and compassion, with cognitive behavioral techniques (Avants & Margolin, 2004). Meditation may displace unhealthy ways of dealing with stress and anxiety, including the use of drugs and alcohol. Especially if accompanied by cognitive therapy, meditation is more effective than attempts at suppressing thoughts about desiring drugs (Kavanagh, Andrade, & May, 2004).

In describing his clinical work with addiction, Marlatt (2002) notes that several Buddhist teachings facilitate a therapeutic result. The idea of impermanence emphasizes that no drug "high" can last permanently. The eightfold path offers a curriculum for the gradual and multifaceted changes that need to be made. The Buddhist concept of the "Middle Way" offers an important insight for those who have relapsed from sobriety. By recognizing a difference between one episode and a full-blown return to being controlled by the drug, the addict has more hope of combating the disorder.

Although Buddhist principles in general and meditation in particular are promising for treating addicted people, the idea needs further research to determine whether it is effective, and if so, how it should be implemented. One study of a small sample of randomly assigned residents in recovery found no improvement for substance abuse patients with 8 weeks of mindfulness meditation training, when it was added to standard treatment (Alterman et al., 2004). Perhaps that was not long enough.

THE DIALOGUE BETWEEN BUDDHISM AND SCIENTIFIC PSYCHOLOGY

Science and religion have not always been happy partners. In the name of religion, scientific theories of the solar system (Copernicus), of evolution (Darwin), and of the so-called big bang that started the universe have all been criticized, and sometimes their supporters were persecuted. Scientists have also sometimes demeaned religious proponents.

Buddhism, however, is, among the world's religions, distinctly receptive to science (Young-Eisendrath, 2003). Buddhism provides insights into higher-order spiritual and moral issues, as do other great religions, but as one consequence of its renunciation of attachments, it does not cling to a particular set of scientific beliefs. Thus it remains receptive to new scientific knowledge (Ratanakul, 2002).

The dialogue between Buddhism (and other religions, too) and the science and practice of psychology is important; each gains from the interaction. What does Buddhism, or religion more generally, have to gain from discussions with psychology?

The Dalai Lama argues that mature ethics depend on a correct understanding of human nature (Bstan-dzin-rgya-mtsho, 1999, 2001) and psychology contributes to this understanding.

Psychology, for its part, gains from the long Buddhist tradition of systematic observation of consciousness through meditation, offering a far more developed technique than the introspectionist methods of early psychology. From these observations based on meditation, psychologists could devise better ways of observing subjective experience, an area that has been relatively neglected in recent years (Lancaster, 1997; Young-Eisendrath, 2003). Using the familiar psychological technique of questionnaires, psychology attempts to quantify Buddhist concepts, including nonattachment (Sahdra, Shaver, & Brown, 2010) and mindfulness (Buchheld, Grossman, & Walach, 2001). Undoubtedly there are still many lessons to be learned as Buddhism and psychology, with other sciences, continue their conversations. How exciting is this dialogue!

Summary

- Buddhism, although a religion, makes many statements that are closer to psychology than to religion as Westerners understand religion.
- It describes the universal human condition of *suffering* and its causes, and it offers methods for ending suffering, in teachings called the *Four Noble Truths* and the *Eightfold Path*.
- Clinging to the idea of stability, including a stable self, is said to be ignorant and a cause of suffering.
- Buddhism is a religious tradition that has developed religious practices, especially *meditation*, based on understandings of phenomena that are of interest to personality theory: thought, the self, emotion, behavior and its consequences, to name a few.
- Meditation is now used by some Western psychotherapists and medical practitioners in conjunction with other therapeutic interventions to deal with stress, anxiety, and many other disorders.
- Neuroscientists studying meditating monks and other meditating subjects have found that the practice does change brain functioning in various ways, depending on the type of meditation and experience of the meditator.
- These effects support the Buddhist claim of increased positive emotions from meditation.
- Benefits to physical health and to society are claimed to result from individual spiritual practice and development.
- Psychotherapists have incorporated meditation into their practice, including treatments for addiction, and neuroscientists are exploring the relationship of meditation to brain functioning.
- Changes in consciousness are central to the Buddhist approach.

Thinking about Buddhist Psychology

1. Which theories from earlier in the book are most similar to Buddhist psychology? How are they similar? How are they different?
2. Why do you suppose that Buddhist ideas have become popular among some therapists?
3. Compare and contrast the idea of the self in Buddhism with ideas that have been presented earlier in this text (e.g., Horney, Allport, Bandura, Rogers). Do you think that Western psychology's ideas of the self are based on illusion?
4. Can you propose a method for testing whether the concept of "past lives" is factually accurate? If so, how? If not, does it have value as a metaphor for experience, or should it be discarded?
5. Do you agree that Buddhism has a role to play within psychology, or should it be kept strictly as a religion?
6. Do you think a person who has trouble focusing attention and who is easily distracted (e.g., by sounds when taking an exam) would be helped more by concentrative meditation or by mindfulness meditation? Why?
7. Discuss the challenges and benefits of applying a theory to a different culture than that in which it was formulated. Do you think it makes sense to apply Buddhist ideas to Western culture? What about applying Western psychological ideas to Eastern cultures?

Study Questions

1. If Buddhism is a religion, why is it of interest to psychologists? Which psychologists, historically, have been interested in it?
2. Describe the life of Siddhartha Gautama and his role in the history of Buddhism.
3. What are the Four Noble Truths?
4. What are some of the translations of "suffering"? What are the implications of these translations for psychological statements?
5. What is the Eightfold Path?
6. What does Buddhism teach about the self?
7. Discuss stability versus change from a Buddhist viewpoint.
8. What is the relationship between the mind (especially intention) and behavior, in the Buddhist approach?
9. What is karma?
10. Explain the concept of dependent origination. How does this relate to the idea that there are multiple causes for events?
11. Does Buddhism describe the body and mind as separate, or not?
12. How does meditation aim to change consciousness?
13. What is Enlightenment? How is it different from Awakening?
14. How does Buddhism view emotions? In particular, what is the Buddhist attitude toward anger?
15. How does Buddhism view compassion? What produces compassion? What are its implications for interpersonal relationships?
16. Compare neuroscience research on emotion with Buddhist ideas.
17. Describe claims of the power of meditation to produce peace. Do you believe these claims? Why or why not?
18. What does Buddhism say about the individual in a community?
19. What is a *koan*?
20. Describe meditation. How is mindfulness meditation different from concentrative meditation?
21. Describe research, especially neuroscience research, on meditation. Does it support the Buddhist model?
22. What health claims are made for mediation?
23. How have psychotherapists used meditation? What are its effects on psychological problems, such as addiction?

17

Conclusion

Chapter Overview

Choosing or Combining Theories
Theories as Metaphors
Summary

---

paradigm

*a general framework
that provides direction
to a field of science,
within which theoretical
concepts are extended
and empirical work is
conducted*

Many theories have been devised to explain personality. Some have seen a historical rise and fall in popularity, while others continue to inspire research or application or both. If there were widespread agreement in the field of personality on which theoretical concepts were most useful, we could say that a dominant **paradigm** prevailed (Kuhn, 1970). A common paradigm would guide personality researchers in their choice of research questions and methods. However, no such agreement exists, as the diversity of theories in this text attests. No one perspective has been able to replace the others by demonstrating its clear superiority in explaining and predicting relevant observations. Indeed, lack of agreement about which observations are relevant makes it difficult to imagine the kind of direct scientific competition that would allow a critical test among theories.

Multiplicity of theory is not necessarily undesirable (Koch, 1981). Having a number of limited-range theories, each developing concepts to understand a relatively narrow range of phenomena, may at some stages of scientific development lead to faster advances than a more comprehensive, but less precise, theory. Now, though, personality seems to be moving toward more communication among its component parts. Developmental processes of learning are building on biological foundations that include descriptions of individual differences. Trait descriptions are being considered in an integrated way with dynamics of social interactions (e.g., Walter Mischel's theory). Emotions and subjective experience are being considered in their cultural context. Perhaps we will not attain the status of an integrated, comprehensive paradigm for personality, but increasingly, the convergences rather than the conflicts among perspectives are receiving attention.

CHOOSING OR COMBINING THEORIES

How many theories of personality are needed? Should we try to select the one best theory or devise a new single theory to guide the field? Or is it better to have the coexistence of several theories? Various opinions have been offered.

Eclecticism

eclecticism

*combining ideas from a
variety of theories*

One way of dealing with the diversity of theories is to advocate **eclecticism**. To be eclectic is to value selected contributions from diverse theories, without accepting any theory completely. For example, we could value psychoanalytic understanding of symbolism in art while also accepting the usefulness of behavioral methods of treating phobias. It certainly seems reasonable to use the best-available theoretical tool when trying to understand a particular issue or when choosing the best form of therapy for a particular client (cf. Lazarus, 1989), so it is not surprising that many mental health professionals, as well as other personality psychologists, consider themselves to be eclectic (Jensen, Bergin, & Greaves, 1990). After all, various theories have different strengths and weaknesses. Eclecticism has limitations as a theory, however; it does not provide a systematic framework for understanding personality, so it cannot be verified as an overall theory. It does not offer a rationale for deciding when to select from among the diverse models.

Pluralism

Various paradigms can coexist, each maintaining its theoretical distinctiveness. This is theoretical **pluralism**. Psychology is a pluralistic discipline (Walsh & Peterson, 1985), and many psychologists consider this to be desirable. Terry Smith (1983) argues that it would be undesirable to focus entirely on one theoretical approach because we cannot be certain which would be most productive:

pluralism
the coexistence of various theories without attempting to combine them

> Given our current lack of knowledge, we should not be staking everything on what, through the dark glass of our ignorance, looks to be the best available alternative; but rather we should take a more experimental approach ... and ask what alternatives are worth trying. Presumably there will be more than one. (p. 148)

Premature integration makes it difficult to define theoretical concepts clearly, and that impedes research and theoretical progress (London, 1988; Russell, 1986). So a pluralistic approach tends to separate the field into separate silos, with limited intercommunication.

Unified Theory

As sciences mature, they develop integrated theories. There have been many calls for the development of a multilevel unified theory that incorporates the various levels of explanation that personality psychologists have explored (e.g., biological, cognitive, and social). Arthur Staats (1981, 1991, 1996) argues that the time has come for psychology to develop a **unified theory**.

Several attempts to integrate theories have been made. Dollard and Miller, for example, combined psychoanalysis with learning theory, and many behaviorists since have advocated behaviorism as the unifying paradigm for all of personality theory (cf. Ardila, 1992). Convergence has also been explored between psychoanalysis and personal construct theory (Warren, 1990), between Adlerian individual psychology and behaviorism (Pratt, 1985), and between the theories of Erikson and Kelly (Neimeyer & Rareshide, 1991). Modern psychodynamic theory, which describes unconscious aspects of interpersonal relationships, has untapped implications for currently popular social cognitive theories (Westen, 1991, 1998b).

unified theory
a theory that combines diverse aspects from various approaches, indicating how they are organized and related

One way to make sense of the diversity of theories is to recognize that they explain different phenomena, often at different levels. A unified theory will then be a **multilevel theory** (e.g., Hyland, 1985; Staats & Eifert, 1990). It would begin with biological inheritance and take into account learning and cultural influences in development, recognizing both external implications and subjective experience. Individual differences would be explored, without presuming that a personality typology alone suffices.

multilevel theory
a unified theory that integrates various levels of explanation (e.g., biological, cognitive, social)

THEORIES AS METAPHORS

We often express our thoughts by using metaphors (figures of speech that imply comparisons). For example, we may refer to the elderly as experiencing the "sunset of their years" or to bad news as a "bitter pill." Scientific theories can also be understood as metaphors (Pepper, 1942). Here are some metaphors that relate to various personality theories.

The Mechanistic Metaphor

mechanistic metaphor

an image that calls attention to the immediate, direct forces that determine personality and behavior

The **mechanistic metaphor** presumes that personality is determined with the same external, decisive determinism that propels physical objects through space. It has been called "the dominant world view in Western civilization" (Sarbin, 1986). This metaphor, adopted from the physical sciences (Rychlak, 1984; Wolman, 1971), historically appealed to psychologists because it made psychology seem more rigorous. The mechanistic metaphor underlies theories as diverse as Freudian theory and behaviorism (although Theodore Sarbin suggests that Freud's warring id, ego, and superego departed from the mechanistic model).

However, the mechanistic metaphor is generally dismissed today as an outdated metaphor borrowed from the physical sciences, specifically eighteenth-century Newtonian physics (Atwood & Maltin, 1991; Oppenheimer, 1956; Slife, 1981). In that metaphor, objects did not move unless they were acted on by outside forces, and then the change was continuous, in proportion to the outside force. With Einstein's formulation of the interrelationship between energy and matter (his famous $E = mc^2$ equation) and with the development of quantum theory, all that has changed. In modern physics, energies within matter can produce change without outside intervention, and change can occur in discontinuous quantum leaps within the atom (Einstein & Infeld, 1938/1961). In contrast to the false dichotomy between the person and the environment (and other false dichotomies, such as between free will and determinism or mind and matter), the new physics proposes an integrated field approach (Midgley & Morris, 1988). If a mechanistic metaphor is inadequate for understanding physical matter, should it be the model for personality?

The Organic Metaphor

organic metaphor

an image that calls attention to the potential for growth and form that is inherent within every person, nurtured by growth-producing circumstances

What about a biological metaphor? The **organic metaphor** compares personality with the growth of plants and animals. Rogers used this metaphor when he described the actualizing tendency, and it is also the underlying metaphor of Erikson's epigenetic principle. Potentials for development are located by this metaphor within the person rather than externally. The environment is seen not as a determining force, as in the mechanistic metaphor, but rather as an environment either conducive to the inherent growth of the personality or an impediment, just as a seed may fall on good or poor soil. This metaphor emphasizes the potential inherent in every person, as part of his or her nature. The role of the environment is to nurture growth, not to cause it.

The Information-Processing Metaphor

information-processing metaphor

an image that calls attention to the cognitive aspects of personality, which can take many forms and therefore can produce many personality outcomes

The **information-processing metaphor** emphasizes cognition and calls attention to people's capacity to function differently, depending on what they think. It influenced the development of cognitive theories, such as those of Kelly, Bandura, and Mischel. The "consciousness revolution" (Sperry, 1988, 1990) regards higher mental functioning, including subjective experience, as causal. Unlike the organic metaphor, which implies only one healthy potential, this metaphor recognizes multiple potentials without focusing only on external determinants (as the mechanistic metaphor does). It recognizes developmental change because personal constructs (like computer programs) can develop and change over time.

The Narrative Metaphor

narrative metaphor

an image that calls attention to the stories people create that give meaning and direction to their lives

Theodore Sarbin (1986) suggests that the **narrative metaphor** underlies much of psychology. Personality can be thought of as the story of a person's life. When personality changes, we in effect rewrite our life stories, perhaps changing the future or telling the past from a different viewpoint. A narrative has a plot, characters, time progression, and important episodes. So does the story of a person's life. The dramatic role playing of George Kelly's theory obviously fits this metaphor.

Narratives distinguish human experience from descriptions of inanimate matter and so provide an alternative to the mechanistic metaphor of physical science. Are they too much like nonscientific fields, like literature and religion, for example?

If we do not test them, surely narrative metaphors can be nonscientific, but the same is true of other metaphors. If we test these metaphors, using the scientific methods of operational definitions and hypothesis testing, making sure that our observations are based on appropriate subjects and are replicated adequately, there is no reason why narrative metaphors cannot be the basis of a scientific theory. They may, in fact, suggest hypotheses overlooked by other metaphors.

The Metaphor of the Emergent Self

The **emergent self metaphor** suggests that a self-directed, willful personality emerges from the more deterministic and predictable forces described by the earlier metaphors. In science fiction, computers and robots are sometimes portrayed as evolving to a willful state, reflecting this image that self-will can emerge from parts that are, in less complex form, determined. This metaphor describes Adler's emphasis on choice and striving, as well as humanistic psychology's discussions of free will. It highlights people's purposeful behavior (cf. Sappington, 1990; Ziller, 1990). It can be considered **teleological** to convey that it focuses attention on the direction toward which a person is moving rather than on the past forces that are determining the present.

> Roger Sperry (1988) has argued that micro-control from neurological processes now is accompanied with macro-control from higher levels, from emergent mental processes. This higher control can be called **emergent determinism**. Joseph Rychlak's (1977, 1986, 1988) logical learning theory proposes the concept of a telosponse, "behavior done for the sake of a premised reason (purpose, intention, etc.)" (Rychlak, 1984, p. 92). He compares his approach to aspects of several of the theories included in this text: "the Freudian wish, the Adlerian prototype, the Jungian archetype, [and] the Kellyian construct" (Rychlak, 1986, p. 757), as well as the humanists Rogers and Maslow (Rychlak, 1977). Gian Vittorio Caprara (1996) proposes that personality is an emergent self-regulatory system.

> For many psychologists, teleology is incompatible with science, which requires the assumption of determinism. In response, Joseph Rychlak (1977, 1984) charges that psychologists have not adequately differentiated between theory and method. Although experimentation requires a causal rather than a teleological model, theory does not. To exclude teleological concepts (e.g., purpose and free will) from theory, from this viewpoint, is unnecessarily limiting.

The Metaphor of the Transcendent Self

The **transcendent self metaphor** is suggested by Jung's mysticism, by the suggestions of experience beyond individual ego that Maslow and Rogers mentioned, and by the Buddhist approach. It implies that individuals are not so separate and self-contained as we usually assume them to be, but rather they are connected in some plane of shared experience. This metaphor, however, has few advocates within Western personality theory, which is still struggling to understand the experience of individuals.

The Metaphor of Chaos and Complexity

In other fields, an approach called **complexity theory** has been developing to explain complicated systems, such as the weather, the immune system, and economic ups and downs (Mitchell, 2009). A precursor of complexity theory, chaos theory holds that events are determined, but even very minor variations in earlier conditions can have dramatic effects on the outcome. Practically speaking, outcomes may not be predictable. A well-known example of chaos theory from early twentieth-century physics is Heisenberg's uncertainty principle in quantum mechanics, stating that it isn't possible to measure the position of a subatomic particle while also knowing its momentum; one or the other must remain uncertain. Like the proverbial straw that broke the camel's back, or the flap of a butterfly's wings thousands of miles away that can theoretically trigger a tornado (the "butterfly effect"), an extraordinary event that seems to come from nowhere is in theory predictable from very detailed equations.

---

emergent self metaphor
an image that calls attention to the higher-order characteristics of purpose and will that are produced by the culmination of lower-order deterministic forces

teleological
viewing phenomena in terms of their overall purpose, design, or intent (rather than in terms of the mechanisms by which they occur)

emergent determinism
causation or determinism from higher mental processes, such as thought, in contrast to lower-order determinism, such as from neurological process

transcendent self metaphor
an image that calls attention to the shared experience of people that is not limited by their individual separateness

complexity theory
theory to account for complicated phenomena, that combines a very large number of predictors and accounts for unusual, emergent phenomena that would not be anticipated based on other observations

Practically speaking, the impossibility of sufficiently precise measurement of initial conditions, combined with the difficulty of fully developing a model for any particular application, prevents detailed prediction of particular events. These qualities make sense for the field of personality, which seeks—and finds—general principles but is unlikely to be able to fully predict individuals.

We get some glimpse of the importance of subtle initial conditions in a phenomenon described by Malcolm Gladwell (2008), based on what sociologists call "accumulative advantage" or more poetically called the "Matthew Effect" by Thomas Merton. That is, children who are the oldest in their school classes, because of the arbitrary date when a child begins elementary school, start out with a small advantage because of their age-related greater maturity. Over time, this small advantage is compounded, and they are more likely than the younger children in their classes to excel in a variety of competitive endeavors, including education and professional sports. The initial small advantage of being a few months older does not dissipate with time, but compounds.

Complexity theories develop models that combine a large variety of input variables in order to predict outcomes. These outcomes are not the gradual, familiar outcomes such as a gradual increase in development, or a predictable response to a single stimulus. Complex models can account for what seem to be anomalies or exceptions. In personality theory, the promise is that such complex models could predict the breakdown of a previously well-adjusted personality, or the transformation from one identity to another. Considerable theoretical development is needed, though, before such models can be devised, and they will require extensive use of mathematics and computers.

A lesson from complexity theories is that we should be aware that predictions that seem reliably repeated may not hold in other circumstances—other contexts, other populations, for example. Against a backdrop of reliable prediction, we should not be surprised by exceptions. They don't invalidate our theories, but are the very nature of complex systems—such as personality.

Summary

- The field of personality, although it has many perspectives and theories, lacks a shared *paradigm* to direct research.
- Alternative solutions to the dilemma of many theories include *eclecticism*, which selects aspects from various theories; *unified theory*, which aims for an integrated and systematic theory combining diverse elements; and *pluralism*, which allows diverse theories to exist while maintaining their separate integrity.
- Several metaphors have been applied to personality theories, including the mechanistic metaphor, the organic metaphor, the information-processing metaphor, the narrative metaphor, the metaphor of the emergent self, the metaphor of the transcendent self, and the metaphor of chaos and complexity.

Thinking about Personality Theory

1. Which metaphor do you consider most appropriate for personality theory? Why?
2. Can you suggest any additional metaphors for personality theory?
3. In your opinion, what issues are most important for personality theorists and researchers to examine next?

Study Questions

1. What is a theoretical paradigm? Does personality theory have a dominant paradigm?
2. Summarize the current status of personality theory.
3. Discuss the ways in which one can deal with theoretical diversity, including eclecticism, pluralism, and the search for a unified theory.
4. Describe the mechanistic metaphor of personality.
5. Describe the organic metaphor of personality.
6. Describe the information-processing metaphor of personality.
7. Describe the narrative metaphor of personality.
8. Describe the emergent self metaphor of personality.
9. Describe the transcendent self metaphor of personality.
10. Describe the metaphor of chaos and complexity.

GLOSSARY

16PF Cattell's questionnaire designed to measure the major source traits of normal personality

act frequency approach measuring personality traits by assessing the frequency of prototypical behaviors

active imagination technique for exploring the unconscious by encouraging waking fantasies

actual self what a person really is at a given time, seen objectively

actualizing tendency the force for growth and development that is innate in all organisms

adaptation coping with the external world

aggressive drive one of Adler's terms for positive striving, emphasizing anger and competitiveness

Agreeableness factor of personality, typified by a friendly, compliant personality

amplification elaboration of dream images as a step toward dream interpretation

amygdala brain area involved in fear, theorized (by Kagan) to contribute to inhibited temperament

anal character personality type resulting from fixation at age 1 to 3, characterized by orderliness, parsimony, and obstinacy

anal stage the second psychosexual stage of development, from age 1 to 3

anatta no-self; the doctrine that there is, in reality, no fixed, stable, enduring self (although the illusion of one may be constructed from fleeting impressions)

anima the femininity that is part of the unconscious of every man

animus the masculinity that is part of the unconscious of every woman

anticipatory response tendency of responses that precede reward to occur earlier and earlier in the behavioral sequence

applied research research intended for practical use

applied value the ability of a theory to guide practical uses

arbitrary rightness secondary adjustment technique in which a person rigidly declares that his or her own view is correct

archetype a primordial image in the collective unconscious; an innate pattern that influences experience of the real world

attachment (Buddhism) craving for a variety of things, including physical objects and even the self; the source of suffering (according to the Second Noble Truth)

attachment (psychoanalysis) bonds of affection in which an infant turns to the mother or other caretaker for comfort and security; by extension, close interpersonal styles in adulthood

attentional processes noticing the model's behavior (a prerequisite for learning by modeling)

autonomy the positive pole of the second psychosocial stage

auxiliary function the second most developed function of an individual's personality

Awakening a transformation from ordinary consciousness in which a person recognizes the true nature of things and the path to spiritual progress

basic anxiety feeling of isolation and helplessness resulting from inadequate parenting in infancy

basic behavioral repertoires (BBRs) learned behaviors fundamental to later learning of more complex behavior, in three categories: language-cognitive, emotional-motivational, and sensory-motor

basic hostility feeling of anger by the young child toward the parents, which must be repressed

basic need a fundamental deficiency need

basic research research intended to develop theory

behavior modification the application of learning principles to therapy

Behavioral Activation System (BAS) in Gray's model, tendency of personality related to the approaching of rewarding experiences

behavioral genetic approach approach that investigates the genetic and environmental contributions to behavior

Behavioral Inhibition System (BIS) in Gray's model, tendency of personality related to reactions to aversive stimuli

behavior-outcome expectancy expectancy about what will happen if a person behaves in a particular way

being motivation higher-level motivation in which the need for self-actualization predominates

Big Five the five-factor model of personality, consisting of Extraversion, Agreeableness, Neuroticism, Conscientiousness, and Openness

blind spots secondary adjustment technique in which a person is unaware of behavior inconsistent with the idealized self-image

B-love nonpossessive love, characteristic of a self-actualized person

bodhisattva a spiritually enlightened person who remains in the world to help others on their spiritual path

Buddha Awakened one; the term often refers to Siddhartha Gautama (Sakyamuni Buddha), who lived in India about 2,500 years ago; in some forms of Buddhism, it is held that everyone can attain buddha status (become a buddha) by following the path, although it may take more than one lifetime to achieve this

CAPS model the Cognitive Affective Personality System model that Mischel offers as an alternative to an overly generalized trait model of personality

cardinal trait a pervasive personality trait that dominates nearly everything a person does

care ability to nurture the development of the next generation; the basic virtue developed during the seventh psychosocial stage

case study an intensive investigation of a single individual

castration anxiety fear that motivates male development at age 3 to 5

catharsis therapeutic effect of a release of emotion when previously repressed material is made conscious

central trait one of the half dozen or so traits that best describe a particular person

Choice Corollary statement that people choose the pole of a construct that promises greater possibility of extending and defining the system of constructs

circumspection the first stage in the C-P-C Cycle, in which various constructs are tentatively explored

client-centered therapy therapy based on the belief that the person seeking help is the best judge of the direction that will lead to growth

cognitive affective unit (CAU) cognitive factors within a person, comprising cognitive and emotional aspects, that influence how a person adapts to the environment; (later terminology than cognitive person variables, in Mischel's theory)

cognitive complexity elaborateness of a person's construct system, reflected in a large number of different constructs

cognitive person variables cognitive factors within a person, less global than traits, which influence how an individual adapts to the environment

collective efficacy the sense that a group can do what is to be done

collective unconscious the inherited unconscious

collectivism values, predominant in some cultures, of social cooperation and group goals

common trait a trait characterizing many people (i.e., a trait considered from the nomothetic point of view)

Commonality Corollary statement describing similarity between people

compartmentalization secondary adjustment technique in which incompatible behaviors are not simultaneously recognized

compensation principle of the relationship between the unconscious and consciousness, by which the unconscious provides what is missing from consciousness to make a complete whole

competence sense of workmanship, of perfecting skills; the basic virtue developed during the fourth psychosocial stage

competencies person variables concerned with what a person is able to do

complexes emotionally charged networks of ideas (such as those resulting from unresolved conflicts)

complexity theory theory to account for complicated phenomena, that combines a very large number of predictors and accounts for unusual, emergent phenomena that would not be anticipated based on other observations

comprehensiveness the ability of a theory to explain a broad variety of observations

concentrative meditation a form of meditation in which attention is focused on a particular object, such as the breath or a word or phrase (mantra), one of the best known being the mantra *om*

concrete construct a construct that cannot be extended to include new elements

condensation combining of two or more images; characteristic of primary processes (e.g., in dreams)

conditions of worth the expectations a person must live up to before receiving respect and love

conflict a situation in which cues for two incompatible responses are provided

confluence learning learning behaviors that satisfy more than one motivation

congruence a feeling of consistency between the real self and the ideal self

Conscientiousness factor of personality, typified by hard work, orderliness, and self-discipline

conscious aware; cognizant; mental processes of which a person is aware

consistency paradox the mismatch between intuition, which says that people are consistent, and research findings, which say they are not

constitutional trait a trait influenced by heredity

construct a concept used in a theory

construct validity the usefulness of a theoretical term, evidenced by an accumulation of research findings

Construction Corollary Kelly's statement that people anticipate replications of events

constructive alternativism the assumption that people can interpret the world in a variety of ways

continuous reinforcement (CR) schedule a reinforcement schedule in which every response is reinforced

control the third stage in the C-P-C Cycle; the way in which the person acts

control group in an experiment, the group not exposed to the experimental treatment

conversion hysteria form of neurosis in which psychological conflicts are expressed in physical symptoms (without actual physical damage)

copying learning to behave in the same way as a model, but not in response to the same cues as the model, in order to be rewarded by perceived similarity to the model

core constructs constructs central to a person's identity and existence

correlation coefficient a measure of the association between two variables, in which 0 indicates no association, and +1 or −1 a strong association (positive or negative)

correlation matrix a chart of the correlations between all pairs of a set of variables

correlational research research method that examines the relationships among measurements

countertransference the analyst's reaction to the patient, as distorted by unresolved conflicts

C-P-C Cycle the three-step process leading to effective action

creative self the person who acts to determine his or her own life

Creativity Cycle the process of changing constructs by loosening and tightening them

crystallized intelligence intelligence influenced by education, so it measures what has been learned

cue what a person notices, which provides a discriminative stimulus for learning

cultural evolution evolution through transmitted learning from one generation to another

Culture Fair Intelligence Test a test designed to measure fluid intelligence only

cynicism secondary adjustment technique in which the moral values of society are rejected

defense mechanisms ego strategies for coping with unconscious conflict

deficiency motivation motivation at lower levels of development

delay of gratification the ability to give up immediate gratifications for larger, more distant rewards

delusion ignorance or false beliefs about the nature of reality

denial primitive defense mechanism in which material that produces conflict is simply repressed

dependent variable the effect in an experimental study

deprecation complex unhealthy way of seeking superiority by belittling others

desacralization loss of a sense of the sacred or spiritual

description theoretical task of identifying the units of personality, with particular emphasis on the differences between people

despair the negative pole of the eighth psychosocial stage

determinism the assumption that phenomena have causes that can be discovered by empirical research

development formation or change (of personality) over time

dharma the true, intrinsic nature of things

Dichotomy Corollary statement that constructs are bipolar

disconfirmation evidence against a theory; observations that contradict the predictions of a hypothesis

discrimination responding only to particular cues

discrimination learning learning to respond differentially, depending on environmental stimuli

displacement defense mechanism in which energy is transferred from one object or activity to another

D-love selfish love, characteristic of a person who is not self-actualized

dominant function a person's predominant psychological function

dominant response a person's most likely response in a given situation

drive what a person wants, which motivates learning

dubkha suffering, which is accepted in the First Noble Truth

dynamic lattice Cattell's diagram to show motivational dynamics

dynamics the motivational aspect of personality

eclectic combining ideas from a variety of theories

eclecticism combining ideas from a variety of theories

ego the most mature structure of personality; mediates intrapsychic conflict and copes with the external world

ego-extensions objects or people that help define a person's identity or sense of self

ego inflation overvaluation of ego consciousness, without recognizing its limited role in the psyche

Eightfold Path the method for achieving an end of suffering, described in the Fourth Noble Truth

elaborative choice a choice that allows a construct system to be extended; the Choice Corollary says this choice will be selected

elusiveness secondary adjustment technique in which a person avoids commitment to any opinion or action

emergenic traits phenotypic traits caused by a constellation of many genes and so may not appear to run in families

emergent determinism causation or determinism from higher mental processes, such as thought, in contrast to lower-order determinism, such as from neurological process

emergent self metaphor an image that calls attention to the higher-order characteristics of purpose and will that are produced by the culmination of lower-order deterministic forces

empathic understanding the ability of the therapist to understand the subjective experience of the client

empirical based on scientific observations

encoding strategies person variables concerned with how a person construes reality

encounter group growth-enhancing technique in which a group of people openly and honestly express their feelings and opinions

Enlightenment higher stage of consciousness that results from following the Eightfold Path; sometimes also used synonymously with Awakening

environmental-mold trait a trait influenced by learning

epigenetic principle the principle for psychosocial development, based on a biological model, in which parts emerge in order of increasing differentiation

erg a constitutional dynamic source trait

Eros the life instinct

Eupsychia a utopian society in which individual and societal needs are both met and where society supports individual development

evolutionary psychology the perspective that applies the evolutionary principles of natural selection to understanding human psychology, including personality

evolved psychological mechanisms specific psychological processes that have evolved because they solved particular adaptive problems (e.g., sexual jealousy, dealing with the problem of paternal uncertainty)

excessive self-control secondary adjustment technique in which emotions are avoided

expansive solution attempting to solve neurotic conflict by seeking mastery; moving against people

expectancies subjective beliefs about what will happen in a particular situation (including behavior outcomes, stimulus outcomes, and self-efficacies)

Experience Corollary Kelly's statement about personality development

experimental group in an experiment, the group exposed to the experimental treatment

expressive traits traits concerned with the style or tempo of a person's behavior

externalization defense mechanism in which conflicts are projected outside

extinction reduction in the frequency of a nonrewarded response; reduction in the rate of responding when reinforcement ends

Extraversion factor (in several factor theories) of personality, typified by sociability, cheerfulness, and activity

extraversion tolerance for high levels of stimulation because of a strong nervous system that inhibits incoming stimulation, leading to sociability in Eysenck's theory

extrinsic religious orientation attitude in which religion is seen as a means to a person's other goals (such as status or security)

facets a more precisely focused aspect of any of the Big Five factors

facilitator the leader of an encounter group

factor a statistically derived, quantitative dimension of personality that is broader than most traits

factor analysis statistical procedure for determining a smaller number of dimensions in a data set from a large number of variables

family constellation the configuration of family members, including the number and birth order of siblings

feeling psychological function in which decisions are based on the emotions they arouse

fictional finalism a person's image of the goal of his or her striving

fidelity ability to sustain loyalties freely pledged; the basic virtue developed during the fifth psychosocial stage

Fight-Flight System (FFS) biological personality factor proposed by Gray that produces rage and panic

fixation failure to develop normally through a particular developmental stage

fixed-role therapy Kelly's method of therapy, based on role playing

flow a state of deep engagement in an activity that is characteristic of creative individuals.

fluid intelligence the part of intelligence that is the innate ability to learn, without including the effects of specific learning

Four Noble Truths that there is suffering, that it has a cause, that suffering can cease, and that there is a path to end suffering

Fragmentation Corollary statement describing the inconsistency of people

free association psychoanalytic technique in which the patient says whatever comes to mind, permitting unconscious connections to be discovered

Freudian slip a psychologically motivated error in speech, hearing, behavior, and so forth (e.g., forgetting the birthday of a disliked relative)

frustration-aggression hypothesis the hypothesis that frustration always leads to aggression, and aggression is always caused by frustration

fully functioning Rogers's term for a mentally healthy person

functional analysis preparatory to behavior modification, careful observation to identify the stimuli and reinforcements influencing behavior

functional autonomy a trait's independence of its developmental origins

Fundamental Postulate Kelly's main assumption, which stresses the importance of psychological constructs

generalization responding to stimuli that were not present during learning as though they were the discriminative stimuli present during learning

generativity the positive pole of the seventh psychosocial stage

genital character healthy personality type

genital stage the adult psychosexual stage

genotype the inherited genetic profile of an individual

gerotranscendence the ninth stage of psychosocial development, referring to the very elderly

growth centers places where people come together to develop their full potential (e.g., Esalen)

guilt the negative pole of the third psychosocial stage

guru teacher; spiritual adviser

harm avoidance biological dimension proposed by Cloninger that inhibits behavior; related to serotonin levels

heritability the extent to which a trait is influenced by genetics; the statistic that shows what proportion of the variability of a trait in a particular population is associated with genetic variability

hierarchy of needs ordered progression of motives, from basic physical needs upward to motives of the most developed human beings

hope fundamental conviction in the trustworthiness of the world; the basic virtue developed during the first psychosocial stage

hostility continuing to try to validate constructs that have already been invalidated

human potential movement social trend to foster the full development of individuals, reflected in the development of growth centers and in transformation of social institutions

hungry ghosts (*pretas*) one of several realms of existence in Buddhist teaching, characterized by persistent, unsatisfied cravings

hypothesis a prediction to be tested by research

I Ching ancient Chinese method of fortune-telling

id the most primitive structure of personality; the source of psychic energy

ideal self what a person feels he or she ought to be like

idealized self an image of what a person wishes to be

identification defense mechanism in which a person fuses or models after another person

identity sense of sameness between one's meaning for oneself and one's meaning for others in the social world; the positive pole of the fifth psychosocial stage

identity achievement status representing optimal development during the fifth (adolescent) psychosocial stage

identity confusion the negative pole of the fifth psychosocial stage

identity diffusion the negative pole of the fifth psychosocial stage (earlier terminology)

identity foreclosure inadequate resolution of the fifth psychosocial stage, in which an identity is accepted without adequate exploration

idiographic focusing on one individual

imitation learning by observing the actions of others

implicit theories of personality ideas about personality that are held by ordinary people (not based on formal theory)

inclusive fitness the evolutionary principle that traits that increase the survival of the individual and his or her genetic relatives will become more frequent by natural selection

independent variable in an experiment, the cause that is manipulated by the researcher

individual differences qualities that make one person different from another

individual trait a trait that characterizes only the one person who has it (i.e., a trait considered from the idiographic point of view)

individualism values, predominant in many Western cultures, of individual goals and achievement (in contrast to shared group goals and cooperation)

Individuality Corollary Kelly's assertion that different people use different constructs

individuation the process of becoming a fully developed person, with all psychic functions developed

industry the positive pole of the fourth psychosocial stage

inferiority the negative pole of the fourth psychosocial stage

inferiority complex stagnation of growth in which difficulties seem too immense to be overcome

information processing metaphor an image that calls attention to the cognitive aspects of personality, which can take many forms and therefore can produce many personality outcomes

inhibited type temperament type (described by Kagan) that is shy and nonassertive around strangers, proposed to have high levels of norepinephrine and an activation of the amygdala

initiative the positive pole of the third psychosocial stage

Inner Directed Supports scale of the Personal Orientation Inventory measuring a person's tendency to obtain support from himself or herself rather than from other people

insight conscious recognition of one's motivation and unconscious conflicts

integrity the positive pole of the eighth psychosocial stage

intellectualization defense mechanism in which a person focuses on thinking and avoids feeling

intimacy the positive pole of the sixth psychosocial stage

intrapsychic conflict conflict within the personality, as between id desires and superego restrictions

intrinsic motivation motivation to perform an activity for its inherent satisfaction (rather than as a means to some other goal)

intrinsic religious orientation attitude in which religion is accepted for its own sake rather than as a means to an end

intuition psychological function in which material is perceived with a broad perspective, emphasizing future possibilities rather than current details

isolation (Erikson) the negative pole of the sixth psychosocial stage

isolation (psychoanalysis) defense mechanism in which conflictful material is kept disconnected from other thoughts

jackass theory Kelly's phrase to indicate that his theory concerns the "nature of the animal" rather than of the environment

jackdaw eclecticism considering concepts from diverse theories, without making careful selection from and evaluation of these concepts

karma intentional or willed activity, which produces consequences (positive or negative, depending on the action)

kin altruism the principle that natural selection favors those who risk their own lives or welfare to improve the survival and reproductive prospects of their genetic relatives

koan in Zen Buddhism, a riddle that is posed for the purpose of overcoming preconceptions and so furthering spiritual enlightenment

latent content the hidden, unconscious meaning of a dream

L-data objective information about the life history of the individual

learning dilemma a situation in which existing responses are not rewarded, which leads to change

libido psychic energy, derived from sexuality

loosening applying constructs in ways that seem not to make sense, such as in brainstorming and free association

love ability to form an intimate mutual relationship with another person; the basic virtue developed during the sixth psychosocial stage

Mahayana Buddhism the major East Asian Buddhist tradition, which pays particular attention to the Buddha and to devotional practices that assist others to follow his path to Enlightenment

mandala symbolic representation of the whole psyche, emphasizing circles and/or squares

manifest content the surface meaning of a dream

man-the-scientist Kelly's metaphor for human personality

masculine protest one of Adler's terms for positive striving, emphasizing manliness

matched dependent behavior learning to make the same response as a model, in response to a cue from the model

mechanistic metaphor an image that calls attention to the immediate, direct forces that determine personality and behavior

meditation a practice in which attention is consciously regulated to enhance serenity and well-being

metaerg environmental-mold dynamic source traits; includes sentiments and attitudes

metamotivated motivated by needs at the top of the hierarchy

method centered an approach to science that emphasizes procedure over content

Middle Way description of the path to Enlightenment by avoiding extremes, such as extreme asceticism or extreme self-indulgence

mindfulness meditation a form of meditation in which thoughts are observed but not judged

mistrust the negative pole of the first psychosocial stage

modeling learning by observing others; also called vicarious learning

Modulation Corollary statement that the permeability of constructs sets limits to construction possibilities

moral disengagement failure to regulate one's behavior to live up to high moral standards

moratorium period provided by society when an adolescent is sufficiently free of commitments to be able to explore identity; also, a stage of identity development when such exploration is occurring, before identity achievement

motivational process deciding whether it is worthwhile to behave as a model has behaved

motor reproduction process being able to do what one has seen a model do

moving against interpersonal orientation emphasizing hostility

moving away interpersonal orientation emphasizing separateness from others

moving toward interpersonal orientation emphasizing dependency

multilevel theory a unified theory that integrates various levels of explanation (e.g., biological, cognitive, social)

Multiple Abstract Variance Analysis (MAVA) statistical technique for assessing how much of a trait is determined by heredity and how much by environment

multivariate a research strategy that includes many variables

Myers-Briggs Type Indicator (MBTI) psychological test for measuring the psychic functions in an individual

narcissism unhealthy self-focus that impairs the ability to have healthy, empathic relationships with other people

narrative metaphor an image that calls attention to the stories people create that give meaning and direction to their lives

negative identity identity based on socially devalued roles

negative reinforcer an outcome stimulus that ends when a response occurs; it has the effect of increasing the rate of responding

neglect parental behavior in which a child's needs are not adequately met

Neuroticism factor of personality in the Five Factor model, typified by negative emotionality

neuroticism tendency toward high levels of emotional arousal; the second factor in Eysenck's factor model

nirvana the goal of spiritual development, in which there is no attachment, and therefore suffering has ended

nomothetic involving comparisons with other individuals; research based on groups of people

novelty seeking biological trait proposed by Cloninger that activates people to explore new things; related to dopamine levels

numinous experience of spiritual or transpersonal energies

object relations term used in psychoanalysis for relationships with people, based originally on the idea that people serve as objects to satisfy libidinal drives

Oedipus conflict conflict that males experience from age 3 to 5 involving sexual love for the mother and aggressive rivalry with the father

Openness factor of personality, typified by artistic, imaginative, and intellectual interests

operant conditioning learning in which the frequency of responding is influenced by the consequences that are contingent on a response

operant responses behaviors freely emitted by an organism

operational definition procedure for measuring a theoretical construct

oral character personality type resulting from fixation in the first psychosexual stage; characterized by optimism, passivity, and dependency

oral stage the first psychosexual stage of development, from birth to age 1

organic metaphor an image that calls attention to the potential for growth and form that is inherent within every person, nurtured by growth-producing circumstances

organismic valuing process inner sense within a person, which guides him or her in the directions of growth and health

Organization Corollary describes the hierarchical relationships among constructs

outcome expectations the belief about what desirable or undesirable things will occur if a behavior is successfully performed

oxytocin hormone released by nursing females and in sexual intercourse; thought to promote caretaking and cuddling

pampering parental behavior in which a child is overindulged or spoiled

paradigm a basic theoretical model, shared by various theorists and researchers; a general framework that provides direction to a field of science, within which theoretical concepts are extended and empirical work is conducted

parapraxis (plural: **-es**) a psychologically motivated error, more commonly called a *Freudian slip*

parental investment the expenditure of time and resources to reproduce each child, especially emphasizing the amount of one's reproductive potential that is expended for each child

partial reinforcement schedule a reinforcement schedule in which only some responses are reinforced

paternal uncertainty evolutionary proposal that men cannot be sure they are the biological fathers of the children born to their mates

peak experiences mystical states of consciousness, characteristic of many but not all self-actualized people

peripheral constructs constructs not central to one's identity

permeable construct a construct that can be extended to include new elements

persona a person's social identity

personal construct (Kelly) a person's concept for predicting events

personal constructs (Mischel) trait terms that people use to describe themselves and other people

Personal Orientation Inventory the most popular measure of self-actualization

personal unconscious that part of the unconscious derived from an individual's experience

personality for Gordon Allport, "the dynamic organization within the individual of those psychophysical systems that determine his unique adjustment to the environment"; the underlying causes within the person of individual behavior and experience

personality coefficient the average relationship between self-report personality measures and behavior, estimated by Mischel at $r = 0.30$

person-centered Rogers's orientation to therapy and education, which focuses on the experience of the client or student rather than the therapist or teacher

phallic stage the third psychosexual stage of development, from age 3 to 5

phenotype the developed characteristics that can be observed in an individual, based on both genetic and environmental influences

pleasure principle the id's motivation to seek pleasure and to avoid pain

pluralism the coexistence of various theories without attempting to combine them

positive psychology current movement in psychology that emphasizes healthy functioning, with concern for immediate experience and positive emotions such as happiness

positive reinforcer an outcome stimulus that is presented contingent on a response and that has the effect of increasing the rate of responding

preconscious mental content of which a person is currently unaware but that can readily be made conscious

preemption the second stage in the C-P-C Cycle, in which a construct is selected

prepotent currently most powerful; said of a need that because it is unmet is most powerful at the moment

preverbal construct a construct that is not conscious

primary process unconscious mental functioning in which the id predominates; characterized by illogical, symbolic thought

primary reinforcer a reinforcer that is not learned (i.e., innate)

prizing characteristic of a good therapist, which involves positively valuing the client; also called unconditional positive regard

problem centered an approach to science that emphasizes subject matter over procedure

Process Scale measuring instrument to assess how far along an individual is to the goal of becoming a fully functioning person

profile the pattern of a person's scores on several parts of a personality test

projection defense mechanism in which a person's own unacceptable impulse is incorrectly thought to belong to someone else

projective test a test that presents ambiguous stimuli such as inkblots or pictures, so responses will be determined by the test taker's unconscious

propriate striving effort based on a sense of selfhood or identity

proprium all aspects of a person that make for unity; a person's sense of self or ego

prototype a typical example of an object or type of person; a "fuzzy concept" typical of the categories people use in perceiving others

psychoanalysis Freud's theory and its application in therapy

psychobiography the application of a personality theory to the study of an individual's life; different from a case study because of its theoretical emphasis

psychological behaviorism behavioral theory, proposed by Staats, that includes traditional personality concerns (e.g., emotion, testing) as well as behavior

psychological type a person's characteristic pattern of major personality dimensions (introversion-extraversion, thinking-feeling, and sensation-intuition)

psychosocial Erikson's approach to development, offered as an alternative to Freud's psychosexual approach

Psychoticism in Eysenck's model, factor related to nonconformity or social deviance

punishment a stimulus contingent on a response and that has the effect of decreasing the rate of responding

purpose orientation to attain goals through striving; the basic virtue developed during the third psychosocial stage

Q-data data from self-report tests or questionnaires

quantitative measures measures that permit expression of various amounts of something, such as a trait

quest orientation religious orientation that seeks answers to existential-religious questions

Range Corollary statement that a construct applies only to some events, not to all

range of convenience the events to which a construct applies

rate of responding the number of responses emitted in a period of time; a change in this rate is taken as evidence of learning

rational coper a stage in middle childhood in which problem-solving ability is important to one's sense of self

rationalization (Freud) defense mechanism in which reasonable, conscious explanations are offered rather than true unconscious motivations

rationalization (Horney) secondary adjustment technique in which a person explains behaviors in socially acceptable ways

reaction formation defense mechanism in which a person thinks or behaves in a manner opposite to the unacceptable unconscious impulse

real self the self that contains the actualizing tendency; the vital, unique center of the self, which has growth potential

reality principle the ego's mode of functioning in which there is appropriate contact with the external world

rebirth continuation of the effects of karma in previous lifetimes into the present

reciprocal altruism the evolutionary principle whereby members of a group take risks to help the survival and reproductive prospects of others, even nonrelatives, with the (not necessarily conscious) expectation of being helped in return

reciprocal determinism the interacting mutual influences of the person, the environment, and the behavior

relational approach approach in modern psychoanalysis that emphasizes interpersonal relationships

reliability consistency, as when a measurement is repeated at another time or by another observer, with similar results

repression defense mechanism in which unacceptable impulses are made unconscious

resignation solution attempting to solve neurotic conflict by seeking freedom; moving away from people

resiliency the strength to survive stressful situations or those in which one is mistreated, without experiencing the usual negative consequences of such experiences

response (Dollard & Miller) what a person does, which can be learned

response (Skinner) a discrete behavior by an organism

response hierarchy list of all the responses a person could make in a given situation, arranged from most likely to least likely

resultant hierarchy a response hierarchy after it has been modified by learning

retention process remembering what a model has done

reward what a person gets as a result of a response in the learning sequence, which strengthens responses because of its drive-reducing effect

reward dependence biological dimension proposed by Cloninger that maintains behavior through seeking rewards; related to norepinephrine levels

ritual cultural practice or tradition that supports ego strengths

ritualism an individual's maladaptive repetitive actions intended to make up for weak aspects of ego development

Role Construct Repertory (REP) Test instrument for measuring a person's constructs

root metaphor the underlying assumptions of a theoretical position, expressed in terms of an image

same behavior a person's behavior being the same as that of a model, considering the cues and reinforcements as well as the response

samsara the wheel of suffering, in which the consequences of unenlightened action lock a person into a cycle of rebirth instead of permitting liberation to nirvana

sangha a community living in harmony and awareness

satellite relationships side relationships, which supplement a person's primary committed relationship

schedule of reinforcement the specific contingency between a response and a reinforcement

scientific method the method of knowing based on systematic observation

secondary process conscious mental functioning in which the ego predominates; characterized by logical thought

secondary reinforcer a reinforcer that is learned

secondary trait a trait that influences a limited range of behaviors

second-order factor analysis factor analysis in which the data are factor scores (rather than raw data); produces more general personality factors

Self the total integrated personality

self as knower a stage in adulthood in which a person integrates the self into a unified whole

self-actualization development of a person's full potential

self-effacing solution attempting to solve neurotic conflict by seeking love; moving toward people

self-efficacy expectancies (or self-efficacy) subjective beliefs about what a person will be able to do

self-regulatory systems and plans ways that a person works on complicated behavior (e.g., by setting goals and by self-criticism)

self-system personal constructs that people use to describe themselves; cognitive structures and subfunctions for perceiving, evaluating, and regulating behavior (not a psychic agent that controls action)

sensation psychological function in which material is perceived concretely, in detail

sensation seeking trait, proposed by Zuckerman, of seeking varied, novel, complex and intense sensations and experiences, even if that requires risk

shadow the unconscious complement to a person's conscious identity, often experienced as dangerous and evil

shame the negative pole of the second psychosocial stage

shaping reinforcement of successive approximations of a response to increase the frequency of a response that originally has a zero base rate

Siddhartha Gautama the historical Buddha, whose spiritual journey provided the foundation for Buddhism; also called Sakyamuni

Skinner box a device that provides a controlled environment for measuring learning

slot movement abrupt change from one pole of a construct to its opposite, often precipitated by stress

social interest innate potential to live cooperatively with other people

Sociality Corollary statement that describes understanding another person or being understood as a prerequisite for a social process with that person

socially useful type a personality that is well adjusted

source traits basic, underlying personality traits

specification equation mathematical expression that shows how personality and situational variables combine to predict a specific behavior

spontaneous recovery return of a response that was previously extinguished

stagnation the negative pole of the seventh psychosocial stage

stimulus generalization occurrence of a response to a stimulus other than the one that was a cue during learning

stimulus-outcome expectancies expectancies about how events will develop in the world, i.e., what events will follow other environmental stimuli

strong nervous system in Pavlov's theory, a nervous system that forms stronger conditioned responses and tolerates higher intensities of stimulation; said by other theorists to produce extraversion

style of life a person's consistent way of striving

subjective stimulus value how much an outcome is valued by an individual

subjective well-being how happy or satisfied an individual is with his or her life

sublimation defense mechanism in which impulses are expressed in socially acceptable ways

subsidiation the pattern of interrelationships among ergs, metaergs, and sentiments (as diagrammed in the dynamic lattice)

superego structure of personality that is the internal voice of parental and societal restrictions

superiority complex a neurotic belief that one is better than others

superiority striving effort to achieve improvement in oneself

superordinate construct a construct that applies broadly and subsumes lower-order constructs

suppression willfully putting thoughts out of consciousness

surface traits traits as defined simply at the level of observable behavior

synchronicity the acausal principle, in which events are determined by transpersonal forces instead of by causes generally understood by science

Taoist Science Maslow's alternative to the traditional scientific method, emphasizing values and subjectivity (instead of objectivity)

T-data data collected from objective tests, such as reaction times

teleological viewing phenomena in terms of their overall purpose, design, or intent (rather than in terms of the mechanisms by which they occur)

temperament consistent styles of behavior and emotional reactions present from early life onward, presumably caused by biological factors; innate emotional aspects of personality; the biologically based foundation of personality, including such characteristic patterns of behavior as emotionality, activity, and sociability

test validity desirable characteristic of a test, indicating it actually does measure what it is intended to measure

Thanatos the death instinct

theoretical proposition theoretical statement about relationships among theoretical constructs

theory a conceptual tool, consisting of systematically organized constructs and propositions, for understanding certain specified phenomena

thinking psychological function in which decisions are based on logic

third force Maslow's term for his theory, emphasizing its opposition to psychoanalysis and behaviorism

threat awareness of imminent comprehensive change in one's core structures

Time Competence a scale of the Personal Orientation Inventory that measures a person's concern with the present rather than the past or future

time-out procedure a procedure or environment in which no reinforcements are given in an effort to extinguish unwanted behavior

trait a characteristic of a person that makes a person unique, with a unique style of adapting to stimuli in the world; personality characteristic that makes one person different from another and/or that describes an individual's personality

trait (Cattell) that which defines what a person will do in a particular situation

trait-versus-situation debate the controversy over which explains more of the variation in behavior: traits or situations (that is, personality or the environment)

transcendent function the process of integrating all opposing aspects of personality into a unified whole

transcendent self metaphor an image that calls attention to the shared experience of people that is not limited by their individual separateness

transference in therapy, the patient's displacement onto the therapist of feelings based on earlier experiences (e.g., with the patient's own parents)

transformation modification of psychic energy to higher purposes (e.g., through ritual)

true experimental research research strategy that manipulates a cause to determine its effect

trust the positive pole of the first psychosocial stage

type a category of people with similar characteristics

tyranny of the shoulds inner demands to live up to the idealized self

unconditional positive regard accepting and valuing a person without requiring particular behaviors as a prerequisite

unconscious mental processes of which a person is unaware

unified theory a theory that combines diverse aspects from various approaches, indicating how they are organized and related

unifying philosophy of life an attitude or set of values, often religious, that gives coherence and meaning to life

uninhibited type temperament type (described by Kagan) that is outgoing and low in fear, proposed to have lower sympathetic nervous system activity

unique trait a trait that only one person has (also called individual trait)

unitas multiplex the Latin phrase indicating that a person makes a unified whole out of many diverse aspects of personality

validation confirmation of an anticipation by events

validity desirable characteristic of a test, indicating it actually does measure what it is intended to measure

variable in research, a measurement of something across various people (or times or situations), which takes on different values

verifiable the ability of a theory to be tested by empirical procedures, resulting in confirmation or disconfirmation

vicarious learning learning by observing others, without being directly rewarded oneself

weak nervous system in Pavlov's theory, a nervous system that forms weaker conditioned responses and does not tolerate high intensities of stimulation; said by other theorists to produce introversion

will conviction that what one wants to happen can happen; the basic virtue developed during the second psychosocial stage

wisdom mature sense of the meaningfulness and wholeness of experience; the basic virtue developed during the eighth psychosocial stage

womb envy men's envy of women's reproductive capacity (the complement of Freud's penis envy)

Word Association Test method devised by Jung to reveal complexes by asking people to say whatever comes to mind when they hear a word

yoga spiritual practice; various forms exist

zazen **meditation** sitting meditation; practiced in Zen Buddhism

Zen Buddhism type of Buddhism found particularly in Japan, which uses koans to overcome limitations of thought

REFERENCES

Abraham, K. (1986). Ego identity differences among Anglo-American and Mexican-American adolescents. *Journal of Adolescence, 9,* 151–167.

Abramowitz, J. S., Tolin, D. F., & Street, G. P. (2001). Paradoxical effects of thought suppression: A meta-analysis of controlled studies. *Clinical Psychology Review, 21,* 683–703.

Ackerman, P. L., Bowen, K. R., Beier, M. E., & Kanfer, R. (2001). Determinants of individual differences and gender differences in knowledge. *Journal of Educational Psychology, 93,* 797–825.

Acklin, M. W., Bibb, J. L., Boyer, P., & Jain, V. (1991). Early memories as expressions of relationship paradigms: A preliminary investigation. *Journal of Personality Assessment, 57,* 177–192.

Acklin, M. W., Sauer, A., Alexander, G., & Dugoni, B. (1989). Predicting depression using earliest childhood memories. *Journal of Personality Assessment, 53,* 51–59.

Adams, H. E., Wright, L. W., Jr., & Lohr, B. A. (1996). Is homophobia associated with homosexual arousal? *Journal of Abnormal Psychology, 105,* 440–445.

Adams-Webber, J. (1990). Personal construct theory and cognitive science. *International Journal of Personal Construct Psychology, 3,* 415–421.

Adler, A. (1927). *Understanding human nature* (W. B. Wolfe, Trans.). New York: Fawcett. (Original work published 1921)

Adler, A. (1929). *The practice and theory of individual psychology* (P. Radin, Trans.) (2nd ed.). London: Routledge & Kegan Paul. (Original work published 1923)

Adler, A. (1964). *Social interest: A challenge to mankind.* New York: Capricorn. (Original work published 1936)

Adler, A. (1982a). The fundamental views of Individual Psychology. *Individual Psychology, 38,* 3–6. (Original work published 1935)

Adler, A. (1982b). The progress of mankind. *Individual Psychology, 38,* 13–17. (Original work published 1937)

Adler, A. (1988a). The child's inner life and a sense of community. *Individual Psychology, 44,* 417–423. (Original work published 1917)

Adler, A. (1988b). Personality as a self-consistent unity. *Individual Psychology, 44,* 431–440. (Original work published 1932)

Adler, A. (1998). Understanding children with emotional problems [based on 1932–1933 lectures]. *Journal of Humanistic Psychology, 38,* 121–127.

Aftanas, L., & Golosheykin, S. (2005). Impact of regular meditation practice on EEG activity at rest and during evoked negative emotions. *International Journal of Neuroscience, 115,* 893–909.

Agger, E. M. (1988). Psychoanalytic perspectives on sibling relationships. *Psychoanalytic Inquiry, 8,* 3–30.

Agor, W. H. (1991). How intuition can be used to enhance creativity in organizations. *Journal of Creative Behavior, 25,* 11–19.

Ainsworth, M. D. S. (1972). Attachment and dependency. In J. L. Gewirtz (Ed.), *Attachment and dependency* (pp. 97–137). Washington, DC: Winston.

Ainsworth, M. D. S., Blehar, M. C., Waters, E., & Wall, S. (1978). *Patterns of attachment: A psychological study of the Strange Situation.* Hillsdale, NJ: Erlbaum.

Aitken, R. (1990). *The gateless barrier: The Wu-Men Kuan (Mumonkan).* San Francisco, CA: North Point Press.

Aknin, L. B., Norton, M. I., & Dunn, E. W. (2009). From wealth to well-being? Money matters, but less than people think. *Journal of Positive Psychology, 4,* 523–527.

Alessandri, G., Caprara, G. V., Eisenberg, N., & Steca, P. (2009). Reciprocal relations among self-efficacy beliefs and pro-sociality across time. *Journal of Personality, 77,* 1229–1259.

Alessi, G. (1992). Models of proximate and ultimate causation in psychology. *American Psychologist, 47,* 1359–1370.

Alexander, I. E. (1988). Personality, psychological assessment, and psychobiography. *Journal of Personality, 56,* 265–294.

Alexander, I. E. (1990). *Personology: Method and content in personality assessment and psychobiography.* Durham, NC: Duke University Press.

Allan, J., & Brown, K. (1993). Jungian play therapy in elementary schools. *Elementary School Guidance and Counseling, 28,* 30–41.

Allen, D. (2001). *Getting things done: The art of stress-free productivity.* New York: Viking.

Allers, C. T., White, J., & Hornbuckle, D. (1990). Early recollections: Detecting depression in the elderly. *Individual Psychology, 46,* 61–66.

Allport, G. W. (1931). What is a trait of personality? *Journal of Abnormal and Social Psychology, 25,* 368–371.

Allport, G. W. (1937a). The functional autonomy of motives. *American Journal of Psychology, 50,* 141–156.

Allport, G. W. (1937b). *Personality: A psychological interpretation.* New York: Henry Holt.

Allport, G. W. (1940). The psychologist's frame of reference. *Psychological Bulletin, 37,* 1–28.

Allport, G. W. (1950a). *The individual and his religion.* New York: Macmillan.

Allport, G. W. (1950b). *The nature of personality: Selected papers.* Cambridge, MA: Addison-Wesley.

Allport, G. W. (1954). *The nature of prejudice.* Cambridge, MA: Addison-Wesley.

Allport, G. W. (1955). *Becoming: Basic considerations for a psychology of personality.* New Haven, CT: Yale University Press.

Allport, G. W. (1959). Religion and prejudice. *Crane Review, 2,* 1–10.

Allport, G. W. (1961). *Pattern and growth in personality.* New York: Holt, Rinehart & Winston.

Allport, G. W. (1962). Prejudice: Is it societal or personal? *Journal of Social Issues, 18*(2), 120–134.

Allport, G. W. (1963). Behavioral science, religion, and mental health. *Journal of Religion and Health, 2,* 187–197.

Allport, G. W. (1964). Mental health: A generic attitude. *Journal of Religion and Health, 4,* 7–21.

Allport, G. W. (Ed.). (1965). *Letters from Jenny.* New York: Harcourt Brace Jovanovich.

Allport, G. W. (1966a). The religious context of prejudice. *Journal for the Scientific Study of Religion, 5,* 447–457.

Allport, G. W. (1966b). Traits revisited. *American Psychologist, 21,* 1–10.

Allport, G. W. (1967). Gordon W. Allport. In E. G. Boring & G. Lindzey (Eds.), *A history of psychology in autobiography* (Vol. 5, pp. 3–25). Englewood Cliffs, NJ: Prentice-Hall.

Allport, G. W., & Allport, F. H. (1921). Personality traits: Their classification and measurement. *Journal of Abnormal and Social Psychology, 16,* 6–40.

Allport, G. W., & Odbert, H. S. (1936). Trait-names: A psycholexical study. *Psychological Monographs, 47* (Whole No. 211).

Allport, G. W., & Postman, L. (1947). *The psychology of rumor.* New York: Henry Holt.

Allport, G. W., & Ross, J. M. (1967). Personal religious orientation and prejudice. *Journal of Personality and Social Psychology, 5,* 432–443.

Allport, G. W., & Vernon, P. E. (1931). *A study of values.* Boston, MA: Houghton Mifflin.

Allport, G. W., & Vernon, P. E. (1933). *Studies in expressive movement.* New York: Macmillan.

Allport, G. W., Vernon, P. E., & Lindzey, G. (1951). *Study of values: A scale for measuring the dominant interests in personality* (Rev. ed.). New York: Houghton Mifflin.

Alterman, A. I., Koppenhaver, J. M., Mulholland, E., Ladden, L. J., & Baime, M. J. (2004). Pilot trial of effectiveness of mindfulness meditation for substance abuse patients. *Journal of Substance Use, 9,* 259–268.

Altman, N. (1994). A perspective on child psychoanalysis 1994: The recognition of relational theory and technique in child treatment. *Psychoanalytic Psychology, 11,* 383–395.

Alvarez, A. N., & Helms, J. E. (2001). Racial identity and reflected appraisals as influences on Asian Americans' racial adjustment. *Cultural Diversity and Ethnic Minority Psychology, 7,* 217–231.

Amaral, D. G. (2002). The primate amygdala and the neurobiology of social behavior: Implications for understanding social anxiety. *Biological Psychiatry, 51,* 11–17.

Ambrose, S. E. (1987). *Nixon: Vol. 1. The education of a politician, 1913–1962.* New York: Simon & Schuster.

Ambrose, S. E. (1989). *Nixon: Vol. 2. The triumph of a politician, 1962–1972.* New York: Simon & Schuster.

American Psychiatric Association. (1994). *Diagnostic and statistical manual of mental disorders* (4th ed.). Washington, DC: Author.

American Psychological Association. (1957). The American Psychological Association Distinguished Scientific Contribution Awards for 1956. *American Psychologist, 12,* 125–133.

American Psychological Association. (1973). Distinguished Professional Contribution Award for 1972. *American Psychologist, 28,* 71–74.

American Psychological Association. (1981). Awards for distinguished scientific contributions: 1980. Albert Bandura. *American Psychologist, 36,* 27–34.

American Psychological Association. (1990). Citation for outstanding lifetime contribution to psychology: Presented to B. F. Skinner, August 10, 1990. *American Psychologist, 45,* 1204–1205.

American Psychological Association. (1992). American Psychological Association citation for outstanding lifetime contribution to psychology: Presented to Neal E. Miller, August 16, 1991. *American Psychologist, 47,* 847.

American Psychological Association. (1997). Gold medal award for life achievement in psychological science. *American Psychologist, 52,* 797–799.

Andresen, J. (2000). Meditation meets behavioral medicine: The story of experimental research on meditation. In J. Andresen & R. K. C. Forman (Eds.), *Cognitive models and spiritual maps: Interdisciplinary explorations of religious experience* (pp. 17–73). Bowling Green, OH: Imprint Academic.

Anderson, C. A., Benjamin, A. J., Jr., & Bartholow, B. D. (1998). Does the gun pull the trigger? Automatic priming effects of weapon pictures and weapon names. *Psychological Science, 9,* 308–314.

Andersen, S. M., & Klatzky, R. L. (1987). Traits and social stereotypes: Levels of categorization in person perception. *Journal of Personality and Social Psychology, 53,* 235–246.

Anderson, W. (1975). The self-actualization of Richard M. Nixon. *Journal of Humanistic Psychology, 15*(1), 27–34.

Andrews, J. D. (1989). Psychotherapy of depression: A self-confirmation model. *Psychological Review, 96,* 576–607.

Andrews, P. W. (2001). The psychology of social chess and the evolution of attribution mechanisms: Explaining the fundamental attribution error. *Evolution and Human Behavior, 22,* 11–29.

Angelou, M. (1969). *I know why the caged bird sings.* New York: Bantam.

Angelou, M. (1974). *Gather together in my name.* New York: Bantam.

Angelou, M. (1976). *Singin' and swingin' and gettin' merry like Christmas.* New York: Bantam.

Angelou, M. (1981). *The heart of a woman.* New York: Bantam.

Angelou, M. (1986). *All God's children need traveling shoes.* New York: Vintage.

Angelou, M. (1993). *Wouldn't take nothing for my journey now.* New York: Random House.

Angelou, M. (1998). *Even the stars look lonesome.* New York: Bantam.

Angelou, M. (2002). *A song flung up to heaven.* New York: Random House.

Angleitner, A., Buss, D. M., & Demtröder, A. I. (1990). A cross-cultural comparison using the act frequency approach (AFA) in West Germany and the United States. *European Journal of Personality, 4,* 187–207.

Annis, H. M. (1990). Relapse to substance abuse: Empirical findings within a cognitive-social learning approach. *Journal of Psychoactive Drugs, 22,* 117–124.

Ansbacher, H. L. (1982). Alfred Adler's views on the unconscious. *Individual Psychology, 38,* 32–41.

Ansbacher, H. L. (1988). Dreikurs's four goals of children's disturbing behavior and Adler's social interest-activity typology. *Individual Psychology, 44,* 282–289.

Ansbacher, H. L. (1989). Adlerian psychology: The tradition of brief psychotherapy. *Individual Psychology, 45,* 26–33.

Ansbacher, H. L. (1990). Alfred Adler, pioneer in prevention of mental disorders. *Journal of Primary Prevention, 11,* 37–68.

Ansbacher, H. L. (1992). Alfred Adler, pioneer in prevention of mental disorders. *Individual Psychology, 48,* 3–34.

Ansbacher, H. L., & Ansbacher, R. R. (Eds.). (1956). *The individual psychology of Alfred Adler: A systematic presentation in selections from his writings.* New York: Harper Torchbooks.

Apostal, R., & Marks, C. (1990). Correlations between the Strong-Campbell and Myers-Briggs scales of introversion-extraversion and career interests. *Psychological Reports, 66,* 811–816.

Ardila, R. (1992). Toward unity in psychology: The experimental synthesis of behaviour. *International Journal of Psychology, 27,* 299–310.

Arnau, R. C., Green, B. A., Rosen, D. H., Gleaves, D. H., & Melancon, J. G. (2003). Are Jungian preferences really categorical? An empirical investigation using taxometric analysis. *Personality and Individual Differences, 34,* 233–251.

Arndt, J., Greenberg, J., Solomon, S., Pyszczynski, T., & Simon, L. (1997). Suppression, accessibility of death-related thoughts, and cultural worldview defense: Exploring the psychodynamics of terror management. *Journal of Personality and Social Psychology, 73,* 5–18.

Arnett, P. A., & Newman, J. P. (2000). Gray's three-arousal model: An empirical investigation. *Personality and Individual Differences, 28,* 1171–1189.

Arnold, L. E. (2001). Alternative treatments for adults with attention-deficit hyperactivity disorder (ADHD). In J. Wasserstein, L. E. Wolf, & F. F. LeFever (Eds.), *Adult attention deficit disorder: Brain mechanisms and life

outcomes* (pp. 310–341, Annals of the New York Academy of Sciences, Vol. 931). New York: New York Academy of Sciences.

Aron, A., & Westbay, L. (1996). Dimensions of the prototype of love. *Journal of Personality and Social Psychology, 70,* 535–551.

ASAP Sports (February 19, 2010). Transcript: Tiger's public statement. Downloaded August 10, 2011, from http://www.tigerwoods.com/news/article/201002198096934/news/

Asendorpf, J. B., & Wilpers, S. (1998). Personality effects on social relationships. *Journal of Personality and Social Psychology, 74,* 1531–1544.

Atkinson, R. (1991). A new myth of humanity. *Humanistic Psychologist, 19,* 354–358.

Atwood, J. D., & Maltin, L. (1991). Putting Eastern philosophies into Western psychotherapies. *American Journal of Psychotherapy, 45,* 368–382.

Aubé, J. (2008). Balancing concern for other with concern for self: Links between unmitigated communion, communion, and psychological well-being. *Journal of Personality, 76,* 101–134.

Austin, J. H. (1998). *Zen and the brain: Toward an understanding of meditation and consciousness.* Cambridge, MA: MIT Press.

Austin, J. T., & Vancouver, J. B. (1996). Goal constructs in psychology: Structure, process, and content. *Psychological Bulletin, 120,* 338–375.

Avants, S. K., & Margolin, A. (2004). Development of spiritual self-schema (3-S) therapy for the treatment of addictive and HIV risk behavior: A convergence of cognitive and Buddhist psychology. *Journal of Psychotherapy Integration, 14,* 253–289.

Avila, C. (2001). Distinguishing BIS-mediated and BAS-mediated disinhibition mechanisms: A comparison of disinhibition models of Gray (1981, 1987) and of Patterson and Newman (1993). *Journal of Personality and Social Psychology, 80,* 311–324.

Avila, C., & Parcet, M. A. (2001). Personality and inhibitory deficits in the stop-signal task: The mediating role of Gray's anxiety and impulsivity. *Personality and Individual Differences, 31,* 975–986.

Ayduk, O., Mendoza-Denton, R., Mischel, W., Downey, G., Peake, P. K., & Rodriguez, M. (2000). Regulating the interpersonal self: Strategic self-regulation for coping with rejection sensitivity. *Journal of Personality and Social Psychology, 79,* 776–792.

Ayduk, O., Mischel, W., & Downey, G. (2002). Attentional mechanisms linking rejection to hostile reactivity: The role of "hot" versus "cool" focus. *Psychological Science, 13,* 443–448.

Aylesworth, A. B., Goodstein, R. C., & Kalra, A. (1999). Effect of archetypal embeds on feelings: An indirect route to affecting attitudes? *Journal of Advertising, 28,* 73–81.

Bache, C. H. (1981). On the emergence of perinatal symptoms in Buddhist meditation. *Journal for the Scientific Study of Religion, 20,* 339–350.

Baird, L. L. (1990). A 24-year longitudinal study of the development of religious ideas. *Psychological Reports, 66,* 479–482.

Baker, J. A., Dilly, L. J., Aupperlee, J. L., & Patil, S. A. (2003). The developmental context of school satisfaction: Schools as psychologically healthy environments. *School Psychology Quarterly, 18,* 206–221.

Baker, R. (1993). Some reflections on humour in psychoanalysis. *International Journal of Psychoanalysis, 74,* 951–960.

Balay, J., & Shevrin, H. (1988). The subliminal psychodynamic activation method: A critical review. *American Psychologist, 43,* 161–174.

Baldwin, A. C., Critelli, J. W., Stevens, L. C., & Russell, S. (1986). Androgyny and sex role measurement: A personal construct approach. *Journal of Personality and Social Psychology, 51,* 1081–1088.

Bandura, A. (1961). Psychotherapy as a learning process. *Psychological Bulletin, 58,* 143–159.

Bandura, A. (1965a). Behavioral modifications through modeling procedures. In L. Krasner & L. Ullmann (Eds.), *Research in behavior modification* (pp. 310–340). New York: Holt, Rinehart & Winston.

Bandura, A. (1965b). Influences of models' reinforcement contingencies on the acquisition of imitative responses. *Journal of Personality and Social Psychology, 1,* 589–595.

Bandura, A. (1965c). Vicarious processes: A case of no-trial learning. In L. Berkowitz (Ed.), *Advances in experimental social psychology* (Vol. 2, pp. 1–55). New York: Academic Press.

Bandura, A. (1969). Social learning of moral judgments. *Journal of Personality and Social Psychology, 11,* 275–279.

Bandura, A. (1973). *Aggression: A social learning analysis.* Englewood Cliffs, NJ: Prentice-Hall.

Bandura, A. (1977). Self-efficacy: Toward a unifying theory of behavioral change. *Psychological Review, 84,* 191–215.

Bandura, A. (1978). The self system in reciprocal determinism. *American Psychologist, 33,* 344–358.

Bandura, A. (1980). Gauging the relationship between self-efficacy judgment and action. *Cognitive Therapy and Research, 4,* 263–268.

Bandura, A. (1984a). Recycling misconceptions of perceived self-efficacy. *Cognitive Therapy and Research, 8,* 231–255.

Bandura, A. (1984b). Representing personal determinants in causal structures. *Psychological Review, 91,* 508–511.

Bandura, A. (1986a). Fearful expectations and avoidant actions as coeffects of perceived self-inefficacy. *American Psychologist, 41,* 1389–1391.

Bandura, A. (1986b). *Social foundations of thought and action: A social cognitive theory.* Englewood Cliffs, NJ: Prentice-Hall.

Bandura, A. (1989a). Human agency in social cognitive theory. *American Psychologist, 44,* 1175–1184.

Bandura, A. (1989b). Regulation of cognitive processes through perceived self-efficacy. *Developmental Psychology, 25,* 729–735.

Bandura, A. (1990a). Perceived self-efficacy in the exercise of control over AIDS infection. *Evaluation and Program Planning, 13,* 9–17.

Bandura, A. (1990b). Selective activation and disengagement of moral control. *Journal of Social Issues, 46*(1), 27–46.

Bandura, A. (1991a). Human agency: The rhetoric and the reality. *American Psychologist, 46,* 157–162.

Bandura, A. (1991b). Social cognitive theory of self-regulation. *Organizational Behavior and Human Decision Processes, 50,* 248–287.

Bandura, A. (1998). Exploration of fortuitous determinants of life paths. *Psychological Inquiry, 9,* 95–115.

Bandura, A. (1999a). Moral disengagement in the perpetration of inhumanities. *Personality and Social Psychology Review, 3,* 193–209.

Bandura, A. (1999b). A sociocognitive analysis of substance abuse: An agentic perspective. *Psychological Science, 10,* 214–217.

Bandura, A. (2000). Exercise of human agency through collective efficacy. *Current Directions in Psychological Science, 9,* 75–78.

Bandura, A. (2001a). The changing face of psychology at the dawning of a globalization era. *Canadian Psychology, 42,* 12–24.

Bandura, A. (2001b). Social cognitive theory: An agentic perspective. *Annual Review of Psychology, 52,* 1–26.

Bandura, A. (2002). Social cognitive theory in cultural context. *Applied Psychology: An International Review, 51,* 269–290.

Bandura, A. (2007). Albert Bandura. In G. Lindzey & W. H. Runyan (Eds.), *A history of psychology in autobiography* (Vol. 9, pp. 43–75). Washington, DC: American Psychological Association.

Bandura, A., Adams, N. E., & Beyer, J. (1977). Cognitive processes mediating behavioral change. *Journal of Personality and Social Psychology, 35,* 125–139.

Bandura, A., Adams, N. E., Hardy, A. B., & Howells, G. N. (1980). Tests of the generality of self-efficacy theory. *Cognitive Therapy and Research, 4,* 39–66.

Bandura, A., & Barab, P. G. (1973). Processes governing disinhibitory effects through symbolic modeling. *Journal of Abnormal Psychology, 82,* 1–9.

Bandura, A., Blanchard, E. B., & Ritter, B. (1969). The relative efficacy of desensitization and modeling approaches for inducing behavioral, affective, and attitudinal changes. *Journal of Personality and Social Psychology, 13,* 173–199.

Bandura, A., Caprara, G. V., Barbaranelli, C., Pastorelli, C., & Regalia, C. (2001). Sociocognitive self-regulatory mechanisms governing transgressive behavior. *Journal of Personality and Social Psychology, 80,* 125–135.

Bandura, A., Cioffi, D., Taylor, C. B., & Brouillard, M. E. (1988). Perceived self-efficacy in coping with cognitive stressors and opioid activation. *Journal of Personality and Social Psychology, 55,* 479–488.

Bandura, A., Grusec, J. E., & Menlove, F. L. (1966). Observational learning as a function of symbolization and incentive set. *Child Development, 37,* 499–506.

Bandura, A., Grusec, J. E., & Menlove, F. L. (1967a). Some social determinants of self-monitoring reinforcement systems. *Journal of Personality and Social Psychology, 5,* 449–455.

Bandura, A., Grusec, J. E., & Menlove, F. L. (1967b). Vicarious extinction of avoidance behavior. *Journal of Personality and Social Psychology, 5,* 16–23.

Bandura, A., Jeffery, R. W., & Wright, C. L. (1974). Efficacy of participant modeling as a function of response induction aids. *Journal of Abnormal Psychology, 83,* 56–64.

Bandura, A., & Jourden, F. J. (1991). Self-regulatory mechanisms governing the impact of social comparison on complex decision making. *Journal of Personality and Social Psychology, 60,* 941–951.

Bandura, A., & McDonald, F. J. (1963). The influence of social reinforcement and the behavior of models in shaping children's moral judgments. *Journal of Abnormal Psychology, 67,* 274–281.

Bandura, A., & Menlove, F. L. (1968). Factors determining vicarious extinction of avoidance behavior through symbolic modeling. *Journal of Personality and Social Psychology, 8,* 99–108.

Bandura, A., & Mischel, W. (1965). Modification of self-imposed delay of reward through exposure to live and symbolic models. *Journal of Personality and Social Psychology, 2,* 698–705.

Bandura, A., O'Leary, A., Taylor, C. B., Gauthier, J., & Gossard, D. (1987). Perceived self-efficacy and pain control: Opioid and nonopioid mechanisms. *Journal of Personality and Social Psychology, 53,* 563–571.

Bandura, A., Reese, L., & Adams, N. E. (1982). Microanalysis of action and fear arousal as a function of differential levels of perceived self-efficacy. *Journal of Personality and Social Psychology, 43,* 5–21.

Bandura, A., Ross, D., & Ross, S. A. (1963a). A comparative test of the status envy, social power, and secondary reinforcement theories of identificatory learning. *Journal of Abnormal and Social Psychology, 67,* 527–534.

Bandura, A., Ross, D., & Ross, S. A. (1963b). Vicarious reinforcement and imitative learning. *Journal of Abnormal and Social Psychology, 67,* 601–607.

Bandura, A., Taylor, C. B., Williams, S. L., Mefford, I. N., & Barchas, J. D. (1985). Catecholamine secretion as a function of perceived coping self-efficacy. *Journal of Consulting and Clinical Psychology, 53,* 406–414.

Bandura, A., & Whalen, C. K. (1966). The influence of antecedent reinforcement and divergent modeling cues on patterns of self-reward. *Journal of Personality and Social Psychology, 3,* 373–382.

Bandura, A., & Wood, R. (1989). Effect of perceived controllability and performance standards on self-regulation of complex decision making. *Journal of Personality and Social Psychology, 56,* 805–814.

Bannister, D. (1975). Personal construct theory psychotherapy. In D. Bannister (Ed.), *Issues and approaches in the psychological therapies* (pp. 31–47). Chichester, UK: Wiley.

Bannister, D., & Salmon, P. (1966). Schizophrenic thought disorder: Specific or diffuse? *British Journal of Medical Psychology, 39,* 215–219.

Barenbaum, N. B. (1997). The case(s) of Gordon Allport. *Journal of Personality, 65,* 743–755.

Barenbaum, N. B. (2000). How social was personality? The Allports' "connection" of social and personality psychology. *Journal of the History of the Behavioral Sciences, 36,* 471–487.

Barends, A., Westen, D., Leigh, J., Silbert, D., & Byers, S. (1990). Assessing affect-tone of relationship paradigms from TAT and interview data. *Psychological Assessment, 2,* 329–332.

Barnes, V. A., Treiber, F. A., & Davis, H. (2001). Impact of Transcendental Meditation® on cardiovascular function at rest and during acute stress in adolescents with high normal blood pressure. *Journal of Psychosomatic Research, 51,* 597–605.

Barnes, V. A., Treiber, F. A., & Johnson, M. H. (2004). Impact of transcendental meditation on ambulatory blood pressure in African-American adolescents. *American Journal of Hypertension, 17,* 366–369.

Baron, S. H., & Pletsch, C. (Eds.). (1985). *Introspection in biography.* Hillsdale, NJ: Erlbaum.

Barresi, J. (1999). On becoming a person. *Philosophical Psychology, 12,* 79–98.

Barrett, D., & Fine, H. J. (1990). The Gnostic syndrome: Anorexia nervosa. *Psychoanalytic Psychotherapy, 4,* 263–270.

Barrett, L. F., & Pietromonaco, P. R. (1997). Accuracy of the five-factor model in predicting perceptions of daily social interactions. *Personality and Social Psychology Bulletin, 23,* 1173–1187.

Barrick, M. R., & Mount, M. K. (1991). The Big Five personality dimensions and job performance: A meta-analysis. *Personnel Psychology, 44,* 1–26.

Barrick, M. R., & Mount, M. K. (1996). Effects of impression management and self-deception on the predictive validity of personality constructs. *Journal of Applied Psychology, 81,* 261–272.

Barrick, M. R., Mount, M. K., & Strauss, J. P. (1993). Conscientiousness and performance of sales representatives: Test of the mediating effects of goal setting. *Journal of Applied Psychology, 78,* 715–722.

Barrick, M. R., Patton, G. K., & Haugland, S. N. (2000). Accuracy of interviewer judgements of job applicant personality traits. *Personnel Psychology, 53,* 925–951.

Barry, B., & Stewart, G. L. (1997). Composition, process, and performance in self-managed groups: The role of personality. *Journal of Applied Psychology, 82,* 62–78.

Barry, G. M. (1991). Consulting with contrary types. *Organization Development Journal, 9*(1), 61–66.

Bartussek, D., Diedrich, O., Naumann, E., & Collet, W. (1993). Introversion-extraversion and event-related potential (ERP): A test of J. A. Gray's theory. *Personality and Individual Differences, 14,* 565–574.

Bass, M. L., Curlette, W. L., Kern, R. M., & McWilliams, A. E., Jr. (2002). Social interest: A meta-analysis of a multidimensional construct. *Journal of Individual Psychology, 58,* 4–34.

Bates, J. E., & Wachs, T. D. (Eds.). (1994). *Temperament: Individual differences at the interface of biology and behavior.* Washington, DC: American Psychological Association.

Batson, C. D. (1976). Religion as prosocial: Agent or double agent? *Journal for the Scientific Study of Religion, 15,* 29–45.

Batson, C. D. (1990). Good Samaritans—or priests and Levites? Using William James as a guide in the study of religious prosocial motivation. *Personality and Social Psychology Bulletin, 16,* 758–768.

Batson, C. D., Eidelman, S. H., & Higley, S. L. (2001). "And who is my neighbor?" II: Quest religion as a source of universal compassion. *Journal for the Scientific Study of Religion, 40,* 39–50.

Batson, C. D., Floyd, R. B., Meyer, J. M., & Winner, A. L. (1999). "And who is my neighbor?": Intrinsic religion as a source of universal compassion. *Journal for the Scientific Study of Religion, 38,* 445–457.

Batson, C. D., & Schoenrade, P. A. (1991a). Measuring religion as quest: I. Validity concerns. *Journal for the Scientific Study of Religion, 30,* 416–429.

Batson, C. D., & Schoenrade, P. A. (1991b). Measuring religion as quest: II. Reliability concerns. *Journal for the Scientific Study of Religion, 30,* 430–447.

Batson, C. D., Schoenrade, P., & Ventis, W. L. (1993). *Religion and the individual.* New York: Oxford University Press.

Baumeister, R. F. (1991). On the stability of variability: Retest reliability of metatraits. *Personality and Social Psychology Bulletin, 17,* 633–639.

Baumeister, R. F. (1997). Esteem threat, self-regulatory breakdown, and emotional distress as factors in self-defeating behavior. *Review of General Psychology, 1,* 145–174.

Baumeister, R. F., Bratslavsky, E., Muraven, M., & Tice, D. M. (1998). Ego depletion: Is the active self a limited resource? *Journal of Personality and Social Psychology, 74,* 1252–1265.

Baumeister, R. F., Dale, K., & Sommer, K. L. (1998). Empirical findings in modern social psychology: Reaction formation, projection, displacement, undoing, isolation, sublimation, and denial. *Journal of Personality, 68,* 1081–1124.

Baumeister, R. F., Heatherton, T. F., & Tice, D. M. (1993). When ego threats lead to self-regulation failure: Negative consequences of high self-esteem. *Journal of Personality and Social Psychology, 64,* 141–156.

Baumeister, R. F., Masicampo, E. J., & Vohs, K. D. (2011). Do conscious thoughts cause behavior? *Annual Review of Psychology, 62,* 331–361.

Baumeister, R. F., Smart, L., & Boden, J. M. (1996). Relation of threatened egotism to violence and aggression: The dark side of high self-esteem. *Psychological Review, 103,* 5–33.

Baumeister, R. F., & Tice, D. M. (1988). Metatraits. *Journal of Personality, 56,* 571–598.

Baumrind, D. (1971). Current patterns of parental authority. *Developmental Psychology Monograph, 4*(1), part 2.

Becker, E. (1973). *The denial of death.* New York: Free Press.

Beebe, J. (1996). Jungian illumination of film. *Psychoanalytic Review, 83,* 579–587.

Beebe, J. (2008). Individuation in the light of Chinese philosophy. *Psychological Perspectives, 51,* 70–86.

Beebe, J., Cambray, J., & Kirsch, T. B. (2001). What Freudians can learn from Jung. *Psychoanalytic Psychology, 18,* 213–242.

Beermann, U., & Ruch, W. (2009). How virtuous is humor? What we can learn from current instruments. *Journal of Positive Psychology, 4,* 528–539.

Behrends, R. S. (1986). The integrated personality: Maximal utilization of information. *Journal of Humanistic Psychology, 26*(1), 27–59.

Bell, A. J., & Cook, H. (1998). Empirical evidence for a compensatory relationship between dream content and repression. *Psychoanalytic Psychology, 15,* 154–163.

Belsky, J. (1993). Etiology of child maltreatment: A developmental-ecological analysis. *Psychological Bulletin, 114,* 413–434.

Benjafield, J. G. (2008). George Kelly: Cognitive psychologist, humanistic psychologist, or something else entirely? *History of Psychology, 11,* 239–262.

Benjamin, L. T., Jr., & Dixon, D. N. (1996). Dream analysis by mail: An American woman seeks Freud's advice. *American Psychologist, 51,* 461–468.

Benjamin, P., & Looby, J. (1998). Defining the nature of spirituality in the context of Maslow's and Rogers's theories. *Counseling and Values, 42*(2), 92–100.

Benson, H., Malhotra, M. S., Goldman, R. F., Jacobs, G. D., & Hopkins, P. J. (1990). Three case reports of the metabolic and electroencephalographic changes during advanced Buddhist meditation techniques. *Behavioral Medicine, 16,* 90–95.

Berant, E., Mikulincer, M., & Shaver, P. R. (2008). Mothers' attachment style, their mental health, and their children's emotional vulnerabilities: A 7-year study of children with congenital heart disease. *Journal of Personality, 76,* 31–66.

Bereczkei, T. (2000). Evolutionary psychology: A new perspective in the behavioral sciences. *European Psychologist, 5,* 175–190.

Berkowitz, L. (1962). *Aggression: A social psychological analysis.* New York: McGraw-Hill.

Berkowitz, L. (1983). Aversively stimulated aggression: Some parallels and differences in research with animals and humans. *American Psychologist, 38,* 1135–1144.

Berkowitz, L. (1989). Frustration-aggression hypothesis: Examination and reformulation. *Psychological Bulletin, 106,* 59–73.

Berkowitz, L., & LePage, A. (1967). Weapons as aggression-eliciting stimuli. *Journal of Personality and Social Psychology, 7,* 202–207.

Berman, S., Ozkaragoz, T., Young, R. M., & Noble, E. P. (2002). D2 dopamine receptor gene polymorphism discriminates two kinds of novelty seeking. *Personality and Individual Differences, 33,* 867–882.

Berr, S. A., Church, A. H., & Waclawski, J. (2000). The right relationship is everything: Linking personality preferences to managerial behaviors. *Human Resource Development Quarterly, 11*(2), 133–157.

Berzonsky, M. D. (1989). The self as a theorist: Individual differences in identity formation. *International Journal of Personal Construct Psychology, 2,* 363–376.

Berzonsky, M. D. (1992). "Can we see ourselves changing? Toward a personal construct model of adult development": Commentary. *Human Development, 35,* 76–80.

Berzonsky, M. D., & Neimeyer, G. J. (1988). Identity status and personal construct systems. *Journal of Adolescence, 11,* 195–204.

Berzonsky, M. D., Rice, K. G., & Neimeyer, G. J. (1990). Identity status and self-construct systems: Process × structure interactions. *Journal of Adolescence, 13,* 251–263.

Bettelheim, B. (1976). *The uses of enchantment: The meaning and importance of fairy tales.* New York: Knopf.

Bhikkhu, T. (Trans.). (1994). Tittha Sutta: Various sectarians (1) [Translation from the Pali canon of *Udana 6.4, Sutta Pitaka*]. Available online at http://www.accesstoinsight.org/tipitaka/kn/ud/ud.6.04.than.html

Bieling, P. J., Summerfeldt, L. J., Israeli, A. L., & Antony, M. M. (2004). Perfectionism as an explanatory construct in comorbidity of Axis I disorders. *Journal of Psychopathology and Behavioral Assessment, 26,* 193–201.

Bieri, J. (1955). Cognitive complexity-simplicity and predictive behavior. *Journal of Abnormal and Social Psychology, 51,* 263–268.

Bilgrave, D. P., & Deluty, R. H. (1998). Religious beliefs and therapeutic orientations of clinical and counseling psychologists. *Journal for the Scientific Study of Religion, 37,* 329–349.

Binder, L. M., Dixon, M. R., & Ghezzi, P. M. (2000). A procedure to teach self-control to children with attention deficit hyperactivity disorder. *Journal of Applied Behavior Analysis, 33,* 233–237.

Birch, M. (1998). Through a glass darkly: Questions about truth and memory. *Psychoanalytic Psychology, 15,* 34–48.

Blackmore, S. (1994). Psi in psychology. *Skeptical Inquirer, 18,* 351–355.

Blagrove, M. (1993). The structuralist analysis of dream series. *Journal of Mental Imagery, 17*(3 & 4), 77–90.

Blankfield, R. P. (1991). Suggestion, relaxation, and hypnosis as adjuncts in the care of surgery patients: A review of the literature. *American Journal of Clinical Hypnosis, 33,* 172–186.

Blatt, S. J. (1995). The destructiveness of perfectionism: Implications for the treatment of depression. *American Psychologist, 50,* 1003–1020.

Block, J. (1993). Studying personality the long way. In D. C. Funder, R. D. Parke, C. Tomlinson-Keasey, & K. Widaman (Eds.), *Studying lives through time: Personality and development* (pp. 4–41). Washington, DC: American Psychological Association.

Block, J. (1995). A contrarian view of the five-factor approach to personality description. *Psychological Bulletin, 117,* 187–215.

Block, J. H., & Block, J. (1980). The role of ego-control and ego-resiliency in the organization of behavior. In W. A. Collins (Ed.), *The Minnesota Symposia on Child Psychology: Vol. 13. Development of cognition, affect, and social relations.* (pp. 39–101). Hillsdale, NJ: Erlbaum.

Bloland, S. E. (2005). *In the shadow of fame: A memoir by the daughter of Erik H. Erikson.* New York: Viking.

Blomberg, J., Lazar, A., & Sandell, R. (2001). Long-term outcome of long-term psychoanalytically oriented therapies: First findings of the Stockholm outcome of psychotherapy and psychoanalysis study. *Psychotherapy Research, 11,* 361–382.

Blum, H. P. (1994). Dora's conversion syndrome: A contribution to the prehistory of the Holocaust. *Psychoanalytic Quarterly, 63,* 518–535.

Blume, E. S. (1995). The ownership of truth. *Journal of Psychohistory, 23*(2), 131–140.

Bodden, J. C. (1970). Cognitive complexity as a factor in appropriate vocational choice. *Journal of Counseling Psychology, 17,* 364–368.

Boden, J. M., & Baumeister, R. F. (1997). Repressive coping: Distraction using pleasant thoughts and memories. *Journal of Personality and Social Psychology, 73,* 45–62.

Bogg, T. (2008). Conscientiousness, the transtheoretical model of change, and exercise: A neo-socioanalytic integration of trait and social-cognitive frameworks in the prediction of behavior. *Journal of Personality, 76,* 775–801.

Bohart, A. C. (1991). The missing 249 words: In search of objectivity. *Psychotherapy, 28,* 497–503.

Bohart, A. C., & Greenberg, L. S. (Eds.). (1997). *Empathy reconsidered: New directions in psychotherapy.* Washington, DC: American Psychological Association.

Bohart, A. C., O'Hara, M., & Leitner, L. M. (1998). Empirically violated treatments: Disenfranchisement of humanistic and other psychotherapies. *Psychotherapy Research, 8*(2), 141–157.

Bolton, L. R., Becker, L. K., & Barber, L. K. (2010). Big Five trait predictors of differential counterproductive work behavior dimensions. *Personality and Individual Differences, 49,* 537–541.

Bonanno, G. A., & Kaltman, S. (2000). The assumed necessity of working through memories of traumatic experiences. In P. R. Dubenstein & J. M. Masling (Eds.). *Psychodynamic perspectives on sickness and health* (pp. 165–200). Washington, DC: American Psychological Association.

Bonanno, G. A., Keltner, D., Holen, A., & Horowitz, M. J. (1995). When avoiding unpleasant emotions might not be such a bad thing: Verbal-autonomic dissociation and midlife conjugal bereavement. *Journal of Personality and Social Psychology, 69,* 975–989.

Bonanno, G. A., Moskowitz, J. T., Papa, A., & Folkman, S. (2005). Resilience to loss in bereaved spouses, bereaved parents, and bereaved gay men. *Journal of Personality and Social Psychology, 88,* 827–843.

Bond, M. (1995). The development and properties of the Defense Style Questionnaire. In H. R. Conte & R. Plutchik (Eds.), *Ego defenses: Theory and measurement* (pp. 202–220). New York: Wiley.

Bondarenko, A. F. (1999). My encounter with Carl Rogers: A retrospective view from the Ukraine. *Journal of Humanistic Psychology, 39*(1), 8–14.

Boon, J. C., & Davis, G. M. (1987). Rumours greatly exaggerated: Allport and Postman's apocryphal study. *Canadian Journal of Behavioural Science, 19,* 430–440.

Boorstein, S. (2000). Transpersonal psychotherapy. *American Journal of Psychotherapy, 54,* 408–423.

Bores-Rangel, E., Church, A. T., Szendre, D., & Reeves, C. (1990). Self-efficacy in relation to occupational consideration and academic performance in high school equivalency students. *Journal of Counseling Psychology, 37,* 407–418.

Borkenau, P. (1990). Traits as ideal-based and goal-derived social categories. *Journal of Personality and Social Psychology, 58,* 381–396.

Borkenau, P., Riemann, R., Spinath, F. M., & Angleitner, A. (2006). Genetic and environmental influences on person × situation profiles. *Journal of Personality, 74,* 1451–1479.

Borkenhagen, A., Klapp, B. F., Brähler, E., & Schoeneich, F. (2008). Differences in the psychic representation of the body in bulimic and anorexic patients: A study with the body grid. *Journal of Constructivist Psychology, 21,* 60–81.

Bornstein, R. F. (1992). The dependent personality: Developmental, social, and clinical perspectives. *Psychological Bulletin, 112,* 3–23.

Bornstein, R. F. (1996). Beyond orality: Toward an object relations/interactionist reconceptualization of the etiology and dynamics of dependency. *Psychoanalytic Psychology, 13,* 177–203.

Bornstein, R. F. (1997). Dependent personality disorder in the DSM-IV and beyond. *Clinical Psychology: Science and Practice, 4,* 175–187.

Bornstein, R. F. (1998). Interpersonal dependency and physical illness: A meta-analytic review of retrospective and prospective studies. *Journal of Research in Personality, 32,* 480–497.

Bornstein, R. F. (2000). From oral fixation to object relations: Changing perspectives on the psychodynamics of interpersonal dependency and illness. In P. R. Duberstein & J. M. Masling (Eds.), *Psychodynamic perspectives on sickness and health* (pp. 3–37). Washington, DC: American Psychological Association.

Bornstein, R. F., & Masling, J. M. (Eds.). (2005). *Scoring the Rorschach: Seven validated systems.* Mahwah, NJ: Erlbaum.

Bosma, H. A., & Kunnen, E. S. (2008). Identity-in-context is not yet identity development-in-context. *Journal of Adolescence, 31,* 281–289.

Bottome, P. (1947). *Alfred Adler: Apostle of freedom* (J. Linton & R. Vaughan, Trans.). London: Faber & Faber.

Bouchard, G., Lussier, Y., & Sabourin, S. (1999). Personality and marital adjustment: Utility of the five-factor model of personality. *Journal of Marriage and the Family, 61,* 651–660.

Bouchard, T. J., Jr., & Loehlin, J. C. (2001). Genes, evolution, and personality. *Behavior Genetics, 31,* 243–273.

Bowen, M. V. B. (1996). The myth of nondirectiveness: The case of Jill. In B. A. Farber, D. C. Brink, & P. M. Raskin (Eds.), *The psychotherapy of Carl Rogers: Cases and commentary* (pp. 84–94). New York: Guilford.

Bowers, K. S. (1994). A review of Ernest R. Hilgard's books on hypnosis, in commemoration of his 90th birthday. *Psychological Science, 5,* 186–189.

Bowers, K. S., & Farvolden, P. (1996). Revisiting a century-old Freudian slip—from suggestion disavowed to the truth repressed. *Psychological Bulletin, 119,* 355–380.

Bowlby, J. (1988). Developmental psychiatry comes of age. *American Journal of Psychiatry, 145,* 1–10.

Bowler, M. C., Bowler, J. L., & Phillips, B. C. (2009). The Big-5 ± 2? The impact of cognitive complexity on the factor structure of the five-factor model. *Personality and Individual Differences, 47,* 979–984.

Boyer, P. (2000). Evolutionary psychology and cultural transmission. *American Behavioral Scientist, 43,* 987–1000.

Boyes, M. E., & French, D. J. (2009). Having a Cyberball: Using a ball-throwing game as an experimental social stressor to examine the relationship between neuroticism and coping. *Personality and Individual Differences, 47,* 396–401.

Boyle, G. J. (1989). Re-examination of the major personality-type factors in the Cattell, Comrey and Eysenck scales: Were the factor solutions by Noller et al. optimal? *Personality and Individual Differences, 10,* 1289–1299.

Boyle, G. J., & Cattell, R. B. (1984). Proof of situational sensitivity of mood states and dynamic traits—ergs and sentiments—to disturbing stimuli. *Personality and Individual Differences, 5,* 541–548.

Bradley, C. L., & Marcia, J. E. (1998). Generativity-stagnation: A five-category model. *Journal of Personality, 66,* 39–64.

Brebner, J. (2000). Comment: "The personality theories of H. J. Eysenck and J. A. Gray: A comparative review." [G. Matthews and K. Gilliland (1999), *Personality and*

Individual Differences, 26, 583–626.] *Personality and Individual Differences, 28,* 1191–1192.

Bremner, J. D., Krystal, J. H., Charney, D. S., & Southwick, S. M. (1996). Neural mechanisms in dissociative amnesia for childhood abuse: Relevance to the current controversy surrounding the "false memory syndrome." *American Journal of Psychiatry, 153,* 71–82.

Bremner, J. D., Krystal, J. H., Southwick, S. M., & Charney, D. S. (1995). Functional neuroanatomical correlates of the effects of stress on memory. *Journal of Traumatic Stress, 8,* 527–553.

Brems, C., & Johnson, M. E. (1990). Reexamination of the Bem Sex-Role Inventory: The interpersonal BSRI. *Journal of Personality Assessment, 55,* 484–498.

Brennan, K. A., & Shaver, P. R. (1998). Attachment styles and personality disorders: Their connections to each other and to parental divorce, parental death, and perceptions of parental caregiving. *Journal of Personality, 66,* 835–878.

Brenneis, C. B. (2000). Evaluating the evidence: Can we find authenticated recovered memory? *Psychoanalytic Psychology, 17,* 61–77.

Brent, D. A. (1989). The psychological autopsy: Methodological considerations for the study of adolescent suicide. *Suicide and Life Threatening Behavior, 19,* 43–57.

Breuer, J., & Freud, S. (1955). Studies on hysteria. In J. Strachey (Ed. and Trans.), *The standard edition of the complete psychological works of Sigmund Freud* (Vol. 2). London: Hogarth Press. (Original work published 1895)

Brewer, M. B. (1999). The psychology of prejudice: Ingroup love or outgroup hate? *Journal of Social Issues, 55,* 429–444.

Brickman, A. L., Yount, S. E., Blaney, N. T., Rothberg, S. T., & De-Nour, A. K. (1996). Personality traits and long-term health status: The influence of neuroticism and conscientiousness on renal deterioration in Type-1 diabetes. *Psychosomatics: Journal of Consultation Liaison Psychiatry, 37,* 459–468.

Bringhurst, N. C. (2001). How assessing personality type can benefit you and your practice. *Journal of Financial Planning, 14*(1), 104–113.

Brock, D. (1996). *The seduction of Hillary Rodham.* New York: Free Press.

Brodley, B. T. (1996). Uncharacteristic directiveness: Rogers and the "anger and hurt" client. In B. A. Farber, D. C. Brink, & P. M. Raskin (Eds.), *The psychotherapy of Carl Rogers: Cases and commentary* (pp. 310–321). New York: Guilford.

Brody, G. H. (1998). Sibling relationship quality: Its causes and consequences. *Annual Review of Psychology, 49,* 1–24.

Brody, N. (1987). Introduction: Some thoughts on the unconscious. *Personality and Social Psychology Bulletin, 13,* 293–298.

Broehl, W. G., Jr., & McGee, V. E. (1981). Content analysis in psychohistory: A study of three lieutenants in the Indian Mutiny, 1957–1958. *Journal of Psychohistory, 8,* 281–306.

Brogden, H. E. (1972). Some observations on two methods in psychology. *Psychological Bulletin, 77,* 431–437.

Bronk, K. C., Hill, P. L., Lapsley, D. K., Talib, T. L., & Finch, H. (2009). Purpose, hope, and life satisfaction in three age groups. *Journal of Positive Psychology, 4,* 500–510.

Brown, C., & Lewis, M. J. (2003). Psychosocial development in the elderly: An investigation into Erikson's ninth stage. *Journal of Aging Studies, 17,* 415–426.

Bruggemann, J. M., & Barry, R. J. (2002). Eysenck's P as a modulator of affective and electrodermal responses to violent and comic film. *Personality and Individual Differences, 32,* 1029–1048.

Bruhn, A. R. (1990). Cognitive-perceptual theory and the projective use of autobiographical memory. *Journal of Personality Assessment, 55,* 95–114.

Bruhn, A. R. (1992a). The Early Memories Procedure: A projective test of autobiographical memory, Part 1. *Journal of Personality Assessment, 58,* 1–15.

Bruhn, A. R. (1992b). The Early Memories Procedure: A projective test of autobiographical memory, Part 2. *Journal of Personality Assessment, 58,* 326–346.

Bruner, J. S. (1956). A cognitive theory of personality. *Contemporary Psychology, 1,* 355–359.

Brunstein, J. C., Schultheiss, O. C., & Grässmann, R. (1998). Personal goals and emotional well-being: The moderating role of motive dispositions. *Journal of Personality and Social Psychology, 75,* 494–508.

Bstan-dzin-rgya-mtsho, Dalai Lama XIV. (1989). *Ocean of wisdom: Guidelines for living.* San Francisco, CA: Harper & Row.

Bstan-dzin-rgya-mtsho, Dalai Lama XIV. (1990). *Freedom in exile: The autobiography of the Dalai Lama.* New York: HarperCollins.

Bstan-dzin-rgya-mtsho, Dalai Lama XIV. (1999). *Ethics for the new millennium.* New York: Riverhead Books.

Bstan-dzin-rgya-mtsho, Dalai Lama XIV. (2000). *A simple path: Basic Buddhist teachings by His Holiness the Dalai Lama* (G. T. Junpa, Trans.; D. Side, Ed.). London: Thorsons.

Bstan-dzin-rgya-mtsho, Dalai Lama XIV. (2001). Understanding our fundamental nature. In R. J. Davidson & A. Harrington (Eds.), *Visions of compassion: Western scientists and Tibetan Buddhists examine human nature* (pp. 66–80). Cary, NC: Oxford University Press.

Bstan-dzin-rgya-mtsho, Dalai Lama XIV. (2003). Cultivating peace as an antidote to violence: Sincere practice is important for promotion of religious harmony. *Vital Speeches of the Day,* 742–743. [Speech delivered to the Washington National Cathedral, Washington, DC, September 11, 2003].

Bstan-dzin-rgya-mtsho, Dalai Lama XIV, & Cutler, H. C. (1998). *The art of happiness: A handbook for living.* New York: Riverhead Books.

Bubenzer, D. L., Zimpfer, D. G., & Mahrle, C. L. (1990). Standardized individual appraisal in agency and private practice: A survey. *Journal of Mental Health Counseling, 12,* 51–66.

Buchheld, N., Grossman, P., & Walach, H. (2001). Meditation-based psychotherapy: The development of the Freiburg Mindfulness Inventory (FMI). *Journal for Meditation, 1,* 5–23.

Buckingham, R. M. (2002). Extraversion, neuroticism and the four temperaments of antiquity: An investigation of physiological reactivity. *Personality and Individual Differences, 32,* 225–246.

Buckmaster, L. R., & Davis, G. A. (1985). ROSE: A measure of self-actualization and its relationship to creativity. *Journal of Creative Behavior, 19,* 30–37.

Bucko, R. A. (2000). The sacred pipe: An archetypal theology. *American Indian Quarterly, 24,* 311–312.

Burn, S. M., & Busso, J. (2005). Ambivalent sexism, scriptural literalism, and religiosity. *Psychology of Women Quarterly, 29,* 412–418.

Burns, C. E., Heiby, E. M., & Tharp, R. G. (1983). A verbal behavior analysis of auditory hallucinations. *Behavior Analyst, 6,* 133–143.

Burr, V., & Butt, T. W. (1989). A personal construct view of hypnosis. *British Journal of Experimental and Clinical Hypnosis, 6,* 85–90.

Burrell, M. J., & Jaffe, A. J. (1999). Personal meaning, drug use, and addiction: An evolutionary constructivist perspective. *Journal of Constructivist Psychology, 12,* 41–63.

Burris, C. T., & Jackson, L. M. (1999). Hate the sin/love the sinner, or love the hater? Intrinsic religion and responses to partner abuse. *Journal for the Scientific Study of Religion, 38,* 160–174.

Burris, C. T., Jackson, L. M., Tarpley, W. R., & Smith, G. J. (1996). Religion as quest: The self-directed pursuit of meaning. *Personality and Social Psychology Bulletin, 22,* 1068–1076.

Burris, C. T., & Tarpley, W. R. (1998). Religion as being: Preliminary validation of the Immanence scale. *Journal of Research in Personality, 32,* 55–79.

Burry, P. J. (2008). *Living with "The Gloria Films": A daughter's memory.* Ross-on-Wye, UK: PCCS Books.

Busch, H., & Hofer, J. (2011). Identity, prosocial behavior, and generative concern in German and Cameroonian Nso adolescents. *Journal of Adolescence, 34,* 629–638.

Bushman, B. J., & Baumeister, R. F. (1998). Threatened egotism, narcissism, self-esteem, and direct and displaced aggression: Does self-love or self-hate lead to violence? *Journal of Personality and Social Psychology, 75,* 219–229.

Bushman, B. J., Baumeister, R. F., Thomaes, S., Ryu, E., Begeer, S., & West. S. G. (2009). Looking again, and harder, for a link between low self-esteem and aggression. *Journal of Personality, 77,* 427–446.

Busjahn, A., Faulhaber, H. D., Freier, K., & Luft, F. C. (1999). Genetic and environmental influences on coping styles: A twin study. *Psychosomatic Medicine, 61,* 469–475.

Buss, A., & Plomin, R. (1975). *A temperament theory of personality development.* New York: Wiley-Interscience.

Buss, D. M. (1988). The evolution of human intrasexual competition: Tactics of mate attraction. *Journal of Personality and Social Psychology, 54,* 616–628.

Buss, D. M. (1989). Sex differences in human mate preferences: Evolutionary hypotheses tested in 37 cultures. *Behavioral and Brain Sciences, 12,* 1–49.

Buss, D. M. (1995). Evolutionary psychology: A new paradigm for psychological science. *Psychological Inquiry, 6,* 1–30.

Buss, D. M. (1997). Evolutionary foundations of personality. In R. Hogan, J. Johnson, & S. Briggs (Eds.), *Handbook of personality psychology* (pp. 317–344). San Diego, CA: Academic Press.

Buss, D. M. (1999). Human nature and individual differences: The evolution of personality. In L. A. Pervin & O. P. John (Eds.), *Handbook of personality: Theory and research* (2nd ed., pp. 31–56). New York: Guilford.

Buss, D. M. (2000). The evolution of happiness. *American Psychologist, 55,* 15–23.

Buss, D. M. (2008). Human nature and individual differences: Evolution of human personality. In O. P. John, R. W. Robins, & L. A. Pervin (Eds.), *Handbook of personality: Theory and research* (3rd ed., pp. 29–60). New York: Guilford.

Buss, D. M., & Craik, K. H. (1980). The frequency concept of dispositions: Dominance and dominant acts. *Journal of Personality, 48,* 379–392.

Buss, D. M., & Craik, K. H. (1983). The act frequency approach to personality. *Psychological Review, 90,* 105–126.

Buss, D. M., & Craik, K. H. (1985). Why not measure that trait? Alternative criteria for identifying important dispositions. *Journal of Personality and Social Psychology, 48,* 934–946.

Buss, D. M., Haselton, M. G., Shackelford, T. K., Bleske, A. L., & Wakefield, J. C. (1998). Adaptations, exaptations, and spandrels. *American Psychologist, 53,* 533–548.

Buss, D. M., Larsen, R. J., Westen, D., & Semmelroth, J. (1992). Sex differences in jealousy: Evolution, physiology, and psychology. *Psychological Science, 3,* 251–255.

Buss, D. M., & Schmitt, D. P. (1993). Sexual strategies theory: An evolutionary perspective on human mating. *Psychological Review, 100,* 204–232.

Buss, D. M., & Shackelford, T. K. (1997). Susceptibility to infidelity in the first year of marriage. *Journal of Research in Personality, 31,* 193–221.

Busseri, M. A., Choma, B. L., & Sadava, S. W. (2009). "As good as it gets" or "The best is yet to come"? How optimists and pessimists view their past, present, and anticipated future life satisfaction. *Personality and Individual Differences, 47,* 352–356.

Bussey, K., & Bandura, A. (1999). Social cognitive theory of gender development and differentiation. *Psychological Review, 106,* 676–713.

Butcher, J. N., & Rouse, S. V. (1996). Personality: Individual differences and clinical assessment. *Annual Review of Psychology, 47,* 87–111.

Butler, A. C., Chapman, J. E., Forman, E. M., & Beck, A. T. (2004). The empirical status of cognitive-behavioral therapy: A review of meta-analyses. *Clinical Psychology Review, 26,* 17–31.

Butler, J. M., & Haigh, G. V. (1954). Changes in the relation between self-concepts and ideal concepts consequent upon client-centered counseling. In C. R. Rogers & R. F. Dymond (Eds.), *Psychotherapy and personality change* (pp. 55–75). Chicago, IL: University of Chicago Press.

Butt, T. (1998). Sedimentation and elaborative choice. *Journal of Constructivist Psychology, 11,* 265–281.

Butz, D. A., & Plant, E. A. (2009). Prejudice control and interracial relations: The role of motivation to respond without prejudice. *Journal of Personality, 77,* 1311–1341.

Cacioppo, J. T., Petty, R. E., Feinstein, J. A., & Jarvis, W. B. G. (1996). Dispositional differences in cognitive motivation: The life and times of individuals varying in need for cognition. *Psychological Bulletin, 119,* 197–253.

Cahill, C., Llewelyn, S. P., & Pearson, C. (1991). Long-term effects of sexual abuse which occurred in childhood: A review. *British Journal of Clinical Psychology, 30,* 117–130.

Cahn, B. R., & Polich, J. (2006). Meditation states and traits: EEG, ERP, and neuroimaging studies. *Psychological Bulletin, 132,* 180–211.

Cain, D. J. (1987). Carl Rogers's life in review. *Person-Centered Review, 2,* 476–506.

Campbell, J. (1949). *The hero with a thousand faces.* New York: Pantheon.

Campbell, J. (1972). *Myths to live by.* New York: Viking.

Campbell, J., Schermer, J. A., Villani, V. C., Nguyen, B., Vickers, L., & Vernon, P. A. (2009). A behavioral genetic study of the dark triad of personality and moral development. *Twin Research and Human Genetics, 12,* 132–136.

Campbell, J. B., & Heller, J. F. (1987). Correlations of extraversion, impulsivity and sociability with sensation seeking and MBTI-introversion. *Personality and Individual Differences, 8,* 133–136.

Campbell, J. F. (1988). The primary personality factors of younger adolescent Hawaiians. *Genetic, Social, and General Psychology Monographs, 114,* 141–171.

Campos, L. S., Otta, E., & Siqueira, J. O. (2002). Sex differences in mate selection strategies: Content analyses and responses to personal advertisements in Brazil. *Evolution and Human Behavior, 23,* 395–406.

Cangemi, J. P. (1984). The real purpose of higher education: Developing self-actualizing personalities. *Education, 105,* 151–154.

Cann, D. R., & Donderi, D. C. (1986). Jungian personality typology and the recall of everyday and archetypal dreams. *Journal of Personality and Social Psychology, 50,* 1021–1030.

Cantor, N., & Mischel, W. (1979a). Prototypes in person perception. In L. Berkowitz (Ed.), *Advances in experimental social psychology* (Vol. 12, pp. 3–52). New York: Academic Press.

Cantor, N., & Mischel, W. (1979b). Prototypicality and personality: Effects on free recall and personality impressions. *Journal of Research in Personality, 13,* 187–205.

Cantril, H., & Allport, G. W. (1935). *The psychology of radio.* New York: Harper.

Caprara, G. V. (1996). Structures and processes in personality psychology. *European Psychologist, 1,* 14–26.

Caprara, G. V., Barbaranelli, C., Bermudez, J., Maslach, C., & Ruch, W. (2000). Multivariate methods for the comparison of factor structures in cross-cultural research: An illustration with the Big Five Questionnaire. *Journal of Cross-Cultural Psychology, 31,* 437–464.

Caprara, G. V., Vecchione, M., Capanna, C., & Mebane, M. (2009). Perceived political self-efficacy: Theory, assessment, and applications. *European Journal of Social Psychology, 39,* 1002–1020.

Carich, M. S., & Willingham, W. (1987). The roots of family systems theory in individual psychology. *Individual Psychology, 43,* 71–78.

Carkhuff, R. R. (1969). *Human and helping relations* (Vols. 1 & 2). New York: Holt, Rinehart & Winston.

Carlsen, M. B. (1996). Engaging synergy: Kindred spirits on the edge. *Journal of Humanistic Psychology, 36*(3), 85–102.

Carlson, J. G. (1985). Recent assessments of the Myers-Briggs Type Indicator. *Journal of Personality Assessment, 49,* 356–365.

Carlson, L. E., Speca, M., Patel, K. D., & Goodey, E. (2004). Mindfulness-based stress reduction in relation to quality of life, mood, symptoms of stress and levels of cortisol, dehydroepiandrosterone sulfate (DHEAS) and melatonin in breast and prostate cancer outpatients. *Psychoneuroendocrinology, 29,* 448–474.

Carlson, M., & Mulaik, S. A. (1993). Trait ratings from descriptions of behavior as mediated by components of meaning. *Multivariate Behavioral Research, 28,* 111–159.

Carlson, R. (1971). Where is the person in personality research? *Psychological Bulletin, 75,* 203–219.

Carlson, R. (1981). Studies in script theory: I. Adult analogs of a childhood nuclear scene. *Journal of Personality and Social Psychology, 40,* 501–510.

Carlson, R. (1988). Exemplary lives: The uses of psychobiography for theory development. *Journal of Personality, 56,* 105–138.

Carp, C. E. (1998). Clown therapy: The creation of a clown character as a treatment intervention. *Arts in Psychotherapy, 25,* 245–255.

Carter, O. L., Presti, D. E., Callistemon, C., Ungerer, Y., Lin, G. B., & Pettigrew, J. D. (2005a). Meditation alters perceptual rivalry in Tibetan Buddhist monks. *Current Biology, 15,* R412–R413.

Carter, O. L., Presti, D. E., Callistemon, C., Ungerer, Y., Lin, G. B., & Pettigrew, J. D. (2005b). Supplemental data: Meditation alters perceptual rivalry in Tibetan Buddhist monks. *Current Biology, 15,* R1.

Cartwright, D. (1989). Concurrent validation of a measure of transcendental powers. *Journal of Parapsychology, 53,* 43–59.

Carver, C. S., Meyer, B., & Antoni, M. H. (2000). Responsiveness to threats and incentives, expectancy of recurrence, and distress and disengagement: Moderator effects in women with early stage breast cancer. *Journal of Consulting and Clinical Psychology, 68,* 965–975.

Carver, C. S., & White, T. L. (1994). Behavioral inhibition, behavioral activation, and affective responses to impending reward and punishment: The BIS/BAS Scales. *Journal of Personality and Social Psychology, 67,* 319–333.

Caseley-Rondi, G., Merikle, P. M., & Bowers, K. S. (1994). Unconscious cognition in the context of general anesthesia. *Consciousness and Cognition, 3,* 166–195.

Caseras, X., Torrubia, R., & Farre, J. M. (2001). Is the Behavioural Inhibition System the core vulnerability for Cluster C personality disorders? *Personality and Individual Differences, 31,* 349–359.

Caspi, A. (2000). The child is father of the man: Personality continuities from childhood to adulthood. *Journal of Personality and Social Psychology, 78,* 158–172.

Caspi, A., Elder, G. H., & Bem, D. J. (1987). Moving against the world: Life-course patterns of explosive children. *Developmental Psychology, 23,* 308–313.

Caspi, A., McClay, J., Moffitt, T., Mill, J., Martin, J., Craig, I., Taylor, A., & Pulton, R. (2002). Role of genotype in the cycle of violence in maltreated children. *Science, 297,* 851–854.

Catina, A., Gitzinger, I., & Hoeckh, H. (1992). Defense mechanisms: An approach from the perspective of personal construct psychology. *Personal Construct Psychology, 5,* 249–257.

Cattell, H. E. P., & Schuerger, J. M. (2003). *Essentials of 16PF assessment.* Hoboken, NJ: Wiley.

Cattell, R. B. (1937). *The fight for our national intelligence.* London: King.

Cattell, R. B. (1943a). The description of personality: Basic traits resolved into clusters. *Journal of Abnormal and Social Psychology, 38,* 476–506.

Cattell, R. B. (1943b). The description of personality: I. Foundations of trait measurement. *Psychological Review, 50,* 559–594.

Cattell, R. B. (1950). *Personality: A systematic theoretical and factual study.* New York: McGraw-Hill.

Cattell, R. B. (1957). *Personality and motivation structure and measurement.* Yonkers, NY: World.

Cattell, R. B. (1960). The multiple abstract variance analysis equations and solutions: For nature-nurture research on continuous variables. *Psychological Review, 67,* 353–372.

Cattell, R. B. (1964). *Personality and social psychology.* San Diego, CA: Robert R. Knapp.

Cattell, R. B. (1965). *The scientific analysis of personality.* Baltimore, MD: Penguin.

Cattell, R. B. (1971). *Abilities: Their structure, growth and action.* Boston, MA: Houghton Mifflin.

Cattell, R. B. (1973). *Personality and mood by questionnaire.* San Francisco, CA: Jossey-Bass.

Cattell, R. B. (1974). Raymond B. Cattell. In G. Lindzey (Ed.), *A history of psychology in autobiography* (Vol. 6, pp. 59–100). Englewood Cliffs, NJ: Prentice-Hall.

Cattell, R. B. (1979). *Personality and learning theory: Vol. 1. The structure of personality in its environment.* New York: Springer-Verlag.

Cattell, R. B. (1984). The voyage of a laboratory, 1928–1984. *Multivariate Behavioral Research, 19,* 121–174.

Cattell, R. B. (1990). Advances in Cattellian personality theory. In L. A. Pervin (Ed.), *Handbook of personality: Theory and research* (pp. 101–110). New York: Guilford.

Cattell, R. B., Boyle, G. J., & Chant, D. (2002). Enriched behavioral prediction equation and its impact on structured learning and the dynamic calculus. *Psychological Review, 109,* 202–205.

Cattell, R. B., Eber, H. W., & Tatsuoka, M. M. (1970). *Handbook for the 16 Personality Factor Questionnaire.* Champaign, IL: IPAT.

Celani, D. P. (1999). Applying Fairbairn's object relations theory to the dynamics of the battered woman. *American Journal of Psychotherapy, 53,* 60–73.

Cervone, D. (1999). Evolutionary psychology and explanation in personality psychology. *American Behavioral Scientist, 43,* 1001–1014.

Cervone, D., Caldwell, T. L., Fiori, M., Orom, H., Shadel, W. G., Kassel, J. D., & Artistico, D. (2008). What underlies appraisals? Experimentally testing a knowledge-and-appraisal model of personality architecture among smokers contemplating high-risk situations. *Journal of Personality, 76,* 929–967.

Chambers, W. V., Olson, C., Carlock, J., & Olson, D. (1986). Clinical and grid predictions of inconsistencies in individuals' personal constructs. *Perceptual and Motor Skills, 62,* 649–650.

Chandler, H. M., Alexander, C. N., & Heaton, D. P. (2005). The Transcendental Meditation program and postconventional self-development: A 10-year longitudinal study. *Journal of Social Behavior and Personality, 17,* 93–121.

Chang, E. C. (1998). Cultural differences, perfectionism, and suicidal risk in a college population: Does social problem solving still matter? *Cognitive Therapy and Research, 22,* 237–254.

Chaplin, C. (1964). *My autobiography.* New York: Simon & Schuster.

Chaplin, W. F., John, O. P., & Goldberg, L. R. (1988). Conceptions of states and traits: Dimensional attributes with ideals as prototypes. *Journal of Personality and Social Psychology, 54,* 541–557.

Chapman, J. P., Chapman, L. J., & Kwapil, T. R. (1994). Does the Eysenck Psychoticism Scale predict psychosis? A ten year longitudinal study. *Personality and Individual Differences, 17,* 369–375.

Chappell, D. W. (2003). Buddhist social principles. In K. H. Dockett, G. R. Dudley-Grant, & C. P. Bankart (Eds.), *Psychology and Buddhism: From individual to global community* (pp. 259–274). Secaucus, NJ: Kluwer Academic.

Cheek, J. (1982). Aggregation, moderator variables, and the validity of personality tests: A peer-rating study. *Journal of Personality and Social Psychology, 43,* 1254–1269.

Chen, T. (1999). *The fundamentals of meditation practice.* (L. To, Trans.; S. Landberg & F. G. French, Eds.). Available online at http://www.buddhanet.net/pdf_file/chanmed1.pdf

Cheng, S. H., & Kuo, W. H. (2000). Family socialization of ethnic identity among Chinese American pre-adolescents. *Journal of Comparative Family Studies, 31,* 463–484.

Chetwynd, T. (1982). *A dictionary of symbols.* London: Paladin.

Chida, Y., & Hamer, M. (2008). Chronic psychosocial factors and acute physiological responses to laboratory-induced stress in healthy populations: A quantitative review of 30 years of investigations. *Psychological Bulletin, 134,* 829–885.

Chomsky, N. (1959). Review of Skinner's verbal behavior. *Language, 35,* 26–58.

Church, A. T., & Katigbak, M. S. (2000). Trait psychology in the Philippines. *American Behavioral Scientist, 44,* 73–94.

Church, A. T., Katigbak, M. S., & del Prado, A. M. (2010). Cultural similarities and differences in perceived affordances of situations for Big Five behaviors. *Journal of Research in Personality, 44,* 78–90.

Chusmir, L. H. (1989). Behavior: A measure of motivation needs. *Psychology: A Journal of Human Behavior, 26*(2 & 3), 1–10.

Ciardiello, J. A. (1985). Beethoven: Modern analytic views of the man and his music. *Psychoanalytic Review, 72,* 129–147.

Cirlot, J. E. (1971). *A dictionary of symbols* (2nd ed.) (J. Sage, Trans.). New York: Philosophical Library.

Claridge, G., & Davis, C. (2001). What's the use of neuroticism? *Personality and Individual Differences, 31,* 383–400.

Clark, J. M., & Paivio, A. (1989). Observational and theoretical terms in psychology: A cognitive perspective on scientific language. *American Psychologist, 44,* 500–512.

Clark, L. A., & Watson, D. (1999). Temperament: A new paradigm for trait psychology. In L. A. Pervin & O. P. John (Eds.), *Handbook of personality: Theory and research* (2nd ed., pp. 399–423). New York: Guilford.

Clark, P. A. (1985). *Individual education: Application of Adler's personality theory.* (ERIC Document Reproduction Service No. EJ325150)

Clarke, S., & Pearson, C. (2000). Personal constructs of male survivors of childhood sexual abuse receiving cognitive analytic therapy. *British Journal of Medical Psychology, 73,* 169–177.

Clinton, H. R. (2003). *Living history.* New York: Scribner.

Cloninger, C. R. (1986). A unified biosocial theory of personality and its role in the development of anxiety states. *Psychiatric Developments, 3,* 167–226.

Cloninger, C. R. (1987a). Neurogenetic adaptive mechanism in alcoholism. *Science, 236,* 410–416.

Cloninger, C. R. (1987b). A systematic method for clinical description and classification of personality variants: A proposal. *Archives of General Psychiatry, 44,* 573–588.

Cloninger, C. R., Sigvardsson, S., & Bohman, M. (1988). Childhood personality predicts alcohol abuse in young adults. *Alcoholism Clinical and Experimental Research, 12,* 494–505.

Cloninger, C. R., & Svrakic, D. M. (1997). Integrative psychobiological approach to psychiatric assessment and treatment. *Psychiatry, 60,* 120–141.

Coccaro, E. F., Siever, L. J., Klar, H. M., Maurer, G., Cochrane, K., Cooper, T. B., Mohs, R. C., & Davis, K. L. (1989). Serotonergic studies in patients with affective and personality disorders. *Archives of General Psychiatry, 46,* 587–599.

Cohen, A. B., Hall, D. E., Koenig, H. G., & Meador, K. G. (2005). Social versus individual motivation: Implications for normative definitions of religious orientation. *Personality and Social Psychology Review, 9,* 48–61.

Cohen, A. B., & Hill, P. C. (2007). Religion as culture: Religious individualism and collectivism among American Catholics, Jews, and Protestants. *Journal of Personality, 75,* 709–742.

Cohen, C. R., Chartrand, J. M., & Jowdy, D. P. (1995). Relationships between career indecision subtypes and ego identity development. *Journal of Counseling Psychology, 42,* 440–447.

Cohen, D. (1997). *Carl Rogers: A critical biography.* London: Constable.

Coles, R. (1970). *Erik H. Erikson: The growth of his work.* Boston, MA: Little, Brown.

Collaer, M. L., & Hines, M. (1995). Human behavioral sex differences: A role for gonadal hormones during early development? *Psychological Bulletin, 118,* 55–107.

Compeau, D., Higgins, C. A., & Huff, S. (1999). Social cognitive theory and individual reactions to computing technology: A longitudinal study. *MIS Quarterly, 23,* 145–158.

Congdon, E., & Canli, T. (2008). A neurogenetic approach to impulsivity. *Journal of Personality, 76,* 1447–1483.

Conrad, H. S. (1932). The validity of personality ratings of preschool children. *Journal of Educational Psychology, 23,* 671–680.

Contrada, R. J., Cather, C., & O'Leary, A. (1999). Personality and health: Dispositions and processes in disease susceptibility and adaptation to illness. In L. A. Pervin & O. P. John (Eds.), *Handbook of personality: Theory and research* (2nd ed., pp. 576–604). New York: Guilford.

Conway, M. A., & Pleydell-Pearce, C. W. (2000). The construction of autobiographical memories in the self-memory system. *Psychological Review, 107,* 261–288.

Cook, J. M., Biyanova, T., & Coyne, J. C. (2009). Influential psychotherapy figures, authors, and books: An internet survey of over 2,000 psychotherapists. *Psychotherapy Theory, Research, Practice, Training, 46,* 42–51.

Coolidge, F. L., Moor, C. J., Yamazaki, T. G., Stewart, S. E., & Segal, D. L. (2001). On the relationship between Karen Horney's tripartite neurotic type theory and personality disorder features. *Personality and Individual Differences, 30,* 1287–1400.

Coolidge, F. L., Segal, D. L., Benight, C. C., & Danielian, J. (2004). The predictive power of Horney's psychoanalytic approach: An empirical study. *American Journal of Psychoanalysis, 64,* 363–374.

Cooper, S. H. (1998). Changing notions of defense within psychoanalytic theory. *Journal of Personality, 66,* 947–964.

Corcoran, K. O., & Mallinckrodt, B. (2000). Adult attachment, self-efficacy, perspective taking, and conflict resolution. *Journal of Counseling and Development, 78,* 473–483.

Cornett, C. (2000). Ideas and identities: The life and work of Erik Erikson [Book review]. *Clinical Social Work Journal, 28,* 123–128.

Corr, P. J., Pickering, A. D., & Gray, J. A. (1997). Personality, punishment, and procedural learning: A test of J. A. Gray's anxiety theory. *Journal of Personality and Social Psychology, 73,* 337–344.

Corsini, R. J. (1989). *Manual: Corsini 4-R System of Individual Education.* Chicago, IL: North American Society of Adlerian Psychology.

Costa, P. T., Jr., & McCrae, R. R. (1985). *The NEO Personality Inventory manual.* Odessa, FL: Psychological Assessment Resources.

Costa, P. T., Jr., & McCrae, R. R. (1988). From catalog to classification: Murray's needs and the five-factor model. *Journal of Personality and Social Psychology, 55,* 258–265.

Costa, P. T., Jr., & McCrae, R. R. (1992a). Four ways five factors are basic. *Personality and Individual Differences, 13,* 653–665.

Costa, P. T., Jr., & McCrae, R. R. (1992b). *Revised NEO Personality Inventory (NEO-PI-R) and NEO Five-Factor Inventory (NEO-FFI) professional manual.* Odessa, FL: Psychological Assessment Resources.

Costa, P. T., Jr., McCrae, R. R., & Dye, D. A. (1991). Facet scales for agreeableness and conscientiousness: A revision of the NEO Personality Inventory. *Personality and Individual Differences, 12,* 887–898.

Côté, J. E. (1993). Foundations of a psychoanalytic social psychology: Neo-Eriksonian propositions regarding the relationship between psychic structure and cultural institutions. *Developmental Review, 13,* 31–53.

Côté, J. E., & Levine, C. (1988a). A critical examination of the ego identity status paradigm. *Developmental Review, 8,* 147–184.

Côté, J. E., & Levine, C. (1988b). On critiquing the identity status paradigm: A rejoinder to Waterman. *Developmental Review, 8,* 209–218.

Côté, J. E., & Levine, C. (1988c). The relationship between ego identity status and Erikson's notions of institutionalized moratoria, value orientation stage, and ego dominance. *Journal of Youth and Adolescence, 17,* 81–99.

Côté, J. E., & Levine, C. (1989). An empirical test of Erikson's theory of ego identity formation. *Youth and Society, 20,* 388–414.

Côté, J. E., & Levine, C. G. (1992). The genesis of the humanistic academic: A second test of Erikson's theory of identity formation. *Youth and Society, 23,* 387–410.

Covington, C. (2001). The future of analysis. *Journal of Analytical Psychology, 46,* 325–334.

Cowan, D. A. (1989). An alternative to the dichotomous interpretation of Jung's psychological functions: Developing more sensitive measurement technology. *Journal of Personality Assessment, 53,* 459–471.

Coward, H. (1989). Jung's conception of the role of religion in psychological development. *Humanistic Psychologist, 17,* 265–273.

Craig, R. J., Loheidi, R. A., Rudolph, B., Leifer, M., & Rubin, N. (1998). Relationship between psychological needs and the five-factor model of personality classification. *Journal of Research in Personality, 32,* 519–527.

Craik, K. H. (1988). Assessing the personalities of historical figures. In W. M. Runyan (Ed.), *Psychology and historical interpretation.* New York: Oxford University Press.

Cramer, D. (1985). Psychological adjustment and the facilitative nature of close personal relationships. *British Journal of Medical Psychology, 58,* 165–168.

Cramer, D. (1986). An item factor analysis of the revised Barrett-Lennard Relationship Inventory. *British Journal of Guidance and Counselling, 14,* 314–325.

Cramer, D. (1990a). Disclosure of personal problems, self-esteem, and the facilitativeness of friends and lovers. *British Journal of Guidance and Counselling, 18,* 186–196.

Cramer, D. (1990b). Self-esteem and close relationships: A statistical refinement. *British Journal of Social Psychology, 29,* 189–191.

Cramer, P. (1997). Evidence for change in children's use of defense mechanisms. *Journal of Personality, 65,* 233–247.

Cramer, P. (1998a). Freshman to senior year: A follow-up study of identity, narcissism, and defense mechanisms. *Journal of Research in Personality, 32,* 156–172.

Cramer, P. (1998b). Threat to gender representation: Identity and identification. *Journal of Personality, 66,* 335–357.

Cramer, P. (2000). Defense mechanisms in psychology today: Further processes for adaptation. *American Psychologist, 55,* 637–646.

Cramer, P. (2001). Identification and its relation to identity development. *Journal of Personality, 69,* 667–688.

Cramer, P. (2002). Defense mechanisms, behavior, and affect in young adulthood. *Journal of Personality, 70,* 103–126.

Cramer, P., & Blatt, S. J. (1990). Use of the TAT to measure change in defense mechanisms following intensive psychotherapy. *Journal of Personality Assessment, 54,* 236–251.

Cramer, P., & Block, J. (1998). Preschool antecedents of defense mechanism use in young adults: A longitudinal study. *Journal of Personality and Social Psychology, 74,* 159–169.

Crandall, J. E. (1991). A scale for social interest. *Individual Psychology, 47,* 106–114. (Original work published 1975)

Crick, F., & Mitchison, G. (1986). REM sleep and neural nets. *Journal of Mind and Behavior, 7,* 229–250.

Crick, N. R., & Dodge, K. A. (1994). A review and reformulation of social information-processing mechanisms in children's social adjustment. *Psychological Bulletin, 115,* 74–101.

Critchfield, T. S., & Kollins, S. H. (2001). Temporal discounting: Basic research and the analysis of socially important behavior. *Journal of Applied Behavior Analysis, 34,* 101–122.

Crockett, J. B., & Crawford, R. L. (1989). The relationship between Myers-Briggs Type Indicator (MBTI) Scale scores and advising style preferences of college freshmen. *Journal of College Student Development, 30,* 154–161.

Cronbach, L. J. (1957). The two disciplines of scientific psychology. *American Psychologist, 12,* 671–684.

Cronbach, L. J. (1975). Beyond the two disciplines of scientific psychology. *American Psychologist, 30,* 116–127.

Cronbach, L. J., & Meehl, P. E. (1955). Construct validity in psychological tests. *Psychological Bulletin, 52,* 281–302.

Csikszentmihalyi, M. (1996). *Creativity: Flow and the psychology of discovery and invention.* New York: HarperCollins.

Cummins, P. (1992). Construing the experience of sexual abuse. *Journal of Personal Construct Psychology, 5,* 355–365.

Curtis, J. M., & Cowell, D. R. (1993). Relation of birth order and scores on measures of pathological narcissism. *Psychological Reports, 72,* 311–315.

Dahlsgaard, K., Peterson, C., & Seligman, M. E. P. (2005). Shared virtue: The convergence of valued human strengths across culture and history. *Review of General Psychology, 9,* 203–213.

Dalton, R, (2004, October 21). Quarrel over book leads to call for misconduct inquiry. *Nature, 431*(7011), 889.

Daly, M. (1978). *Gyn/Ecology: The metaethics of radical feminism.* Boston, MA: Beacon Press.

Damasio, A. R. (1994). *Descartes' error: Emotion, reason, and the human brain.* New York: Putnam.

Daniels, M. (1988). The myth of self-actualization. *Journal of Humanistic Psychology, 28*(1), 7–38.

Darwin, C. (1909). The origin of species. In *Harvard classics* (Vol. 11). New York: P. F. Collier. (Original work published 1859)

Das, A. K. (1989). Beyond self-actualization. *International Journal for the Advancement of Counselling, 12,* 13–27.

David, J. P., Green, P. J., Martin, R., & Suls, J. (1997). Differential roles of neuroticism, extraversion, and event desirability for mood in daily life: An integrative model of top-down and bottom-up influences. *Journal of Personality and Social Psychology, 73,* 149–159.

Davidow, S., & Bruhn, A. R. (1990). Earliest memories and the dynamics of delinquency: A replication study. *Journal of Personality Assessment, 54,* 601–616.

Davidson, K., & MacGregor, M. W. (1998). A critical appraisal of self-report defense mechanism measures. *Journal of Personality, 66,* 965–992.

Davidson, R. J. (2000). Affective style, psychopathology, and resilience: Brain mechanisms and plasticity. *American Psychologist, 55,* 1196–1214.

Davidson, R. J. (2001). Toward a biology of positive affect and compassion. In R. J. Davidson & A. Harrington (Eds.), *Visions of compassion: Western scientists and Tibetan Buddhists examine human nature* (pp. 107–130). Cary, NC: Oxford University Press.

Davidson, R. J. (2003). Darwin and the neural basis of emotion and affective style. *Annals of the New York Academy of Sciences, 1000,* 316–336.

Davidson, R. J. (2005). Emotion regulation, happiness, and the neuroplasticity of the brain. *Advances, 21*(3 & 4), 25–29.

Davidson, R. J., Ekman, P., Saron, C. D., Senulis, J. A., & Friesen, W. V. (1990). Approach-withdrawal and cerebral asymmetry: I. Emotional expression and brain physiology. *Journal of Personality and Social Psychology, 58,* 330–341.

Davidson, R. J., & Fox, N. A. (1989). Frontal brain asymmetry predicts infants' response to maternal separation. *Journal of Abnormal Psychology, 98,* 127–131.

Davidson, R. J., Kabat-Zinn, J., Schumacher, J., Rosenkranz, M., Muller, D., Santorelli, S. F., Urbanowskik, F., Harrington, A., Bonus, K., & Sheridan, J. F. (2003). Alterations in brain and immune function produced by mindfulness meditation. *Psychosomatic Medicine, 65,* 564–570.

Davidson, R. J., Putnam, K. M., & Larson, C. L. (2000). Dysfunction in the neural circuitry of emotion regulation—A possible prelude to violence. *Science, 289,* 591–594.

Davies, J. L., & Alexander, C. N. (2005). Alleviating political violence through reducing collective tension: Impact assessment analyses of the Lebanon war. *Journal of Social Behavior and Personality, 17,* 285–338.

Davis, D. L., Grove, S. J., & Knowles, P. A. (1990). An experimental application of personality type as an analogue for decision-making style. *Psychological Reports, 66,* 167–175.

Davis, T. (1986). Book reviews. *Individual Psychology, 42,* 133–142.

Davis-Berman, J. (1990). Physical self-efficacy, perceived physical status, and depressive symptomatology in older adults. *Journal of Psychology, 124,* 207–215.

Dawes, R. M. (1994). *House of cards: Psychology and psychotherapy built on myth.* New York: Free Press.

Dawis, R. V. (1996). Vocational psychology, vocational adjustment, and the workforce: Some familiar and unanticipated consequences. *Psychology, Public Policy, and Law, 2,* 229–248.

Dawson, G., Panagiotides, H., Klinger, L. G., & Hill, D. (1992). The role of frontal lobe functioning in the development of infant self-regulatory behavior. *Brain and Cognition, 20,* 152–175.

de Nicolas, A. T. (1998). The biocultural paradigm: The neural connection between science and mysticism. *Experimental Gerontology, 33,* 169–182.

de Quervain, D. J. F., Roozendaal, B., & McGaugh, J. L. (1998). Stress and glucocorticoids impair retrieval of long-term spatial memory. *Nature, 394,* 787–790.

De Raad, B. (1998). Five big, Big Five issues: Rationale, content, structure, status, and crosscultural assessment. *European Psychologist, 3,* 113–124.

de Silva, P. (1990). Buddhist psychology: A review of theory and practice. *Current Psychology, 9,* 236–254.

de St. Aubin, E. (1998). Truth against the world: A psycho-biographical exploration of generativity in the life of Frank Lloyd Wright. In D. P. McAdams & E. de St. Aubin (Eds.), *Generativity and adult development: How and why we care for the next generation* (pp. 391–427). Washington, DC: American Psychological Association.

de Vries, R. E., de Vries, A., & Feij, J. A. (2009). Sensation seeking, risk-taking, and the HEXACO model of personality. *Personality and Individual Differences, 47,* 536–540.

de Waal, F. B. M. (2002). Evolutionary psychology: The wheat and the chaff. *Current Directions in Psychological Science, 11,* 187–191.

de Waal, F. B. M. (2008). Putting the altruism back into altruism: The evolution of empathy. *Annual Review of Psychology, 59,* 279–300.

Deary, I. J., Johnson, W., & Houlihan, L. M. (2009). Genetic foundations of human intelligence. *Human Genetics, 126,* 215–232.

DeCarvalho, R. J. (1989). Contributions to the history of psychology: LXII. Carl Rogers' naturalistic system of ethics. *Psychological Reports, 65,* 1155–1162.

DeCarvalho, R. J. (1990a). Contributions to the history of psychology: LXIX. Gordon Allport on the problem of method in psychology. *Psychological Reports, 67,* 267–275.

DeCarvalho, R. J. (1990b). The growth hypothesis and self-actualization: An existential alternative. *Humanistic Psychologist, 18,* 252–258.

DeCarvalho, R. J. (1990c). A history of the "third force" in psychology. *Journal of Humanistic Psychology, 30*(4), 22–44.

DeCarvalho, R. J. (1990d). Who coined the term "humanistic psychology"? *Humanistic Psychologist, 18,* 350–351.

DeCarvalho, R. J. (1991a). Gordon Allport and humanistic psychology. *Journal of Humanistic Psychology, 31*(3), 8–13.

DeCarvalho, R. J. (1991b). The humanistic paradigm in education. *Humanistic Psychologist, 19,* 88–104.

DeCarvalho, R. J. (1992). The humanistic ethics of Rollo May. *Journal of Humanistic Psychology, 32*(1), 7–18.

Deci, E. L. (1975). *Intrinsic motivation.* New York: Plenum.

Decker, P. J., & Nathan, B. N. (1985). *Behavior modeling training: Principles and applications.* New York: Praeger.

DeGrandpre, R. J. (2000). A science of meaning: Can behaviorism bring meaning to psychological science? *American Psychologist, 55,* 721–739.

DeHoff, S. L. (1998). In search of a paradigm for psychological and spiritual growth: Implications for psychotherapy and spiritual direction. *Pastoral Psychology, 46,* 333–346.

Delmonte, M. M. (1984). Psychometric scores and meditation practice: A literature review. *Personality and Individual Differences, 5,* 559–563.

Demanchick, S. P., & Kirschenbaum, H. (2008). Carl Rogers and the CIA. *Journal of Humanistic Psychology, 48,* 6–31.

DeNeve, K. M., & Cooper, H. (1998). The happy personality: A meta-analysis of 137 personality traits and subjective well-being. *Psychological Bulletin, 124,* 197–229.

Dennison, L., Moss-Morris, R., & Chalder, T. (2009). A review of psychological correlates of adjustment in patients with multiple sclerosis. *Clinical Psychology Review, 29,* 141–153.

Desharnais, R., Bouillon, J., & Godin, G. (1986). Self-efficacy and outcome expectations as determinants of exercise adherence. *Psychological Reports, 59,* 1155–1159.

Dien, D. (1992). Gender and individuation: China and the West. *Psychoanalytic Review, 79,* 105–119.

Diener, E., Emmons, R. A., Larsen, R. J., & Griffin, S. (1985). The Satisfaction with Life Scale. *Journal of Personality Assessment, 49,* 71–75.

Diener, E., Suh, E. M., Lucas, R. E., & Smith, H. L. (1999). Subjective well-being: Three decades of progress. *Psychological Bulletin, 125,* 276–302.

Digman, J. M. (1989). Five robust trait dimensions: Development, stability, and utility. *Journal of Personality, 57,* 195–214.

Digman, J. M. (1990). Personality structure: Emergence of the five-factor model. *Annual Review of Psychology, 41,* 417–440.

Digman, J. M. (1997). Higher-order factors of the Big Five. *Journal of Personality and Social Psychology, 73,* 1246–1256.

Dillen, L., Siongers, M., Helskens, D., & Verhofstadt-Denève, L. (2009). When puppets speak: Dialectical psychodrama within developmental child psychotherapy. *Journal of Constructivist Psychology, 22,* 55–82.

Dimsdale, J. E., & Mills, P. J. (2002). An unanticipated effect of meditation on cardiovascular pharmacology and physiology. *American Journal of Cardiology, 90,* 908–909.

Dinkmeyer, D., & Dinkmeyer, D., Jr. (1989). Adlerian psychology. *Psychology, 26,* 26–34.

Dinkmeyer, D., & McKay, G. (1976). *Systematic training for effective parenting.* Circle Pines, MN: American Guidance Service.

Dinkmeyer, D., McKay, G., & Dinkmeyer, J. (1982). *The next step: Effective parenting through problem solving.* Circle Pines, MN: American Guidance Service.

Dinsmoor, J. A. (1992). Setting the record straight: The social views of B. F. Skinner. *American Psychologist, 47,* 1454–1463.

Distel, M. A., Trull, T. J., Willemsen, G., Vink, J. M., Derom, C. A., Lynskey, M., Martin, N. G., & Boomsma, D. I. (2009). The five factor model of personality and borderline personality disorder: A genetic analysis of comorbidity. *Biological Psychiatry, 66,* 1131–1138.

Dockett, K. H. (2003). Buddhist empowerment: Individual, organizational, and societal transformation. In K. H. Dockett, G. R. Dudley-Grant, & C. P. Bankart (Eds.), *Psychology and Buddhism: From individual to global community* (pp. 173–196). Secaucus, NJ: Kluwer Academic.

Dockett, K. H., & North-Schulte, D. (2003). Transcending self and other: Mahayana principles of integration. In S. Muramoto & P. Young-Eisendrath (Eds.), *Awakening and insight: Zen Buddhism and psychotherapy* (pp. 215–238). New York: Brunner-Routledge.

Dolce, J. J. (1987). Self-efficacy and disability beliefs in behavioral treatment of pain. *Behaviour Research and Therapy, 25,* 289–299.

Dollard, J. (1949). *Criteria for the life history: With analyses of six notable documents.* New York: Peter Smith.

Dollard, J., & Miller, N. E. (1950). *Personality and psychotherapy: An analysis in terms of learning, thinking, and culture.* New York: McGraw-Hill.

Dollard, J., Miller, N. E., Doob, L. W., Mowrer, O. H., Sears, R. R., et al. (1939). *Frustration and aggression.* New Haven, CT: Yale University Press.

Dollinger, S. J., Leong, F. T. L., & Ulicni, S. K. (1996). On traits and values: With special reference to openness to experience. *Journal of Research in Personality, 30,* 23–41.

Dominguez, M. M., & Carton, J. S. (1997). The relationship between self-actualization and parenting style. *Journal of Social Behavior and Personality, 12,* 1093–1100.

Domino, G., & Affonso, D. D. (1990). A personality measure of Erikson's life stages: The Inventory of Psychosocial Balance. *Journal of Personality Assessment, 54,* 576–588.

Donahue, E. M., Robins, R. W., Roberts, B. W., & John, O. P. (1993). The divided self: Concurrent and longitudinal effects of psychological adjustment and social roles on self-concept differentiation. *Journal of Personality and Social Psychology, 64,* 834–846.

Donahue, M. J. (1985). Intrinsic and extrinsic religiousness: Review and meta-analysis. *Journal of Personality and Social Psychology, 48,* 400–419.

Donaldson, S. I., & Ko, I. (2010). Positive organizational psychology, behavior, and scholarship: A review of the emerging literature and evidence base. *Journal of Positive Psychology, 5,* 177–191.

Donnellan, M. B., Burt, S. A., Levendosky, A. A., & Klump, K. L. (2008). Genes, personality, and attachment in adults: A multivariate behavioral genetic analysis. *Personality and Social Psychology Bulletin, 34,* 3–16.

Dreikurs, R. (1950). *Fundamentals of Adlerian psychology.* Chicago, IL: Alfred Adler Institute.

Dreikurs, R. (1982). Adleriana. *Individual Psychology, 38,* 7. (Original work published 1940)

Dreikurs, R., & Soltz, V. (1964). *Children: The challenge.* New York: Hawthorn.

Drigotas, S. M., & Barta, W. (2001). The cheating heart: Scientific explorations of infidelity. *Current Directions in Psychological Science, 10,* 177–180.

Drob, S. L. (1999). Jung and the Kabbalah. *History of Psychology, 2,* 102–118.

Dubow, E. F., Huesmann, L. R., & Eron, L. D. (1987). Childhood correlates of adult ego development. *Child Development, 58,* 859–869.

Duckworth, A. L., Quinn, P. D., & Seligman, M. E. P. (2009). Positive predictors of teacher effectiveness. *Journal of Positive Psychology, 6,* 540–547.

Dudley-Grant, G. R. (2003). Buddhism, psychology, and addiction theory in psychotherapy. In K. H. Dockett, G. R. Dudley-Grant, & C. P. Bankart (Eds.), *Psychology and Buddhism: From individual to global community* (pp. 105–124). Secaucus, NJ: Kluwer Academic.

Duncan, L. E. (2010). Using group consciousness theories to understand political activism: Case studies of Barack Obama, Hillary Clinton, and Ingo Hasselbach. *Journal of Personality, 78,* 1601–1636.

Duncan, R. C., Konefal, J., & Spechler, M. M. (1990). Effect of neurolinguistic programming training on self-actualization as measured by the Personal Orientation Inventory. *Psychological Reports, 66,* 1323–1330.

Dweck, C. S., & Leggett, E. L. (1988). A social-cognitive approach to motivation and personality. *Psychological Review, 95,* 256–273.

Dyck, L. R., Caron, A., & Aron, D. (2006). Working on the positive emotional attractor through training in health care. *Journal of Management Development, 25,* 671–688.

Dzewaltowski, D. A. (1989). Toward a model of exercise motivation. *Journal of Sport and Exercise Psychology, 11,* 251–269.

Eacott, M. J., & Crawley, R. A. (1998). The offset of childhood amnesia: Memory for events that occurred before age 3. *Journal of Experimental Psychology: General, 127,* 22–33.

Eagle, M. (1997). Contributions of Erik Erikson. In Erik Erikson's clinical contributions: A symposium in memorial tribute. *Psychoanalytic Review, 84,* 337–347.

Eagle, M. N. (1996). Attachment research and psychoanalytic theory. In J. M. Masling & R. F. Bornstein (Eds.), *Psychoanalytic perspectives on developmental psychology* (Ch. 4, pp. 105–149). Washington, DC: American Psychological Association.

Eagly, A. H. (1987). *Sex differences in social behavior: A social-role interpretation.* Hillsdale, NJ: Erlbaum.

Eagly, A. H., & Wood, W. (1991). Explaining sex differences in social behavior: A meta-analytic perspective. *Personality and Social Psychology Bulletin, 17,* 306–315.

Ebstein, R. P. (2006). The molecular genetic architecture of human personality: Beyond self-report questionnaires. *Molecular Psychiatry, 11,* 427–445.

Eden, D., & Zuk, Y. (1995). Seasickness as a self-fulfilling prophecy: Raising self-efficacy to boost performance at sea. *Journal of Applied Psychology, 80,* 628–635.

Edinger, E. F. (1968). An outline of analytical psychology. *Quadrant, 1,* 1–12.

Edinger, E. F. (1972). *Ego and archetype: Individuation and the religious function of the psyche.* New York: Putnam.

Edinger, E. F. (1999). *Archetype of the apocalypse: A Jungian study of the book of Revelation.* Chicago, IL: Open Court.

Egan, S., & Stelmack, R. M. (2003). A personality profile of Mount Everest climbers. *Personality and Individual Differences, 34,* 1491–1494.

Egan, V., & Taylor, D. (2010). Shoplifting, unethical consumer behaviour, and personality. *Personality and Individual Differences, 48,* 878–883.

Einstein, A., & Infeld, L. (1961). *The evolution of physics: The growth of ideas from early concepts to relativity and quanta.* New York: Simon & Schuster. (Original work published 1938)

Eisenberger, R., Armeli, S., & Pretz, J. (1998). Can the promise of reward increase creativity? *Journal of Personality and Social Psychology, 74,* 704–714.

Ekehammar, B., & Akrami, N. (2007). Personality and prejudice: From Big Five personality factors to facets. *Journal of Personality, 75,* 899–925.

Ekman, P. (1993). Facial expression and emotion. *American Psychologist, 48,* 376–379.

Ekman, P., Davidson, R. J., & Friesen, W. V. (1990). The Duchenne smile: II. Emotional expression and brain physiology. *Journal of Personality and Social Psychology, 58,* 342–353.

Ekman, P., Davidson, R. J., Ricard, M., & Wallace, B. A. (2005). Buddhist and psychological perspectives on emotion and well-being. *Current Directions in Psychological Science, 14,* 59–63.

Elizabeth, P. (1983). Comparison of psychoanalytic and a client-centered group treatment model on measures of anxiety and self-actualization. *Journal of Counseling Psychology, 30,* 425–428.

Ellenberger, H. F. (1970). *The discovery of the unconscious: The history and evolution of dynamic psychiatry.* New York: Basic Books.

Ellenberger, H. F. (1991). The story of Helene Preiswerk: A critical study with new documents. *History of Psychiatry, 2*(5, Pt 1), 41–52.

Elliott, D., Amerikaner, M., & Swank, P. (1987). Early recollections and the Vocational Preference Inventory as predictors of vocational choice. *Individual Psychology, 43,* 353–359.

Elliott, J. E. (1992). Compensatory buffers, depression, and irrational beliefs. *Journal of Cognitive Psychotherapy, 6,* 175–184.

Ellis, A. (1989). Using rational-emotive therapy (RET) as crisis intervention: A single session with a suicidal client. *Individual Psychology, 45,* 75–81.

Elms, A. C. (1988). Freud as Leonardo: Why the first psycho-biography went wrong. *Journal of Personality, 56,* 19–40.

Elovitz, P. H. (2008). A comparative psychohistory of McCain and Obama. *Journal of Psychohistory, 36,* 98–143.

Elovitz, P. H. (2010). Messianic hopes, anger, fantasy, fear, and disappointment in Obama's presidency. *Journal of Psychohistory, 38,* 102–123.

Elson, M. (Ed.). (1987). *The Kohut seminars on self psychology and psychotherapy with adolescents and young adults.* New York: Norton.

Emavardhana, T., & Tori, C. D. (1997). Changes in self-concept, ego defense mechanisms, and religiosity following seven-day Vipassana meditation retreats. *Journal for the Scientific Study of Religion, 36,* 194–206.

Emmons, R. A. (1997). Motives and life goals. In R. Hogan, J. Johnson, & S. Briggs (Eds.), *Handbook of personality psychology* (pp. 485–512). San Diego, CA: Academic Press.

Emmons, R. A. (2006). Spirituality: Recent progress. In M. Csikszentmihalyi & I. S. Csikszentmihalyi (Eds.), *A life worth living: Contributions to positive psychology* (pp. 62–81). New York: Oxford University Press.

Emmons, R. A., Diener, E., & Larsen, R. J. (1985). Choice of situations and congruence models of interactionism. *Personality and Individual Differences, 6,* 693–705.

Endler, N. S., & Magnusson, D. (Eds.). (1976). *Interactional psychology and personality.* New York: Wiley.

Engle, R. W., Tuholski, S. W., Laughlin, J. E., & Conway, A. R. A. (1999). Working memory, short-term memory, and general fluid intelligence: A latent-variable approach. *Journal of Experimental Psychology: General, 128,* 309–331.

Epel, E. S., Bandura, A., & Zimbardo, P. G. (1999). Escaping homelessness: The influences of self-efficacy and time perspective on coping with homelessness. *Journal of Applied Social Psychology, 29,* 575–596.

Epstein, J. A., Botvin, G. J., & Diaz, T. (1999). Social influence and psychological determinants of smoking among inner-city adolescents. *Journal of Child and Adolescent Substance Abuse, 8,* 1–19.

Epstein, R. (1991). Skinner, creativity, and the problem of spontaneous behavior. *Psychological Science, 2,* 362–370.

Epstein, S., & O'Brien, E. J. (1985). The person-situation debate in historical and current perspective. *Psychological Bulletin, 98,* 513–537.

Epting, F. R. (1984). *Personal construct counselling and psychotherapy.* New York: Wiley.

Epting, F. R., & Leitner, L. M. (1992). Humanistic psychology and personal construct theory. *Humanistic Psychologist, 20,* 243–259.

Erdle, S., Irwing, P., Rushton, J. P., & Park, J. (2010). The General Factor of Personality and its relation to Self-Esteem in 628,640 Internet respondents. *Personality and Individual Differences, 48,* 343–346.

Erikson, E. H. (1950). *Childhood and society.* New York: Norton.

Erikson, E. H. (1951). Statement to the committee on privilege and tenure of the University of California concerning the California loyalty oath. *Psychiatry, 14,* 243–245.

Erikson, E. H. (1958). *Young man Luther: A study in psycho-analysis and history.* New York: Norton.

Erikson, E. H. (1959). Identity and the life cycle. Selected papers. *Psychological Issues, 1* (Monograph 1). New York: International Universities Press.

Erikson, E. H. (1961). The roots of virtue. In J. Huxley (Ed.), *The humanist frame* (pp. 145–165). New York: Harper & Brothers.

Erikson, E. H. (1963). *Childhood and society* (2nd ed.). New York: Norton.

Erikson, E. H. (1964). *Insight and responsibility: Lectures on the ethical implications of psychoanalytic insight.* New York: Norton.

Erikson, E. H. (1968). *Identity: Youth and crisis.* New York: Norton.

Erikson, E. H. (1969). *Gandhi's truth: On the origins of militant nonviolence.* New York: Norton.

Erikson, E. H. (1975). *Life history and the historical moment.* New York: Norton.

Erikson, E. H. (1982). *The life cycle completed: A review.* New York: Norton.

Erikson, E. H. (1988). Youth: Fidelity and diversity. *Daedalus, 117*(3), 1–24. (Original work published 1962)

Erikson, E. H. (1997). *The life cycle completed: Extended version with new chapters on the ninth stage by Joan M. Erikson.* New York: Norton.

Erikson, E. H., Erikson, J. M., & Kivnick, H. Q. (1986). *Vital involvement in old age.* New York: Norton.

Eriksson, C. (1992). Social interest/social feeling and the evolution of consciousness. *Individual Psychology, 48,* 277–287.

Essex, M. J., Klein, M. H., Cho, E., & Kalin, N. H. (2002). Maternal stress beginning in infancy may sensitize children to later stress exposure: Effects on cortisol and behavior. *Biological Psychiatry, 52,* 776–784.

Essig, T. S., & Russell, R. L. (1990). Analyzing subjectivity in therapeutic discourse: Rogers, Perls, Ellis and Gloria revisited. *Psychotherapy, 27,* 271–281.

Etzioni, A. (1998). Voluntary simplicity: Characterization, select psychological implications and societal consequences. *Journal of Economic Psychology, 19,* 619–643.

Evans, D. E., & Rothbart, M. K. (2008). A two-factor model of temperament. *Personality and Individual Differences, 47,* 565–570.

Evans, R. I. (1981). *Dialogue with Gordon Allport.* New York: Praeger.

Evans, R. I. (1989). *Albert Bandura: The man and his ideas—A dialogue.* New York: Praeger.

Exner, J. E., & Andronikof-Sanglade, A. (1992). Rorschach changes following brief and short-term therapy. *Journal of Personality Assessment, 59,* 59–71.

Eysenck, H. J. (1967). *The biological basis of personality.* Springfield, IL: Thomas.

Eysenck, H. J. (1990a). Biological dimensions of personality. In L. A. Pervin (Ed.), *Handbook of personality: Theory and research* (pp. 244–276). New York: Guilford.

Eysenck, H. J. (1990b). Genetic and environmental contributions to individual differences: The three major dimensions of personality. *Journal of Personality, 58,* 245–261.

Eysenck, H. J. (1991). Dimensions of personality: 16, 5, or 3?—Criteria for a taxonomic paradigm. *Personality and Individual Differences, 12,* 773–790.

Eysenck, H. J. (1992). Four ways five factors are not basic. *Personality and Individual Differences, 13,* 667–673.

Eysenck, H. J. (1993). Creativity and personality: Suggestions for a theory. *Psychological Inquiry, 4,* 147–178.

Eysenck, H. J. (1994). Creativity and personality: Word association, origence, and psychoticism. *Creativity Research Journal, 7,* 209–216.

Eysenck, H. J., & Eysenck, M. W. (1985). *Personality and individual differences: A natural science approach.* New York: Plenum.

Eysenck, H. J., & Eysenck, S. B. G. (1975). *Manual of the Eysenck Personality Questionnaire.* San Diego, CA: Educational and Industrial Testing Service.

Eysenck, H. J., & Eysenck, S. B. G. (1991). *Manual of the Eysenck personality scales.* London: Hodder & Stoughton.

Fabrega, H., Jr. (1990). The concept of somatization as a cultural and historical product of Western medicine. *Psychosomatic Medicine, 52,* 653–672.

Fairfield, B. (1990). Reorientation: The use of hypnosis for lifestyle change. *Individual Psychology, 46,* 451–458.

Falbo, T. (1987). Only children in the United States and China. *Applied Social Psychology Annual, 7,* 159–183.

Falkenström, F. (2009). Studying mindfulness in experienced meditators: A quasi-experimental approach. *Personality and Individual Differences, 48,* 305–310.

Fanon, F. (1967). *Black skin, white masks.* New York: Grove Press.

Feeney, B. C., & Kirkpatrick, L. A. (1996). Effects of adult attachment and presence of romantic partners on physiological responses to stress. *Journal of Personality and Social Psychology, 70,* 255–270.

Fehr, B., & Russell, J. A. (1991). The concept of love viewed from a prototype perspective. *Journal of Personality and Social Psychology, 60,* 425–438.

Feiring, C. (1984). Behavioral styles in infancy and adulthood: The work of Karen Horney and attachment theorists collaterally considered. *American Journal of Psychoanalysis, 44,* 197–208.

Felix, A. (2010). *Sonia Sotomayor: The true American dream.* New York: Berkley Books. (Kindle Version). Retrieved from www.amazon.com

Ferguson, C. J. (2010). Genetic contributions to antisocial personality and behavior: A meta-analytic review from an evolutionary perspective. *Journal of Social Psychology, 150,* 160–180.

Ferguson, E., Sanders, A., O'Hehir, F., & James, D. (2000). Predictive validity of personal statements and the role of the five-factor model of personality in relation to medical training. *Journal of Occupational and Organizational Psychology, 73,* 321–344.

Fernald, P. S. (2000). Carl Rogers: Body-centered counselor. *Journal of Counseling and Development, 78,* 172–179.

Fink, B., & Penton-Voak, I. (2002). Evolutionary psychology of facial attractiveness. *Current Directions in Psychological Science, 11,* 154–158.

Finkelhor, D., Hotaling, G., Lewis, I. A., & Smith, C. (1990). Sexual abuse in a national survey of adult men and women: Prevalence, characteristics, and risk factors. *Child Abuse and Neglect, 14,* 19–28.

Finn, M., & Rubin, J. B. (2000). Psychotherapy with Buddhists. In P. S. Richards & A. E. Allen (Eds.), *Handbook of psychotherapy and religious diversity* (pp. 317–340). Washington, DC: American Psychological Association.

First People. (n.d.). A Cherokee legend: Two wolves. Available online at http://www.firstpeople.us/FP-Html-Legends/TwoWolves-Cherokee.html

Fischer, A. H., & Mosquera, P. M. R. (2001). What concerns men? Women or other men? A critical appraisal of the evolutionary theory of sex differences in aggression. *Psychology, Evolution and Gender, 3,* 5–25.

Fisher, J. D., & Fisher, W. A. (1992). Changing AIDS-risk behavior. *Psychological Bulletin, 111,* 455–474.

Fisher, S., & Greenberg, R. P. (1977). *The scientific credibility of Freud's theories and therapy.* New York: Basic Books.

Fisher, W. W. (2001). Functional analysis of precurrent contingencies between mands and destructive behavior. *Behavior Analyst Today, 2,* 176–181.

Fitzpatrick, J. J. (1976). Erik H. Erikson and psychohistory. *Bulletin of the Menninger Clinic, 40,* 295–314.

Fivush, R. (2010). The development of autobiographical memory. *Annual Review of Psychology, 62,* 559–582.

Fleeson, W. (2001). Toward a structure- and process-integrated view of personality: Traits as density distributions of states. *Journal of Personality and Social Psychology, 80,* 1011–1027.

Fleeson, W. (2007). Situation-based contingencies underlying trait-content manifestation in behavior. *Journal of Personality, 75,* 825–861.

Fleeson, W., & Noftle, E. E. (2008). Where does personality have its influence? A supermatrix of consistency concepts. *Journal of Personality, 76,* 1356–1385.

Flere, S., & Lavrič, M. (2008). Is intrinsic religious orientation a culturally specific American Protestant concept? The fusion of intrinsic and extrinsic religious orientation among non-Protestants. *European Journal of Social Psychology, 38,* 521–530.

Flett, G. L., Hewitt, P. L., Blankstein, K. R., & Gray, L. (1998). Psychological distress and the frequency of perfectionistic thinking. *Journal of Personality and Social Psychology, 75,* 1363–1381.

Florin, P., Mednick, M., & Wandersman, A. (1986). Cognitive social learning variables and the characteristics of leaders. *Journal of Applied Social Psychology, 16,* 808–830.

Flynn, J. R. (1987). Massive IQ gains in 14 nations: What IQ tests really measure. *Psychological Bulletin, 101,* 171–191.

Fodor, E. M., & Roffe-Steinrotter, D. (1998). Rogerian leadership style and creativity. *Journal of Research in Personality, 32,* 236–242.

Fonagy, P. (2008). A genuinely developmental theory of sexual enjoyment and its implications for psychoanalytic technique. *Journal of the American Psychoanalytic Association, 56,* 11–36.

Fonagy, P., & Moran, G. S. (1990). Studies on the efficacy of child psychoanalysis. *Journal of Consulting and Clinical Psychology, 58,* 684–695.

Fonagy, P., & Target, M. (2007). The rooting of the mind in the body: New links between attachment theory and psychoanalytic thought. *Journal of the American Psychoanalytic Association, 55,* 411–456.

Ford, J. G., & Maas, S. (1989). On actualizing person-centered theory: A critique of textbook treatments of Rogers's motivational constructs. *Teaching of Psychology, 16,* 30–31.

Ford, T. E. (2000). Effects of sexist humor on tolerance of sexist events. *Personality and Social Psychology Bulletin, 26,* 1094–1107.

Fordham, F. (1966). *An introduction to Jung's psychology* (3rd ed.). Baltimore, MD: Penguin Books.

Forest, J. J. (1987). Effects on self-actualization of paperbacks about psychological self-help. *Psychological Reports, 60,* 1243–1246.

Forey, W. F., Christensen, O. J., & England, J. T. (1994). Teacher burnout: A relationship with Holland and Adlerian typologies. *Individual Psychology, 50,* 3–17.

Forster, J. R. (1992). Eliciting personal constructs and articulating goals. *Journal of Career Development, 18,* 175–185.

Fosse, R., Stickgold, R., & Hobson, J. A. (2001). Brain-mind states: Reciprocal variation in thoughts and hallucinations. *Psychological Science, 12,* 30–36.

Fowers, B. J., Mollica, C. O., & Procacci, E. N. (2010). Constitutive and instrumental goal orientations and their relations with eudaimonic and hedonic well-being. *Journal of Positive Psychology, 5,* 139–153.

Fraley, C. R., & Brumbaugh, C. C. (2007). Adult attachment and preemptive defenses: Converging evidence on the role of defensive exclusion at the level of encoding. *Journal of Personality, 75,* 1033–1050.

Francis, D., & Meaney, M. J. (1999). Maternal care and development of stress responses. *Current Opinion in Neurobiology, 9,* 128–134.

Francis, L. J., & Bourke, R. (2003). Personality and religion: Applying Cattell's model among secondary school pupils. *Current Psychology: Developmental, Learning, Personality, Social, 22,* 125–137.

Frank, G. (1999). Freud's concept of the superego: Review and assessment. *Psychoanalytic Psychology, 16,* 448–463.

Frank, G. (2008). A response to "The relevance of Sigmund Freud for the 21st century." *Psychoanalytic Psychology, 25,* 375–379.

Frank, J. D. (1982). Therapeutic components shared by all psychotherapies. In J. H. Harvey & M. M. Parks (Eds.), *Psychotherapy research and behavior change* (Vol. 1, pp. 5–37). Washington, DC: American Psychological Association.

Frankel, F. H. (1987). Significant developments in medical hypnosis during the past 25 years. *International Journal of Clinical and Experimental Hypnosis, 35,* 231–247.

Franken, I. H. A. (2002). Behavioral approach system (BAS) sensitivity predicts alcohol craving. *Personality and Individual Differences, 32,* 349–355.

Franklin, A. J. (1999). Invisibility syndrome and racial identity development in psychotherapy and counseling African American men. *Counseling Psychologist, 27,* 761–793.

Freese, J., Powell, B., & Steelman, L. C. (1999). Rebel without a cause effect: Birth order and social attitudes. *American Sociological Review, 64,* 207–231.

Freud, A. (1935). *Psychoanalysis for teachers and parents* (B. Low, Trans.). New York: Emerson Books.

Freud, A. (1966). *The ego and the mechanisms of defense* (Rev. ed.). New York: International Universities Press. (Original work published 1936)

Freud, S. (1953). Character and anal eroticism. In J. Strachey (Ed. and Trans.), *The standard edition of the complete psychological works of Sigmund Freud* (Vol. 9, pp. 169–175). London: Hogarth Press. (Original work published 1908)

Freud, S. (1953). The interpretation of dreams. In J. Strachey (Ed. and Trans.), *The standard edition of the complete psychological works of Sigmund Freud* (Vols. 4 & 5). London: Hogarth Press. (Original work published 1900)

Freud, S. (1957). Leonardo da Vinci and a memory of his childhood. In J. Strachey (Ed. and Trans.), *The standard edition of the complete psychological works of Sigmund Freud* (Vol. 11, pp. 59–137). London: Hogarth Press. (Original work published 1910)

Freud, S. (1958). *On creativity and the unconscious.* New York: Harper & Row. (Original work published 1925)

Freud, S. (1962a). The aetiology of hysteria. In J. Strachey (Ed. and Trans.), *The standard edition of the complete psychological works of Sigmund Freud* (Vol. 3, pp. 187–221). London: Hogarth Press. (Original work published 1896)

Freud, S. (1962b). *The ego and the id* (J. Riviere, Trans.; J. Strachey, Ed.). New York: Norton. (Original work published 1923)

Freud, S. (1962c). Three essays on the theory of sexuality. In J. Strachey (Ed. and Trans.), *Sigmund Freud: Three essays on the theory of sexuality* (pp. 1–130). New York: Basic Books. (Original work published 1905)

Freud, S. (1963a). *An autobiographical study* (J. Strachey, Trans.). New York: Norton. (Original work published 1935)

Freud, S. (1963b). *Jokes and their relation to the unconscious* (J. Strachey, Ed. and Trans.). New York: Norton. (Original work published 1916)

Freud, S. (1966a). *The complete introductory lectures on psychoanalysis* (J. Strachey, Ed. and Trans.). New York: Norton. (Original work published 1933)

Freud, S. (1966b). Project for a scientific psychology. In J. Strachey (Ed. and Trans.), *The standard edition of the complete psychological works of Sigmund Freud* (Vol. 1, pp. 283–397). London: Hogarth Press. (Original work published 1895)

Freud, S. (1978). The psychogenesis of a case of homosexuality in a woman. In P. Reif (Ed.) & B. Low & R. Gabler (Trans.), *Sexuality and the psychology of love.* New York: Macmillan. (Original work published 1920)

Freud, S., & Bullitt, W. C. (1966). *Thomas Woodrow Wilson: A psychological study.* Boston, MA: Houghton Mifflin.

Freyd, J. J. (1994). Betrayal trauma: Traumatic amnesia as an adaptive response to childhood abuse. *Ethics and Behavior, 4,* 307–329.

Freyd, J. J. (1996). *Betrayal trauma: The logic of forgetting childhood abuse.* Cambridge, MA: Harvard University Press.

Frick, W. B. (1993). Subpersonalities: Who conducts the orchestra? *Journal of Humanistic Psychology, 33*(2), 122–128.

Frick, W. B. (2000). Remembering Maslow: Reflections on a 1968 interview. *Journal of Humanistic Psychology, 40*(2), 128–147.

Friedman, H. S., & Booth-Kewley, S. (1987). Personality, Type A behavior, and coronary heart disease: The role of emotional expression. *Journal of Personality and Social Psychology, 53,* 783–792.

Friedman, M. (1982). Comment on the Rogers-May discussion of evil. *Journal of Humanistic Psychology, 22,* 93–96.

Friedman, M. (1994). Reflections on the Buber-Rogers dialogue. *Journal of Humanistic Psychology, 34*(1), 46–65.

Froehle, T. C. (1989). Personal construct threat as a mediator of performance anxiety in a beginning course in counseling techniques. *Journal of College Student Development, 30,* 536–540.

Froh, J. J., Kashdan, T. B., Ozimkowski, K. M., & Miller, N. (2009). Who benefits the most from a gratitude intervention in children and adolescents? Examining positive affect as a moderator. *Journal of Positive Psychology, 4,* 408–422.

Fromm, M. (1993). What students really learn: Students' personal constructions of learning items. *International Journal of Personal Construct Psychology, 6,* 195–208.

Fuchsman, K. (2009). Barack Obama and the cycle of American liberalism. *Journal of Psychohistory, 37,* 145–159.

Fudin, R. (1986). Subliminal psychodynamic activation: Mommy and I are not yet one. *Perceptual and Motor Skills, 63,* 1159–1179.

Fudin, R. (2001). Problems in Silverman's work indicate the need for a new approach to research on subliminal psychodynamic activation. *Perceptual and Motor Skills, 92*(3, Pt 1), 611–622.

Fuller, J. L. (1960). Behavior genetics. *Annual Review of Psychology, 11,* 41–70.

Fuller, R. C. (1982). Carl Rogers, religion, and the role of psychology in American culture. *Journal of Humanistic Psychology, 22,* 21–32.

Fuller-Rowell, T. E., Burrow, A. L., & Ong, A. D. (2011). Changes in racial identity among African American college students following the election of Barack Obama. *Developmental Psychology, 47,* 1608–1618.

Fulton, A. S., Gorsuch, R. L., & Maynard, E. A. (1999). Religious orientation, antihomosexual sentiment, and fundamentalism among Christians. *Journal for the Scientific Study of Religion, 38,* 14–22.

Funder, D. C. (1991). Global traits: A neo-Allportian approach to personality. *Psychological Science, 2,* 31–39.

Furnham, A. (1990). The fakeability of the 16PF, Myers-Briggs and FIRO-B personality measures. *Personality and Individual Differences, 11,* 711–716.

Furnham, A. (1991). Personality and occupational success: 16PF correlates of cabin crew performance. *Personality and Individual Differences, 12,* 87–90.

Furnham, A., Moutafi, J., & Baguma, P. (2002). A cross-cultural study on the role of weight and waist-to-hip ratio on female attractiveness. *Personality and Individual Differences, 32,* 729–745.

Furnham, A., & Stringfield, P. (1993). Personality and work performance: Myers-Briggs Type Indicator correlates of managerial performance in two cultures. *Personality and Individual Differences, 14,* 145–153.

Gaensbauer, T. J., & Jordan, L. (2009). Psychoanalytic perspectives on early trauma: Interviews with thirty analysts who treated an adult victim of a circumscribed trauma in early childhood. *Journal of the American Psychoanalytic Association, 57,* 947–977.

Gaines, S. O., & Reed, E. S. (1995). Prejudice: From Allport to DuBois. *American Psychologist, 50,* 96–103.

Galassi, J. P., & Akos, P. (2004). Developmental advocacy: Twenty-first century school counseling. *Journal of Counseling and Development, 82,* 146–157.

Gallagher, M. W., & Lopez, S. J. (2009). Positive expectancies and mental health: Identifying the unique contributions of hope and optimism. *Journal of Positive Psychology, 4,* 548–556.

Gallo, E. (1994). Synchronicity and the archetypes. *Skeptical Inquirer, 18,* 396–403.

Galvin, M., Shekhar, A., Simon, J., Stilwell, B., Ten Eyck, R., Laite, G., Karwisch, G., & Blix, S. (1991). Low dopamine beta-hydroxylase: A biological sequela of abuse and neglect? *Psychiatry Research, 39,* 1–11.

Gandhi, M. K. (1957). *An autobiography: The story of my experiments with truth.* Boston, MA: Beacon Press.

Gangestad, S. W., & Simpson, J. A. (1990). Toward an evolutionary theory of female sociosexual variation. *Journal of Personality, 58,* 69–96.

Gara, M. A., Rosenberg, S., & Mueller, D. R. (1989). Perception of self and other in schizophrenia. *International Journal of Personal Construct Psychology, 2,* 253–270.

Garces-Foley, K. (2003). Buddhism, hospice, and the American way of dying. *Review of Religious Research, 44,* 341–353.

Garcia, M. E., Schmitz, J. M., & Doerfler, L. A. (1990). A fine-grained analysis of the role of self-efficacy in self-initiated attempts to quit smoking. *Journal of Consulting and Clinical Psychology, 58,* 317–322.

Garcia-Coll, C., Kagan, J., & Reznick, J. S. (1984). Behavioral inhibition in young children. *Child Development, 55,* 1005–1009.

Garden, A. M. (1991). The purpose of burnout: A Jungian interpretation. *Journal of Social Behavior and Personality, 6,* 73–93.

Garland, D. J., & Barry, J. R. (1990). Personality and leader behaviors in collegiate football: A multidimensional approach to performance. *Journal of Research in Personality, 24,* 355–370.

Garnier, H. E., & Stein, J. A. (1998). Values and the family: Risk and protective factors for adolescent problem behaviors. *Youth and Society, 30,* 89–120.

Garrett, K. R. (1985). Elbow room in a functional analysis: Freedom and dignity regained. *Behaviorism, 13,* 21–36.

Garrow, D. J. (1986). *Bearing the cross: Martin Luther King, Jr., and the Southern Christian Leadership Conference.* New York: Vintage Books.

Gaskins, R. W. (1999). "Adding legs to a snake": A reanalysis of motivation and the pursuit of happiness from a Zen Buddhist perspective. *Journal of Educational Psychology, 91,* 204–215.

Gattuso, S., & Saw, C. (1998). Humanistic education in gerontology—a case study using narrative. *Educational Gerontology, 24,* 279–285.

Gedo, P. M. (1999). Single case studies in psychotherapy research. *Psychoanalytic Psychology, 16,* 274–280.

Geen, R. G. (1997). Psychophysiological approaches to personality. In R. Hogan, J. Johnson, & S. Briggs (Eds.), *Handbook of personality psychology* (pp. 387–414). San Diego, CA: Academic Press.

Geher, G. (2000). Perceived and actual characteristics of parents and partners: A test of a Freudian model of mate selection. *Current Psychology, 19*(3), 194–214.

Geller, L. (1982). The failure of self-actualization theory: A critique of Carl Rogers and Abraham Maslow. *Journal of Humanistic Psychology, 22*(2), 56–73.

Genia, V. (1993). A psychometric evaluation of the Allport-Ross I/E Scales in a religiously heterogeneous sample. *Journal for the Scientific Study of Religion, 32,* 284–290.

Genoni, T., Jr. (1994). American Psychological Association statement addresses the debate over assisted memory. *Skeptical Inquirer, 18,* 342–343.

George, J. M., & Zhou, J. (2001). When openness to experience and conscientiousness are related to creative behavior: An interactional approach. *Journal of Applied Psychology, 86,* 513–524.

Geppert, U., & Halisch, F. (2001). Genetic vs. environmental determinants of traits, motives, self-referential cognitions, and volitional control in old age: First results from the Munich Twin Study (GOLD). In A. Efklides, J. Kuhl, & R. M. Sorrentino (Eds.), *Trends and prospects in motivation research* (pp. 359–387). New York: Kluwer Academic.

Ghorbani, N., Watson, P. J., & Mirhasani, V. S. (2007). Religious commitment in Iran: Correlates and factors of Quest and Extrinsic Religious Orientations. *Archive for the Study of Religion, 29,* 245–257.

Ghorpade, J., Lackritz, J. R., & Singh, G. (2006). Intrinsic religious orientation among minorities in the United States: A research note. *International Journal for the Psychology of Religion, 16,* 51–62.

Ghose, L. (2004). A study in Buddhist psychology: Is Buddhism truly pro-detachment and anti-attachment? *Contemporary Buddhism, 5,* 105–120.

Giese-Davis, J., & Spiegel, D. (2001). Suppression, repressive-defensiveness, restraint, and distress in metastatic breast cancer: Separable or inseparable constructs? *Journal of Personality, 69,* 417–449.

Gigerenzer, G. (1991). From tools to theories: A heuristic of discovery in cognitive psychology. *Psychological Review, 98,* 254–267.

Gilligan, C. (1982). *In a different voice.* Cambridge, MA: Harvard University Press.

Gilman, R., & Huebner, S. (2003). A review of life satisfaction research with children and adolescents. *School Psychology Quarterly, 18,* 192–205.

Gilman, S. L. (2001). Karen Horney, M. D., 1885–1952. *American Journal of Psychiatry, 158,* 1205.

Girelli, S. A., & Stake, J. E. (1993). Bipolarity in Jungian type theory and the Myers-Briggs Type Indicator. *Journal of Personality Assessment, 60,* 290–301.

Gladwell, M. (2008). *Outliers: The story of success.* New York: Little, Brown, and Company.

Gleaves, D. H., & Hernandez, E. (1999). Recent reformulations of Freud's development and abandonment of his seduction theory: Historical/scientific clarification or a continued assault on truth? *History of Psychology, 2,* 324–354.

Gleser, G. C., & Ihilevich, D. (1969). An objective instrument for measuring defense mechanisms. *Journal of Consulting and Clinical Psychology, 33,* 51–60.

Glucksman, M. L. (2000). Affect dysregulation: Defense or deficit? *Journal of the American Academy of Psychoanalysis, 28,* 263–273.

Goebel, B. L., & Boeck, B. E. (1987). Ego integrity and fear of death: A comparison of institutionalized and independently living older adults. *Death Studies, 11,* 193–204.

Goertzel, M. G., Goertzel, V., & Goertzel, T. G. (1978). *Three hundred eminent personalities.* San Francisco, CA: Jossey-Bass.

Gold, I., & Stoljar, D. (1999). A neuron doctrine in the philosophy of neuroscience. *Behavioral and Brain Sciences, 22,* 809–830.

Goldberg, L. R. (1981). Language and individual differences: The search for universals in personality lexicons. In L. Wheeler (Ed.), *Review of personality and social psychology* (Vol. 2, pp. 141–165). Beverly Hills, CA: Sage.

Goldberg, L. R. (1982). From Ace to Zombie: Some explorations in the language of personality. In C. D. Spielberger & J. N. Butcher (Eds.), *Advances in personality assessment* (Vol. 1, pp. 203–234). Hillsdale, NJ: Erlbaum.

Goldberg, L. R. (1992). The development of markers for the big five factor structure. *Psychological Assessment, 4,* 26–42.

Goldfried, M. R. (2007). What has psychotherapy inherited from Carl Rogers? *Psychotherapy: Theory, Research, Practice, Training, 44,* 249–252.

Goldfried, M. R., Greenberg, L. S., & Marmar, C. (1990). Individual psychotherapy: Process and outcome. *Annual Review of Psychology, 41,* 659–688.

Goldman, L. (1996). Mind, character, and the deferral of gratification. *Educational Forum, 60,* 135–140.

Goldsmith, J. Z., Mosher, J. K., Stiles, W. B., & Greenberg, L. S. (2008). Speaking with the client's voices: How a person-centered therapist used reflections to facilitate assimilation. *Person-Centered and Experiential Psychotherapies, 7,* 155–172.

Goldwert, M. (1986). Childhood seduction and the spiritualization of psychology: The case of Jung and Rank. *Child Abuse and Neglect, 10,* 555–557.

Goleman, D. (2004). *Destructive emotions: A scientific dialogue with the Dalai Lama.* Westminster, MD: Bantam Books.

Gomez, A., & Gomez, R. (2002). Personality traits of the behavioural approach and inhibition systems: Associations with processing of emotional stimuli. *Personality and Individual Differences, 32,* 1299–1316.

Gonçalves, M. M., Matos, M., & Santos, A. (2009). Narrative therapy and the nature of "innovative moments" in the construction of change. *Journal of Constructivist Psychology, 22,* 1–23.

Gondola, J. C., & Tuckman, B. W. (1985). Effects of a systematic program of exercise on selected measures of creativity. *Perceptual and Motor Skills, 60,* 53–54.

Goodspeed, R. B., & DeLucia, A. G. (1990). Stress reduction at the worksite: An evaluation of two methods. *American Journal of Health Promotion, 4,* 333–337.

Goodstein, L. (2003, September 18). Dalai Lama says terror may need a violent reply. *New York Times,* p. A18.

Goodwin, R. D., Cox, B. J., & Clara, I. (2006). Neuroticism and physical disorders among adults in the community: Results from the National Comorbidity Survey. *Journal of Behavioral Medicine, 29,* 229–238.

Goossens, L. (2001). Global versus domain-specific statuses in identity research: A comparison of two self-report measures. *Journal of Adolescence, 24,* 681–699.

Gordon, C. R., Ben-Aryeh, H., Spitzer, O., Doweck, I., Gonen, A., Melamed, Y., & Shupak, A. (1994). Seasickness susceptibility, personality factors, and salivation. *Aviation, Space, and Environmental Medicine, 65,* 610–614.

Gorsuch, R. L., & McPherson, S. E. (1989). Intrinsic/extrinsic measurement: I/E-revised and single-item scales. *Journal for the Scientific Study of Religion, 28,* 348–354.

Gosling, S. D., John, O. P., Robins, R. W., & Craik, K. H. (1998). Do people know how they behave? Self-reported act frequencies compared with on-line codings by observers. *Journal of Personality and Social Psychology, 74,* 1337–1349.

Gould, D., Hodge, K., Peterson, K., & Giannini, J. (1989). An exploratory examination of strategies used by elite coaches to enhance self-efficacy in athletes. *Journal of Sport and Exercise Psychology, 11,* 128–140.

Gramzow, R. H., Sedikides, C., Panter, A. T., Sathy, V., Harris, J., & Insko, C. A. (2004). Patterns of self-regulation and the Big Five. *European Journal of Personality, 18,* 367–385.

Grand, S., & Alpert, J. L. (1993). The core trauma of incest: An object relations view. *Professional Psychology: Research and Practice, 24,* 330–334.

Grant, A, M., Curtayne, L., & Burton, G. (2009). Executive coaching enhances goal attainment, resilience and workplace well-being: A randomized controlled study. *Journal of Positive Psychology, 4,* 396–407.

Gray, J. (1999). Ivan Petrovich Pavlov and the conditioned reflex. *Brain Research Bulletin, 50,* 433.

Gray, J. A. (1987). *The psychology of fear and stress.* Cambridge, UK: Cambridge University Press.

Graziano, W. G., Jensen-Campbell, L. A., & Hair, E. C. (1996). Perceiving interpersonal conflict and reacting to it: The case for agreeableness. *Journal of Personality and Social Psychology, 70,* 820–835.

Greasley, P. (2000). Handwriting analysis and personality assessment: The creative use of analogy, symbolism, and metaphor. *European Psychologist, 5,* 44–51.

Greenberg, J. R. (1986). Theoretical models and the analyst's neutrality. *Contemporary Psychoanalysis, 22,* 89–106. (Reprinted, with Editors' Introduction and Afterword, in S. A. Mitchell & L. Aron (1999). *Relational psychoanalysis: The emergence of a tradition* (pp. 131–152). Hillsdale, NJ: Analytical Press.)

Greenberg, J., & Mitchell, S. (1983). *Object relations in psychoanalytic theory.* Cambridge, MA: Harvard University Press.

Greenberg, R. P., & Fisher, S. (1978, September). Testing Dr. Freud. *Human Behavior,* pp. 28–33.

Greenwald, A. G. (1992). New look 3: Unconscious cognition reclaimed. *American Psychologist, 47,* 766–779.

Greever, K. B., Tseng, M. S., & Friedland, B. U. (1973). Development of the Social Interest Index. *Journal of Consulting and Clinical Psychology, 41,* 454–458.

Gregory, A. M., Caspi, A., Moffitt, T. E., Milne, B. J., Poulton, R., & Sears, M. R. (2009). Links between anxiety and allergies: Psychobiological reality or possible methodological bias? *Journal of Personality, 77,* 348–361.

Gregory, T., Nettlebeck, T., & Wilson, C. (2010). Openness to experience, intelligence, and successful ageing. *Personality and Individual Differences, 48,* 895–899.

Greitemeyer, T., Osswald, S., Fischer, P., & Frey, D. (2007). Civil courage: Implicit theories, related concepts, and measurement. *Journal of Positive Psychology, 2,* 115–119.

Grey, W. (1994). Philosophy and the paranormal. Part 1: The problem of "psi." *Skeptical Inquirer, 18,* 142–149.

Gross, J. J. (1999). Emotion and emotion regulation. In L. A. Pervin & O. P. John (Eds.), *Handbook of personality: Theory and research* (2nd ed., pp. 525–552). New York: Guilford.

Gross, J. J., & Levenson, R. W. (1993). Emotional suppression: Physiology, self-report, and expressive behavior. *Journal of Personality and Social Psychology, 64,* 970–986.

Gross, J. J., & Levenson, R. W. (1997). Hiding feelings: The acute effects of inhibiting negative and positive emotion. *Journal of Abnormal Psychology, 106,* 95–103.

Grossman, P., Niemann, L., Schmidt, S., & Walach, H. (2004). Mindfulness-based stress reduction and health benefits: A meta-analysis. *Journal of Psychosomatic Research, 57,* 35–43.

Grotstein J. S. (1993). A reappraisal of W. R. D. Fairbairn. *Bulletin of the Menninger Clinic, 57,* 421–450.

Grove, W. M., & Meehl, P. E. (1996). Comparative efficiency of informal (subjective, impressionistic) and formal (mechanical, algorithmic) prediction procedures: The clinical-statistical controversy. *Psychology, Public Policy, and Law, 2,* 293–323.

Gruber, H. E. (1989). The evolving systems approach to creative work. In D. B. Wallace & H. E. Gruber (Eds.), *Creative people at work: Twelve cognitive case studies* (pp. 3–43). New York: Oxford University Press.

Gruen, A. (1998). Reductionistic biological thinking and the denial of experience and pain in developmental theories. *Journal of Humanistic Psychology, 38*(2), 84–102.

Grünbaum, A. (2008). Popper's fundamental misdiagnosis of the scientific defects of Freudian psychoanalysis and of their bearing on the theory of demarcation. *Psychoanalytic Psychology, 25,* 574–589.

Grusec, J., & Mischel, W. (1966). Model's characteristics as determinants of social learning. *Journal of Personality and Social Psychology, 4,* 211–215.

Guastello, D. D., & Guastello, S. J. (2002, June). Birth category effects on the Gordon Personal Profile variables. *Journal of Articles in Support of the Null Hypothesis, 1*(1) [Electronic journal]. Retrieved June 28, 2002, from http://www.jasnh.com/a1.htm

Gundrum, M., Lietaer, G., & Van Hees-Matthijssen, C. (1999). Carl Rogers' responses in the 17th session with Miss Mun: Comments from a process-experiential and psychoanalytic perspective. *British Journal of Guidance and Counselling, 27,* 461–482.

Gustafson, R. (1986). Alcohol, frustration, and aggression: An experiment using the balanced placebo design. *Psychological Reports, 59,* 207–218.

Guydish, J., Jackson, T. T., Markley, R. P., & Zelhart, P. F. (1985). George A. Kelly: Pioneer in rural school psychology. *Journal of School Psychology, 23,* 297–304.

Haaken, J. (1993). From Al-Anon to ACOA: Codependence and the reconstruction of caregiving. *Signs, 18,* 321–345.

Hagemann, D., Hewig, J., Walter, C., Schankin, A., Danner, D., & Naumann, E. (2009). Positive evidence for Eysenck's arousal hypothesis: A combined EEG and MRI study with multiple measurement occasions. *Personality and Individual Differences, 47,* 717–721.

Haidt, J., & Rodin, J. (1999). Control and efficacy as interdisciplinary bridges. *Review of General Psychology, 3,* 317–337.

Halisch, F., & Geppert, U. (2001). Motives, personal goals, and life satisfaction in old age: First results from the Munich Twin Study (GOLD). In A. Efklides, J. Kuhl, & R. M. Sorrentino (Eds.), *Trends and prospects in motivation research* (pp. 389–409). New York: Kluwer Academic.

Hall, C. S. (1966). *The meaning of dreams.* New York: McGraw-Hill.

Hall, C. S., & Nordby, V. J. (1973). *A primer of Jungian psychology.* New York: Mentor Books.

Hall, S. S. (2003, September 14). Is Buddhism good for your health? *New York Times Magazine,* p. 46.

Halpern, D. F. (1997). Sex differences in intelligence: Implications for education. *American Psychologist, 10,* 1091–1102.

Hamilton, W. D. (1964). The genetical evolution of social behavior: I and II. *Journal of Theoretical Biology, 7,* 1–52.

Hammack, P. L. (2010). The political psychology of personal narrative: The case of Barack Obama. *Analyses of Social Issues and Public Policy, 10,* 182–206.

Hampson, S. E. (1998). When is an inconsistency not an inconsistency? Trait reconciliation in personality description and impression formation. *Journal of Personality and Social Psychology, 74,* 102–117.

Han, J. J., Leichtman, M. D., & Wang, Q. (1998). Autobiographical memory in Korean, Chinese, and American children. *Developmental Psychology, 34,* 701–713.

Hankoff, L. D. (1987). The earliest memories of criminals. *International Journal of Offender Therapy and Comparative Criminology, 31,* 195–201.

Hanlon, R. P., Jr. (2000). The use of typology in financial planning. *Journal of Financial Planning, 13*(7), 96–112.

Hanna, F. J. (1996). Community feeling, empathy, and intersubjectivity: A phenomenological framework. *Individual Psychology, 52,* 22–30.

Hardaway, R. A. (1990). Subliminally activated symbiotic fantasies: Facts and artifacts. *Psychological Bulletin, 107,* 177–195.

Harmon-Jones, E., & Allen, J. J. B. (1997). Behavioral activation sensitivity and resting frontal EEG asymmetry: Covariation of putative indicators related to risk for mood disorders. *Journal of Abnormal Psychology, 106,* 159–163.

Harmon-Jones, E., & Allen, J. J. B. (1998). Anger and frontal brain activity: EEG asymmetry consistent with approach motivation despite negative affective valence. *Journal of Personality and Social Psychology, 74,* 1310–1316.

Harrell, W. J., Jr. (2010). "The reality of American life has strayed from its myths": Barack Obama's *The Audacity of Hope* and the discourse of the American reclamation jeremiad. *Journal of Black Studies, 41,* 164–183.

Harren, V. A., Kass, R. A., Tinsley, H. E. A., & Moreland, J. R. (1979). Influence of gender, sex-role attitudes, and cognitive complexity on gender-dominant career choices. *Journal of Counseling Psychology, 26,* 227–234.

Harrington, D. M. (1993). Child-rearing antecedents of suboptimal personality development: Exploring aspects of Alice Miller's concept of the *poisonous pedagogy.* In D. C. Funder, R. D. Parke, C. Tomlinson-Keasey, & K. Widaman (Eds.), *Studying lives through time: Personality and development* (pp. 289–313). Washington, DC: American Psychological Association.

Harrington, D. M., Block, J. H., & Block, J. (1987). Testing aspects of Carl Rogers's theory of creative environments: Child-rearing antecedents of creative potential in young adolescents. *Journal of Personality and Social Psychology, 52,* 851–856.

Harrington, R., & Loffredo, D. A. (2001). The relationship between life satisfaction, self-consciousness, and the Myers-Briggs Type Inventory dimensions. *Journal of Psychology, 135,* 439–450.

Harris, C. R. (2002). Sexual and romantic jealousy in heterosexual and homosexual adults. *Psychological Science, 13,* 7–12.

Harris, S. (2004). *The end of faith: Religion, terror, and the future of reason.* New York: Norton.

Hart, D., Keller, M., Edelstein, W., & Hofmann, V. (1998). Childhood personality influences on social-cognitive development: A longitudinal study. *Journal of Personality and Social Psychology, 74,* 1278–1289.

Harter, J. K., Schmidt, F. L., & Keyes, C. L. M. (2003). Well-being in the workplace and its relationship to business outcomes: A review. In C. L. M. Keyes & J. Haidt (Eds.), *Flourishing: Positive psychology and the life well-lived* (pp. 205–224). Washington, DC: American Psychological Association.

Hartmann, E. (1998). Nightmare after trauma as a paradigm for all dreams: A new approach to the nature and functions of dreaming. *Psychiatry: Interpersonal and Biological Processes, 61,* 223–238.

Hartmann, E., Zborowski, M., Rosen, R., & Grace, N. (2001). Contextualizing images in dreams: More intense after abuse and trauma. *Dreaming: Journal of the Association for the Study of Dreams, 11,* 115–126.

Hartmann, H. (1958). *Ego psychology and the problem of adaptation* (D. Rapaport, Trans.). New York: International Universities Press. (Original work published 1939)

Hattie, J., & Cooksey, R. W. (1984). Procedures for assessing the validities of tests using the "known-groups" method. *Applied Psychological Measurement, 8,* 295–305.

Haule, J. R. (2000). Jung's practice of analysis: A Euro-American parallel to Ch'an Buddhism. *Journal of Individual Psychology, 56,* 353–365.

Hayden, J. (1993). The condom race. *Journal of American College Health, 42*(3), 133–136.

Hayden, T., & Mischel, W. (1976). Maintaining trait consistency in the resolution of behavioral inconsistency: The wolf in sheep's clothing? *Journal of Personality, 44,* 109–132.

Hayes, R. P. (2003). Classical Buddhist model of a healthy mind. In K. H. Dockett, G. R. Dudley-Grant, & C. P. Bankart (Eds.), *Psychology and Buddhism: From individual to global community* (pp. 161–170). Secaucus, NJ: Kluwer Academic.

Hays, R. D., & Ellickson, P. L. (1990). How generalizable are adolescents' beliefs about pro-drug pressures and resistance self-efficacy? *Journal of Applied Social Psychology, 20,* 321–340.

Hazan, C., & Shaver, P. (1987). Romantic love conceptualized as an attachment process. *Journal of Personality and Social Psychology, 52,* 511–524.

Hazan, C., & Shaver, P. (1994). Attachment as an organizational framework for research on close relationships. *Psychological Inquiry, 5,* 1–22.

Headey, B., Schupp, J., Tucci, I., & Wagner, G. G. (2010). Authentic happiness theory supported by impact of religion on life satisfaction: A longitudinal analysis with data for Germany. *Journal of Positive Psychology, 5,* 73–82.

Heckhausen, H., & Beckmann, J. (1990). Intentional action and action slips. *Psychological Review, 97,* 36–48.

Heggestad, E. D., & Morrison, M. J. (2008). An inductive exploration of the social effectiveness construct space. *Journal of Personality, 76,* 839–873.

Hegland, S. M., & Galejs, I. (1983). Developmental aspects of locus of control in preschool children. *Journal of Genetic Psychology, 143,* 229–239.

Heine, S. J., & Buchtel, E. E. (2009). Personality: The universal and the culturally specific. *Annual Review of Psychology, 60,* 369–394.

Heiserman, A., & Cook, H. (1998). Narcissism, affect, and gender: An empirical examination of Kernberg's and Kohut's theories of narcissism. *Psychoanalytic Psychology, 15,* 74–92.

Heisig, J. W. (2002). Jung, Christianity, and Buddhism. In S. Muramoto & P. Young-Eisendrath (Eds.), *Awakening and insight: Zen Buddhism and psychotherapy* (pp. 45–66). New York: Brunner-Routledge.

Heller, D., Watson, D., & Ilies, R. (2006). The dynamic process of life satisfaction. *Journal of Personality, 74,* 1421–1450.

Helms, J. E. (1990). *Black and White racial identity: Theory, research, and practice.* Westport, CT: Greenwood Press.

Helson, R., & Picano, J. (1990). Is the traditional role bad for women? *Journal of Personality and Social Psychology, 59,* 311–320.

Helson, R., & Wink, P. (1987). Two conceptions of maturity examined in the findings of a longitudinal study. *Journal of Personality and Social Psychology, 53,* 531–541.

Henning, K., Ey, S., & Shaw, D. (1998). Perfectionism, the imposter phenomenon and psychological adjustment in medical, dental, nursing and pharmacy students. *Medical Education, 32,* 456–464.

Henry, J. (1967). Discussion of Erikson's eight ages of man. In *Current Issues in Psychiatry* (Vol. 2). New York: Science House.

Herek, G. M. (1987). Religious orientation and prejudice: A comparison of racial and sexual attitudes. *Personality and Social Psychology Bulletin, 13,* 34–44.

Hermans, H. J. M. (1987). The dream in the process of valuation: A method of interpretation. *Journal of Personality and Social Psychology, 53,* 163–175.

Hermans, H. J. M. (1988). On the integration of nomothetic and idiographic research methods in the study of personal meaning. *Journal of Personality, 56,* 785–812.

Hermans, H. J. M., & Oles, P. K. (1996). Value crisis: Affective organization of personal meanings. *Journal of Research in Personality, 30,* 457–482.

Herrera, H. (1983). *Frida: A biography of Frida Kahlo.* New York: HarperCollins.

Herrnstein, R. J., Nickerson, R. S., de Sánchez, M., & Swets, J. A. (1986). Teaching thinking skills. *American Psychologist, 41,* 1279–1289.

Herron, R. E., & Cavanaugh, K. L. (2005). Can the Transcendental Meditation program reduce the medical expenditures of older people? A longitudinal cost-reduction study in Canada. *Journal of Social Behavior and Personality, 17,* 415–442.

Hettman, D. W., & Jenkins, E. (1990). Volunteerism and social interest. *Individual Psychology, 46,* 298–303.

Heubeck, B. G., Wilkinson, R. B., & Cologon, J. (1998). A second look at Carver and White's (1994) BIS/BAS scales. *Personality and Individual Differences, 25,* 785–800.

Hewitt, P. L., Flett, G. L., & Ediger, E. (1996). Perfectionism and depression: Longitudinal assessment of a specific vulnerability hypothesis. *Journal of Abnormal Psychology, 105,* 276–280.

Hewitt, P. L., Newton, J., Flett, G. L., & Callander, L. (1997). Perfectionism and suicide ideation in adolescent psychiatric patients. *Journal of Abnormal Child Psychology, 25,* 95–101.

Heyduk, R. G., & Fenigstein, A. (1984). Influential works and authors in psychology: A survey of eminent psychologists. *American Psychologist, 39,* 556–559.

Hicks, J. A., & King, L. A. (2009). Positive mood and social relatedness as information about meaning in life. *Journal of Positive Psychology, 4,* 471–482.

Hicks, L. E. (1985). Is there a disposition to avoid the fundamental attribution error? *Journal of Research in Personality, 19,* 436–456.

Higgins, E. T. (1997). Beyond pleasure and pain. *American Psychologist, 52,* 1280–1300.

Hilgard, E. R. (1976). Neodissociation theory of multiple cognitive control systems. In G. E. Schwartz & D. Shapiro (Eds.), *Consciousness and self-regulation: Advances in research* (Vol. 1, pp. 137–171). New York: Plenum.

Hilgard, E. R. (1994). Neodissociation theory. In S. J. Lynn & J. W. Rhue, *Dissociation: Clinical, theoretical and research perspectives* (pp. 32–51). New York: Guilford.

Hill, C. E., & Corbett, M. M. (1993). A perspective on the history of process and outcome research in counseling psychology. *Journal of Counseling Psychology, 40*, 3–24.

Hills, P., & Argyle, M. (2001). Emotional stability as a major dimension of happiness. *Personality and Individual Differences, 31*, 1357–1364.

Hillstrom, E. (1984). Human personality: Deterministic or merely predictable? *Journal of Psychology and Christianity, 3*, 42–48.

Hobson, J. A. (1988). *The dreaming brain.* New York: Basic Books.

Hobson, J. A., & Leonard, J. (2001). *Out of its mind: Psychiatry in crisis.* Cambridge, MA: Perseus.

Hobson, J. A., & McCarley, R. W. (1977). The brain as a dream state generator: An activation-synthesis hypothesis of the dream process. *American Journal of Psychiatry, 134*, 1335–1348.

Hodapp, V., Heiligtag, U., & Störmer, S. W. (1990). Cardiovascular reactivity, anxiety and anger during perceived controllability. *Biological Psychology, 30*, 161–170.

Hofer, J., Busch, H., Chasiotis, A., Kärtner, J., & Campos, D. (2008). Concern for generativity and its relation to implicit pro-social power motivation, generative goals, and satisfaction with life: A cross-cultural investigation. *Journal of Personality, 76*, 1–30.

Hofer, J., Busch, H., Chasiotis, A., & Kiessling, F. (2006). Motive congruence and interpersonal identity status. *Journal of Personality, 74*, 511–541.

Hoffman, E. (1997). *The drive for self: Alfred Adler and the founding of individual psychology.* Reading, MA: Addison-Wesley.

Hoffman, E. (2009). Rollo May on Maslow and Rogers: "No theory of evil." *Journal of Humanistic Psychology, 49*, 484–485.

Hoffman, E., & Muramoto, S. (2007). Peak-experiences among Japanese youth. *Journal of Humanistic Psychology, 47*, 524–540.

Hoffman, L., Karush, R. K., Garfinkle, M. S., Roose, S. P., & Cherry, S. (2009). A cross-sectional survey of child and adolescent analysts in New York City. *Journal of the American Psychoanalytic Association, 57*, 911–917.

Hoffman, L. W. (1991). The influence of the family environment on personality: Accounting for sibling differences. *Psychological Bulletin, 110*, 187–203.

Hofstetter, C. R., Sallis, J. F., & Hovell, M. F. (1990). Some health dimensions of self-efficacy: Analysis of theoretical specificity. *Social Science and Medicine, 31*, 1051–1056.

Hogan, M. (2010). [Review of the book *Beyond revenge: The evolution of the forgiveness instinct,* by M. McCullough]. *Journal of Positive Psychology, 5*, 97–100.

Hogan, R., Hogan, J., & Roberts, B. W. (1996). Personality measurement and employment decisions: Questions and answers. *American Psychologist, 51*, 469–477.

Holland, J. G. (1992). B. F. Skinner (1904–1990) [obituary]. *American Psychologist, 47*, 665–667.

Holland, J. L. (1996). Exploring careers with a typology: What we have learned and some new directions. *American Psychologist, 51*, 397–406.

Holland, J. M., & Neimeyer, R. A. (2009). The efficacy of personal construct therapy as a function of the type and severity of the presenting problem. *Journal of Constructivist Psychology, 22*, 170–185.

Hollis, J. (2000). *The archetypal imagination.* College Station, TX: Texas A & M University Press.

Hom, H. L., & Knight, H. (1996). Delay of gratification: Mothers' predictions about four attentional techniques. *Journal of Genetic Psychology, 157*, 180–190.

Honos-Webb, L., Harrick, E. A., Stiles, W. B., & Park, C. L. (2000). Assimilation of traumatic experiences and physical-health outcomes: Cautions for the Pennebaker paradigm. *Psychotherapy: Theory, Research, Practice, Training, 37*, 307–314.

Hook, J. N., Worthington, E. L., Jr., Davis, D. E., Jennings, D. J., II, & Gartner, A. L. (2010). Empirically supported religious and spiritual therapies. *Journal of Clinical Psychology, 66*, 46–72.

Hopkins, J. R. (1995). Erik Homburger Erikson (1902–1994) [obituary]. *American Psychologist, 50*, 796–797.

Horley, J. (1991). Values and beliefs as personal constructs. *International Journal of Personal Construct Psychology, 4*, 1–14.

Horn, J. (1984). Genetical underpinnings. *Multivariate Behavioral Research, 19*, 307–309.

Horn, J. (2001). Raymond Bernard Cattell (1905–1998) [obituary]. *American Psychologist, 56*, 71–72.

Horner, A. J. (1994). In search of ordinariness: The dissolution of false pride. *American Journal of Psychoanalysis, 54*, 87–93.

Horner, M. S. (1972). Toward an understanding of achievement-related conflicts in women. *Journal of Social Issues, 28*(2), 157–175.

Horney, K. (1937). *The neurotic personality of our time.* New York: Norton.

Horney, K. (1939). *New ways in psychoanalysis.* New York: Norton.

Horney, K. (1945). *Our inner conflicts: A constructive theory of neurosis.* New York: Norton.

Horney, K. (1950). *Neurosis and human growth: The struggle toward self-realization.* New York: Norton.

Horney, K. (1967a). The flight from womanhood: The masculinity complex in women as viewed by men and by women.

In H. Kelman (Ed.), *Feminine psychology* (pp. 54–70). New York: Norton. (Original work published 1926)

Horney, K. (1967b). On the genesis of the castration complex in women. In H. Kelman (Ed.), *Feminine psychology* (pp. 37–53). New York: Norton. (Original work published 1923)

Horney, K. (1967c). Inhibited femininity: Psychoanalytical contribution to the problem of frigidity. In H. Kelman (Ed.), *Feminine psychology* (pp. 71–83). New York: Norton. (Original work published 1926)

Horney, K. (1967d). The neurotic need for love. In H. Kelman (Ed.), *Feminine psychology* (pp. 245–258). New York: Norton. (Original work published 1937)

Horney, K. (1967e). The problem of feminine masochism. In H. Kelman (Ed.), *Feminine psychology* (pp. 214–233). New York: Norton. (Original work published 1935)

Horsburgh, V. A., Schermer, J. A., Veselka, L., & Vernon, P. A. (2009). A behavioural genetic study of mental toughness and personality. *Personality and Individual Differences, 46,* 100–105.

Horton, R. S., & Sedikides, C. (2009). Narcissistic responding to ego threat: When the status of the evaluator matters. *Journal of Personality, 77,* 1493–1525.

Horwitz, N. M. (2001). Why do people stay in hateful relationships? The concept of malignant vindictiveness. *American Journal of Psychoanalysis, 61,* 143–160.

Houston, B. K., Smith, M. A., & Cates, D. S. (1989). Hostility patterns and cardiovascular reactivity to stress. *Psychophysiology, 26,* 337–342.

Howard, G. S. (1985). The role of values in the science of psychology. *American Psychologist, 40,* 255–265.

Howard, G. S. (1988). Kelly's thought at age 33: Suggestions for conceptual and methodological refinements. *International Journal of Personal Construct Psychology, 1,* 263–272.

Howard, G. S. (1991). Culture tales: A narrative approach to thinking, cross-cultural psychology, and psychotherapy. *American Psychologist, 46,* 187–197.

Howard, J. A., Blumstein, P., & Schwartz, P. (1986). Sex, power, and influence tactics in intimate relationships. *Journal of Personality and Social Psychology, 51,* 102–109.

Howard, S. C. (2011). Manifestations of nommo: Afrocentric analysis of President Barack Obama. *Journal of Black Studies, 42,* 737–750.

Howell, R. H., Owen, P. D., & Nocks, E. C. (1990). Increasing safety belt use: Effects of modeling and trip length. *Journal of Applied Social Psychology, 20,* 254–263.

Howell, R. T., & Hill, G. (2009). The mediators of experiential purchases: Determining the impact of psychological needs satisfaction and social comparison. *Journal of Positive Psychology, 4,* 511–522.

Hoyle, R. H., Fejfar, M. C., & Miller, J. D. (2000). Personality and sexual risk taking: A quantitative review. *Journal of Personality, 68,* 1203–1231.

Hoyle, R. H., & Sherrill, M. R. (2006). Future orientation in the self-system: Possible selves, self-regulation, and behavior. *Journal of Personality, 74,* 1673–1696.

Hoyt, M. F. (1996). Introduction: Some stories are better than others. In M. F. Hoyt (Ed.). *Constructive therapies* (Vol. 2, pp. 1–32). New York: Guilford.

Huber, J. W., & Altmaier, E. M. (1983). An investigation of the self-statement systems of phobic and nonphobic individuals. *Cognitive Therapy and Research, 7,* 355–362.

Hudson, V. M. (1990). Birth order of world leaders: An exploratory analysis of effects on personality and behavior. *Political Psychology, 11,* 583–601.

Hume, D. K., & Montgomerie, R. (2001). Facial attractiveness signals different aspects of "quality" in women and men. *Evolution and Human Behavior, 22,* 93–112.

Huntley, C. W., & Davis, F. (1983). Undergraduate study of value scores as predictors of occupation 25 years later. *Journal of Personality and Social Psychology, 45,* 1148–1155.

Huston, H. L., Rosen, D. H., & Smith, S. M. (1999). Evolutionary memory. In D. Rosen & M. Luebbert (Eds.), *The evolution of the psyche.* Westport, CT: Praeger.

Hutton, P. H. (1983). The psychohistory of Erik Erikson from the perspective of collective mentalities. *Psychohistorical Review, 12,* 18–25.

Hyland, M. E. (1985). Do person variables exist in different ways? *American Psychologist, 40,* 1003–1010.

Iacoboni, M. (2009). Imitation, empathy, and mirror neurons. *Annual Review of Psychology, 60,* 653–670.

Immelman, A. (1993). The assessment of political personality: A psychodiagnostically relevant conceptualization and methodology. *Political Psychology, 14,* 725–741.

Ingram, D. H. (2001). The Hofgeismar lectures: A contemporary overview of Horneyan psychoanalysis. *American Journal of Psychoanalysis, 61,* 113–141.

Integrating Buddhist philosophy with cognitive and behavioral practice [Special series]. (2002). *Cognitive and Behavioral Practice, 9,* 38–78.

Ivancevich, J. M., Matteson, M. T., & Gamble, G. O. (1987). Birth order and the Type A coronary behavior pattern. *Individual Psychology, 43,* 42–49.

Ivey, A. E. (1971). *Microcounseling: Innovations in interviewing training.* Springfield, IL: Thomas.

Izadikhah, Z., Jackson, C. J., & Loxton, N. (2010). An integrative approach to personality: Behavioural Approach System, mastery approach orientation and environmental cues in the prediction of work performance. *Personality and Individual Differences, 48,* 590–595.

Izard, C. E. (1991). *The psychology of emotions.* New York: Plenum Press.

Jackson, T. T., Markley, R. P., Zelhart, P. F., & Guydish, J. (1988). Contributions to the history of psychology: XLV. Attitude research: George A. Kelly's use of polar adjectives. *Psychological Reports, 62,* 47–52.

Jacobo, M. C. (2001). Revolutions in psychoanalytic theory of lesbian development: Dora to dykes and back again. *Psychoanalytic Psychology, 18,* 667–683.

Jacobsen, T., Edelstein, W., & Hofmann, V. (1994). A longitudinal study of the relation between representations of attachment in childhood and cognitive functioning in childhood and adolescence. *Developmental Psychology, 30,* 112–124.

Jaffe, L. S. (1992). The impact of theory on psychological testing: How psychoanalytic theory makes diagnostic testing more enjoyable and rewarding. *Journal of Personality Assessment, 58,* 621–630.

Jakupcak, M., Lisak, D., & Roemer, L. (2002). The role of masculine ideology and masculine gender role stress in men's perpetration of relationship violence. *Psychology of Men and Masculinity, 3,* 97–106.

Jankowicz, A. D. (1987). Whatever became of George Kelly? Applications and implications. *American Psychologist, 42,* 481–487.

Jankowicz, A. D., & Hisrich, R. (1987). Intuition in small-business lending decisions. *Journal of Small Business Management, 25,* 45–52.

Jason, L. A., & Moritsugu, J. (2003). The role of religion and spirituality in community building. In S. Muramoto & P. Young-Eisendrath (Eds.), *Awakening and insight: Zen Buddhism and psychotherapy* (pp. 197–214). New York: Brunner-Routledge.

Jefferson, T., Jr., Herbst, J. H., & McCrae, R. R. (1998). Associations between birth order and personality traits: Evidence from self-reports and observer ratings. *Journal of Research in Personality, 32,* 498–509.

Jenkins, A. H. (1997). The empathic context in psychotherapy with people of color. In A. C. Bohart & L. S. Greenberg (Eds.), *Empathy reconsidered: New directions in psychotherapy* (pp. 321–341). Washington, DC: American Psychological Association.

Jenkins, K. B., & Cos, G. (2010). A time for change and a candidate's voice: Pragmatism and the rhetoric of inclusion in Barack Obama's 2008 presidential campaign. *American Behavioral Scientist, 54*(3), 184–202.

Jensen, J. P., Bergin, A. E., & Greaves, D. W. (1990). The meaning of eclecticism: New survey and analysis of components. *Professional Psychology: Research and Practice, 21,* 124–130.

Jerskey, B. A., Panizzon, M. S., Jacobson, K. C., Neale, M. C., Grant, M. D., Schultz, M., Eisen, S. A., Tsuang, M. T., & Lyons, M. J. (2010). Marriage and divorce: A genetic perspective. *Personality and Individual Differences, 49,* 473–478.

Ji, C. C., & Ibrahim, Y. (2007). Islamic doctrinal orthodoxy and religious orientations: Scale development and validation. *International Journal for the Study of Religion, 17,* 189–208.

Joe, V. C., McGee, S. J., & Dazey, D. (1977). Religiousness and devaluation of a rape victim. *Journal of Clinical Psychology, 33,* 64.

John, O. P. (1990). The "Big Five" factor taxonomy: Dimensions of personality in the natural language and in questionnaires. In L. A. Pervin (Ed.), *Handbook of personality: Theory and research* (pp. 66–100). New York: Guilford.

John, O. P., Angleitner, A., & Ostendorf, F. (1988). The lexical approach to personality: A historical review of trait taxonomic research. *European Journal of Personality, 2,* 171–203.

John, O. P., Naumann, L. P., & Soto, C. J. (2008). Paradigm shift to the integrative Big Five trait taxonomy. In O. P. John, R. W. Robins, & L. A. Pervin (Eds.), *Handbook of personality: Theory and research* (3rd ed., pp. 114–158). New York: Guilford Press.

Johnson, A. M., Vernon, P. A., & Feiler, A. R. (2008). Behavioral genetic studies of personality: An introduction and review of the results of 50+ years of research. In G. J. Boyle, G. Matthews, & D. H. Saklofske (Eds.), *The Sage handbook of personality theory and assessment: Personality theories and models* (Vol. 1, pp. 145–173). Thousand Oaks, CA: Sage.

Johnson, B. T., & Nichols, D. R. (1998). Social psychologists' expertise in the public interest: Civilian morale research during World War II. *Journal of Social Issues, 54,* 53–77.

Johnson, N. B. (1991). Primordial image and the archetypal design of art. *Journal of Analytical Psychology, 36,* 371–392.

Johnson, S. L., Sandrow, D., Meyer, B., Winters, R., Miller, I., Solomon, D., & Keitner, G. (2000). Increases in manic symptoms after life events involving goal attainment. *Journal of Abnormal Psychology, 109,* 721–727.

Johnson, W. (2010). Extending and testing Tom Bouchard's experience producing drive theory. *Personality and Individual Differences, 49,* 296–301.

Jones, D. (1999). Evolutionary psychology. *Annual Review of Anthropology, 28,* 553–575.

Jones, E. E., & Nisbett, R. E. (1972). The actor and the observer: Divergent perceptions of the causes of behavior. In E. E. Jones, D. E. Kanouse, H. H. Kelley, R. E. Nisbett, S. Valins, & B. Weiner (Eds.), *Attribution: Perceiving the causes of behavior.* Morristown, NJ: General Learning Press.

Jones, E. E., & Windholz, M. (1990). The psychoanalytic case study: Toward a method for systematic inquiry. *Journal of the American Psychoanalytic Association, 38,* 985–1015.

Jones, M. M. (1980). Conversion reaction: Anachronism or evolutionary form? A review of the neurologic, behavioral, and psychoanalytic literature. *Psychological Bulletin, 87,* 427–441.

Jones, T. L., & Prinz, R. J. (2005). Potential roles of parental self-efficacy in parent and child adjustment: A review. *Clinical Psychology Review, 25,* 341–363.

Jones, W. H., Couch, L., & Scott, S. (1997). Trust and betrayal: The psychology of getting along and getting ahead. In R. Hogan, J. Johnson, & S. Briggs (Eds.), *Handbook of personality psychology* (pp. 465–482). San Diego, CA: Academic Press.

Joubert, C. E. (1989). Birth order and narcissism. *Psychological Reports, 64,* 721–722.

Joyce, P. R., McHugh, P. C., Light, K. J., Rowe, S., Miller, A. L., & Kennedy, M. A. (2009). Relationships between angry-impulsive personality traits and genetic polymorphisms of the dopamine transporter. *Biological Psychiatry, 66,* 717–721.

Judge, T. A., Higgins, C. A., Thoresen, C. J., & Barrick, M. R. (1999). The big five personality traits, general mental ability, and career success across the life span. *Personnel Psychology, 52,* 621–652.

Judge, T. A., Martocchio, J. J., & Thoresen, C. J. (1997). Five-factor model of personality and employee absence. *Journal of Applied Psychology, 82,* 745–755.

Jung, C. G. (1954). Marriage as a psychological relationship. In C. G. Jung, *The development of personality* (pp. 187–201) (W. McGuire, Ed.; R. F. C. Hull, Trans.). Princeton, NJ: Princeton University Press. (Original work published 1931)

Jung, C. G. (1959). *Aion: Researches into the phenomenology of the self* (2nd ed.) (R. F. C. Hull, Trans.). Princeton, NJ: Princeton University Press.

Jung, C. G. (1960a). *The psychogenesis of mental disease* (R. F. C. Hull, Trans.). Princeton, NJ: Princeton University Press.

Jung, C. G. (1960b). *Synchronicity: An acausal connecting principle* (R. F. C. Hull, Trans.). Princeton, NJ: Princeton University Press.

Jung, C. G. (1961). *Memories, dreams, reflections* (A. Jaffe, Ed.; R. Winston & C. Winston, Trans.). New York: Random House.

Jung, C. G. (1964). *Civilization in transition* (R. F. C. Hull, Trans.). Princeton, NJ: Princeton University Press.

Jung, C. G. (1968a). *Alchemical studies* (R. F. C. Hull, Trans.). Princeton, NJ: Princeton University Press.

Jung, C. G. (1968b). *Psychology and alchemy* (2nd ed.) (R. F. C. Hull, Trans.). Princeton, NJ: Princeton University Press. (Original work published 1944)

Jung, C. G. (1969). *Four archetypes: Mother, rebirth, spirit, trickster* (R. F. C. Hull, Trans.). Princeton, NJ: Princeton University Press.

Jung, C. G. (1970). *Mysterium coniunctionis: An inquiry into the separation and synthesis of psychic opposites in alchemy* (2nd ed.) (R. F. C. Hull, Trans.). Princeton, NJ: Princeton University Press.

Jung, C. G. (1971). *Psychological types* (R. F. C. Hull and H. G. Baynes, Trans.). Princeton, NJ: Princeton University Press.

Jung, C. G. (1973). *Experimental researches* (L. Stein & D. Riviere, Trans.). Princeton, NJ: Princeton University Press.

Jung, C. G. (1974). The practical use of dream-analysis. In C. G. Jung, *Dreams* (pp. 87–109) (W. McGuire, Ed.; R. F. C. Hull, Trans.). Princeton, NJ: Princeton University Press.

Jung, C. G. (1987). The association method: Lecture III. *American Journal of Psychology, 100,* 489–509. (Original work published 1910)

Jung, C. G. (1989). *Analytical psychology: Notes of the seminar given in 1925.* Princeton, NJ: Princeton University Press.

Kagan, J. (1990). Validity is local. *American Psychologist, 45,* 294–295.

Kagan, J. (1994). *Galen's prophecy: Temperament in human nature.* New York: Westview Press.

Kahle, L. R., & Chiagouris, L. (Eds.). (1997). *Values, lifestyles, and psychographics.* Mahwah, NJ: Erlbaum.

Kahn, E. (1996). The intersubjective perspective and the client-centered approach: Are they one at their core? *Psychotherapy, 33,* 30–42.

Kahn, E. (1999). A critique of nondirectivity in the person-centered approach. *Journal of Humanistic Psychology, 39*(4), 94–110.

Kahn, J. (2006, July 2). Last stop, Lhasa: Rail link ties remote Tibet to China. *New York Times.* pp. 1, 8.

Kaliski, E. M., Rubinson, L., Lawrance, L., & Levy, S. R. (1990). AIDS, runaways, and self-efficacy. *Family and Community Health, 13*(1), 65–72.

Kamilar, S. (2002). A Buddhist psychology. In R. P. Olson (Ed.), *Religious theories of personality and psychotherapy: East meets West* (pp. 85–139). New York: Haworth Press.

Kandel, E. R. (1999). Biology and the future of psychoanalysis: A new intellectual framework for psychiatry revisited. *American Journal of Psychiatry, 156,* 505–524.

Kanfer, R., Wanberg, C. R., & Kantrowitz, T. M. (2001). Job search and employment: A personality-motivational analysis and meta-analytic review. *Journal of Applied Psychology, 86,* 837–855.

Kaplan, H. A. (1997). Moral outrage: Virtue as a defense. *Psychoanalytic Review, 84,* 55–71.

Kaplan, S. J., & Schoeneberg, L. A. (1987). Personality theory: The rabbinic and Adlerian paradigm. *Individual Psychology, 43,* 315–318.

Kappe, R., & van der Flier, H. (2010). Using multiple and specific criteria to assess the predictive validity of the Big Five personality factors on academic performance. *Journal of Research in Personality, 44,* 142–145.

Karliner, R., Westrich, E. K., Shedler, J., & Mayman, M. (1996). Bridging the gap between psychodynamic and scientific psychology: The Adelphi Early Memory Index. In J. M. Masling & R. F. Bornstein (Eds.), *Psychoanalytic perspectives on developmental psychology* (Ch. 2, pp. 43–67). Washington, DC: American Psychological Association.

Karney, B. R., & Bradbury, T. N. (1995). The longitudinal course of marital quality and stability: A review of theory, method, and research. *Psychological Bulletin, 118,* 3–34.

Karten, Y. J. G., Olariu, A., & Cameron, H. A. (2005). Stress in early life inhibits neurogenesis in adulthood. *Trends in Neurosciences, 28,* 171–172.

Kasamatsu, A., & Hirai, T. (1973). An electroencephalographic study on the Zen meditation (zazen). *Journal of the American Institute of Hypnosis, 14,* 107–114.

Kaser-Boyd, N. (1993). Rorschachs of women who commit homicide. *Journal of Personality Assessment, 60,* 458–470.

Kast, V. (1996). The clinical use of fairy tales by a "classical" Jungian analyst. *Psychoanalytic Review, 83,* 509–523.

Kavanagh, D. J., Andrade, J., & May, J. (2004). Beating the urge: Implications of research into substance-related desires. *Addictive Behaviors, 29,* 1359–1372.

Keefer, L., & Blanchard, E. B. (2002). A one year follow-up of relaxation response meditation as a treatment for irritable bowel syndrome. *Behaviour Research and Therapy, 40,* 541–546.

Keijsers, G. P. J., Schaap, C. P. D. R., & Hoogduin, C. A. L. (2000). The impact of interpersonal patient and therapist behavior on outcome in cognitive-behavior therapy. *Behavior Modification, 24,* 264–297.

Kelly, A. E., & Nauta, M. M. (1997). Reactance and thought suppression. *Personality and Social Psychology Bulletin, 23,* 1123–1132.

Kelly, B. D. (2008). Buddhist psychology, psychotherapy and the brain: A critical introduction. *Transcultural Psychiatry, 45,* 5–30.

Kelly, G. A. (1955). *The psychology of personal constructs* (Vols. 1 & 2). New York: Norton.

Kelly, G. A. (1958). Man's construction of his alternatives. In G. Lindzey (Ed.), *The assessment of human motives* (pp. 33–64). New York: Holt, Rinehart & Winston.

Kelly, G. A. (1962). Sin and psychotherapy. Temple University Symposium on Psychotherapy, Philadelphia, March 9, 1962. Reprinted in B. Maher (Ed.), *Clinical psychology and personality: The selected papers of George Kelly* (1969, pp. 165–188). New York: Wiley.

Kelly, G. A. (1963a). The autobiography of a theory. Reprinted in B. Maher (Ed.), *Clinical psychology and personality: The selected papers of George Kelly* (1969, pp. 46–65). New York: Wiley.

Kelly, G. A. (1963b). Nonparametric factor analysis of personality theories. *Journal of Individual Psychology, 19,* 115–147. Reprinted in B. Maher (Ed.), *Clinical psychology and personality: The selected papers of George Kelly* (1969, pp. 301–332). New York: Wiley.

Kelly, G. A. (1964). The language of hypotheses: Man's psychological instrument. *Journal of Individual Psychology, 20,* 137–152. Reprinted in B. Maher (Ed.), *Clinical psychology and personality: The selected papers of George Kelly* (1969, pp. 147–162). New York: Wiley.

Kelly, G. A. (1969). Humanistic methodology in psychological research. In B. Maher (Ed.), *Clinical psychology and personality: The selected papers of George Kelly* (pp. 133–146). New York: Wiley.

Kelman, H. C. (1999). The interdependence of Israeli and Palestinian national identities: The role of the other in existential conflicts. *Journal of Social Issues, 55,* 581–600.

Kendler, H. H. (2002). A personal encounter with psychology (1937–2002). *History of Psychology, 5,* 52–84.

Kernberg, P. F. (1994). Mechanisms of defense: Development and research perspectives. *Bulletin of the Menninger Clinic, 58,* 55–87.

Kerr, M., Lambert, W. W., & Bem, D. J. (1996). Life course sequelae of childhood shyness in Sweden: Comparison with the United States. *Developmental Psychology, 32,* 1100–1105.

Keutzer, C. S. (1984). The power of meaning: From quantum mechanics to synchronicity. *Journal of Humanistic Psychology, 24*(1), 80–94.

Kewman, D. G., & Tate, D. G. (1998). Suicide in SCI: A psychological autopsy. *Rehabilitation Psychology, 43,* 143–151.

Khan, Z. H., & Watson, P. J. (2004). Religious orientation and the experience of *Eid-ul-Azha* among Pakistani Muslims. *Journal for the Scientific Study of Religion, 43,* 537–545.

Khan, Z. H., Watson, P. J., & Habib, F. (2005). Muslim attitudes toward religion, religious orientation and empathy among Pakistanis. *Mental Health, Religion, and Culture, 8,* 49–61.

Kihlstrom, J. (1985). Conscious, subconscious, unconscious: A cognitive perspective. In K. S. Bowers & D. Meichenbaum (Eds.), *The unconscious reconsidered* (pp. 149–211). New York: Wiley.

Kihlstrom, J. F. (1987). The cognitive unconscious. *Science, 237,* 1445–1452.

Kihlstrom, J. F. (1990). The psychological unconscious. In L. A. Pervin (Ed.), *Handbook of personality: Theory and research* (pp. 445–464). New York: Guilford.

Kihlstrom, J. F. (1994). Hypnosis, delayed recall, and the principles of memory. *International Journal of Clinical and Experimental Hypnosis, 42,* 337–345.

Kihlstrom, J. F. (1995). The trauma-memory argument. *Consciousness and Cognition, 4,* 65–67.

Kihlstrom, J. F., Barnhardt, T. M., & Tataryn, D. J. (1992). The psychological unconscious: Found, lost, and regained. *American Psychologist, 47,* 788–791.

Killgore, W. D. S. (2000). Academic and research interest in several approaches to psychotherapy: A computerized search of literature in the past 16 years. *Psychological Reports, 87,* 717–720.

Kim, J. E., Nesselroade, J. R., & Featherman, D. L. (1996). The state component in self-reported worldviews and religious beliefs of older adults: The MacArthur successful aging studies. *Psychology and Aging, 11,* 396–407.

Kimble, G. A. (1984). Psychology's two cultures. *American Psychologist, 39,* 833–839.

Kimble, G. A. (1994). A new formula for behaviorism. *Psychological Review, 101,* 254–258.

Kim-Prieto, C., & Diener, E. (2009). Religion as a source of variation in the experience of positive and negative emotions. *Journal of Positive Psychology, 4,* 447–460.

King, L. A., & Hicks, J. A. (2009). Detecting and construing meaning in life events. *Journal of Positive Psychology, 4,* 317–330.

King, L. A., & Napa, C. K. (1998). What makes a good life? *Journal of Personality and Social Psychology, 75,* 156–165.

King, L. A., Walker, L. M., & Broyles, S. J. (1996). Creativity and the five-factor model. *Journal of Research in Personality, 30,* 189–203.

King, M. L., Jr. (1968). The role of the behavioral scientist in the civil rights movement. *American Psychologist, 23,* 180–186.

King, N. (1987). *Everybody loves Oprah! Her remarkable life story.* New York: William Morrow and Company.

Kirmayer, L. J. (1992). From the witches' hammer to the Oedipus complex: Castration anxiety in Western society. *Transcultural Psychiatric Research Review, 29,* 133–158.

Kirsch, I., & Lynn, S. J. (1995). The altered state of hypnosis: Changes in the theoretical landscape. *American Psychologist, 50,* 846–858.

Kirsch, I., & Lynn, S. J. (1998). Dissociation theories of hypnosis. *Psychological Bulletin, 123,* 100–115.

Kirsch, I., Montgomery, G., & Sapirstein, G. (1995). Hypnosis as an adjunct to cognitive behavioral psychotherapy: A meta-analysis. *Journal of Consulting and Clinical Psychology, 63,* 214–220.

Kirschenbaum, D. S. (1985). Proximity and specificity of planning: A position paper. *Cognitive Therapy and Research, 9,* 489–506.

Kirsner, D. (2007). "Do as I say, not as I do": Ralph Greenson, Anna Freud, and superrich patients. *Psychoanalytic Psychology, 24,* 475–486.

Klayman, J., & Ha, Y. (1987). Confirmation, disconfirmation, and information in hypothesis testing. *Psychological Review, 94,* 211–228.

Klein, M. (1946). Notes on some schizoid mechanisms. In M. Klein, P. Heimann, S. Isaacs, & J. Riviere (Eds.), *Developments in psychoanalysis.* London: Hogarth Press.

Klein, S. (2006). (S. Lehmann, Trans.). *The science of happiness: How our brains make us happy—and what we can do to get happier.* New York: Marlowe & Company.

Klimstra, T. A., Crocetti, E., Hale, W. W., Kolman, A. I. M., Fortanier, E., & Meeus, W. H. J. (2011). Identity formation in juvenile delinquents and clinically referred youth. *European Review of Applied Psychology, 61*(3), 123–130.

Klohnen, E. C., & Bera, S. (1998). Behavioral and experiential patterns of avoidantly and securely attached women across adulthood: A 31-year perspective. *Journal of Personality and Social Psychology, 74,* 211–223.

Kluckhohn, C., & Murray, H. A. (1953). Personality formation: The determinants. In C. Kluckhohn, H. Murray, & D. Schneider (Eds.), *Personality in nature, society and culture* (pp. 53–67). New York: Knopf.

Knafo, D. (2009). Freud's memory erased. *Psychoanalytic Psychology, 26,* 171–190.

Knierim, T. (n.d.). Introduction to Buddhism. Available online at http://thebigview.com/download/buddhism.pdf

Knight, J. (2004, December 9). Buddhism on the brain. *Nature, 432,* 670.

Knight, K., Elfenbein, M. H., Capozzi, L., Eason, H. A., & Bernardo, M. F. (2000). Relationship of connected and separate knowing to parental style and birth order. *Sex Roles, 43,* 229–240.

Knight, Z. G. (2005). The use of the "corrective emotional experience" and the search for the bad object in psychotherapy. *American Journal of Psychotherapy, 59,* 30–41.

Koch, S. (1981). The nature and limits of psychological knowledge: Lessons of a century qua "science." *American Psychologist, 36,* 257–269.

Kohlmetz, C., Kopiez, R., & Altenmüller, E. (2003). Stability of motor programs during a state of meditation: Electrocortical activity in a pianist playing "Vexations" by Erik Satie continuously for 28 hours. *Psychology of Music, 31,* 173–186.

Kohut, H. (1984). *How does analysis cure?* Chicago, IL: University of Chicago Press.

Konik, J., & Stewart, A. (2004). Sexual identity development in the context of compulsory heterosexuality. *Journal of Personality, 72,* 815–844.

Koran, J. J., & Camp, B. D. (1998). On the effects of modeling. *Curator, 41*(4), 10–12.

Kores, R. C., Murphy, W. D., Rosenthal, T. L., Elias, D. B., & North, W. C. (1990). Predicting outcome of chronic pain treatment via a modified self-efficacy scale. *Behaviour Research and Therapy, 28,* 165–169.

Kraemer, G. W. (1992). A psychobiological theory of attachment. *Behavioral and Brain Sciences, 15,* 493–541.

Kraft, T. (1992). Counteracting pain in malignant disease by hypnotic techniques: Five case studies. *Contemporary Hypnosis, 9,* 123–129.

Kratochwill, T. R., & Martens, B. K. (1994). Applied behavior analysis and school psychology. *Journal of Applied Behavior Analysis, 27,* 3–5.

Kris, E. (1964). *Psychoanalytic explorations in art.* New York: Shocken. (Original work published 1952)

Kroger, J., Martinussen, M., & Marcia, J. E. (2010). Identity status change during adolescence and young adulthood: A meta-analysis. *Journal of Adolescence, 33,* 683–698.

Krosnick, J. A., Betz, A. L., Jussim, L. J., & Lynn, A. R. (1992). Subliminal conditioning of attitudes. *Personality and Social Psychology Bulletin, 18,* 152–162.

Krueger, R. F., & Walton, K. E. (2008). Introduction to the special issue. *Journal of Personality, 76,* 1347–1354.

Kuhn, T. S. (1970). *The structure of scientific revolutions* (2nd ed.). Chicago, IL: University of Chicago Press.

Kull, S. (1983). Nuclear arms and the desire for world destruction. *Political Psychology, 4,* 563–591.

Kupfersmid, J. (1992). The "defense" of Sigmund Freud. *Psychotherapy, 29,* 297–309.

Kurdek, L. A. (1997). The link between facets of neuroticism and dimensions of relationship commitment: Evidence from gay, lesbian, and heterosexual couples. *Journal of Family Psychology, 11,* 503–514.

Kwan, V. S. Y., Bond, M. H., & Singelis, T. M. (1997). Pancultural explanations for life satisfaction: Adding relationship harmony to self-esteem. *Journal of Personality and Social Psychology, 73,* 1038–1051.

Lacks, R. (1980). *Women and Judaism: Myth, history, and struggle.* Garden City, NY: Doubleday.

LaFromboise, T., Coleman, H. L. K., & Gerton, J. (1993). Psychological impact of biculturalism: Evidence and theory. *Psychological Bulletin, 114,* 395–412.

Lambert, N. M., Graham, S. M., Fincham, F. D., & Stillman, T. F. (2009). A changed perspective: How gratitude can affect sense of coherence through positive reframing. *Journal of Positive Psychology, 4,* 461–470.

Lamborn, S. D., Mounts, N. S., Steinberg, L., & Dornbusch, S. (1991). Patterns of competence and adjustment among adolescents from authoritative, authoritarian, indulgent, and neglectful families. *Child Development, 62,* 1049–1065.

Lamiell, J. T. (1997). Individuals and the differences between them. In R. Hogan, J. Johnson, & S. Briggs (Eds.), *Handbook of personality psychology* (pp. 117–141). San Diego, CA: Academic Press.

LaMothe, R., Arnold, J., & Crane, J. (1998). The penumbra of religious discourse. *Psychoanalytic Psychology, 15,* 63–73.

Lancaster, B. L. (1997). On the stages of perception: Towards a synthesis of cognitive neuroscience and the Buddhist abhidhamma tradition. *Journal of Consciousness Studies, 4,* 122–142.

Landfield, A. W. (1982). A construction of fragmentation and unity: The fragmentation corollary. In J. C. Mancuso & J. R. Adams-Webber (Eds.), *The construing person* (pp. 170–197). New York: Praeger.

Landfield, A. W. (1988). Personal science and the concept of validation. *International Journal of Personal Construct Psychology, 1,* 237–249.

Landfield, A. W., & Epting, F. R. (1987). *Personal construct psychology: Clinical and personality assessment.* New York: Human Sciences Press.

Lang, P. J. (1994). The varieties of emotional experience: A meditation on James-Lange theory. *Psychological Review, 101,* 211–221.

Langer, W. (1972). *The mind of Adolph Hitler: The secret wartime report.* New York: Basic Books.

Lang-Takac, E., & Osterweil, Z. (1992). Separateness and connectedness: Differences between the genders. *Sex Roles, 27,* 277–289.

Larsson, H., Viding, E., & Plomin, R. (2008). Callous–unemotional traits and antisocial behavior: Genetic, environmental, and early parenting characteristics. *Criminal Justice and Behavior, 35,* 197–211.

Las Heras, A. (1992). Psychosociology of Jung's parapsychological ability. *Journal of the Society for Psychical Research, 58,* 189–193.

Lasko, J. K. (1954). Parent behavior toward first and second children. *Genetic Psychology Monographs, 49,* 97–137.

Laungani, P. (1997). Replacing client-centred counselling with culture-centred counselling. *Counselling Psychology Quarterly, 10,* 343–351.

Lavy, S., Mikulincer, M., & Shaver, P. R. (2010). Autonomy-proximity imbalance: An attachment theory perspective on intrusiveness in romantic relationships. *Personality and Individual Differences, 48,* 552–556.

Lawrence, L. (1988). The covert seduction theory: Filling the gap between the seduction theory and the Oedipus complex. *American Journal of Psychoanalysis, 48,* 247–250.

Lax, R. F. (1995). Freud's views and the changing perspective on femaleness and femininity: What my female analysands taught me. *Psychoanalytic Psychology, 12,* 393–406.

Lax, R. F. (1997). Father's seduction of daughter entices her into the Oedipal phase: Mother's role in the formation of the girl's superego. *Psychoanalytic Psychology, 24,* 306–316.

Lay, C. H., Knish, S., & Zanatta, R. (1992). Self-handicappers and procrastinators: A comparison of their practice behavior prior to an evaluation. *Journal of Research in Personality, 26,* 242–257.

Lazar, S. W., Kerr, C. E., Wasserman, R. H., Gray, J. R., Greve, D. N., Treatway, M. T., McGarvey, M., Quinn, B. T., Dusek, J. A., Benson, H., Rauch, S. L., Moore, C. I., & Fischl, B. (2005). Meditation experience is associated with increased cortical thickness. *NeuroReport, 16,* 1893–1897.

Lazarsfeld, S. (1991). The courage for imperfection. *Individual Psychology, 47,* 93–96.

Lazarus, A. A. (1989). Why I am an eclectic (not an integrationist). *British Journal of Guidance and Counselling, 17,* 248–258.

Leach, C., Freshwater, K., Aldridge, J., & Sutherland, J. (2001). Analysis of repertory grids in clinical practice. *British Journal of Clinical Psychology, 40,* 225–248.

Leak, G. K., & Fish, S. (1989). Religious orientation, impression management, and self-deception: Toward a clarification of the link between religiosity and social desirability. *Journal for the Scientific Study of Religion, 28,* 355–359.

Leak, G. K., & Gardner, L. E. (1990). Sexual attitudes, love attitudes, and social interest. *Individual Psychology, 46,* 55–60.

Leak, G. K., Gardner, L. E., & Pounds, B. (1992). A comparison of Eastern religion, Christianity, and social interest. *Individual Psychology, 48,* 53–64.

Leak, G. K., Millard, R. J., Perry, N. W., & Williams, D. E. (1985). An investigation of the nomological network of social interest. *Journal of Research in Personality, 19,* 197–207.

Leak, G. K., & Williams, D. E. (1989). Relationship between social interest, alienation, and psychological hardiness. *Individual Psychology, 45,* 369–375.

LeDoux, J. (2002). *Synaptic self: How our brains become who we are.* New York: Viking.

Lee, D. Y., & Uhlemann, M. R. (1984). Comparison of verbal responses of Rogers, Shostrom, and Lazarus. *Journal of Counseling Psychology, 31,* 91–94.

Lee, K., & Ashton, M. C. (2008). The HEXACO personality factors in the indigenous personality lexicons of English and 11 other languages. *Journal of Personality, 76,* 1001–1053.

Lefebure, L. D. (2005). The contribution of H. H. the XIVth Dalai Lama to interfaith education. *Cross Currents, 55,* 83–89.

Leitner, L. M., & Cado, S. (1982). Personal constructs and homosexual stress. *Journal of Personality and Social Psychology, 43,* 869–872.

Leitner, L. M., & Guthrie, A. J. (1993). Validation of therapist interventions in psychotherapy: Clarity, ambiguity, and subjectivity. *International Journal of Personal Construct Psychology, 6,* 281–294.

Leitner, L. M., & Pfenninger, D. T. (1994). Sociality and optimal functioning. *Journal of Constructivist Psychology, 7,* 119–135.

Lemire, D. (1998). Individual psychology and innovation: The de-Freuding of creativity. *Journal of Individual Psychology, 54,* 108–118.

Lennings, C. J. (1996). Adolescent aggression and imagery: Contributions from object relations and social cognitive theory. *Adolescence, 31,* 831–840.

Lent, R. W., & Hackett, G. (1987). Career self-efficacy: Empirical status and future directions. *Journal of Vocational Behavior, 30,* 347–382.

Levant, R. F. (1996). The new psychology of men. *Professional Psychology: Research and Practice, 27,* 259–265.

LeVay, S. (1991). A difference in hypothalamic structure between heterosexual and homosexual men. *Science, 253,* 1034–1037.

Levey, J. (1986). Richard Nixon as elder statesman. *Journal of Psychohistory, 13,* 427–448.

Lewes, L. (1998). A special Oedipal mechanism in the development of male homosexuality. *Psychoanalytic Psychology, 15,* 341–359.

Lewis, C. A. (1993). Oral pessimism and depressive symptoms. *Journal of Psychology, 127,* 335–343.

Lewis, W. A., & Bucher, A. M. (1992). Anger, catharsis, the reformulated frustration-aggression hypothesis, and health consequences. *Psychotherapy, 29,* 385–392.

Lilienfeld, S. O. (2010). Can psychology become a science? *Personality and Individual Differences, 49,* 281–288.

Lindsay, D. S., & Read, J. D. (1995). "Memory work" and recovered memories of childhood sexual abuse: Scientific evidence and public, professional, and personal issues. *Psychology, Public Policy, and Law, 1,* 846–908.

Linley, P. A., Maltby, J., Wood, A. M., Osborne, G., & Hurling, R. (2009). Measuring happiness: The higher order factor structure of subjective and psychological well-being measures. *Personality and Individual Differences, 47,* 878–884.

Linville, P. W. (1985). Self-complexity and affective extremity: Don't put all of your eggs in one cognitive basket. *Social Cognition, 3,* 94–120.

Lisle, L. (1980). *Portrait of an artist: A biography of Georgia O'Keeffe.* New York: Seaview.

Litt, M. D. (1988). Cognitive mediators of stressful experience: Self-efficacy and perceived control. *Cognitive Therapy and Research, 12,* 241–260.

Livesley, W. J., & Jang, K. L. (2008). The behavioral genetics of personality disorder. *Annual Review of Clinical Psychology, 4,* 247–274.

Lockhart, W. H. (1984). Rogers' "necessary and sufficient conditions" revisited. *British Journal of Guidance and Counselling, 12,* 113–123.

Loehlin, J. C. (1984). R. B. Cattell and behavior genetics. *Multivariate Behavioral Research, 19,* 310–321.

Loehlin, J. C. (2010). Environment and the behavior genetics of personality: Let me count the ways. *Personality and Individual Differences, 49,* 302–305.

Loehlin, J. C., McCrae, R. R., & Costa, P. T., Jr. (1998). Heritabilities of common and measure-specific components of the big five personality factors. *Journal of Research in Personality, 32,* 431–453.

Loevinger, J. (1966). The meaning and measurement of ego development. *American Psychologist, 21,* 195–206.

Loevinger, J. (1976). *Ego development: Conceptions and theories.* San Francisco, CA: Jossey-Bass.

Loevinger, J. (1979). Construct validity of the sentence completion test of ego development. *Applied Psychological Measurement, 3,* 281–311.

Loevinger, J. (1985). Revision of the Sentence Completion Test for Ego Development. *Journal of Personality and Social Psychology, 48,* 420–427.

Loewenberg, P. (1988). Psychoanalytic models of history: Freud and after. In W. M. Runyan (Ed.), *Psychology and historical interpretation* (pp. 126–156). New York: Oxford University Press.

Lombardi, D. N., & Elcock, L. E. (1997). Freud versus Adler on dreams. *American Psychologist, 52,* 572–573.

London, P. (1988). Metamorphosis in psychotherapy: Slouching toward integration. *Journal of Integrative and Eclectic Psychotherapy, 7*(1), 3–12.

Lorenzini, R., Sassaroli, S., & Rocchi, M. T. (1989). Schizophrenia and paranoia as solutions to predictive failure. *International Journal of Personal Construct Psychology, 2,* 417–432.

Lorimer, R. (1976). A reconsideration of the psychological roots of Gandhi's Truth. *Psychoanalytic Review, 63,* 191–207.

Lorr, H. (1991). An empirical evaluation of the MBTI typology. *Personality and Individual Differences, 12,* 1141–1146.

Loy, D. R. (2002). *A Buddhist history of the West: Studies in lack.* Albany, NY: State University of New York Press.

Lubinski, D. (1995). Applied individual differences research and its quantitative methods. *Psychology, Public Policy, and Law, 2,* 187–203.

Lubinski, D., Schmidt, D. B., & Benbow, C. P. (1996). A 20-year stability analysis of the Study of Values for intellectually gifted individuals from adolescence to adulthood. *Journal of Applied Psychology, 81,* 443–451.

Lutz, A., Greischar, L. L., Rawlings, N. B., Ricard, M., & Davidson, R. J. (2004). Long-term meditators self-induce high-amplitude gamma synchrony during mental practice. *Proceedings of the National Academy of Sciences, 101*(46), 16369–16373. Available online at http://www.pnas.org/cgi/doi/10.1073/pnas.0407401101

Lykken, D. T., McGue, M., Tellegen, A., & Bouchard, T. J., Jr. (1992). Emergenesis: Genetic traits that may not run in families. *American Psychologist, 47,* 1565–1577.

Lykken, D., & Tellegen, A. (1996). Happiness is a stochastic phenomenon. *Psychological Science, 7,* 186–189.

Lynn, R., Hampson, S. L., & Mullineux, J. C. (1987). A long-term increase in the fluid intelligence of English children. *Nature, 328,* 797.

Lynn, S. J., Lock, T. G., Myers, B., & Payne, D. G. (1997). Recalling the unrecallable: Should hypnosis be used to recover memories in psychotherapy? *Current Directions in Psychological Science, 6,* 79–83.

Lyons, L. S., & Sperling, M. B. (1996). Clinical applications of attachment theory: Empirical and theoretical perspectives. In J. M. Masling & R. F. Bornstein (Eds.), *Psychoanalytic perspectives on developmental psychology* (Ch. 6, pp. 221–256). Washington, DC: American Psychological Association.

Lyubomirsky, S., Sheldon, K. M., & Schkade, D. (2005). Pursuing happiness: The architecture of sustainable change. *Review of General Psychology, 9,* 111–131.

Mabry, C. H. (1993). Gender differences in ego level. *Psychological Reports, 72,* 752–754.

Maccoby, E. E. (2000). Parenting and its effects on children: On reading and misreading behavior genetics. *Annual Review of Psychology, 51,* 1–27.

Maccoby, M. (1995). The two voices of Erich Fromm: Prophet and analyst. *Society, 32*(5), 72–82.

Mack, J. E. (1971). Psychoanalysis and historical biography. *Journal of the American Psychoanalytic Association, 19,* 143–179.

Mack, J. E. (1986). Nuclear weapons and the dark side of mankind. *Political Psychology, 7,* 223–233.

Mackavey, W. R., Malley, J. E., & Stewart, A. J. (1991). Remembering autobiographically consequential experiences: Content analysis of psychologists' accounts of their lives. *Psychology and Aging, 6,* 50–59.

MacLaren, V. V., & Best, L. A. (2010). Nonsuicidal self-injury, potentially addictive behaviors, and the five factor model in undergraduates. *Personality and Individual Differences, 49,* 521–525.

MacLaren, V. V., Best, L. A., Dixon, M. L., & Harrigan, K. A. (2011). Problem gambling and the five factor model in university students. *Personality and Individual Differences, 50,* 335–338.

MacLean, C. R. K., Walton, K. G., Wenneberg, S. R., Levitsky, D. K., Mandarino, J. P., Wazin, R., Hillis, S. L., & Schneider, R. H. (1997). Effects of the transcendental meditation program on adaptive mechanisms: Changes in hormone levels and responses to stress after 4 months of practice. *Psychoneuroendocrinology, 22,* 277–295.

Maddi, S. R., & Costa, P. T., Jr. (1972). *Humanism in personology: Allport, Maslow, and Murray.* Chicago, IL: Aldine Atherton.

Maddi, S. R., Harvey, R. H., Khoshaba, D. M., Fazel, M., & Resurreccion, N. (2009). Hardiness training facilitates performance in college. *Journal of Positive Psychology, 4,* 566–577.

Mahalik, J. R., Cournoyer, R. J., DeFrank, W., Cherry, M., & Napolitano, J. M. (1998). Men's gender role conflict and use of psychological defenses. *Journal of Counseling Psychology, 45,* 247–255.

Mahathera, N. (1982). *Buddhism in a nutshell.* Kandy, Sri Lanka: Buddhist Publication Society. Available online at http://www.buddhanet.net/pdf_file/nutshell.pdf

Mahoney, M. F. (1966). *The meaning in dreams and dreaming: The Jungian viewpoint.* Secaucus, NJ: Citadel Press.

Mahrer, A. R. (2007). To a large extent, the field got it wrong: New learnings from a new look at an old classic. *Psychotherapy: Theory, Research, Practice, Training, 44,* 274–278.

Mahrer, A. R., Nadler, W. P., Stalikas, A., Schachter, H. M., & Sterner, I. (1988). Common and distinctive therapeutic change processes in client-centered, rational-emotive, and experiential psychotherapies. *Psychological Reports, 62,* 972–974.

Maidenbaum, A., & Thomson, L. (1989). Star Trek: In search of the essential John Lennon. *Quadrant, 22*(2), 87–91.

Mair, G. (1994). *Oprah Winfrey: The real story.* New York: Birch Lane Press.

Mair, M. (1988). Psychology as storytelling. *International Journal of Personal Construct Psychology, 1,* 125–137.

Malik, R., Krasney, M., Aldworth, B., & Ladd, H. W. (1996). Effects of subliminal symbiotic stimuli on anxiety reduction. *Perceptual and Motor Skills, 82,* 771–784.

Mallory, M. E. (1989). Q-sort definition of ego identity status. *Journal of Youth and Adolescence, 18,* 399–412.

Malone, M. (1977). *Psychetypes: A new way of exploring personality.* New York: Pocket Books.

Malouff, J. M., Thorsteinsson, E. B., Schutte, N. S., Bhullar, N., & Rooke, S. E. (2010). The Five-Factor Model of personality and relationship satisfaction of intimate partners: A meta-analysis. *Journal of Research in Personality, 44,* 124–127.

Mancuso, J. C. (1998). Can an avowed adherent of personal-construct psychology be counted as a social constructionist? *Journal of Constructivist Psychology, 11,* 205–219.

Manheim, A. R. (1998). The relationship between the artistic process and self-actualization. *Art Therapy, 15*(2), 99–106.

Manian, N., Papdakis, A. A., Strauman, T. J., & Essex, M. J. (2006). The development of children's ideal and ought self-guides: Parenting, temperament, and individual differences in guide strength. *Journal of Personality, 74,* 1619–1645.

Manna, A., Raffone, A., Perrucci, M. G., Nardo, D., Ferretti, A., Tartaro, A., Londei, A., Gratta, C. D., Belardinelli, M. O., & Romani, G. L. (2010). Neural correlates of focused attention and cognitive monitoring in meditation. *Brain Research Bulletin, 82,* 46–56.

Mansfield, V. (1991). The opposites in quantum physics and Jungian psychology: II. Applications. *Journal of Analytical Psychology, 36,* 289–306.

Mansfield, V., & Spiegelman, J. M. (1991). The opposites in quantum physics and Jungian psychology: I. Theoretical foundations. *Journal of Analytical Psychology, 36,* 267–287.

Maoz, Z., & Astorino, A. (1992). The cognitive structure of peacemaking: Egypt and Israel, 1970–1978. *Political Psychology, 13,* 647–662.

Marcia, J. E. (1966). Development and validation of ego-identity status. *Journal of Personality and Social Psychology, 3,* 551–558.

Marcovitz, E. (1982). Jung's three secrets: Slochower on "Freud as Yahweh in Jung's Answer to Job." *American Imago, 39,* 59–72.

Marcus-Newhall, A., Pedersen, W. C., Miller, N., & Carlson, M. (2000). Displaced aggression is alive and well: A meta-analytic review. *Journal of Personality and Social Psychology, 78,* 670–689.

Marks, S. G., & Koepke, J. E. (1994). Pet attachment and generativity among young adults. *Journal of Psychology, 128,* 641–650.

Markus, H. (1977). Self-schemata and processing information about the self. *Journal of Personality and Social Psychology, 35,* 63–78.

Marlatt, G. A. (2002). Buddhist philosophy and the treatment of addictive behavior. *Cognitive and Behavioral Practice, 9,* 44–50.

Marsden, D., & Littler, D. (2000). Exploring consumer product construct systems with the repertory grid technique. *Qualitative Market Research, 3,* 127–143.

Marsh, C. S., & Colangelo, N. (1983). The application of Dabrowski's concept of multilevelness to Allport's concept of unity. *Counseling and Values, 27,* 213–228.

Marshall, G. N. (1991). Levels of analysis and personality: Lessons from the person-situation debate? *Psychological Science, 2,* 427–428.

Martin, R. A., Berry, G. E., Dobranski, T., & Horne, M. (1996). Emotion perception threshold: Individual differences in emotional sensitivity. *Journal of Research in Personality, 30,* 290–305.

Marx, D. M., Brown, J. L., & Steele, C. M. (1999). Allport's legacy and the situational press of stereotypes. *Journal of Social Issues, 55,* 491–502.

Mascha, E. (2008). Political satire and hegemony: A case of "passive revolution" during Mussolini's ascendance to power 1919–1925. *Humor, 21,* 69–98.

Masling, J., Weiss, L., & Rothschild, B. (1968). Relationships of oral imagery to yielding behavior and birth order. *Journal of Consulting and Clinical Psychology, 32,* 89–91.

Maslow, A. H. (1942). Self-esteem (dominance-feeling) and sexuality in women. *Journal of Social Psychology, 16,* 259–294.

Maslow, A. H. (1943). A theory of human motivation. *Psychological Review, 50,* 370–396. Reprinted in R. J. Lowry (Ed.), *Dominance, self-esteem, self-actualization: Germinal papers of A. H. Maslow* (1973, pp. 153–173). Monterey, CA: Brooks/Cole.

Maslow, A. H. (1955). Deficiency motivation and growth motivation. In M. R. Jones (Ed.), *Nebraska symposium on motivation* (pp. 1–30). Lincoln, NE: University of Nebraska Press.

Maslow, A. H. (1958). Emotional blocks to creativity. *Journal of Individual Psychology, 14,* 51–56.

Maslow, A. H. (1962). *Toward a psychology of being.* Princeton, NJ: Van Nostrand.

Maslow, A. H. (1964). Synergy in the society and in the individual. *Journal of Individual Psychology, 20,* 153–164.

Maslow, A. H. (1966). *The psychology of science: A reconnaissance.* New York: Harper & Row.

Maslow, A. H. (1968a, July). A conversation with Abraham H. Maslow. *Psychology Today,* pp. 34–37, 54–57.

Maslow, A. H. (1968b). *Toward a psychology of being* (2nd ed.). New York: Van Nostrand.

Maslow, A. H. (1970). *Religions, values, and peak-experiences.* New York: Viking.

Maslow, A. H. (1976). *The farther reaches of human nature* (2nd ed.). New York: Viking.

Maslow, A. H. (1987). *Motivation and personality* (3rd ed.). New York: Harper & Row. (Original work published 1954)

Maslow, A. H. (with Stephens, D. C., & Heil, G.). (1998). *Maslow on management.* New York: Wiley.

Mason, L. I., Alexander, C. N., Travis, F. T., Marsh, G., Orme-Johnson, D. W., Gackenbach, J., Mason, D. C., Rainforth, M. & Walton, K. G. (1997). Electrophysiological correlates of higher states of consciousness during sleep in long-term practitioners of the Transcendental Meditation program. *Sleep, 20,* 102–110.

Massarik, F. (1992). The humanistic core of industrial/organizational psychology. *Humanistic Psychologist, 20,* 389–396.

Massaro, T. M. (1997). The meanings of shame: Implications for legal reform. *Psychology, Public Policy, and Law, 3,* 645–704.

Masson, J. M. (1984). *The assault on truth: Freud's suppression of the seduction theory.* New York: Farrar, Straus & Giroux.

Mastey, D. (2010). Slumming and/as self-making in Barack Obama's Dreams from my father. *Journal of Black Studies, 40,* 484–501.

Matsumoto, D. (2007). Culture, context, and behavior. *Journal of Personality, 75,* 1285–1320.

Matta, K. F., & Kern, G. M. (1991). Interactive videodisc instruction: The influence of personality on learning. *International Journal of Man-Machine Studies, 35,* 541–552.

Mattoon, M. A. (1978). *Applied dream analysis: A Jungian approach.* New York: Wiley.

Mauro, C. F., & Harris, Y. R. (2000). The influence of maternal child-rearing attitudes and teaching behaviors on preschoolers' delay of gratification. *Journal of Genetic Psychology, 161,* 292–306.

May, R. (1982). The problem of evil: An open letter to Carl Rogers. *Journal of Humanistic Psychology, 22,* 10–21.

May, R. (1991). *The cry for myth.* New York: Norton.

Mayes, C. (1999). Reflecting on the archetypes of teaching. *Teaching Education, 10*(2), 3–16.

Mazzucchelli, T. G., Kane, R. T., & Rees, C. S. (2010). Behavioral activation interventions for well-being: A meta-analysis. *Journal of Positive Psychology, 5,* 105–121.

McAdams, D. P. (1990). Unity and purpose in human lives: The emergence of identity as a life story. In A. I. Rabin, R. A. Zucker, R. A. Emmons, & S. Frank (Eds.), *Studying persons and lives* (pp. 148–200). New York: Springer-Verlag.

McAdams, D. P., & de St. Aubin, E. (1992). A theory of generativity and its assessment through self-report, behavioral acts, and narrative themes in autobiography. *Journal of Personality and Social Psychology, 62,* 1003–1015.

McAdams, D. P., Diamond, A., de St. Aubin, E., & Mansfield, E. (1997). Stories of commitment: The psychosocial construction of generative lives. *Journal of Personality and Social Psychology, 72,* 678–694.

McArdle, J. J., & Cattell, R. B. (1994). Structural equation models of factorial invariance in parallel proportional profiles and oblique cofactor problems. *Multivariate Behavioral Research, 29,* 63–113.

McCaulley, M. H. (1990). The Myers-Briggs Type Indicator: A measure for individuals and groups. *Measurement and Evaluation in Counseling and Development, 22,* 181–195.

McClelland, D. C. (1955). Comments on Professor Maslow's paper. In M. R. Jones (Ed.), *Nebraska symposium on motivation* (pp. 31–37). Lincoln, NE: University of Nebraska Press.

McClelland, D. C., Koestner, R., & Weinberger, J. (1989). How do self-attributed and implicit motives differ? *Psychological Review, 96,* 690–702.

McClelland, D. C., & Winter, D. G. (1969). *Motivating economic achievement.* New York: Free Press.

McCourt, K., Bouchard, T. J., Jr., Lykken, D. T., Tellegen, A., & Keyes, M. (1999). Authoritarianism revisited: Genetic and environmental influences examined in twins reared apart and together. *Personality and Individual Differences, 27,* 985–1014.

McCrae, R. R. (1990). Traits and trait names: How well is openness represented in natural languages? *European Journal of Personality, 4,* 119–129.

McCrae, R. R. (1991). The five-factor model and its assessment in clinical settings. *Journal of Personality Assessment, 57,* 399–414.

McCrae, R. R. (2000). Trait psychology and the revival of personality and culture studies. *American Behavioral Scientist, 44,* 10–31.

McCrae, R. R., & Costa, P. T., Jr. (1982). Comparison of EPI and psychoticism scales with measures of the five-factor model of personality. *Personality and Individual Differences, 6,* 587–597.

McCrae, R. R., & Costa, P. T., Jr. (1984). *Emerging lives, enduring dispositions: Personality in adulthood.* Boston, MA: Little, Brown.

McCrae, R. R., & Costa, P. T., Jr. (1987). Validation of the five-factor model of personality across instruments and observers. *Journal of Personality and Social Psychology, 52,* 81–90.

McCrae, R. R., & Costa, P. T., Jr. (1988). Recalled parent-child relations and adult personality. *Journal of Personality, 56,* 417–434.

McCrae, R. R., & Costa, P. T., Jr. (1989). Reinterpreting the Myers-Briggs Type Indicator from the perspective of the five-factor model of personality. *Journal of Personality, 57,* 17–40.

McCrae, R. R., & Costa, P. T., Jr. (1991). Adding Liebe und Arbeit: The full five-factor model and well-being. *Personality and Social Psychology Bulletin, 17,* 227–232.

McCrae, R. R., & Costa, P. T., Jr. (2008). The five-factor theory of personality. In O. P. John, R. W. Robins, & L. A. Pervin (Eds.), *Handbook of personality: Theory and research* (3rd ed., pp. 159–181). New York: Guilford Press.

McCrae, R. R., Costa, P. T., Jr., Del Pilar, G. H., Rolland, J. P., & Parker, W. D. (1998). Cross-cultural assessment of the five-factor model: The revised NEO personality inventory. *Journal of Cross-Cultural Psychology, 29,* 171–188.

McCrae, R. R., Costa, P. T., Jr., & Piedmont, R. L. (1993). Folk concepts, natural language, and psychological constructs: The California Psychological Inventory and the five-factor model. *Journal of Personality, 61,* 1–26.

McCroskey, J. C., Heisel, A. D., & Richmond, V. P. (2001). Eysenck's big three and communication traits: Three correlational studies. *Communication Monographs, 68,* 360–366.

McCullagh, P. (1986). Model status as a determinant of observational learning and performance. *Journal of Sport Psychology, 8,* 319–331.

McCullough, M. (2008). *Beyond revenge: The evolution of the forgiveness instinct.* San Francisco, CA: Jossey-Bass.

McDargh, J. (2000). Spiritual conceptions of love. In A. E. Kazdin (Ed.), *Encyclopedia of Psychology* (Vol. 5, pp. 85–87). New York: Oxford University Press.

McGowan, D. (1994). *What is wrong with Jung.* Buffalo, NY: Prometheus Books.

McGrath, J. (1986). *Freud's discovery of psychoanalysis: The politics of hysteria.* Ithaca, NY: Cornell University Press.

McGue, M., & Lykken, D. T. (1992). Genetic influence on risk of divorce. *Psychological Science, 3,* 368–373.

McGuire, W. (Ed.). (1974). *The Freud/Jung letters: The correspondence between Sigmund Freud and C. G. Jung* (R. Manheim & R. F. C. Hull, Trans.). Princeton, NJ: Princeton University Press.

McKee, K. J., Wilson, F., Chung, M. C., Hinchliff, S., Goudie, F., Elford, H., & Mitchell, C. (2005). Reminiscence, regrets and activity in older people in residential care: Associations with psychological health. *British Journal of Clinical Psychology, 44,* 543–561.

McNamara, L., & Ballard, M. E. (1999). Resting arousal, sensation seeking, and music preference. *Genetic, Social and General Psychology Monographs, 125,* 229–251.

McPherson, F. M., Barden, V., & Buckley, F. (1970). The use of "psychological" constructs by affectively flattened schizophrenics. *British Journal of Medical Psychology, 43,* 291–293.

McPherson, F. M., & Buckley, F. (1970). Thought-process disorder and personal construct subsystems. *British Journal of Social and Clinical Psychology, 9*, 380–381.

McPherson, F. M., & Gray, A. (1976). Psychological construing and psychological symptoms. *British Journal of Medical Psychology, 49*, 73–79.

McWilliams, S. A. (1993). Construct no idols. *International Journal of Personal Construct Psychology, 6*, 269–280.

Meditation in psychotherapy. (2005, April). *Harvard Mental Health Letter, 21*(10), 1–4.

Meier, B. P., Robinson, M. D., Carter, M. S., & Hinsz, V. B. (2010). Are sociable people more beautiful? A zero-acquaintance analysis of agreeableness, extraversion, and attractiveness. *Journal of Research in Personality, 44*, 293–296.

Mendolia, M., Moore, J., & Tesser, A. (1996). Dispositional and situational determinants of repression. *Journal of Personality and Social Psychology, 70*, 856–867.

Mendoza-Denton, R., Ayduk, O., Mischel, W., Shoda, Y., & Testa, A. (2001). Person × situation interactionism in self-encoding (*I Am…When…*): Implications for affect regulation and social information processing. *Journal of Personality and Social Psychology, 80*, 533–544.

Mendoza-Denton, R., & Goldman-Flythe, M. (2009). Personality and racial/ethnic relations: A perspective from Cognitive–Affective Personality System (CAPS) theory. *Journal of Personality, 77*, 1261–1282.

Merenda, P. F. (1987). Toward a four-factor theory of temperament and/or personality. *Journal of Personality Assessment, 51*, 367–374.

Mesquida, C. G., & Wiener, N. I. (1996). Human collective aggression: A behavioral ecology perspective. *Ethology and Sociobiology, 17*, 247–262.

Metcalfe, J., & Mischel, W. (1999). A hot/cool-system analysis of delay of gratification: Dynamics of willpower. *Psychological Review, 106*, 3–19.

Meyer-Bahlburg, H. F. L., Ehrhardt, A. A., Rosen, L. R., Gruen, R. S., Veridiano, N. P., Vann, F. H., & Neuwalder, H. F. (1995). Prenatal estrogens and the development of homosexual orientation. *Developmental Psychology, 31*, 12–21.

Michalon, M. (2001). "Selflessness" in the service of the ego: Contributions, limitations, and dangers of Buddhist psychology for Western psychotherapy. *American Journal of Psychotherapy, 55*, 202–218.

Michalski, R. L., & Shackelford, T. K. (2010). Evolutionary personality psychology: Reconciling human nature and individual differences. *Personality and Individual Differences, 48*, 509–516.

Mickelson, K. D., Kessler, R. C., & Shaver, P. R. (1997). Adult attachment in a nationally representative sample. *Journal of Personality and Social Psychology, 73*, 1092–1106.

Midence, K., & Hargreaves, I. (1997). Psychosocial adjustment in male-to-female transsexuals: An overview of the research evidence. *Journal of Psychology, 131*, 602–614.

Midgley, B. D., & Morris, E. K. (1988). The integrated field: An alternative to the behavior-analytic conceptualization of behavioral units. *Psychological Record, 38*, 483–500.

Mikulincer, M. (1998a). Adult attachment style and individual differences in functional versus dysfunctional experiences of anger. *Journal of Personality and Social Psychology, 74*, 513–524.

Mikulincer, M. (1998b). Attachment working models and the sense of trust: An exploration of interaction goals and affect regulation. *Journal of Personality and Social Psychology, 74*, 1209–1224.

Miletic, M. P. (2002). The introduction of a feminine psychology to psychoanalysis: Karen Horney's legacy. *Contemporary Psychoanalysis, 38*, 287–299.

Mill, J. (1984). High and low self-monitoring individuals: Their decoding skills and empathic expression. *Journal of Personality, 52*, 372–388.

Miller, A. J., & Worthington, E. L., Jr. (2010). Sex differences in forgiveness and mental health in recently married couples. *Journal of Positive Psychology, 5*, 12–23.

Miller, C. (2001). Childhood animal cruelty and interpersonal violence. *Clinical Psychology Review, 21*, 735–749.

Miller, D. B. (1999). Racial socialization and racial identity: Can they promote resiliency for African American adolescents? *Adolescence, 34*, 493–501.

Miller, E. M. (2000). Homosexuality, birth order, and evolution: Toward an equilibrium reproductive economics of homosexuality. *Archives of Sexual Behavior, 29*, 1–34.

Miller, G. (1969). Psychology as a means of promoting human welfare. *American Psychologist, 24*, 1063–1075.

Miller, J. B. (1976). *Toward a new psychology of women.* Boston, MA: Beacon Press.

Miller, M. E. (2002). Zen and psychotherapy: From neutrality, through relationship, to the emptying space. In S. Muramoto & P. Young-Eisendrath (Eds.), *Awakening and insight: Zen Buddhism and psychotherapy* (pp. 81–92). New York: Brunner-Routledge.

Miller, M. J., Smith, T. S., Wilkinson, L., & Tobacyk, J. (1987). Narcissism and social interest among counselors-in-training. *Psychological Reports, 60*, 765–766.

Miller, N. E. (1941). An experimental investigation of acquired drives. Abstract of paper presented at the 49th Annual Meeting of the American Psychological Association, September 3–6, 1941. *Psychological Bulletin, 38*, 534–535.

Miller, N. E. (1985). Some professional and scientific problems and opportunities for biofeedback. *Biofeedback and Self Regulation, 10*, 3024.

Miller, N. E. (1989). Biomedical foundations for biofeedback. *Advances, 6*(3), 30–36.

Miller, N. E. (1992a). Some examples of psychophysiology and the unconscious. *Biofeedback and Self Regulation, 17*, 3–16.

Miller, N. E. (1992b). Studies of fear as an acquirable drive: I. Fear as motivation and fear-reduction as reinforcement in the learning of new responses. *Journal of Experimental Psychology: General, 121,* 6–11. (Original work published 1948)

Miller, N. E., & Dollard, J. (1941). *Social learning and imitation.* New Haven, CT: Yale University Press.

Miller, N. E., & Dworkin, B. R. (1977). Effects of learning on visceral functions: Biofeedback. *New England Journal of Medicine, 296,* 1274–1278.

Miller, T. Q., Smith, T. W., Turner, C. W., Guijarro, M. L., & Hallet, A. J. (1996). Meta-analytic review of research on hostility and physical health. *Psychological Bulletin, 119,* 322–348.

Minarik, M. L., & Ahrens, A. H. (1996). Relations of eating and symptoms of depression and anxiety to the dimensions of perfectionism among undergraduate women. *Cognitive Therapy and Research, 20,* 155–169.

Mind and Life Institute. (2006). The Cultivating Emotional Balance program. Available online at http://www.mindandlife. org/ceb.program.html

Minton, H. L. (1968). Contemporary concepts of power and Adler's views. *Journal of Individual Psychology, 24,* 46–55.

Mischel, H. N., & Mischel, W. (1983). The development of children's knowledge of self-control strategies. *Child Development, 54,* 603–619.

Mischel, W. (1966). Theory and research on the antecedents of self-imposed delay of reward. In B. Maher (Ed.), *Progress in experimental personality research* (Vol. 3, pp. 85–132). New York: Academic Press.

Mischel, W. (1968). *Personality and assessment.* New York: Wiley.

Mischel, W. (1973). Toward a cognitive social learning reconceptualization of personality. *Psychological Review, 80,* 252–283.

Mischel, W. (1974). Processes in delay of gratification. In L. Berkowitz (Ed.), *Advances in experimental social psychology* (Vol. 7, pp. 249–292). New York: Academic Press.

Mischel, W. (1977). The interaction of person and situation. In D. Magnusson & N. S. Endler (Eds.), *Personality at the crossroads: Current issues in interactional psychology* (pp. 333–352). Hillsdale, NJ: Erlbaum.

Mischel, W. (1981a). *Introduction to personality* (3rd ed.). New York: Holt, Rinehart & Winston.

Mischel, W. (1981b). Personality and cognition: Something borrowed, something new? In N. Cantor & J. F. Kihlstrom (Eds.), *Personality, cognition, and social interaction.* Hillsdale, NJ: Erlbaum.

Mischel, W. (1983a). Alternatives in the pursuit of the predictability and consistency of persons: Stable data that yield unstable interpretations. *Journal of Personality, 51,* 578–604.

Mischel, W. (1983b). Delay of gratification as process and as person variable in development. In D. Magnusson & V. P. Allen (Eds.), *Human development: An interactional perspective* (pp. 149–165). New York: Academic Press.

Mischel, W. (1984a). Convergences and challenges in the search for consistency. *American Psychologist, 39,* 351–364.

Mischel, W. (1984b). On the predictability of behavior and the structure of personality. In R. A. Zucker, J. Aronoff, & A. I. Rabin (Eds.), *Personality and the prediction of behavior* (pp. 269–305). New York: Academic Press.

Mischel, W. (1992). Looking for personality. In S. Koch & D. E. Leary (Eds.), *A century of psychology as science* (pp. 515–526). Washington, DC: American Psychological Association.

Mischel, W. (2004). Toward an integrative science of the person. *Annual Review of Psychology, 55,* 1–22.

Mischel, W. (2007). Walter Mischel. In G. Lindzey & W. M. Runyan (Eds.), *A history of psychology in autobiography* (Vol. 9, pp. 229–267). Washington, DC: American Psychological Association.

Mischel, W., & Baker, N. (1975). Cognitive appraisals and transformations in delay behavior. *Journal of Personality and Social Psychology, 31,* 254–261.

Mischel, W., & Ebbesen, E. B. (1970). Attention in delay of gratification. *Journal of Personality and Social Psychology, 16,* 329–337.

Mischel, W., Ebbesen, E. B., & Zeiss, A. R. (1972). Cognitive and attentional mechanisms in delay of gratification. *Journal of Personality and Social Psychology, 21,* 204–218.

Mischel, W., & Liebert, R. M. (1966). Effects of discrepancies between observed and imposed reward criteria on their acquisition and transmission. *Journal of Personality and Social Psychology, 3,* 45–53.

Mischel, W., Mendoza-Denton, R., & Hong, Y. Y. (2009). Toward an integrative CAPS approach to racial/ethnic relations. *Journal of Personality, 77,* 1365–1379.

Mischel, W., & Moore, B. (1973). Effects of attention to symbolically presented rewards on self-control. *Journal of Personality and Social Psychology, 28,* 172–179.

Mischel, W., & Peake, P. K. (1982). Beyond déjà vu in the search for cross-situational consistency. *Psychological Review, 89,* 730–755.

Mischel, W., & Peake, P. K. (1983). Some facets of consistency: Replies to Epstein, Funder, and Bem. *Psychological Review, 90,* 394–402.

Mischel, W., & Shoda, Y. (1995). A cognitive-affective system theory of personality: Reconceptualizing situations, dispositions, dynamics, and invariance in personality structure. *Psychological Review, 102,* 246–268.

Mischel, W., & Shoda, Y. (1998). Reconciling processing dynamics and personality dispositions. *Annual Review of Psychology, 49,* 229–258.

Mischel, W., Shoda, Y., & Peake, P. K. (1988). The nature of adolescent competencies predicted by preschool delay of gratification. *Journal of Personality and Social Psychology, 54,* 687–696.

Mischel, W., Shoda, Y., & Rodriguez, M. L. (1989). Delay of gratification in children. *Science, 244,* 933–938.

Mischel, W., & Staub, E. (1965). Effects of expectancy on working and waiting for larger rewards. *Journal of Personality and Social Psychology, 2,* 625–633.

Mischel, W., Zeiss, R., & Zeiss, A. (1974). Internal-external control and persistence: Validation and implications of the Stanford Preschool Internal-External Scale. *Journal of Personality and Social Psychology, 29,* 265–278.

Mitchell, M. (2009). *Complexity: A guided tour.* New York: Oxford University Press. (Kindle Version). Available online at www.amazon.com

Mitchell, S. A. (1999). The wings of Icarus: Illusion and the problem of narcissism. In S. A. Mitchell & L. Aron (Eds.), *Relational psychoanalysis: The emergence of a tradition* (pp. 153–179). Hillsdale, NJ: Analytical Press. (Reprinted from *Contemporary Psychoanalysis, 22,* 107–132, 1970)

Mitchell, S. A., & Aron, L. (Eds.). (1999). *Relational psychoanalysis: The emergence of a tradition.* Hillsdale, NJ: Analytic Press.

Mongrain, M. (1998). Parental representations and support-seeking behaviors related to dependency and self-criticism. *Journal of Personality, 66,* 151–173.

Monk-Turner, E. (2003). The benefits of meditation: Experimental findings. *Social Science Journal, 40,* 465–470.

Monte, C. F. (1980). *Beneath the mask: An introduction to theories of personality* (2nd ed.). New York: Henry Holt.

Moodley, R. (2000). The *Right to be Desperate* and *Hurt and Anger* in the presence of Carl Rogers: A racial/psychological identity approach. *Counselling Psychology Quarterly, 13,* 353–364.

Moore, M. K., & Neimeyer, R. A. (1991). A confirmatory factor analysis of the Threat Index. *Journal of Personality and Social Psychology, 60,* 122–129.

Moran, J. R., Fleming, C. M., Somervell, P., & Manson, S. M. (1999). Measuring bicultural ethnic identity among American Indian adolescents: A factor analytic study. *Journal of Adolescent Research, 14,* 405–426.

Morçöl, G., & Asche, M. (1993). Repertory grid in problem structuring: A case illustration. *International Journal of Personal Construct Psychology, 6,* 371–390.

Morgan, A. C. (1997). The application of infant research to psychoanalytic theory and therapy. *Psychoanalytic Psychology, 14,* 315–336.

Moritz, C. (Ed.). (1974). Miller, Neal Edgar. *Current biography yearbook* (pp. 276–279). New York: W. H. Wilson.

Morse, C., Bockoven, J., & Bettesworth, A. (1988). Effects of DUSO-2 and DUSO-2-revised on children's social skills and self-esteem. *Elementary School Guidance and Counseling, 22,* 199–205.

Morvay, Z. (1999). Horney, Zen, and the real self: Theoretical and historical connections. *American Journal of Psychoanalysis, 59,* 25–35.

Mosak, H. H., & Dreikurs, R. (2000). Spirituality: The fifth life task. *Individual Psychologist, 5,* 16–11. Reprinted in *Journal of Individual Psychology, 56,* 257–265. (Original work published 1967)

Moskowitz, D. S. (1990). Convergence of self-reports and independent observers: Dominance and friendliness. *Journal of Personality and Social Psychology, 58,* 1096–1106.

Moustakas, C. (1986). Origins of humanistic psychology. *Humanistic Psychologist, 14,* 122–123.

Mozdzierz, G. J., Greenblatt, R. L., & Murphy, T. J. (1988). Further validation of the Sulliman Scale of Social Interest and the Social Interest Scale. *Individual Psychology, 44,* 30–34.

Mullen, M. K. (1994). Earliest recollections of childhood: A demographic analysis. *Cognition, 52,* 55–79.

Multon, K. D., Brown, S. D., & Lent, R. W. (1991). Relation of self-efficacy beliefs to academic outcomes: A meta-analytic investigation. *Journal of Counseling Psychology, 38,* 30–38.

Munter, P. O. (1975). The medical model revisited: A humanistic reply. *Journal of Personality Assessment, 39,* 4.

Muramoto, S. (2002). Buddhism, religion and psychotherapy in the world today. In S. Muramoto & P. Young-Eisendrath (Eds.), *Awakening and insight: Zen Buddhism and psychotherapy* (pp. 15–29). New York: Brunner-Routledge.

Muraven, M., Tice, D. M., & Baumeister, R. F. (1998). Self-control as limited resource: Regulatory depletion patterns. *Journal of Personality and Social Psychology, 74,* 774–789.

Murray, H. A. (1938). *Explorations in personality.* New York: Oxford University Press.

Murray, H. A. (1943, October). Analysis of the personality of Adolph Hitler: With predictions of his future behavior and suggestions for dealing with him now and after Germany's surrender. Confidential report to the Office of Strategic Services. Available online at http://library.lawschool.cornell.edu/WhatWeHave/SpecialCollections/Donovan/Hitler/index.cfm

Murray, J. B. (1990). Review of research on the Myers-Briggs Type Indicator. *Perceptual and Motor Skills, 70,* 1187–1202.

Muslin, H., & Desai, P. (1984). Ghandi [sic] and his fathers. *Psychohistory Review, 12,* 7–18.

Myers, D. G., & Diener, E. (1995). Who is happy? *Psychological Science, 6,* 10–19.

Myers, I. B., & McCaulley, M. H. (1985). *Manual: A guide to the development and use of the Myers-Briggs Type Indicator.* Palo Alto, CA: Consulting Psychologists Press.

Myers, L. B., Brewin, C. R., & Power, M. J. (1998). Repressive coping and the directed forgetting of emotional material. *Journal of Abnormal Psychology, 107,* 141–148.

Myers, S. (2000). Empathic listening: Reports on the experience of being heard. *Journal of Humanistic Psychology, 40*(2), 148–173.

Nahmias, E. (2005). Agency, authorship, and illusion. *Consciousness and Cognition, 14,* 771–785.

Naifeh, S. C. (2001). Carl Gustav Jung, M.D., 1875–1961. *American Journal of Psychiatry, 158,* 173.

Nash, M. R. (1987). What, if anything, is regressed about hypnotic age regression? A review of the empirical literature. *Psychological Bulletin, 102,* 42–52.

Natsoulas, T. (1993). Freud and consciousness: VIII. Conscious psychical processes perforce involve higher-order consciousness—intrinsically or concomitantly? A current issue. *Psychoanalysis and Contemporary Thought, 16,* 597–631.

Natsoulas, T. (1994). A rediscovery of consciousness. *Consciousness and Cognition, 3,* 223–245.

Navarick, D. J. (1998). Impulsive choice in adults: How consistent are individual differences? *Psychological Record, 48,* 665–674.

Neff, K. D., Pisitsungkagarn, K., & Hsieh, Y. P. (2008). Self-compassion and self-construal in the United States, Thailand, and Taiwan. *Journal of Cross-Cultural Psychology, 39,* 267–285.

Neff, K. D., & Vonk, R. (2009). Self-compassion versus global self-esteem: Two different ways of relating to oneself. *Journal of Personality, 77,* 23–50.

Neher, A. (1996). Jung's theory of archetypes: A critique. *Journal of Humanistic Psychology, 36,* 61–91.

Neimeyer, G. J. (1988). Cognitive integration and differentiation in vocational behavior. *Counseling Psychologist, 16,* 440–475.

Neimeyer, G. J. (1992). Personal constructs in career counseling and development. *Journal of Career Development, 18*(3), 163–173.

Neimeyer, G. J., & Khouzam, N. (1985). A repertory grid study of restrained eaters. *British Journal of Medical Psychology, 58,* 365–367.

Neimeyer, G. J., & Rareshide, M. B. (1991). Personal memories and personal identity: The impact of ego identity on autobiographical memory recall. *Journal of Personality and Social Psychology, 60,* 562–569.

Neimeyer, R. A. (1985a). Actualization, integration, and fear of death: A test of the additive model. *Death Studies, 9,* 235–244.

Neimeyer, R. A. (1985b). Personal constructs in clinical practice. In P. C. Kendall (Ed.), *Advances in cognitive behavioral research and therapy* (Vol. 4, pp. 275–339). New York: Academic Press.

Neimeyer, R. A. (1987). An orientation to personal construct therapy. In R. A. Neimeyer & G. J. Neimeyer (Eds.), *Personal construct therapy casebook* (pp. 3–19). New York: Springer.

Neimeyer, R. A. (1992). Constructivist approaches to the measurement of meaning. In G. J. Neimeyer (Ed.), *Constructivist assessment: A casebook* (pp. 58–103). Newbury Park, CA: Sage.

Neimeyer, R. A. (1993). An appraisal of constructivist psychotherapies. *Journal of Consulting and Clinical Psychology, 61,* 221–234.

Neimeyer, R. A. (1994). The role of client-generated narratives in psychotherapy. *International Journal of Personal Construct Psychology, 7,* 229–242.

Neimeyer, R. A. (1999). Narrative strategies in grief therapy. *Journal of Constructivist Psychology, 12,* 65–85.

Neimeyer, R. A. (2001). Unfounded trust: A constructivist meditation. *American Journal of Psychotherapy, 55,* 364–371.

Neimeyer, R. A., Moore, M. K., & Bagley, K. J. (1988). A preliminary factor structure for the Threat Index. *Death Studies, 12,* 217–225.

Neimeyer, R. A., & Neimeyer, G. J. (Eds.). (1987). *Personal construct therapy casebook.* New York: Springer.

Neiss, M. B., Stevenson, J., Legrand, L. N., Iacono, W. G., & Sedikides, C. (2009). Self-esteem, negative emotionality, and depression as a common temperamental core: A study of mid-adolescent twin girls. *Journal of Personality, 77,* 327–346.

Nelson, D. V., Friedman, L. C., Baer, P. E., Lane, M., & Smith, F. E. (1989). Attitudes to cancer: Psychometric properties of fighting spirit and denial. *Journal of Behavioral Medicine, 12,* 341–355.

Nelson, L. S., & Roberge, L. P. (1993). The relationship between psychological type and preference for career services: Implications for career development strategies. *College Student Journal, 27,* 312–321.

Neumann, E. (1963). *The great mother: An analysis of the archetype* (2nd ed.). Princeton, NJ: Princeton University Press.

Nevis, E. C. (1983). Using an American perspective in understanding another culture: Toward a hierarchy of needs for the People's Republic of China. *Journal of Applied Behavioral Science, 19,* 249–264.

Newman, D. L., Tellegen, A., & Bouchard, T. J., Jr. (1998). Individual differences in adult ego development: Sources of influence in twins reared apart. *Journal of Personality and Social Psychology, 74,* 985–995.

Newman, L. S., Duff, K. J., & Baumeister, R. F. (1997). A new look at defensive projection: Thought suppression, accessibility, and biased person perception. *Journal of Personality and Social Psychology, 72,* 980–1001.

Newman, L. S., Higgins, E. T., & Vookles, J. (1992). Self-guide strength and emotional vulnerability: Birth order as a moderator of self-affect relations. *Personality and Social Psychology Bulletin, 18,* 402–411.

Neyer, F. J., & Lahnart, J. (2007). Relationships matter in personality development: Evidence from an 8-year longitudinal study across young adulthood. *Journal of Personality, 75,* 535–568.

Nez, D. (1991). Persephone's return: Archetypal art therapy and the treatment of a survivor of abuse. *Arts in Psychotherapy, 18*(2), 123–130.

Nhat Hanh, T. (1996). *Being peace.* Berkeley, CA: Parallax Press.

Nhat Hanh, T. (2001). *Anger.* New York: Riverhead Books.

Nicholson, I. (1997). Humanistic psychology and the intellectual identity: The "open" system of Gordon Allport. *Journal of Humanistic Psychology, 37*(3), 61–79.

Nicholson, I. (2007). Baring the soul: Paul Bindrim, Abraham Maslow and "nude psychotherapy." *Journal of the History of the Behavioral Sciences, 43,* 337–359.

Nicholson, I. A. M. (1998). Gordon Allport, character, and the "culture of personality," 1897–1937. *History of Psychology, 1,* 52–68.

Nichtern, S. (1985). Gandhi: His adolescent conflict of mind and body. *Adolescent Psychiatry, 12,* 17–23.

Nidich, R. J., Nidich, S. I., & Alexander, C. N. (2005). Moral development and natural law. *Journal of Social Behavior and Personality, 17,* 137–149.

Nidich, S. I., Schneider, R. H., Nidich, R. J., Foster, G., Sharma, H., Salerno, J., Goodman, R., & Alexander, C. N. (2005). Effect of the Transcendental Meditation program on intellectual development in community-dwelling older adults. *Journal of Social Behavior and Personality, 17,* 217–226.

Niemiec, C. P., Ryan, R. M., Patrick, H., Deci, E. L., & Williams, G. C. (2010). The energization of health-behavior change: Examining the associations among autonomous self-regulation, subjective vitality, depressive symptoms, and tobacco abstinence. *Journal of Positive Psychology, 5,* 122–138.

Nigg, J. T., Lohr, N. E., Westen, D., Gold, L. J., & Silk, K. R. (1992). Malevolent object representations in borderline personality disorder and major depression. *Journal of Abnormal Psychology, 101,* 61–67.

Nixon, R. M. (1962). *Six crises.* Garden City, NY: Doubleday.

Nixon, R. M. (1990). *In the arena: A memoir of victory, defeat, and renewal.* New York: Simon & Schuster.

Noll, R. (1994). *The Jung cult: Origins of a charismatic movement.* Princeton, NJ: Princeton University Press.

Norman, W. T. (1963). Toward an adequate taxonomy of personality attributes: Replicated factor structure in peer nomination personality ratings. *Journal of Abnormal and Social Psychology, 66,* 574–583.

Oates, S. B. (1982). *Let the trumpet sound: The life of Martin Luther King, Jr.* New York: Mentor Books.

Obama, B. (2004). *Dreams from my father: A story of race and inheritance.* New York: Three Rivers Press. (Originally published in 1995)

Obama, B. (2006). *The audacity of hope: Thoughts on reclaiming the American dream.* New York: Three Rivers Press.

Obama, B. (2008). *Change we can believe in: Barack Obama's plan to renew America's promise.* Edinburgh, NY: Canongate.

Ochberg, R. L. (1988). Life stories and the psychosocial construction of careers. *Journal of Personality, 56,* 173–204.

Ochse, R., & Plug, C. (1986). Cross-cultural investigation of the validity of Erikson's theory of personality development. *Journal of Personality and Social Psychology, 50,* 1240–1252.

O'Connell, A. N. (1980). Karen Horney: Theorist in psychoanalysis and feminine psychology. *Psychology of Women Quarterly, 5,* 81–93.

O'Connell, A. N., & Russo, N. F. (1980). Models for achievement: Eminent women in psychology. *Psychology of Women Quarterly, 5,* 6–10.

O'Connell, W. (1990). Natural high theory and practice (NHTP) as a model of Adlerian holism. *Individual Psychology, 46,* 263–269.

O'Connor, P. J., & Jackson, C. (2008). Learning to be saints or sinners: The indirect pathway from sensation seeking to behavior through mastery orientation. *Journal of Personality, 76,* 733–752.

O'Driscoll, A. (2007). The growing influence of mindfulness on the work of the counseling psychologist: A review. *Counselling Psychology Review, 24,* 16–23.

O'Leary, A. (1985). Self-efficacy and health. *Behavior Research and Therapy, 23,* 437–452.

O'Leary, A. (1992). Self-efficacy and health: Behavioral and stress-physiological mediation. *Cognitive Therapy and Research, 16,* 229–245.

O'Leary, K. D., & Drabman, R. (1971). Token reinforcement programs in the classroom: A review. *Psychological Bulletin, 75,* 379–398.

O'Neill, R. M., & Bornstein, R. F. (1990). Oral-dependence and gender: Factors in help-seeking response set and self-reported psychopathology in psychiatric inpatients. *Journal of Personality Assessment, 55,* 28–40.

O'Neill, R. M., Greenberg, R. P., & Fisher, S. (1992). Humor and anality. *Humor: International Journal of Humor Research, 5,* 283–291.

O'Roark, A. M. (1990). Comment on Cowan's interpretation of the Myers-Briggs Type Indicator and Jung's psychological functions. *Journal of Personality Assessment, 55,* 815–817.

Oishi, S. (2004). Personality *in* culture: A neo-Allportian view. *Journal of Research in Personality, 38,* 68–74.

Olds, D. D. (1992). Consciousness: A brain-centered, informational approach. *Psychoanalytic Inquiry, 12,* 419–444.

Oliver, P. H., Guerin, D. W., & Goffman, J. K. (2009). Big five parental personality traits, parenting behaviors, and adolescent behavior problems: A mediation model. *Personality and Individual Differences, 47,* 631–636.

Olson, B. (1999). *Hell to pay: The unfolding story of Hillary Rodham Clinton.* Washington, DC: Regnery.

Olson, E. E. (1990). The transcendent function in organizational change. *Journal of Applied Behavioral Science, 26,* 69–81.

Oppenheimer, R. (1956). Analogy in science. *American Psychologist, 11,* 127–135.

Orbach, I. (1997). A taxonomy of factors related to suicidal behavior. *Clinical Psychology: Science and Practice, 4,* 208–224.

Orlofsky, J. L. (1978). The relationship between intimacy and antecedent personality components. *Adolescence, 13,* 419–441.

Orne, M. T. (1959). The nature of hypnosis: Artifact and essence. *Journal of Abnormal and Social Psychology, 58,* 277–299.

Orne, M. T. (1971). Hypnosis, motivation, and the ecological validity of the psychological experiment. In W. J. Arnold &

M. M. Page (Eds.), *Nebraska symposium on motivation, 1970* (pp. 187–265). Lincoln, NE: University of Nebraska Press.

Otto, R. K., Poythress, N., Starr, L., & Darkes, J. (1993). An empirical study of the reports of APA's peer review panel in the congressional review of the U.S.S. Iowa incident. *Journal of Personality Assessment, 61,* 425–442.

Owen, D. (2001). *The chosen one: Tiger Woods and the dilemma of greatness.* New York: Simon and Schuster.

Ozer, E. M., & Bandura, A. (1990). Mechanisms governing empowerment effects: A self-efficacy analysis. *Journal of Personality and Social Psychology, 58,* 472–486.

Paige, J. M. (1966). Letters from Jenny: An approach to the clinical analysis of personality structure by computer. In P. J. Stone, D. C. Dunphy, M. S. Smith, & D. M. Ogilvie (Eds.), *The General Inquirer: A computer approach to content analysis* (pp. 431–451). Cambridge, MA: MIT Press.

Palmer, E. C., & Carr, K. (1991). Dr. Rogers, meet Mr. Rogers: The theoretical and clinical similarities between Carl and Fred Rogers. *Social Behavior and Personality, 19,* 39–44.

Pam, A., & Rivera, J. A. (1995). Sexual pathology and dangerousness from a Thematic Apperception Test protocol. *Professional Psychology: Research and Practice, 26,* 72–77.

Pancer, S. M., Hunsberger, B., Pratt, M. W., & Alisat, S. (2000). Cognitive complexity of expectations and adjustment to university in the first year. *Journal of Adolescent Research, 15,* 38–57.

Pandora, K. (1998). "Mapping the new mental world created by radio": Media messages, cultural politics, and Cantril and Allport's *The Psychology of Radio. Journal of Social Issues, 54,* 7–27.

Paniagua, F. A. (1987). "Knowing" the world within the skin: A remark on Skinner's behavioral theory of knowledge. *Psychological Reports, 61,* 741–742.

Paranjpe, A. C. (1998). *Self and identity in modern psychology and Indian thought.* New York: Kluwer Academic.

Paris, B. J. (1999). Karen Horney's vision of the self. *American Journal of Psychoanalysis, 59,* 157–166.

Park, C., Cohen, L. H., & Herb, L. (1990). Intrinsic religiousness and religious coping as life stress moderators for Catholics versus Protestants. *Journal of Personality and Social Psychology, 59,* 562–574.

Park, H. S., & Murgatroyd, W. (1998). Relationship between intrinsic-extrinsic religious orientation and depressive symptoms in Korean Americans. *Counselling Psychology Quarterly, 11,* 315–324.

Park, N., Peterson, C, & Ruch, W. (2009). Orientations to happiness and life satisfaction in twenty-seven nations. *Journal of Positive Psychology, 4,* 273–279.

Patai, R. (1967). *The Hebrew goddess.* New York: Avon Books.

Paterson, D. G. (1999). A provocative treatise. *Journal of Higher Education, 70,* 621–623.

Patterson, D. R., Everett, J. J., Burns, G. L., & Marvin, J. A. (1992). Hypnosis for the treatment of burn pain. *Journal of Consulting and Clinical Psychology, 60,* 713–717.

Patton, C. J. (1992). Fear of abandonment and binge eating: A subliminal psychodynamic activation investigation. *Journal of Nervous and Mental Disease, 180,* 484–490.

Paul, R. (1985). Freud and the seduction theory: A critical examination of Masson's "The assault on truth." *Journal of Psychoanalytic Anthropology, 8,* 161–187.

Paulhus, D. L., Fridhandler, B., & Hayes, S. (1997). Psychological defense: Contemporary theory and research. In R. Hogan, J. Johnson, & S. Briggs (Eds.), *Handbook of personality psychology* (pp. 543–579). San Diego, CA: Academic Press.

Pavot, W., & Diener, E. (2008). The Satisfaction with Life Scale and the emerging construct of life satisfaction. *Journal of Positive Psychology, 3,* 137–152.

Payne, R. L. (2000). Eupsychian management and the millennium. *Journal of Managerial Psychology, 15,* 219–226.

Peake, P. K., & Mischel, W. (1984). Getting lost in the search for large coefficients: Reply to Conley. *Psychological Review, 91,* 497–501.

Pelzer, D. (1995). *A child called "it": One child's courage to survive.* Deerfield Beach, FL: Health Communications.

Pelzer, D. (1997). *The lost boy: A foster child's search for the love of a family.* Deerfield Beach, FL: Health Communications.

Pelzer, D. (1999). *A man named Dave: A story of triumph and forgiveness.* New York: Plume.

Pelzer, D. (2000). *Help yourself: Celebrating the rewards of resilience and gratitude.* New York: Dutton.

Pelzer, D. (2004). *The privilege of youth: A teenager's story of longing for acceptance and friendship.* New York: Dutton.

Pennebaker, J. (1993). Putting stress into words: Health, linguistic, and therapeutic implications. *Behavioral Research Therapy, 31,* 539–548.

Pennebaker, J. W., Colder, M., & Sharp, L. K. (1990). Accelerating the coping process. *Journal of Personality and Social Psychology, 58,* 528–537.

Pepper, S. C. (1942). *World hypotheses: A study in evidence.* Berkeley, CA: University of California Press.

Perlini, A. H., Haley, A., & Buczel, A. (1998). Hypnosis and reporting biases: Telling the truth. *Journal of Research in Personality, 32,* 13–32.

Perlman, M. (1983). Phaethon and the thermonuclear chariot. *Spring: An Annual of Archetypal Psychology and Jungian Thought* (pp. 87–108). Zürich, Switzerland: Spring.

Perluss, B. (2008). Climbing the alchemical mountain. *Psychological Perspectives, 51,* 87–107.

Perry J. C., & Ianni, F. F. (1998). Observer-rated measures of defense mechanisms. *Journal of Personality, 66,* 994–1024.

Peters, M. L., Flink, I. K., Boersma, K., & Linton, S. J. (2010). Manipulating optimism: Can imagining a best possible self be used to increase positive future expectancies? *Journal of Positive Psychology, 5,* 204–211.

Peterson, B. E. (2006). Generativity and successful parenting: An analysis of young adult outcomes. *Journal of Personality, 74,* 847–869.

Peterson, B. E., & Klohnen, E. C. (1995). Realization of generativity in two samples of women at midlife. *Psychology and Aging, 10,* 20–29.

Peterson, B. E., Smirles, K. A., & Wentworth, P. A. (1997). Generativity and authoritarianism: Implications for personality, political involvement, and parenting. *Journal of Personality and Social Psychology, 72,* 1202–1216.

Peterson, B. E., & Stewart, A. J. (1990). Using personal and fictional documents to assess psychosocial development: A case study of Vera Brittain's generativity. *Psychology and Aging, 5,* 400–411.

Peterson, B. E., & Stewart, A. J. (1996). Antecedents and contexts of generativity motivation at midlife. *Psychology and Aging, 11,* 21–33.

Peterson, C. (1993). Helpless behavior. *Behaviour Research and Therapy, 31,* 289–295.

Peterson, C. (2006). The Values in Action (VIA) classification of strengths. In M. Csikszentmihalyi & I. S. Csikszentmihalyi (Eds.), *A life worth living: Contributions to positive psychology* (pp. 29–48). New York: Oxford University Press.

Peterson, C., Seligman, M. E. P., & Vaillant, G. E. (1988). Pessimistic explanatory style is a risk factor for physical illness: A thirty-five-year longitudinal study. *Journal of Personality and Social Psychology, 55,* 23–27.

Peterson-Cooney, L. (1987). Time-concentrated instruction as an immediate risk to self-actualization. *Psychological Reports, 61,* 183–190.

Petrie, K. J., Booth, R. J., & Pennebaker, J. W. (1998). The immunological effects of thought suppression. *Journal of Personality and Social Psychology, 75,* 1264–1272.

Pettigrew, T. F. (1999). Gordon Willard Allport: A tribute. *Journal of Social Issues, 55,* 415–427.

Phillips, A. S., Long, R. G., & Bedeian, A. G. (1990). Type A status: Birth order and gender effects. *Individual Psychology, 46,* 365–373.

Phillips, J. M., & Gully, S. M. (1997). Role of goal orientation, ability, need for achievement, and locus of control in the self-efficacy and goal-setting process. *Journal of Applied Psychology, 82,* 792–802.

Phillips, K. L. (1980). The riddle of change. In G. Epstein (Ed.), *Studies in non-deterministic psychology* (pp. 229–253). New York: Human Sciences Press.

Phillips, K., & Matheny, A. P., Jr. (1997). Evidence for genetic influence on both cross-situation and situation-specific components of behavior. *Journal of Personality and Social Psychology, 73,* 129–138.

Pichot, P. (1984). Centenary of the birth of Hermann Rorschach. *Journal of Personality Assessment, 48,* 591–596.

Pickering, A. D. (1997). The conceptual nervous system and personality: From Pavlov to neural networks. *European Psychologist, 2,* 139–163.

Piers, C. (1998). Contemporary trauma theory and its relation to character. *Psychoanalytic Psychology, 15,* 14–33.

Pietikainen, P., & Ihanus, J. (2003). On the origins of psychoanalytic psychohistory. *History of Psychology, 6,* 171–194.

Piliavin, J. A. (2003). Doing well by doing good: Benefits for the benefactor. In C. L. M. Keyes & J. Haidt (Eds.), *Flourishing: Positive psychology and the life well-lived* (pp. 227–247). Washington, DC: American Psychological Association.

Ploubidis, G. B., & Grundy, E. (2009). Personality and all cause mortality: Evidence for indirect links. *Personality and Individual Differences, 47,* 203–208.

Pois, R. A. (1990). The case for clinical training and challenges to psychohistory. *Psychohistory Review, 18,* 169–187.

Polivy, J. (1998). The effects of behavioral inhibition: Integrating internal cues, cognition, behavior, and affect. *Psychological Inquiry, 9,* 181–204.

Pollock, P. H., & Kear-Colwell, J. J. (1994). Women who stab: A personal construct analysis of sexual victimization and offending behaviour. *British Journal of Medical Psychology, 67,* 13–22.

Popper, K. R. (1962). *Conjectures and refutations.* New York: Basic Books.

Porter, S. S., & Inks, L. W. (2000). Cognitive complexity and salesperson adaptability: An exploratory investigation. *Journal of Personal Selling and Sales Management, 20,* 15–21.

Pratt, A. B. (1985). Adlerian psychology as an intuitive operant system. *Behavior Analyst, 8,* 39–51.

Pratt, M. W., Danso, H. A., Arnold, M. L., Norris, J. E., & Filyer, R. (2001). Adult generativity and the socialization of adolescents: Relations to mothers' and fathers' parenting beliefs, styles, and practices. *Journal of Personality, 69,* 89–120.

Prerost, F. J. (1989). Humor as an intervention strategy during psychological treatment: Imagery and incongruity. *Psychology, 26,* 34–40.

Price, M. E., Cosmides, L., & Tooby, J. (2002). Punitive sentiment as an anti-free rider psychological device. *Evolution and Human Behavior, 23,* 203–231.

Primavera, J. P., III, & Kaiser, R. S. (1992). Non-pharmacological treatment of headache: Is less more? *Headache, 32,* 393–395.

Proctor, C. L., Linley, P. A., & Maltby, J. (2009). Youth life satisfaction: A review of the literature. *Journal of Happiness Studies, 10,* 583–630.

Progoff, I. (1975). *At a journal workshop.* New York: Dialogue House Library.

Protinsky, H. (1988). Identity formation: A comparison of problem and nonproblem adolescents. *Adolescence, 23,* 67–72.

Pryor, D. B., & Tollerud, T. R. (1999). Applications of Adlerian principles in school settings. *Professional School Counseling, 2,* 299–304.

Pulkkinen, L. (1992). Life-styles in personality development. *European Journal of Personality, 6,* 139–155.

Qirko, H. (2004). Altruistic celibacy, kin-cue manipulation, and the development of religious institutions. *Zygon, 39,* 681–706.

Quay, H. C. (1997). Inhibition and attention deficit hyperactivity disorder. *Journal of Abnormal Child Psychology, 25,* 7–13.

Quinn, S. (1988). *A mind of her own: The life of Karen Horney.* Reading, MA: Addison-Wesley.

Rachman, A. W., Yard, M. A., & Kennedy, R. E. (2009). Noninterpretative measures in the analysis of trauma. *Psychoanalytic Psychology, 26,* 259–273.

Raggatt, P. (2006). Putting the Five-Factor Model into context: Evidence linking Big Five traits to narrative identity. *Journal of Personality, 74,* 1321–1348.

Rapaport, D. (1959). Introduction: A historical survey of psychoanalytic ego psychology. In E. H. Erikson, *Identity and the life cycle: Selected papers. Psychological Issues, 1* (pp. 5–17). New York: International Universities Press.

Raskin, J. D., & Epting, F. R. (1993). Personal construct theory and the argument against mental illness. *International Journal of Personal Construct Psychology, 6,* 351–369.

Ratanakul, P. (2002). Buddhism and science: Allies or enemies? *Zygon, 37,* 115–120.

Rathunde, K. (2001). Toward a psychology of optimal human functioning: What positive psychology can learn from the "experimental turns" of James, Dewey, and Maslow. *Journal of Humanistic Psychology, 41,* 135–141.

Reinsdorf, W. (1993–1994). Schizophrenia, poetic imagery and metaphor. *Imagination, Cognition and Personality, 13,* 335–345.

Reis, H. T., Lin, Y., Bennett, M. E., & Nezlek, J. B. (1993). Change and consistency in social participation during early adulthood. *Developmental Psychology, 29,* 633–645.

Reis, S. M., & Renzulli, J. S. (2004). Current research on the social and emotional development of gifted and talented students: Good news and future possibilities. *Psychology in the Schools, 41,* 119–130.

Reiser, M. F. (2001). The dream in contemporary psychiatry. *American Journal of Psychiatry, 158,* 351–359.

Remnick, D. (2010). *The bridge: The life and rise of Barack Obama.* New York: Alfred A. Knopf.

Rendon, M. (1988). A cognitive unconscious? *American Journal of Psychoanalysis, 48,* 291–293.

Repp, A. (1994). Comments on functional analysis procedures for school-based behavior problems. *Journal of Applied Behavior Analysis, 27,* 409–411.

Reuter, M., Schmitz, A., Corr, P., & Hennig, J. (2006). Molecular genetics support Gray's personality theory: The interaction of COMT and DRD2 polymorphisms predicts the behavioural approach system. *International Journal of Neuropsychopharmacology, 9,* 155–166.

Revelle, W., & Oehlberg, K. (2008). Integrating experimental and observational personality research—The contributions of Hans Eysenck. *Journal of Personality, 76,* 1387–1414.

Rhodewalt, F., Madrian, J. C., & Cheney, S. (1998). Narcissism, self-knowledge, organization, and emotional reactivity: The effect of daily experience on self-esteem and affect. *Personality and Social Psychology Bulletin, 24,* 75–87.

Rhodewalt, F., & Morf, C. C. (1998). On self-aggrandizement and anger: A temporal analysis of narcissism and affective reactions to success and failure. *Journal of Personality and Social Psychology, 74,* 672–685.

Rholes, W. S., Simpson, J. A., Blakely, B. S., Lanigan, L., & Allen, E. A. (1997). Adult attachment styles, the desire to have children, and working models of parenthood. *Journal of Personality, 65,* 357–385.

Richards, A. C., & Combs, A. W. (1992). Education and the humanistic challenge. *Humanistic Psychologist, 20,* 372–388.

Richards, J. M., Beal, W. E., Seagal, J. D., & Pennebaker, J. W. (2000). Effects of disclosure of traumatic events on illness behavior among psychiatric prison inmates. *Journal of Abnormal Psychology, 109,* 156–160.

Richards, P. S., & Bergin, A. E. (1997). *A spiritual strategy for counseling and psychotherapy.* Washington, DC: American Psychological Association.

Richardson, F. C., & Manaster, G. J. (1997). Back to the future: Alfred Adler on freedom and commitment. *Individual Psychology, 53,* 286–309.

Richman, J. (2001). Humor and creative life styles. *American Journal of Psychotherapy, 55,* 420–428.

Rideout, C. A., & Richardson, S. A. (1989). A teambuilding model: Appreciating differences using the Myers-Briggs Type Indicator with developmental theory. *Journal of Counseling and Development, 67,* 529–533.

Riedel, H. P. R., Heiby, E. M., & Kopetskie, S. (2001). Psychological behaviorism theory of bipolar disorder. *Psychological Record, 51,* 507–532.

Rilling, J. K., & Sanfey, A. G. (2011). The neuroscience of social decision-making. *Annual Review of Psychology, 62,* 1–17.

Rilling, M. (2000). John Watson's paradoxical struggle to explain Freud. *American Psychologist, 55,* 301–312.

Risemberg, R., & Zimmerman, B. J. (1992). Self-regulated learning in gifted students. *Roeper Review, 15,* 98–101.

Ritskes, R., Ritskes-Hoitinga, M., Stodkilde-Jorgensen, H., Baerentsen, K., & Hartman, T. (2003). MRI scanning during Zen meditation: The picture of enlightenment? *Constructivism in the Human Sciences, 8,* 85–90.

Roberts, B. W. (2007). Contextualizing personality psychology. *Journal of Personality, 75,* 1071–1082.

Roberts, B. W., & Donahue, E. M. (1994). One personality, multiple selves: Integrating personality and social roles. *Journal of Personality, 62,* 199–218.

Roberts, R. E., Phinney, J. S., Masse, L. C., Chen, Y. R., Roberts, C. R., & Romero, A. (1999). The structure of ethnic identity of young adolescents from diverse ethnocultural groups. *Journal of Early Adolescence, 19,* 301–322.

Robins, C. J. (2002). Zen principles and mindfulness practice in dialectical behavior therapy. *Cognitive and Behavioral Practice, 9,* 50–57.

Robinson, M. D., & Wilkowski, B. M. (2006). Loving, hating, vacillating: Agreeableness, implicit self-esteem, and neurotic conflict. *Journal of Personality, 74,* 935–977.

Robinson, O. C., Demetre, J. D., & Corney, R. (2010). Personality and retirement: Exploring the links between the Big Five personality traits, reasons for retirement and the experience of being retired. *Personality and Individual Differences, 48,* 792–797.

Rodriguez, M. L., Mischel, W., & Shoda, Y. (1989). Cognitive person variables in the delay of gratification of older children at risk. *Journal of Personality and Social Psychology, 57,* 358–367.

Roemer, W. W. (1987). An application of the interpersonal models developed by Karen Horney and Timothy Leary to Type A-B behavior patterns. *American Journal of Psychoanalysis, 47,* 116–130.

Rogeness, G. A., & McClure, E. B. (1996). Development and neurotransmitter-environmental interactions. *Development and Psychopathology, 8,* 183–199.

Rogers, C. R. (1942a). *Counseling and psychotherapy: Newer concepts in practice.* Boston, MA: Houghton Mifflin.

Rogers, C. R. (1942b). The use of electrically recorded interviews in improving psychotherapeutic techniques. *American Journal of Orthopsychiatry, 12,* 429–434.

Rogers, C. R. (1951). *Client-centered therapy.* Boston, MA: Houghton Mifflin.

Rogers, C. R. (1954). Towards a theory of creativity. *ETC: A Review of General Semantics, 11,* 249–260.

Rogers, C. R. (1955). Persons or science: A philosophical question. *American Psychologist, 10,* 267–278.

Rogers, C. R. (1956). Intellectualized psychotherapy. *Contemporary Psychology, 1,* 355–358.

Rogers, C. R. (1957a). The necessary and sufficient conditions of therapeutic personality change. *Journal of Consulting Psychology, 21,* 95–103.

Rogers, C. R. (1957b). Personal thoughts on teaching and learning. *Merrill-Palmer Quarterly, 3,* 241–243.

Rogers, C. R. (1959). A theory of therapy, personality, and interpersonal relationships, as developed in the client-centered framework. In S. Koch (Ed.), *Psychology: A study of a science: Vol. 3. Formulations of the person and the social context* (pp. 185–256). New York: McGraw-Hill.

Rogers, C. R. (1961). *On becoming a person: A therapist's view of psychotherapy.* Boston, MA: Houghton Mifflin.

Rogers, C. R. (1964). Toward a modern approach to values: The valuing process in the mature person. *Journal of Abnormal and Social Psychology, 68,* 160–167.

Rogers, C. R. (1967). Carl R. Rogers. In E. G. Boring & G. Lindzey (Eds.), *A history of psychology in autobiography* (Vol. 5, pp. 341–384). New York: Appleton-Century-Crofts.

Rogers, C. R. (1968). Some thoughts regarding the current presuppositions of the behavioral sciences. In W. Coulson & C. R. Rogers (Eds.), *Man and the science of man* (pp. 55–72). Columbus, OH: Chas. E. Merrill.

Rogers, C. R. (1969). *Freedom to learn: A view of what education might become.* Columbus, OH: Merrill.

Rogers, C. R. (1970). *Carl Rogers on encounter groups.* New York: Harper & Row.

Rogers, C. R. (1973). Some new challenges. *American Psychologist, 28,* 379–387.

Rogers, C. R. (1974a). Can learning encompass both ideas and feelings? *Education, 95,* 103–114.

Rogers, C. R. (1974b). The project at Immaculate Heart: An experiment in self-directed change. *Education, 95,* 172–196.

Rogers, C. R. (1974c). In retrospect: Forty-six years. *American Psychologist, 29,* 115–123.

Rogers, C. R. (1977). *Carl Rogers on personal power.* New York: Delacorte Press.

Rogers, C. R. (1979). The foundations of the person-centered approach. *Education, 100,* 98–107.

Rogers, C. R. (1980). *A way of being.* Boston, MA: Houghton Mifflin.

Rogers, C. R. (1982a). A psychologist looks at nuclear war: Its threat, its possible prevention. *Journal of Humanistic Psychology, 22*(4), 9–20.

Rogers, C. R. (1982b). Reply to Rollo May's letter to Carl Rogers. *Journal of Humanistic Psychology, 22*(4), 85–89.

Rogers, C. R. (1983). *Freedom to learn for the 80's.* Columbus, OH: Merrill.

Rogers, C. R. (1986a). Rogers, Kohut, and Erickson: A personal perspective on some similarities and differences. *Person-Centered Review, 1,* 125–140.

Rogers, C. R. (1986b). The Rust workshop. *Journal of Humanistic Psychology, 26*(3), 23–45.

Rogers, C. R. (1986c). Transference. *Person-Centered Review, 2,* 182–188.

Rogers, C. R. (1987). Comments on the issue of equality in psychotherapy. *Journal of Humanistic Psychology, 27*(1), 38–40.

Rogers, C. R., & Ryback, D. (1984). One alternative to nuclear planetary suicide. *Counseling Psychologist, 12,* 3–12.

Rogers, C. R., & Skinner, B. F. (1956). Some issues concerning the control of human behavior. *Science, 124,* 1057–1066.

Romanoff, B. (1999). Meaning reconstruction in the wake of loss [Book review]. *Death Studies, 23,* 465–472.

Roscoe, B., & Peterson, K. L. (1982). Teacher and situational characteristics which enhance learning and development. *College Student Journal, 16,* 389–394.

Rosen, D. H. (1993). *Transforming depression: Healing the soul through creativity.* New York: Penguin.

Rosen, D. H. (1996). *The Tao of Jung: The way of integrity.* New York: Penguin.

Rosen, D. H., Smith, S. M., Huston, H. L., & Gonzalez, G. (1991). Empirical study of associations between symbols and their meanings: Evidence of collective unconscious (archetypal) memory. *Journal of Analytical Psychology, 36,* 211–228.

Rosen, J. B., & Schulkin, J. (1998). From normal fear to pathological anxiety. *Psychological Review, 105,* 325–350.

Rosenberg, B. G. (2000). Birth order and personality: Is Sulloway's treatment a radical rebellion or is he preserving the status quo? *Politics and the Life Sciences, 19,* 170–172.

Rosenberg, S. D., Schnurr, P. P., & Oxman, T. E. (1990). Content analysis: A comparison of manual and computerized systems. *Journal of Personality Assessment, 54,* 298–310.

Rosenman, S. (1989). Guardians, ferrets and defilers of the treasure: The Masson-Freudians controversy. *Journal of Psychohistory, 16,* 297–321.

Rosenstein, D. S., & Horowitz, H. A. (1996). Adolescent attachment and psychopathology. *Journal of Consulting and Clinical Psychology, 64,* 244–253.

Ross, L. (1977). The intuitive psychologist and his shortcomings: Distortions in the attribution process. In L. Berkowitz (Ed.), *Advances in experimental social psychology* (Vol. 10, pp. 173–220). New York: Academic Press.

Rothbaum, F., & Weisz, J. R. (1994). Parental caregiving and child externalizing behavior in nonclinical samples: A meta-analysis. *Psychological Bulletin, 116,* 55–74.

Rotter, J. B. (1966). Generalized expectancies for internal versus external control of reinforcement. *Psychological Monographs, 80* (Whole No. 609).

Rotter, J. B. (1990). Internal versus external control of reinforcement: A case history of a variable. *American Psychologist, 45,* 489–493.

Rowan, J. (2007). On leaving Flatland and honoring Maslow. *Humanistic Psychologist, 35,* 73–79.

Rowland, R. C., & Jones, J. M. (2007). Recasting the American Dream and American politics: Barack Obama's keynote address to the 2004 Democratic National Convention. *Quarterly Journal of Speech, 93,* 425–448.

Rubin, K. H. (1998). Social and emotional development from a cultural perspective. *Developmental Psychology, 34,* 611–615.

Rugel, R. P., & Barry, D. (1990). Overcoming denial through the group: A test of acceptance theory. *Small Group Research, 21,* 45–58.

Runco, M. A., Ebersole, P., & Mraz, W. (1991). Creativity and self-actualization. *Journal of Social Behavior and Personality, 6*(5), 161–167.

Runyan, W. M. (1981). Why did Van Gogh cut off his ear? The problem of alternative explanations in psychobiography. *Journal of Personality and Social Psychology, 40,* 1070–1077.

Runyan, W. M. (1982). The psychobiography debate: An analytical review. In L. Wheeler (Ed.), *Review of personality and social psychology* (Vol. 3, pp. 225–253). Beverly Hills, CA: Sage.

Runyan, W. M. (1983). Idiographic goals and methods in the study of lives. *Journal of Personality, 51,* 413–437.

Runyan, W. M. (1988). *Psychology and historical interpretation.* New York: Oxford University Press.

Runyon, R. S. (1984). Freud and Adler: A conceptual analysis of their differences. *Psychoanalytic Review, 71,* 413–421.

Rushton, J. P., Bons, T. A., & Hur, Y. M. (2008). The genetics and evolution of the general factor of personality. *Journal of Research in Personality, 42,* 1173–1185.

Rushton, J. P., & Irwing, P. (2009a). A General Factor of Personality (GFP) from the Multidimensional Personality Questionnaire. *Personality and Individual Differences, 47,* 571–576.

Rushton, J. P., & Irwing, P. (2009b). A General Factor of Personality in 16 sets of the Big Five, the Guilford–Zimmerman Temperament Survey, the California Psychological Inventory, and the Temperament and Character Inventory. *Personality and Individual Differences, 47,* 558–564.

Russell, R. L. (1986). The inadvisability of admixing psychoanalysis with other forms of psychotherapy. *Journal of Contemporary Psychotherapy, 16,* 76–86.

Ruvolo, A. P., & Brennan, C. J. (1997). What's love got to do with it? Close relationships and perceived growth. *Personality and Social Psychology Bulletin, 23,* 814–823.

Ryan, R. M., & Deci, E. L. (2000). Self-determination theory and the facilitation of intrinsic motivation, social development, and well-being. *American Psychologist, 55,* 68–78.

Ryan, R. M., Rigby, S., & King, K. (1993). Two types of religious internalization and their relations to religious orientations and mental health. *Journal of Personality and Social Psychology, 65,* 586–596.

Ryback, D. (1983). Jedi and Jungian forces. *Psychological Perspectives, 14,* 238–244.

Rychlak, J. F. (1977). *The psychology of rigorous humanism.* New York: Wiley-Interscience.

Rychlak, J. F. (1984). Newtonianism and the professional responsibility of psychologists: Who speaks for humanity? *Professional Psychology: Research and Practice, 15,* 82–95.

Rychlak, J. F. (1986). Logical learning theory: A teleological alternative in the field of personality. *Journal of Personality, 54,* 734–762.

Rychlak, J. F. (1988). *The psychology of rigorous humanism* (2nd ed.). New York: New York University Press.

Rychlak, J. F. (1998). How Boulder biases have limited possible theoretical contributions to psychotherapy. *Clinical Psychology: Science and Practice, 5,* 233–241.

Ryff, C. D. (1989). Happiness is everything, or is it? Explorations on the meaning of psychological well-being. *Journal of Personality and Social Psychology, 57,* 1069–1081.

Sabido, M. (1981). *Towards the social use of soap operas.* Mexico City, Mexico: Institute for Communication Research.

Sabol, S. Z., Nelson, M. L., Fisher, C., Gunzerath, L., Brody, C. L., Hu, S., Sirota, L. A., Marcus, S. E., Greenberg, B. D., Lucas, F. R., IV, Benjamin, J., Murphy, D. L., & Hamer, D. H. (1999). A genetic association for cigarette smoking behavior. *Health Psychology, 18,* 7–13.

Sackett, S. J. (1998). Career counseling as an aid to self-actual-ization. *Journal of Career Development, 24,* 235–244.

Sahdra, B. K., Shaver, P. R., & Brown, K. W. (2010). A scale to measure nonattachment: A Buddhist complement to western research on attachment and adaptive functioning. *Journal of Personality Assessment, 92,* 116–127.

Salmon, C. A., & Daly, M. (1998). Birth order and familial sentiment: Middleborns are different. *Evolution and Human Behavior, 19,* 299–312.

Salmon, D., & Fenning, P. (1993). A process of mentorship in school consultation. *Journal of Educational and Psychological Consultation, 4*(1), 69–87.

Salmon, D., & Lehrer, R. (1989). School consultant's implicit theories of action. *Professional School Psychology, 4,* 173–187.

Salovey, P., & Mayer, J. D. (1990). Emotional intelligence. *Imagination, Cognition and Personality, 9,* 185–211.

Sandler, I. N., Schoenfelder, E. N., Wolchik, S. A., & MacKinnon, D. P. (2011). Long-term impact of prevention programs to promote effective parenting: Lasting effects but uncertain processes. *Annual Review of Psychology, 62,* 299–329.

Sanger, M. (1971). *Margaret Sanger: An autobiography.* New York: Dover. (Original work published 1938)

Sansone, C., & Thoman, D. B. (2006). Maintaining activity engagement: Individual differences in the process of self-regulating emotion. *Journal of Personality, 74,* 1697–1720.

Sappington, A. A. (1990). Recent psychological approaches to the free will versus determinism issue. *Psychological Bulletin, 108,* 19–29.

Saraswati, N. (2002, May). Balancing the emotions. *Yoga Magazine.* Available online at http://www.yogamag.net/archives/2002/3may02/balemo.shtml

Sarbin, T. R. (1986). The narrative as a root metaphor for psychology. In T. R. Sarbin (Ed.), *Narrative psychology: The storied nature of human conduct* (pp. 3–21). New York: Praeger.

Sarchione, C. D., Cuttler, M. J., Muchinsky, P. M., & Nelson-Gray, R. O. (1998). Prediction of dysfunctional job behaviors among law enforcement officers. *Journal of Applied Psychology, 83,* 904–912.

Saucier, G. (2009). Recurrent personality dimensions in inclusive lexical studies: Indications for a Big Six structure. *Journal of Personality, 77,* 1577–1614.

Saucier, G., Bel-Bahar, T., & Fernandez, C. (2007). What modifies the expression of personality tendencies? Defining basic domains of situation variables. *Journal of Personality, 75,* 479–503.

Saucier, G., & Skrzypińska, K. (2006). Spiritual but not religious? Evidence for two independent dimensions. *Journal of Personality, 74,* 1257–1292.

Saunders, P., & Skar, P. (2001). Archetypes, complexes and self-organization. *Journal of Analytical Psychology, 46,* 305–323.

Sax, K. W., & Strakowski, S. M. (1998). Enhanced behavioral response to repeated d-amphetamine and personality traits in humans. *Biological Psychiatry, 44,* 1192–1195.

Schachter, S. (1963). Birth order, eminence, and higher education. *American Sociological Review, 3,* 757–767.

Schaefer, S. M., Jackson, D. C., Davidson, R. J., Aguirre, G. K., Kimberg, D. Y., & Thompson-Schill, S. L. (2002). Modulation of amygdalar activity by the conscious regulation of negative emotion. *Journal of Cognitive Neuroscience, 14,* 913–921.

Schaum, M. (2000). "Erasing angel": The Lucifer-trickster figure in Flannery O'Connor's short fiction. *Southern Literary Journal, 33*(1), 1–26.

Scheflin, A. W., & Brown, D. (1996). Repressed memory or dissociative amnesia: What the science says. *Journal of Psychiatry and Law, 24,* 143–188.

Schepeler, E. (1990). The biographer's transference: A chapter in psychobiographical epistemology. *Biography, 13,* 111–129.

Scherr, A. (2001). Leonardo Da Vinci, Sigmund Freud, and fear of flying. *Midwest Quarterly, 42,* 115–132.

Schlamm, L. (2007). C. G. Jung and numinous experience: Between the known and the unknown. *European Journal of Psychotherapy and Counselling, 9,* 403–414.

Schmidt, F. L., & Hunter, J. E. (1998). The validity and utility of selection methods in personnel psychology: Practical and theoretical implications of 85 years of research findings. *Psychological Bulletin, 124,* 262–274.

Schmidt, L. A., Fox, N. A., Rubin, K. H., Hu, S., & Hamer, D. H. (2002). Molecular genetics of shyness and aggression in preschoolers. *Personality and Individual Differences, 33,* 227–238.

Schmitt, D. R. (1984). Interpersonal relations: Cooperation and competition. *Journal of the Experimental Analysis of Behavior, 42,* 377–383.

Schmutte, P. S., & Ryff, C. D. (1997). Personality and well-being: Reexamining methods and meanings. *Journal of Personality and Social Psychology, 73,* 549–559.

Schnaitter, R. (1987). Behaviorism is not cognitive and cogni-tivism is not behavioral. *Behaviorism, 15,* 1–11.

Schneider, R. H., Alexander, C. N., Staggers, F., Rainforth, M., Salerno, J. W., Hartz, A., Arndt, S., Barnes, V. A., & Nidich, S. I. (2005). Long-term effects of stress reduction on mortality in persons ≥55 years of age with systemic hypertension. *American Journal of Cardiology, 95,* 1060–1064.

Schnell, R. L. (1980). Contributions to psychohistory: IV. Individual experience in historiography and psychoanalysis: Significance of Erik Erikson and Robert Coles. *Psychological Reports, 46,* 591–612.

Schnell, T. (2009). The Sources of Meaning and Meaning in Life Questionnaire (SoMe): Relations to demographics and well-being. *Journal of Positive Psychology, 4,* 483–499.

Schott, R. L. (1992). Abraham Maslow, humanistic psychology, and organization leadership: A Jungian perspective. *Journal of Humanistic Psychology, 32*(1), 106–120.

Schramski, T. G., & Giovando, K. (1993). Sexual orientation, social interest, and exemplary practice. *Individual Psychology, 49,* 199–204.

Schueller, S. M. (2010). Preferences for positive psychology exercises. *Journal of Positive Psychology, 5,* 192–203.

Schurr, K. T., Ruble, V., Palomba, C., Pickerill, B., & Moore, D. (1997). Relationships between the MBTI and selected aspect of Tinto's model for college attrition. *Journal of Psychological Type, 40,* 31–34.

Schwartz, D. (1999). Is a gay Oedipus a Trojan horse? Commentary on Lewes's "A special Oedipal mechanism in the development of male homosexuality." *Psychoanalytic Psychology, 16,* 88–93.

Schwartz, L. K., & Simmons, J. P. (2001). Contact quality and attitudes toward the elderly. *Educational Gerontology, 27,* 127–137.

Schwartz, M. D., Taylor, K. L., & Willard, K. S. (2003). Prospective association between distress and mammography utilization among women with a family history of breast cancer. *Journal of Behavioral Medicine, 26,* 105–117.

Schwartz, M. D., Taylor, K. L., Willard, K. S., Siegel, J. E., Lamdan, R. M., & Moran, K. (1999). Distress, personality, and mammography utilization among women with a family history of breast cancer. *Health Psychology, 18,* 327–332.

Schwartz, S. J., Dunkel, C. S., & Waterman, A. S. (2009). Terrorism: An identity theory perspective. *Studies in Conflict and Terrorism, 32,* 537–559.

Scott, J. (2011). *A singular woman: The untold story of Barack Obama's mother.* New York: Penguin.

Scott, N. E., & Borodovsky, L. G. (1990). Effective use of cultural role taking. *Professional Psychology: Research and Practice, 21,* 167–170.

Sears, D. O. (1986). College sophomores in the laboratory: Influences of a narrow data base on social psychology's view of human nature. *Journal of Personality and Social Psychology, 51,* 515–530.

Seeman, T. E., Dubin, L. F., & Seeman, M. (2003). Religiosity/spirituality and health: A critical review of the evidence for biological pathways. *American Psychologist, 58,* 53–63.

Segura, D. A., & Pierce, J. L. (1993). Chicana/o family structure and gender personality: Chodorow, familism, and psychoanalytic sociology revisited. *Signs, 19,* 62–91.

Seligman, M. E. (1992). *Helplessness: On depression, development, and death* (Rev. ed.). New York: W. H. Freeman.

Seligman, M. E. P., & Csikszentmihalyi, M. (2000). Positive psychology: An introduction. *American Psychologist, 55,* 5–14.

Sewell, K. W. (1996). Constructional risk factors for a posttraumatic stress response after a mass murder. *Journal of Constructivist Psychology, 9,* 97–107.

Sewell, K. W., Cromwell, R. L., Farrell-Higgins, J., Palmer, R., Ohlde, C., & Patterson, T. W. (1996). Hierarchical elaboration in the conceptual structures of Vietnam combat veterans. *Journal of Constructivist Psychology, 9,* 79–96.

Sexton, H. (1993). Exploring a psychotherapeutic change sequence: Relating process to intersessional and posttreatment outcome. *Journal of Consulting and Clinical Psychology, 61,* 128–136.

Sexton, T. L., & Tuckman, B. W. (1991). Self-beliefs and behavior: The role of self-efficacy and outcome expectation over time. *Personality and Individual Differences, 12,* 725–736.

Shafran, R., & Mansell, W. (2001). Perfectionism and psychopathology: A review of research and treatment. *Clinical Psychology Review, 21,* 879–906.

Shapiro, B. L. (1991). The use of personal construct theory and the repertory grid in the development of case reports of children's science learning. *International Journal of Personal Construct Psychology, 4,* 251–271.

Shapiro, K. (2002). Freudian slipage [Book review]. *Commentary, 113,* 60–63.

Shapiro, S. B. (1997). The UCSB Confluent Education Program: Its essence and demise. *Journal of Humanistic Psychology, 37*(3), 80–105.

Shapiro, S. B. (1998). *The place of confluent education in the human potential movement: A historical perspective.* Lanham, MD: University Press of America.

Shapiro, S. L., Astin, J. A., Bishop, S. R., & Cordova, M. (2005). Mindfulness-based stress reduction for health care professionals: Results from a randomized trial. *International Journal of Stress Management, 12,* 164–176.

Sharpsteen, D. J., & Kirkpatrick, L. A. (1997). Romantic jealousy and adult romantic attachment. *Journal of Personality and Social Psychology, 72,* 627–640.

Shatz, S. M. (2004). The relationship between Horney's three neurotic types and Eysenck's PEN model of personality. *Personality and Individual Differences, 37,* 1255–1261.

Shaver, P. R., & Brennan, K. A. (1992). Attachment styles and the "big five" personality traits: Their connections with each other and with romantic outcomes. *Personality and Social Psychology Bulletin, 18,* 536–545.

Shean, G. (2001). A critical look at the assumptions of cognitive therapy. *Psychiatry, 64,* 158–164.

Sheard, M., & Golby, J. (2009). Investigating the "rigid persistence paradox" in professional rugby union football. *International Journal of Sport and Exercise Psychology, 7,* 101–114.

Shelton, S. H. (1990). Developing the construct of general self-efficacy. *Psychological Reports, 66,* 987–994.

Sherman, R., & Dinkmeyer, D. (1987). *Systems of family therapy: An Adlerian integration.* New York: Brunner/Mazel.

Shoda, Y., Mischel, W., & Peake, P. K. (1990). Predicting adolescent cognitive and self-regulatory competencies from preschool delay of gratification: Identifying diagnostic conditions. *Developmental Psychology, 26,* 978–986.

Shoda, Y., Mischel, W., & Wright, J. C. (1989). Intuitive interactionism in person perception: Effects of situation-behavior relations on dispositional judgments. *Journal of Personality and Social Psychology, 56,* 41–53.

Shoda, Y., Mischel, W., & Wright, J. C. (1994). Intraindividual stability in the organization and patterning of behavior: Incorporating psychological situations into the idiographic analysis of personality. *Journal of Personality and Social Psychology, 67,* 674–687.

Shore, J. (2003). A Buddhist model of the human self: Working through the Jung-Hisamatsu discussion. In P. Young-Eisendrath (Ed.), *Awakening and insight: Zen Buddhism and psychotherapy* (pp. 29–42). Florence, KY: Routledge.

Shostrom, E. L. (1964). An inventory for the measurement of self-actualization. *Educational and Psychological Measurement, 24,* 207–217.

Shostrom, E. L. (Producer). (1965). *Three approaches to psychotherapy* (part 1) [Motion picture]. Orange, CA: Psychological Films.

Shostrom, E. L. (1972). *Freedom to be: Experiencing and expressing your total being.* Englewood Cliffs, NJ: Prentice-Hall.

Shostrom, E. L. (1975). Rejoinder to Anderson's article. *Journal of Humanistic Psychology, 15*(1), 35.

Shulman, D. G., & Ferguson, G. R. (1988). An experimental investigation of Kernberg's and Kohut's theories of narcissism. *Journal of Clinical Psychology, 44,* 445–451.

Siegel, B. (1982). Penis envy: From anatomical deficiency to narcissistic disturbance. *Bulletin of the Menninger Clinic, 46,* 363–376.

Siegel, P., & Weinberger, J. (1998). Capturing the "Mommy and I are one" merger fantasy: The oneness motive. In R. F. Bornstein & J. M. Masling (Eds.), *Empirical perspectives on the psychoanalytic unconscious* (pp. 71–97). Washington, DC: American Psychological Association.

Silverman, D. K. (1998). The tie that binds: Affect regulation, attachment, and psychoanalysis. *Psychoanalytic Psychology, 15,* 187–212.

Silverman, L. H. (1976). Psychoanalytic theory: "The reports of my death are greatly exaggerated." *American Psychologist, 31,* 621–635.

Silverman, L. H. (1983). The subliminal psychodynamic activation method: Overview and comprehensive listing of studies. In J. Masling (Ed.), *Empirical studies of psychoanalytic theories* (Vol. 1, pp. 69–100). Hillsdale, NJ: Analytic Press.

Silverman, L. H., Bronstein, A., & Mendelsohn, E. (1976). The further use of the subliminal psychodynamic activation method for the experimental study of the clinical theory of psychoanalysis: On the specificity of relationships between manifest psychopathology and unconscious conflict. *Psychotherapy: Theory, Research and Practice, 13,* 2–16.

Silverman, L. H., Frank, S. G., & Dachinger, P. (1974). A psychoanalytic reinterpretation of the effectiveness of systematic desensitization: Experimental data bearing on the role of merging fantasies. *Journal of Abnormal Psychology, 83,* 313–318.

Silverman, L. H., Kwawer, J. S., Wolitzky, C., & Coron, M. (1973). An experimental study of aspects of the psychoanalytic theory of male homosexuality. *Journal of Abnormal Psychology, 82,* 178–188.

Silverman, L. H., Martin, A., Ungaro, R., & Mendelsohn, E. (1978). Effect of subliminal stimulation of symbiotic fantasies on behavior modification treatment of obesity. *Journal of Consulting and Clinical Psychology, 46,* 432–441.

Silverman, L. H., Ross, D. L., Adler, J. M., & Lustig, D. A. (1978). Simple research paradigm for demonstrating subliminal psychodynamic activation: Effects of Oedipal stimuli on dart-throwing accuracy in college males. *Journal of Abnormal Psychology, 87,* 341–357.

Silverstein, S. M. (1993). Methodological and empirical considerations in assessing the validity of psychoanalytic theories of hypnosis. *Genetic, Social, and General Psychology Monographs, 119,* 5–54.

Simmonds, J. G. (2006). The oceanic feeling and a sea change: Historical challenges to reductionist attitudes to religion and spirit from within psychoanalysis. *Psychoanalytic Psychology, 23,* 128–142.

Simonton, D. K. (1998). Mad King George: The impact of personal and political stress on mental and physical health. *Journal of Personality, 66,* 443–466.

Sin, N. L., & Lyubomirsky, S. (2009). Enhancing well-being and alleviating depressive symptoms with positive psychology interventions: A practice-friendly meta-analysis. *Journal of Clinical Psychology: In Session, 65,* 467–487.

Sinclair, S., Pappas, J., & Lun, J. (2009). The interpersonal basis of stereotype-relevant self-views. *Journal of Personality, 77,* 1343–1364.

Singer, J. (1994). *Boundaries of the soul: The practice of Jung's psychology* (Rev. ed.). New York: Anchor.

Singh, N. N., Wahler, R. G., Adkins, A. D., & Myers, R. E. (2003). Soles of the feet: A mindfulness-based self-control intervention for aggression by an individual with mild mental retardation and mental illness. *Research in Developmental Disabilities, 24,* 158–169.

Sipps, G. J., & Alexander, R. A. (1987). The multifactorial nature of extraversion-introversion in the Myers-Briggs Type Indicator and Eysenck Personality Inventory. *Educational and Psychological Measurement, 47,* 543–552.

Sizemore, C. C., & Huber, R. J. (1988). The twenty-two faces of Eve. *Individual Psychology, 44,* 53–62.

Skinner, B. F. (1938). *The behavior of organisms.* New York: Appleton-Century.

Skinner, B. F. (1945, October). Baby in a box. *Ladies' Home Journal,* p. 30.

Skinner, B. F. (1948). *Walden two.* New York: Macmillan.

Skinner, B. F. (1950). Are theories of learning necessary? *Psychological Review, 57,* 193–216.

Skinner, B. F. (1953a). *Science and human behavior.* New York: Free Press.

Skinner, B. F. (1953b). Some contributions to an experimental analysis of behavior and to psychology as a whole. *American Psychologist, 8,* 69–78.

Skinner, B. F. (1957). *Verbal behavior.* New York: Appleton-Century-Crofts.

Skinner, B. F. (1958). *Notebooks* (R. Epstein, Ed.). Englewood Cliffs, NJ: Prentice-Hall.

Skinner, B. F. (1963). Behaviorism at fifty. *Science, 140,* 951–958.

Skinner, B. F. (1967). Autobiography. In E. G. Boring & G. Lindzey (Eds.), *A history of psychology in autobiography* (Vol. 5, pp. 385–413). New York: Appleton-Century-Crofts.

Skinner, B. F. (1971). *Beyond freedom and dignity.* New York: Knopf.

Skinner, B. F. (1972). *Cumulative record: A selection of papers* (3rd ed.). New York: Appleton-Century Crofts.

Skinner, B. F. (1975). The steep and thorny way to a science of behavior. *American Psychologist, 30,* 42–49.

Skinner, B. F. (1976). *Particulars of my life.* New York: Knopf.

Skinner, B. F. (1979). *The shaping of a behaviorist.* New York: Knopf.

Skinner, B. F. (1990). Can psychology be a science of mind? *American Psychologist, 45,* 1206–1210.

Slade, P. D., & Owens, R. G. (1998). A dual process model of perfectionism based on reinforcement theory. *Behavior Modification, 22,* 372–390.

Slife, B. D. (1981). Psychology's reliance on linear time: A reformulation. *Journal of Mind and Behavior, 2,* 27–46.

Slote, W. H. (1992). Oedipal ties and the issue of separation-individuation in traditional Confucian societies. *Journal of the American Academy of Psychoanalysis, 20,* 435–453.

Smith, B. W., Tooley, E. M., Christopher, P. J., & Kay, V. S. (2010). Resilience as the ability to bounce back from stress: A neglected personal resource? *Journal of Positive Psychology, 5,* 166–176.

Smith, C. P. (Ed.). (1992). *Handbook of thematic content analysis.* New York: Cambridge University Press.

Smith, D. (1982). Trends in counseling and psychotherapy. *American Psychologist, 37,* 802–809.

Smith, H. (1985). The sacred unconscious, with footnotes on self-actualization and evil. *Journal of Humanistic Psychology, 25*(3), 65–80.

Smith, M. B. (1973). On self-actualization: A transambivalent examination of a focal theme in Maslow's psychology. *Journal of Humanistic Psychology, 13*(2), 17–33.

Smith, M. B. (1990). Humanistic psychology. *Journal of Humanistic Psychology, 30*(4), 6–21.

Smith, T. L. (1983). Skinner's environmentalism: The analogy with natural selection. *Behaviorism, 11,* 133–153.

Smyth, J. M. (1998). Written emotional expression: Effect sizes, outcome types, and moderating variables. *Journal of Consulting and Clinical Psychology, 66,* 174–184.

Sneed, C. D., McCrae, R. R., & Funder, D. C. (1998). Lay conceptions of the five-factor model and its indicators. *Personality and Social Psychology Bulletin, 24,* 115–126.

So, K., & Orme-Johnson, D. W. (2001). Three randomized experiments on the longitudinal effects of the Transcendental Meditation technique on cognition. *Intelligence, 29,* 419–440.

Sohier, R. (1985–1986). Homosexual mutuality: Variation on a theme by Erik Erikson. *Journal of Homosexuality, 12*(2), 25–38.

Sohlberg, S., Billinghurst, A., & Nylén, S. (1998). Moderation of mood change after subliminal symbiotic stimulation: Four experiments contributing to the further demystification of Silverman's "Mommy and I are one" findings. *Journal of Research in Personality, 32,* 33–54.

Sohlberg, S., Samuelberg, P., Sidén, Y., & Thörn, C. (1998). Caveat medicus—Let the subliminal healer beware: Two experiments suggesting conditions when the effects of Silverman's *Mommy and I are one* phrase are negative. *Psychoanalytic Psychology, 15,* 93–114.

Sohn, D., & Lamal, P. A. (1982). Self-reinforcement: Its reinforcing capability and its clinical utility. *Psychological Record, 32,* 179–203.

Soldz, S., & Vaillant, G. E. (1999). The Big Five personality traits and the life course: A 45-year longitudinal study. *Journal of Research in Personality, 33,* 208–232.

Somer, O., & Goldberg, L. R. (1999). The structure of Turkish trait-descriptive adjectives. *Journal of Personality and Social Psychology, 76,* 431–450.

Sommers-Flanagan, J. (2007). The development and evolution of person-centered expressive art therapy: A conversation with Natalie Rogers. *Journal of Counseling and Development, 85,* 120–125.

Soresi, S., & Nota, L. (2000). A social skill training for persons with Down's syndrome. *European Psychologist, 5,* 33–43.

Spanos, N. P. (1994). Multiple identity enactments and multiple personality disorder: A sociocognitive perspective. *Psychological Bulletin, 116,* 143–165.

Spanos, N. P., Burgess, C. A., Cocco, L., & Pinch, N. (1993). Reporting bias and response to difficult suggestions in highly hypnotizable hypnotic subjects. *Journal of Research in Personality, 27,* 270–284.

Spanos, N. P., Sims, A., de Faye, B., Mondoux, T. J., & Gabora, N. J. (1992–1993). A comparison of hypnotic and nonhypnotic treatments for smoking. *Imagination, Cognition and Personality, 12,* 12–43.

Sperling, M. B., & Berman, W. H. (1991). An attachment classification of desperate love. *Journal of Personality Assessment, 56,* 45–55.

Sperling, M. B., Berman, W. H., & Fagen, G. (1992). Classification of adult attachment: An integrative taxonomy from attachment and psychoanalytic theories. *Journal of Personality Assessment, 59,* 239–247.

Sperry, R. W. (1988). Psychology's mentalist paradigm and the religion/science tension. *American Psychologist, 43,* 607–613.

Sperry, R. W. (1990). Structure and significance of the consciousness revolution. *Person-Centered Review, 5,* 120–129.

Spielberg, S. (Director), & Lustig, B. (Producer). (1993). *Schindler's list* [Motion picture]. Hollywood: Universal Pictures.

Spink, K. (1997). *Mother Teresa: A complete authorized biography.* New York: HarperCollins.

Spitz, R. A. (1945). Hospitalism. *Psychoanalytic Study of the Child, 2,* 53–74.

Staats, A. W. (1968). *Learning, language, and cognition.* New York: Holt, Rinehart & Winston.

Staats, A. W. (1971). *Child learning, intelligence and personality.* New York: Harper and Row.

Staats, A. W. (1975). *Social behaviorism.* Homewood, IL: Dorsey.

Staats, A. W. (1981). Social behaviorism, unified theory, unified theory construction methods, and the Zeitgeist of separatism. *American Psychologist, 36,* 239–256.

Staats, A. W. (1986). Behaviorism with a personality: The paradigmatic behavioral assessment approach. In R. O. Nelson & S. C. Hayes (Eds.), *Conceptual foundations of behavioral assessment* (pp. 242–296). New York: Guilford.

Staats, A. W. (1988). Skinner's theory and the emotion-behavior relationship: Incipient change with major implications. *American Psychologist, 43,* 747–748.

Staats, A. W. (1991). Unified positivism and unification psychology: Fad or new field? *American Psychologist, 46,* 899–912.

Staats, A. W. (1993). Personality theory, abnormal psychology, and psychological measurement: A psychological behaviorism. *Behavior Modification, 17,* 8–42.

Staats, A. W. (1996). *Behavior and personality: Psychological behaviorism.* New York: Springer.

Staats, A. W., & Burns, G. L. (1981). Intelligence and child development: What intelligence is and how it is learned and functions. *Genetic Psychology Monographs, 104,* 237–301.

Staats, A. W., & Burns, G. L. (1982). Emotional personality repertoire as cause of behavior: Specification of personality and interaction principles. *Journal of Personality and Social Psychology, 43,* 873–881.

Staats, A. W., & Eifert, G. H. (1990). The paradigmatic behaviorism theory of emotions. *Clinical Psychology Review, 10,* 539–566.

Staats, A. W., Gross, M. C., Guay, P. F., & Carlson, C. C. (1973). Personality and social systems and attitude-reinforcer-discriminative theory: Interest (attitude) formation, function, and measurement. *Journal of Personality and Social Psychology, 26,* 251–261.

Staats, A. W., & Heiby, E. M. (1985). Paradigmatic behaviorism's theory of depression: Unified, explanatory, and heuristic. In S. Reiss & R. R. Bootzin (Eds.), *Theoretical issues in behavior therapy* (pp. 279–330). New York: Academic Press.

Stajkovic, A. D., & Luthans, F. (1998). Self-efficacy and work-related performance: A meta-analysis. *Psychological Bulletin, 124,* 240–261.

Stallings, M. C., Hewitt, J. K., Cloninger, C. R., Heath, A. C., & Eaves, L. J. (1996). Genetic and environmental structure of the Tridimensional Personality Questionnaire: Three or four temperament dimensions? *Journal of Personality and Social Psychology, 70,* 127–140.

Stansfeld, S., Head, J., Bartley, M., & Fonagy, P. (2008). Social position, early deprivation and the development of attachment. *Social Psychiatry and Psychiatric Epidemiology, 43,* 516–526.

Staudinger, U. M., Fleeson, W., & Baltes, P. B. (1999). Predictors of subjective physical health and global well-being: Similarities and differences between the United States and Germany. *Journal of Personality and Social Psychology, 76,* 305–319.

Stava, L. J., & Jaffa, M. (1988). Some operationalizations of the neodissociation concept and their relationship to hypnotic susceptibility. *Journal of Personality and Social Psychology, 54,* 989–996.

Steblay, N. M., & Bothwell, R. K. (1994). Evidence for hypnotically refreshed testimony: The view from the laboratory. *Law and Human Behavior, 18,* 635–651.

Steele, C. M., & Josephs, R. A. (1990). Alcohol myopia: Its prized and dangerous effects. *American Psychologist, 45,* 921–933.

Steffney, J. (1975). Symbolism and death in Jung and Zen Buddhism. *Philosophy East and West, 25,* 175–185.

Stein, H. (1988). Twelve stages of creative Adlerian psychotherapy. *Individual Psychology, 44,* 138–143.

Stein, H. T., & Edwards, M. E. (1998). Alfred Adler: Classical theory and practice. In P. Marcus & A. Rosenberg (Eds.), *Psychoanalytic versions of the human condition and clinical practice: Philosophies of life and their impact on practice* (pp. 64–93). New York: New York University Press.

Steinem, G. (1986). *Marilyn: Norma Jeane.* New York: Signet.

Steklis, H. D., & Walter, A. (1991). Culture, biology, and human nature: A mechanistic approach. *Human Nature, 2,* 137–169.

Stelmack, R. M. (1997). The psychophysics and psychophysiology of extraversion and arousal. In H. Nyborg (Ed.), *The scientific study of human nature: Tribute to Hans J. Eysenck at eighty* (pp. 388–403). New York: Pergamon.

Stenberg, G., Johansson, M., Olsson, A., Lindgren, M., & Rosen, I. (2000). Semantic processing without conscious identification: Evidence from event-related potentials. *Journal of Experimental Psychology: Learning, Memory, and Cognition, 26,* 973–1004.

Stephens, R. S., Wertz, J. S., & Roffman, R. A. (1995). Self-efficacy and marijuana cessation: A construct validity analysis. *Journal of Consulting and Clinical Psychology, 63,* 1022–1031.

Stern, P. J. (1976). *The haunted prophet.* New York: Delta Books.

Stevens, A. (1995). Jungian psychology, the body, and the future. *Journal of Analytical Psychology, 40,* 353–364.

Stewart, A. J., Franz, C., & Layton, L. (1988). The changing self: Using personal documents to study lives. *Journal of Personality, 56,* 41–74.

Stewart, R. B., Verbrugge, K. M., & Beilfuss, M. C. (1998). Sibling relationships in early adulthood: A typology. *Personal Relationships, 5,* 59–74.

Stewart, V., & Stewart, A. (1982). *Business applications of repertory grid*. London: McGraw-Hill.

Stock, J., & Cervone, D. (1990). Proximal goal-setting and self-regulatory processes. *Cognitive Therapy and Research, 14,* 483–498.

Stoeber, J., Otto, K., & Dalbert, C. (2009). Perfectionism and the Big Five: Conscientiousness predicts longitudinal increases in self-oriented perfectionism. *Personality and Individual Differences, 47,* 363–368.

Stone, A. A., Schwartz, J. E., Neale, J. M., Shiffman, S., Marco, C. A., Hickcox, M., Paty, J., Porter, L. S., & Cruise, L. J. (1998). A comparison of coping assessed by ecological momentary assessment and retrospective recall. *Journal of Personality and Social Psychology, 74,* 1670–1680.

Stone, L. (1981). *The past and the present*. Boston, MA: Routledge & Kegan Paul.

Stone, M. H. (2009). Theorist orientation from diagnosing a case of suicide. *Journal of Individual Psychology, 65,* 34–46.

Storm, L., & Thalbourne, M. A. (2001). Studies of the I Ching: I. A replication. *Journal of Parapsychology, 65,* 105–124.

Strathearn, L., Li, J., Fonagy, P., & Montague, P. R. (2008). What's in a smile Maternal brain responses to infant facial cues. *Pediatrics, 122,* 40–51.

Stratton, G. M. (2005). *Anger: Its religious and moral significance*. New York: Macmillan. (Reprinted electronic version from PsycBOOKS, Accession No. 2005–00637–000) (Original work published 1923)

Strelau, J. (1997). The contribution of Pavlov's typology of CNS properties to personality research. *European Psychologist, 2,* 125–138.

Stroebe, M, Schut, H., & Stroebe, W. (2006). Who benefits from disclosure? Exploration of attachment style differences in the effects of expressing emotions. *Clinical Psychology Review, 26,* 66–85.

Strube, M. J., & Ota, S. (1982). Type A coronary-prone behavior pattern: Relationship to birth order and family size. *Personality and Social Psychology Bulletin, 8,* 317–323.

Sudak, H. S. (2000). Current theories of psychoanalysis [Book review]. *American Journal of Psychiatry, 157,* 300–301.

Suedfeld, P., & Bluck, S. (1993). Changes in integrative complexity accompanying significant life events: Historical evidence. *Journal of Personality and Social Psychology, 64,* 124–130.

Suedfeld, P., Corteen, R. S., & McCormick, C. (1986). The role of integrative complexity in military leadership: Robert E. Lee and his opponents. *Journal of Applied Social Psychology, 16,* 498–507.

Sugiyama, M. S. (2001). New science, old myth: An evolutionary critique of the Oedipal paradigm. *Mosaic: A Journal for the Interdisciplinary Study of Literature, 34,* 121–136.

Suh, E. M. (2007). Downsides of an *overly* context-sensitive self: Implications from the culture and subjective well-being research. *Journal of Personality, 75,* 1321–1343.

Sullivan, H. S. (1953). *The interpersonal theory of psychiatry*. New York: Norton.

Sulloway, F. J. (1979). *Freud, biologist of the mind: Beyond the psychoanalytic legend*. New York: Basic Books.

Sulloway, F. J. (1996). *Born to rebel: Birth order, family dynamics, and creative lives*. New York: Vintage Books.

Sumedho, B. (1992). *The four noble truths*. Hertfordshire, UK: Amaravati. Available online at http://www.buddhanet.net/pdf_file/4nobltru.pdf

Summers, A. (1985). *Goddess: The secret lives of Marilyn Monroe*. New York: New American Library.

Sundberg, N. D. (1965). *The sixth mental measurements yearbook* (pp. 322–325). Highland Park, NJ: Gryphon Press.

Sutton, S. K., & Davidson, R. J. (1997). Prefrontal brain asymmetry: A biological substrate of the behavioral approach and inhibition systems. *Psychological Science, 8,* 204–210.

Swansbrough, R. H. (1994). A Kohutian analysis of President Bush's personality and style in the Persian Gulf crisis. *Political Psychology, 15,* 227–276.

Sweeny, T. J., & Myers, J. E. (1986). Early recollections: An Adlerian technique with older people. *Clinical Gerontologist, 4,* 3–12.

Swickert, R. J., & Gilliland, K. (1998). Relationship between the brainstem auditory evoked response and extraversion, impulsivity, and sociability. *Journal of Research in Personality, 32,* 314–330.

Symonds, A. (1991). Gender issues and Horney theory. *American Journal of Psychoanalysis, 51,* 301–312.

Taga, K. A., Friedman, H. S., & Martin, L. R. (2009). Early personality traits as predictors of mortality risk following conjugal bereavement. *Journal of Personality, 77,* 669–690.

Talbot, R., Cooper, C. L., & Ellis, B. (1991). Uses of the dependency grid for investigating social support in stressful situations. *Stress Medicine, 7*(3), 171–180.

Tamdgidi, M. H. (2008). Thich Nhat Hanh's sociological imagination. *Human Architecture: Journal of the Sociology of Self-Knowledge, 6,* vii–x.

Tamir, M., Robinson, M. D., & Solberg, E. C. (2006). You may worry, but can you recognize threats when you see them?: Neuroticism, threat identifications, and negative affect. *Journal of Personality, 74,* 1482–1505.

Tangney, J. P. (1990). Assessing individual differences in proneness to shame and guilt: Development of the Self-Conscious Affect and Attribution Inventory. *Journal of Personality and Social Psychology, 59,* 102–111.

Tangney, J. P. (1994). The mixed legacy of the superego: Adaptive and maladaptive aspects of shame and guilt. In M. J. Masling & R. F. Bornstein (Eds.), *Empirical perspectives on object relations theory*. Washington, DC: American Psychological Association.

Tangney, J. P., & Dearing, R. L. (2004). Gender differences in morality. In R. F. Bornstein & J. M. Masling (Eds.), *The psychodynamics of gender and gender role*. Washington, DC: American Psychological Association.

Tangney, J. P., Hill-Barlow, D., Wagner, P. E., Marschall, D. E., Borenstein, J. K., Sanftner, J., Mohr, T., & Gramzow,

R. (1996). Assessing individual differences in constructive versus destructive responses to anger across the lifespan. *Journal of Personality and Social Psychology, 70,* 780–796.

Tart, C. T. (1992). Perspectives on scientism, religion, and philosophy provided by parapsychology. *Journal of Humanistic Psychology, 32*(2), 70–100.

Taub, J. M. (1998). Eysenck's descriptive and biological theory of personality: A review of construct validity. *International Journal of Neuroscience, 94*(3–4), 145–198.

Taylor, E. (2000). "What is man, psychologist, that thou art so unmindful of him?": Henry A. Murray on the historical relation between classical personality theory and humanistic psychology. *Journal of Humanistic Psychology, 40,* 29–42.

Taylor, J. C., & Romanczyk, R. G. (1994). Generating hypotheses about the function of student problem behavior by observing teacher behavior. *Journal of Applied Behavior Analysis, 27,* 251–265.

Taylor, J. G. (2002). Paying attention to consciousness. *Trends in the Cognitive Sciences, 6,* 206–210.

Tegano, D. W. (1990). Relationship of tolerance of ambiguity and playfulness to creativity. *Psychological Reports, 66,* 1047–1056.

Teixeira, B. (1987). Comments on ahimsa (nonviolence). *Journal of Transpersonal Psychology, 19,* 1–17.

Tenopyr, M. L. (1995). The complex interaction between measurement and national employment. *Psychology, Public Policy, and Law, 2,* 348–362.

Terrill, R. E. (2009). Unity and duality in Barack Obama's "A more perfect union." *Quarterly Journal of Speech, 95,* 363–386.

Tesser, A. (1993). The importance of heritability in psychological research: The case of attitudes. *Psychological Review, 100,* 129–142.

Teti, D. M., & Gelfand, D. M. (1991). Behavioral competence among mothers of infants in the first year: The mediational role of maternal self-efficacy. *Child Development, 62,* 918–929.

The Transcendental Meditation Program. (2005). Available online at http://www.tm.org/

Thom, D. P., & Coetzee, C. H. (2004). Identity development of South African adolescents in a democratic society. *Society in Transition, 35,* 183–193.

Thompson, B., & Borrello, G. M. (1986). Construct validity of the Myers-Briggs Type Indicator. *Educational and Psychological Measurement, 46,* 745–752.

Thompson, T., Steffert, T., & Gruzelier, J. (2009). Effects of guided immune-imagery: The moderating influence of openness to experience. *Personality and Individual Differences, 47,* 789–794.

Thomson, N. F., & Martinko, M. J. (1995). The relationship between MBTI types and attributional style. *Journal of Psychological Type, 35,* 22–30.

Thomson, R. F. (2000). Zazen and psychotherapeutic presence. *American Journal of Psychotherapy, 54,* 531–548.

Thorne, B. M., Fyfe, J. H., & Carskadon, T. G. (1987). The Myers-Briggs Type Indicator and coronary heart disease. *Journal of Personality Assessment, 51,* 545–554.

Thurston, J. R., & Mussen, P. H. (1951). Infant feeding gratification and adult personality. *Journal of Personality, 19,* 449–458.

Tiberius, V., & Hall, A. (2010). Normative theory and psychological research: Hedonism, eudaimonism, and why it matters. *Journal of Positive Psychology, 5,* 212–225.

Ticho, E. A. (1982). The alternate schools and the self. *Journal of the American Psychoanalytic Association, 30,* 849–862.

Tiger Woods profile. (2006). Downloaded August 31, 2006 from http://www.tigerwoods.com/content/default.sps?iType=6266

Tloczynski, J. (1993). Is the self essential? Handling reductionism. *Perceptual and Motor Skills, 76,* 723–732.

Tloczynski, J., Knoll, C., & Fitch, A. (1997). The relationship among spirituality, religious ideology, and personality. *Journal of Psychology and Theology, 25,* 208–213.

Tobacyk, J. J., & Downs, A. (1986). Personal construct threat and irrational beliefs as cognitive predictors of increases in musical performance anxiety. *Journal of Personality and Social Psychology, 51,* 779–782.

Tobey, L. H., & Bruhn, A. R. (1992). Early memories and the criminally dangerous. *Journal of Personality Assessment, 59,* 137–152.

Todd, J. T., & Morris, E. K. (1992). Case histories in the great power of steady misrepresentation. *American Psychologist, 47,* 1441–1453.

Tomarken, A. J., Davidson, R. J., & Henriques, J. B. (1990). Resting frontal brain asymmetry predicts affective responses to films. *Journal of Personality and Social Psychology, 59,* 791–801.

Tomarken, A. J., Davidson, R. J., Wheeler, R. E., & Doss, R. (1992). Psychometric properties of resting anterior EEG asymmetry: Temporal stability and internal consistency. *Psychophysiology, 29,* 576–592.

Tomasello, M. (1999). The human adaptation for culture. *Annual Review of Anthropology, 28,* 509–529.

Tomori, C., & Bavelas, J. B. (2007). Using microanalysis of communication to compare solution-focused and client-centered therapies. *Journal of Family Psychotherapy,18,* 25–43.

Tori, C. D., & Bilmes, M. (2002). Multiculturalism and psychoanalytic psychology: The validation of a defense mechanisms measure in an Asian population. *Psychoanalytic Psychology, 19,* 701–721.

Torrey, J. W. (1987). Phases of feminist re-vision in the psychology of personality. *Teaching of Psychology, 14,* 155–160.

Townsend, F. (2000). Taking *Born to Rebel* seriously: The need for independent review. *Politics and the Life Sciences, 19,* 205–210.

Trappey, C. (1996). A meta-analysis of consumer choice and subliminal advertising. *Psychology and Marketing, 13,* 517–530.

Travis, F. (2001). Autonomic and EEG patterns distinguish transcending from other experiences during Transcendental Meditation practice. *International Journal of Psychophysiology, 42,* 1–9.

Travis, F., & Pearson, C. (2000). Pure consciousness: Distinct phenomenological and physiological correlates of "consciousness itself." *International Journal of Neuroscience, 100,* 77–89.

Travis, F., Tecce, J., Arenander, A., & Wallace, R. K. (2002). Patterns of EEG coherence, power and contingent negative variation characterize the integration of transcendental and waking states. *Biological Psychology, 61,* 293–319.

Treadway, M., & McCloskey, M. (1987). Cite unseen: Distortions of the Allport and Postman rumor study in the eyewitness testimony literature. *Law and Behavior, 11,* 19–25.

Triandis, H. C. (1996). The psychological measurement of cultural syndromes. *American Psychologist, 51,* 407–415.

Triandis, H. C. (2001). Individualism-collectivism and personality. *Journal of Personality, 69,* 907–924.

Triandis, H. C., McCusker, C., & Hui, C. H. (1990). Multimethod probes of individualism and collectivism. *Journal of Personality and Social Psychology, 59,* 1006–1020.

Tribich, D., & Messer, S. (1974). Psychoanalytic character type and status of authority as determiners of suggestibility. *Journal of Consulting and Clinical Psychology, 42,* 842–848.

Trivers, R. (1972). Parental investment and sexual selection. In B. Campbell (Ed.), *Sexual selection and the descent of man: 1871–1971* (pp. 136–179). Chicago, IL: Aldine.

Trull, T. J., Useda, J. D., Holcomb, J., Doan, B. T., Axelrod, S. R., Stern, B. L., & Gershuny, B. S. (1998). A structured interview for the assessment of the five-factor model of personality. *Psychological Assessment, 10,* 229–240.

Trungpa, C. (2005). *The sanity we are born with: A Buddhist approach to psychology.* Boston, MA: Shambhala.

Tryon, W. W. (1990). Why paradigmatic behaviorism should be retitled psychological behaviorism. *Behavior Therapist, 13,* 127–128.

Tsang, J., & McCullough, M. E. (2003). Measuring religious constructs: A hierarchical approach to construct organization and scale selection. In S. J. Lopez & C. R. Snyder (Eds.), *Positive psychological assessment: A handbook of models and measures* (pp. 345–360). Washington, DC: American Psychological Association.

Tsang, J. A., & Rowatt, W. C. (2007). The relationship between religious orientation, right-wing authoritarianism, and implicit sexual prejudice. *International Journal for the Psychology of Religion, 17,* 99–120.

Tucker, I. F. (1991). Predicting scores on the Rathus Assertiveness Schedule from Myers-Briggs Type Indicator categories. *Psychological Reports, 69,* 571–576.

Tucker, J. S., Friedman, H. S., Schwartz, J. E., Cirqui, M. H., Tomlinson-Keasey, C., Wingard, D. L., & Martin, L. R. (1997). Parental divorce: Effects on individual behavior and longevity. *Journal of Personality and Social Psychology, 73,* 381–391.

Tuckman, B. W. (1990). Group versus goal-setting effects on the self-regulated performance of students differing in self-efficacy. *Journal of Experimental Education, 58,* 291–298.

Tudor, K., & Worrall, M. (1994). Congruence reconsidered. *British Journal of Guidance and Counselling, 22,* 197–206.

Turk, B. (1990). Kids with courage. *Individual Psychology, 46,* 178–183.

Turkheimer, E. (1998). Heritability and biological explanation. *Psychological Review, 105,* 782–791.

Turpin, M., Dallos, R., Owen, R., & Thomas, M. (2009). The meaning and impact of head and neck cancer: An interpretative phenomenological and repertory grid analysis. *Journal of Constructivist Psychology, 22,* 24–54.

Turvey, C., & Salovey, P. (1993–1994). Measures of repression: Converging on the same construct? *Imagination, Cognition and Personality, 13,* 279–289.

Tuten, T. L., & August, R. A. (1998). Understanding consumer satisfaction in services settings: A bidimensional model of service strategies. *Journal of Social Behavior and Personality, 13,* 553–564.

Twenge, J. M. (2000). The age of anxiety? Birth cohort change in anxiety and neuroticism, 1952–1993. *Journal of Personality and Social Psychology, 79,* 1007–1021.

Twenge, J. M. (2001). Birth cohort changes in extraversion: A cross-temporal meta-analysis, 1966–1993. *Personality and Individual Differences, 30,* 735–748.

Twenge, J. M., & Campbell, W. K. (2001). Age and birth cohort differences in self-esteem: A cross-temporal meta-analysis. *Personality and Social Psychology Review, 5,* 321–344.

Twomey, H. B., Kaslow, N. J., & Croft, S. (2000). Childhood maltreatment, object relations, and suicidal behavior in women. *Psychoanalytic Psychology, 17,* 313–335.

Tyson, P. (2009a). Child development and child psychoanalysis: Research and education. *Journal of the American Psychoanalytic Association, 57,* 871–879.

Tyson, P. (2009b). Research in child psychoanalysis: Twenty-five-year follow-up of a severely disturbed child. *Journal of the American Psychoanalytic Association, 57,* 919–945.

Utay, J. M., & Utay, C. M. (1996). Applications of Adler's theory in counseling and education. *Journal of Instructional Psychology, 23,* 251–256.

Vaillant, G. E. (1971). Theoretical hierarchy of adaptive ego mechanisms. *Archives of General Psychiatry, 24,* 107–118.

Vaillant, G. E. (1992). The historical origins and future potential of Sigmund Freud's concept of the mechanisms of defence. *International Review of Psychoanalysis, 19,* 35–50.

Vaillant, G. E. (1993). *The wisdom of the ego.* Cambridge, MA: Harvard University Press.

Vaillant, G. E. (1994). Ego mechanisms of defense and personality psychopathology. *Journal of Abnormal Psychology, 103,* 44–50.

Vaillant, G. E. (2000). Adaptive mental mechanisms and their role in a positive psychology. *American Psychologist, 55,* 89–98.

Vaillant, G. E. (2002). Quantum change: When epiphanies and sudden insights transform ordinary lives [Book review]. *American Journal of Psychiatry, 159,* 1620–1621.

Vaillant, G. E. (2003). Mental health. *American Journal of Psychiatry, 160,* 1373–1384.

Vaillant, G. E., & Davis, J. T. (2000). Social/emotional intelligence and midlife resilience in schoolboys with low tested intelligence. *American Journal of Orthopsychiatry, 70,* 215–222.

Van Boven, L. (2005). Experientialism, materialism, and the pursuit of happiness. *Review of General Psychology, 9,* 132–142.

van der Kolk, B. A., & Fisler, R. (1995). Dissociation and the fragmentary nature of traumatic memories: Overview and exploratory study. *Journal of Traumatic Stress, 8,* 505–525.

Van Eenwyk, J. R. (1997). *Archetypes and strange attractors: The chaotic world of symbols.* Toronto, Canada: Inner City Books.

van IJzendoorn, M. H., & Bakermans-Kranenburg, M. J. (1996). Attachment representations in mothers, fathers, adolescents, and clinical groups: A meta-analytic search for normative data. *Journal of Consulting and Clinical Psychology, 64,* 8–21.

Van Kalmthout, M. A. (1995). The religious dimension of Rogers's work. *Journal of Humanistic Psychology, 35*(4), 23–39.

Vanheule, S., & Verhaeghe, P. (2009). Identity through a psychoanalytic looking glass. *Theory and Psychology, 19,* 391–411.

Vannoy, S. D., & Hoyt, W. T. (2004). Evaluation of an anger therapy intervention for incarcerated adult males. *Journal of Offender Rehabilitation, 39*(2), 39–57.

vanOyen Witvliet, C., Knoll, R, W., Hinman, N. G., & DeYoung, P. A. (2010). Compassion-focused reappraisal, benefit-focused reappraisal, and rumination after an interpersonal offense: Emotion regulation implications for subjective emotion, linguistic responses, and physiology. *Journal of Positive Psychology, 5,* 226–242.

Vaughn, C. M., & Pfenninger, D. T. (1994). Kelly and the concept of developmental stages. *Journal of Constructivist Psychology, 7,* 177–190.

Vázquez, C., & Hervás, G. (2010). Perceived benefits after terrorist attacks: The role of positive and negative emotions. *Journal of Positive Psychology, 5,* 154–163.

Veenvliet, S. G. (2008). Intrinsic religious orientation and religious teaching: Differential judgments toward same-gender sexual behavior and gay men and lesbians. *International Journal for the Psychology of Religion, 18,* 53–65.

Velmans, M. (1991). Is human information processing conscious? *Behavioral and Brain Sciences, 14,* 651–726.

Verhulst, B., Hatemi, P. K., & Martin, N. G. (2010). The nature of the relationship between personality traits and political attitudes. *Personality and Individual Differences, 49,* 306–316.

Vernon, P. A., Martin, R. A., Schermer, J. A., & Mackie, A. (2008). A behavioral genetic investigation of humor styles and their correlations with the Big-5 personality dimensions. *Personality and Individual Differences, 44,* 1116–1125.

Vernon, P. A., Petrides, K. V., Bratko, D., & Schermer, J. A. (2008). A behavioral genetic study of trait emotional intelligence. *Emotion, 8,* 635–642.

Vernon, P. A., Villani, V. C., Schermer, J. A., Kirilovic, S., Martin, R. A., Petrides, K. V., Spector, T. D., & Cherkas, L. F. (2010). Genetic and environmental correlations between trait emotional intelligence and humor styles. *Journal of Individual Differences, 30,* 130–137.

Vervoort, L., Wolters, L. H., Hogendoorn, S. M., de Haan, E., Boer, F., & Prins, P. J. M. (2010). Sensitivity of Gray's Behavioral Inhibition System in clinically anxious and non-anxious children and adolescents. *Personality and Individual Differences, 48,* 629–633.

Viney, L. L. (1981). Experimenting with experience: A psychotherapeutic case study. *Psychotherapy, 18,* 271–278.

Viney, L. L. (1992). Can we see ourselves changing? Toward a personal construct model of adult development. *Human Development, 35,* 65–75.

Vleioras, G., & Bosma, H. A. (2005). Are identity styles important for psychological well-being? *Journal of Adolescence, 28,* 397–409.

Volkan, V. D., Itzkowitz, N., & Dod, A. W. (1997). *Richard Nixon: A psychobiography.* New York: Columbia University Press.

von Franz, M. L. (1964). Conclusion: Science and the unconscious. In C. G. Jung (Ed.), *Man and his symbols* (pp. 304–310). Garden City, NY: Doubleday.

Vyse, S. A. (1990). Adopting a viewpoint: Psychology majors and psychological theory. *Teaching of Psychology, 17,* 227–230.

Waite, R. G. L. (1977). *The psychopathic God: Adolf Hitler.* New York: Basic Books.

Walach, H., Buchheld, N., Buttenmüller, V., Kleinknecht, N., & Schmidt, S. (2006). Measuring mindfulness—The Freiburg Mindfulness Inventory (FMI). *Personality and Individual Differences, 40,* 1543–1555.

Waldron, R. (1987). *Oprah!* New York: St. Martin's Press.

Walker, B. M. (1990). Construing George Kelly's construing of the person-in-relation. *International Journal of Personal Construct Psychology, 3,* 41–50.

Walker, B. M. (1992). Values and Kelly's theory: Becoming a good scientist. *International Journal of Personal Construct Psychology, 5,* 259–269.

Walker, B. M., & Winter, D. A. (2007). The elaboration of personal construct psychology. *Annual Review of Psychology, 58,* 453–477.

Walker, C. J. (2010). Experiencing flow: Is doing it together better than doing it alone? *Journal of Positive Psychology, 5,* 3–11.

Wallach, M. A. (2004). Humanism's heritage [Review of *Escape from Freedom* (2nd ed.)]. *PsychCRITIQUES.* Originally published in *Contemporary Psychology: APA Review of Books,* 1996, *41*(1), 7–11.

Wallach, M. A., & Wallach, L. (1983). *Psychology: Sanction for selfishness.* San Francisco, CA: Freeman.

Wallis, C. (2005, January 9). The new happiness. *Time, 165*(3), A2–A9.

Walsh, B. W., & Peterson, L. E. (1985). Philosophical foundations of psychological theories: The issue of synthesis. *Psychotherapy, 2,* 145–153.

Walsh, R. (1988). Two Asian psychologies and their implications for Western psychotherapists. *American Journal of Psychotherapy, 42,* 543–560.

Walsh, R., & Shapiro, S. L. (2006). The meeting of meditative disciplines and Western psychology. *American Psychologist, 61,* 227–239.

Wang, Q. (2001). Culture effects on adults' earliest childhood recollection and self-description: Implications for the relation between memory and the self. *Journal of Personality and Social Psychology, 81,* 220–233.

Ward, E. A. (1993). Generalizability of psychological research from undergraduates to employed adults. *Journal of Social Psychology, 133,* 513–519.

Ward, R. A., & Loftus, E. F. (1985). Eyewitness performance in different psychological types. *Journal of General Psychology, 112,* 191–200.

Warren, B. (1990). Psychoanalysis and personal construct theory: An exploration. *Journal of Psychology, 124,* 449–463.

Warren, B. (1991). Concepts, constructs, cognitive psychology, and personal construct theory. *Journal of Psychology, 125,* 525–536.

Warren, W. G. (1990a). Is personal construct psychology a cognitive psychology? *International Journal of Personal Construct Psychology, 3,* 393–414.

Warren, W. G. (1990b). Personal construct theory and the Aristotelian and Galileian modes of thought. *International Journal of Personal Construct Psychology, 3,* 263–280.

Waterman, A. S. (1990). Personal expressiveness: Philosophical and psychological foundations. *Journal of Mind and Behavior, 11,* 47–73.

Waterman, A. S., Schwartz, S. J., Zamboanga, B. L., Ravert, R. D., Williams, M. K., Agocha, V. B., Kim, S. Y., & Donnellan, M. B. (2010). The Questionnaire for Eudaimonic Well-Being: Psychometric properties, demographic comparisons, and evidence of validity. *Journal of Positive Psychology, 5,* 41–61.

Watkins, C. E., Jr., & Hector, M. (1990). A simple test of the concurrent validity of the Social Interest Index. *Journal of Personality Assessment, 55,* 812–814.

Watson, B. (Trans.) (1968). *The complete works of Chuang Tzu.* New York: Columbia University Press.

Watson, D., & Clark, L. A. (1997). Extraversion and its positive emotional core. In R. Hogan, J. Johnson, & S. Briggs (Eds.), *Handbook of personality psychology* (pp. 767–793). San Diego, CA: Academic Press.

Watson, J. B. (1970). *Behaviorism.* New York: Norton. (Original work published 1924)

Watson, J. C., & Rennie, D. L. (1994). Qualitative analysis of clients' subjective experience of significant moments during the exploration of problematic reactions. *Journal of Counseling Psychology, 41,* 500–509.

Watson, P. J., Hood, R. W., Morris, R. J., & Hall, J. R. (1984). Empathy, religious orientation, and social desirability. *Journal of Psychology, 117,* 211–216.

Watts, R. E. (1992). Biblical agape as a model of social interest. *Individual Psychology, 48,* 35–40.

Watts, R. E. (1996). Social interest and the core conditions: Could it be that Adler influenced Rogers? *Journal of Humanistic Counseling, Education, and Development, 34*(4), 165–170.

Wax, M. L. (2000). Oedipus as normative? Freud's complex, Hook's query, Malinowski's Trobrianders, Stoller's anomalies. *Journal of the American Academy of Psychoanalysis, 28,* 117–132.

Weaver, L. (2008). Facilitating change in men who are violent towards women: Considering the ethics and efficacy of a person-centered approach. *Person-Centered and Experiential Psychotherapies, 7,* 173–184.

Webster-Stratton, C. (1998). Preventing conduct problems in Head Start children: Strengthening parenting competencies. *Journal of Consulting and Clinical Psychology, 66,* 715–730.

Wegner, D. M., Erber, R., & Zanakos, S. (1993). Ironic processes in the mental control of mood and mood-related thought. *Journal of Personality and Social Psychology, 65,* 1093–1104.

Wegner, D. M., Schneider, D. J., Carter, S. R., & White, T. L. (1987). Paradoxical effects of thought suppression. *Journal of Personality and Social Psychology, 53,* 5–13.

Wegner, D. M., & Wheatley, T. (1999). Apparent mental causation: Sources of the experience of will. *American Psychologist, 54,* 480–492.

Wehr, G. (1987). *Jung: A biography* (D. M. Weeks, Trans.). Boston, MA: Shambhala.

Weinberg, R. S., Hughes, H. H., Critelli, J. W., England, R., & Jackson, A. (1984). Effects of preexisting and manipulated self-efficacy on weight loss in a self-control program. *Journal of Research in Personality, 18,* 352–358.

Weiner, I. B., & Exner, J. E., Jr. (1991). Rorschach changes in long-term and short-term psychotherapy. *Journal of Personality Assessment, 56,* 453–465.

Weinrach, S. G. (1990). Rogers and Gloria: The controversial film and the enduring relationship. *Psychotherapy, 27,* 282–290.

Weinrach, S. G. (1991). Rogers' encounter with Gloria: What did Rogers know and when? *Psychotherapy, 28,* 504–506.

Weiss, A., Bates, T. C., & Luciano, M. (2008). Happiness is a personal(ity) thing: The genetics of personality and well-being in a representative sample. *Psychological Science, 19,* 205–210.

Wellman, J. A., Czopp, A. M., & Geers, A. L. (2009). The egalitarian optimist and the confrontation of prejudice. *Journal of Positive Psychology, 4,* 389–395.

Wells-Parker, E., Miller, D. I., & Topping, J. S. (1990). Development of control-of-outcome scales and self-efficacy scales for women in four life roles. *Journal of Personality Assessment, 54,* 564–575.

Wenneberg, S. R., Schneider, R. H., Walton, K. G., Maclean, C. R. K., Levitsky, D. K., Salerno, J. W., Wallace, R. K., Mandarino, J. V., Rainforth, M. V., & Waziri, R. (1997). A controlled study of the effects of the Transcendental Meditation® program on cardiovascular reactivity and ambulatory blood pressure. *International Journal of Neuroscience, 89,* 15–28.

Wenzlaff, R. M., & Wegner, D. M. (2000). Thought suppression. *Annual Review of Psychology, 51,* 59–91.

Wertheimer, M. (1978). Humanistic psychology and the humane but tough-minded psychologist. *American Psychologist, 33,* 739–745.

West, S. G. (1986). Methodological developments in personality research: An introduction. *Journal of Personality, 54,* 1–17.

Westen, D. (1991). Social cognition and object relations. *Psychological Bulletin, 109,* 429–455.

Westen, D. (1998). Unconscious thought, feeling, and motivation: The end of a century-long debate. In R. F. Bornstein & J. M. Masling (Eds.), *Empirical perspectives on the psychoanalytic unconscious* (pp. 1–43). Washington, DC: American Psychological Association.

Westen, D., Gabbard, G. O., & Ortigo, K. M. (2008). Psychoanalytic approaches to personality. In O. P. John, R. W. Robins, & L. A. Pervin (Eds.), *Handbook of personality: Theory and research* (3rd ed., pp. 61–113). New York: Guilford Press.

Westen, D., Klepser, J., Ruffins, S. A., Silverman, M., Lifton, N., & Boekamp, J. (1991). Object relations in childhood and adolescence: The development of working representations. *Journal of Consulting and Clinical Psychology, 59,* 400–409.

Westen, D., & Morrison, K. (2001). A multidimensional meta-analysis of treatments for depression, panic, and generalized anxiety disorder: An empirical examination of the status of empirically supported therapies. *Journal of Consulting and Clinical Psychology, 69,* 875–899.

Westen, D., Muderrisoglu, S., Fowler, C., Shedler, J., & Koren, D. (1997). Affect regulation and affective experience: Individual differences, group differences, and measurement using a Q-sort procedure. *Journal of Consulting and Clinical Psychology, 65,* 429–439.

Westkott, M. (1986a). *The feminist legacy of Karen Horney.* New Haven, CT: Yale University Press.

Westkott, M. (1986b). Historical and developmental roots of female dependency. *Psychotherapy, 23,* 213–220.

Westkott, M. (1989). Female relationship and the idealized self. *American Journal of Psychoanalysis, 49,* 239–250.

Westkott, M. (1998). Horney, Zen, and the real self. *American Journal of Psychoanalysis, 58,* 287–301.

Wheeler, P. (2001). The Myers-Briggs Type Indicator and applications to accounting education research. *Issues in Accounting Education, 16,* 125–150.

Wheeler, S. (2000). What makes a good counsellor? An analysis of ways in which counsellor trainers construe good and bad counselling trainees. *Counselling Psychology Quarterly, 13,* 65–83.

Whitbourne, S. K., Zuschlag, M. K., Elliot, L. B., & Waterman, A. S. (1992). Psychosocial development in adulthood: A 22-year sequential study. *Journal of Personality and Social Psychology, 63,* 260–271.

White, T. H. (1975). *Breach of faith: The fall of Richard Nixon.* New York: Atheneum.

Whitfield, C. L. (1995). How common is traumatic forgetting? *Journal of Psychohistory, 23*(2), 119–130.

Wickett, J. C., Vernon, P. A., & Lee, D. H. (2000). Relationships between factors of intelligence and brain volume. *Personality and Individual Differences, 29,* 1095–1122.

Wiedenfeld, S. A., O'Leary, A., Bandura, A., Brown, S., Levine, S., & Raska, K. (1990). Impact of perceived self-efficacy in coping with stressors on components of the immune system. *Journal of Personality and Social Psychology, 59,* 1082–1094.

Wiederman, M. W., & Kendall, E. (1999). Evolution, sex, and jealousy: Investigation with a sample from Sweden. *Evolution and Human Behavior, 20,* 121–128.

Wiese, M. R. R., & Kramer, J. J. (1988). Parent training research: An analysis of the empirical literature 1975–1985. *Psychology in the Schools, 25,* 325–330.

Wiggins, J. S. (1984). Cattell's system from the perspective of mainstream personality theory. *Multivariate Behavioral Research, 19,* 176–190.

Wiggins, J. S., & Trapnell, P. D. (1997). Personality structure: The return of the big five. In R. Hogan, J. Johnson, & S. Briggs (Eds.), *Handbook of personality psychology* (pp. 737–765). San Diego, CA: Academic Press.

Wild, C. (1965). Creativity and adaptive regression. *Journal of Personality and Social Psychology, 2,* 161–169.

Wilhelm, H. (1960). *Change: Eight lectures on the I Ching.* Princeton, NJ: Princeton University Press.

Wilkins, P. (2000). Unconditional positive regard considered. *British Journal of Guidance and Counselling, 28,* 23–36.

Wilkinson, W. W. (2004). Religiosity, authoritarianism, and homophobia: A multidimensional approach. *International Journal for the Psychology of Religion, 14,* 55–67.

Williams, P., with Tribe, A. (2000). *Buddhist thought: A complete introduction to the Indian tradition.* London: Routledge.

Williams, S. L., Kinney, P. J., Harap, S. T., & Liebmann, M. (1997). Thoughts of agoraphobic people during scary tasks. *Journal of Abnormal Psychology, 106,* 511–520.

Williams, S. S., Kimble, D. L., Covell, N. H., Weiss, L. H., Newton, K. J., Fisher, J. D., & Fisher, W. A. (1992). College students use implicit personality theory instead of safer sex. *Journal of Applied Social Psychology, 22,* 921–933.

Wills, T. A., Windle, M., & Cleary, S. D. (1998). Temperament and novelty seeking in adolescent substance use: Convergence of dimensions of temperament with constructs from Cloninger's theory. *Journal of Personality and Social Psychology, 74,* 387–406.

Winston, A. S., & Baker, J. E. (1985). Behavior analytic studies of creativity: A critical review. *Behavior Analyst, 8,* 191–205.

Winter, D. A. (1993). Slot rattling from law enforcement to lawbreaking: A personal construct theory exploration of police stress. *International Journal of Personal Construct Psychology, 6,* 253–267.

Winter, D. G. (1993). Power, affiliation, and war: Three tests of a motivational model. *Journal of Personality and Social Psychology, 65,* 532–545.

Winter, D. G. (1996). Gordon Allport and the legend of "Rinehart." *Journal of Personality, 64,* 263–273.

Winter, D. G. (1997). Allport's life and Allport's psychology. *Journal of Personality, 65,* 723–731.

Winter, D. G., & Carlson, L. A. (1988). Using motive scores in the psychobiographical study of an individual: The case of Richard Nixon. *Journal of Personality, 56,* 75–103.

Winter, D. G., Hermann, M. G., Weintraub, W., & Walker, S. G. (1991a). The personalities of Bush and Gorbachev at a distance: Follow-up on predictions. *Political Psychology, 12,* 457–464.

Winter, D. G., Hermann, M. G., Weintraub, W., & Walker, S. G. (1991b). The personalities of Bush and Gorbachev measured at a distance: Procedures, portraits, and policy. *Political Psychology, 12,* 215–245.

Winter, D. G., John, O. P., Stewart, A. J., Klohnen, E. C., & Duncan, L. E. (1998). Traits and motives: Toward an integration of two traditions in personality research. *Psychological Review, 105,* 230–250.

Winter, S. (1999). *Freud and the institution of psychoanalytic knowledge.* Stanford, CA: Stanford University Press.

Wiseman, H., & Rice, L. N. (1989). Sequential analyses of therapist-client interaction during change events: A task-focused approach. *Journal of Consulting and Clinical Psychology, 57,* 281–286.

Woike, B. A., Osier, T. J., & Candela, K. (1996). Attachment styles and violent imagery in thematic stories about relationships. *Personality and Social Psychology Bulletin, 22,* 1030–1034.

Wojcik, J. V. (1988). Social learning predictors of the avoidance of smoking relapse. *Addictive Behaviors, 13,* 177–180.

Wolfenstein, E. V. (1993). Mr. Moneybags meets the Rat Man: Marx and Freud on the meaning of money. *Political Psychology, 14,* 279–308.

Wollman, N., & Stouder, R. (1991). Believed efficacy and political activity: A test of the specificity hypothesis. *Journal of Social Psychology, 13,* 557–566.

Wolman, B. B. (1971). Does psychology need its own philosophy of science? *American Psychologist, 26,* 877–886.

Wood, R., & Bandura, A. (1989a). Impact of conceptions of ability on self-regulatory mechanisms and complex decision making. *Journal of Personality and Social Psychology, 56,* 407–415.

Wood, R., & Bandura, A. (1989b). Social cognitive theory of organizational management. *Academy of Management Review, 14,* 361–384.

Wood, R., Bandura, A., & Bailey, T. (1990). Mechanisms governing organizational performance in complex decision-making environments. *Organizational Behavior and Human Decision Processes, 46,* 181–201.

Woodward, B., & Bernstein, C. (1976). *The final days.* New York: Avon Books.

Wright, J. C., & Mischel, W. (1987). A conditional approach to dispositional constructs: The local predictability of social behavior. *Journal of Personality and Social Psychology, 53,* 1159–1177.

Wright, J. C., & Mischel, W. (1988). Conditional hedges and the intuitive psychology of traits. *Journal of Personality and Social Psychology, 55,* 454–469.

Wright, T. M., & Reise, S. P. (1997). Personality and unrestricted sexual behavior: Correlations of sociosexuality in Caucasian and Asian college students. *Journal of Research in Personality, 31,* 166–192.

Wright, W. J. (1985). Personality profiles of four leaders of the German Lutheran Reformation. *Psychohistory Review, 14,* 12–22.

Wurgaft, L. D. (1976). Erik Erikson: From Luther to Gandhi. *Psychoanalytic Review, 63,* 209–233.

Yamamoto, S. (2003). Environmental problems and Buddhist ethics: From the perspective of the consciousness-only doctrine. In S. Muramoto & P. Young-Eisendrath (Eds.), *Awakening and insight: Zen Buddhism and psychotherapy* (pp. 239–257). New York: Brunner-Routledge.

Yapko, M. D. (1994). Suggestibility and repressed memories of abuse: A survey of psychotherapists' beliefs. *American Journal of Clinical Hypnosis, 36*(3), 163–171.

Yeh, C. J., & Hwang, M. Y. (2000). Interdependence in ethnic identity and self: Implications for theory and practice. *Journal of Counseling and Development, 78,* 420–429.

Ying, Y. (2001). Migration and cultural orientation: An empirical test of the psychoanalytic theory in Chinese Americans. *Journal of Applied Psychoanalytic Studies, 3,* 409–430.

Yogev, S. (1983). Judging the professional woman: Changing research, changing values. *Psychology of Women Quarterly, 7,* 219–234.

Young-Bruehl, E. (Ed.). (1990). *Freud on women: A reader.* New York: Norton.

Young-Eisendrath, P. (2002). The transformation of human suffering: A perspective from psychotherapy and Buddhism. In S. Muramoto & P. Young-Eisendrath (Eds.), *Awakening and insight: Zen Buddhism and psychotherapy* (pp. 67–80). New York: Brunner-Routledge.

Young-Eisendrath, P. (2003). Suffering from biobabble: Searching for a science of subjectivity. In K. H. Dockett, G. R. Dudley-Grant, & C. P. Bankart (Eds.), *Psychology and Buddhism: From individual to global community* (pp. 125–138). Secaucus, NJ: Kluwer Academic.

Zawadzki, B., & Strelau, J. (2010). Structure of personality: Search for a general factor viewed from a temperament perspective. *Personality and Individual Differences, 49,* 77–82.

Zayas, V., Mischel, W., Shoda, Y., & Aber, J. L. (2011). Roots of adult attachment: Maternal caregiving at 18 months predicts adult peer and partner attachment. *Social Psychological and Personality Science, 2,* 289–297.

Zborowski, M. J., & McNamara, P. (1998). Attachment hypothesis of REM sleep: Toward an integration of psychoanalysis, neuroscience, and evolutionary psychology and the implications for psychopathology research. *Psychoanalytic Psychology, 15,* 115–140.

Zhou, X., Saucier, G., Gao, D., & Liu, J. (2009). The factor structure of Chinese personality terms. *Journal of Personality, 77,* 363–400.

Ziller, R. C. (1990). Environment-self behavior: A general theory of personal control. *Journal of Social Behavior and Personality, 5,* 227–242.

Zimmerman, M. A. (1989). The relationship between political efficacy and citizen participation: Construct validation studies. *Journal of Personality Assessment, 53,* 554–566.

Zimmerman, M. A., & Warschausky, S. (1998). Empowerment theory for rehabilitation research: Conceptual and methodological issues. *Rehabilitation Psychology, 43,* 3–16.

Zolten, A. J. (1989). Constructive integration of learning theory and phenomenological approaches to biofeedback training. *Biofeedback and Self-Regulation, 14,* 89–99.

Zosky, D. L. (1999). The application of object relations theory to domestic violence. *Clinical Social Work Journal, 27,* 55–69.

Zuckerman, M. (1994). *Behavioral expressions and biosocial bases of sensation seeking.* New York: Cambridge University Press.

Zuckerman, M., & Kuhlman, D. M. (2000). Personality and risk-taking: Common biosocial factors. *Journal of Personality, 68,* 999–1029.

Zuckerman, M., Kuhlman, D. M., & Camac, C. (1988). What lies beyond E and N? Factor analyses of scales believed to measure basic dimensions of personality. *Journal of Personality and Social Psychology, 54,* 96–107.

Zupp, A. (2004, January/February). Why won't the Dalai Lama pick a fight? *Humanist,* pp. 5–6.

Zuriff, G. E. (1985). *Behaviorism: A conceptual reconstruction.* New York: Columbia University Press.

Zuroff, D. C. (1986). Was Gordon Allport a trait theorist? *Journal of Personality and Social Psychology, 51,* 993–1000.

Zvoch, K. (1999). Family type and investment in education: A comparison of genetic and stepparent families. *Evolution and Human Behavior, 20,* 453–464.

Zweig, C., & Wolf, S. (1997). *Romancing the shadow: A guide to soul work for a vital, authentic life.* New York: Ballantine.

CREDITS

AUTHOR INDEX

SUBJECT INDEX